BIG ISLAND
O F   H A W A I I
HANDBOOK

INCLUDING HAWAII VOLCANOES NATIONAL PARK,
THE KONA COAST, AND WAIPIO VALLEY

D0369750

BIG ISLAND
OF HAWAII
HANDBOOK

INCLUDING HAWAII VOLCANOES NATIONAL PARK, THE KONA COAST, AND WAIPIO VALLEY

SECOND EDITION

J.D. BISIGNANI

MOON
PUBLICATIONS INC.

BIG ISLAND OF HAWAII HANDBOOK
SECOND EDITION
Published by
Moon Publications, Inc.
P.O. Box 3040
Chico, California 95927-3040, USA

Printed by
Colorcraft Ltd., Hong Kong

Please send all comments,
corrections, additions,
amendments, and critiques to:

**J.D. BISIGNANI
MOON PUBLICATIONS, INC.
P.O. BOX 3040
CHICO, CA 95927-3040, USA**

Printing History
  1st edition—September 1990
    Reprinted April 1992
  2nd edition – June 1994
    Reprinted September 1994
    Reprinted March 1995
    Reprinted November 1995

Library of Congress Cataloging in Publication Data
  Bisignani, J.D., 1947-
    Big Island of Hawaii Handbook/J.D. Bisignani -- 2nd ed.
      p. cm.
    Includes bibliographical references and index.
    ISBN 1-56691-006-4 :
    1. Hawaii Island (Hawaii)—Guidebooks.
    I. Title, II. Title: Big island handbook.
    DU628.H28B57   1994   93-39522
    919.69'1044—dc20   CIP

Editor: Don Root
Copy Editor: Elizabeth Kim
Production & Design: Nancy Kennedy, David Hurst
Cartographers: Bob Race, Brian Bardwell
Index: Mark Arends

Cover Art: *Whisper of the Night Wind* by Roy Tabora,
courtesy of Kahn Galleries, 4569 Kukui St., Kapaa, Kauai, HI 96746

Distributed in United States by Publishers Group West.
Printed in Hong Kong.

Although the author and publisher have made every effort to ensure that the information was correct at the
time of going to press, the author and publisher do not assume and hereby disclaim any liability to any party
for any loss or damage caused by errors, omissions, or any potential travel disruption due to labor or financial
difficulty, whether such errors or omissions result from negligence, accident, or any other cause.

WARNING: Nothing in this book is intended to be used for navigation. Mariners are advised to consult official
sailing directions and nautical charts.

to *Madame Pele and all women of heart*

ACKNOWLEDGMENTS

Writing the acknowledgments for a book is supercharged with energy. It's a time when you look forward, hopefully, to a bright future for your work, and a time when you reflect on all that has gone into producing it. Mostly it's a time to say thank you. Thank you for the grace necessary to carry out the task, and thank you to all the wonderful people whose efforts have helped so much along the way. To the following people, I offer my most sincere thank you.

Firstly, to the Moon staff, professionals every one. As time has passed, and one book has followed another, they've become amazingly adept at their work, to the point where their mastery is a marvel to watch.

I would also like to thank the following people for their special help and consideration: Dr. Greg Leo, an adventurer and environmentalist who has done remarkable field research and provided me with invaluable information about the unique flora and fauna of Hawaii; Roger Rose of the Bishop Museum; Lee Wild, Hawaiian Mission Houses Museum; Marilyn Nicholson, State Foundation of Culture and the Arts; the Hawaii Visitors Bureau; Donna Jung, Donna Jung and Associates, who has showed confidence in me since day one; Haunani Vieira, Dollar Rent A Car; Keoni Wagner, Hawaiian Airlines; Jim and John Costello; Dr. Terry and Nancy Carolan; Elizabeth Demotte, Ritz-Carlton Mauna Lani; Barbara Schonley, Destination Molokai; Elisa Josephsohn, Public Relations; Faith Ogawa, for helping me keep the faith; Carol Zahorsky, Four Seasons Resort; Joyce Matsumoto, Halekulani; Jeanne Datz, Hilton Hotels; Nancy Daniels, Kahala Hilton; Dianne Doer, Kona Hilton; Rudy Bosma, Lanai City Service; Donn Takahashi and Carol Dawson, Maui Prince Hotel; Dennis Costa, Maui Hill; Kim Marshall, Grand Wailea Resort; Sheila Donnelly, Diana Reutter, Julie Char, Sweetie Aiwohi Nelson, Deborah Sharkey of Sheila Donnelly & Associates; Sandi Kato-Klutke, Aston Kauai Beach Villa; Barbara Sheehan, Sheraton Moana Surfrider; Sally Proctor, Aston Hotels; Norm Manzione, Suntrips; Renee Cochran and Will Titus, Colony Resorts; Linda Darling-Mann, Coco Palms Resort. To all of you, my deepest aloha.

CONTENTS

MAPS

MAP SYMBOLS

━━━━ FREEWAY

──── MAIN HIGHWAY

──── SECONDARY ROAD

─ ─ ─ JEEP TRAIL

─·─·─ FOOT TRAIL

 HIGHWAY NUMBER

 WATER

 MOUNTAIN

 LARGE TOWN OR CITY

O TOWN OR VILLAGE

 POINT OF INTEREST

• STATE OR BEACH PARK

 HEIAU

▲ CAMPGROUND

● HOTEL/ACCOMMODATION

✈ AIRPORT

CHARTS

SPECIAL TOPICS

ABBREVIATIONS

4WD = four-wheel drive
HVB = Hawaii Visitors Bureau
incl. = included
p/d = per day
p/h = per hour

p/w = per week
RT = roundtrip
St. Mon. = State Monument
YH = youth hostel

IS THIS BOOK OUT OF DATE?

In today's world, things change so rapidly that it's impossible for one person to keep up with everything happening in any one place. This is particularly true in Hawaii, where situations are always in flux. Travel books are like automobiles: they require fine tuning and frequent overhauls to keep in shape. Help us keep this book in shape! We require input from our readers so that we can continue to provide the best, most current information available. Please write to let us know about any inaccuracies, new information, or misleading suggestions. Although we try to make our maps as accurate as possible, errors do occur. If you have any suggestions for improvement or places that should be included, please let us know about them.

We especially appreciate letters from female travelers, visiting expatriates, local residents, and hikers and outdoor enthusiasts. We also like hearing from experts in the field as well as from local hotel owners and individuals wishing to accommodate visitors from abroad.

As you travel through the islands, keep notes in the margins of this book. Notes written on the spot are always more accurate than those put down on paper later. If you take a photograph during your trip that you feel might be included in future editions, please send it to us. Send only good slide duplicates or glossy black-and-white prints. Drawings and other artwork are also appreciated. If we use your photo or drawing, you'll be mentioned in the credits and receive a free copy of the book. Keep in mind, however, that the publisher cannot return any materials unless you include a self-addressed, stamped envelope. Moon Publications will own the rights on all material submitted. Address your letter to:

J.D. Bisignani
Moon Publications
P.O. Box 3040
Chico, CA 95927-3040, USA

BOB RACE

INTRODUCTION

The island of Hawaii is grand in so many ways. Its two nicknames, "The Orchid Island" and "The Volcano Island," are both excellent choices: the island produces more of the delicate blooms than anywhere else on earth; and Pele, the fire goddess who makes her mythological home here, regularly sends rivers of lava from the world's largest and most active volcanoes. However, to the people who live here, Hawaii has only one real nickname, "The Big Island." Big isn't necessarily better, but when you combine it with beautiful, uncrowded, traditional, and inexpensive, it's hard to beat.

The Big Island was the first to be inhabited by the Polynesian settlers, yet it's geologically the youngest of the Hawaiian Islands at barely a million years old. Like all the islands in the Hawaiian chain, it's a mini-continent whose geographical demarcations are much more apparent because of its size. There are parched deserts, steaming fissures, jet-black sand beaches, raw semi-cooled lava flows, snow-covered mountains, entire forests encased in hardened stone, and lush valleys where countless waterfalls break through the rock faces of 1,000-foot-tall chasms. There are small working villages that time has passed by, the state's most tropical city, and an arid coast stretching over 90 miles where the sun is guaranteed to shine. You'll find some of the islands' least expensive accommodations as well as some of the world's most exclusive resorts.

Historically, the Big Island is loaded with religious upheavals, the births and deaths of great people, vintage missionary homes and churches, reconstructed *heiau,* and even a royal palace. Here is the country's largest privately owned ranch, where cowboy life is the norm; America's only coffee plantations; and enclaves of the counterculture, where people with alternative lifestyles are still trying to keep the faith of the '60s.

Sportspeople love it here, too. The Big Island is a mecca for triathletes and offers snow skiing in season, plenty of camping and hiking, and the best marlin waters in all the oceans of the world.

There are direct flights to the Big Island, where the fascination of perhaps not "old" Hawaii, but definitely "simple" Hawaii, still lingers.

OVERVIEW

Hilo on the east coast and Kailua-Kona on the west are the two ports of entry to the Big Island. At opposite ends of the island as well as of the cultural spectrum, the two have a friendly rivalry. It doesn't matter at which one you arrive, because a trip to the Big Island without visiting both is unthinkable. Better yet, split your stay and use each as a base while you tour. The Big Island is the only Hawaiian island big enough that you can't drive around it comfortably in one day, nor should you try. Each of the six districts is interesting enough to spend at least one day exploring.

Hilo And Vicinity

Hilo is the oldest port of entry, the most tropical town in Hawaii, and the only major city built on the island's windward coast. The city is one tremendous greenhouse where exotic flowers and tropical plants are a normal part of the landscape, and entire blocks canopied by adjoining banyans are taken for granted. The town, which hosts the yearly Merrie Monarch Festival, boasts an early morning fish market, Japanese gardens, the Lyman House Museum, and a profusion of natural phenomena, including Rainbow Falls and Boiling Pots. Plenty of rooms in Hilo are generally easily available, and its variety of restaurants will titillate anyone's taste buds. Both go easy on the pocketbook while maintaining high standards.

Saddle Road begins just outside of Hilo. It slices directly across the island through a most astonishing high valley or "saddle" separating the mountains of Mauna Loa and Mauna Kea. Passable, but the bane of car-rental companies, it heads 13,796 feet up to the top of Mauna Kea, where a series of astronomical observatories peer into the heavens through the clearest air on earth.

Northeast

Hamakua refers to the entire northeast coast, where streams, wind, and pounding surf have chiseled the lava into towering cliffs and precipitous valleys known locally by the unromantic name of "gulches." All the flatlands here are awash in a green sea of sugarcane. A spur road from the forgotten town of Honomu leads to

copter over lava

J.D. BISIGNANI

Akaka Falls, whose waters tumble over a 442-foot cliff—the highest sheer drop of water in Hawaii. North along the coastal road is Honokaa, a one-street town of stores, restaurants, and crafts shops. The main road bears left here to the cowboy town of Waimea, but a smaller road inches farther north. It dead-ends at the top of Waipio Valley, cradled by cliffs on three sides with its mouth wide open to the sea. The valley is reachable only by foot, 4WD vehicle, or horseback. On its verdant floor a handful of families live simply by raising taro, a few head of cattle, and horses. Waipio was a burial ground of Hawaiian *ali'i*, where *kahuna* traditionally came to commune with spirits. The enchantment of this "power spot" remains.

Southeast

Puna lies south of Hilo and makes up the majority of the southeast coast. Here are the greatest lava fields that have spewed from Kilauea, the heart of Volcanoes National Park. An ancient flow embraced a forest in its fiery grasp, entombing trees that stand like sentinels today in Lava Tree State Monument. Cape Kumukahi, a pointed lava flow that reached the ocean in 1868, is officially the easternmost point in Hawaii. Just below it is a string of beaches featuring ebony-black sand. Past the small village of Kalapana, the road skirts the coast before it dead-ends where it has been covered over by lava. Chain of Craters Road is now passable only *from* Hawaii Volcanoes National Park. Wahaula Visitor Center has been torched by lava, but the Wahaula Heiau, where human sacrifice was introduced to the islands, survived and can be reached on foot if conditions permit. Chain of Craters Road spills off the mountain through a forbidding, yet vibrant, wasteland of old lava flows until it comes to the sea, where this living volcano fumes and throbs. Atop the vol-

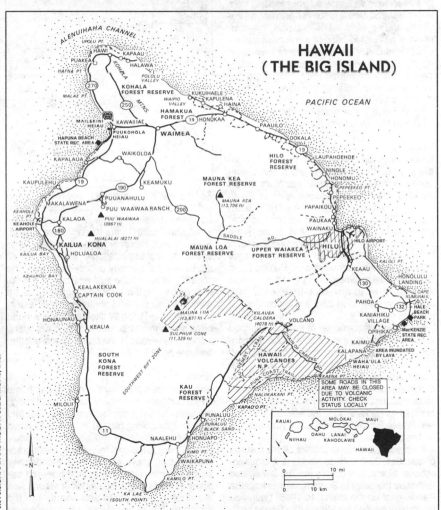

cano, miles of hiking trails crisscross the park and lead to the very summit of Mauna Loa. You can view the natural phenomena of steaming fissures, boiling mud, Devastation Trail, and Thurston Lava Tube, large enough to accommodate a subway train. Here, too, you can lodge or dine at Volcano House, a venerable inn carved into the rim of the crater.

Kau, the southern tip of the island, is primarily a desert. On well-marked trails leading from the main road you'll discover ancient petroglyphs and an eerie set of footprints, the remnants of an ill-fated band of warriors who were smothered under the moist ash of a volcanic eruption and whose demise marked the ascendancy of Kamehameha the Great. Here are some lovely beaches and state parks you'll have virtually to yourself. A tiny road leads to Ka Lae ("South Point"), the most southerly piece of ground in the United States.

Kona

Kona, the west coast, is in every way the opposite of Hilo. It's dry, sunny, and brilliant, with large expanses of old barren lava flows. When watered, the rich soil blossoms, as in South Kona, renowned for its diminutive coffee plantations. The town of Captain Cook, named after the intrepid Pacific explorer, lies just above the very beach where he was slain because of a terrible miscommunication two centuries ago. Ironically, nearby is the restored Pu'uhonua o Honaunau Heiau, where mercy and forgiveness were rendered to any *kapu*-breaker or vanquished warrior who made it into the confines of this safe refuge.

Kailua-Kona is the center of Kona. The airport is just north and here is a concentration of condos and hotels. The town itself boasts an array of art and designer shops; world-class triathletes come here to train, and charter boats depart in search of marlin. Within Kailua is Mokuaikaua Church, a legacy of the very first packet of missionaries to arrive in the islands; and Hulihee Palace, vacation home of the Kamehameha line of kings.

Northward, the Kona District offers a string of beaches. Just outside Kailua is a clothing-optional beach, one of very few in Hawaii, and farther up the coast in South Kohala is Hapuna Beach, best on the island. In 1965, Laurence Rockefeller opened the Mauna Kea Resort here.

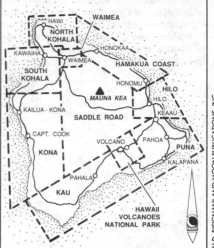

BIG ISLAND REGIONS

©J.D. BISIGNANI AND MOON PUBLICATIONS, INC.

For the last three decades, this resort, along with its sculptured, coast-hugging golf course, has been considered one of the finest in the world. Just south is the Kona Village Resort, whose guests can arrive at a private airstrip to spend the night in a "simple" grass shack on the beach. Its serenity is broken only by the soothing music of the surf and by the not-so-melodious singing of "Kona nightingales," a pampered herd of wild donkeys that frequents this area. The Hilton Waikoloa Village is here, billed as the most fabulous resort on earth, and just down the road is the Mauna Lani, another first-rate hotel.

North

North Kohala is primarily the peninsular thumb on the northern extremity of the island, although the area does dip south along the coast and eastward into rolling hills. At its base is Waimea (Kamuela), center of the enormous Parker Ranch. Here in the cool mountains, cattle graze in chest-high grass and *paniolo,* astride their sturdy mounts, ride herd in time-honored tradition. Hunters range the slopes of Mauna Kea in search of wild goats and boars, and the Fourth of July is boisterously acknowledged by the wild whoops of cowboys at the world-class Parker Ranch Rodeo. Along the coast are beach parks, empty except for an occasional local family picnic. A series of *heiau* dot the coast, and on the northernmost tip a broad plain overlooking a sweeping panorama marks the birthplace of Kamehameha the Great. The main town up here is Hawi, holding on after the sugar companies pulled out a few years ago. Down the road is Kapaau, where Kamehameha's statue resides in fulfillment of a *kahuna* prophecy. Along this little-traveled road, a handful of artists offer their crafts in small shops. At road's end is the overlook of Pololu Valley, where a steep descent takes you to secluded beaches and camping in an area once frequented by some of the most powerful sorcerers in the land.

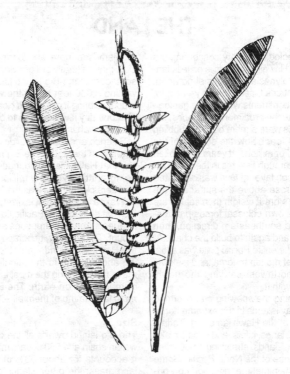

heliconia

DIANA LASICH HARPER

DIANA LASICH HARPER

THE LAND

The modern geological theory concerning the formation of the Hawaiian Islands is no less fanciful than the Polynesian legends sung about it. Science maintains that 30 million years ago, while the great continents were being geologically tortured into their rudimentary shapes, the Hawaiian Islands were a mere ooze of bubbling magma 20,000 feet below the surface of the primordial sea. For millions of years this molten rock flowed up through fissures in the sea floor. Slowly, layer upon layer of lava was deposited until an island rose above the surface of the sea. The island's great weight then sealed the fissures, whose own colossal forces progressively crept in a southeastern direction, then burst out again and again to build the chain. At the same time, the entire Pacific plate was afloat on a giant sea of molten magma, and it slowly glided to the northwest carrying the newly formed islands with it.

In the beginning the spewing crack formed Kure and Midway islands in the extreme northwestern sector of the Hawaiian chain. Today, more than 130 islands, islets, and shoals make up the Hawaiian Islands, stretching 1,600 miles across an expanse of the North Pacific. Some geologists maintain that the "hot spot" now primarily under the Big Island remains relatively stationary, and that the 1,600-mile spread of the Hawaiian archipelago is due to a northwest drifting effect of about three to five inches per year. Still, with the center of activity under the Big Island, Mauna Loa and Kilauea volcanoes

regularly add more land to the only state in the U.S. that is literally still growing. About 30 miles southeast of the Big Island is Loihi Seamount, waiting 3,000 feet below the waves. Frequent eruptions bring it closer and closer to the surface until one day it will emerge to become the newest Hawaiian island.

Science and *The Kumulipo* oral history differ sharply on the age of the Big Island. Scientists say that Hawaii is the youngest of the islands, being a little over one million years old; the chanters claim that it was the first "island-child" of Wakea and Papa. It is, irrefutably, closest to the "hot spot" on the Pacific floor, evidenced by Kilauea's frequent eruptions and by Loihi Seamount. The geology, geography, and location of the Hawaiian Islands, and their ongoing drifting and building in the middle of the Pacific, make them among the most fascinating pieces of real estate on earth. The Big Island is the *most* fascinating of them all—it is truly unique.

Size

The Big Island dwarfs all the others in the Hawaiian chain at 4,038 square miles and growing. It accounts for about 63% of the state's total land mass; the other islands could fit within it two times over. With 266 miles of coastline, the island stretches about 95 miles from north to south and 80 miles from east to west. Cape Kumukahi is the easternmost point in the state, and Ka Lae ("South Point") is the southernmost point in the country.

The Mountains

The tremendous volcanic peak of **Mauna Kea** ("White Mountain"), located in north-central Hawaii, has been extinct for over 4,000 years. Its seasonal snowcap earns Mauna Kea its name and reputation as a good skiing area in winter. Over 18,000 feet of mountain below the surface rises straight up from the ocean floor— making Mauna Kea actually 31,796 feet tall, a substantial 2,768 feet taller than Mt. Everest; some consider it the tallest mountain in the world. At 13,796 feet above sea level, it is without doubt the tallest peak in the Pacific. Near its top, at 13,020 feet, is **Lake Waiau,** the highest lake in the state and third highest in the country. Mauna Kea was obviously a sacred mountain to the Hawaiians, and its white dome was a welcome beacon to seafarers. On its slope is the largest adze quarry in Polynesia, from which high-quality basalt was taken to be fashioned into prized tools. The atmosphere atop the mountain, which sits mid-Pacific far from pollutants, is the most rarefied and cleanest on earth. The clarity makes Mauna Kea a natural for astronomical observatories. The complex of telescopes on its summit is internationally staffed and provides data to scientists around the world.

The **Kohala Mountains** to the northwest are the oldest. This section looks more like the other Hawaiian islands, with deep gorges and valleys along the coast and a forested interior. As you head east toward Waimea from Kawaihae on Route 19, for every mile that you travel you pick up about 10 inches of rainfall per year. This becomes obvious as you begin to pass little streams and rivulets running from the mountains.

Mount Hualalai at 8,271 feet is the backdrop to Kailua-Kona. It's home to many of the Big Island's endangered birds and supports many of the region's newest housing developments. Just a few years ago, Mt. Hualalai was thought to be extinct, since the last time it erupted was in 1801. Recently, volcanologists using infrared technology have discovered the mountain to be red-hot again. The U.S. Geological Survey has listed this sleeper as the fourth most dangerous volcano in the U.S., because when it does erupt, it's expected to produce a tremendous amount of lava that will pour rapidly down its steep sides. The scientists, whose opinion is seconded by local Hawaiians, say that the mountain will blow within the next 10 years. The housing developers don't say anything.

Even though **Mauna Loa** ("Long Mountain") measures a respectable 13,677 feet, its height isn't its claim to fame. This active volcano, 60 miles long by 30 wide, is comprised of 10,000 cubic miles of iron-hard lava, making it the densest and most massive mountain on earth. In 1950, a tremendous lava flow belched from Mauna Loa's summit, reaching an astonishing rate of 6,750,000 cubic yards per hour. Seven lava rivers flowed for 23 days, emitting over 600 million cubic yards of lava that covered 35 square miles. There were no injuries, but the villages of Kaapuna and Honokua were partially destroyed along with the Magoo Ranch.

Kilauea, whose pragmatic name means "The Spewing," is the world's most active volcano. In the last hundred years, it has erupted on the average once every 11 months. The Hawaiians believed that the goddess Pele inhabited every volcano in the Hawaiian chain, and that her home is now Halemaumau Crater in Kilauea Caldera. Kilauea is the most scientifically watched volcano in the world, with a permanent observatory built right into the crater rim. When it erupts, the flows are so predictable that observers run toward the mountain, not away from it! The flows, however, can burst from fis-

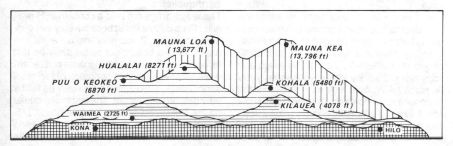

sures far from the center of the crater in areas that don't seem "active." This occurs mainly in the Puna District. In 1959, Kilauea Iki Crater came to life after 91 years, and although the flow wasn't as massive as others, it did send blazing fountains of lava 1,900 feet into the air. Kilauea has been very active within the last few years, with eruptions occurring at least once a month and expected to continue. Most activity has been from a yet unnamed vent below Pu'uo. You might be lucky enough to see this phenomenon while visiting.

Island Builders

The Hawaiians worshiped Madame Pele, the fire goddess. Her name translates equally as "volcano," "fire pit," or "eruption of lava." When she was angry, she complained by spitting fire which cooled and formed land. Volcanologists say that the islands are huge mounds of cooled basaltic lava surrounded by billions of polyp skeletons which have formed coral reefs. The Hawaiian Islands are shield volcanoes that erupt gently and form an elongated dome much like a turtle shell. The Big Island is a perfect example of this. Once the lava is above the surface of the sea, its tremendous weight seals the fissure below. Eventually the giant tube that carried lava to the surface sinks in on itself and forms a caldera, as evidenced atop Kilauea. More eruptions occur periodically, and they cover the already existing island like frosting on a titanic cake. Wind and water take over next and relentlessly sculpt the raw lava into deep crevices and cuts that become valleys. The once-smooth Kohala Mountains, once a single, smooth block typical of a shield volcano, are now a jagged, multispired mountain range due to this process.

Lava

Lava flows in two distinct types, for which the Hawaiian names have become universal geological terms: a'a and pa'hoehoe. They're easily distinguished in appearance, but chemically they're the same. A'a' is extremely rough and spiny and will quickly tear up your shoes if you do much hiking over it. Also, if you have the misfortune to fall down, you'll immediately know why they call it a'a. Pa'hoehoe, a billowy, ropy lava that looks like burned pancake batter, can mold itself into fantastic shapes. Examples of

both lavas are frequently encountered on various hikes throughout the Big Island. Other lava oddities that you may spot are peridots (green, gemlike stones called "Pele's Diamonds"); clear, feldsparlike, white cotton candy called "Pele's hair"; and gray lichens known as "Hawaiian snow" covering the older flows. For a full account of recent lava flows and eruptions, see pp. 216-217.

Tsunamis

"Tsunami" is the Japanese word for "tidal wave." It ranks up there with the worst of them in sparking horror in human beings. But if you were to count up all the people in Hawaii who have been swept away by tidal waves in the last 50 years, the toll wouldn't come close to those killed on bicycles in only a few Mainland cities in just five years. A Hawaiian tsunami is actually a seismic sea wave that has been generated by an earthquake that could easily have originated thousands of miles away in South America or Alaska. Some waves have been clocked at speeds up to 500 mph. The safest place during a tsunami, besides high ground well away from beach areas, is out on the open ocean where even an enormous wave is perceived only as a large swell—a tidal wave is only dangerous when it is opposed by land. Hilo has been struck with the two worst tidal waves in modern history. A giant wave smashed the islands on April 1, 1946, and swept away 159 people and over 1,300 homes; Hilo sustained most of these losses. Again, on May 23, 1960, Hilo took the brunt of a wave that rumbled through the business district, killing 61 people. There is an elaborate warning system throughout the island; warning procedures and inundation maps are listed in the front of the telephone directory.

Earthquakes

These rumblings are also a concern in Hawaii and offer a double threat because they can generate tsunamis. If you ever feel a tremor and are close to a beach, get as far away as fast as possible. The Big Island, because of its active volcanoes, experiences hundreds of technical earthquakes, although 99% can only be felt by very delicate equipment. The last major quake on the Big Island occurred in late Nov. 1975, reaching 7.2 on the Richter scale and causing many millions of dollars' worth of damage in the

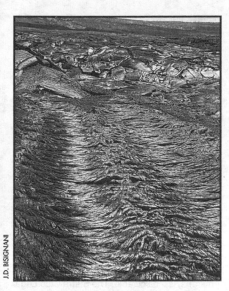

pa'hoehoe *lava*

island's southern regions. The only loss of life occurred when a beach collapsed and two people from a large camping party were drowned.

Beaches, Ponds, And The Coast

The Big Island takes the rap for having poor beaches—this isn't true! They are certainly few and far between, but they are spectacular. Hawaii is big and young, so distances are greater than on other islands, and the wave action hasn't had enough time to grind the new lava into sand. The Kona and Kohala coast beaches, along with a few nooks and crannies around Hilo, are gorgeous. Puna's beaches are incredible black sand, and the southern part of the island has a string of hidden beaches enjoyed only by those intrepid enough to get to them. Full listings are found in the various travel chapters under "Beaches."

Makalawena, just north of Keahole airport on a rough coastal trail, has a beautiful white-sand beach. Inland is its associated wetland pond, probably the most important one on the Big Island. This fragile and archaeologically important area is managed by the Bishop Estate, tel. 322-6088. Currently entry is not allowed, except with a U.S. Fish and Wildlife Service official or a state biologist. However, the Sierra Club and Audubon Society are permitted to enter, and you can arrange to accompany them on a field trip. If you wish to visit this beautiful area, consider contacting these organizations long before your trip to the Big Island. The second most important body of water is near Honokohau Beach. For details see p. 240.

Protecting The Coral Reef

Currently controversy is raging over an attempt to place anchoring pins in the hard lava rock just off the Kailua-Kona Coast. Boats could latch onto them, and by doing so would not drag their anchors across the fragile coral reef, as is now the case. The Dive Council in Kona isn't known for agreeing on many issues because they represent so many different factions, but on this issue they agree unanimously that the pins should be put in place. So, they collectively decided to make a move in favor of the pins, which have been used successfully all over the world. The process is environmentally sound, and in fact the technology specifically needed for drilling in lava rock was worked out at the University of Hawaii. After three years elapsed, during which the Department of Land and Natural Resources debated whether it was their responsibility or that of the Hawaii Department of Transportation to implement the program, the Dive Council went ahead and put in the pins, without the moorings. Upstaged, the Department of Land and Natural Resources was furious and at meetings tried to find a scapegoat at which they could throw their bureaucratic book. They would be better served spending their energies protecting the reef.

In a separate issue, the Department of Land and Natural Resources is attempting to trade 450 acres of state land surrounding Kua Bay (just north of the airport in Kona). This magnificent area has a secluded beach that is very popular with local people, and is well documented as having significant archaeological sites. In return, from international land developers, they will receive 340 acres of rocky coastal land that isn't nearly as beautiful, and coincidentally would be difficult to develop as a resort.

Geothermal Controversy

Pele's blood-red lava is cool compared to the uncompromising debate now sizzling between natives' rights groups allied with environmentalists, and geothermal advocates who view the the the Big Island's molten core as an infinite source of power. Governor John D. Waihee, with strong support from the state's legislators, has sanctioned the construction of a geothermal well within the 27,000 acres that make up the **Wao Kele O Puna Rainforest**—the *only* tropical lowland rainforest in the United States! Another 20 power plants will bore into the east rift of Kilauea Volcano, and all will require huge steam collection systems, power plants, power lines, and towers that will march across the most expansive and pristine panoramas that the island has to offer. Adding to the magnitude of this engineering feat (the largest developmental plan of any type ever attempted in Hawaii) will be a deep ocean cable stretching from the Big Island to Maui, and on to Oahu. Transversing an unstable ocean canyon over 6,500 feet deep, the cable, with an estimated cost of $3 billion, will lie at more than seven times the depth of any cable laid thus far anywhere in the world. The major developers, Hawaii's Campbell Estates, and True Geothermal of Casper, Wyoming, envision generating about 500 megawatts of electricity, about four times the amount needed by the Big Island at the present rate of consumption. The power will be used to further develop Kona, on the Big Island; the substantial excess will be exported to Oahu and Maui. Residents of Puna, where the development will occur, can see no benefit in despoiling their homes and environment in order to fuel the ravenous demands generated by tourism on the islands.

One of the constituents of the anti-geothermal coalition, the **Pele Defense Fund**, views the development as a desecration of the land according to traditional religion, believing that each well is a puncture wound in Pele's side. To these local people, many of whom are native Hawaiians who trace their lineage directly to Pele, and who feel protected by her, the drilling amounts to no less than sacrilege. Having recently lost a local court battle claiming that the area has religious significance, they plan to carry on the fight all the way to the Supreme Court. The Pele Defense Fund points out that the wells are being drilled over extremely unstable land that is susceptible to a rampaging lava flow at any time. A destroyed well could

pump incalculable volumes of hydrogen sulfide gas into the atmosphere. They also contend that most of the jobs at the sites are low-paying maintenance jobs that will hardly benefit the local economy, and that the higher-paying managerial positions will be given to new arrivals brought in from the Mainland.

To environmentally aware botanists and entomologists, the despoiling of any of the precious and dwindling rainforest is a nightmare (see "Tropical Rainforests" on pp. 17-18). Even one footfall in a 2,000-year-old bog-floored rainforest can take months and even years to disappear. Native species of plants could be made extinct through the introduction of foreign species inadvertently carried by workers and machinery, while the ruts left by construction could become stagnant pools breeding mosquito larvae that affect native birds. The destruction caused by heavy trucks, earth-moving machinery, site deforestation, and the constant maintenance of the site, in these fragile environs, is incalculable. The Sierra Club Legal Defense Fund has been attempting to force the Environmental Protection Agency, Army Corps of Engineers, U.S. Geological Survey, Department of Energy, and National Park Service— the federal agencies involved in the project—to prepare an environmental impact statement which, unbelievably, has not been done to date! The Sierra Club seeks a moratorium placed on construction until a study is done. All scientists agree that once a rainforest is destroyed, or disturbed, it is virtually gone forever.

Proponents of the geothermal power plants point to the fact that Hawaii is *the* most oil-dependent state in America. They say that the building of the pollution-free plants will save millions of barrels of oil over the years, reduce air pollutants, and help reduce the threat to Hawaii's coastline due to oil spills. Ormat Energy Systems of Sparks, Nevada, who purchased Puna Geothermal Venture, the previous plant operator, claims that its geothermal technology provides for a "closed system" that will pump any residual geothermal brine and steam back into the earth, while absolutely eliminating any foul smell of hydrogen sulfide gas. Opponents say that the vast majority of Hawaii's imported petroleum is used for automobiles and aircraft, and that the development of alternative sources of power like solar and wind energy, along with increased conservation, could easily make up for the purported savings.

The real issue in the development of geothermal electrical power generation on the Big Island is the priorities of modern American society: power and profits now for large developers and corporations, or the preservation of the earth's wild places for future generations. Neither seems able to wait.

Environmental Resource Groups

Anyone interested in Hawaii's environmental issues could contact the following for more information: **Hawaii Green Movement,** Box 61508, Honolulu, HI 96839; **Sierra Club Legal Defense Fund,** 212 Merchant St., Suite 202, Honolulu, HI 96813, tel. 599-2436; **Pele Defense Fund,** Box 404, Volcano, HI 96875, tel. 935-1663; **Rainforest Action Network,** 301 Broadway, Suite A, San Francisco, CA 94133, tel. (415) 398-4404.

Environment Hawaii, 733 Bishop St., Honolulu, HI 96813, tel. 934-0115, individual subscription rate $35 per year, is a savvy monthly newsletter that focuses on environmental and political issues facing Hawaii today. The well-researched and concisely written newsletter attempts to be fair to all parties concerned, explaining both sides to most controversies. Short on preaching and long on common sense, *Environment Hawaii* is an excellent resource for anyone interested in sociopolitical and environmental issues.

For environmental tours see "Getting Around."

CLIMATE

The average temperature around the island varies between 72 and 78° F. Summers raise the temperature to the mid-80s and winters cool off to the low 70s. Both Kona and Hilo seem to maintain a year-round average of about 80 degrees. As usual, it's cooler in the higher elevations, and Waimea (Kamuela) sees most days in the mid-60s to low 70s, while Volcanoes maintains a steady 60 degrees. Atop Mauna Kea, the temperature rarely climbs above 50° or dips below 30, while the summit of Mauna Loa is about 10 degrees warmer.

Rainfall

Weatherwise the Big Island's climate varies not so much in temperature, but precipitation. Hawaii has some of the wettest and driest coastal (tourist) areas in the islands. The line separating wet from dry can be dramatic. Waimea, for example, has an actual dry and wet side of town, as if a boundary line split the town in two! Houses on the dry side are at a premium. Kona and Hilo are opposites. The Kona Coast is almost guaranteed to be sunny and bright, receiving as little as 15 inches of rainfall per year. Both Kona and the Kau Desert to the south are in the rain shadow of Mauna Loa, and most rain clouds coming from east to west are pierced by its summit before they ever reach Kona. Hilo is wet, with predictable afternoon and evening showers—they make the entire town blossom.

Though this reputation keeps many tourists away, the rain's predictability makes it easy to avoid a drenching while exploring the town. Hilo does get as much as 150 inches of rainfall per year, with a record of 153.93 inches set in 1971. It also holds the dubious honor of being the town with the most rainfall recorded by the National Weather Service in a 24-hour period—a drenching 22.3 inches in Feb. 1979.

"So Good" Weather

The ancient Hawaiians had words to describe climatic specifics such as rain, wind, fog, and even snow, but they didn't have a general word for "weather." The reason is that the weather is just about the same throughout the year and depends more on where you are on any given island than on what season it is. The Hawaiians did distinguish between *kau* (summer, May-Oct.) and *hoo'ilo* (winter, Nov.-April), but this distinction included social, religious, and even navigational factors, far beyond a mere distinction of weather variations.

The average daytime temperature throughout Hawaii is about 80° F (26° C), with the average winter (January) day registering 78°, and the average summer (August) day raising the thermometer only seven degrees to 85. Nighttime temperatures drop less than 10 degrees. Altitude, however, does drop temperatures about three degrees for every 1,000 feet; if you

AVERAGE MAXIMUM/MINIMUM TEMPERATURE AND RAINFALL

TOWN		JAN.	MARCH	MAY	JUNE	SEPT.	NOV.
Hilo	high	79	79	80	82	82	80
	low	62	62	61	70	70	65
	rain	11	15	7	10	10	15
Kona	high	80	81	81	82	82	81
	low	62	64	65	68	68	63
	rain	4	3	2	0	2	1

temperature in °F, rainfall in inches

intend to visit the mountain peaks of Mauna Loa and Mauna Kea (both over 10,000 feet), expect the temperature to be at least 30 degrees cooler than at sea level. Recently snows lasted atop Mauna Kea well into June, with nighttime temperatures well below freezing; the hottest day ever recorded was in 1931 in the Puna District of the Big Island—a scorching (for Hawaii) 100 degrees.

The Trade Winds
Temperatures in the 50th state are both constant and moderate because of the trade winds. These breezes are so prevailing that the northeast sides of the islands are always referred to as **windward,** regardless of where the wind happens to blow on any given day. You can count on the trades to be blowing on an average of 300 days per year, hardly missing a day during summer, and occurring half the time in winter. They blow throughout the day but are strong during the heat of the afternoon, then weaken at night. Just when you need a cooling breeze, there they are, and when the temperature drops at night, it's as if someone turned down a giant fan.

The trade winds are also a factor in keeping down the humidity. They will suddenly disappear, however, usually in winter, and might not resume for a few weeks. The Tropic of Cancer runs through the center of Hawaii, yet the latitude's famed oppressively hot and muggy weather is joyfully absent in the islands. Honolulu, on the same latitude as sweaty Hong

Kong and Havana, has only a 50-60% daily humidity factor.

Kona Winds
Kona means "leeward" in Hawaiian, and when the trades stop blowing, these southerly winds often take over. To anyone from Hawaii, "*kona* wind" is a euphemism for bad weather, for it brings in hot, sticky air. Luckily, *kona* winds are most common Oct.-April, when they appear roughly half the time. The temperatures drop slightly during the winter so these hot winds are tolerable, and even useful for moderating the thermometer. In the summer they are awful, but luckily again they hardly ever blow during this season.

A *kona* storm is another matter. These subtropical low-pressure storms develop west of the Hawaiian Islands, and as they move east draw winds up from the south. Usual only in winter, they can cause considerable damage to crops and real estate. There is no real pattern to *kona* storms—some years they come every few weeks while in other years they don't appear at all.

Bad Weather
With all this talk of ideal weather it might seem as if there isn't any bad. Read on. When a storm does hit an island, conditions can be bleak and miserable. The worst storms are in the winter and often have the warped sense of humor to drop their heaviest rainfalls on areas that are normally quite dry. It's not infrequent for a storm

WIND AND WAVES

SHORE   BREAKERS   SWELLS   CHOPS   RIPPLES   WIND

to dump more than three inches of rain an hour; this can go as high as 10, making Hawaiian rainfalls some of the heaviest on earth.

Hawaii has also been hit with some walloping hurricanes in the last few decades. There haven't been many but they've been destructive. The vast majority of hurricanes originate far to the southeast off the Pacific coasts of Mexico and Latin America. Most pass harmlessly south of Hawaii but some, swept along by *kona* winds, strike the islands. The most recent and destructive was Hurricane Iniki, which battered the islands in 1992. It had its greatest effect on Niihau, the Poipu Beach area of Kauai, and the leeward coast of Oahu.

No alien land in all the world has any deep, strong charm for me, but that one; no other land could so longingly and beseechingly haunt my sleeping and waking, through half a lifetime, as that one has done. Other things leave me, but it abides.

—Mark Twain, c. 1889

DIANA LASICH HARPER

FLORA AND FAUNA

THE MYSTERY OF MIGRATION

Anyone who loves a mystery will be intrigued by the speculation about how plants and animals first came to Hawaii. Most people's idea of an island paradise includes swaying palms, dense mysterious jungles ablaze with wildflowers, and luscious fruits just waiting to be plucked. In fact, for millions of years the Hawaiian chain consisted of raw and barren islands where no plants grew and no birds sang. Why? Because they are geological orphans that spontaneously popped up in the middle of the Pacific Ocean. The islands, more than 2,000 miles from any continental landfall, were therefore isolated from the normal ecological spread of plants and animals. Even the most tenacious travelers of the flora and fauna kingdoms would be sorely tried in crossing the mighty Pacific. Those that made it by pure chance found a totally foreign ecosystem. They had to adapt or perish. The survivors evolved quickly, and many plants and birds became so specialized that they were not only limited to specific islands in the chain but to habitats that frequently encompassed a single isolated valley. It was as if after traveling so far, and finding a niche, they never budged again. Luckily, the soil of Hawaii was virgin and rich, the competition from other plants or animals was nonexistent, and the climate was sufficiently varied and nearly perfect for most growing things.

The evolution of plants and animals on the isolated islands was astonishingly rapid. A tremendous change in environment, coupled with a limited gene pool, accelerated natural selection. For example, many plants lost their protective thorns and spines because there were no grazing animals or birds to destroy them. Before settlement, Hawaii had no fruits, vegetables, coconut palms, edible land animals, conifers, mangroves, or banyans. Tropical flowers, wild and vibrant as we know them today, were relatively few. In a land where thousands of orchids now brighten every corner, there were only four native varieties, the least in any of the 50 states. Today, the indigenous plants and animals have the highest rate of extinction anywhere on earth. By the beginning of this century, native plants growing below 1,500 feet in elevation were almost completely extinct or totally replaced by introduced species. The land and its living things have been greatly transformed by humans and their agriculture. This inexorable process began when Hawaii was the domain of its original Polynesian settlers, then greatly accelerated when the land was inundated by Western peoples.

The indigenous plants and birds of the Big Island have suffered the same fate as those of the other Hawaiian Islands; they're among the most endangered species on earth and disappearing at an alarming rate. There are some sanctuaries on the Big Island where native species still live, but they must be vigorously protected. Do your bit to save them; enjoy but do not disturb.

PLANTS, FLOWERS, AND TREES

Hawaii's indigenous and endemic plants, flowers, and trees are both fascinating and beautiful, but unfortunately, like everything else that was native, they are quickly disappearing. The majority of flora considered exotic by visitors was introduced either by the original Polynesians or by later white settlers. The Polynesians who colonized Hawaii brought foodstuffs, including coconuts, bananas, taro, breadfruit, sweet potatoes, yams, and sugarcane. They also carried along gourds to use as containers, *awa* to make a basic intoxicant, and the ti plant to use for offerings or to string into *hula* skirts. Non-Hawaiian settlers over the years have brought mangos, papayas, passion fruit, pineapples, and the other tropical fruits and vegetables associated with the islands. Also, most of the flowers, including protea, plumeria, anthuriums, orchids, heliconia, ginger, and most hibiscus, have come

from every continent on earth. Tropical America, Asia, Java, India, and China have contributed their most beautiful and delicate blooms. Hawaii is blessed with national and state parks, gardens, undisturbed rainforests, private reserves, and commercial nurseries that offer an exhaustive botanical survey of the island. The following is a sampling of the common native and introduced flora that add dazzling color and exotic tastes to the landscape.

Native Trees

Koa and **ohia** are two indigenous trees still seen on the Big Island. Both have been greatly reduced by the foraging of introduced cattle and goats, and through logging and forest fires. The koa, a form of acacia, is Hawaii's finest native tree. It can grow to over 70 feet high and has a strong, straight trunk which can measure more than 10 feet in circumference. Koa is a very quickly growing legume that fixes nitrogen in the soil. It is believed that the tree originated in Africa, where it was very damp. It then migrated to Australia, where it was very dry, which caused the elimination of leaves so that all that was left were bare stems which could survive in the desert climate. When koa came to the Pacific islands, instead of reverting to the true leaf, it just broadened its leaf stem into sickle-shaped, leaf-like foliage that produces an inconspicuous, pale-yellow flower. When the tree is young or damaged it will revert to the original feathery, fernlike leaf that evolved in Africa millions of years ago. The koa does best in well-drained soil in deep forest areas, but scruffy specimens will grow on poorer soil. The Hawaiians used koa as the main log for their dugout canoes, and elaborate ceremonies were performed when a log was cut and dragged to a canoe shed. Koa wood was also preferred for paddles, spears, even surfboards. Today it is still, unfortunately, considered an excellent furniture wood, and although fine specimens can be found in the reserve of Hawaii Volcanoes National Park, loggers elsewhere are harvesting the last of the big trees.

The ohia is a survivor, and therefore the most abundant of all the native Hawaiian trees. Coming in a variety of shapes and sizes, it grows as miniature trees in wet bogs or 100-foot giants on cool, dark slopes at higher elevations. This tree is often the first life in new lava flows.

koa

LOUISE FOOTE

ohia-lehua

The ohia produces a tuftlike flower—usually red, but occasionally orange, yellow, or white, the latter being very rare and elusive—that resembles a natural pompon. The flower was considered sacred to Pele; it was said that she would cause a rainstorm if you picked ohia blossoms without the proper prayers. The flowers were fashioned into *lei* that resembled feather boas. The strong, hard wood was used to make canoes, poi bowls, and especially temple images. Ohia logs were also used as railroad ties and shipped to the Mainland from Pahoa. It's believed that the "golden spike" linking rail lines between the U.S. East and West coasts was driven into a Puna ohia log when the two railroads came together in Ogden, Utah.

Other Flora
The Hawaiians called the **prickly pear cactus** *panini,* which translates as "very unfriendly," undoubtedly because of the sharp spines covering the flat, thick leaves. The cactus is typical of those found in Mexico and the southwestern United States. It was introduced to Hawaii before 1810 and established itself coincidentally with the cattle brought in at the time; *panini* is

very common in North Kohala, especially on the Parker Ranch lands. It is assumed that Don Marin, a Spanish advisor to Kamehameha I, was responsible for importing the plant. Perhaps the early *paniolo* (cowboy) felt lonely without it. The *panini* can grow to heights of 15 feet and is now considered a pest, but nonetheless looks as if it belongs. It develops small and delicious pear-shaped fruits. Hikers who decide to pick the fruit should be careful of small, yellowish bristles that can burrow under the skin and irritate. The fruit turns into beautiful yellow and orange flowers measuring three inches across. An attempt is being made to control the cactus in *paniolo* country. *El cosano rojo,* the red worm found in the bottom of Mexican tequila, has been introduced to destroy the plant. It burrows into the cactus and eats the hardwood center, causing the plant to wither and die.

More species of **lobelia** grow in Hawaii than anywhere else in the world. A common garden flower elsewhere, in Hawaii it grows to tree height. You'll see some unique species covered with hair or with spikes. The lobelia flower is tiny and resembles a miniature orchid with curved and pointed ends, like the beak of the native *i'iwi.* This bird feeds on the flower's nectar; it's obvious that both evolved in Hawaii together and exhibit the strange phenomenon of nature mimicking nature.

The Big Island has more species of **gesneriad,** the African violet family, than anywhere else on earth. Many don't have the showy flowers that you normally associate with African violets

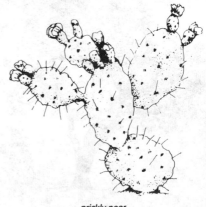

DIANA LASICH HARPER

prickly pear

J.D. BISIGNANI

Fiddlehead ferns are prevalent along trails where the lava has weathered.

but have evolved into strange species with huge, fuzzy leaves.

The **puahanul,** meaning "many flowers," is Hawaii's native hydrangea; it is common in the upland forests of the Big Island.

Ferns

If you travel to Volcanoes National Park you will find yourself deep in an amazing, high-altitude tropical rainforest. This unique forest exists because of the 120 inches of annual rainfall, which turns the raw lava into a lush forest. Besides stands of ohia and koa, you'll be treated to a primordial display of ferns. All new fronds on ferns are called "fiddleheads" because of the way they unfurl and resemble the scrolls of violin heads. Fiddleheads were eaten by Hawaiians during times of famine. The most common ferns are *hapuu,* a rather large tree fern, and *amauamau,* a smaller type with a more simple frond. A soft, furry growth around the base of the stalks is called *pulu.* At one time *pulu* was collected for stuffing mattresses, and a factory was located atop Volcanoes. But *pulu* breaks down and forms a very fine dust after a few years, so it never really became generally accepted for mattresses.

At high altitudes, young ferns and other plants will often produce new growth that turns bright red as protection against the sun's ultraviolet rays. You'll see it on new foliage before it hardens. Hawaiians called this new growth *liko.* Today, people still make *lei* from *liko* because it has so many subtle and beautiful colors. Ohia *liko* is a favorite for *lei* because it is so striking.

Tropical Rainforests

When it comes to pure and diverse natural beauty, the U.S. is one of the finest pieces of real estate on earth. As if purple mountains' majesty and fruited plains weren't enough, it even received a tiny, living emerald of tropical rainforest. A tropical rainforest is where the earth takes a breath and exhales pure sweet oxygen through its vibrant green canopy. Located in the territories of Puerto Rico and the Virgin Islands and in the state of Hawaii, these forests comprise only one-half of one percent of the world's total, and they must be preserved. The U.S. Congress passed two bills in 1986 designed to protect the unique biological diversity of its tropical areas, but their destruction has continued unabated. The lowland rainforests of Hawaii, populated mostly by native ohia, are being razed. Landowners slash, burn, and bulldoze them to create more land for cattle and agriculture and, most distressingly, for wood chips to generate electricity! Introduced wild boar gouge the forest floor, exposing sensitive roots and leaving tiny, fetid ponds where mosquito larvae thrive. Feral goats roam the forests like hoofed locusts and strip all vegetation within reach.

Maui's Nature Conservancy Preserve in Waikamoi has managed to fence in a speck of this forest, keeping it safe from these animals for the time being. Almost half the birds classified in the U.S. as endangered live in Hawaii, and almost all of these make their homes in the rainforests. For example, Maui's rainforests have yielded the *poouli,* a new species of bird discovered only in 1974. Another forest survey in 1981 rediscovered the Bishop's *o'o,* a bird thought to be extinct at the turn of the century. We can only lament the passing of the rainforests that have already fallen to ignorance, but if this ill-fated destruction continues on a global level, we will be lamenting our own passing. We must nurture the rainforests that remain, and with simple enlightenment, let them be.

BIRDS

One of the great tragedies of natural history is the continuing demise of Hawaiian birdlife. Perhaps only 15 original species of birds remain of the more than 70 native families that thrived before the coming of humans. Since the arrival of Captain Cook in 1778, 23 species have become extinct, with 31 more in danger. And what's not known is how many species were wiped out before the coming of white explorers. Experts believe that the Hawaiians annihilated about 40 species, including seven other species of geese besides the *nene*, a rare one-legged owl, ibis, lovebirds, sea eagles, and hunting creepers—all gone before Captain Cook arrived. Hawaii's endangered birds account for more than 50% of the birds listed in the U.S. Sport Fisheries and Wildlife's *Red Book* (which cites rare and endangered animals). In the last 200 years, more than four times as many birds have become extinct in Hawaii as in all of North America. These figures unfortunately suggest that a full 40% of Hawaii's endemic birds no longer exist. Almost all of Oahu's native birds are gone and few indigenous Hawaiian birds can be found on any island below the 3,000-foot level.

Native birds have been reduced in number because of multiple factors. The original Polynesians helped wipe out many species. They altered large areas for farming, and used fire to destroy patches of pristine forests. Also, bird feathers were highly prized for the making of *lei*, for featherwork in capes and helmets, and for the large *kahili* fans that indicated rank among the *ali'i*. Introduced exotic birds and the new diseases they carried are another major reason for reduction of native bird numbers, along with predation by the mongoose and rat—especially upon ground-nesting birds. Bird malaria and bird pox are also devastating to the native species. Mosquitoes, unknown in Hawaii until a ship named the *Wellington* introduced them at Lahaina in 1826 through larvae carried in its water barrels, infect most native birds, causing a rapid reduction in birdlife. Feral pigs rooting deep in the rainforests knock over ferns and small trees, creating fetid pools in which mosquito larvae thrive. However, the most damaging factor by far is the assault upon native forests by agriculture and land developers. The vast majority of Hawaiian birds evolved into specialists. They lived in only one small area and ate a very limited number of plants or insects, which once removed or altered soon killed the birds.

You'll spot birds all over the Big Island, from the coastal areas to the high mountain slopes. Some are found on other islands as well, but the ones listed below are found only or mainly on the Big Island. Every bird listed is either threatened or endangered.

Hawaii's Own

The *nene*, or Hawaiian goose, deserves special mention because it is Hawaii's state bird and is making a comeback from the edge of extinction. The *nene* is found only on the slopes of Mauna Loa, Hualalai, and Mauna Kea on the Big Island, and in Haleakala Crater on Maui. It was extinct on Maui until a few birds were returned there in 1957, but some experts maintain that the *nene* lived naturally only on the Big Island. *Nene* are raised at the Wildfowl Trust in Slimbridge, England, which placed the first birds at Haleakala; and at the Hawaiian Fish and Game Station at Pohakuloa, along the Saddle Road on Hawaii. By the 1940s, fewer than 50 birds lived in the wild. Now approximately 125 birds

MARY ANN ABEL

The nene, the state bird, lives only on Haleakala on Maui and on the slopes of Mauna Loa and Mauna Kea.

The **Hawaiian crow,** or *alala,* is reduced to less than 12 birds living on the slopes of Hualalai and Mauna Loa above the 3,000-foot level. It looks like the common raven but has a more melodious voice and sometimes dull brown feathers. The *alala* breeds in early spring, and the greenish-blue, black-flecked eggs hatch from April to June. It is extremely nervous while nesting and any disturbance will cause it to abandon its young.

The **Hawaiian hawk** *('io)* primarily lives on the slopes of Mauna Loa and Mauna Kea below 9,000 feet. It travels from there to other parts of the island and can often be seen kiting in the skies over Hawaii Volcanoes National Park, upland from Kailua-Kona, and in remote spots like Waimanu Valley. This noble bird, the royalty of the skies, symbolized the *ali'i.* The *'io* population was once dwindling, and many scientists feared that the bird was headed for extinction. The hawk exists only on the Big Island for reasons that are not entirely clear. The good news is that the *'io* is making a dramatic comeback, also for reasons that are still unclear. Speculation has it that it may be gaining resistance to some diseases, including malaria, or that it may have learned how to prey on the introduced rats, or even that it may be adapting to life in macadamia nut groves and other alternate habitats.

The ***akiapola'au*** is a five-inch yellow bird hardly bigger than its name. It lives mainly on the eastern slopes in ohia and koa forests above 3,500 feet. It has a long, curved upper beak for probing and a smaller lower beak that it uses woodpecker-fashion. The *akiapola'au* opens its mouth wide, strikes the wood with its lower beak, and then uses the upper beak to scrape out any larvae or insects. Listen for the distinctive rapping sound to spot this melodious singer. The *akiapola'au* can be seen at the Hakalau Fish and Wildlife Preserve; south of Powerline Road off the Saddle Road; and along the Pu'u O'o Volcano Trail from Volcanoes National Park.

Marine Birds
Two coastal birds that breed on the high slopes of Hawaii's volcanoes and feed on the coast are the **Hawaiian petrel** *('ua'u)* and the **Newell shearwater** *('a'o).* The *'ua'u* lives on the barren high slopes and craters, where it nests in burrows or under stones. Breeding season lasts from mid-March to mid-October. Only one chick

'io

live on Haleakala and 500 on the Big Island. Although the birds can be raised successfully in captivity, their life in the wild is still in question.

The *nene* is believed to be a descendant of the Canadian goose, which it resembles. Geese are migratory birds that form strong kinship ties, mating for life. It's speculated that a migrating goose became disabled, and along with its loyal mate, remained in Hawaii. The *nene* is smaller than its Canadian cousin, has lost a great deal of webbing in its feet, and is perfectly at home away from water, foraging and nesting on rugged and bleak lava flows.

Good places to view *nene* are in Volcanoes National Park at Kipuka Nene Campground (see p. 226), Summit Caldera, Devastation Trail, and at Volcanoes Golf Course, at dawn and dusk. They gather at the golf course because they love to feed on grasses. The places to view them on the Kona side are at Puulani, a housing development north of Kailua-Kona; or at Kaloka Mauka, another housing development on the slopes of Mt. Hualalai. At the top of the road up Mt. Hualalai is a trail, a good place to see the *nene.* Unfortunately, as the housing developments proliferate and the residents invariably acquire dogs and cats, the *nene* will disappear. The *nene* is a perfect symbol of Hawaii: let it be, and it will live.

is born and nurtured on regurgitated squid and fish. The *'ua'u* suffers heavily from predation. The *'a'o* prefers the forested slopes of the interior. It breeds from April-Nov., and spends its days at sea and nights inland. Feral cats and dogs reduce its numbers considerably.

Forest Birds

The following birds are found in the upland forests of the Big Island. The **elepaio** is found on other islands but is also spotted in Volcanoes National Park. This long-tailed (often held upright), five-inch brown bird (appearance can vary considerably) can be coaxed to come within touching distance of the observer. Sometimes it will sit on lower branches above your head and scold you. This bird was the special *amakua* (personal spirit) of canoe builders in ancient lore. Fairly common in the rainforest, it is basically a flycatcher.

The **amakihi** and **iiwi** are endemic birds not endangered at the moment. The *amakihi* is one of the most common native birds; yellowish green, it frequents the high branches of the ohia, koa, and sandalwood looking for insects, nectar, or fruit. It is less specialized than most other Hawaiian birds, the main reason for its continued existence. The *iiwi* is a bright red bird with a salmon-colored, hooked bill. It's found on Hawaii in the forests above 2,000 feet. It too feeds on a variety of insects and flowers. The *iiwi* is known for a harsh voice that sounds like a squeaking hinge, but it's also capable of a melodious song. The *iiwi* can be spotted at the top of Kaloka Mauka (a housing development north of Kailua-Kona), at Powerline Road, which goes south off the Saddle Road, and at Pu'u O'o Trail in Volcanoes National Park.

The **apapane** is abundant on Hawaii, especially atop Volcanoes, and being the most common native bird, is the easiest to see. It's a chubby, red-bodied bird about five inches long with a black bill, legs, wingtips, and tail feathers. It's quick and flitty and has a wide variety of calls and songs, from beautiful warbles to mechanical buzzes. Its feathers were sought by Hawaiians to produce distinctive capes and helmets for the *ali'i*.

The **Hawaiian thrush** *(oma'o)* is a fairly common bird found above 3,000 feet in the windward forests of Hawaii. This eight-inch gray bird is a good singer, often seen perching with distinctive drooping wings and a shivering body. The *oma'o* is probably descended from Townsend's solitaire. The best place to look for it is at the Thurston Lava Tube (see p. 221), where you can see it doing its baby-bird shivering-and-shaking act. A great mimic, it can sound like a cat or even like an old-fashioned radio with stations changing as you turn the dial. Another good place to see the *oma'o* is along Powerline Road, off the Saddle Road.

The **akepa** is a four- to five-inch bird. The male is a brilliant orange to red, the female a drab green and yellow. It is found mainly on Hualalai and in windward forests.

The six-inch, bright yellow **palila** is found only on Hawaii in the forests of Mauna Kea above 6,000 feet. It depends exclusively upon *mamane* trees for survival, eating its pods, buds, and flowers. *Mamane* seedlings are destroyed by feral sheep. The Department of Land and Natural Resources for some inexplicable reason attempted to introduce sheep on the land that is the main refuge for the *palila,* which greatly endangered the bird's survival. The Sierra Club and Audubon Society immediately sued to prevent this enviornmental fiasco, and were successful in winning their case in the local courts. The Department of Land and Natural resources insisted on fighting the decision all the way to the

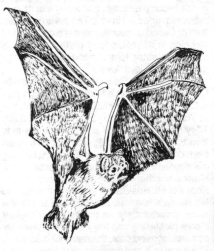

hoary bat

Supreme Court. They lost, and reluctantly got rid of the sheep. But instead of letting a bad decision fade away, they compounded their folly by introducing a different type of sheep. They were sued again, lost again, and again fought it all the way to the Supreme Court, wasting taxpayers money every laborious inch of the way. As goes the *mamane,* so goes the *palila.* As goes the *palila,* so goes humanity's attempt to live in harmony with nature.

The *po'ouli* is a dark-brown, five-inch bird with a black mask and dark-brown feet. Its tail is short, and it sports a conical bill. It was saved from extinction through efforts of the Sierra Club and Audubon Society, who successfully had it listed as the newest addition to the Federal List of Endangered Species. The bird has one remaining stronghold deep in the forests of Maui.

OTHER HAWAIIAN ANIMALS

Hawaii had only two indigenous mammals, the monk seal (found throughout the islands) and the hoary bat (found mainly on the Big Island). The remainder of the Big Island's mammals are transplants. But like anything else, including people, that has been in the islands long enough, they have taken on characteristics that make them "local."

The following animals are found primarily on the Big Island. The **Hawaiian hoary bat** (ope 'ape'a) is a cousin of the Mainland bat, a strong flier that made it to Hawaii eons ago and developed its own species. Its tail has a whitish coloration, hence its name. Small populations of the bat are found on Maui and Kauai, but the greatest numbers of them are on the Big Island, where they have been spotted even on the upper slopes of Mauna Loa and Mauna Kea. The hoary bat has a 13-inch wingspan. Unlike other bats, it is a solitary creature, roosting in trees. It gives birth to twins in early summer and can often be spotted over Hilo and Kealakekua bays just around sundown.

The **feral dog** *(ilio)* is found on all the islands but especially on the slopes of Mauna Kea, where packs chase feral sheep. Poisoned and shot by local ranchers, its numbers are diminishing. Black dogs, thought to be more tender, are still eaten in some Hawaiian and Filipino communities.

The **feral sheep** is an escaped descendant of animals brought to the islands by Captain Vancouver in the 1790s, and of merinos brought to the island later and raised for their exceptional woolly fleece. It exists only on the Big Island, on the upper slopes of Mauna Loa, Mauna Kea, and Hualalai; by the 1930s, its numbers topped 40,000 head. The fleece is a buff brown, and its two-foot-wide curved horns are often sought as hunting trophies. Feral sheep are responsible for the overgrazing of young *mamane* trees, necessary to the endangered bird, *palila.* In 1979, a law was passed to exterminate or remove the sheep from Mauna Kea so that the native *palila* could survive.

The **mouflon sheep** was introduced to Lanai and Hawaii to cut down on overgrazing and serve as trophy animals. This Mediterranean sheep can interbreed with feral sheep to produce a hybrid. It lives on the upper slopes of Mauna Loa and Mauna Kea. Unfortunately, its introduction has not been a success. No evidence concludes that the smaller family groups of mouflon cause less damage than the herding feral sheep, and hunters reportedly don't like the meat as much as feral mutton.

The **feral donkey,** better known as the "Kona nightingale," came to Hawaii as a beast of burden. Domesticated donkeys are found on all islands, but a few wild herds still roam the Big Island along the Kona Coast, especially near the exclusive Kona Village Resort at Kaupulehu.

Feral cattle were introduced by Captain Vancouver, who gave a few domesticated head to Kamehameha; immediately a *kapu* (taboo) against killing them went into effect for 10 years. The lush grasses of Hawaii were perfect and the cattle flourished; by the early 1800s they were out of control and were hunted and exterminated. Finally, Mexican cowboys were brought to Hawaii to teach the locals how to be range hands. From this legacy sprang the Hawaiian *paniolo.*

Drosophila, The Hawaiian Fly
Most people hardly pay attention to flies, unless one lands on the plate lunch. But geneticists from throughout the world, and especially from the University of Hawaii, make a special pilgrimage to the Volcano area of the Big Island and to Maui just to study the native Hawaiian drosophila. This critter is related to the fruit fly

and housefly, but there are hundreds of native species that are singularly unique. The Hawaiian ecosystem is very simple and straightforward, so geneticists can trace the evolutionary changes from species to subspecies through mating behavior. The scientists compare the species between the two islands, and chart the differences. Major discoveries in evolutionary genetics have been made through these studies.

MARINE LIFE

The **humpback whale** migrates to Hawaiian waters yearly, arriving in late December and departing by mid-March. The best places to view it are along the South Kona Coast, especially at Kealakekua Bay and Ka Lae ("South Point"), with many sightings off the Puna coast around Isaac Hale Beach Park.

Hawaii Volcanoes National Park stretches from the top of Mauna Kea all the way down to the sea. It is here, around Apua Point, that three of the last-known nesting sites of the very endangered **hawksbill turtle** are found. This creature has been ravished in the Pacific, where it is ruthlessly hunted for its shell which is made into women's jewelry, especially combs. It is illegal to bring items made from turtle shell into the U.S., but the hunt goes on.

Billfish
Although these magnificent game fish occur in various South Sea and Hawaiian waters, catching them is easiest in the clear, smooth waters off the Kona Coast. The billfish—swordfish, sailfish, marlin, and a'u—share two distinctive common features: a long, spearlike or swordlike snout, and a prominent dorsal fin. The three main species of billfish caught are the blue, striped, and black marlin. Of these three, the **blue marlin** is the leading game fish in Kona waters. The blue has tipped the scales at well over 1,000 pounds, but the average fish weighs in at 300-400 pounds. When alive, this fish is a striking cobalt blue, but death brings a color change to slate blue. It feeds on skipjack tuna; throughout the summer, fishing boats look for

schools of tuna as a tip-off to blues in the area. The **black marlin** is the largest and most coveted catch for blue-water anglers. This solitary fish is infrequently found in the banks off Kona. Granddaddies can weigh 1,800 pounds, but the average is a mere 200. The **striped marlin** is the most common commercial billfish, a highly prized food served in finer restaurants and often sliced into *sashimi*. Its coloration is a remarkable royal blue. Its spectacular leaps when caught gives it a great reputation as a fighter. The striped marlin is smaller than the other marlins, so a 100-pounder is a very good catch. For more information see "Sports and Recreation" on pp. 78-80.

THE HAKALAU FOREST NATIONAL WILDLIFE REFUGE

The Hakalau Forest National Wildlife Refuge, tel. 969-9909, is a joint effort of the Nature Conservancy and the U.S. Fish and Wildlife Service, who have acquired a large tract of rainforest off the Saddle Road that goes all the way up to the Parker Ranch lands. It's upland forest and scrub that drifts down into solid rainforest. These two agencies are working hand-in-hand to reconvert the area into natural habitat. Efforts include fencing; ridding the area of cattle, pigs, feral dogs, and cats; and replanting with koa while removing introduced and exotic foliage. It's a tremendous task that's mainly being shouldered by Dick Watts and his helper, John Emig, rangers with the U.S. Fish and Wildlife Service. The refuge is not adequately staffed to accept visits by the general public at this time. Exceptions are made for working scientists or people who would like to volunteer for an ongoing project. If you *truly* have a dedication to help and aren't afraid to get your hands dirty, contact Dick for a very rewarding experience. The logistics of setting up your visit require that you be willing to work for at least an entire day in physically demanding conditions. The refuge is very beautiful, a diamond in the rough, that encompasses an incredible rainforest unlike any on the Big Island.

HISTORY

THE ROAD FROM TAHITI

Until the 1820s, when New England missionaries began a phonetic rendering of the Hawaiian language, the past was kept vividly alive only by the sonorous voices of special *kahuna* who chanted the sacred *mele*. The chants were beautiful, flowing word pictures that captured the essence of every aspect of life. These *mele* praised the land *(mele aina)*, royalty *(mele ali'i)*, and life's tender aspects *(mele aloha)*. Chants were dedicated to friendship, hardship, and favorite children. Entire villages sometimes joined together to compose a *mele*—every word was chosen carefully, and the wise old *kapuna* would decide if the words were lucky or unlucky. Some *mele* were bawdy or funny on the surface but contained secret meanings, often bitingly sarcastic, that ridiculed an inept or cruel leader. The most important chants took listeners back into the dim past before people lived in Hawaii. From these genealogies *(ko'ihonua),* the *ali'i* derived the right to rule, since these chants went back to the gods Wakea and Papa from whom the *ali'i* were directly descended.

The Kumulipo

The great genealogies, finally compiled in the late 1800s by order of King Kalakaua, were collectively known as *The Kumulipo, A Hawaiian Creation Chant,* basically a Polynesian account of Genesis. Other chants related to the beginning of this world, but *The Kumulipo* sums it all up and is generally considered the best. The chant relates that after the beginning of time, there is a period of darkness. The darkness, however, mysteriously brims with spontaneous life; during this period plants and animals are born, as well as Kumulipo, the man, and Po'ele, the woman. In the eighth chant darkness gives way to light and the gods descend to earth. Wakea is "the sky father" and Papa is "the earth mother," whose union gives birth to the islands of Hawaii. First born is Hawaii, followed by Maui, then Kahoolawe. Apparently, Papa becomes bushed after three consecutive births and decides to vacation in Tahiti. While Papa is away recovering from postpartum depression and working on her tan, Wakea gets lonely and takes Kaula as his second wife; she bears him the island-child of Lanai. Not fully cheered up, but getting the hang of it, Wakea takes a third wife, Hina, who promptly bears the island of Molokai. Meanwhile, Papa gets wind of these shenanigans, returns from Polynesia, and retaliates by taking up with Lua, a young and virile god. She soon gives birth to the island of Oahu. Papa and Wakea finally decide that they really are meant for each other and reconcile to conceive Kauai, Niihau, Kaula, and Nihoa. These two progenitors are the source from which the *ali'i* ultimately traced their lineage, and from which they derived their god-ordained power to rule.

Basically, there are two major genealogical families: the **Nana'ulu**, who became the royal *ali'i* of Oahu and Kauai; and the **Ulu**, who provided the royalty of Maui and Hawaii. The best sources of information on Hawaiian myth and legend are Martha Beckwith's *Hawaiian Mythology* and the monumental three-volume opus *An Account of the Polynesian Race* compiled by Abraham Fornander from 1878-85. Fornander, after settling in Hawaii, married an *ali'i* from Molokai and had an illustrious career as a newspaperman, Maui circuit judge, and finally Supreme Court justice. For years Fornander sent scribes to every corner of the kingdom to listen to the elder *kupuna*. They returned with firsthand accounts, which he dutifully recorded.

The Big Island plays a significant role in Hawaii's history. A long list of "firsts" have occurred here. Historians generally believe (backed up by the oral tradition) that the Big Island was the first in the Hawaiian chain to be settled by the Polynesians. The dates now used are A.D. 600-700. Hawaii is geographically the closest island to Polynesia; Mauna Loa and especially Mauna Kea, with its white summit, present easily spotted landmarks. Psychologically, the Polynesian wayfarers would have been very attracted to Hawaii as a lost homeland. Compared to Tahiti and most other South Sea islands (except Fiji), it's huge. It *looked* like the promised land. Some may wonder why the Polynesians chose to live atop an obviously active volcano and not bypass it for a more congenial island. The volcanism of the Big Island is comparatively gentle; the lava flows follow predictable routes and rarely turn killer. The animistic Hawaiians would have been drawn to live where the godly forces of nature were so apparent. The mana (power) would be exceptionally strong, and therefore the *ali'i* would be great. Human sacrifice was introduced to Hawaii at Wahaula Heiau in the Puna District in the 13th century, and from there

LOUISE FOOTE

The Polynesians, attuned to every nuance in their environment, noticed that a migratory land bird called the golden plover arrived from the north every year. They reasoned that since the plover was not a seabird, there must be land to the north.

luakini (human-sacrifice temples) spread throughout the islands.

The Great Navigators

No one knows exactly when the first Polynesians arrived in Hawaii, but the great deliberate migrations from the southern islands seems to have taken place A.D. 500-800; anthropologists keep pushing the date backward as new evidence becomes available. Even before that, however, it's reasonable to assume that the first people to set foot on Hawaii were probably fishermen, or perhaps defeated warriors whose canoes were blown hopelessly northward into unfamiliar waters. They arrived by a combination of extraordinary good luck and an uncanny ability to sail and navigate without instruments, using the sun by day and the moon and rising stars by night. They could feel the water and determine direction by swells, tides, and currents. The movements of fish and cloud formations were also utilized to give direction. Since their arrival was probably an accident, they were unprepared to settle on the fertile but barren lands, having no stock animals, plant cuttings, or women. Forced to return southward, undoubtedly many lost their lives at sea, but a few wild-eyed stragglers must have made it home to tell tales of a paradise to the north where land was plentiful and the sea bounteous. This is affirmed

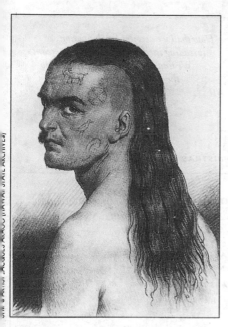

by ancient navigational chants from Tahiti, Moorea, and Bora Bora, which passing from father to son revealed how to follow the stars to the "heavenly homeland in the north." Possibly a few migrations followed, but it's known that for centuries there was no real reason for a mass exodus, so the chants alone remained and eventually became shadowy legend.

From Where They Came

It's generally agreed that the first planned migrations were from the violent cannibal islands that Spanish explorers called the Marquesas, 11 islands in extreme eastern Polynesia. The islands themselves are harsh and inhospitable, breeding a toughness into these people which enabled them to withstand the hardships of long, unsure ocean voyages and years of resettlement. Marquesans were a fiercely independent people whose chiefs could rise from the ranks because of bravery or intelligence. They must have also been a savage-looking lot. Both men and women tattooed themselves in complex blue patterns from head to foot. The warriors carried massive, intricately designed ironwood war clubs and wore carved whale teeth in slits in

their earlobes, which became stretched to the shoulders. They shaved the sides of their heads with sharks' teeth, tied their hair in two topknots that looked like horns, and rubbed their heavily muscled and tattooed bodies with scented coconut oils. Their cults worshiped mummified ancestors; the bodies of warriors of defeated neighboring tribes were consumed. They were masters at building great double-hulled canoes launched from huge canoe sheds. Two hulls were fastened together to form a catamaran, and a hut in the center provided shelter in bad weather. The average voyaging canoe was 60-80 feet long and could comfortably hold an extended family of about 30 people. These small family bands carried all the staples they would need in the new lands.

The New Lands

For five centuries the Marquesans settled and lived peacefully on the new land, as if Hawaii's aloha spirit overcame most of their fierceness. The tribes coexisted in relative harmony, especially since there was no competition for land. Cannibalism died out. There was much coming and going between Hawaii and Polynesia as new people came to settle for hundreds of years. Then, it appears that in the 12th century a deliberate exodus of warlike Tahitians arrived and subjugated the settled islanders. They came to conquer. This incursion had a terrific significance on the Hawaiian religious and social system. Oral tradition relates that a Tahitian priest, Paao, found the mana of the Hawaiian chiefs to be low, signifying that their gods were weak. Paao built a *heiau* at Wahaula on the Big Island, then introduced the warlike god Ku and the rigid *kapu* system through which the new rulers became dominant. Voyages between Tahiti and Hawaii continued for about 100 years and Tahitian customs, legends, and language became the Hawaiian way of life. Then suddenly, for no recorded or apparent reason, the voyages discontinued and Hawaii returned to total isolation.

The islands remained forgotten for almost 500 years until the indomitable English seaman, Capt. James Cook, sighted Oahu on Jan. 18, 1778 and stepped ashore at Waimea on Kauai two days later. At that time Hawaii's isolation was so complete that even the Polynesians had forgotten about it. On an earlier voyage, Tupaia, a high priest from Raiatea, had

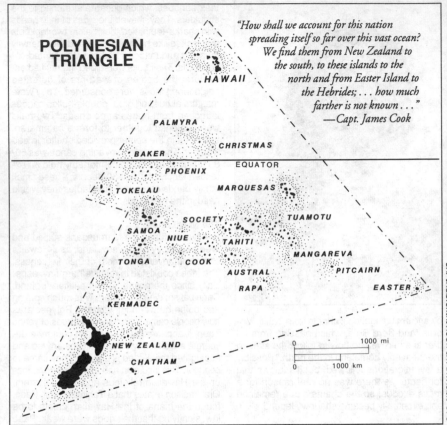

POLYNESIAN TRIANGLE

"How shall we account for this nation spreading itself so far over this vast ocean? We find them from New Zealand to the south, to these islands to the north and from Easter Island to the Hebrides; . . . how much farther is not known . . ."
—*Capt. James Cook*

HAWAII

PALMYRA

CHRISTMAS

BAKER

EQUATOR

PHOENIX

TOKELAU

MARQUESAS

SOCIETY

TUAMOTU

SAMOA

NIUE

TAHITI

TONGA

COOK

MANGAREVA

AUSTRAL

PITCAIRN

RAPA

EASTER

KERMADEC

NEW ZEALAND

CHATHAM

0   1000 mi
0   1000 km

© J.D. BISIGNANI AND MOON PUBLICATIONS, INC.

accompanied Captain Cook as he sailed throughout Polynesia. Tupaia demonstrated his vast knowledge of existing archipelagos throughout the South Pacific by naming over 130 islands and drawing a map that included the Tonga group, the Cook Islands, the Marquesas, even tiny Pitcairn, a rock in far eastern Polynesia where the mutinous crew of the *Bounty* found solace. In mentioning the Marquesas, Tupaia said, *"He ma'a te ka'ata,"* which means "Food is man" or simply "Cannibals!" But remarkably absent from Tupaia's vast knowledge was the existence of Easter Island, New Zealand, and Hawaii.

The next waves of people to Hawaii would be white, and the Hawaiian world would be changed quickly and forever.

THE WORLD DISCOVERS HAWAII

The late 18th century was an extraordinary time in Hawaiian history. Monumental changes seemed to happen all at once. First, Capt. James Cook, a Yorkshire farm boy fulfilling his destiny as the all-time greatest Pacific explorer, found Hawaii for the rest of the world. For better or worse, it could no longer be an isolated Polynesian homeland. For the first time in Hawaiian history, a charismatic leader named Kamehameha emerged, and after a long civil war united all the islands into one centralized kingdom. The death of Captain Cook in Hawaii marked the beginning of a long series of tragic misunderstandings between whites and natives. When Kamehameha died, the old religious system of *kapu* came to an end, leaving the Hawaiians in a spiritual vortex. Many takers arrived to fill the void: missionaries after souls, whalers after their prey and a good time, traders and planters after profits and a home. The islands were opened and devoured like ripe fruit. Powerful nations, including Russia, Great Britain, France, and the United States, yearned to bring this strategic Pacific jewel under their own influence. The 19th century brought the demise of the Hawaiian people as a dominant political force in their own land and with it the end of Hawaii as a sovereign monarchy. An almost bloodless yet bitter military coup followed by a brief Hawaiian Republic ended in annexation by the United States. As the U.S. became completely entrenched politically and militarily, a new social and economic order was founded on the plantation system. Amazingly rapid population growth occurred with the importation of plantation workers from Asia and Europe, which yielded a unique cosmopolitan blend of races like nowhere else on earth. By the dawning of the 20th century, the face of old Hawaii had been altered forever; the "sacred homeland in the north" was hurled into the modern age. The attack on Pearl Harbor saw a tremendous loss of life and brought Hawaii closer to the U.S. by a baptism of blood. Finally, on Aug. 21, 1959, after 59 years as a "territory," Hawaii officially became the 50th state of the Union.

Captain Cook Sights Hawaii

In 1776 Capt. James Cook set sail for the Pacific from Plymouth, England on his third and final expedition into this still vastly unexplored region of the world. On a fruitless quest for the fabled Northwest Passage across the North American continent, he sailed down the coast of Africa, rounded the Cape of Good Hope, crossed the Indian Ocean, and traveled past New Zealand, Tasmania, and the Friendly Islands (where an unsuccessful plot was hatched by the *friendly* natives to murder him). On Jan. 18, 1778, Captain Cook's 100-foot flagship HMS *Resolution* and its 90-foot companion HMS *Discovery* sighted Oahu. Two days later, they sighted Kauai and went ashore at the village of Waimea on Jan. 20, 1778. Though anxious to get on with his mission, Cook decided to make a quick sortie to investigate this new land and reprovision his

ships. He did, however, take time to remark in his diary about the close resemblance of these newfound people to others he had encountered as far south as New Zealand, and marveled at their widespread habitation across the Pacific.

The first trade was some brass medals for a mackerel. Cook also stated that he had never before met natives so astonished by a ship, and that they had an amazing fascination for iron, which they called *toe*, Hawaiian for "adze." There is even some conjecture that a Spanish ship under one Captain Gaetano had landed in Hawaii as early as the 16th century, trading a few scraps of iron that the Hawaiians valued even more than the Europeans valued gold. It was also noted that the Hawaiian women gave themselves freely to the sailors with the apparent good wishes of the island men. This was actually a ploy by the *kahuna* to test if the white newcomers were gods or men—gods didn't need women. These sailors proved immediately mortal. Cook, who was also a physician, tried valiantly to keep the 66 men (out of 112) who had measurable cases of V.D. away from the women. The task proved impossible as women literally swarmed the ships; when Cook returned less than a year later, it was logged that signs of V.D. were already apparent on some natives' faces.

Cook was impressed with the Hawaiians' swimming ability and with their well-bred manners. They had happy dispositions and sticky fingers, stealing any object made of metal, especially nails. The first item stolen was a butcher's cleaver. An unidentified native grabbed it, plunged overboard, swam to shore, and waved his booty in triumph. The Hawaiians didn't seem to care for beads and were not at all impressed with a mirror. Cook provisioned his ships by trading chisels for hogs, while common sailors gleefully traded nails for sex. Landing parties were sent inland to fill casks with fresh water. On one such excursion a Mr. Williamson, who was eventually drummed out of the Royal Navy for cowardice, unnecessarily shot and killed a native. After a brief stop on Niihau, the ships sailed away, but both groups were indelibly impressed with the memory of each other.

Cook Returns

Almost a year later, when winter weather forced Cook to return from the coast of Alaska, his discovery began to take on far-reaching signifi-

HAWAII STATE ARCHIVES

Capt. James Cook

cance. Cook had named Hawaii the Sandwich Islands, in honor of one of his patrons, John Montague, the Earl of Sandwich. On this return voyage, he spotted Maui on Nov. 26, 1778. After eight weeks of seeking a suitable harbor, the ships bypassed it, but not before the coastline was duly drawn by Lt. William Bligh, one of Cook's finest and most trusted officers. (Bligh would find his own drama almost 10 years later as commander of the infamous HMS *Bounty*.) The *Discovery* and *Resolution* finally found safe anchorage at Kealakekua Bay on the Kona coast of the Big Island. It is very lucky for history that on board was Mr. Anderson, ship's chronicler, who left a handwritten record of the strange and tragic events that followed. Even more important were the drawings of John Webber, ship's artist, who rendered invaluable impressions in superb drawings and etchings. Other noteworthy men aboard were George Vancouver, who would lead the first British return to Hawaii after Cook's death and introduce many fruits, vegetables, cattle, sheep, and goats; and James Burney, who would become a long-standing leading authority on the Pacific.

The Great God Lono Returns

By all accounts Cook was a humane and just captain, greatly admired by his men. Unlike many other supremacists of that time, he was known to have a respectful attitude toward any people he discovered, treating them as equals and recognizing the significance of their cultures. Not known as a violent man, he would use his superior weapons against natives only in an absolute case of self-defense. His hardened crew had been at sea facing untold hardship for almost three years; returning to Hawaii was truly like reentering paradise.

A strange series of coincidences sailed with Cook into Kealakekua Bay on Jan. 16, 1779. It was *makahiki* time, a period of rejoicing and festivity dedicated to the fertility god of the earth, Lono. Normal *kapu* days were suspended and willing partners freely enjoyed each other sexually, as well as dancing, feasting, and the islands' version of Olympic games. It was long held in Hawaiian legend that the great god Lono would return to earth. Lono's image was a small wooden figure perched on a tall, mastlike crossbeam; hanging from the crossbeam were long, white sheets of tapa. Who else could Cook be but Lono, and what else could his ships with their masts and white sails be but his sacred floating *heiau?* This explained the Hawaiians' previous fascination with his ships, but to add to the remarkable coincidence, Kealakekua Harbor happened to be considered Lono's private sacred harbor. Natives from throughout the land prostrated themselves and paid homage to the returning god. Cook was taken ashore and brought to Lono's sacred temple, where he was afforded the highest respect. The ships badly needed fresh supplies so the Hawaiians readily gave all they had, stretching their own provisions to the limit. To the sailors' delight, this included full measures of the aloha spirit.

The Fatal Misunderstandings

After an uproarious welcome and generous hospitality for over a month, it became obvious that the newcomers were beginning to overstay their welcome. During the interim a seaman named William Watman died, convincing the Hawaiians that the *haole* were indeed mortals, not gods. Watman was buried at Hikiau Heiau, where a plaque commemorates the event to this day. Incidents of petty theft began to increase dramatically. The lesser chiefs indicated it was time to leave by "rubbing the Englishmen's bellies." Inadvertently many *kapu* were broken by the English, and once-friendly relations became strained. Finally, the ships sailed away on Feb. 4, 1779.

After plying terrible seas for only a week, *Resolution's* foremast was damaged. Cook sailed back into Kealakekua Bay, dragging the mast ashore on Feb. 13. The natives, now totally hostile, hurled rocks at the sailors. Orders were given to load muskets with ball; firearms had previously only been loaded with shot and a light charge. Confrontations increased when some Hawaiians stole a small boat and Cook's men set after them, capturing the fleeing canoe which held an *ali'i* named Palea. The English treated him roughly; to the Hawaiians horror, they even smacked him on the head with a paddle. The Hawaiians then furiously attacked the marines, who abandoned the small boat.

Cook Goes Down

Next the Hawaiians stole a small cutter from the *Discovery* that had been moored to a buoy and partially sunk to protect it from the sun. For the first time Captain Cook became furious. He ordered Captain Clerk of the *Discovery* to sail to the southeast end of the bay and stop any canoe trying to leave Kealakekua. Cook then made a fatal error in judgment. He decided to take nine armed marines ashore in an attempt to convince the venerable King Kalaniopuu to accompany him back aboard ship, where he would hold him for ransom in exchange for the cutter. The old king agreed, but his wife prevailed upon him not to trust the *haole*. Kalaniopuu sat down on the beach to think while the tension steadily grew.

Meanwhile, a group of marines fired upon a canoe trying to leave the bay. A lesser chief, Nookemai, was killed. The crowd around Cook and his men reached an estimated 20,000. Warriors outraged by the killing of the chief armed themselves with clubs and protective straw-mat armor. One bold warrior advanced on Cook and struck him with his *pahoa*. In retaliation, Cook drew a tiny pistol lightly loaded with shot and fired at the warrior. His bullets spent themselves on the straw armor and fell harmlessly to the ground. The Hawaiians went wild. Lt. Molesworth Phillips, in charge of the nine marines, began a withering fire; Cook himself slew two natives.

Overpowered by sheer numbers, the marines headed for boats standing offshore, while Lieutenant Phillips lay wounded. It is believed that Captain Cook, the greatest seaman ever to

enter the Pacific, stood helplessly in knee-deep water instead of making for the boats because he could not swim! Hopelessly surrounded, he was knocked on the head. Countless warriors then passed a knife around and hacked and mutilated his lifeless body. A sad Lieutenant King lamented in his diary, "Thus fell our great and excellent commander."

The Final Chapter

Captain Clerk, now in charge, settled his men and prevailed upon the Hawaiians to return Cook's body. On the morning of Feb. 16 a grisly piece of charred meat was brought aboard: the Hawaiians, according to their custom, had afforded Cook the highest honor by baking his body in an underground oven to remove the flesh from the bones. On Feb. 17 a group of Hawaiians in a canoe taunted the marines by brandishing Cook's hat. The English, strained to the limit and thinking that Cook was being desecrated, finally broke. Foaming with blood-lust, they leveled their cannons and muskets on shore and shot anything that moved. It is believed that Kamehameha the Great was wounded in this flurry, along with four *ali'i;* 25 *makaainana* (commoners) were killed. Finally, on Feb. 21, 1779, the bones of Capt. James Cook's hands, skull, arms, and legs were returned and tearfully buried at sea. A common seaman, one Mr. Zimmerman, summed up the feelings of all who sailed under Cook when he wrote, ". . . he was our leading star." The English sailed next morning after dropping off their Hawaiian girl-friends who were still aboard.

Captain Clerk, in bad health, carried on with the fruitless search for the Northwest Passage. He died and was buried at the Siberian village of Petropavlovisk. England was at war with upstart colonists in America, so the return of the expedition warranted little fanfare. The *Resolution* was converted into an army transport to fight the pesky Americans; the once proud *Discovery* was reduced to a convict ship ferrying inmates to Botany Bay, Australia. Mrs. Cook, the great captain's steadfast and chaste wife, lived to the age of 93, surviving all her children. She was given a stipend of 200 pounds per year and finished her days surrounded by Cook's mementos, observing the anniversary of his death to the very end by fasting and reading from the Bible.

THE UNIFICATION OF OLD HAWAII

Hawaii was already in a state of political turmoil and civil war when Cook arrived. In the 1780s the islands were roughly divided into three kingdoms: venerable Kalaniopuu ruled Hawaii and the Hana district of Maui; wily and ruthless warrior-king Kahekili ruled Maui, Kahoolawe, Lanai, and later Oahu; and Kaeo, Kahekili's brother, ruled Kauai. War ravaged the land until a remarkable chief, Kamehameha, rose and subjugated all the islands under one rule. Kamehameha initiated a dynasty that would last for about 100 years, until the independent monarchy of Hawaii forever ceased to be. To add a zing to this brewing political stew, Westerners and their technology were beginning to come in ever-increasing numbers. In 1786, Captain LaPerouse and his French exploration party landed in what's now LaPerouse Bay near Lahaina, foreshadowing European attention to the islands. In 1786 two American captains, Portlock and Dixon, made landfall in Hawaii. Also, it was known that a fortune could be made on the fur trade between the Pacific Northwest and Canton, China; stopping in Hawaii could make it feasible. After this was reported, the fate of Hawaii was sealed.

Hawaii under Kamehameha was ready to enter its "golden age." The social order was medieval, with the *ali'i* as knights owing their military allegiance to the king, and the serflike *makaainana* paying tribute and working the lands. The priesthood of *kahuna* filled the posts of advisors, sorcerers, navigators, doctors, and historians. This was Polynesian Hawaii at its apex. But like the uniquely Hawaiian silversword, the old culture blossomed, and as soon as it did, began to wither. Ever since, all that was purely Hawaiian has been supplanted by the relentless foreign influences that began bearing down upon it.

Young Kamehameha

The greatest native son of Hawaii, Kamehameha, was born under mysterious circumstances in the Kohala District, probably in 1753. He was royal born to Keoua Kupuapaikalaninui, the chief of Kohala, and Kekuiapoiwa, a chieftess from Kona. Accounts vary, but one claims that before his birth, a *kahuna* prophesied that this child would grow to be a "killer of chiefs." Be-

King Kamehameha

HAWAII STATE ARCHIVES

cause of this, the local chiefs conspired to murder the infant. When Kekuiapoiwa's time came, she secretly went to the royal birthing stones near Mookini Heiau and delivered Kamehameha. She entrusted her baby to a manservant and instructed him to hide the child. He headed for the rugged and remote coast around Kapaau. Here Kamehameha was raised in the mountains, mostly by men. Always alone, he earned the nickname "the lonely one."

Kamehameha was a man noticed by everyone; there was no doubt he was a force to be reckoned with. He had met Captain Cook when the *Discovery* unsuccessfully tried to land at Hana on Maui. While aboard, he made a lasting impression, distinguishing himself from the multitude of natives swarming the ships by his royal bearing. Lt. James King, in a diary entry, remarked that Kamehameha was a fierce-looking man, almost ugly, but that he was obviously intelligent, observant, and very good-natured. Kamehameha received his early military training from his uncle Kalaniopuu, the great king of Hawaii and Hana who fought fierce battles against Alapai, the usurper who stole his hereditary lands. After regaining Hawaii, Kalaniopuu returned to his Hana district and turned his attention to conquering all of Maui. During this period young Kamehameha distinguished himself as a ferocious warrior and earned the nickname of "the hard-shelled crab," even though old Kahekili, Maui's king, almost annihilated Kalaniopuu's army at the sand hills of Wailuku.

When the old king neared death, he passed on the kingdom to his son Kiwalao. He also, however, empowered Kamehameha as the keeper of the family war god Kukailimoku: Ku of the Bloody Red Mouth, Ku the Destroyer. Oddly enough, Kamehameha had been born not 500 yards from Ku's great *heiau* at Kohala, and had heard the chanting and observed the ceremonies dedicated to this fierce god from his first breath. Soon after Kalaniopuu died, Kamehameha found himself in a bitter war that he did not seek against his two cousins, Kiwalao and his brother Keoua, with the island of Hawaii at stake. The skirmishing lasted nine years until Kamehameha's armies met the two brothers at Mokuohai in an indecisive battle in which Kiwalao was killed. The result was a shaky truce with Keoua, a much-embittered enemy. During this fighting, Kahekili of Maui conquered Oahu, where he built a house of the skulls and bones of his adversaries as a reminder of his omnipotence. He also extended his will to Kauai by marrying his half-brother to a high-ranking chieftess of that island. A new factor would resolve this stalemate of power—the coming of the *haole*.

The Olowalu Massacre

In 1790 the American merchant ship *Ella Nora,* commanded by Yankee Capt. Simon Metcalfe, was looking for a harbor after its long voyage from the Pacific Northwest. Following a day behind was the *Fair American,* a tiny ship sailed by Metcalfe's son Thomas and a crew of five. Simon Metcalfe, perhaps by necessity, was a stern and humorless man who would broach no interference. While his ship was anchored at Olowalu, a beach area about five miles east of Lahaina, some natives slipped close in their canoes and stole a small boat, killing a seaman in the process. Metcalfe decided to trick the Hawaiians by first negotiating a truce and then unleashing full fury upon them. Signaling he was willing to trade, he invited canoes of innocent natives to visit his ship. In the meantime, he ordered that all cannons and muskets be readied with scatter shot. When the canoes were within hailing distance, he ordered his crew to

fire at will. Over 100 people were slain; the Hawaiians remembered this killing as "the day of spilled brains." Metcalfe then sailed away to Kealakekua Bay and in an unrelated incident succeeded in insulting Kameiamoku, a ruling chief, who vowed to annihilate the next *haole* ship that he saw.

Fate sent him the *Fair American* and young Thomas Metcalfe. The little ship was entirely overrun by superior forces. In the ensuing battle, the mate, Isaac Davis, so distinguished himself by open acts of bravery that his life alone was spared. Kameiamoku later turned over both Davis and the ship to Kamehameha. Meanwhile, while harbored at Kealakekua, the senior Metcalfe sent John Young to reconnoiter. Kamehameha, having learned of the capture of the *Fair American,* detained Young so he could not report, and Metcalfe, losing patience, marooned his own man and sailed off to Canton. (Metcalfe never learned of the fate of his son Thomas, and was later killed with another son while trading with the Native Americans along the Pacific coast of the Mainland.) Kamehameha quickly realized the significance of his two captives and the *Fair American* with its brace of small cannons. He appropriated the ship and made Davis and Young trusted advisors, eventually raising them to the rank of chief. They would all play a significant role in the unification of Hawaii.

Kamehameha The Great

Later in 1790, supported by the savvy of Davis and Young and the cannons from the *Fair American* which he mounted on carts, Kamehameha invaded Maui, using Hana as his power base. The island's defenders under Kalaniekupule, son of Kahekili who was lingering on Oahu, were totally demoralized, then driven back into the deathtrap of Iao Valley. There, Kamehameha's forces annihilated them. No mercy was expected and none given, although mostly commoners were slain with no significant *ali'i* falling to the victors. So many were killed in this sheer-walled, inescapable valley that the battle was called *"ka pani wai"* which means "the damming of the waters"—literally with dead bodies.

While Kamehameha was fighting on Maui, his old nemesis Keoua was busy running amok back on Hawaii, again pillaging Kamehameha's lands. The great warrior returned home flushed with victory, but in two battles could not subdue Keoua. Finally, Kamehameha had a prophetic dream in which he was told that Ku would lead him to victory over all the lands of Hawaii if he would build a *heiau* to the war god at Kawaihae. Even before the temple was finished, old Kahekili attempted to invade Waipio, Kamehameha's stronghold. But Kamehameha summoned Davis and Young, and with the *Fair American* and an enormous fleet of war canoes defeated Kahekili at Waimanu. Kahekili had no choice but to accept the indomitable Kamehameha as the king of Maui, although he himself remained the administrative head until his death in 1794.

Now only Keoua remained in the way and he would be defeated not by war, but by the great mana of Ku. While Keoua's armies were crossing the desert on the southern slopes of Kilauea, the fire goddess Pele trumpeted her disapproval and sent a huge cloud of poisonous gas and mud-ash into the air. It descended upon and instantly killed the middle legions of Keoua's armies and their families. The footprints of this ill-fated army remain to this day outlined in the mud-ash as clearly as if they were deliberately encased in wet cement. Keoua's intuition told him that the victorious mana of the gods had swung to Kamehameha and that his own fate was sealed. Kamehameha sent word that he wanted Keoua to meet with him at Ku's newly dedicated temple in Kawaihae. Both knew that Keoua must die. Riding proudly in his canoe, the old nemesis came gloriously outfitted in the red-and-gold feathered cape and helmet signifying his exalted rank. When he stepped ashore he was felled by Kamehameha's warriors. His body was ceremoniously laid upon the altar along with 11 others who were slaughtered and dedicated to Ku, of the Maggot-dripping Mouth.

Increasing Contact

By the time Kamehameha had won the Big Island, Hawaii was becoming a regular stopover for numerous ships seeking the lucrative sandalwood trade with China. In Feb. 1791, Capt. George Vancouver, still seeking the Northwest Passage, returned to Kealakekua where he was greeted by a throng of 30,000. The captain at once recognized Kamehameha, who was wearing a Chinese dressing gown that he had received in tribute from another chief who in turn

had received it directly from the hands of Cook himself. The diary of a crewmember, Thomas Manby, relates that Kamehameha, missing his front teeth, was more fierce-looking than ever as he approached the ship in an elegant double-hulled canoe sporting 46 rowers. The king invited all to a great feast prepared for them on the beach. Kamehameha's appetite matched his tremendous size. It was noted that he ate two sizable fish, a king-sized bowl of poi, a small pig, and an entire baked dog. Kamehameha personally entertained the English by putting on a mock battle in which he deftly avoided spears by rolling, tumbling, and catching them in midair, all the while hurling his own spear a great distance. The English reciprocated by firing cannon bursts into the air, creating an impromptu fireworks display. Kamehameha requested from Vancouver a full table setting with which he was provided, but his request for firearms was prudently denied. Captain Vancouver became a trusted advisor of Kamehameha, and told him about the white man's form of worship. He even interceded for Kamehameha

Capt. George Vancouver

with his headstrong queen, Kaahumanu, and coaxed her from her hiding place under a rock when she sought refuge at Pu'uhonua O Honaunau. The captain gave gifts of beef cattle, fowl, and breeding stock of sheep and goats. The ship's naturalist, Archibald Menzies, was the first *haole* to climb Mauna Kea; he also introduced a large assortment of fruits and vegetables. The Hawaiians were cheerful and outgoing, and showed remorse when they indicated that the remainder of Cook's bones had been buried at a temple close to Kealakekua. John Young, by this time firmly entrenched into Hawaiian society, made no request to sail away with Vancouver. During the next two decades of Kamehameha's rule, the French, Russians, English, and Americans discovered the great whaling waters off Hawaii. Their increasing visits shook and finally tumbled the ancient religion and social order of *kapu*.

Finishing Touches

After Keoua was laid to rest, it was only a matter of time until Kamehameha consolidated his power over all of Hawaii. In 1794 the old warrior Kahekili of Maui died and gave Oahu to his son, Kalanikupule, while Kauai and Niihau went to his brother Kaeo. In wars between the two, Kalanikupule was victorious, though he did not possess the grit of his father nor the great mana of Kamehameha. He had previously murdered a Captain Brown, who had anchored in Honolulu, and seized his ship, the *Jackal*. With the aid of this ship, Kalanikupule now determined to attack Kamehameha. However, while en route, the sailors regained control of their ship and cruised to the Big Island to inform and join with Kamehameha. An army of 16,000 was raised and sailed for Maui, where they met only token resistance, destroyed Lahaina, pillaged the countryside, and subjugated Molokai in one bloody battle.

The war canoes sailed next for Oahu and the final showdown. The great army landed at Waikiki, and though defenders fought bravely, giving up Oahu by the inch, they were steadily driven into the surrounding mountains. The beleaguered army made its last stand at Nuuanu Pali, a great precipice in the mountains behind present-day Honolulu. Kamehameha's warriors mercilessly drove the enemy into the great abyss. Kalanikupule, who hid in the mountains,

was captured after a few months and sacrificed to Ku, the Snatcher of Lands, thereby ending the struggle for power.

Kamehameha put down a revolt on Hawaii in 1796. The king of Kauai, Kaumuali, accepting the inevitable, recognized Kamehameha as supreme ruler without suffering the ravages of a needless war. Kamehameha, for the first time in Hawaiian history, was the undisputed ruler of all the islands of "the heavenly homeland in the north."

Kamehameha's Rule

Kamehameha was as gentle in victory as he was ferocious in battle. Under his rule which lasted until his death on May 8, 1819, Hawaii enjoyed a peace unlike any the warring islands had ever known. The king moved his royal court to Lahaina, where in 1803 he built the "Brick Palace," the first permanent building of Hawaii. The benevolent tyrant also enacted the "Law of the Splintered Paddle." This law, which protected the weak from the exploitation of the strong, had its origins in an incident of many years before. A brave defender of a small overwhelmed village had broken a paddle over Kamehameha's head and taught the chief—literally in one stroke—about the nobility of the commoner.

However, just as Old Hawaii reached its "golden age," its demise was at hand. The relentless waves of *haole* both innocently and determinedly battered the old ways into the ground. With the foreign ships came prosperity and fanciful new goods after which the *ali'i* lusted. The *makaainana* were worked mercilessly to provide sandalwood for the China trade. This was the first "boom" economy to hit the islands, but it set the standard of exploitation that would follow. Kamehameha built an observation tower in Lahaina to watch for ships, many of which were his own returning laden with riches from the world at large. In the last years of his life Kamehameha returned to his beloved Kona Coast, where he enjoyed the excellent fishing renowned to this day. He had taken Hawaii from the darkness of warfare into the light of peace. He died true to the religious and moral *kapu* of his youth, the only ones he had ever known, and with him died a unique way of life. Two loyal retainers buried his bones after the baked flesh had been ceremoniously stripped away. A secret burial cave was chosen so that no one could desecrate the

the great Queen Kaahumanu, by ship's artist Louis Choris from the Otto Von Kotzebue expedition, circa 1816

HAWAII STATE ARCHIVES

remains of the great chief, thereby absorbing his mana. The tomb's whereabouts remains unknown, and disturbing the dead remains one of the strictest *kapu* to this day. The Lonely One's kingdom would pass to his son, Liholiho, but true power would be in the hands of his beloved but feisty wife Kaahumanu. As Kamehameha's spirit drifted from this earth, two forces sailing around Cape Horn would forever change Hawaii: the missionaries and the whalers.

MISSIONARIES AND WHALERS

The year 1819 was of the utmost significance in Hawaiian history. It marked the death of Kamehameha, the overthrow of the ancient *kapu* system, the arrival of the first "whaler" in Lahaina, and the departure of Calvinist missionaries from New England determined to convert the heathen islands. Great changes began to rattle the old order to its foundations. With the *kapu* system and all of the ancient gods abandoned (except for the fire goddess Pele of Kilauea), a great void permeated the souls of the Hawaiians. In the coming decades Hawaii, also coveted by Russia, France, and England, was finally consumed by America. The islands had the first American school, printing press, and newspaper *(The Polynesian)* west of the Mississippi. Lahaina, in its heyday, became the world's greatest whaling port, accommodating over 500 ships during its peak years.

The Royal Family

Maui's Hana District provided Hawaii with one of its greatest queens, Kaahumanu, born in 1768 in a cave within walking distance of Hana Harbor. At the age of 17 she became the third of Kamehameha's 21 wives and eventually the love of his life. At first she proved to be totally independent and unmanageable, and was known to openly defy her king by taking numerous lovers. Kamehameha placed a *kapu* on her body and even had her attended by horribly deformed hunchbacks in an effort to curb her carnal appetites, but she continued to flaunt his authority. Young Kaahumanu had no love for her great, lumbering, unattractive husband, but in time (even Captain Vancouver was pressed into service as a marriage counselor) she learned to love him dearly. She in turn became his favorite wife, although she remained childless throughout her life. Kamehameha's first wife was the supremely royal Keopuolani, who so outranked even him that the king himself had to approach her naked and crawling on his belly. Keopuolani produced the royal children Liholiho and Kauikeaouli, who became King Kamehameha II and III, respectively. Just before Kamehameha I died in 1819 he appointed Liholiho his successor, but he also had the wisdom to make Kaahumanu the *kuhina nui* or queen regent. Initially, Liholiho was weak and became a drunkard. Later he became a good ruler, but he was always supported by his royal mother Keopuolani and by the ever-formidable Kaahumanu.

Kapu Is *Pau*

Kaahumanu was greatly loved and respected by the people. On public occasions, she donned Kamehameha's royal cloak and spear: so attired and infused with the king's mana, she demonstrated that she was the real leader of Hawaii. For six months after Kamehameha's death, Kaahumanu counseled Liholiho on what he must do. The wise *kuhina nui* knew that the old ways were *pau* ("finished") and that Hawaii could not hope to function in a rapidly changing world under the *kapu* system. In Nov. 1819, Kaahumanu and Keopuolani prevailed upon Liholiho to break two of the oldest and most sacred *kapu* by eating with women and by allowing women to eat previously forbidden foods such as bananas and certain fish. Heavily fortified with strong drink and attended by other high-ranking chiefs and a handful of foreigners, Kaahumanu and Liholiho ate together in public. This feast became known as *Ai Noa* ("free eating"). As the first morsels passed Kaahumanu's lips, the ancient gods of Hawaii tumbled. Throughout the land, revered *heiau* were burned and abandoned and the idols knocked to the ground. Now the people had nothing but their weakened inner selves to rely on. Nothing and no one could answer their prayers; their spiritual lives were empty and in shambles.

Missionaries

Into this spiritual vortex sailed the brig *Thaddeus* on April 4, 1820. It had set sail from Boston on Oct. 23, 1819, lured to the Big Island by Henry Opukahaia, a local boy born at Napoopoo in 1792. Coming ashore at Kailua-Kona, the reverends Bingham and Thurston were granted a one-year trial missionary period by King Liholiho. They established themselves on the Big Island and Oahu and from there began the transformation of Hawaii. The missionaries were people of God, but also practical-minded Yankees. They brought education, enterprise, and most importantly, unlike the transient seafarers, a commitment to stay and build. By 1824 the new faith had such a foothold that Chieftess Keopuolani climbed to the firepit atop Kilauea and defied Pele. This was even more striking than the previous breaking of the food *kapu* because the strength of Pele could actually be seen. Keopuolani ate forbidden *ohelo* berries and cried out, "Jehovah is my God." Over the next decades the governing of Hawaii slipped away from the Big Island and moved to the new port cities of Lahaina and later, Honolulu. In 1847, the Parker Ranch began with a two-acre grant given to John Parker. He coupled this with 360 acres given to his *ali'i* wife Kipikane by the land division known as the Great *Mahele*.

Rapid Conversions

The year 1824 also marked the death of Keopuolani, who was given a Christian burial. She had set the standard by accepting Christianity, and a number of the *ali'i* had followed the queen's lead. Liholiho had sailed off to England, where he and his wife contracted measles and died. Their bodies were returned by the British in 1825, on the HMS *Blonde* captained by Lord Byron, cousin of *the* Lord Byron. During these years, Kaahumanu allied herself with Rev. Richards, pastor of the first mission in the Islands, and together they wrote Hawaii's first code of laws based upon the Ten Commandments. Foremost was the condemnation of murder, theft, brawling, and the desecration of the Sabbath by work or play. The early missionaries had the best of intentions, but like all zealots they were blinded by the singlemindedness that was also their greatest ally. They weren't surgically selective in their destruction of native beliefs. *Anything* native was felt to be inferior, and they set about wiping out all traces of the old ways. In their rampage they reduced the Hawaiian culture to ashes, plucking self-will and determination from the hearts of a once-proud people. More so than the whalers, they terminated the Hawaiian way of life.

The Early Seamen

A good portion of the common seamen of the early 19th century came from the dregs of the Western world. Many a whoremongering drunkard had awoken from a stupor and found himself on the pitching deck of a ship, discovering to his dismay that he had been "pressed into naval service." For the most part these sailors were a filthy, uneducated, lawless rabble. Their present situation was dim, their future hopless, and they would live to be 30 if they were lucky and didn't die from scurvy or a thousand other miserable fates. They snatched brief pleasure in every port and jumped ship at every opportunity, especially in an easy berth like Lahaina. They displayed the worst elements of Western culture—which the Hawaiians naively mimicked. In exchange for aloha they gave drunkenness, sloth, and insidious death by disease. By the 1850s the population of native Hawaiians tumbled from the estimated 300,000 reported by Captain Cook in 1778 to barely 60,000. Common conditions such as colds, flu, venereal disease, and sometimes smallpox and cholera decimated the Hawaiians, who had no natural immunities to these foreign ailments. By the time the missionaries arrived, *hapa haole* children were common in Lahaina streets.

The earliest merchant ships to the Islands were owned or skippered by lawless opportunists who had come seeking sandalwood after first filling their holds with furs from the Pacific Northwest. Aided by *ali'i* hungry for manufactured goods and Western finery, they raped Hawaiian forests of this fragrant wood so coveted in China. Next, droves of sailors came in search of whales. The whalers, decent men at home, left their morals back in the Atlantic and lived by the slogan "no conscience east of the Cape." The delights of Hawaii were just too tempting for most.

Two Worlds Tragically Collide

The 1820s were a time of confusion and soul-searching for the Hawaiians. When Kamehameha II died the kingdom passed to Kauikeaouli (Kamehameha III), who made his lifelong residence in Lahaina. The young king was only nine years old when the title passed to him, but his power was secure because Kaahumanu was still a vibrant *kuhina nui*. The young prince, more so than any other, was raised in the cultural confusion of the times. His childhood was spent during the very cusp of the change from old ways to new, and he was often pulled in two directions by vastly differing beliefs. Since he was royal born, he was bound by age-old Hawaiian tradition to mate and produce an heir with the highest-ranking *ali'i* in the kingdom. This mate happened to be his younger sister, the Princess Nahienaena. To the old Hawaiian advisors, this arrangement was perfectly acceptable and encouraged. To the increasingly influential missionaries, incest was an unimaginable abomination in the eyes of God. The problem was compounded by the fact that Kamehameha III and Nahienaena were drawn to each other and were deeply in love. The young

Kamehameha III

HAWAII STATE ARCHIVES

king could not stand the mental pressure imposed by conflicting worlds. He became a teenage alcoholic too royal to be restrained by anyone in the kingdom, and his bouts of drunkenness and womanizing were both legendary and scandalous.

Meanwhile, Nahienaena was even more pressured because she was a favorite of the missionaries, baptized into the church at age 12. She too vacillated between the old and the new. At times a pious Christian, at others she drank all night and took numerous lovers. As the prince and princess grew into their late teens, they became even more attached to each other and hardly made an attempt to keep their relationship from the missionaries. Whenever possible, they lived together in a grass house built for the princess by her father.

In 1832, the great Kaahumanu died, leaving the king on his own. In 1833, at the age of 18, Kamehameha III announced that the "regency" was over and that all the lands in Hawaii were his personally, and that he alone was the ultimate law. Almost immediately, however, he decreed that his half-sister Kinau would be "premier," signifying that he would leave the actual running of the kingdom in her hands. Kamehameha III fell into total drunken confusion, until one night he attempted suicide. After this episode he seemed to straighten up a bit and mostly kept a low profile. In 1836, Princess Nahienaena was convinced by the missionaries to take a husband. She married Leleiohoku, a chief from the Big Island, but continued to sleep with her brother. It is uncertain who fathered the child, but Nahienaena gave birth to a baby boy in Sept. 1836. The young prince survived for only a few hours, and Nahienaena never recovered from her convalescence. She died in Dec. 1836 and was laid to rest in the mausoleum next to her mother, Keopuolani, on the royal island in Mokuhina Pond (still in existence in modern-day Lahaina). After the death of his sister, Kamehameha III became a sober and righteous ruler. Often seen paying his respects at the royal mausoleum, he ruled longer than any other king until his death in 1854.

The Missionaries Prevail

In 1823, the first mission was established in Lahaina under the pastorage of Rev. Richards and his wife. Within a few years, many of the notable ali'i had been, at least in appearance, converted to Christianity. By 1828 the cornerstones for Wainee Church, the first stone church on the island, were laid just behind the palace of Kamehameha III. The struggle between missionaries and whalers centered around public drunkenness and the servicing of sailors by native women. The normally God-fearing whalers had signed on for perilous duty that lasted up to three years, and when they anchored in Lahaina they demanded their pleasure. The missionaries were instrumental in placing a curfew on sailors and prohibiting native women from boarding ships, which had become customary. These measures certainly did not stop the liasons between sailor and wahine, but they did impose a modicum of social sanction and tolled the end of the wide-open days. The sailors were outraged; in 1825 the crew from the Daniel attacked the home of the meddler, Rev. Richards. A year later a similar incident occurred. In 1827, confined and lonely sailors from the whaler John Palmer fired their cannons at Rev. Richards' newly built home.

Slowly the tensions eased, and by 1836 many sailors were regulars at the Seamen's Chapel adjacent to the Baldwin home. Unfortunately, even the missionaries couldn't stop the pesky mosquito from entering the islands through the port of Lahaina. The mosquitoes arrived from Mexico in 1826 aboard the merchant ship Wellington. They were inadvertently carried as larvae in the water barrels and democratically pestered everyone in the islands from that day forward, regardless of race, religion, or creed.

Foreign Influence

By the 1840s Honolulu was becoming the center of commerce in the islands; when Kamehameha III moved the royal court there from Lahaina, the ascendant fate of the new capital was guaranteed. In 1843, Lord Paulet, commander of the warship Carysfort, forced Kamehameha III to sign a treaty ceding Hawaii to the British. London, however, repudiated this act, and Hawaii's independence was restored within a few months when Queen Victoria sent Admiral Thomas as her personal agent of good intentions. The king memorialized the turn of events by a speech in which he uttered the phrase, Ua mau ke ea o ka aina i ka pono ("The life of the land is preserved in righteousness"), now Hawaii's motto. The French used similar bullying tactics to force an unfavorable treaty on the Hawaiians in 1839; as part of these heavy-handed negotiations they exacted a payment of $20,000 and the right of Catholics to enjoy religious freedom in the islands. In 1842 the U.S. recognized and guaranteed Hawaii's independence without a formal treaty, and by 1860 over 80% of the islands' trade was with America.

The Great Mahele

In 1840 Kamehameha III ended his autocratic rule and instituted a constitutional monarchy. This brought about the Hawaiian Bill of Rights, but the most far-reaching change was the transition to private ownership of land. Formerly, all land belonged to the ruling chief, who gave wedge-shaped parcels called ahupua'a to lesser chiefs to be worked for him. The commoners did all the real labor, their produce heavily taxed by the ali'i. The fortunes of war, the death of a chief, or the mere whim of a superior could force a commoner off the land. The Hawaiians, however, could not think in terms of "owning" land. No one could *possess* land; one could only *use* land, and its *ownership* was a strange foreign concept. (As a result, naive Hawaiians gave up their lands for a song to unscrupulous traders, which remains an integral, unrectified problem to this day.) In 1847 Kamehameha III and his advisors separated the lands of Hawaii into three groupings: crown land (belonging to the king), government land (belonging to the chiefs), and the people's land (the largest parcels). In 1848, 245 *ali'i* entered their land claims in the *Mahele Book,* assuring them ownership. In 1850 the commoners were given title in fee simple to the lands they cultivated and lived on as tenants, not including house lots in towns. Commoners without land could buy small *kuleana* (farms) from the government at 50 cents per acre. In 1850, foreigners were also allowed to purchase land in fee simple, and the ownership of Hawaii from that day forward slipped steadily from the hands of its indigenous people.

KING SUGAR

The sugar industry began at Hana, Maui in 1849. A whaler named George Wilfong hauled four blubber pots ashore and set them up on a rocky hill in the middle of 60 acres he had planted in sugar. A team of oxen turned "crushing rollers" and the cane juice flowed down an open trough into the pots, under which an attending native kept a roaring fire burning. Wilfong's methods of refining were crude but the resulting high-quality sugar turned a neat profit in Lahaina. The main problem was labor. The Hawaiians, who made excellent whalers, were basically indentured workers. They became extremely disillusioned with their contracts, which could last up to 10 years. Most of their wages were eaten up by manufactured commodities sold at the company store, and it didn't take long for them to realize that they were little more than slaves. At every opportunity they either left the area or just refused to work.

Imported Labor
The **Masters and Servants Act of 1850,** which allowed importation of laborers under the contract system, ostensibly guaranteed an endless supply of cheap labor for the plantations. Chinese laborers were imported, but were too enterprising to remain in the fields for a meager $3 per month. They left as soon as opportunity permitted, and went into business as small merchants and retailers. In the meantime, Wilfong had sold out, releasing most of the Hawaiians previously held under contract, and his plantation fell into disuse. In 1860 two Danish brothers, August and Oscar Unna, bought land at Hana to raise sugar. They solved the labor problem by importing Japanese laborers who were extremely hard-working and easily managed. The workday lasted 10 hours, six days a week, for a salary of $20 per month with housing and medical care thrown in. Plantation life was very structured, with stringent rules governing even bedtimes and lights out. A worker was fined for being late or for smoking on the job. Even the Japanese couldn't function under these circumstances, and improvements in benefits and housing were slowly gained.

Sugar Grows
The demand for "Sandwich Island Sugar" grew as California was populated during the gold rush, and increased dramatically when the American Civil War demanded a constant supply. The only sugar plantations on the Mainland were small plots confined to the Confederate states, whose products would hardly be bought by the Union and whose fields, later in the war, were destroyed. By the 1870s it was clear to the planters, still mainly New Englanders, that the U.S. was their market; they tried often to gain closer ties and favorable tariffs. The Americans also planted rumors that the British were interested in annexing Hawaii; this put pressure on the U.S. Congress to pass the long-desired **Reciprocity Act,** which would exempt sugar from import duty. It finally passed in 1875, in exchange for U.S. long-range rights to the strategic naval port of Pearl Harbor, among other concessions. These agreements gave increased political power to a small group of American planters whose outlooks were similar to those of the post-Civil War South, where a few powerful whites were the virtual masters of a multitude of dark-skinned laborers. Sugar was now big business and the Hana District alone exported almost 3,000 tons per year. All of Hawaii would have to reckon with the "sugar barons."

Changing Society

The sugar plantation system changed life in Hawaii physically, spiritually, politically, and economically. Now boatloads of workers came not only from Japan, but from Portugal, Germany, and even Russia. The white-skinned workers were most often the field foremen *(luna)*. With the immigrants came new religions, new animals and plants, unique cuisines, and a plantation language known as *pidgin*, or better yet, *da'kine*. Many Asians and, to a lesser extent, the other groups, including the white plantation owners, intermarried with Hawaiians. A new class of people properly termed "cosmopolitan" but more familiarly and aptly known as "locals" was emerging. These were the people of multiple race backgrounds who couldn't exactly say *what* they were but it was clear to all just *who* they were. The plantation owners became the new "chiefs" of Hawaii who could carve up the land and dispense favors. The Hawaiian monarchy was soon eliminated.

A KINGDOM PASSES

The fate of Lahaina's Wainee Church through the years has been a symbol of the political and economic climate of the times. Its construction heralded the beginning of missionary dominance in 1828. It was destroyed by a tornado or "ghost wind" in 1858, just when whaling began to falter and the previously dominant missionaries began losing their control to the merchants and planters. In 1894, Wainee Church was burned to the ground by royalists supporting the besieged Queen Liliuokalani. Rebuilding was begun in 1897—while Hawaii was a republic ruled by the sugar planters—with a grant from H.P. Baldwin. It wasn't until 1947 that Wainee was finally completed and remodeled.

The Beginning Of The End

Like the Hawaiian people themselves, the Kamehameha dynasty in the mid-1800s was dying from within. King Kamehameha IV (Alexander Liholiho) ruled 1854-63; his only child died in 1862. He was succeeded by his older brother Kamehameha V (Lot Kamehameha) who ruled until 1872. With his passing the Kamehameha line ended. William Lunalilo, elected king in 1873 by popular vote, was of royal,

Queen Liliuokalani

but not Kamehameha, lineage. He died after only a year in office, and being a bachelor left no heirs. He was succeeded by David Kalakaua, known far and wide as "The Merrie Monarch," who made a world tour and was well received wherever he went. He built Iolani Palace in Honolulu and was personally in favor of closer ties with the U.S., helping push through the Reciprocity Act. Kalakaua died in 1891 and was replaced by his sister Lydia Liliuokalani, last of the Hawaiian monarchs.

The Revolution

When Liliuokalani took office in 1891, the native population was at a low of 40,000 and she felt that the U.S. had too much influence over her homeland. She was known to personally favor the English over the Americans. She attempted to replace the liberal constitution of 1887 (adopted by her pro-American brother) with an autocratic mandate in which she would have had much more political and economic control of the islands. When the McKinley Tariff of 1890 brought a decline in sugar profits, she made no attempt to improve the situation. Thus, the planters saw her as a political obstacle to their economic growth; most of Hawaii's American planters and merchants were in favor of a rebellion. She would have to go! A central spokesperson and firebrand was Lorrin Thurston, a Honolulu publisher who, with a central core of about 30 men, challenged the Hawaiian monarchy. Although Liliuokalani rallied some support and had a small military potential in her personal guard, the coup was ridiculously easy—it took only one casualty. Captain John Good shot a Hawaiian policeman in the arm and that did it. Naturally, the conspirators could not have succeeded without some solid assurances from a secret contingent in the U.S. Congress as well as outgoing President Benjamin Harrison, who favored Hawaii's annexation. Marines from the *Boston* went ashore to "protect American lives," and on Jan. 17, 1893, the Hawaiian monarchy came to an end.

The provisional government was headed by Sanford B. Dole, who became president of the Hawaiian Republic. Liliuokalani surrendered not to the conspirators but to U.S. Ambassador John Stevens. She believed that the U.S. government, which had assured her of Hawaiian independence, would be outraged by the overthrow and would come to her aid. Incoming President Grover Cleveland *was* outraged and Hawaii wasn't immediately annexed as expected. When queried about what she would do with the conspirators if she were reinstated, Liliuokalani said that they would be hung as traitors. The racist press of the times, which portrayed the Hawaiians as half-civilized, bloodthirsty heathens, publicized this widely. Since the conspirators were the leading citizens of the land, the queen's words proved untimely. In Jan. 1895 a small, ill-fated counterrevolution headed by Liliuokalani failed, and she was placed under house arrest in Iolani Palace. Officials of the republic insisted that she use her married name (Mrs. John Dominis) to sign the documents forcing her to abdicate her throne. She was also forced to swear allegiance to the new republic. Liliuokalani went on to write *Hawaii's Story* and the lyric ballad "Aloha O'e." She never forgave the conspirators and remained "queen" to the Hawaiians until her death in 1917.

Annexation

The overwhelming majority of Hawaiians opposed annexation and desired to restore the monarchy. But they were prevented from voting by the new republic because they couldn't meet the imposed property and income qualifications—a transparent ruse by the planters to control the majority. Most *haole* were racist and believed that the "common people" could not be entrusted with the vote because they were childish and incapable of ruling themselves. The fact that the Hawaiians had existed quite well for 1,000 years before the white man even reached Hawaii was never considered. The Philippine theater of the Spanish-American War also prompted annexation. One of the strongest proponents was Alfred Mahon, a brilliant naval strategist who, with support from Theodore Roosevelt, argued that the U.S. military must have Hawaii in order to be a viable force in the Pacific. In addition, Japan, victorious in its recent war with China, protested the American intention to annex, and in so doing prompted even moderates to support annexation for fear that the Japanese themselves coveted the prize. On July 7, 1898, President McKinley signed the annexation agreement, and this "tropical fruit" was finally put into America's basket.

MODERN TIMES

Hawaii entered the 20th century totally transformed from what it had been. The old Hawaiian language, religion, culture, and leadership were all gone; Western dress, values, education, and recreation were the norm. Native Hawaiians were now unseen citizens who lived in dwindling numbers in remote areas. The plantations, new centers of social order, had a strong Asian flavor; more than 75% of their work force was Asian. There was a small white middle class, an all-powerful white elite, and a single political party ruled by that elite. Education, however, was always highly prized, and by the turn of the century all racial groups were encouraged to attend school. By 1900, almost 90% of Hawaiians were literate (far above the national norm) and schooling was mandatory for all children between ages six and 15. Intermarriage was accepted, and there was a mixing of the races like nowhere else on earth. The military became increasingly important to Hawaii. It brought in money and jobs, dominating the island economy. The Japanese attack on Pearl Harbor,

Honolulu Star-Bulletin 1st EXTRA

8 PAGES—HONOLULU, TERRITORY OF HAWAII, U. S. A., SUNDAY, DECEMBER 7, 1941—8 PAGES ★ PRICE FIVE CENTS

WAR!

(Associated Press by Transpacific Telephone)

SAN FRANCISCO, Dec. 7.—President Roosevelt announced this morning that Japanese planes had attacked Manila and Pearl Harbor.

OAHU BOMBED BY JAPANESE PLANES

The Honolulu Star Bulletin *banner headline announces the beginning of U.S. involvement in WW II on Sunday, Dec. 7, 1941.*

which began U.S. involvement in WW II, bound Hawaii to America forever. Once the islands had been baptized by blood, the average Mainlander felt that Hawaii was American soil. A movement among Hawaiians to become part of the Union began to grow. They wanted a real voice in Washington, not merely a voteless delegate as provided under their territory status. Hawaii became the 50th state in 1959 and the jumbo-jet revolution of the 1960s made it easily accessible to growing numbers of tourists from all over the world.

Military History

A few military strategists realized the importance of Hawaii early in the 19th century, but most didn't recognize the advantages until the Spanish-American War. It was clearly an unsinkable ship in the middle of the Pacific from which the U.S. could launch military operations. Troops were stationed at Camp McKinley, at the foot of Diamond Head, the main military compound until it became obsolete in 1907. Pearl Harbor was first surveyed in 1872 by General Schofield. Later, a military base named in his honor, Schofield Barracks, was a main military post in central Oahu. It first housed the U.S. 5th Cavalry in 1909 and was heavily bombed by the Japanese at the outset of WW II. Pearl Harbor, first dredged in 1908, was officially opened on Dec. 11, 1911. The first warship to enter was the

cruiser *California*. Ever since, the military has been a mainstay of island economy. Unfortunately, there has been long-standing bad blood between locals and military personnel. Each group has tended to look down upon the other.

Pearl Harbor Attack

On the morning of Dec. 7, 1941, the Japanese carrier *Akagi*, flying the battle flag of the famed Admiral Togo of the Russo-Japanese War, received and broadcast over its PA system island music from Honolulu station KGMB. Deep in the bowels of the ship a radio man listened for a much different message, coming thousands of miles from the Japanese mainland. When the ironically poetic message "east wind rain" was received, the attack was launched. At the end of the day, 2,325 U.S. servicemen and 57 civilians were dead; 188 planes were destroyed; 18 major warships were sunk or heavily damaged; and the U.S. was in the war. Japanese casualties were ludicrously light. The ignited conflict would rage for four years until Japan, through Nagasaki and Hiroshima, was vaporized into total submission. At the end of hostilities, Hawaii would never again be considered separate from America.

Statehood

A number of economic and political reasons explain why the ruling elite of Hawaii desired statehood, but put simply, the vast majority of people who lived there, especially after WW II, considered themselves Americans. The first serious mention of making "The Sandwich Islands" a state was in the 1850s under President Franklin Pierce, but it wasn't taken seriously until the monarchy was overthrown in the 1890s. For the next 50 years statehood proposals were made repeatedly to Congress, but there was stiff opposition, especially from the southern states. With Hawaii a territory, an import quota system beneficial to Mainland producers could be enacted on produce, especially sugar. Also, there was prejudice against creating a state in a place where the majority of the populace was not white. This situation was illuminated by the infamous Massie Rape Case of 1931 (see pp. 56-57), which went down as one of the greatest miscarriages of justice in American history.

During WW II, Hawaii was placed under martial law, but no serious attempt to intern the Japanese population was made, as in California.

There were simply too many Japanese, who went on to gain the respect of the American people by their outstanding fighting record during the war. Hawaii's own 100th Battalion became the famous 442nd Regimental Combat Team, which gained notoriety by saving the Lost Texas Battalion during the Battle of the Bulge and went on to be *the* most decorated battalion in all of WW II. When these GIs returned home, *no one* was going to tell them that they were not loyal Americans. Many of these AJAs (Americans of Japanese Ancestry) took advantage of the GI Bill and received higher education. They were from the common people, not the elite, and they rallied grass-roots support for statehood. When the vote finally occurred, approximately 132,900 voted in favor of statehood with only 7,800 votes against. Congress passed the Hawaii State Bill on March 12, 1959, and on Aug. 21, 1959, President Eisenhower announced that Hawaii was officially the 50th state.

GOVERNMENT

The only difference between the government of the state of Hawaii and those of other states is that it's "streamlined," and in theory more efficient. There are only two levels of government: the state and the county. With no town or city governments to deal with, considerable bureaucracy is eliminated. Hawaii, in anticipation of becoming a state, drafted a constitution in 1950 and was ready to go when statehood came. Politics and government are taken seriously in the Aloha State, which consistently turns in the best national voting record per capita. For example, in the first state elections 173,000 of 180,000 registered voters voted—a whopping 94% of the electorate. In the election to ratify statehood, hardly a ballot went uncast, with 95% of the voters opting for statehood. The bill carried every island of Hawaii except Niihau, where, coincidentally, most of the people (total population 250 or so) are of relatively pure Hawaiian blood. The U.S. Congress passed the Hawaii State Bill on March 12, 1959, and on Aug. 21, 1959, President Eisenhower proclaimed Hawaii the 50th state.

The present governor is John Waihee III, first Hawaiian governor in the United States. Mr. Waihee has held this office since 1986.

County Of Hawaii

The county of Hawaii is almost entirely Democratic with a token Republican state senator or representative here and there. Of the 25 State Senatorial Districts, Hawaii County is represented by three. The First District is the whole southern part of the island, from Puna to Kailua; its representative is one of the few Republicans holding office on the island. The Second District is mainly Hilo. The Third District takes in the whole northern section and is a shared district with East Maui. The combination of these two areas has been traditional, even from old Hawaiian times.

Of 51 seats in the State House of Representatives, Hawaii County has six. The Sixth District is again shared with East Maui and takes in most of South Kohala. At this time, all representatives are Democrats, except for a Republican representing Kailua-Kona, Fifth District.

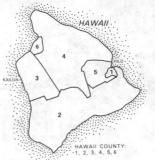

SENATORIAL DISTRICTS

HAWAII

3
HILO
1
KAILUA
MAUI
3
2
HAWAII COUNTY: 1, 2, 3

HOUSE DISTRICTS

HAWAII

6
4
HILO
KAILUA
3
5
2
HAWAII COUNTY:
1, 2, 3, 4, 5, 6

© J.D. BISIGNANI AND MOON PUBLICATIONS, INC.

ECONOMY

Hawaii's mid-Pacific location makes it perfect for two primary sources of income: tourism and the military. Tourists come in anticipation of endless golden days on soothing beaches, while the military is provided with the strategic position of an unsinkable battleship. Each economic sector nets Hawaii about $4 billion annually, money which should keep flowing smoothly and even increasing into the foreseeable future. These revenues remain mostly aloof from the normal ups and downs of the Mainland U.S. economy. Together they make up 60% of the islands' income, and both attract either gung-ho enthusiasts or rabidly negative detractors. The remaining 40% comes in descending proportions from manufacturing, construction, and agriculture (mainly sugar and pineapples). As long as the sun shines and the balance of global power requires a military presence, the economic stability of Hawaii is guaranteed.

TOURISM

"The earthly paradise! Don't you want to go to it? Why, of course!" This was the opening line of *The Hawaiian Guide Book* by Henry Whitney which appeared in 1875. In print for 25 years, it sold for 60 cents during a time when a roundtrip sea voyage between San Francisco and Honolulu cost $125. The technique is a bit dated, but the human desires remain the same: some of us seek paradise, all seek escape, some are drawn to play out a drama in a beautiful setting. Tourists have been coming to Hawaii ever since steamship service began in the 1860s. Until WW II, luxury liners carried the financial elite on exclusive voyages to the islands. By the 1920s 10,000 visitors a year were spending almost $5 million—cementing the bond between Hawaii and tourism.

A $25,000 prize offered by James Dole of pineapple fame sparked a trans-Pacific air race in 1927. The success of the aerial daredevils who answered the challenge proved that commercial air travel to Hawaii was feasible. Two years later, **Hawaiian Air** was offering regularly scheduled flights between all of the major islands. By 1950, airplanes had captured over 50% of the transportation market, and ocean voyages were relegated to "specialty travel" catering to the elite. By 1960 the large airbuses made their debut; 300,000 tourists arrived on eight designated airlines. The Boeing 747 began operating in 1969. These enormous planes could carry hundreds of passengers at reasonable rates, so travel to Hawaii became possible for the average-income person. In 1970, two million arrived, and by 1990 close to six million passengers arrived on 22 international air carriers. The first hotel in Hawaii was the **Volcano House,** which overlooked Kilauea Crater and was built in 1866.

Over 3,000 island residents are directly employed by the hotel industry, and many more indirectly serve the tourists. Of the slightly more than 7,000 hotel rooms, the greatest concentration is in Kona. The Kona hotels have the lowest occupancy rate in the state, rarely rising above 60%. Of the major islands, Hawaii receives the fewest tourists annually, only about 7,000 on any given day.

Tourists: Who, When, And Where

Tourism-based income outstripped pineapples and sugar by the mid-'60s and the boom was on. Most visitors (75%) are Americans, and the largest numbers come from the West Coast. Sun-seeking refugees from frigid Alaska, however, make up the greatest proportional number, according to population figures. The remaining arrivals are, in descending order, from Japan, Canada, Australia, and England. Europe, as a whole, sends proportionately fewer visitors than North America or Asia, while the fewest come from South America. The Japanese market is constantly growing and by the year 1990 over a million Japanese visitors per year are expected. This is particularly beneficial to the tourist market because the average Western tourist spends about $100 per day, while a Japanese counterpart spends just over $300 per day. (However, the average Japanese tourist stays only about five days, which is shorter than the typical visit.) Up until very recently the Japanese traveled only in groups and primarily stayed on Oahu. Now the trend is to travel independently or to come with a group and then peel off, with a hefty percentage heading for the "Neighbor Islands" (all islands other than Oahu).

The typical visitor is slightly affluent, and female visitors outnumber males three to two. The average age (35) is a touch higher than in most vacation areas because it reflects an inflated proportion of retirees heading for Hawaii, especially Honolulu, to fulfill lifelong "dream" vacations. A typical stay lasts about 12 days, down from a month in the 1950s; a full 50% are repeat visitors. On any given day there are about 70,000 travelers on Oahu, 15,000 on Maui, and about 7,000 each on Kauai and Hawaii. Molokai and Lanai get so few visitors that the figures are hardly counted. In 1964 only 10% of the islands' hotel rooms were on the Neighbor Islands, but by 1966 the figure jumped

to 25%, with more than 70% of the tourists opting to visit the Neighbor Islands. Today four out of 10 hotel rooms are on the Neighbor Islands and that figure should reach 50% shortly.

Joaquin Miller, the 19th-century poet of the Sierra, said, "I tell you my boy, the man who has not seen the Sandwich Islands, in this one great ocean's warm heart, has not seen the world." The times have certainly changed, but the sentiments of most visitors to Hawaii remain the same.

Tourism-related Problems

Tourism is both boon and blight to Hawaii. It is the root cause of two problems: one environmental, the other socioeconomic. The environmental impact is obvious and best described by the lament in songstress Joni Mitchell's "Big Yellow Taxi": "They paved paradise and put up a parking lot." Put simply, tourism can draw too many people to an area and overburden it. In the process, it stresses the land and destroys the natural beauty that attracted people in the first place. Tourists come to Hawaii for what has been called its "ambient resource": a balanced collage of indulgent climate, invigorating waters, intoxicating scenery, and exotic people all wrapped up neatly in one area which can both soothe and excite. It is in the best interest of Hawaii to preserve this "resource."

Like the land, humans are stressed by tourism. Local people, who once took the "Hawaiian lifestyle" for granted, become displaced and estranged in their own land. Some areas, predominantly along gorgeous beaches that were average- to low-income communities, are now overdeveloped, with prices going through the roof. The locals are not only forced to move out, but often must come back as service personnel in the tourist industry and cater to the very people who displaced them. At one time the psychological blow was softened because, after all, the newcomers were merely benign tourists who would stay a short time, spend a wad of money, and leave.

Today, condos are being built and a different sort of visitor is arriving. Many condo owners are well-educated businesspeople and professionals in above-average income brackets. The average condo owner is a Mainlander who purchases one as a second or retirement home. These people are not islanders and have a tough

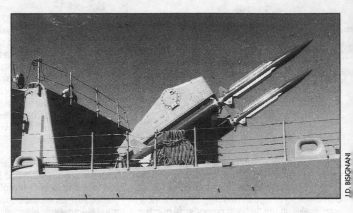

Missiles stand ready to defend America's unsinkable "Battleship Hawaii."

J.D. BISIGNANI

time relating to the locals, who naturally feel resentment. Moreover, since they don't *leave* like normal tourists, they use community facilities, find those special nooks and crannies for shopping or sunbathing that were once the exclusive domain of locals, and have a say as voters in community governments. The islanders become more and more disenfranchised. Many believe that the new order instigated by tourism is similar to what has always existed in Hawaii: a few from the privileged class being catered to by many from the working class. In a way it's an extension of the plantation system, but instead of carrying pineapples, most islanders find themselves carrying luggage, cocktails, or broiled fish. One argument, however, remains undeniable: whether it's people or pineapples, one has to make a living. The days of a little grass shack on a sunny beach aren't gone; it's just that you need a wallet full of credit cards to afford one.

THE MILITARY

Hawaii is the most militarized state in the U.S.: all five services are represented. Camp H.M. Smith, overlooking Pearl Harbor, is the headquarters of CINCPAC (Commander in Chief Pacific), which is responsible for 70% of the earth's surface, from California to the east coast of Africa and to both poles. The U.S. military presence dates back to 1887, when Pearl Harbor was given to the Navy as part of the Sugar Reciprocity Treaty. The sugar planters were given favorable duty-free treatment for their sugar,

while the U.S. Navy was allowed exclusive rights to one of the best harbors in the Pacific. In 1894, when the monarchy was being overthrown by the sugar planters, the USS *Boston* sent a contingency of U.S. Marines ashore to "keep order," which really amounted to a show of force backing the revolution. The Spanish-American War saw U.S. troops billeted at Camp McKinley at the foot of Diamond Head, and Schofield Barracks opened to receive the 5th Cavalry in 1909. Pearl Harbor's flames ignited WW II, and there has been no looking back since then.

Just under 200 army personnel are stationed on the Big Island, with about the same number of dependents. Most of these people are attached to the enormous Pohakuloa Military Reserve in the center of the island; a lesser number are at a few minor installations around Hilo and at Kilauea.

The Military Has No Aloha
Not everyone is thrilled by the strong military presence in Hawaii. Two factions, native Hawaiians and antinuclear groups, are downright angry. Radical contingencies of native Hawaiian-rights groups consider Hawaii an independent country, besieged and "occupied" by the U.S. government. They date their loss of independence to Liliuokalani's overthrow in 1894. The vast majority of ethnic Hawaiians, though they consider themselves Americans, are concerned about loss of their rightful homelands with no financial reparation, and about continuing destruction of and disregard for their traditional religious and historical sites. A long list of griev-

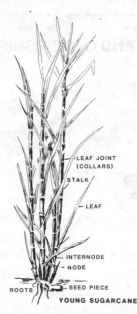

LEAF JOINT (COLLARS)
STALK
LEAF
INTERNODE
NODE
ROOTS — SEED PIECE
YOUNG SUGARCANE

LOUISE FOOTE

Anyone interested in the nuclear controversy can contact the following organizations: Catholic Action of Hawaii, 1918 University Ave., Honolulu, HI 96822; U.S. Nuclear Free Pacific Network, 942 Market St., Rm. 711, San Francisco, CA 94102; or *Kahuliau* ("an independent newspaper focusing on Hawaii and Pacific issues"), Box 61337, Honolulu, HI 96822.

AGRICULTURE

The Big Island's economy is the state's most agriculturally based. Over 6,000 farmhands, horticultural workers, and *paniolo* work the land to produce over half of the state's vegetables and melons and over 75% of the fruit, especially papaya. The Big Island also produces 33 million pounds of macadamia nuts, the state's entire crop except for what's produced by small farms here and there on the other islands. And 300 or more horticultural farms produce the largest number of orchids and anthuriums in the state, leaving the Big Island awash in color and fragrance. In the hills, entrepreneurs raise *pakalolo* (marijuana), which has become the state's most productive cash crop.

Sugar
Hawaii is the state's largest sugar grower, with over 90,000 acres in cane. These produce four million tons of refined sugar, 40% of the state's output. The majority of sugar land is along the Hamakua Coast, long known for its abundant water supply. At one time, the cane was even transported to the mills by water flumes. Another large pocket of cane fields is found on the southern part of the island, mostly in Puna.

Coffee
The Kona District is a splendid area for raising coffee; it gives the beans a beautiful tan. Lying in Mauna Loa's rain shadow, it gets dewy mornings followed by sunshine and an afternoon cloud shadow. This coffee has long been accepted as gourmet quality, and is sold in the better restaurants throughout Hawaii and in fine coffee shops around the world. It's a dark, full-bodied coffee with a rich aroma. Approximately 650 small farms produce nearly $4 million a year in coffee revenue. Few, however, make it a full-time business.

ances is cited by native Hawaiian action groups, but the best and clearest example is the controversy over the sacred island, Kahoolawe, which is used as a bombing target by the U.S. Navy.

A major controversy raised by the military presence focuses on Hawaii as a nuclear target. The ultimate goal of the antinuclear protestors is to see the Pacific, and the entire world, free from nuclear arms. They see Hawaii as a big target used by the international power merchants on the Mainland as both pawn and watchdog—if war breaks out, they say, the Hawaiian Islands will be reduced to cinders. The military naturally counters that a strong Hawaii is a deterrent to nuclear war and that Hawaii is not only a powerful offensive weapon, but one of the best-defended regions of the world. Unfortunately, when you are on an island there is no place to go: like a boxer in a ring, you can run, but you can't hide. Also, the military has been recently cited for disposing of stockpiles of chemical weapons by incineration on Johnston Island, a military installation southwest of the Big Island. Because there was no environmental impact study, scientists fear that wind and currents could carry the pollutants to the main Hawaiian islands, destroying delicate coral reefs along the way.

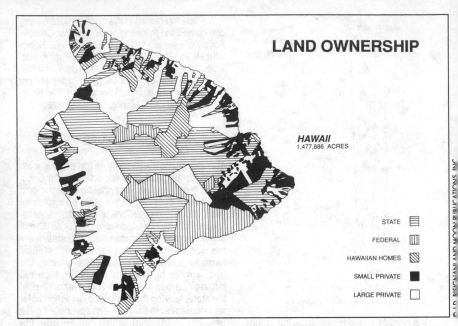

LAND OWNERSHIP

HAWAII
1,477,886 ACRES

STATE
FEDERAL
HAWAIIAN HOMES
SMALL PRIVATE
LARGE PRIVATE

© JD. BISCHAN AND MOON PUBLICATIONS, INC

Cattle

Hawaii's cattle ranches produce over 18 million pounds of beef per year, 65% of the state's total. More than 360 independent ranches are located on the island, but they are dwarfed both in size and production by the massive Parker Ranch, which alone is three-quarters the size of Oahu.

THE "BIG FIVE"

Until statehood, Hawaii was ruled economically by a consortium of corporations known as the "Big Five": **C. Brewer and Co.**, sugar, ranching, and chemicals, founded in 1826; **Theo. H. Davies & Co.**, sugar, investments, insurance, and transportation, founded in 1845; **Amfac Inc.** (originally H. Hackfield Inc.—a German firm that changed its name and ownership during the anti-German sentiment of WW I to American Factors), sugar, insurance, and land development, founded in 1849; **Castle and Cooke Inc.**, (Dole) pineapple, food packing, and land development, founded in 1851; and **Alexander and Baldwin Inc.**, shipping, sugar, and pineapple, founded in 1895. This

economic oligarchy ruled Hawaii with a velvet glove and a steel grip.

With members on all important corporate boards, they controlled all major commerce, including banking, shipping, insurance, hotel development, agriculture, utilities, and wholesale and retail merchandising. Anyone trying to buck the system was ground to dust, finding it suddenly impossible to do business in the islands. The Big Five were made up of the islands' oldest and most well-established *haole* families; all included bloodlines from Hawaii's own nobility. They looked among themselves for suitable husbands and wives, so that breaking in from the outside even through marriage was hardly possible. The only time they were successfully challenged prior to statehood was when Sears, Roebuck and Co. opened a store on Oahu. Closing ranks, the Big Five decreed that their steamships would not carry Sears's freight. When Sears threatened to buy its own steamship line, the Big Five relented.

Actually, statehood, and more to the point, tourism, broke their oligarchy. After 1960 too much money was at stake for Mainland-based corporations to ignore. Eventually the grip of the Big Five was loosened, but they are still enormously powerful and richer than ever. These days, however, they don't control everything; now their power is land. With only five other major landholders, they control 65% of the privately held land in Hawaii.

LAND OWNERSHIP

Landwise, Hawaii is a small pie, and its slices are not at all well divided. Of the state's 6,425 square miles of land, the six main inhabited islands make up 98% of it. (This figure does not include Niihau, which is privately owned by the Robinson family and inhabited by some of the last remaining pure-blooded Hawaiians; nor does it include Kahoolawe, the uninhabited U.S. Navy bombing target just off Maui's south shore.) Of the 4,045,511 acres that make up the inhabited islands, 36% is owned by the state

and 10% by the federal government; the remaining 54% is in private hands. But only 40 owners, with 5,000 or more acres each, own 75% of all private lands. Moreover, only 10 private concerns own two-thirds of these lands. To be more specific, Castle and Cooke Inc. owns 99% of Lanai, while 40-60% of Maui, Oahu, Molokai, Kauai, and Hawaii is owned by less than a dozen private parties. The largest private landowner is the Kamehameha Schools/ Bishop Estate, which recently lost a Supreme Court battle that ended with a ruling allowing the state of Hawaii to acquire privately owned land for "the public good."

More than in any other state, Hawaii's landowners tend to lease land instead of selling it, and many private homes are on rented ground. Many feel that with land prices going up all the time, only the very rich land developers will be able to purchase, and the "people" of Hawaii will become even more land-poor.

JACQUES ARAGO, CIRCA 1819 (HAWAII STATE ARCHIVES)

PEOPLE

Nowhere else on earth can you find such a kaleidoscopic mixture of people. Every major race is
accounted for, and over 50 ethnic groups are
represented throughout the islands, making
Hawaii the most racially integrated state in the
U.S. Its population of one million includes 120,000
permanently stationed military personnel and
their dependents. It is the only state where whites
are not the majority. About 60% of the people living in Hawaii were born there, 25% were born
on the Mainland U.S., and 15% are foreign-born.

The population of Hawaii has been growing
steadily in recent times, but it fluctuated wildly in
times past. In 1876 it ebbed to its lowest, with
only 55,000 permanent residents in the islands.
This was the era of large sugar plantations; their
constant demand for labor was the primary
cause of the importation of various peoples from
around the world, which is what led to Hawaii's
racially integrated society. WW II saw Hawaii's
population swell from 400,000 just prior to the
war to 900,000 during the war. Naturally,
500,000 were military personnel who left at

war's end, but many returned to settle after getting a taste of island living.

Of the one million people in the islands today,
800,000 live on Oahu, with over half of these
living in the Honolulu Metropolitan Area. The
rest of the population is distributed as follows:
93,000 on Hawaii, with 36,000 living in Hilo;
63,000 on Maui, with the largest concentration,
23,000, in Wailuku/Kahului; 40,000 on Kauai,
including 230 pure-blooded Hawaiians on Niihau; 6,000 on Molokai; and just over 2,000 on
Lanai. The population density, statewide, is 156
people per square mile, slightly less than California's 183 people per square mile. The population is not at all evenly distributed, with Oahu
claiming about 1,600 people per square mile,
and Hawaii barely 25 residents per square mile.
City dwellers outnumber those living in the country by four to one.

Population Figures
With 100,000 people or so, the Big Island has
the second-largest island population in Hawaii,

just under 10% of the state's total. However, it has the smallest population density of the main islands, with barely 25 people per square mile. Hilo has the largest population with 38,000 residents, followed by Kailua-Kona with under 10,000, and Captain Cook with 2,500 or so. The ethnic breakdown of the 100,000 people is as follows: 34% Caucasian, 27% Japanese, 19% Hawaiian, 14% Filipino, 2% Chinese, 4% other.

THE HAWAIIANS

The study of the native Hawaiians is ultimately a study in tragedy because it ends in their demise as a viable people. When Captain Cook first sighted Hawaii in 1778, there were an estimated 300,000 natives living in relative harmony with their ecological surroundings; within 100 years a scant 50,000 demoralized and dejected Hawaiians existed almost as wards of the state. Today, although 115,000 people claim varying degrees of Hawaiian blood, experts say that fewer than 1,000 are pure Hawaiian, and this is stretching it.

It's easy to see why people of Hawaiian lineage can be bitter over what they have lost, being strangers in their own land now, much like Native Americans. The overwhelming majority of "Hawaiians" are of mixed heritage, and the wisest take the best from all worlds. From the Hawaiian side comes simplicity, love of the land, and acceptance of people. It is the Hawaiian legacy of aloha that remains immortal and adds that special elusive quality that *is* Hawaii.

Polynesian Roots

The Polynesians' original stock is muddled and remains an anthropological mystery, but it's believed that they were nomadic wanderers who migrated from both the Indian subcontinent and Southeast Asia through Indonesia, where they learned to sail and navigate on protected waterways. As they migrated they honed their sailing skills until they could take on the Pacific, and as they moved, they absorbed people from other cultures and races until they had coalesced into what we now know as Polynesians.

Abraham Fornander, still considered a major authority on the subject, wrote in his 1885 *Account of the Polynesian Race* that he believed the Polynesians started as a white (Aryan) race

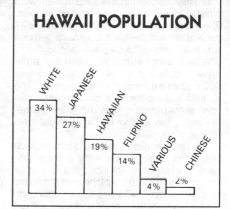

that was heavily influenced by contact with the Cushite Chaldeo-Arabian civilization. He estimated their arrival in Hawaii at A.D. 600, based on Hawaiian genealogical chants. Modern science seems to bear this date out, although it remains skeptical about his other surmises. According to others, the intrepid Polynesians who actually settled Hawaii are believed to have come from the Marquesas Islands, 1,000 miles southeast of Hawaii. The Marquesans were cannibals known for their tenacity and strength, attributes that would serve them well.

The Caste System

Hawaiian society was divided into rankings by a strict caste system determined by birth, and from which there was no chance of escaping. The highest rank was the *ali'i,* the chiefs and royalty. The impeccable genealogies of the *ali'i* were traced back to the gods themselves, and the chants *(mo'o ali'i)* were memorized and sung by professionals (called *ku'auhau)* who were themselves *ali'i.* Ranking passed from both father and mother, and custom dictated that the first mating of an *ali'i* be with a person of equal status.

A *kahuna* was a highly skilled person whose advice was sought before any major project was undertaken, such as building a house, hollowing a canoe log, or even offering a prayer. The *mo'o kahuna* were the priests of Ku and Lono, and they were in charge of praying and following rituals. They were very powerful *ali'i* and kept strict secrets and laws concerning their various functions.

Besides this priesthood of *kahuna*, there were other *kahuna* who were not *ali'i* but commoners. The two most important were the healers *(kahuna lapa'au)* and the black magicians *(kahuna ana'ana)*, who could pray a person to death. The *kahuna lapa'au* had a marvelous pharmacopia of herbs and spices that could cure over 250 diseases common to the Hawaiians. The *kahuna ana'ana* could be hired to cast a love spell over a person or cause his or her untimely death. They seldom had to send out a reminder of payment!

The common people were called the *makaainana*, "the people of land"—the farmers, artisans, and fishermen. The land that they lived on was owned by the *ali'i*, but they were not bound to it. If the local *ali'i* was cruel or unfair, the *makaainana* had the right to leave and reside on another's lands. The *makaainana* mostly loved their local *ali'i* much like a child loves a parent, and the feeling was reciprocal. *Makaainana* who lived close to the *ali'i* and could be counted on as warriors in times of trouble were called *kanaka no lua kaua*, "a man for the heat of battle." They were treated with greater favor than those who lived in the backcountry, *kanaka no hii kua*, whose lesser standing opened them up to discrimination and cruelty. All *makaainana* formed extended families called *ohana* who usually lived on the same section of land, called *ahupua'a*. Those farmers who lived inland would barter their produce with the fishermen who lived on the shore, and thus all shared equally in the bounty of land and sea.

A special group called *kauwa* was a landless, untouchable caste confined to living on reservations. Their origins were obviously Polynesian, but they appeared to be descendants of castaways who had survived and become perhaps the aboriginals of Hawaii before the main migrations. It was *kapu* for anyone to go onto *kauwa* lands, and doing so meant instant death. If a human sacrifice was needed, the *kahuna* would simply summon a *kauwa*, who had no recourse but to mutely comply. To this day, to call someone *kauwa*, which now supposedly only means servant, is still considered a fight-provoking insult.

Kapu And Day-to-day Life

Occasionally there were horrible wars, but mostly the people lived quiet and ordered lives based on a strict caste society and the *kapu* system. Famine was known but only on a regional level, and the population was kept in check by birth control, crude abortions, and the distasteful practice of infanticide, especially of baby girls. The Hawaiians were absolutely loving and nurturing par-ents under most circumstances, and would even take in a *hanai* (adopted child or oldster), a lovely practice that lingers to this day.

A strict division of labor existed among men and women. Men were the only ones permitted to have anything to do with taro: this foodstuff was so sacred that there were a greater number of *kapu* concerning taro than concerning man himself. Men pounded poi and served it to the women. Men also were the fishermen and the builders of houses, canoes, irrigation ditches, and walls. Women tended to other gardens and shoreline fishing, and were responsible for making tapa cloth. The entire family lived in the common house called the *hale noa*.

Certain things were kapu between the sexes. Primarily, women could not enter the *mua* (man's house), nor could they eat with men. Certain foods such as pork, coconut, red fish, and bananas were forbidden to women, and it was *kapu* for a man to have intercourse before going fishing, engaging in battle, or attending a religious ceremony. Young boys lived with the women until they underwent a circumcision rite called *pule ipu*. After this was performed, they were required to keep the *kapu* of men. A true Hawaiian settlement required a minimum of five huts: the men's eating hut; women's menstruation hut; women's eating hut; communal sleeping hut; and prayer hut. Without these five separate structures, Hawaiian "society" could not happen, since the *ia kapu* (forbidden eating between men and women) could not be observed. *Ali'i* could also declare a *kapu*, and often did so. Certain lands or fishing areas were temporarily made *kapu* so that they could revitalize. Even today, it is *kapu* for anyone to remove all the *opihi* (a type of limpet) from a rock. The great King Kamehameha I even placed a *kapu* on the body of his notoriously unfaithful child bride, Kaahumanu. It didn't work! The greatest *kapu (kapu moe)* was afforded to the highest ranking *ali'i*: anyone coming into their presence had to prostrate themselves. Lesser ranking *ali'i* were afforded the *kapu noho*: lessers had to sit or kneel in their presence. Commoners could

JOHN WEBBER (HAWAII STATE ARCHIVES)

not let their shadows fall upon an *ali'i* or enter their house except through a special door. Breaking a *kapu* meant immediate death.

Fatal Flaws

Less than 100 years after Captain Cook's arrival, King Kalakaua found himself with only 48,000 Hawaiian subjects, down more than 80%. Wherever the king went, he would beseech his people, *"Hooulu lahui,"* "Increase the race," but it was already too late. It was as if nature herself had turned her back on these once-proud people. Many of their marriages were barren and in 1874 when only 1,400 children were born, a full 75% died in infancy. The Hawaiians could do nothing but watch as their race faded from existence.

The Causes Of Decline

The ecological system of Hawaii has always been exceptionally fragile and this included its people. When the first whites arrived they found a great people who were large, strong, and virile. But when it came to fighting off the most minor diseases, the Hawaiians proved as delicate as hothouse flowers. To exacerbate the situation, the Hawaiians were totally uninhibited toward sexual intercourse between willing partners, and they engaged in it openly and with

abandon. Unfortunately, the sailors who arrived were full of syphilis and gonorrhea. The Hawaiian women brought these diseases home and, given the nature of Hawaiian society at the time, they spread like wildfire. By the time the missionaries came in 1820 and helped to halt the unbridled fornication, they estimated the native population at only 140,000, less than half of what it had been only 40 years since initial contact! In the next 50 years measles, mumps, influenza, and tuberculosis further ravaged the people. Furthermore, Hawaiian men were excellent sailors, and it's estimated that during the whaling years at least 25% of all able-bodied Hawaiian men sailed away, never to return.

But the coup de grace that really ended the Hawaiian race, as such, was that all racial newcomers to the islands were attracted to the Hawaiians and the Hawaiians were in turn attracted to them. With so many interracial marriages, the Hawaiians literally bred themselves out of existence. By 1910, there were still twice as many full-blooded Hawaiians as mixed-bloods, but by 1940 mixed-blooded Hawaiians were the fastest-growing group, and full-blooded the fastest declining.

Hawaiians Today

Many of the Hawaiians who moved to the cities became more and more disenfranchised. Their folk society stressed openness and a giving nature, but downplayed the individual and the ownership of private property. These cultural traits made them easy targets for the users and schemers until they finally became either apathetic or angry. Most surveys reveal that although Hawaiians number only 12% of the population, they account for almost 50% of the financially destitute families and about half of all arrests and illegitimate births. Niihau, a privately owned island, is home to about 250 pure-blooded Hawaiians, representing the largest concentration of them, per capita, in the islands. The Robinson family, which owns the island, restricts visitors to invited guests only.

The second-largest concentration is on Molokai, where 2,700 Hawaiians, living mostly on 40-acre *kuleana* of Hawaiian Homes Lands, make up 45% of that island's population. The majority of mixed-blooded Hawaiians, 80,000 or so, live on Oahu, where they are particularly strong in the hotel and entertainment fields.

People of Hawaiian extraction are still a delight to meet, and anyone so lucky as to be befriended by one long regards this friendship as the highlight of his or her travels. The Hawaiians have always given their aloha freely to all the peoples of the world, and it is we who must acknowledge this precious gift.

THE CHINESE

Next to Yankees from New England, the Chinese are the oldest migrant group in Hawaii, and their influence has far outshone their meager numbers. They brought to Hawaii, along with their individuality, Confucianism, Taoism, and Buddhism, although many have long since become Christians. The Chinese population of 57,000 makes up only six percent of the state's total, and the majority (52,000) reside on Oahu. As an ethnic group they account for the least amount of crime, the highest per capita income, and a disproportionate number of professionals.

The First Chinese
No one knows his name, but an unknown Chinese immigrant is credited with being the first person in Hawaii to refine sugar. This Asian-wanderer tried his hand at crude refining on Lanai in 1802. Fifty years later the sugar plantations desperately needed workers, and the first Chinese brought to Hawaii under the newly passed Masters and Servants Act were 195 coolies from Amoy, who arrived in 1852. These conscripts were contracted for three to five years and given $3 per month plus room and board. This was for 12 hours a day, six days a week, and even in 1852 these wages were the pits. The Chinese almost always left the plantations the minute their contracts expired. They went into business for themselves and promptly monopolized the restaurant and small-shop trades.

The Chinese Niche
Although many people in Hawaii considered all Chinese ethnically the same, they were actually quite different. The majority came from Guangdong Province in southern China. They were two distinct ethnic groups: the Punti made up 75% of the immigrants, and the Hakka made up the remainder. In China, they remained separate from each other, never mixing; in Hawaii,

they mixed out of necessity. For one, hardly any Chinese women came over at first, and the ones who followed were at a premium and gladly accepted as wives, regardless of ethnic background. The Chinese were also one of the first groups who willingly intermarried with the Hawaiians, from whom they gained a reputation for being exceptionally caring spouses.

The Chinese accepted the social order and kept a low profile. For example, during the turbulent labor movements of the 1930s and '40s in Hawaii, the Chinese community produced not one labor leader, radical intellectual, or left-wing politician. When Hawaii became a state, one of the two senators elected was Hiram Fong, a racially mixed Chinese. Since statehood, the Chinese community has carried on business as usual as they continue to rise both economically and socially.

THE JAPANESE

Most scholars believe that (inevitably) a few Japanese castaways floated to Hawaii long before Captain Cook arrived, and might have introduced the iron with which the islanders seemed to be familiar before the white explorers arrived. The first official arrivals from Japan were ambassadors sent by the Japanese shogun to negotiate in Washington; they stopped en route at Honolulu in March 1860. But it was as plantation workers that the Japanese were brought en masse to the islands. A small group arrived in 1868, and mass migration started in 1885.

In 1886, because of famine, the Japanese government allowed farmers mainly from southern Honshu, Kyushu, and Okinawa to emigrate. Among these were members of Japan's little-talked-about untouchable caste, called *eta* or *burakumin* in Japan and *chorinbo* in Hawaii. They gratefully seized this opportunity to better their lot, an impossibility in Japan. The first Japanese migrants were almost all men. Between 1897 and 1908 migration was steady, with about 70% of the immigrants being men. Afterwards, migration slowed because of a "gentlemen's agreement," a euphemism for racism against the "yellow peril." By 1900 there were over 60,000 Japanese in the islands, constituting the largest ethnic group.

The Japanese-American GIs returned as "our boys."

AJAs, Americans Of Japanese Ancestry

Parents of most Japanese children born before WW II were *issei* (first generation), who considered themselves apart from other Americans and clung to the notion of "we Japanese." Their children, the *nisei* or second generation, were a different matter altogether. In one generation they had become Americans, and they put into practice the high Japanese virtues of obligation, duty, and loyalty to the homeland; that homeland was now unquestionably America. After Pearl Harbor was bombed, the FBI kept close tabs on the Japanese community, and the menace of the "enemy within" prompted the decision to place Hawaii under martial law for the duration of the war. It has since been noted that not a single charge of espionage or sabotage was ever reported against the Japanese community in Hawaii during the war.

AJAs As GIs

Although Japanese had formed a battalion during WW I, they were insulted by being considered unacceptable as American soldiers in WW II. Some Japanese-Americans volunteered to serve in labor battalions, and because of their flawless work and loyalty, it was decided to put out a call for a few hundred volunteers to form a combat unit. Over 10,000 signed up! AJAs formed two distinguished units in WW II: the 100th Infantry Battalion, and later the 442nd Regimental Combat Team. They landed in Italy at Salerno and even fought from Guadalcanal to Okinawa. They distinguished themselves by becoming *the* most decorated unit in American military history.

The AJAs Return

Many returning AJAs took advantage of the G.I. Bill and received college educations. The "Big Five" corporations (see pp. 48-49) for the first time accepted former AJA officers as executives, and the old order was changed. Many Japanese became involved with Hawaiian politics and the first elected to Congress was Daniel Inouye, who had lost an arm fighting in WW II. Hawaii's past governor, George Ariyoshi, elected in 1974, was the country's first Japanese-American to reach such a high office. Most Japanese, even as they climb the economic ladder, tend to remain Democrats.

Today, one out of every two political offices in Hawaii is held by a Japanese-American. In one of those weird quirks of fate, it is now the Hawaiian Japanese who are accused by other ethnic groups of engaging in unfair political practices—nepotism and reverse discrimination. Many of these accusations against AJAs are undoubtedly motivated by jealousy, but the AJAs' record in social fairness issues is not without blemish; true to their custom of family loyalty, they do stick together.

There are now 240,000 people in Hawaii of Japanese ancestry, one-quarter of the state's population. They are the least likely of any ethnic group in Hawaii to marry outside of their group—especially the men—and they enjoy a higher-than-average standard of living.

CAUCASIANS

White people have a distinction separating them from all other ethnic groups in Hawaii: they are lumped together as one. You can be anything from a Protestant Norwegian dockworker to a Greek Orthodox shipping tycoon, but if your skin is white, in Hawaii you're a *haole*. What's more, you could have arrived at Waikiki from Missoula, Montana, in the last 24 hours, or your *kamaaina* family can go back five generations, but again, if you're white, you're a *haole*.

The word *"haole"* has a floating connotation that depends upon the spirit in which it's used. It can mean everything from a derisive "honky" or "cracker" to nothing more than "white person." The exact Hawaiian meaning is clouded, but some say it meant "a man of no background," because white men couldn't chant a genealogical *kanaenae* telling the Hawaiians who they were. The word eventually evolved to mean "foreign white man" and today, simply "white person."

White History

Next to Hawaiians themselves, white people have the oldest stake in Hawaii. They've been there as settlers in earnest since the missionaries of the 1820s, and were established long before any other migrant group. From last century until statehood, old *haole* families owned and controlled everything, and although they were generally benevolent, philanthropic, and paternalistic, they were also racist. They were established *kamaaina* families, many of whom made up the boards of the Big Five corporations or owned huge plantations and formed an inner social circle that was closed to the outside. Many managed to find mates from among close family acquaintances.

Their paternalism, which they accepted with grave responsibility, at first only extended to the Hawaiians, who saw them as replacing their own *ali'i*. Asians were considered primarily instruments of production. These supremacist attitudes tended to drag on in Hawaii until quite recent times. They are today responsible for the sometimes sour relations between white and nonwhite people in the islands. Today, all individual white people are resented to a certain degree because of these past acts, even though they personally were in no way involved.

White Plantation Workers

In the 1880s the white landowners looked around and felt surrounded and outnumbered by Asians, so they tried to import white people for plantation work. None of their schemes seemed to work out. Europeans were accustomed to a much higher wage scale and better living conditions than were provided on the plantations. Although only workers and not considered the equals of the ruling elite, they still were expected to act like a special class. They were treated preferentially, which meant higher wages for the same jobs performed by Asians. Some of the imported workers included: 600 Scandinavians in 1881; 1,400 Germans from 1881-85; 400 Poles from 1897-98; and 2,400 Russians from 1909-12. Many proved troublesome, like the Poles and Russians who staged strikes after only months on the job. Many quickly moved to the Mainland. A contingency of Scots, who first came as mule skinners, did become successful plantation managers and supervisors. The Germans and Scandinavians were well received and climbed the social ladder rapidly, becoming professionals and skilled workers.

The Depression years, not as economically bad in Hawaii as in the continental U.S., brought many Mainland whites seeking opportunity, mostly from the South and the West. These new people were even more racist toward brown-skinned people and Asians than the *kamaaina haole*, and they made matters worse. They also competed more intensely for jobs. The racial tension generated during this period came to a head in 1932 with the infamous "Massie Rape Case."

The Massie Rape Case

Thomas Massie, a naval officer, and his young wife, Thalia, attended a party at the Officers Club. After drinking and dancing all evening, they got into a row and Thalia rushed out in a huff. A few hours later, Thalia was at home, confused and hysterical, claiming to have been raped by some local men. On the most circumstantial evidence, Joseph Kahahawai and four friends of mixed ethnic background were accused. In a highly controversial trial rife with racial tensions, the verdict ended in a hung jury.

While a new trial was being set, Kahahawai and his friends were out on bail. Seeking revenge, Thomas Massie and Grace Fortescue, Thalia's mother, kidnapped Joseph Kahahawai with a plan of extracting a confession from him. They were aided by two enlisted men assigned to guard Thalia. While questioning Joseph, they killed him and attempted to dump his body in the sea but were apprehended. Another controversial trial—this time for Mrs. Fortescue, Massie, and the accomplices—followed. Clarence Darrow, the famous lawyer, sailed to Hawaii to defend them. For killing Kahahawai, these people served *one hour* of imprisonment in the judge's private chambers. The other four, acquitted with Joseph Kahahawai, maintain innocence of the rape to this day. Later, the Massies divorced, and Thalia went on to become a depressed alcoholic who took her own life.

The Portuguese

The last time anyone looked, Portugal was still attached to the European continent, but for some anomalous reason the Portuguese weren't considered *haole* in Hawaii for the longest time. About 12,000 arrived between 1878 and 1887 and another 6,000 came between 1906 and 1913. Accompanied during this period by 8,000 Spanish, they were considered one and the same. Most of the Portuguese were illiterate peasants from Madeira and the Azores, and the Spanish hailed from Andalusia. They were very well received, and because they were white but not *haole,* they made a perfect "buffer" ethnic group. Committed to staying in Hawaii, they rose to be skilled workers—the *"luna* class" on the plantations. However, they deemphasized education and became very racist toward Asians, regarding them as a threat to their job security.

By 1920, the 27,000 Portuguese made up 11% of the population. After that they tended to blend with the other ethnic groups and weren't counted separately. Portuguese men tended to marry within their ethnic group, but a good portion of Portuguese women married other white men and became closer to the *haole* group, while another large portion chose Hawaiian mates and grew further away. Although they didn't originate pidgin English (see "Language"), the unique melodious quality of their native tongue did give pidgin that certain lilt it has today. Also, the ukulele ("jumping flea") was closely patterned after the *cavaquinho,* a Portuguese stringed folk instrument.

The Caucasian Population

Today Caucasians make up the largest racial group in the islands at 33% (about 330,000) of the population. There are heavy white concentrations throughout Oahu, especially in Waikiki, Kailua-Kaneohe, and around Pearl City. The white population is the fastest growing in the islands because most people resettling in Hawaii are white Americans predominantly from the West Coast.

FILIPINOS AND OTHERS

The Filipinos who came to Hawaii brought high hopes of amassing personal fortunes and returning home as rich heroes; for most it was a dream that never came true. Filipinos had been American nationals ever since the Spanish-American War of 1898, and as such weren't subject to immigration laws that curtailed the importation of other Asian workers at the turn of this century. The first to arrive were 15 families in 1906, but a large number came in 1924 as strikebreakers. The majority were illiterate peasants called *Ilocanos* from the northern Philippines, with about 10% Visayans from the central cities. The Visayans were not as hardworking or thrifty, but were much more sophisticated. From the first, Filipinos were looked down upon by all the other immigrant groups, and were considered particularly uncouth by the Japanese. The value they placed on education was the least of any group, and even by 1930 only about half could speak rudimentary English, the majority remaining illiterate. They were billeted in the worst housing, performed the most menial jobs, and were the last hired and first fired.

One big difference between Filipinos and other groups was that the men brought no Filipino women to marry, so they clung to the idea of returning home. In 1930 there were 30,000 men and only 360 women. This hopeless situation led to a great deal of prostitution and homosexuality; many of these terribly lonely bachelors would feast and drink on weekends and engage in their gruesome but exciting pastime of cockfighting on Sundays. When some did manage to find wives, their mates were inevitably part Hawaiian. Today, there are still plenty of old Filipino bachelors who never managed to get home, and the Sunday cockfights remain a way of life.

The Filipinos constitute 14% of Hawaii's population (140,000), with almost 90% living on Oahu. Many visitors to Hawaii mistake Filipinos for Hawaiians because of their dark skin, and this is a minor irritant to both groups. Some streetwise Filipinos even claim to be Hawaiians, because being Hawaiian is "in" and goes over well with the tourists, especially the young women tourists. For the most part, these people are hard-working, dependable laborers who do tough work for little recognition. They remain low on the social totem pole and have not yet organized politically to stand up for their rights.

Other Groups

About 10% of Hawaii's population is made up of a conglomerate of other ethnic groups. Of these, the largest is Korean, with 14,000 people. About 8,000 Koreans came to Hawaii from 1903 until 1905, when their government halted emigration. During the same period about 6,000 Puerto Ricans arrived, but they have become so assimilated that only 4,000 people in Hawaii today consider themselves Puerto Rican. There were also two attempts made last century to import other Polynesians to strengthen the dying Hawaiian race, but they were failures. In 1869 only 126 central Polynesian natives could be

lured to Hawaii, and from 1878 to 1885 2,500 Gilbert Islanders arrived. Both groups became immediately disenchanted with Hawaii. They pined away for their own islands and departed for home as soon as possible.

Today, however, 12,000 Samoans have settled in Hawaii, and with more on the way they are the fastest-growing minority in the state. For unexplainable reasons, Samoans and native Hawaiians get along extremely poorly and have the worst racial tensions and animosity of any groups. The Samoans ostensibly should represent the archetypical Polynesians that the Hawaiians are seeking, but it doesn't work that way. Samoans are criticized by Hawaiians for their hot tempers, lingering feuds, and petty jealousies. They're clannish and are often the butt of "dumb" jokes. This racism seems especially ridiculous, but that's the way it is.

Just to add a bit more exotic spice to the stew, there are about 10,000 blacks, a few thousand Native Americans, and a smattering of Vietnamese refugees living on the Islands.

LANGUAGE

Hawaii is part of America and people speak English there, but that's not the whole story. If you turn on the TV to catch the evening news, you'll hear "Walter Cronkite" English, unless of course you happen to tune in to a Japanese-language broadcast designed for tourists from that country. You can easily pick up a Chinese-language newspaper or groove to the music on a Filipino radio station, but let's not confuse the issue. All your needs and requests at airports, car-rental agencies, restaurants, hotels, or wherever you happen to travel will be completely understood, as well as answered, in English. However, when you happen to overhear islanders speaking, what they're saying will sound somewhat familiar but you won't be able to pick up all the words, and the beat and melody of the language will be noticeably different.

Hawaii, like New England, the deep South, and the Midwest, has its own unmistakable linguistic regionalism. All the ethnic peoples who make up Hawaii have enriched the English spoken there with words, expressions, and subtle shades of meaning that are commonly used and understood throughout the islands. The

greatest influence on English has come from the Hawaiian language itself, and words such as aloha, *hula*, and muumuu are familiarly used and understood by most Americans.

Other migrant peoples, especially the Chinese, Japanese, and Portuguese, influenced the local dialect to such an extent that the simplified plantation lingo they spoke has become known as "pidgin." A fun and enriching part of the "island experience" is picking up a few words of Hawaiian and pidgin. English is the official language of the state, business, education, and perhaps even the mind; but pidgin is the language of the people, the emotions, and life, while Hawaiian remains the language of the heart and the soul.

Note: Many Hawaiian words are commonly used in English, appear in English dictionaries, and therefore would ordinarily be subject to the rules of English grammar. The Hawaiian language, however, does not pluralize nouns by adding an "s"; the singular and plural are differentiated in context. For purposes of this book, and to highlight rather than denigrate the Hawaiian culture, the Hawaiian style of pluralization will be followed for common Hawaiian words. The following are some examples of plural Hawaiian nouns treated this way in this book: *haole* (not haoles), *hula, kahuna, lei, nene*.

PIDGIN

The dictionary definition of pidgin is: a simplified language with a rudimentary grammar used as a means of communication between people speaking different languages. Hawaiian pidgin is a little more complicated than that. It had its roots during the plantation days of last century when white owners and *luna* (foremen) had to communicate with recently arrived Chinese, Japanese, and Portuguese laborers. It was designed as a simple language of the here and now, and was primarily concerned with the necessary functions of working, eating, and sleeping. It has an economical noun-verb-object structure (not necessarily in that order).

Hawaiian words make up most of pidgin's non-English vocabulary. It includes a good smattering of Chinese, Japanese, and Samoan; the distinctive rising inflection is provided by the melodious Mediterranean lilt of the Portuguese. Pidgin is not a stagnant language. It's kept alive by hip new words introduced by people who are "so radical," or especially by slang words introduced by teenagers. It's a colorful English, like "jive" or "ghettoese" spoken by American blacks, and is as regionally unique as the speech of Cajuns from Louisiana's bayous. *Makaainana* of all socioethnic backgrounds can at least understand pidgin. Most islanders are proud of it, while some consider it a low-class jargon. The Hawaiian House of Representatives has given pidgin an official sanction, and most people feel that it adds a real local style and should be preserved.

Pidgin Lives

Pidgin is first learned at school where all students, regardless of background, are exposed to it. The pidgin spoken by young people today is "fo' real" different from that of their parents. It's no longer only plantation talk but has moved to the streets and picked up some sophistication. At one time there was an academic movement to exterminate it, but that idea died away with

the same thinking that insisted on making left-handed people write with their right hand. It is strange, however, that pidgin has become the unofficial language of Hawaii's grass-roots movement, when it actually began as a white owners' language which was used to supplant Hawaiian and all other languages brought to the islands.

Although hip young *haole* use pidgin all the time, it has gained the connotation of being the language of the nonwhite locals, and is part of the "us against them" way of thinking. All local people, *haole* or not, do consider pidgin their own island language, and don't really like it when it's used by *malihini* (newcomers). If you're in the islands long enough, you don't have to bother learning pidgin; it'll learn you. There's a book sold all over the islands called *Pidgin to da Max*, written by (you guessed it) a *haole* from Nebraska named Doug Simonson. You might not be able to understand what's being said by locals speaking pidgin (that's usually the idea), but you should be able to *feel* what's being meant.

HAWAIIAN

The Hawaiian language sways like a palm tree in a gentle wind. Its words are as melodious as a love song. Linguists say that you can learn a lot about people through their language; when you hear Hawaiian you think of gentleness and love, and it's hard to imagine the ferocious side so evident in Hawaii's past. With its many Polynesian root words easily traced to Indonesian and Malay, Hawaiian is obviously from this same stock. The Hawaiian spoken today is very different from old Hawaiian. Its greatest metamorphosis occurred when the missionaries began to write it down in the 1820s. There is a movement to reestablish the Hawaiian language, and courses in it are offered at the University of Hawaii. Many scholars have put forth translations of Hawaiian, but there are endless, volatile disagreements in the academic sector about the real meanings of Hawaiian words. Hawaiian is no longer spoken as a language except on Niihau, and the closest tourists will come to it are in place-names, street names, and words that have become part of common usage, such as aloha and *mahalo*. A few old Hawaiians still speak it at home and

CAPSULE PIDGIN

The following are a few commonly used words and expressions that should give you an idea of pidgin. It really can't be written properly, merely approximated, but for now, *"Brah, study da' kine an' bimbye you be hele on, brah! O.K.? Lesgo."*

an' den—and then?; big deal; so what's next; how boring

bimbye—after a while; bye and bye. "Bimbye, you learn pidgin."

blalah—brother, but refers to a large, heavy set, good-natured Hawaiian man

brah—all the bro's in Hawaii are brahs; brother; pal. Used to call someone's attention. One of the most common words used even among people who are not acquainted. After a fill-up at a gas station, a person would say "Tanks, brah."

cockaroach—steal; rip off. If you really want to find out what *cockaroach* means, just leave your camera on your beach blanket when you take a little dip.

da' kine—a catch-all word of many meanings that epitomizes the essence of pidgin. *Da' kine* is easily used as a euphemism and is substituted whenever the speaker is at a loss for a word or just wants to generalize. It can mean: you know?; whatchamacallit; of that type.

geev um—give it to them; give them hell; go for it. Can be used as an encouragement. If a surfer is riding a great wave, the people on the beach might yell, "Geev um, brah!"

hana ho—again. Especially after a concert, the audience shouts "Hana ho!" (One more!).

hele on—right on!; hip; with it; groovy

howzit?—as in "howzit brah?"; what's happening?; how is it going? The most common greeting, used in place of the more formal "How do you do?"

hu hu—angry! "You put the make on the wrong da' kine wahine brah, and you in da' kine trouble, if you get one big Hawaiian blalah plenty hu hu."

kapu—a Hawaiian word meaning "forbidden." If *kapu* is written on a gate or posted on a tree, it means "No trespassing." *Kapu*-breakers are still very unpopular in the islands.

lesgo—Let's go! Do it!

li'dis an' li'dat—like this or that; a catch-all grouping used especially if you want to avoid details; like, ya' know?

lolo buggah—stupid or crazy guy (person). Words to a tropical island song go, "I want to find the lolo who stole my pakalolo."

mo' bettah—real good!; great idea. An island sentiment used to be "Mo' bettah you *come* Hawaii." Now it has subtly changed to "Mo' bettah you *visit* Hawaii."

ono—number one! delicious; great; groovy. "Hawaii is ono, brah!"

pakalolo—literally "crazy smoke"; marijuana; grass; reefer. "Hey, brah! Maui-wowie da' kine ono pakalolo."

pakiki head—stubborn; bull-headed

pau—a Hawaiian word meaning finished; done; over and done with. *Pau hana* means end of work or quitting time. Once used by plantation workers, now used by everyone.

stink face—basically frowning at someone; using facial expression to show displeasure. Hard looks. What you'll get if you give local people a hard time.

swell head—burned up; angry

talk story—spinning yarns; shooting the breeze; throwing the bull; a rap session. If you're lucky enough to be around to hear *kapuna* (elders) "talk story," you can hear some fantastic tales in the tradition of old Hawaii.

tita—sister, but only used to describe a fun-loving, down-to-earth country girl

waddascoops—what's the scoop?; what's up?; what's happening?

there are sermons in Hawaiian at some local churches. Kawaiahao Church in downtown Honolulu is the most famous of these. (See the Glossary for a list of commonly used Hawaiian words.)

Wiki Wiki Hawaiian

Thanks to the missionaries, the Hawaiian language is rendered phonetically using only 12 letters. They are the five vowels, a-e-i-o-u, sounded as they are in Italian; and seven consonants, h-k-l-m-n-p-w, sounded exactly as they are in English. Sometimes "w" is pronounced as "v," but this only occurs in the middle of a word and always follows a vowel. A consonant is always followed by a vowel, forming two-letter syllables, but vowels are often found in pairs or even triplets. A slight oddity about Hawaiian is the glottal stop. This is an abrupt break in sound in the middle of a word such as "oh-oh" in English, and is denoted with an apostrophe ('). A good example is *ali'i*; or even better, the Oahu town of Ha'iku, which actually means "abrupt break."

Pronunciation Key

For those unfamiliar with the sounds of Italian or other Romance languages, the vowels are sounded as follows:

A —in stressed syllables, long **a** as in **"ah"** (that feels good!). For example, Haleakala (Hah lay ah kah lah.) Unstressed syllables get a short "a" as in "again" or "above." For example, Kamehameha (**Ka**meh**a**meh**a**).

E —short **e** as in p**e** n or d**e**nt (H**a**le). Long **e** sounded as "ay" as in sw**ay** or d**ay**. For example, the Hawaiian goose (**nene**) is a "nay nay," not a "knee knee."

I —a long **i** as in s**ee** or w**e** (Hawa**ii** or p**a**l**i**).

O —round **o** as in n**o** or **oh** (k**o**a, or **o**n**o**).

U —round **u** as in d**o** or st**ew** (ka**pu**, or **Pu**na).

Diphthongs

There are also eight vowel pairs known as "diphthongs" (ae-ai-ao-au-ei-eu-oi-ou). These are the sounds made by gliding from one vowel to another within a syllable. The stress is placed on the first vowel. In English, examples would be

THE ALPHABET.

VOWELS.	Names.	SOUND.	
		Ex. in Eng.	Ex. in Hawaii.
A a	---â	as in *father*,	la—sun.
E e	---a	— *tete*,	hemo—cast off.
I i	---e	— *marine*,	maiie—quiet.
O o	---o	— *over*,	ono—sweet.
U u	---oo	—*rule*,	nui—large.

CONSONANTS.	Names.	CONSONANTS.	Names.
B b	be	**N n**	nu
D d	de	**P p**	pi
H h	he	**R r**	ro
K k	ke	**T t**	ti
L l	la	**V v**	vi
M m	mu	**W w**	we

The following are used in spelling foreign words:

| F f | fe | S s | se |
| G g | ge | Y y | yi |

soil and euphoria. Common examples in Hawaiian are *lei* (lay) and *heiau.*

Stress

The best way to learn which syllables are stressed in Hawaiian is by listening closely. It becomes obvious after a while. There are also some vowel sounds that are held longer than others; these can occur at the beginning of a word, such as the first "a" in *aina,* or in the middle of a word, like the first "a" in *lanai.* Again, it's a matter of tuning your ear and paying attention. No one is going to give you a hard time if you mispronounce a word. It's good, however, to pay close attention to the pronunciation of street and place-names because many Hawaiian words sound alike and a misplaced vowel here or there could be the difference between getting where you want to go and getting lost.

CAPSULE HAWAIIAN

The list on the following pages is merely designed to give you a "taste" of Hawaiian and to provide a basic vocabulary of words in common usage which you are likely to hear. Becoming familiar with them is not a strict necessity, but they will definitely enhance your experience and make it more congenial when talking with local people. You'll soon notice that many islanders spice their speech with certain words, especially when they're speaking "pidgin," and you too can use them just as soon as you feel comfortable. You might even discover some Hawaiian words that are so perfectly expressive they'll become a regular part of your vocabulary. Many Hawaiian words have actually made it into the English dictionary. Place names, historical names, and descriptive terms used throughout the text may not appear in the lists below, but will be cited in the glossary at the back of the book. Also see "Pidgin" in the "Language" section, "Food," and "Getting Around" for applicable Hawaiian words and phrases in these categories. The definitions given are not exhaustive, but are generally considered the most common.

BASIC VOCABULARY

a'a—rough clinker lava. *A'a* has become the correct geological term to describe this type of lava found anywhere in the world.

ae—yes

akamai—smart; clever; wise

ali'i—a Hawaiian chief or noble

aloha—the most common greeting in the islands; can mean both hello and goodbye, welcome or farewell. It also can mean romantic love, affection or best wishes.

aole—no

hale—house or building; often combined with other words to name a specific place such as Haleakala ("House of the Sun"), or Hale Pai at Lahainaluna, meaning "printing house"

hana—work; combined with *pau* means end of work or quitting time

haole—a word that at one time meant foreigner, but now means a white person or Caucasian. Many etymological definitions have been put forth, but none satisfies everyone. Some feel that it signified a person without a background, because the first white men could not chant their genealogies as was common to Hawaiians.

hapa—half, as in a mixed-blooded person being referred to as *hapa haole*

hapai—pregnant. Used by all ethnic groups when a *keiki* is on the way.

heiau—a traditional Hawaiian temple. A platform made of skillfully fitted rocks, upon which structures were built and offerings made to the gods.

holomuu—an ankle-length dress that is much more fitted than a muumuu and is often worn on formal occasions

hoolaulea—any happy event, but especially a family outing or picnic

hoomalimali—sweet talk; flattery

huhu—angry; irritated; mad

hui—a group; meeting; society; often used to refer to Chinese businesspeople or family members who pool their money to get businesses started

hula—a native Hawaiian dance in which the rhythm of the islands is captured in swaying hips and the stories told by lyrically moving hands

huli huli—barbecue, as in *huli huli* chicken

imu—underground oven filled with hot rocks and used for baking; the main cooking feature at a luau, used to steam-bake pork and other succulent dishes. Traditionally the tending of the *imu* was for men only.

ipo—sweetheart; lover; girl- or boyfriend

kahuna—priest; sorcerer; doctor; skillful person. *Kahuna* had tremendous power in old Hawaii which they used for both good and evil. The *kahuna ana'ana* was a feared individual because he practiced "black magic" and could pray a person to death, while a *kahuna lapa'au* was a medical practitioner bringing aid and comfort to the people.

kalua—means roasted underground in an *imu*. A favorite island food is *kalua* pork.

kamaaina—a child of the land; an old-timer; a longtime island resident of any ethnic background; a resident of Hawaii or native son or daughter. Hotels and airlines often offer discounts called "*kamaaina* rates" to anyone who can prove island residency.

kane—means man, but is used to signify a husband or boyfriend. Written on a door, it means "Men's Room."

kapu—forbidden; taboo; keep out; do not touch

kapuna—a grandparent or old-timer; usually means someone who has gained wisdom. The statewide school system now invites *kapuna* to talk to the children about the old ways and methods.

kaukau—slang word meaning food or chow; grub. Some of the best eating in Hawaii is from "*kaukau* wagons," which are trucks from which plate lunches and other morsels are sold.

keiki—child or children; used by all ethnic groups. "Have you hugged your *keiki* today?"

kokua—help; as in "Your *kokua* is needed to keep Hawaii free from litter."

kona wind—a muggy subtropical wind that blows from the south and hits the leeward side of the islands. It usually brings sticky hot weather and one of the few times when air-conditioning will be appreciated.

lanai—veranda or porch. You'll pay more for a hotel room if it has a lanai with an ocean view.

lei—a traditional garland of flowers or vines; one of Hawaii's most beautiful customs. Given at any auspicious occasion, but especially when arriving or leaving Hawaii.

limu—varieties of edible seaweed gathered from the shoreline. It makes an excellent salad and is used to garnish many island dishes—a favorite at luaus.

lomilomi—traditional Hawaiian massage; also, a vinegared salad made of raw salmon, chopped onions, and spices

lua—the toilet; head; bathroom

luau—a Hawaiian feast featuring poi, *imu*-baked pork and other traditional foods. A good luau provides some of the best gastronomical delights in the world.

mahalo—thanks; thank you. *Mahalo nui* means big thanks or thank you very much.

mahu—a homosexual; often used derisively like "fag" or "queer"

makai—toward the sea; used by most islanders when giving directions

malihini—what you are if you have just arrived: a newcomer; a tenderfoot; a recent arrival

manauahi—free; gratis; extra

manini—stingy; tight; a Hawaiianized word taken from the name of Don Francisco *Marin,* who was instrumental in bringing many fruits and plants to Hawaii. He was known for never sharing any of the bounty from his substantial gardens on Vineyard Street in Honolulu, therefore his name came to mean "stingy."

mauka—toward the mountains; used by most islanders when giving directions

mauna—mountain; often combined with other words to be more descriptive, as in Mauna Kea ("White Mountain")

moana—the ocean; the sea. Many businesses, hotels, and places have *moana* as part of their names.

muumuu—the garment introduced by the missionaries to cover the nakedness of the Hawaiians; a "Mother Hubbard," a long dress with a high neckline that has become fashionable attire for almost any occasion in Hawaii

ohana—a family; the fundamental social division; extended family; now used to denote a social organization with "grass roots," as in the "Protect Kahoolawe Ohana"

okolehau—literally "iron bottom"; a traditional booze made from ti root. *Okole* means "rear end" and *hau* means "iron," which was descriptive of the huge blubber pots in which *okolehau* was made. Also, if you drink too much it'll surely knock you on your *okole*.

ono—delicious; delightful; the best. *Ono ono* means "extra or absolutely" delicious.

opu—belly; stomach

pa'hoehoe—smooth, ropey lava that looks like burnt pancake batter. *Pa'hoehoe* is now the correct geological term used to describe this type of lava found anywhere in the world.

pakalolo—"crazy smoke"; marijuana; grass; smoke; dope

pali—a cliff; precipice. Hawaii's geology makes them quite common. The most famous are the *pali* of Oahu where a major battle was fought.

paniolo—a Hawaiian cowboy; derived from the Spanish *espaniola*. The first cowboys brought in during the early 19th century were Mexicans from California.

pau—finished; done; completed; often combined into *pau hana,* which means end of work or quitting time

pilau—stink; smells bad; stench

pilikia—trouble of any kind, big or small; bad times

poi—a glutinous paste made from the pounded corm of taro which, slightly fermented, has a light sour taste. Purplish in color, it is a staple at luaus, where it is called one-, two-, or three-finger poi, depending upon its thickness.

pono—righteous or excellent

puka—a hole of any size. *Puka* is used by all island residents and can be employed when talking about a tiny *puka* in a rubber boat or a *puka* (tunnel) through a mountain.

punee—bed; narrow couch; used by all ethnic groups. To recline on a *punee* on a breezy lanai is a true island treat.

pu pu—an appetizer; a snack; hors d'oeuvres; can be anything from cheese and crackers to sushi. Oftentimes, bars or nightclubs offer them free.

pupule—crazy; nuts; out of your mind

tapa—a traditional paper cloth made from beaten bark. Intricate designs were stamped in using beaters, and color was added with natural dyes. The tradition was lost in Hawaii but is now making a comeback, and provides some of the most beautiful folk art in the islands.

tutu—grandmother; granny; older woman; used by all as a term of respect and endearment

ukulele—*uku* means "flea" and *lele* means "jumping." Thus ukulele means "jumping flea," which was the way the Hawaiians perceived the quick finger movements used on the banjo-type Portuguese folk instrument called a *cavaquinho.* The ukulele quickly became synonymous with the islands.

wahine—young woman; female; girl; wife; used by all ethnic groups. When written on a door, means "Women's Room."

wai—fresh water; drinking water

wela—hot. *Wela kahao* is a "hot time" or "making whoopee."

wiki—quickly; fast; in a hurry; often seen as *wiki wiki* ("very fast"), as in "Wiki wiki Messenger Service"

USEFUL PHRASES

Aloha ahiahi—Good evening.
Aloha au ia oe—I love you!
Aloha kakahiaka—Good morning.
Aloha nui loa—much love; fondest regards
Hauoli la hanau—Happy birthday.

Hauoli makahiki hou—Happy New Year.
Komo mai—please come in; enter; welcome
Mele kalikimaka—Merry Christmas.
Okole maluna—bottoms up; salute; cheers; kampai

In what other land save this one is the commonest form
of greeting not 'Good Day,' . . . but 'Love?' . . . Aloha . . .
It is the positive affirmation of one's own heart giving.

—Jack London, 1916

By permission Wm. Ellis, circa 1791 (Hawaii State Archives)

RELIGION

The Lord saw fit to keep His island paradise secret from humans for a few million years, but once we finally arrived we were awfully thankful. Hawaii sometimes seems like a floating tabernacle; everywhere you look there's a church, temple, shrine, or *heiau*. The islands are either a very holy place, or there's a powerful lot of sinning going on that would require so many houses of prayer. Actually, it's just America's "right to worship" concept fully employed in microcosm. All the peoples who came to Hawaii brought their own forms of devotion. The Polynesian Hawaiians praised the primordial creators, Wakea and Papa, from whom their pantheon of animistically inspired gods sprang. Obviously to a modern world these old gods would never do. Unfortunately for the old gods, there were simply too many of them, and belief in them was looked upon as mere superstition, the folly of semicivilized pagans. So the famous missionaries of the 1820s brought Congregational Christianity and the "true path" to heaven.

Inconveniently, the Catholics, Mormons, Reformed Mormons, Adventists, Episcopalians, Unitarians, Christian Scientists, Lutherans, Dap-

tists, Jehovah's Witnesses, Salvation Army, and every other major and minor denomination of Christianity that followed in their wake brought their own brands of enlightenment and never quite agreed with each other. Chinese and Japanese immigrants established the major sects of Buddhism, Confucianism, Taoism, and Shintoism. Allah is praised, the Torah is chanted in Jewish synagogues, and nirvana is available at a variety of Hindu temples. If the spirit moves you, a Hare Krishna devotee will be glad to point you in the right direction and give you a free flower for only a dollar or two. If the world is still too much with you, you might find peace at a Church of Scientology, or meditate at a kundalini yoga institute, or perhaps find relief at a local assembly of Baha'i. Anyway, rejoice, because in Hawaii you'll not only find paradise, you might even find salvation.

HAWAIIAN BELIEFS

The Polynesian Hawaiians worshiped nature. They saw its forces manifested in a multiplicity of forms to which they ascribed godlike powers, and based daily life on this animistic philosophy. Handpicked and specially trained storytellers chanted the exploits of the gods. These ancient tales, kept alive in a special oral tradition called *moolelo,* were recited only by day. Entranced listeners encircled the chanter; in respect for the gods and in fear of their wrath, they were forbidden to move once the tale was begun. This was serious business where a person's life could be at stake. It was not like the telling of *kaao,* which were simple fictions, tall tales, and yarns of ancient heroes related for amusement and to pass the long nights. Any object, animate or inanimate, could be a god. All could be infused with mana, especially a dead body or respected ancestor.

Ohana had personal family gods called *amakua* on whom they called in times of danger or strife. There were children of gods called *kupua* who were thought to live among humans and were distinguished either for their beauty and strength or for their ugliness and terror. It was told that processions of dead *ali'i,* called "Marchers of the Night," wandered through the land of the living and unless you were properly protected it could mean death if they looked upon you. There were simple ghosts known as *akua lapu* who merely frightened people. Forests, waterfalls, trees, springs, and a thousand forms of nature were the manifestations of *akua li'i,* "little spirits" who could be invoked at any time for help or protection. It made no difference who or what you were in old Hawaii; the gods were ever-present and they took a direct and active role in your life.

Behind all of these beliefs was an innate sense of natural balance and order. It could be interpreted as positive-negative, yin-yang, plus-minus, life-death, light-dark, whatever, but the main idea was that everything had its opposite. The time of darkness when only the gods lived was *po* . When the great gods descended to the earth and created light, this was *ao* and humanity was born. All of these *moolelo* are part of the *Kumulipo,* the great chant that records the Hawaiian version of creation. From the time the gods descended and touched the earth at Ku Moku on Lanai, the genealogies were kept. Unlike the Bible, these included the noble families of female as well as male *ali'i.*

Note: For more information regarding life in pre-contact Hawaii see pp. 51-53.

THE STRIFES OF MAUI

Of all the heroes and mythological figures of Polynesia, Maui is the best known. His "strifes" are like the great Greek epics, and they make excellent tales of daring that elders loved to relate to youngsters around the evening fire. Maui was abandoned by his mother, Hina of Fire, when he was an infant. She wrapped him in her hair and cast him upon the sea where she expected him to die, but he lived and returned home to become her favorite. She knew then that he was a born hero and had strength far beyond that of ordinary mortals. His first exploit was to lift the sky. In those days the sky hung so low that humans had to crawl around on all fours. A seductive young woman approached Maui and asked him to use his great strength to lift the sky. In fine heroic fashion, the big boy agreed, if the beautiful woman would euphemistically "give him a drink from her gourd." He then obliged her by lifting the sky, and he might even have made the earth move for her once or twice.

More Land
The territory of mankind was small at that time. Maui decided that more land was needed, so he conspired to "fish up islands." He descended into the land of the dead and petitioned an ancestress to fashion him a hook from her jawbone. She obliged and created the mythical hook, *Manai ikalani.* Maui then secured a sacred *alae* bird that he intended to use for bait and bid his brothers to paddle him far out to sea. When he arrived at the deepest spot, he lowered *Manai ikalani* baited with the sacred bird, and his sister, Hina of the Sea, placed it into the mouth of "Old One Tooth," who held the land fast to the bottom of the waters. Maui then exhorted his brothers to row, but warned them not to look back. They strained at the oars with all their might and slowly a great land mass arose. One brother, overcome by curiosity, looked back, and when he did so, the land shattered into all of the islands of Polynesia.

Further Exploits
Maui still desired to serve mankind. People were without fire, the secret of which was held by the sacred *alae* birds, who learned it from Maui's

far distant mother. Hina of Fire gave Maui her burning fingernails, but he oafishly kept dropping them into streams until all had fizzled out and he had totally irritated his generous progenitor. She pursued him, trying to burn him to a cinder; Maui chanted for rain to put out her scorching fires. When she saw that they were being quenched, she hid her fire in the barks of special trees and informed the mud hens where they could be found, but first made them promise never to tell humans. Maui knew of this and captured a mud hen, threatening to wring its scrawny, traitorous neck unless it gave up the secret. The bird tried trickery and told Maui first to rub together the stems of sugarcane, then banana and even taro. None worked, and Maui's determined rubbing is why these plants have hollow roots today.

Finally, with Maui's hands tightening around the mud hen's gizzard, the bird confessed that fire could be found in the *hau* tree and also the sandalwood, which Maui named *ili aha* ("fire bark") in its honor. He then rubbed all the feathers off the mud hen's head for being so deceitful, which is why their crowns are featherless today.

The Sun Is Snared

Maui's greatest deed, however, was in snaring the sun and exacting a promise that it would go slower across the heavens. The people complained that there were not enough daylight hours to fish or farm. Maui's mother could not dry her tapa cloth because the sun rose and set so quickly. She asked her son to help. Maui went to his blind grandmother, who lived on the slopes of Haleakala and was responsible for cooking the sun's bananas, which he ate every day in passing. She told him to personally weave 16 strong ropes with nooses from his sister's hair. Some say these came from her head, but other versions insist that it was no doubt Hina's pubic hair that had the power to hold the sun god. Maui positioned himself with the rope, and as each of the 16 rays of the sun came across Haleakala, he snared them until the sun was defenseless and had to bargain for his life. Maui agreed to free him if he promised to go more slowly. From that time forward the sun agreed to move slowly and Haleakala ("The House of the Sun") became his home.

HEIAU AND IDOLS

A *heiau* is a Hawaiian temple. The basic *heiau* was a masterfully built and fitted rectangular stone wall that varied in size from about as big as a basketball court to as big as a football field. Once the restraining outer walls were built, the interior was backfilled with smaller stones and the top dressing was expertly laid and then rolled, perhaps with a log, to form a pavement-like surface. All that remains of Hawaii's many *heiau* are the stone platforms. The buildings upon them, made from perishable wood, leaves, and grass, have long since disappeared.

Some *heiau* were dreaded temples where human sacrifices were made. Tradition says that this barbaric custom began at Wahaula Heiau on the Big Island in the 12th century and was introduced by a ferocious Tahitian priest named Paao. Other *heiau,* such as Pu'uhonua o Honaunau, also on the Big Island, were temples of refuge where the weak, widowed, orphaned, and vanquished could find safety and sanctuary.

Idols

The Hawaiian people worshiped gods who took the form of idols fashioned from wood, feathers, or stone. The eyes were made from shells and until these were inlaid, the idol was dormant. The hair used was often human hair, and the arms and legs were usually flexed. The mouth was either gaping or formed a wide figure-eight lying on its side, and more likely than not was lined with glistening dog teeth. Small figures made of woven basketry were expertly covered with feathers. Red and yellow feathers were favorites taken from specific birds by men whose only work was to roam the forests in search of them.

Ghosts

The Hawaiians had countless superstitions and ghost legends, but two of the more interesting involve astral travel of the soul and the "Marchers of the Night." The soul, *uhane,* was considered by Hawaiians to be totally free and independent of its body, *kino.* The soul could separate, leaving the body asleep or very drowsy. This disincorporated soul *(hihi'o)* could visit people and was considered quite different from a *lapu* or ordinary spirit of a dead person. A *kahuna* could immediately recognize if a person's *uhane* had left the body, and a special wreath was placed upon the head to protect the person and to facilitate reentry.

If confronted by an apparition, you could test to see if it was indeed dead or still alive by placing leaves of an *ape* plant upon the ground. If the leaves tore when they were walked upon, the spirit was merely human, but if they remained intact it was a ghost. Or you could sneak up and startle the vision, and if it disappeared it was a ghost. Also, if no reflection of the face appeared when it drank water from an offered calabash, it was a ghost. Unfortunately, there were no instructions to follow once you had determined that you indeed had a ghost on your hands. Maybe it was better not to know! Some people would sprinkle salt and water around their houses, but this kept away evil spirits, not ghosts.

There are also many stories of *kahuna* restoring a soul to a dead body. First they had to catch it and keep it in a gourd. They then placed beautiful tapa and fragrant flowers and herbs about the body to make it more enticing. Slowly, they would coax the soul out of the gourd until it reentered the body through the big toe.

Death Marchers

One inexplicable phenomenon that many people attest to is *ka huakai o ka po,* "Marchers of the Night." This march of the dead is fatal if you gaze upon it unless one of the marchers happens to be a friendly ancestor who will protect you. The peak time for "the march" is 7:30 p.m.-2 a.m. The marchers can be dead *ali'i* and warriors, the gods themselves, or the lesser *amakua*. When the *amakua* march there is usually chanting and music. *Ali'i* marches are more somber. The entire procession, lit by torches, often stops at the house of a relative and might even carry him or her away. When the gods themselves march, there is often thunder, lightning, and heavy seas. The sky is lit with torches, and they walk six abreast, three gods and three goddesses. If you get in the way of a march, remove your clothing and prostrate yourself. If the marching gods or *amakua* happen to be ones to which you prayed, you might be spared. If it's a march of the *ali'i,* you might make it if you lie face upward and feign death. If you *do* see a death march, the last thing that you'll worry about is lying naked on the ground looking ridiculous.

MISSIONARIES ONE AND ALL

In Hawaii, when you say "missionaries," it's taken for granted you're referring to the small and determined band of Congregationalists who arrived aboard the brig *Thaddeus* in 1820, and the follow-up groups called "companies" or "packets" that reinforced them. They were sent from Boston by the American Board of Commissioners for Foreign Missions (ABCFM), which learned of the supposed sad and godless plight of the Hawaiian people through returning sailors and especially through the few Hawaiians who had come to America to study.

The person most instrumental in bringing the missionaries to Hawaii was a young man named Opukahaia. He was an orphan befriended by a ship's captain and taken to New England, where he studied theology. Obsessed with the desire to return home and save his people from certain damnation, Opukahaia wrote accounts of life in Hawaii that were published and widely read. These accounts were directly responsible for the formation of the Pioneer Company to the Sandwich Islands Missions in 1819. Unfortunately, Opukahaia died in New England from typhus the year before they left.

"Civilizing" Hawaii

The first missionaries had the straightforward task of bringing the Hawaiians out of paganism and into Christianity and civilization. They met with terrible hostility—not from the natives, but from the sea captains and traders who were very happy with the open debauchery and wanton whoremongering that was status quo in the Hawaii of 1820. Many direct confrontations between these two factions even included the cannonading of missionaries' homes by American sea captains who were denied the customary visits of island women, thanks to meddlesome "do-gooders." The most memorable of these incidents involved "Mad Jack" Percival, the captain of the USS *Dolphin,* who bombed a church in Kahaina to show his rancor. In actuality, the truth of the situation was much closer to the sentiments of James Jarves, who wrote, "The missionary was a far more useful and agreeable man than his Catholicism would indicate; and the trader was not so bad a man as the missionary would make him out to be." The missionaries' primary aim might have been conversion, but the most fortuitous by-product was education, which raised the consciousness of every Hawaiian, regardless of religious affiliation. In 40 short years Hawaii was considered a civilized nation well on its way into the modern world, and the American Board of Missions officially ended its support in 1863.

Non-Christians
By the turn of the century, both Shintoism and Buddhism, brought by the Japanese and Chinese, were firmly established in Hawaii. The first official Buddhist temple was Hongpa Hongwanji, established on Oahu in 1889. All the denominations of Buddhism account for 17% (170,000 parishioners) of the island's religious total, and there are about 50,000 Shintoists. The Hindu religion has perhaps 2,000 adherents, and about the same number of Jewish people live throughout Hawaii with only one synagogue, Temple Emanuel, on Oahu. The largest number of people in Hawaii (300,000) remains unaffiliated, and about 10,000 people are in new religious movements and lesser-known faiths such as Baha'i and Unitarianism.

CONDUCT

ILLEGAL DRUGS

The use and availability of illegal, controlled, and recreational drugs are about the same in Hawaii as throughout the rest of America. Cocaine constitutes the fastest-growing recreational drug and is available on the streets of the main cities, especially Honolulu. Although most dealers are small-time, the drug is brought in by organized crime. The underworld here is mostly populated by men of Asian descent, and recently the Japanese *yakuza* is said to be displaying a heightened involvement in Hawaiian organized crime. Cocaine trafficking fans out from Honolulu.

A new drug menace hitting Hawaii is "ice." Ice is smokable methamphetamine that will wire a user for up to 24 hours. The high lasts longer and the drug is cheaper than cocaine or its derivative, "crack." Users become quickly dependent, despondent, and violent because ice robs them of their sleep as well as their dignity. Its use is particularly prevalent among late-night workers. Many of the violent deaths in Honolulu have been linked to the growing use of ice.

However, the main drug available and commonly used in Hawaii is marijuana, which is locally called *pakalolo*. There are also three varieties of psychoactive mushrooms that contain the hallucinogen psilocybin. They grow wild, but are considered illegal controlled substances.

Pakalolo Growing

About 25 years ago, mostly *haole* hippies from the Mainland began growing pot in the more remote sections of the islands, such as Puna on Hawaii and around Hana on Maui. They discovered what legitimate planters had known for 200 years: plant a broomstick in Hawaii, treat it right, and it'll grow. *Pakalolo,* after all, is a weed, and it grows in Hawaii like wildfire. The locals quickly got into the act when they realized that they, too, could grow a "money tree." As a matter of fact, they began resenting the *haole* usurpers, and a quiet and sometimes dangerous feud has been going on ever since. Much is made of the viciousness of the back-country "growers" of Hawaii. There are tales of booby traps and armed patrols guarding their plants in the hills, but mostly it's a cat-and-mouse game between the authorities and the growers. If you, as a tourist, are tramping about in the forest and happen upon someone's "patch," don't touch anything. Just back off and you'll be okay. Pot has the largest monetary turnover of any crop in the islands, and as such, is now considered a major source of agricultural revenue. There are all kinds of local names and varieties of pot in Hawaii, the most potent being "Kona Gold," "Puna Butter," and "Maui Wowie." These names are all becoming passé. It's possible that a dealer will approach you. Their normal technique is to stroll by and in a barely audible whisper say, "Buds?"

Hawaiian *pakalolo* is sold slightly differently than on the Mainland. The dealers package it in heat-sealed "Seal-a-Meal" plastic bags. The glory days are over, and many deals, especially on the streets, are rip-offs. All passengers leaving Hawaii are subject to a thorough "agricultural inspection," and you can bet they're not only looking for illegal papayas. In 1984 there was an uproar involving a particular post office on the Big Island. It turned out that a staggering 80% of the outgoing packages contained *pakalolo*. The authorities are getting wise.

THEFT AND HASSLES

From the minute you sit behind the wheel of your rental car, you'll be warned not to leave valuables unattended and to lock up your car tighter than a drum. Signs warning about theft at most major tourist attractions help fuel your paranoia. Many hotel rooms offer coin-operated safes so you can lock your valuables away and relax while getting sunburned. Stories abound about purse snatchings and surly locals just itching to give you a hard time. Well, they're all true to a degree, but Hawaii's reputation is much worse than the reality. In Hawaii you'll have to observe two golden laws: if you look for trouble, you'll find it; and a fool and his camera are soon parted.

Theft

The majority of theft in Hawaii is of the "sneak thief" variety. If you leave your hotel door unlocked, a camera sitting on the seat of your rental car, or valuables on your beach towel, you'll be inviting a very obliging thief to pad away with your stuff. You have to learn to take precautions, but they won't be anything like those employed in rougher areas like South America or Southeast Asia; just normal American precautions.

If you must walk alone at night, stay on the main streets in well-lit areas. Always lock your hotel door and windows and place valuable jewelry in the hotel safe. When you leave your hotel for the beach, there is absolutely no reason to carry all your traveler's checks and credit cards or a big wad of money. Just take what you'll need for drinks and lunch. If you're uptight about leaving money in your beach bag, stick it in your bathing suit or bikini. American money is just as negotiable if it is damp. Don't leave your camera or portable stereo on the beach unattended. Ask a person nearby to watch them for you while you go for a dip. Most people won't mind at all, and you can repay the favor.

While sightseeing in your shiny new rental car, which immediately brands you as a tourist, again, don't take more than what you'll need for the day. Why people leave a camera sitting on the seat of their car is a mystery! Many people lock valuables in the trunk, but remember that most good car thieves can "jimmy" it open as quickly as you can open it with your key. If you must, for some reason, leave camera or valuables in your car, lock them in the trunk or consider putting them under the hood. Thieves usually don't look there, and on most modern cars you can only pop the hood with a lever inside the car. It's not fail-safe, but it's worth a try.

Campers face special problems because their entire scene is open to thievery. Most campgrounds don't have any real security, but who, after all, wants to fence an old tent or a used sleeping bag? Many tents have zippers that can be secured with a small padlock. If you want to go trekking and are afraid to leave your gear in the campground, take a large green garbage bag with you. Transport your gear down the trail and then walk off through some thick brush. Put your gear in the garbage bag and bury it under leaves and other light camouflage. That's about

WARNING
DO NOT LEAVE PURSE, WALLET OR CAMERA IN LOCKED OR UNLOCKED CARS

as safe as you can be. You can also use a variation on this technique instead of leaving your valuables in your rental car.

Hassles

Another self-perpetuating myth about Hawaii is that "the natives are restless." An undeniable animosity exists between locals (especially those with some Hawaiian blood) and *haole*. Fortunately, this prejudice is directed mostly at the group and not at the individual. The locals are resentful of those *haole* who came, took their land, and relegated them to second-class citizenship. They realize that this is not the average tourist and they can tell what you are at a glance. Tourists usually are treated with understanding and are given a type of immunity. Besides, Hawaiians are still among the most friendly, giving, and understanding people on earth.

Haole who live in Hawaii might tell you stories of their children having trouble at school. They could even mention an unhappy situation at some schools called "beat-up-a-*haole*" day, and you might hear that if you're a *haole* it's not a matter of "if" you'll be beaten up, but "when." Truthfully, most of this depends upon your attitude and your sensitivity. The locals feel infringed upon, so don't fuel these feelings. If you're at a beach park and there is a group of local people in one area, don't crowd them. If you go into a local bar and you're the only one of your ethnic group in sight, you shouldn't have to be told to leave. Much of the hassle involves drinking. Booze brings out the worst prejudice on all sides. If you're invited to a beach party, and the local guys start getting drunk, make this your exit call. Don't wait until it's too late.

Most trouble seems to be directed toward white men. White women are mostly immune from being beaten up, but they have to beware of the violence of sexual abuse and rape. Although plenty of local women marry white men, it's not a good idea to try to pick up a local girl. If you're known in the area and have been properly introduced, that's another story. Also, women out for the night in bars or discos can be approached if they're not in the company of local guys. If you are with your bikini-clad girl-friend, and a bunch of local guys are, say, drinking beer at a beach park, don't go over and try to be friendly and ask, "What's up?" You, and especially your girlfriend, just might find out. Maintain your own dignity and self-respect by treating others with dignity and respect. Most times you'll reap what you sow.

BOB RACE

OUT AND ABOUT
CAMPING AND HIKING

The Big Island has the best camping in the state, with more facilities and less competition for campsites than on the other islands. Over three dozen parks fringe the coastline and sit deep in the interior; almost half offer camping. The others boast a combination of rugged hikes, easy strolls, self-guided nature walks, swimming, historical sites, and natural phenomena. The ones with campgrounds are state-, county-, and nationally operated, ranging from remote walk-in sites to housekeeping cabins. All, except the national park, require inexpensive camping permits, and although there is usually no problem obtaining sites, always write for reservations well in advance, allowing a minimum of one month for letters to go back and forth.

Note: For camping and hiking offered by organizations focusing on ecotourism, see "Getting Around."

General Information
Most campgrounds have pavilions, fireplaces, toilets (sometimes pit), and running water, but usually no individual electrical hookups. Pavil-

ions often have electric lights, but sometimes campers appropriate the bulbs, so it's wise to carry your own. Drinking water is available, but at times brackish water is used for flushing toilets and for showers, so read all signs regarding water. Backcountry shelters have catchment water, but never hike without an adequate supply of your own. Cooking fires are allowed in established firepits, but no wood is provided. Charcoal is a good idea. When camping in the mountains, be prepared for cold and rainy weather. Women, especially, should never hike or camp alone, and everyone should exercise precaution against theft, though it's not as prevalent as on the other islands.

County Parks
The county-maintained parks are open to the public for day use, and permits are only required for camping (tents or RVs). For information write: Department of Parks and Recreation, County of Hawaii, 25 Aupuni St., Hilo, HI 96720, tel. 961-8311. You can pick up your permits here, but only during business hours Mon.-Friday. If

you'll be arriving after hours or on a weekend, have the permits mailed to you. Branch offices are located at Hale Halawai in Kailua-Kona, tel. 323-3046; at Captain Cook, tel. 323-3046; and at Waimea, tel. 885-5454. Fees are $1 per adult p/d; children 13-17, 50 cents; youngsters free. Pavilions for exclusive use are $5 p/d with kitchen, $2 without.

State Parks And Cabins
Day use of state parks is free, with no permit required, but you will need one for tent camping and for cabins. If you want a cabin, at least one week's notice is required regardless of availability. You can pick up your permit if you arrive during normal business hours, but again it saves time if you do it all by mail. Write: Department of Land and Natural Resources, Division of State Parks, Box 936 (75 Aupuni St.) Hilo, HI 96720, tel. 961-7200.

Cabins or A-frames are offered at Mauna Kea State Recreation Area's Pohakuloa Camp, tel. 935-7237; Hapuna Beach State Recreation Area, tel. 882-7995; Kalopa State Recreation Center, tel. 775-7114; and Niaulani Cabin at Kilauea State Park. Fees and regulations vary slightly so when writing for permits specify exactly which facility you require, for how long, and for how many people. For example, A-frames are a flat $7 per night, while cabins start at $10 s, up to $30 for a party of six.

Hawaii Volcanoes National Park
Both day use and overnight camping at Hawaii Volcanoes National Park are free and no permits are required. The drive-in campgrounds throughout the park can be reserved, but usually operate on a first-come, first-served basis. Your stay is limited to seven days per campground per year. A-frame cabins are provided at Namakani Paio Campground, and arrangements are made through Volcano House, Hawaii Volcanoes National Park, HI 96718, tel. 967-7321. There are free walk-in trail cabins and shelters throughout the park; you can't reserve them and you should expect to share them with other hikers. Coleman stoves and lanterns are sometimes provided (check), but you provide the fuel. Basic bedding and cooking utensils are also there for your convenience. Shelters, in the park along the coast, are three-sided, open affairs that offer only a partial covering against the elements. For information on camping and hiking in the park, write Hawaii Volcanoes National Park, Information Services, Volcano, HI 96718.

Hiking The Big Island
Hiking on the Big Island is stupendous. There's something for everyone, from civilized walks to the breathtaking Akaka Falls to huff-puff treks to the summit of Mauna Loa. The largest number of trails, and the most outstanding according to many, are laced across Volcanoes National Park. After all, this is the world's most active volcano. You can hike across the crater floor, spurred on by the knowledge that it can shake to life at any moment. Or dip down off the mountain and amble the lonely trails in the Kau desert or remnants of the King's Coastal Trail in Puna.

The most important thing to do, before heading out in Volcanoes, is to stop at Park Headquarters and inquire about trail conditions. Make absolutely sure to register, giving the rangers your hiking itinerary. In the event of an eruption, they will be able to locate you and send a helicopter if necessary. Follow this advice; your life may depend upon it! Everyone can enjoy vistas on Devastation Trail or Sulfur Bank or at the Thurston Lava Tube without any danger whatsoever. In the north you'll find Waipio, Waimanu, and Pololu valleys. All offer secluded hiking and camping where you can play Robinson Crusoe on your own beach and gather a variety of island fruits from once-cultivated trees gone wild.

Camping/Hiking Tours
Hawaiian Island Kamping Excursions, Box 726, Pahoa, HI 96778, tel. 965-7293 or (800) 726-4453, offers adventure hiking tours ranging from a 12-day deluxe tour covering the Big Island and Kauai, to a five-day Waimanu Valley escape to this pristine area along the Big Island's north coast. The tours are designed to include a great deal of personal attention, with a maximum of 16 people per group allowed. Tour leaders, intimately versed in the flora, fauna, geology, history, and ancient cosmology of the islands, share their knowledge as you trek along. All interisland flights, accommodations (ranging from tents to condos), and meals are provided. A deposit is required to confirm a place on a tour

BIG ISLAND CAMPGROUNDS

and to receive a packet containing information necesary to make your tour enjoyable.

An organization offering camping and hiking trips to the Big Island is **Wilderness Hawaii,** Box 61692, Honolulu, HI 96839, tel. (808) 737-4697. Lead by Sheena Sandler, Wilderness Hawaii offers courses that range from a 4- to a 12-day sojourn where the experiential journey takes place as much within yourself as on the hiking trail.

Note: For more about ecotourism in Hawaii see that section in "Getting Around," following.

Equipment

Like everything else you take to Hawaii, your camping and hiking equipment should be lightweight and durable. Camping equipment size and weight should not cause a problem with baggage requirements on airlines: if it does, it's a tip off that you'ro hauling too much. Once odd luggage strategy you might consider is to bring along a small **styrofoam cooler** packed with equipment. Substitute food items for the equipment when you get.to Hawaii; if you intend to car-camp successfully and keep food prices down, you'll definitely need a cooler. You can also buy one on arrival for only a few dollars. You'll need a lightweight **tent,** preferably with a rainfly and a sewn-in floor. This will save you from getting wet and miserable, and will keep out mosquitoes, cockroaches, ants, and the few stinging insects in Hawaii. Atop Mauna Loa, where you can expect cold and wind, a tent is a must; in fact you won't be allowed to camp without one. (See p.149.)

Sleeping bags are a good idea, although you can get along at sea level with only a blanket. Down-filled or high-quality synthetic bags are necessary for Mauna Kea, Mauna Loa, or any high-altitude camping—you'll freeze without one. **Camp-stoves** are needed because there's very little wood in some volcanic areas, it's often wet in the deep forest, and open fires are often prohibited. If you'll be car-camping, take along a multi-burner stove; for trekking, a backpacker's stove will be necessary. The grills found at some campgrounds are popular with many families who go often to the beach parks for an open-air dinner. You can buy a very inexpensive charcoal grill at many variety stores throughout Hawaii. It's a great idea to take along a **lantern.** This will give added safety for car-campers. Definitely take a **flashlight,** replacement batteries, and a few small **candles.** A complete **first-aid kit** can mean the difference between life and death, and is worth the extra bulk. Hikers, especially those leaving the coastal areas, should take **rain gear,** a plastic ground cloth, utility knife, compass, safety whistle, mess kit, water purification tablets, canteen, nylon twine, and waterproof matches. You can find plenty of stores that sell, and a few stores that rent, camping equipment; check the Yellow Pages under "Camping Equipment," and "Shopping" in the travel chapters.

Camping equipment is available for rent from **Pacific United Rent All,** 1080 Kilauea Ave., Hilo, tel. 935-2974. It can also be purchased at **Gaspro,** tel. 935-3341 Hilo or 329-7393 Kona; **J&J Sporting,** tel. 329-2610, Kona; **The Surplus Store,** tel. 935-6398 Hilo, 329-1240 Kona.

Safety

There are two things in Hawaii that you must keep your eye on in order to remain safe: humans and nature. The general rule is, the farther you get away from towns, the safer you'll be from human-induced hassles. If possible, don't hike or camp alone, especially if you're a woman. Don't leave your valuables in your tent, and always carry your money, papers, and camera with you (See "Theft and Hassles" in the "Conduct" section). Don't tempt the locals by being overly friendly or unfriendly, and make yourself scarce if they're drinking. While hiking, remember that many trails are well maintained, but trailhead markers are often missing. The trails themselves can be muddy, which can make them treacherously slippery and often knee-deep. Always bring food because you cannot, in most cases, forage from the land. Water in most streams is biologically polluted and will give you bad stomach problems if you drink it without purifying it first by boiling, filtering, or adding purification tablets. For your part, please don't use the streams as a toilet.

Precautions

Always tell a ranger or official of your hiking intentions. Supply an itinerary and your expected route, then stick to it. Twilight is short in the islands, and night sets in rapidly. In June sunrise and sunset are around 6 a.m. and 7 p.m.; in December these occur at 7 a.m. and 6 p.m. If you become lost at night, stay put, light a fire if possible, and stay as dry as you can. Hawaii is made of volcanic rock which is brittle and crumbly. Never attempt to climb steep *pali* (cliffs). Be aware of current lava flows, and heed all posted advice. If lost, walk on ridges and avoid the gulches, which have more obstacles and make it harder for rescuers to spot you. Be careful of elevation sickness, especially on Mauna Loa and Mauna Kea. The best cure is to descend as soon as possible.

Heat can cause you to lose water and salt. If you become woozy or weak, rest, take salt, and drink water as you need it. Remember, it takes much more water to restore a dehydrated person than to keep hydrated; take small, frequent sips. Be mindful of flash floods. Small creeks can turn into raging torrents with upland rains. Never camp in a dry creekbed. Fog is only encountered at elevations of 1,500-5,000 feet, but be careful of disorientation. Generally, stay within your limits, be careful, and enjoy yourself.

Helpful Departments And Organizations

The **Department of Land and Natural Resources,** Division of Forestry and Wildlife, 1151 Punchbowl St., Honolulu, HI 96813, tel. 548-2861, is helpful in providing trail maps, accessibility information, hunting and fishing regulations, and general forest rules. Their "Recreation Map" (for each island) is excellent and free. The following organizations can provide general information on wildlife, conservation, and organized hiking trips: **Hawaiian Trail and Mountain Club,** Box 2238, Honolulu, HI 96804; **Hawaiian Audubon Society,** Box 22832, Honolulu, HI 96822; and **The Sierra Club,** 1100 Alakea St., Honolulu, HI 96813, tel. 538-6616. All the above organizations have branch offices

and affiliates on the Big Island. Write for current information.

Topographical And Nautical Charts, Etc.

For detailed topographical maps, write **U.S. Geological Survey,** Federal Center, Denver, CO 80225. In Hawaii, a wide range of topographical maps can be purchased at **Trans-Pacific Instrument Co.,** 1406 Colburn St., Honolulu, HI 96817, tel. 841-7538. For nautical charts, write **National Ocean Service,** 6501 Lafayette Ave., Riverdale, MD 20737-1199, tel. (301) 436-6990.

Hilo's **Basically Books,** downtown at 46 Waianuenue St., tel. 961-0144, has an unbeatable selection of maps. You can get anywhere you want to go with their nautical charts, road maps, and topographical maps, which include sectionals for serious hikers and trekkers. Their collection covers most of the Pacific.

BOB RACE

SPORTS AND RECREATION

You'll have no problem having fun on the Big Island. Everybody goes outside to play. You can drive golf balls over lagoons, smack tennis balls at over 50 private and public courts, ski, snorkel, windsurf, gallop a horse, bag a wild turkey, or latch on to a marlin that'll tail-walk across a windowpane sea. Choose your sport and have a ball.

DEEP-SEA AND FRESHWATER FISHING

Hawaii has some of the most exciting and productive "blue waters" in all the world. You'll find a sportfishing fleet made up of skippers and crews who are experienced professional anglers. You can also fish from jetties, piers, rocks, or the shore. If rod and reel don't strike your fancy, try the old-fashioned throw net, or take along a spear when you go snorkeling or scuba diving. There's nighttime torch fishing that requires special skills and equipment, and freshwater fishing in public areas. Streams and irrigation ditches yield introduced trout, bass, and catfish. While you're at it, you might want to try crabbing for Kona and Samoan crabs, or working low-tide areas after sundown hunting octopus, a tantalizing island delicacy.

Deep-sea Fishing

Most game-fishing boats work the waters on the calmer Kona side of the island. Some skippers, carrying anglers who are accustomed to the sea, will also work the much rougher windward coasts and island channels where the fish bite just as well. Trolling is the preferred method of deep-sea fishing; this is done usually in waters of 1,000-2,000 fathoms (a fathom is six feet). The skipper will either "area fish," which means running in a crisscross pattern over a known productive area, or "ledge fish," which involves trolling over submerged ledges where the game fish are known to feed. The most advanced marine technology, available on many boats, sends sonar bleeps searching for fish. On deck, the crew and anglers scan the horizon in the age-old Hawaiian tradition—searching for clusters of seabirds feeding on baitfish pursued to the surface by the huge and aggressive game fish. "Still fishing," or "bottom fishing" with hand-lines, yields some tremendous fish.

The Game Fish

The most thrilling game fish in Hawaiian waters is marlin, generically known as "billfish" or *a'u* to the locals. The king of them is the blue marlin, with record catches well over 1,000 pounds. There are also striped marlin and sail-fish, which often go over 200 pounds. The best times for marlin are during spring, summer, and fall. The fishing tapers off in January and picks up again by late February. "Blues" can be caught year-round but, oddly enough, when they stop biting it seems as though the striped marlin pick up. Second to the marlin are tuna. *Ahi* (yellowfin tuna) are caught in Hawaiian waters at depths of 100-1,000 fathoms. They can weigh 300 pounds, but 25-100 pounds is common. There are also *aku* (skipjack tuna) and the delicious *ono*, which average 20-40 pounds.

Mahimahi is another strong, fighting, deep-water game fish abundant in Hawaii. These delicious fish can weigh up to 70 pounds. Shore fishing and baitcasting yield *papio*, a jack tuna. *Akule*, a scad (locally called *halalu*), is a small-ish schooling fish that comes close to shore and is great to catch on light tackle. *Ulua* are shore fish and can be found in tidepools. They're excellent eating, average two to three pounds, and are taken at night or with spears.

O'io are bonefish that come close to shore to spawn. They're caught by baitcasting and bottom fishing with cut bait. They're bony, but they're a favorite for fish cakes and *poki*. *Awa* is a schooling fish that loves brackish water. It can grow up to three feet long, and is a good fighter. A favorite for throw-netters, it's even raised commercially in fishponds. Besides these there are plenty of goatfish, mullet, mackerel, snapper, sharks, and even salmon.

Fishing Boats And Charters

The fishing around the Big Island's Kona Coast ranges from excellent to outstanding! It's legendary for marlin fishing, but there are other fish in the sea. A large fleet of charter boats with skilled captains and tested crews is ready, willing, and competent to take you out. The vast majority are berthed at Honokohau Small Boat Harbor just north of Kailua-Kona (see p. 238). The best times of year for marlin are July-September and Jan.-March (when the generally larger females arrive). August is the optimum month. Rough seas can keep boats in for a few days during December and early January, but by February all are generally out.

You can hire a boat for a private or share charter, staying out for a full day or half day. Boat size varies, but tour anglers per mid-size

boat is about average. Approximate rates are: private, full day $400-600, half day $250-350; share, full day $125, half day $85. Full days are eight hours, half days four, with three-quarter days and overnighters available too. No licenses are required and all gear is provided. Bring your own lunch, beverages, and camera. Some of the best boats with top-notch reputations include *Summer Rain, Notorious,* and *Kona Rainbow.*

To charter a boat contact the individual captains directly, check at your hotel activities desk, or book through one of the following agencies. **Kona Marlin Center** at Honokohau Harbor, tel. 329-7529 or (800) 648-7529, is owned by Jim Dahlberg, who was born and raised on the Big Island. This is the main booking facility in the area. If you're after a company that's knowledgeable about getting you onto a boat that will bring you to waters where you'll have the opportunity to catch one of the twirling and gigantic "big blues," this is the place to come. Other general booking agencies include: **Kona Activities Center** in Kailua-Kona, tel. 329-3171; **Kona Coast Activities** at Honokohau Harbor, tel. 329-2971; **Kona Charter Skippers Assoc.**, Box 806, Kailua-Kona, HI 96740, tel. 329-3600; **Mauna Kea Beach Hotel,** Travel Desk, Box 218, Kamuela, HI 96743, tel. 882-7222; and **Jack's Kona Charters,** tel. 325-7558 or (800) 545-5662, who can put you on any number of boats.

Most boats are berthed at Honokohau Harbor off Route 19, about midway between downtown Kailua and Keahole Airport. Big fish are sometimes still weighed in at Kailua Pier, in front of King Kamehameha Kona Beach Hotel for the benefit of the tourists. But Honokohau Harbor has eclipsed Kailua Pier, which is now tamed and primarily for swimmers, triathletes, and body-boarders. Congestion makes it difficult for charter boats to get in and out so the majority of the trade has moved up to Honokohau (see p. 238).

An excellent publication listing boats and general deep-sea fishing information is *Fins and Fairways, Hawaii,* Box P, Kailua-Kona, HI 96745, tel. 325-6171, published by Capt. Tom Armstrong. This tabloid, available free at newsstands and in hotel/condo lobbies, is filled with descriptions of boats, phone numbers, captains' names, maps, and photos of recent catches. Write for subscription rates.

J.D. BISIGNANI

weigh-in at Honokohau Harbor

Coastal And Freshwater Fishing

You don't have to hire a boat to catch fish! The coastline is productive too. *Ulua* are caught all along the coast south of Hilo, and at South Point and Kealakekua Point. *Papio* and *halalu* are caught in bays all around the island, while *manini* and *ama'ama* hit from Kawaihae to Puako. Hilo Bay is easily accessible to anyone, and the fishing is very exciting, especially at the mouth of the Wailuku River.

Licensed fishing is limited to the **Waiakea Public Fishing Area,** a state-operated facility in downtown Hilo. This 26-acre pond offers a variety of saltwater and brackish-water species. A license is required. You can pick one up at sporting goods stores or at the Division of Conservation and Resources Enforcement Office, 75 Aupuni St., Hilo, HI 96720, tel. 961-7291.

Freshwater Fish

Hawaii has only one native freshwater game fish, the *o'opu*. This goby is an oddball with fused ventral fins. It grows to 12 inches long and is found on all islands, especially Kauai.

Introduced species include largemouth and smallmouth bass, bluegill, catfish, *tucunare,* oscar, carp, and tilapia. The only trout to survive is the rainbow, found only in the streams of Kauai. The *tucunare* is a tough, fighting, good-tasting game fish introduced from South America, similar to the oscar from the same region. Both have been compared to bass, but are of a different family.

The tilapia is from Africa and has become common in Hawaii's irrigation ditches. It is a "mouth breeder" and the young will take refuge in their parents' protective jaws even a few weeks after hatching. The snakehead is an eel-like fish that inhabits the reservoirs and is a great fighter. The channel catfish can grow to over 20 pounds; it bites best after sundown. Or go for carp—with its broad tail and tremendous strength, it's the poor man's game fish. All of these species are best caught with light spinning tackle or with a bamboo pole and trusty old worm.

Fishing Rules

Fishing licenses (freshwater needed only) are good July 1-June 30. Licenses cost $7.50 for nonresidents, $3.50 for tourists (good for 30 days), $3.75 for residents and military personnel, $1.50 for children ages 9-15; they are free to senior citizens. Licenses are obtained from the Division of Conservation and Resources Enforcement (Oahu, tel. 548-8766) or from most sporting goods stores. For free booklets and information write Division of Aquatic Resources, 1151 Punchbowl St., Honolulu, HI 96813. All game fish may be taken year-round, except trout. Trout, only on Kauai, may be taken for 16 days commencing on the first Saturday of August. Thereafter, for the remainder of August and September, trout can be taken only on Saturday, Sunday, and state holidays.

SNORKELING, SCUBA, AND WATERSPORTS

If you think that Hawaii is beautiful above the sea, wait until you explore below. The warm tropical waters and coral growth make it a fascinating haven for reef fish and aquatic plantlife. You'll soon discover that Hawaiian waters are remarkably clear, with excellent visibility. Fish in every fathomable color parade by. Lavender clusters of coral, red and gold coral trees, and over 1,500 different types of shells carpet the ocean floor. In some spots the fish are so accustomed to humans that they'll eat bread from your hand. In other spots, lurking moray eels add the special zest of danger. Sharks and barracuda pose less danger than scraping your knee on the coral or being driven against the rocks by a heavy swell. There are enormous but harmless sea bass and a profusion of sea turtles. All this awaits you below Hawaii's waters.

Hawaii has particularly generous underwater vistas open to anyone donning a mask and fins. Snorkel and dive sites, varying in difficulty and challenge, are accessible from the island. Sites can be totally hospitable, good for families and first-time snorkelers who want an exciting

FRESHWATER FISH

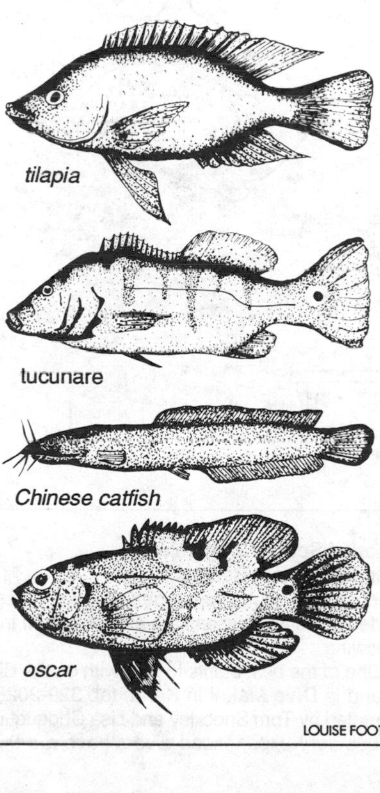

tilapia

tucunare

Chinese catfish

oscar

LOUISE FOOTE

but safe frolic; or they can be accessible only to the experienced diver. Specific sites are listed under "Beaches" in the travel sections.

Scuba
Those in the know consider the deep diving along the steep drop-offs of Hawaii's geologically young coastline some of the best in the state. The ocean surrounding the Big Island has not had a chance to turn the relatively new lava to sand, which makes the visibility absolutely perfect, even to depths of 150 feet or more. There's also 60-70 miles of coral belt around the Big Island, which adds up to a magnificent diving experience. Only advanced divers should attempt deep-water dives, but beginners and snorkelers will have many visual thrills inside the protected bays and coves. (See "Beaches" in the travel sections.)

If you're a scuba diver you'll have to show your C Card before local shops will rent you gear, fill your tanks, or take you on a charter dive. Plenty of outstanding scuba instructors will give you lessons toward certification, and they're especially reasonable because of the stiff competition. Prices vary, but you can take a three- to five-day semiprivate certification course including all equipment for about $275 (instruction book, dive tables, logbook extra charge). Divers unaccustomed to Hawaiian waters should not dive alone regardless of their experience. Most opt for dive tours to special dive grounds guaranteed to please. These vary also, but an *accompanied* single-tank dive where no boat is involved goes for about $75; for a single-tank boat dive, expect to spend $85. There are special charter dives, night dives, and photography dives. Most companies pick you up at your hotel, take you to the site, and return you home. Basic equipment costs $20-30 for the day, and most times you'll only need the top of a wetsuit.

Snorkeling
Scuba diving takes expensive special equipment, skills, and athletic ability. Snorkeling in comparison is much simpler and enjoyable to anyone who can swim. In about 15 minutes you can be taught the fundamentals of snorkeling— you really don't need formal instructions. Other snorkelers or dive-shop attendants can tell you enough to get you started. Because you can breathe without lifting your head, you get great

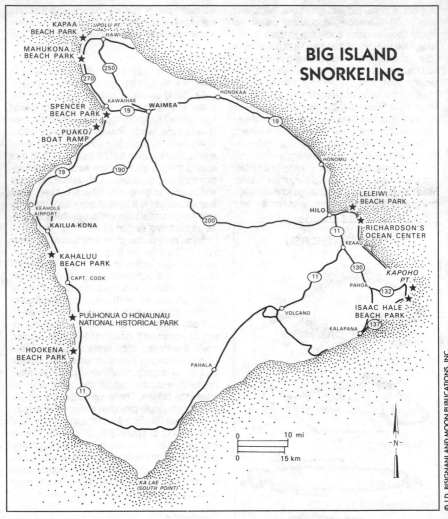

BIG ISLAND SNORKELING

KAPAA BEACH PARK
MAHUKONA BEACH PARK
UPOLU PT.
HAWI
250
270
KAWAIHAE
SPENCER BEACH PARK
WAIMEA
19
PUAKO/ BOAT RAMP
HONOKAA
19
190
HONOMU
19
KEAHOLE AIRPORT
KAILUA-KONA
LELEIWI BEACH PARK
HILO
RICHARDSON'S OCEAN CENTER
200
KEAAU
KAHALUU BEACH PARK
CAPT. COOK
11
11
130
PAHOA
KAPOHO PT.
132
PUUHONUA O HONAUNAU NATIONAL HISTORICAL PARK
VOLCANO
ISAAC HALE BEACH PARK
137
HOOKENA BEACH PARK
KALAPANA
PAHALA
11
0   10 mi
0   15 km
-N-
KA LAE (SOUTH POINT)

© J.D. BISIGNANI AND MOON PUBLICATIONS, INC.

propulsion from the fins and hardly ever need to use your arms. You can go for much greater distances and spend longer periods in the water than if you were swimming. Experienced snorkelers make an art of this sport and you, too, can see and do amazing things with a mask, snorkel, and flippers. Don't, however, get a false sense of invincibility and exceed your limitations. Also see **Snuba** below.

Snorkel/Scuba Companies And Equipment Rentals

Snorkel and scuba rental gear as well as escorted dives and lessons are available from the following.

One of the best outfits to dive with on the Big Island is **Dive Makai** in Kona, tel. 329-2025, operated by Tom Shockley and Lisa Choquette. These very experienced divers have run this service for years and have many dedicated customers. Both Tom and Lisa are conservationists who help preserve the fragile reef. They've worked very hard with the Diver's Council to protect dive sites from fish collectors and to protect the reef from destruction by anchors. Their motto, "We care," is not a trite saying, as they continue to preserve the reef for you and your children.

Another excellent diving outfit is **Jack's Diving Locker,** tel. 329-7585, (800) 345-4807, in the Kona Inn Shopping Village—a responsible outfit that does a good job of watching out for their customers and taking care of the reef. They run diving and snorkeling excursions along the Kona Coast from Kealakekua Bay to Keahole Point, which takes in over 50 dive sites (most of which have permanent moorings to protect the reef from damage by anchoring). Jack's also specializes in snorkel sales and rentals ($7.50 for 24 hours), scuba rentals, certification classes, and dive classes. You can do a five-hour snorkel/sail on the *Blue Dolphin* departing at 8:30 a.m., or on their larger *Na Pali Kai II* (ask for rates).

King Kamehameha Divers in the King Kamehameha Kona Beach Hotel, Kailua-Kona, tel. 329-5662, offers a daily boat charter that gives you a two-tank certified dive with your own gear for $75, $90 with their gear. An introductory dive is $65, and snorkeling is $40. This includes continental breakfast, lunch, and soft drinks. Rental rates for snorkeling gear run $10 for 24 hours, boogie boards $6-10.

Big Island Divers, tel. 329-6068, in the Honokohau Small Boat Harbor, offers a scuba certification course for only $59.95 that's given on four consecutive Saturdays or Wednesdays, so you must intend to stay on the Big Island for that length of time. The normal four-day course costs $450. They also rent complete snorkel gear for only $6 for 24 hours.

Kohala Divers, located along Route 270 in Kawaihae (see p. 304), open daily 8 a.m.-5 p.m., tel. 882-7774, offers scuba certification for $300, snorkel rentals for $10 (24 hours), and scuba rentals for $22. They lead two-tank dives for $75, and will take snorkelers along if they have room on the boat ($15). It's a bit far to go from Kailua-Kona but it's a big savings, and they're the only dive company along the Kohala coast.

Snorkel Bob's, tel. 329-0770, in the parking lot next to the Kona Hilton right in front of Huggo's Restaurant, offers snorkel gear for $15 per week for basic equipment. Upgrading to a comfortable surgical silicone mask with Italian fins is $27. Boogie boards are $9-15 p/d, $22-35 p/w depending on quality.

The **Nautilus Dive Center,** 382 Kamehameha Ave., Hilo, tel. 935-6939, is one of the only dive companies on the Hilo side, and offers a free informative dive map.

Snuba, tel. 326-7446, offers a new underwater concept that is perfect for an introductory underwater adventure. Tethered to a flotation raft bearing a scuba tank, you are unencumbered by the normal scuba equipment and your descent is limited to under 20 feet. For those who feel timid about scuba diving or who just want a new, fun-filled adventure, Snuba might be the answer. Prices are $49 for a beach dive, $40 for a boat dive.

Larger hotels often have snorkel equipment for guests, but if it isn't free, it always costs more than if you rented it from a dive shop. Scuba and snorkel cruises are booked through the various activity centers mentioned under "Sightseeing Tours" (see pp. 140-142), and at your hotel travel desk.

An alternative to boat dives is shore diving. *Shore Diving in Kona* is a great book listing sites, equipment, regulations, and suggestions for successful and safe dives. If your budget is limited and you're an experienced shore diver, it's a way to have a great outing at a reasonable price.

Snorkel/Scuba Dive Boats

Snorkeling, scuba, and snuba excursions are provided by the following: The **Fair Wind,** tel. 322-2788, leaving daily from magnificent Keauhou Bay (Snuba too); **The Body Glove,** tel. 326-7122 (Snuba too); **Capt. Cook VI,** tel. 329-6411; **Kamanu Charters,** tel. 329-2021; **Sea Quest,** tel. 329-7238; and **Captain Beans',** tel. 329-2955. Also see "Ocean Tours," pp. 141-142.

Surfing And Sailboarding

The surfing off the Big Island is rather uninspiring compared to that off the other islands. The reefs are treacherous and the surf is lazy. Some surfers bob around off the north section of Hilo Bay, and sometimes in Kealakekua and Wailua bays on the Kona side. Puna also attracts a few

REEF FISH

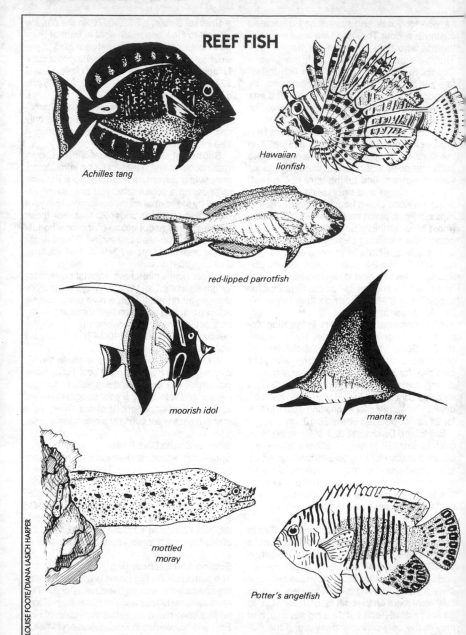

Achilles tang

Hawaiian lionfish

red-lipped parrotfish

moorish idol

manta ray

mottled moray

Potter's angelfish

LOUISE FOOTE/DIANA LASICH HARPER

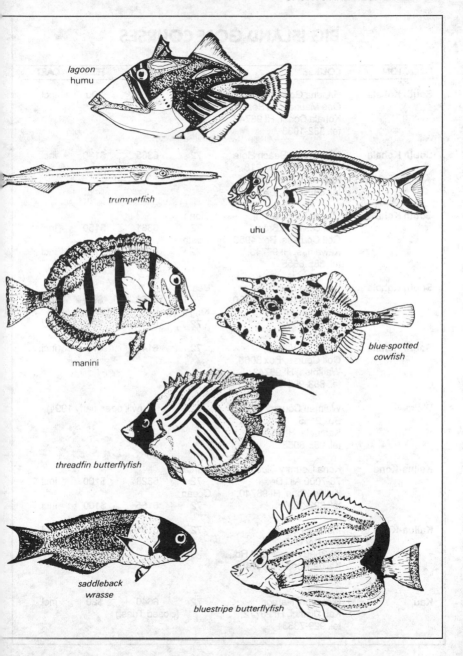

lagoon humu

trumpetfish

uhu

manini

blue-spotted cowfish

threadfin butterflyfish

saddleback wrasse

bluestripe butterflyfish

BIG ISLAND GOLF COURSES

LOCATION	COURSE	PAR	YARDS	FEES	CART
South Kohala	Hapuna Golf Course, One Mauna Kea Beach Dr., Kohala Coast, HI 96743, tel. 882-1035	72	6069	$90	incl.
South Kohala	Mauna Kea Beach Hote Golf Course, Box 218, Kamuela, HI 96743, tel. 882-7222	72	6365	$130	incl.
South Kohala	Mauna Lani Resort, Frances H. I'i Brown Golf Courses, Box 4959, Kawaihae, HI 96743, tel. 885-6655	North 72 South 72	6361 6370	$150 $150	incl. incl.
South Kohala	Waikoloa Beach Golf Courses, Box 5100, Waikoloa, HI 96743, tel. 883-6060	Beach 70 King's 72	5958 6010	$95 $95	incl. incl.
South Kohala	Waikoloa Village Golf Course, Box 3068, Waikoloa, HI 96743, tel. 883-9621	72	6142	$75	incl.
Waimea	Waimea Country Club, Box 2155, Kamuela, HI 96743, tel. 885-8053	72	(will open early 1994)		
Kailua-Kona	Kona Country Club, 78-7000 Ali'i Dr., Kailua-Kona, HI 96740, tel. 322-2595	Mountain 72 Ocean 72	5828 6165	$100 $100	incl. incl.
Kailua-Kona	Makalei Hawaii Country Club, 72-3890 Hawaii Belt Rd., Kailua-Kona, HI 96740, tel. 325-6625	72	6101	$77	incl.
Kau	Discovery Harbor, Kau District, HI 96772, tel. 929-7353	72	6640 (closed Tues.)	$20	incl.

BIG ISLAND GOLF COURSES

LOCATION	COURSE	PAR	YARDS	FEES	CART
Kau	Seamountain Golf Course, Box 85, Pahala, HI 96777, tel. 928-6222	72	6106	$36	$14
Kau	Volcano Golf and Country Club, Box 46, Volcano National Park, HI 96718, tel. 967-7331	72	5936	$52	incl.
Hilo	Hilo Municipal Golf Course, 340 Haihai St., Hilo, HI 96720, tel. 959-7711	71	6320	$6 (weekdays) $8 (weekends and holidays)	$14.50
Hilo	Naniloa Country Club, 120 Banyan Dr., Hilo, HI 96720, tel. 935-3000	36	2875	$35 (9 holes)	$14 (for 18)
Hamakua Coast	Hamakua Country Club, Box 344, Honokaa, HI 96727, tel. 775-7244	33	2520 (9 holes) (no club rental)	$10	(no carts)

off Isaac Hale and Kaimu beaches, and up north off Waipio Valley Beach. However, the winds are great for sailboarding.

Jet-skiing, Parasailing, Etc.
For those interested in thrill rides, **Kona Water Sports,** tel. 329-1593, rents jet skis and conducts water-skiing and parasailing excursions.

SKIING

Bored with sun and surf? Strap the "boards" to your feet and hit the slopes of Mauna Kea. There are no lifts so you'll need a 4WD to get to the top, and someone willing to pick you up again at the bottom. You can rent 4WDs from the car-rental agencies (see "Getting Around," following), but if that seems like too much hassle just contact **Ski Guides Hawaii,** Box 2020, Kamuela, HI 96743, tel. 885-4188 or 889-6747. Here you can rent skis and they'll provide the "lifts" to the top. You can expect snow Dec.-May, but you can't always count on it.

GOLF

The Big Island has some of the most beautiful golf links in Hawaii. Robert Trent Jones Sr. and Jr. have both built exceptional courses here. Dad built the Mauna Kea Beach Hotel course, while the kid built his at the Waikoloa Beach Resort. Both links are in South Kohala, as is another spectacular course at the nearby Mauna Lani. If these are too rich for your blood, you can hit nine holes in Hilo for about $10. How about golfing at Volcano Golf Course, where if you miss a short putt, you can blame it on an earthquake.

TENNIS

Many tennis courts dot the Big Island, and plenty of them are free. County courts are under the control of the Department of Parks and Recreation, which maintains a combination of lighted and unlit courts in Hilo, Kona, and Waimea. Some private and hotel courts are open to the public for a fee, while others restrict play to guests only.

HUNTING

Most people don't think of Hawaii as a place for hunting, but actually it's quite good. Seven species of introduced game mammals and 16 species of game birds are regularly hunted. Not all species of game animals are open on all islands, but every island offers hunting. Huge unpopulated expanses of grassland, forest, and scrubby mountainside are very good for hunting. The Big Island's game includes feral pig, sheep, and goats, plus a variety of pheasant, quail, dove, and wild turkey. Mauna Kea Beach Hotel guests can hunt on the Parker Ranch, while the **McCandless Ranch** near Captain Cook supplies guides for its 30,000 acres. For information contact Steve Arrington, Box 63 G, Captain Cook, HI 96704, tel. 328-2349/2389. Public game lands are located throughout the island; a license is required to take birds and game. For full information, write Division of Forestry and Wildlife, 1643 Kilauea Ave., Box 4849, Hilo, HI 96720, tel. 961-7221.

Gambel's quail

General Hunting Rules
Hunting licenses are mandatory in order to hunt on public, private, or military land anywhere in Hawaii. They're good for one year beginning July 1 and cost $7.50 residents, $15 nonresidents; free to senior citizens. Licenses are available from sporting goods stores and from the various offices of the Division of Forestry and Wildlife (see below). This government organization also sets and enforces the rules, so contact them with any questions. Generally, hunting hours are from a half-hour before sunrise to a half-hour after sunset. At times, there are "checking stations" where the hunter must check in before and after hunting.

Rifles must have a muzzle velocity greater than 1,200-foot-pounds. Shotguns larger than .20 gauge are allowed, and muzzleloaders must have a .45 caliber bore or larger. Bows must have a minimum draw of 45 pounds for straight bows and 30 pounds for compounds. Arrows must be broadheads. The use of hunting dogs is permitted only for certain species of birds and game, and when dogs are permitted, only smaller caliber rifles and shotguns, and spears and knives, may be used—no big bore guns/shotguns. Hunters must wear orange safety cloth on front and back no smaller than a 12-inch square. Certain big-game species are hunted only by lottery selection; contact the Division of Forestry and Wildlife two months in advance. Guide service is not mandatory, but is advised if you're unfamiliar with hunting in Hawaii. You can hunt on private land only with

feral pig

BIG ISLAND TENNIS COURTS

PUBLIC COURTS

Under jursidiction of the Department of Parks and Recreation,
25 Aupuni St., Hilo, HI 96720. Tel. 961-8311.

LOCATION	NAME OF COURT	NO. OF COURTS	LIGHTED
Hilo	Ainaole Park	1	No
Hilo	Hakalau Park	2	No
Hilo	Hilo High School	1	No
Hilo	Hoolulu Park	8	Yes
Hilo	Lincoln Park	4	Yes
Hilo	Mohouli Park	2	No
Hilo	University of Hawaii-Hilo College	2	No
Honokaa	Honokaa Park	2	Yes
Kapaau	Kamehameha Park	2	Yes
Kau	Kau High School	2	Yes
Keaau	Keaau Park	2	No
Kona	Greenwell Park	1	Yes
Kona	Kailua Park (Old Kona Airport)	4	Yes
Kona	Kailua Playground	1	Yes
Kona	Keauhou Park	1	No
Waimea	Waimea Park	2	Yes
Waimea	Hawaii Prep Academy	4	Yes

HOTEL AND PRIVATE COURTS THAT ARE OPEN TO THE PUBLIC

LOCATION	NAME OF COURT	NO. OF COURTS	LIGHTED
Kailua-Kona	King Kamehameha Kona Beach Hotel (fee)	2	Yes
Kailua-Kona	Kona Hilton Beach and Tennis Resort (fee)	4	Yes
Kailua-Kona	Kona Lagoon (fee for nonguests)	2	Yes
Kamuela	Waimea Park	2	Yes
Keauhou-Kona	Keauhou Beach Hotel (fee)	6	Yes
Keauhou-Kona	Kona Surf Hotel Racket Club (fee)	7	Yes
Kona	Country Club Villas	2	No
Pahala	Seamountain Tennis Center (fee)	4	No
Waikoloa	Waikoloa village (fee)	2	Yes

permission, and you must possess a valid hunting license. Guns and ammunition brought into Hawaii must be registered with the chief of police of the corresponding county within 48 hours of arrival.

Information
Hunting rules and regulations are always subject to change. Also, environmental considerations often change bag limits and seasons. Make sure to check with the Division of Forestry and

Wildlife for the most current information. Request "Rules Regulating Game Bird Hunting, Field Trails and Commercial Shooting Preserves," "Rules Regulating Game Mammal Hunting," and "Hunting in Hawaii." Direct inquiries to: Department of Land and Natural Resources, Division of Forestry and Wildlife Office, Box 4849, Hilo 96720, tel. 961-7221.

Game Animals

All game animals on Hawaii have been introduced. Some have adapted admirably and are becoming well entrenched, while the existence of others is still precarious. **Feral pigs** are escaped domestic pigs that have gone wild and are found on all islands except Lanai. The stock is a mixture of original Polynesian pigs and subsequently introduced species. The pigs are hunted with dogs and usually killed with a spear or long knife—not recommended for the timid or tenderhearted. These beasts' four-inch tusks and fighting spirit make them tough and dangerous. **Feral goats** come in a variety of colors. Found on all islands except Lanai, they have been known to cause erosion and are viewed as a pest in some areas, especially on Haleakala. Openly hunted on all islands, their meat when done properly is considered delicious. **Mouflon sheep** are native to Corsica and Sardinia. They do well on Lanai and on the windswept slopes of Mauna Loa and Mauna Kea, where they're hunted at various times by public lottery. **Feral sheep** haunt the slopes of Mauna Kea and Mauna Loa

Explore the Big Island on horseback with a paniolo guide.

at 7,000-12,000 feet. They travel in flocks and destroy vegetation. It takes determination and a good set of lungs to bag one, especially with a bow and arrow.

Game Birds

A number of game birds are found on most of the islands. Bag limits and hunting seasons vary, so check with the Division of Forestry and Wildlife for details. **Ring-necked pheasant** is one of the best game birds; it is found on all the islands. The **kalij pheasant** from Nepal is found only on the Big Island, where the **green pheasant** is also prevalent; some are found on Oahu and Maui. **Francolins,** gray and black, from India and the Sudan, are similar to partridges. They are hunted on all islands with dogs and are great roasted. There are also **chukar** from Tibet, found on the slopes of all islands; a number of **quail,** including the **Japanese and California** varieties; **doves;** and the **wild Rio Grande turkeys** which are found on all islands except

gray francolin

Kauai and Oahu (although a few of the "featherless variety" have been known to walk the streets of Waikiki).

HORSEBACK RIDING

Waipio Naalapa Trail Rides, operated by Sherri Hannum, tel. 775-0419, offers the most unique rides on Hawaii. Sherri and her family have lived in Waipio Valley for 20 years and know its history, geology, and legends intimately. She offers pickup service from Kukuihaele for the half-day rides ($65). Sherri treats guests like family. If you have time, don't miss this wonderful adventure! For full information see p. 194.

Waipio Valley Wagon Tour, tel. 775-9518, owned and operated by Peter Tolin, is a mule-drawn tour of the magnificent Waipio Valley. The two-hour tours leave four times daily at 9 a.m., 10:30 a.m., 12:30 p.m., and 2 or 4 p.m. The cost is $35, children under 12 half price, children two and under free. For full information see p. 195.

H.R.T. Waipio Tour Desk, tel. 775-7291, located in the Hawaiian Holiday Macadamia Nut Factory in Honokaa, offers van and horseback riding through fabulous Waipio Valley (see p. 190). Daily van tours at 9:30 a.m. and 1 p.m. (pick-up service from your hotel costs extra) usually last 90 minutes, including a short shuttle to Waipio, and cost $26 per person. The horseback rides start at the same times but last 2 1/2 hours and cost $65, including transportation from Honokaa to Waipio. Make reservations 24 hours in advance.

Enjoyable rides are also offered by the **Mauna Kea Beach Hotel** (to nonguests also), tel. 882-7222. They have an arrangement with the Parker Ranch, which will supply a *paniolo* to guide you over the quarter-million acres of open range on the slopes of Mauna Kea. The stables are at Parker Ranch headquarters in Waimea.

King's Trail Rides, tel. 323-2388, has offices along Route 11 high above the Kona Coast on the outskirts of Kealakekua. Prices are $50 for a 1 1/2-hour trail ride, $60 for two hours, and $79 for a five-hour adventure, half of which is on horseback (lunch included). After being driven to the 4,200-foot level, you mount up to ride the Kealakekua Ranch lands, a 20,000-acre working spread. This is the "real McCoy!"

NANA LASCH HARPER

ARTS AND CRAFTS

Referring to Hawaii as "paradise" is about as hackneyed as you can get, but when you qualify it as an "artists' paradise" it's the absolute truth. Something about the place evokes art (or at least personal expression) from most people. The islands are like a magnet: they not only draw artists to them, they draw art *from* the artists. The list of literary figures who have visited Hawaii and had something inspirational to say reads like a freshman literature survey: William Henry Dana, Herman Melville, Mark Twain, Robert Louis Stevenson, Jack London, Somerset Maugham, Joaquin Miller, and of course James Michener.

The inspiration comes from the astounding natural surroundings. The land is so beautiful yet so raw; the ocean's power and rhythm is primal and ever-present; the riotous colors of flowers and fruit leap from the deep-green jungle background. Crystal water beads and pale mists turn the mountains into mystic temples, while rainbows come riding on the crests of waves. The stunning variety of faces begging to be rendered appears as if all the world sent delegations to the islands. And in most cases it did! Inspiration is everywhere, as is art, good or bad.

Sometimes the artwork is overpowering in itself and in its sheer volume. Though geared to the tourist market of cheap souvenirs, there is hardly a shop in Hawaii that doesn't sell some item that falls into the general category of "art." You can find everything from carved monkey-face coconut shells to true masterpieces. The Polynesian Hawaiians were master artisans, and their legacy still lives in a wide variety of woodcarvings, basketry, and weavings. The *hula* is art in swaying motion, and the true form is rigorously studied and taken very seriously. There is hardly a resort area that doesn't offer the "bump and grind" tourist's *hula* but even these revues are accompanied by proficient local musicians. Nightclubs offer "slack key" balladeers and island music played on ukuleles, while the sound of Hawaii's own steel guitar spills from many lounges.

Vibrant fabrics that catch the spirit of the islands are rendered into muumuus and aloha shirts at countless local factories. They're almost a mandatory purchase! Pottery, heavily influenced by the Japanese, is well developed at numerous kilns. Local artisans fashion delicate jewelry from coral and olivine, while some ply the whaler's legacy of etching on ivory, called scrimshaw. There is a fine quilt-making tradition, flower art in *lei*, and street artists working in everything from airbrush to glass. The following is an overview; for local offerings please see "Shopping" in the travel chapters.

ARTS TO BUY

Wild Hawaiian shirts or bright muumuus, especially when worn on the Mainland, have the magical effect of making wearers "feel" like they're in Hawaii, while at the same time eliciting spontaneous smiles from passers-by. Maybe it's the colors, or perhaps it's just the "vibe" that signifies "party time" or "hang loose," but nothing says Hawaii like alohawear does. There are more than a dozen fabric houses in Hawaii turning out distinctive patterns, and many dozens of factories creating their own personalized designs. These factories often have attached retail outlets, but in any case you can find hundreds of shops selling alohawear. Aloha shirts were the brilliant idea of a Chinese merchant in Honolulu, who used to hand-tailor them and sell them to the tourists who arrived by ship in the glory days before WW II. They were an instant success. Muumuus or "Mother Hubbards" were the idea of missionaries, who were appalled by Hawaiian women running about *au naturelle* and insisted on covering their new Christian converts from head to foot. Now the roles are reversed, and it's Mainlanders who come to Hawaii and immediately strip down to as little clothing as possible.

Alohawear

At one time exclusively made of cotton, or from manmade yet naturally based rayon, these materials were and still are the best for any tropical clothing. Beware, however: polyester has slowly crept into the market! No material could possibly be worse for the island climate, so when buying your alohawear make sure to check the label for material content. Muumuus now come in various styles and can be worn for the entire spectrum of social occasions in Hawaii. Aloha

shirts are basically cut the same as always, but the patterns have undergone changes, and apart from the original flowers and ferns, modern shirts might depict an island scene in the manner of a silkscreen painting. A basic good-quality muumuu or aloha shirt starts at about $25 and is guaranteed to be worth its price in good times and happy smiles. The connoisseur might want to purchase *The Hawaiian Shirt, Its Art and History* by R. Thomas Steele. It's illustrated with more than 150 shirts that are now considered works of art by collectors the world over.

Scrimshaw

This art of etching and carving on bone and ivory has become an island tradition handed down from the times of the old whaling ships. Although scrimshaw can be found throughout Hawaii, the center remains in the old whaling

DIANA LASICH HARPER

capital of Lahaina, Maui. There along Front Street are numerous shops specializing in scrimshaw. Today, pieces are carved on fossilized walrus ivory that is gathered by Eskimos and shipped to Hawaii. It comes in a variety of shades from pure white to mocha, depending upon the mineral content of the earth in which it was buried. Elephant ivory or whale bone is no longer used because of ecological considerations, but there is a "gray market" in Pacific walrus tusks. Eskimos can legally hunt the walrus.

They then make a few minimal scratches on the tusks which technically qualifies them to be "Native American art" and free of most governmental restrictions. The tusks are then sent to Hawaii as art objects, but the superficial scratches are immediately removed and the ivory is reworked by artisans. Scrimshaw is made into everything from belt buckles to delicate earrings and even into coffee-table centerpieces. The prices can go from a few dollars up into the thousands.

Woodcarvings

One Hawaiian art that has not died out is woodcarving. This art was extremely well developed among the old Hawaiians, who almost exclusively used koa because of its density, strength, and natural luster. It was turned into canoes, woodware, and furniture for the ali'i. Koa is becoming increasingly scarce, though many items are still available—and costly. Milo and monkeypod are also excellent woods for carving and have largely replaced koa. You can buy tikis, bowls, and furniture at numerous shops. Countless inexpensive carved items are sold at variety stores, such as hula dancers or salad servers, but most of these are imported from Asia or the Philippines and can be bought at any variety store.

Weaving

The minute you arrive in Hawaii, you should shell out $2 for a woven beach mat. This is a necessity, not a frivolous purchase, but it definitely won't have been made in Hawaii. What is made in Hawaii is lau hala. This is traditional Hawaiian weaving from the leaves (lau) of the pandanus (hala) tree. These leaves vary greatly in length, with the largest over six feet, and they have a thorny spine that must be removed before they can be worked. The color ranges from light tan to dark brown. The leaves are cut into strips one-eighth- to one-inch wide and are then employed in weaving. Any variety of items can be made or at least covered in lau hala. It makes great purses, mats, baskets, and table mats.

Woven into a hat, it's absolutely superb but should not be confused with a palm-frond hat. A lau hala hat is amazingly supple and even when squashed will pop back into shape. A good one is expensive ($25) and with proper care will last

for years. All lau hala should be given a light application of mineral oil on a monthly basis, especially if it's exposed to the sun. For flat items, iron over a damp cloth and keep purses and baskets stuffed with paper when not in use. Palm fronds also are widely used in weaving. They, too, are a great natural raw material, but not as good as lau hala. Almost any item, such as a beach bag woven from palm, makes a good authentic yet inexpensive gift or souvenir; a wide selection is available in countless shops.

Gift Items

Jewelry is always an appreciated gift, especially if it's distinctive, and Hawaii has some of the most original. The sea provides the basic raw materials of pink, gold, and black coral that is so beautiful it holds the same fascination as gemstones. Harvesting the coral is very dangerous work. The Lahaina beds off Maui have one of the best black coral lodes in the islands, but unlike reef coral, these trees grow at depths bordering the outer limits of a scuba diver's capabilities. Only the best can dive 180 feet after the black coral, and about one diver per year dies in pursuit of it. Conservationists have placed great pressure on the harvesters of these deep corals, and the state of Hawaii has placed strict limits and guidelines on the firms and divers involved.

Pink coral has long been treasured by humans. The Greeks considered it a talisman for good health, and there's even evidence that it has been coveted since the Stone Age. Coral jewelry is on sale at many shops throughout Hawaii. The value comes from the color of the coral and the workmanship.

Puka shells (with small, naturally occurring holes) and opihi shells are also made into jewelry. Many times these items are very inexpensive, yet they are authentic and are great purchases for the price. Hanging macrame planters festooned with seashells are usually quite affordable and are sold at roadside stands along with shells.

Hawaii produces some unique food items that are appreciated by most people. Various-sized jars of macadamia nuts and butters are great gifts, as are tins of rich, gourmet-quality Kona coffee, the only coffee produced in the U.S. Guava, pineapple, passion fruit, and mango are often gift-boxed into assortments of jams, jellies, and spicy chutneys. And for that special

classic hula *troupe*

person in your life, you can bring home island fragrances in bottles of perfumes and colognes in the exotic odors of gardenia, plumeria, and even ginger. All of the above items are reasonably priced, lightweight, and easy to carry.

HULA AND LEI

Hawaiian *hula* was never performed in grass skirts; tapa or ti-leaf skirts were worn. Grass skirts came to Hawaii from the Gilbert Islands, so if you see grass or cellophane skirts in a "*hula* revue," you'll know that it's not traditional. *Hula,* like all artforms, has its own highly specialized techniques. A dancer has to learn how to control every part of his or her body, including the facial expressions, which become very important and help set the mood. The hands are extremely important and provide instant background scenery. For example, if the hands are thrust outward in an aggressive manner, this can signify a battle; if they sway gently overhead, they refer to the gods or the early time of creation. They can easily become rain or clouds or the sun, sea, or moon. You must watch the hands to get the gist of the story, but one comeback to this advice was the classic wisecrack, "You watch the parts you like, and I'll watch the parts I like."

Swaying hips, depending upon their motion, can depict a long walk, a canoe ride, or sexual intercourse. The foot motion can portray a bat-

tle, a walk, or any kind of movement or conveyance. The overall effect is multidirectional synchronized movement.

Correct chanting of the *mele* is an integral part of the performance. These story-chants, combined with the various musical instruments that accompany the dance, make the *hula* very much like opera, and are especially similar in the way the tale is unfolded.

Language Of The *Lei*

Every major island of Hawaii is symbolized by its own *lei,* made from a distinctive flower, shell, or fern. Each island has its own official color as well, which doesn't necessarily correspond to the color of the island's *lei.* The island of Hawaii's *lei* is made from the red (or rare creamy white or orange) ohia-lehua blossom. The ohia-lehua tree grows from sea level to 9,000 feet and produces an abundance of tufted flowers. The official color of Hawaii Island, like the lava from its active volcanoes, is red.

THAT GOOD OLD ISLAND MUSIC

The missionaries usually take a beating for destroying so much Hawaiian culture while civilizing the natives. However, they seem to have done one thing right: they taught the Hawaiians the diatonic scale and immediately opened a door to latent and superbly harmonious talent. Before the missionaries, the Hawaiians knew

HAWAIIAN *LEI*

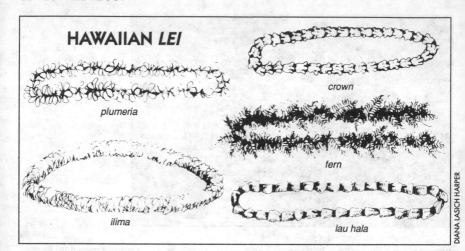

plumeria

crown

fern

ilima

lau hala

DIANA LASICH HARPER

little about melody. Though sonorous, their *mele* were repetitive chants emphasizing historical accuracy rather than music. The Hawaiians, in short, didn't *sing*. But within a few years of the missionaries' arrival, they were belting out good old Christian hymns, and one of their favorite pastimes became group and individual singing.

Early in the 1800s, Spanish *vaqueros* from California were imported to teach the Hawaiians how to be cowboys. With them came guitars and moody ballads. The Hawaiian *paniolo* (cowboys) quickly learned how to punch cows and croon away the long lonely nights on the range. Immigrants who came along a little later in the 19th century, especially from Portugal, helped create a Hawaiian-style music. Their biggest musical contribution was a small, four-stringed instrument called a *braga* or *cavaquinho*. One owned by Augusto Dias was the prototype of a homegrown Hawaiian instrument that became known as the ukulele. "Jumping flea," the translation of "ukulele," is an appropriate name devised by the Hawaiians when they saw how nimble the fingers were as they "jumped" over the strings.

The Merrie Monarch, King Kalakaua, and Queen Liliuokalani were both patrons of the arts who furthered the Hawaiian musical identity at the turn of the century. Kalakaua revived the *hula* and was also a gifted lyricist and balladeer. He wrote the words to "Hawaii Pono," which became the national anthem of Hawaii and later

the state anthem. Liliuokalani wrote the hauntingly beautiful "Aloha Oe," which is often pointed to as the "spirit of Hawaii" in music. Detractors say that its melody is extremely close to the old Christian hymn, "Rock Beside the Sea," but the lyrics are so beautiful and perfectly fitted that this doesn't matter.

Just prior to Kalakaua's reign, a Prussian bandmaster, Capt. Henri Berger, was invited to head the fledgling Royal Hawaiian Band, which he turned into a very respectable ensemble lauded by many visitors to the islands. Berger was open-minded and learned to love Hawaiian music. He collaborated with Kalakaua and other island musicians to incorporate their music into a Western format. He headed the band for 43 years until 1915, and was instrumental in making music a serious pursuit of talented Hawaiians.

Popular Hawaiian Music

Hawaiian music has a unique twang, a special feeling that says to everyone who hears it: "Relax, sit back in the moonlight, watch the swaying palms as the surf sings a lullaby." This special sound is epitomized by the bouncy ukulele, the falsetto voices of Hawaiian crooners, and by the smooth ring of the "steel" or "Hawaiian" guitar. The steel guitar is a variation originated by Joseph Kekuku in the 1890s. Stories abound of how he devised this instrument; the most popular versions say that Joe dropped his comb or pocket knife on his guitar strings and liked what he heard. Driven by the faint rhythm of an inner sound, he went to the machine shop at the Kamehameha School and turned out a steel bar for sliding over the strings. To complete the sound he changed the cat-gut strings to steel and raised them so they wouldn't hit the frets. *Voilà!*—Hawaiian music as the world knows it today.

The first melodious strains of **slack-key guitar** can be traced back to the time of Kamehameha III, when Spanish cowboys (the forerunners of Hawaiian *paniolo*) from California were brought to the kingdom to run the wild cattle that had grown steadily in numbers ever since killing them was made *kapu* by Kamehameha I. The white settlers' gift had become a menace, growing in numbers to the point where they were even attacking grass houses for fodder. The Spanish cowboys roped, branded, and corralled them, and living up to the cowboy image, would pass lonesome nights on the range singing and playing their guitars. The Hawaiians, who made excellent cowboys, and their ears, recently tuned by the missionaries, picked up the melodies accompanied by the strange new instrument, and quickly Hawaiianized them. The Spanish had their way of tuning the guitar, and played difficult and aggressive music that did not sit well with Hawaiians, who were much more gentle and casual in their manners.

Hawaiians soon became adept at making their own music. At first, one person played the melody, but it lacked fullness. There was no body to the sound. So, as one *paniolo* fooled with the melody, another soon learned to play bass, which added depth. But, a player was often alone, and by experimenting learned that he could get the right hand going with the melody, and at the same time could play the bass note with the thumb to improve the sound. Singers also learned that they could "open tune" the guitar to match their rich voices.

Due to *kahunaism*, Hawaiians believed that knowledge was sacred, and what is sacred should be treated with utmost respect, which meant keeping it secret except from sincere apprentices. Guitar playing became a personal artform whose secrets were closely guarded and handed down only to family members, and only to those who showed ability and determination. When old-time slack-key guitar players

were done strumming, they loosened all the strings so that no one could figure out how they had it tuned. If they were playing, and someone came by who was interested and wasn't part of the family, the Hawaiians put the guitar down and placed their foot across the strings until the person went away. As time went on, more and more Hawaiians began to play slack key, and a common repertoire emerged.

An accomplished musician could easily figure out the simple songs, once they had figured out how the family had tuned the guitar. One of the most popular tunings was the "open G." Old Hawaiian folks called it the "taro patch tune." Different songs came out, and if you were in their family and were interested in the guitar, they took the time to sit down and teach you. The way they taught was straightforward, and a test of your sincerity at the same time. The old master would start to play. They just wanted you to listen, get a feel for the music, not any more than that. You brought your guitar and *listened*. When you felt it, you played it, and the knowledge was transferred. Today, only a handful of slack-key guitar players know how to play the classic tunes classically. The best-known and perhaps greatest slack-key player was Gabby Pahinui, with the Sons of Hawaii. He passed away recently, but left many recordings behind. A slack-key master still singing and playing is Raymond Kane. Raymond now teaches a handful of students his wonderful and haunting music. Not one of his students is from his own family, and most are *haole* musicians trying to preserve the classical method of playing.

Hawaiian music received its biggest boost from a remarkable radio program known as "Hawaii Calls." This program sent out its music from the Banyan Court of the Moana Hotel from 1935 until 1975. At its peak in the mid-1950s, it was syndicated on over 700 radio stations throughout the world. Ironically, Japanese pilots heading for Pearl Harbor tuned in island music as a signal beam. Some internationally famous classic tunes came out of the '40s and '50s. Jack Pitman composed "Beyond the Reef" in 1948; over 300 artists have recorded it and it has sold well over 12 million records. Other million-record sellers include: "Sweet Leilani," "Lovely *Hula* Hands," "The Cross-eyed Mayor of Kaunakakai," and "The Hawaiian Wedding Song."

By the 1960s, Hawaiian music began to die. It was just too corny for those turbulent years. Hawaiian music was too light, belonging to the older generation and the good times that followed WW II. One man was instrumental in keeping Hawaiian music alive during this period. Don Ho, with his "Tiny Bubbles," became the token Hawaiian musician of the '60s and early '70s. He's persevered long enough to become a legend in his own time, and his Polynesian Extravaganza still packs them in six nights a week in Honolulu. Al Harrington, "The South Pacific Man," has another Honolulu "big revue" that draws large crowds. Of this type of entertainer, perhaps the most Hawaiian is Danny Kaleikini, who entertains his audience with dances, Hawaiian anecdotes, and tunes on the traditional Hawaiian nose flute.

The Beat Goes On
Beginning in the mid-'70s, islanders began to assert their cultural identity. One of the unifying factors was the coming of age of "Hawaiian" music. It graduated from the "little grass shack" novelty tune and began to include sophisticated jazz, rock, and contemporary rhythms. Accomplished musicians whose roots were in traditional island music began to highlight their tunes with this distinctive sound. The best embellish their arrangements with ukuleles, steel guitars, and traditional percussion and melodic instruments. Some excellent modern recording artists have become island institutions. The local people say that you know if the Hawaiian harmonies are good if they give you "chicken skin."

Each year special music awards, **Na Hoku Hanohano,** or *Hoku* for short, are given to distinguished island musicians. The following are recent *Hoku* winners considered by their contemporaries to be among the best in Hawaii. If they're playing while you're there, don't miss them. **Loyal Garner,** who was awarded *Female Vocalist of the Year* for "I Shall Sing," is a truly wonderful artist. **Del Beazley,** who walked away with top honors for *Male Vocalist of the Year, Contemporary Hawaiian Album, and Song of the Year,* all from his fantastic album "Night and Day," is a wonderful performer. **Makaha Sons Of Niihau** captured a number of *Hoku* for *Best Traditional Hawaiian Album, Best Group, and Album of the Year* for their fantastic work "Ho'oluana." Led by Israel Kamakawiwoole, they

are the best and shouldn't be missed. *Best Contemporary Album* went to **Hawaiian Style Band** for "Vanishing Treasures," while *Single of the Year* was awarded to **Bryan Kessler & Me No Hoa Aloha** for "Heiau," a haunting melody. *Instrumental Album of the Year* was awarded to **Susan Gillespie and Susi Hussong** for "Wedding Music," and *Most Promising Artist* was taken by **Kealohi** for "Kealohi."

Past winners of *Hoku* who have become renowned performers include: **Brothers Cazimero,** who are blessed with beautiful harmonic voices; **Krush,** who are highly regarded for their contemporary sounds; **The Peter Moon Band,** fantastic performers with a strong traditional sound; **Karen Keawehawai'i,** who has a sparkling voice and can be very funny when the mood strikes her; and **Henry Kapono,** formerly of Cecelio and Kapono, who keeps a low profile but is an incredible performer and excellent songwriter. His shows are noncommercial and very special. **Cecilio** is now teamed up with **Maggie Herron;** they are hot together and have a strong following in Honolulu. **The Beamer Brothers** are excellent performers, and can be seen at various nightspots.

Some top-notch performers with a strong following are: Ledward Kaapana; Mango; Oliver Kelly; Ka'eo; Na Leo Pilimehana, whose "Local Boys" recently won a *Hoku* for Best Single; Freitas Brothers; Brickwood Galuteria, who won a double *Hoku* for Best Male Vocalist and Most Promising Artist; and Third Road Delite.

Classical And Chamber Music
A wide assortment of classical and chamber music is offered in Hawaii. The following organizations sponsor concerts throughout the year: Chamber Music Hawaii, 905 Spencer St., No. 404, Honolulu, HI 96822 (tel. 531-6617); Classical Guitar Society of Hawaii, 1229-D Waimanu, Honolulu, HI 96814 (tel. 537-6451); The Ensemble Players Guild, Box 50225, Honolulu, HI 96850 (tel. 735-1173); Hawaii Concert Society, Box 663, Hilo, HI 96721 (tel. 935-5831); Honolulu Symphony Society, 1000 Bishop St., Suite 901, Honolulu, HI 96813 (tel. 537-6171); Kauai Concert Association, 5867 Haaheo Pl., Kapaa, HI 96746 (tel. 822-7593); Maui Philharmonic Society, 2274 S. Kihei Rd., Kihei, HI 96753 (tel. 879-2962).

ART INFORMATION

This section includes the names and addresses of guilds, centers, and organizations that dispense information on Hawaiian arts and crafts.

Arts Council of Hawaii, Box 50225, Honolulu, HI 96850, tel. 524-7120, Karl Ichida, Exec. Director. A citizens' advocacy group for the arts providing technical assistance and information to individuals and groups. Publishes the *Cultural Climate,* a newsletter covering what's happening in the arts of Hawaii. Includes a calendar of events, feature articles, and editorials. Membership fee, $15, Includes newsletter; nonmembers, 50 cents per issue.

Bishop Museum, 1355 Kalihi St., Box 19000-A, Honolulu, HI 96819, tel. 847-3511. The world's *best* museum covering Polynesia and Hawaii. Exhibits, galleries, archives, demonstrations of Hawaiian crafts, and a planetarium. On the premises, Shop Pacifica has a complete selection of books and publications on all aspects of Hawaiian art and culture. Shouldn't be missed.

Contemporary Arts Center, 605 Kapiolani Blvd., Honolulu, HI 96813, tel. 525-8047. Promotes public awareness of contemporary art by providing gallery space, publicity, and exposure for local artists. Also houses a permanent collection and monthly exhibitions.

East Hawaii Cultural Council, Box 1312, Hilo, HI 96721. Publishes the *The Center Newspaper,* a monthly newsletter of what's happening artistically and culturally primarily on the Big Island. Includes a good monthly calendar of events with listings from exhibit openings to movies.

East-West Center Culture Learning Institute, Burns Hall 4076, 1777 East-West Rd., Honolulu, HI 96848, tel. 948-8006. At U of H campus. Dedicated to the sharing, exhibiting and appreciation of arts, culture and crafts from throughout Asia and the Western world. Their bimonthly *Centerviews* includes an events calendar and topical editorials on the Pacific. Free.

East-West Journal, 1633 Kapiolani Blvd., Honolulu, HI 96814. Yearly guide to exhibition galleries featuring the work of locally renowned artists.

Hawaii Craftsmen, Box 22145, Honolulu, HI 96823, tel. 523-1974. Increases awareness of Hawaiian crafts through programs, exhibitions, workshops, lectures, and demonstrations.

Honolulu Academy of Arts, 900 S. Beretania St., Honolulu, HI 96814, tel. 538-3693. Collects, preserves and exhibits works of art. Offers public art education programs related to their collections. Also offers tours, classes, lectures, films, and a variety of publications.

Honolulu Symphony Society, 1000 Bishop St., Honolulu, HI 96813, tel. 537-6171. Provides professional-level music, primarily symphonic concerts.

Pacific Handcrafters Guild, Box 15491, Honolulu, HI 96818, tel. 923-5726. Focuses on developing and preserving handicrafts in Hawaii and the Pacific. They sponsor four major crafts fairs annually.

State Foundation on Culture and the Arts, 335 Merchant St., Room 202, Honolulu, HI 96813, tel. 548-4145. Began by state legislature in 1965 to preserve Hawaii's diverse cultural and artistic heritage. Publishes *Hawaii Cultural Resource Directory,* which lists most of the art organizations, galleries, councils, co-ops, and guilds throughout Hawaii. Very complete.

University of Hawaii at Manoa Art Gallery, 2535 The Mall, Honolulu, HI 96822, tel. 948-6888. Showcases contemporary artwork. Theme changes periodically.

carved koa bowl, traditional style

SHOPPING

The following is an overview of the main shopping areas and where their locations around the island. Almost every town has at least a gas station and market, and they will be listed in the travel chapters under "Shopping." Look there for directions to and descriptions of specific malls, art shops, and boutiques in the area. Supermarkets, health food stores, and local markets are listed in the individual travel chapters, generally in the "Food" sections.

SHOPPING CENTERS

General shopping centers are found in Hilo, Kailua-Kona, Waimea, and Captain Cook. Like most shopping malls, these have a variety of stores whose offerings include apparel, dry goods, sporting goods, food, photography supplies, or outdoor rentals.

Hilo Malls

The main shopping center in Hilo is the **Prince Kuhio Plaza** at 111 E. Puainako. This shoppers' paradise is Hilo's newest and the island's largest shopping mall. An older but still full-service shopping center is **Kaiko'o Mall** at 777 Kilauea Avenue. The **Hilo Shopping Center** is about one-half mile south on Kilauea Ave. at the corner of Kekuanoa Street. This smaller mall has only a handful of local shops. **Puainako Town Center** is located at 2100 Kanoelehua Avenue. **Waiakea Shopping Plaza**, at 100 Kanoelehua Ave., has a small clutch of stores.

Kona Malls

Two commodities that you're guaranteed in Kailua-Kona are plenty of sunshine and plenty of shopping. **Kona Inn Shopping Village** is located in central Kailua at 75-5744 Ali'i Dr. and has more than 40 shops selling everything from fabrics to fruits. **World Square** is smaller and just across the road. **Kona Banyan Court,** also in central Kailua, has a dozen shops with a medley of goods and services. **Kailua Bay Inn Shopping Plaza** is along Ali'i Drive, **Akona Kai Mall** is across from Kailua Pier, while the **Kona Coast Shopping Plaza** and the **North Kona Shopping Center** are both along Palani Road. **Lanihau Center,** at 75-5595 Palani Rd., tel. 329-9333, is one of Kailua-Kona's newest shopping additions. **King Kamehameha Kona Beach Hotel Mall** is an exclusive shopping haven on the first floor of the hotel, while **Rawson Plaza,** at 74-5563 Kaiwi St., is in the industrial area and offers bargains. **Waterfront Row** is a new shopping and food complex at the south end of downtown Kailua-Kona that's done in period architecture with rough-cut lumber.

Keauhou Shopping Village is conveniently located at the corner of Ali'i Dr. and Kamehameha III Rd. at the far end of Kailua-Kona. Here you'll find everything from a post office to a supermarket. Continuing south on Route 11, you'll spot **Kainaliu Village Mall** along the main drag.

Kealakekua Ranch Center, in Captain Cook, is a two-story mall with fashions and general supplies.

Waimea (Kamuela) Malls

After the diversity of shopping malls in Kailua and Hilo, it's like a breath of fresh air to have only one choice. In Waimea try the **Parker Ranch Shopping Center,** which has over 30 shops, including a pharmacy, grocery, and general merchandise. A small herd of shops in this center also features ranch and Western-wear with a Hawaiian twist. **Parker Square Shopping Mall,** along Route 19, has a collection of fine boutiques and shops. **Waimea Shopping Center,** also along Route 19, is one of Waimea's newest shopping malls.

BOOKSTORES

Two aspects of a quality vacation are knowing what you're doing and thoroughly relaxing while doing it. Nothing helps you do this better than a good book. The following stores offer full selections.

Hilo has excellent bookstores (also see shopping malls above). **Basically Books,** downtown at 46 Waianuenue St., tel. 961-0144, has a good selection of Hawaiiana and out-of-print books, and an unbeatable selection of maps. You can get anywhere you want to go with their nautical charts, road maps, and topographical maps, which include sectionals for serious hikers and trekkers. Their collection covers most of the Pacific. They also feature a very good selection of travel books, and flags from countries throughout the world. The **Book Gallery,** tel. 959-7744, at Prince Kuhio Plaza, is a full-selection bookstore featuring Hawaiiana, hardcovers, and paperbacks. **Waldenbooks,** also at Prince Kuhio Plaza, tel. 959-6468, open daily 9 a.m.-9 p.m., is the largest and best-stocked bookstore in the Hilo area. **Bookfinders of Hawaii,** at 150 Haili St., tel. 961-5055, specializes in hard-to-find and out-of-print books. If you want it, they'll get it.

Kailua-Kona bookstores include **Waldenbooks** in Lanihau Center on Palani Rd., tel. 329-0015; **Middle Earth Bookshop** at 75-5719 Ali'i Dr., in the Kona Plaza Shopping Arcade, tel. 329-2123; **Keauhou Village Bookshop** at Keauhou Shopping Village, tel. 322-8111, open Mon.-Fri. 9 a.m.-9 p.m., Sat. 9 a.m.-6 p.m., Sun. 9 a.m.-5 p.m.

Waimea offers books at the **Waimea General Store,** located at the Parker Square Shopping Mall, tel. 885-4479, open Mon.-Sat. 9 a.m.-5 p.m., Sun. 10 a.m.-4 p.m., and at Waimea Shopping Center.

SPECIALTY SHOPS, ART, AND NEAT THINGS

You can stroll in and out of flower shops, T-shirt factories, and a panoply of boutiques offering ceramics, paintings, carvings, and all manner of island handicrafts. Art and crafts shops are always a part of the Big Island's shopping malls, and in even the smallest village you can count on at least one local artist displaying his or her creations. The following list of artists and shops is by no means exhaustive, but for the most part, they are in out-of-the-way places and worth a visit. Art shops and boutiques in specific areas will be covered in the travel sections under "Shopping."

In Hilo, **Hawaiian Handcrafts** at 760 Kilauea Ave., tel. 935-5587, specializes in woodcarvings. **Halemanu Crafts** is a shop at 195 Kinole St. where senior citizens from the Hilo area display their fine *lau hala* weavings. **Sugawara Lauhala and Gift Shop** at 59 Kalakaua St. is a virtually unknown Hilo institution making genuine *lau hala* weavings. The **Crystal Grotto** at 290 Kamehameha Ave., tel. 935-2284, is a metaphysical bookstore filled with crystals, jewelry, videotapes, tarot cards, incense, and oils, and a full line of magnificently crafted beadwork. **Old Town Printer and Stationers** at 201 Kinoole St., open weekdays 8 a.m-5 p.m., has been in business for 35 years selling stationery, office supplies, postcards, notecards, and a terrific selection of calendars. **Sig Zane Design** at 122 Kamehameha Ave., tel. 935-7077, is one of the most unique and distinctive shops on the island. Here, owner and designer Sig Zane creates distinctive island wearables in 100% cotton.

While heading up the Hamakua Coast, make sure to visit **The Hawaiian Artifacts Shop** along the main drag in downtown Honokaa. **Waipio Valley Artworks** in Kukuihaele, tel. 775-0958, showcases exclusive artwork of distinguished island artists.

If you are after an exquisite piece of art, a unique memento, or an inexpensive but distinctive souvenir, make sure to visit the **Volcano Art Center** in Hawaii Volcanoes National Park.

woven palm frond
baskets and hats

J.D. BISIGNANI

In Kona's World Square Shopping Center, visit the **Showcase Gallery** for its offerings of glasswork, beadwork, featherwork, enameling, and shell *lei* from the islands, with emphasis on the Big Island. Across the way, the **Coral Isle Art Shop** presents modern versions of traditional Hawaiian carvings. **Collectors Fine Art** in the Kona Inn Shopping Village is a perfect labyrinth of rooms and hallways showcasing fine art from around the world. Here too, **Crystal Visions** has incense, perfume, metaphysical books, and the channeling of personal and cosmic vibrations through its large selection of crystals, crystal balls, and pyramids. **Kona Inn Jewelry,** for world treasures, is one of the oldest and best-known shops for a square deal in Kona. **Alapaki's,** at Keauhou Shopping Village, sells traditional island arts and crafts. **The Glass Blower,** across from the seawall along Likana Ln., is a very interesting shop where you can watch the artist actually blowing the glass.

The mountain village of Holualoa has become an artists' haven. As you enter the village you'll spot **Kimura's Lauhala Shop,** which has been selling and producing its famous *lau hala* hats ever since local weavers began bartering their creations for groceries in 1915. In town you'll find a converted coffee mill, gaily painted and decorated, that's the home of the **Kona Art Center,** a community art-cooperative run by Robert and Carol Rogers since 1965. The premier shop in town, **Studio 7,** is owned and operated by Hiroki Morinoue, who studied at the

Kona Art Gallery as a young man. The shop showcases Hiroki's work along with that of about 35 Big Island artists, including famous *raku* potter Chiu Leong. A separate shop in the same building is **Goldsmithing by Sam Rosen,** featuring unusual, one-of-a-kind works mostly in gold, silver, and precious stones.

In the nearby village of Kainalu look for **The Blue Ginger Gallery,** tel. 322-3898, that displays the art of owners Jill and David Bever, as well as artists' works from all over the island. **Elizabeth Harris and Co.** in Kealakekua, tel. 323-2447, displays shirts, T-shirts, and dresses made by 13 local seamstresses and artists. The **Kahanahou Hawaiian Foundation,** tel. 322-3901, is along the road in Kealakekua. They deal in ancient Hawaiian handicrafts, including masks, *hula* drums, and *hula* accoutrements.

The Little Grass Shack is an institution in Kealakekua. It looks like a tourist trap, but don't let that stop you from going in and finding some authentic souvenirs, most of which come from the surrounding area. **Tropical Temptations in Kealakekua,** tel. 326-2007, turns the best available grade of local fruits, nuts, and coffee beans into delicious candies. **Country Store Antiques** is next door to the Manago Hotel, just as you're entering Captain Cook. Owned and operated by E.L. Mahre, it's filled to the brim with kerosene lamps, dolls, glassware, old bottles, and Hawaiian antique jewelry.

Along the north shore in Kapaau across from the Kamehameha statue is **Ackerman Gallery**

I and II, where you'll find the work of artist Gary Ackerman along with displays of local pottery, carvings, and one-of-a-kind jewelry. **Hana Koa** is a woodworking shop owned by artist Don Wilkinson. Don, a friendly storehouse of information, lives along Route 250 heading into Hawi from Waimea. Another local artist is **David Gomes,** a guitar and ukulele maker who works in koa. His small shop is located about a half mile on the Kapaau side of the junction of routes 270 and 250.

In the *paniolo* town of Waimea you can pick up downhome cowboy items or sophisticated artwork at the following shops. At the **Parker Ranch Center,** the **Paddock Shop** sells boots, cowboy hats, shirts, skirts, and buckles and bows. **Nikko Natural Fabrics,** in the Kamuela Country Plaza, will dress you in cottons, woollens, and silks, and adorn your walls with batiks and fine fiber arts, tel. 885-7661. In the **Parker Square Center,** along Route 19, the **Gallery of Great Things,** tel. 885-7706, really is loaded with great things—everything from a carousel horse to koa hair sticks. Here too, **Gifts in Mind** has novelty items, and a very good selection of aloha shirts and dresses; **Mango Ranch** sells duds for cowpokes, including bow ties, fancy shirts, and cowboy hats. Across the road **Kamaaina Woods** sells locally created wood handicrafts.

ipu, *a drum used to accompany* hula

SUE STRANGIO EVERETT

FESTIVALS, HOLIDAYS, AND EVENTS

In addition to all the American national holidays, Hawaii celebrates its own festivals, pageants, ethnic fairs, and a multitude of specialized exhibits. They occur throughout the year, some particular to only one island or locality, others, such as Aloha Week and *Lei* Day, celebrated on all the islands. Check local newspapers and the free island magazines for dates. Some of the smaller local happenings are semi-spontaneous, so there's no *exact* date when they're held. These are some of the most rewarding, because they provide the best times to have fun with the local people.

The following events and celebrations are either particular to the Big Island, or they're celebrated here in a special way. Everyone is welcome to join in the fun, and most times the events are either free or nominally priced. There's no better way to enjoy yourself while vacationing than by joining in a local party or happening.

JANUARY

Thump in the New Year with a traditional Japanese **Mochi Pounding Festival** at Volcano Art Center, Volcanoes National Park, Hawaii.

The athletes gear up with the Big Island **Triathlon Invitational** held in late December or early January. This is a three-day event that ranges all over the island and includes an overnight stay at Volcanoes National Park.

During **The Volcano Wilderness Marathon and Rim Runs** the truly energetic run 26 miles through the desolate Kau Desert, while a 10-mile race around the Caldera Crater Rim features over 1,000 participants.

FEBRUARY

Early February
February offers everything from the links to skiing at the **Mauna Kea Ski Meet** atop the Big Island's 13,000-foot volcano—weather and snow conditions dictate the exact time, which can vary from early January to March. Skiers from around the world compete in cup and cross-country skiing.

Mid- To Late February
Enjoy the authentic western flavor of the **Great Waikoloa Horse Races and Rodeo** at Waikoloa Stables, Waikoloa, Hawaii. Major rodeo events draw skilled *paniolo* from around the islands.

The **Annual Keauhou-Kona Triathlon** at Keauhou Bay, Big Island, is open to athletes unable to enter Ironman, and to anyone in good health. Each of its three events is half as long as in the Ironman, and it allows relay-team racing for each grueling segment.

MARCH

Mid-March rumbles in with the **Kona Stampede** at Honaunau Arena, Honaunau, Kona, Hawaii. *Paniolo* provide plenty of action during the full range of rodeo events. For information call 885-7628.

Mid-month features feminine beauty, grace, and athletic ability at the **Miss Aloha Hawaii Pageant** at Hilo Civic Auditorium, Hilo, Hawaii.

The end of March is dedicated to Prince Kuhio, a member of the royal family and Hawaii's first delegate to the U.S. Congress. **Prince Kuhio Day** is a state holiday honoring the prince, held on March 26, his birthday.

APRIL

Wesak, or **Buddha Day,** is on the closest Sunday to April 8, and celebrates the birthday of Gautama Buddha. Ornate offerings of tropical flowers are placed at temple altars throughout Hawaii.

The **Paniolo Ski Meet** features exciting skiing atop the Big Island's Mauna Kea, conditions permitting.

The **Merrie Monarch Festival** in Hilo sways with the best *hula* dancers that the islands' *hula halau* have to offer. Gentle but stiff competition features *hula* in both its ancient (*kahiko*) and modern (*auana*) forms. The festival runs for a week on a variable schedule from year to year. It's immensely popular with islanders, so hotels, cars, and flights are booked solid. For information call 935-9168, or the HVB at 961-5797.

The **Kona Sports Festival,** Kailua-Kona, Hawaii, is a solid week of sports entertainment and frivolity held toward the end of the month.

MAY

May 1 is May Day to the communist world, but in Hawaii red is only one of the colors when everyone dons a *lei* for **Lei Day**. Festivities abound throughout Hawaii.

The **Captain Cook Festival** at Kailua-Kona offers Hawaiian games, music, and fishing.

Look skyward on May 5, **Japanese Boys' Day,** and you'll see paper carp *(koi)* flying from rooftops. Carp symbolize the virtues of strength and courage. The number of *koi* kites corresponds to the number of sons in the family, with the largest, highest *koi* for the eldest, and then down the line.

Filipino Fiesta is a month-long celebration of the islands' Filipino poulation. Food, various festivities, and a beauty contest are part of the fiesta.

Costumed riders from the annals of Hawaiian history ride again at **Hawaii on Horseback.** Horsemanship and a Western flair mark these days held in and around Waimea and the Parker Ranch on the Big Island.

Annual Western Week at Honokaa on the Big Island is a fun-filled week with a Western theme. It includes a cookout, parade, rodeo, and dance.

JUNE

King Kamehameha Day, June 11, is a state holiday honoring Kamehameha the Great, a Big Island native son, with festivities on all islands. Check local papers for times and particulars. Kailua-Kona is hospitable with a *ho'olaule'a* (large, festive party), parades, art demonstrations, entertainment, and contests.

The **Kamehameha Ski Meet** atop Mauna Kea takes place in early June, when bikini-clad contestants add a little extra spice on those bouncy moguls.

Hilo flashes its brilliant colors with the **Annual Hilo Orchid Society Show** at the Hilo Civic Auditorium, and the **Annual Big Island Bonsai Show,** Wailoa Center, Hilo (both sometimes scheduled for early July).

Bon Odori, the Japanese festival of departed souls, features dances and candle-lighting ceremonies held at numerous Buddhist temples throughout the island. These festivities change yearly and can be held anytime from late June to early August.

JULY

The week of the **Fourth of July** offers the all-American sport of rodeo along with parades.

Don't miss the **July 4 Parker Ranch Rodeo and Horseraces,** Paniolo Park, Waimea, Hawaii. The epitome of rodeo by Hawaii's top cowboys is set at the Parker Ranch, the largest privately owned ranch in all of America, including Texas, pardner! Call 885-7655.

Annual Naalehu Rodeo, in Naalehu, includes rodeo events, motorcycle and dune buggy races, luaus, food booths and Hawaiian entertainment.

The **Big Island Marathon** in Hilo consists of a full and half marathon starting and ending at the Hilo Hawaiian Hotel.

Four-person teams of one pro and three amateurs compete in the 54-hole **Mauna Kea Beach Hotel's Annual Pro-Am Golf Tournament** held at the hotel links along the Big Island's Kohala Coast.

The **International Festival of the Pacific** in mid-July features a "Pageant of Nations" in Hilo. Folk dances, complete with authentic costumes from throughout Asia and the Pacific, add a rare excitement to the festivities. Contact the Japanese Chamber of Commerce, tel. 961-6123, for details.

The beauty and grace of one of Hawaii's ethnic groups is apparent at the **Miss Hawaii Filipina Pageant,** Hawaii Naniloa Hotel, Hilo.

The **Annual Honomu Village Fair** starts with a 46-mile Volcano-to-Honomu team relay race followed by "mountainball" and volleyball. There's plenty of local foods, and arts and crafts.

AUGUST

The first August weekend is **Establishment Day.** Traditional *hula* and *lei* workshops are presented at the Big Island's Puukohala Heiau, where traditional artifacts are also on display.

The **Kona Hawaiian Billfish Tournament,** in the waters off Kona, brings American teams seeking entry to the **Annual Hawaiian International Billfish Tournament,** held about one week later. Contact Peter Fithian, tel. 922-9708.

The macadamia nut harvest is celebrated with sporting events, horse racing and a "Harvest Ball" at the **Macadamia Nut Harvest Festival,** Honokaa, Hawaii. Call 755-7792.

August 17 is **Admission Day,** a state holiday recognizing the day that Hawaii became a state.

SEPTEMBER

In early September don't miss the **Parker Ranch Round-Up Rodeo,** Paniolo Park in Waimea.

The **Million Dollar Golden Marlin Fishing Tournament** catches plenty of fishermen at Kailua-Kona.

The **Hawaii County Fair** at Hilo is an old-time fair held on the grounds of Hilo Civic Auditorium.

Aloha Week in late September features festivities on all of the islands as everyone celebrates Hawaii's own "intangible quality," aloha. There are parades, luaus, historical pageants, balls, and various entertainment. The spirit of aloha is infectious and all are welcomed to join in. Check local papers and tourist literature for happenings near you.

OCTOBER

When they really "wanna have fun," super-athletes come to the **Ironman World Triathlon Championship** at Kailua-Kona, Hawaii. A 2.4-mile open-ocean swim, followed by a 112-mile bike ride, and topped off with a full marathon, is their idea of a good day. Ironman Office, tel. 528-2050.

NOVEMBER

Taste the best and only coffee commercially grown in the U.S. at the **Annual Kona Coffee Festival** in Kailua-Kona. Parades, arts and crafts, plus ethnic foods and entertainment are part of the festivities.

The **Annual King Kalakaua Keiki** *Hula* **Festival** is for children from around the state who come to Kailua-Kona to perform their *hula*. Plenty of fun, but the competition is serious.

November 11, **Veterans Day,** is a national holiday celebrated by parades.

Christmas in the Country, atop Hawaii's volcano, is a delight. Merrymakers frolic in the crisp air or relax around a blazing fire, drinking hot toddys. Also, plenty of arts and crafts, food, and Santa for the *keiki*. Volcano Art Center, Hawaii Volcanoes National Park, Hawaii, tel. 976-7676.

The **YWCA Festival of Trees** presents Christmas crafts, ornaments, and decorated trees on display and for sale at the YMCA, Hilo, Hawaii, tel. 935-7141.

DECEMBER

Christmas Fantasyland of Trees at Honokaa is an early showing of gaily decorated trees. The right Christmas spirit auctions them off for charity; tel. 775-0345.

The people of Hilo celebrate a New England Christmas in memory of the missionaries with **A Christmas Tradition.** Held at the Lyman House Memorial Museum, Hilo, tel. 935-5021.

Bodhi Day is ushered in with ceremonies at Buddhist temples to commemorate Buddha's day of enlightenment.

At the **Mauna Kea Beach Hotel's Annual Invitational Golf Tournament,** men and women play at this fabulous golf course on the Kohala Coast, Hawaii, tel. 882-7222.

On **New Year's Eve** hold onto your hat, because they do it up big in Hawaii. The merriment and alcohol flow all over the islands. Firecrackers are illegal, but they go off everywhere. Beware of hangovers and "amateur" drunken drivers.

bird of paradise

DIANA LASICH HARPER

ALPHONSE PELLION, CIRCA 1819 (HAWAII STATE ARCHIVES)

ACCOMMODATIONS

Finding suitable accommodations on Hawaii is never a problem. The 7,000-plus rooms available have the lowest annual occupancy rate of any in the islands at only 65%. Except for the height of the high seasons and during the Merrie Monarch Festival in Hilo, you can count on finding a room at a bargain. Many places offer kitchenettes and long-term discounts as a matter of course. The highest concentration of rooms is strung along Ali'i Dr. in Kailua-Kona—over 4,500 in condos, apartment hotels, and standard hotels. Hilo has almost 2,000 rooms; many of its hotels have "gone condo," and you can get some great deals. The rest are scattered around the island in small villages from Naalehu in the south to Hawi in the north, where you can almost count on being the only off-island guest. You can comfortably stay in the cowboy town of Waimea, or perch above Kilauea Crater at one of the oldest hotel sites in the islands. There are bed and breakfasts, and the camping is superb, with a campsite almost guaranteed at any time.

The Range

The Big Island has a tremendous range of accommodations. A concentration of the world's greatest luxury resorts are within minutes of each other on the Kohala coast: The Mauna Kea Beach Hotel, Mauna Lani, Ritz-Carlton Waikoloa, and Kona Village Resort. The Mauna Kea, built by Laurence Rockefeller, has everything the name implies. The others are just as superb, with hideaway "grass shacks," exquisite art collections as an integral part of the grounds, world-ranked golf courses, and perfect crescent beaches.

Kona has fine hotels like the King Kamehameha Kona Beach Hotel and Kona Hilton in downtown Kailua. Just south towards Keahou is a string of reasonably priced yet luxurious hotels like the Kona Lagoon. Interspersed among the big hotels are little places with homey atmospheres and great rates. Hilo offers the best accommodations bargains. Luxury hotels such as the Hilo Hawaiian and Naniloa Surf are priced like mid-range hotels on the other islands. There are also semi-fleabags in town that pass the basic cleanliness test and go for as little as $20 per day, along with gems like the Dolphin Bay Hotel that gives you so much for your money it's embarrassing. And for a real treat, head to Hawaii Volcanoes National Park and stay at one of the bed and breakfasts tucked away there, or at Volcano House where raw nature has thrilled kings, queens, and luminaries like humorist Mark Twain for over a century.

If you want to get away from everybody else, it's no problem, and you don't have to be rich to do it. Pass-through towns like Captain Cook and Waimea have accommodations at very reasonable prices. You can try a colf growth ro treat in Puna at Kalani Honua Culture Center or at the Wood Valley Buddhist Temple above Pahala. Want ultimate seclusion? Head down to Tom Araki's Hotel or the Treehouse in Waipio Valley, or spend the night at a defunct, century-old girls' boarding school in Kapaau.

Hotels

Even with the wide variety of other accommodations available, most vistors, at least first-timers, tend to stay in hotels. At one time, hotels were the only places to stay, and characters like Mark Twain were berthed at Kilauea's rude Volcano House, while millionaires and nobility sailed for Waikiki, where they stayed in luxury at the Moana Hotel or Royal Hawaiian; both still stand as vintage reminders of days past. Maui's Pioneer Inn dates from the turn of the century, and if you were Hawaii-bound, these and a handful that haven't survived were about all that were offered. Today, there are 60,000 hotel rooms statewide, and every year more hotels are built and older ones renovated. They come in all shapes and sizes, from 10-room, family-run affairs to high-rise giants. A trend turned some into condominiums, while the Neighbor Islands have learned an aesthetic lesson from Waikiki and build low-rise resorts that don't obstruct the view and blend more readily with the surroundings. Whatever accommodations you want, you'll find them in Hawaii.

Types Of Hotel Rooms

Most readily available and least expensive is a bedroom with bath, the latter sometimes shared in the more inexpensive hotels. Some hotels can also offer you a studio, a large sitting room that converts to a bedroom; a suite, a bedroom with sitting room; or an apartment with full kitchen plus at least one bedroom. Kitchenettes are often available, and contain a refrigerator, sink, and stove usually in a small corner nook or fitted together as one space-saving unit. Kitchenettes cost a bit more but save you a bundle by allowing you to prepare some of your own meals. To get that vacation feeling while keeping costs down, eat breakfast in, pack a lunch for the day, and go out to dinner. If you rent a kitchenette, make sure all the appliances work as soon as you arrive. If they don't, notify the front desk immediately, and if the hotel will not rectify the situation ask to be moved or ask for a reduced rate. Hawaii has cockroaches (see p. 144), so put all food away.

Hotel Rates:
Add Nine Percent Room Tax

Every year Hawaiian hotels welcome in the New Year by hiking their rates by about 10%. A room that was $90 this year will be $99 next year, and so on. Hawaii, because of its gigantic tourist flow and tough competition, offers hotel rooms at universally lower rates than those at most developed resort areas around the world. Package deals, especially to Waikiki, almost throw in a week's lodging for the price of an air ticket. The basic **daily rate** is geared toward double occupancy; singles are hit in the pocketbook. Single rates are cheaper than doubles, but never as low as half the double rate; the most you get off is 40%. **Weekly and monthly** rates will save you approximately 10% off the daily rate. Make sure to ask because this information won't be volunteered. Many hotels will charge for a double and then add an additional charge ($3-25) for extra persons. Some hotels, not always the budget ones, let you cram in as many as can sleep on the floor with no additional charge, so again, ask. Others have a policy of **minimum stay,** usually three days, but their rates can be cheaper, and **business/corporate rates** are usually offered to anyone who can at least produce a business card.

Hawaii's **peak season** runs from just before Christmas until after Easter, and then again in early summer. Rooms are at a premium, and peak-season rates are an extra 10% above the normal daily rate. Oftentimes they'll also suspend weekly and monthly rates during peak

Kona Hilton Beach and Tennis Resort

KONA HILTON BEACH AND TENNIS RESORT

season. The **off-peak** season is late summer and fall, when rooms are easy to come by and most hotels offer off-peak rates. Subtract about 10% from the normal rate.

In Hawaiian hotels you always pay more for a good view. Terms vary slightly, but usually "ocean front" means that your room faces the ocean and your view is mostly unimpeded. "Ocean view" is slightly more vague. It could be a decent view, or it could require standing on the dresser and craning your neck to catch a tiny slice of the sea sandwiched between two skyscrapers. Rooms are also designated and priced upward as **standard, superior,** and **deluxe.** As you go up, this could mean larger rooms with more amenities, or can merely signify a better view.

Plenty of hotels offer the **family plan,** which allows children under a certain age to stay in their parents' room free, if they use the existing bedding. If another bed or crib is required, there is an additional charge. Only a limited number of hotels offer the **American plan,** where breakfast and dinner are included with the night's lodging. In many hotels, you're provided with a refrigerator and a heating unit for coffee and tea at no extra charge.

Paying, Deposits, And Reservations

The vast majority of Hawaiian hotels accept foreign and domestic traveler's checks, personal checks preapproved by the management, foreign cash, and most major credit cards. Reservations are always the best policy, and they're easily made through travel agents or directly by contacting the hotel. In all cases, bring documentation of your confirmed reservations with you in case of a mix-up.

Deposits are not always required to make reservations, but they do secure them. Some hotels require the first night's payment in advance. Reservations without a deposit can be legally released if the room is not claimed by 6 p.m. Remember too that letters "requesting reservations" are not the same as "confirmed reservations." In letters, include your dates of stay, type of room you want, and price. Once the hotel answers your letter, *confirm* your reservations with a phone call or follow-up letter and make sure that the hotel sends you a copy of the confirmation. All hotels and resorts have **cancellation requirements** for refunding deposits. The time limit on these can be as little as 24 hours before arrival, to a full 30 days. Some hotels require full **advance payment** for your length of stay, especially during peak season or during times of crowded special events such as the Merrie Monarch Festival in Hilo. Be aware of the time required for a cancellation notice *before* making your reservation deposit, especially when dealing with advance payment. If you have confirmed reservations, especially with a deposit, and there is no room for you, or one that doesn't meet prearranged requirements, you should be given the option of accepting alternate accommodations. You are owed the difference in room rates if there is any. If there is no room whatsoever, the hotel is required to find you one at a comparable hotel and to refund your deposit in full.

Amenities
All hotels have some of them, and some hotels have all of them. Air-conditioning is available in most, but under normal circumstances you won't need it. Balmy trade winds provide plenty of breezes, which flow through louvered windows and doors in many hotels. Casablanca room fans are better. TVs are often included in the rate, but not always. In-room phones are provided, but a service charge is usually tacked on, even for local calls. Swimming pools are very common, even though the hotel may sit right on the beach. There is always a restaurant of some sort, a coffee shop or two, a bar, a cocktail lounge, and sometimes a sundries shop. Some hotels also offer tennis courts or golf courses either as part of the premises or affiliated with the hotel; usually an "activities desk" can book you into a variety of daily outings. Plenty of hotels offer laundromats on the premises, and hotel towels can be used at the beach. Bellhops get about $1 per bag, and maid service is free, though maids are customarily tipped $1-2 per day and a bit more if kitchenettes are involved. Parking is free. Hotels can often arrange special services like babysitters, all kinds of lessons, and special entertainment activities. A few even have bicycles and snorkeling equipment to lend. They'll receive and send mail for you, cash your traveler's checks, and take messages.

Condominiums
The method of paying for and reserving a condo is just about the same as for a hotel. However, requirements for deposits, final payments, and cancellation charges are much stiffer than in hotels. Make absolutely sure you fully understand all of these requirements when you make your reservations. The main qualitative difference between a condo and a hotel is in amenities. At a condo, you're more on your own. You're temporarily renting an apartment, so there won't be any bellhops and rarely a bar, restaurant, or lounge on the premises, though many times you'll find a sundries store. The main lobby, instead of having that grand-entrance feel of many hotels, is more like an apart-

ment-house entrance, although there might be a front desk. Condos can be efficiencies (one big room), but mostly they are one- or multiple-bedroom affairs with a complete kitchen. Reasonable housekeeping items should be provided: linens, all furniture, and a fully equipped kitchen. Most have TVs and phones, but remember that the furnishings provided are up to the owner. You can find brand-new furnishings that are top of the line, right down to "garage sale" bargains. Inquire about the furnishings when you make your reservations. Maid service might be included on a limited basis (for example, once weekly), or you might have to pay extra for it.

Condos usually require a minimum stay, although some will rent on a daily basis, like hotels. Minimum stays when applicable are often three days, but seven is also commonplace, and during peak season, two weeks isn't unheard of. Swimming pools are common, and depending on the "theme" of the condo, you can find saunas, weight rooms, Jacuzzis, and tennis courts. Rates are about 10-15% higher than at comparable hotels, with hardly any difference between doubles and singles. A nominal extra fee is charged for more than two people; condos can normally accommodate four to six guests. You can find clean, decent condos for as little as $200 per week, all the way up to exclusive apartments for well over $1500. Their real advantage is for families, friends who want to share, and especially long-term stays, for which you will always get a special rate. The kitchen facilities save a great deal on dining costs, and it's common to find units with their own mini-washers and dryers. Parking space is ample for guests, and like hotels, plenty of stay/drive deals are offered. You'll find condos all over Hawaii, but they're particularly prevalent on Maui.

Hotel/Condominium Information
The best source of hotel/condo information is the **Hawaii Visitors Bureau.** While planning your trip, either visit one nearby or write to them in Hawaii. (Addresses are given in the "Information and Services" section of the Introduction.) Request a copy of their free and current *Member Accommodation Guide.* This handy booklet lists all the hotel/condo members of the HVB, with addresses, phone numbers, facilities, and rates. General tips are also given.

Hotel/Condo Booking And Reservations

The following is a partial list of booking agents handling a number of properties on the Big Island. They include but are not limited to: **Kona Vacation Resorts,** tel. (800) 367-5168; **Hawaiian Holiday Rentals & Management,** tel. (800) 462-6630; **Hawaii Resort Management,** tel. (800) 553-5053; and **Keahou Property Management,** tel. (800) 745-5662. Many of the B&B agencies listed below can also book you into condominiums.

BED AND BREAKFASTS

Bed-and-breakfast (B&B) inns are hardly a new idea. The Bible talks of the hospitable hosts who opened the gates of their homes and invited the wayfarer in to spend the night. B&Bs have a long tradition in Europe and were commonplace in Revolutionary America. Now, lodging in a private home called a bed and breakfast is becoming increasingly fashionable throughout America, and Hawaii is no exception. Not only can you visit the Big Island, you can "live" there for a time with a host family and share an intimate experience of daily life.

Points To Consider

The primary feature of B&B homes is that every one is privately owned, and therefore uniquely different from every other. The range of B&Bs is as wide as the living standards in America. You'll find everything from a semi-mansion in the most fashionable residential area to a little grass shack offered by a downhome fisherman and his family. This means that it's particularly important for the guest to choose a host family with whom his or her lifestyle is compatible.

Unlike at a hotel or a condo, you'll be living *with* a host (usually a family), although your room will be private, with private baths and separate entrances being quite common. You don't just "check in" to a B&B. In Hawaii you go through agencies (listed below) which act as go-betweens, matching host and guest. Write to them and they'll send you a booklet with a complete description of the B&B, its general location, the fees charged, and a good idea of the lifestyle of your host family. With the reservations application they'll include a questionnaire that will basically determine your profile: Are you single?

Do you have children? Smoker? etc., as well as arrival and departure dates and all pertinent particulars.

Since B&Bs are run by individual families, the times that they will accept guests can vary according to what's happening in their lives. This makes it imperative to write well in advance: three months is good; earlier is too long and too many things can change. Four weeks is about the minimum time required to make all necessary arrangements. Expect a minimum stay (three days is common) and a maximum stay. B&Bs are not long-term housing, although it's hoped that guest and host will develop a friendship and that future stays can be as long as both desire.

B&B Agencies

A top-notch B&B agency is **Bed and Breakfast Hawaii,** operated by Evelyn Warner and Al Davis. They've been running this service since 1978, and their reputation is excellent. B&B Hawaii has a membership fee of $10 yearly. For this they mail you their "Directory of Homes," a periodic "hot sheet" of new listings, and all pertinent guest applications; add $1 handling. Write Bed and Breakfast Hawaii, Box 449, Kapaa, HI 96746, tel. 822-7771 or (800) 733-1632.

One of the most experienced agencies, **Bed And Breakfast Honolulu Statewide,** at 3242 Kaohinanai Dr., Honolulu, HI 96817, tel. 595-7533 or (800) 288-4666, owned and operated by Marylee and Gene Bridges, began in 1982. Since then, they've become masters at finding visitors the perfect accommodations to match their desires, needs, and pocketbooks. Their repertoire of guest homes offers more than 400 rooms, with half on Oahu and the other half scattered around the state. Accommodations from Marylee and Gene are more personally tailored than a hotel room. When you phone, they'll match your needs to their computerized in-house guidelines.

Other well-known agencies include the following: **Go Native Hawaii** will send you a directory and all needed information if you write to them at 65 Halaulani Pl., Box 11418, Hilo, HI, 96721, tel. 935-4178 or (800) 662-8483. **Volcano Reservations,** owned and operated by Graham and Judy Millar, Box 160, Volcano, HI 96785, tel. 967-7244 or (800) 736-7140, is an agency specializing in the Volcano area, but with rentals available throughout the state. **Pacific Hawaii Bed And Breakfast** at 19 Kai Nanal Pl., Kailua, HI 96734, tel. 486-8838 or (800) 999-6026, lists homes throughout the state, but especially around Kailua/Kaneohe on Oahu's upscale windward coast. **Hawaiian Islands Vacation Rentals**, 1277 Mokulua Dr., Kailua, HI 96734, tel. 261-7895 or (800) 258-7895, is owned and operated by Rick Maxey, who can arrange stays on all islands and help with interisland flights and car rental. **Babson's Vacation Rentals and Reservation Service**, 3371 Keha Dr., Kihei, Maui, HI 96753, tel. 874-1166 or (800) 824-6409, is owned and operated by Ann and Bob Babson, a delightful couple who will try hard to match your stay with your budget. **Affordable Paradise**, 226 Pouli Rd., Kailua, HI 96734, tel. 261-1693 or (800) 925-9065, specializes in Oahu B&Bs, but can arrange stays on all islands.

Three agencies specializing in beachfront villas, luxury condominiums, and exclusive estates are **Villas of Hawaii**, 4218 Waialae Ave., Suite 203, Honolulu, HI 96816, tel. 735-9000; and **Vacation Locations Hawaii**, Box 1689, Kihei, HI 96753, tel. 874-0077. Information on B&Bs can also be obtained from the **American Board of Bed and Breakfast Associations**, Box 23294, Washington, D.C. 20026.

Home Exchanges

One other method of staying in Hawaii, open to homeowners, is to offer the use of your home for use of a home in Hawaii. This is done by listing your home with an agency that facilitates the exchange and publishes a descriptive directory. To list your home and to find out what is available, write **Vacation Exchange Club,** 12006 111 Ave., Youngtown, AZ 85363; or Interservice Home Exchange, Box 87, Glen Echo, MD 20812.

Residence Information

If you have been considering moving to the Big Island, or would just like to explore the possibility, contact **The Big Island by Mail,** Box 333, Kailua-Kona, HI 96745, tel. 329-7688. Owner Barbara Uechi will mail you an order blank listing an assortment of books, magazines, and newspapers especially chosen to guide the homeowner or businessperson looking to relocate to Hawaii. She can also offer information on moving and storage, education, building codes, and the economy.

Hostels

The Big Island has two very reasonably priced hostels operating at this time. **Arnott's Lodge,** 98 Apapane Rd., Hilo, HI 96720, tel. 969-7097, (800) 368-8752 mainland, (800) 953-7773 Hawaii, offers a dormitory bunk for $15, and semi-private rooms with a shared bath, kitchen and living room for $26 s, $36 d. Arnott's also offers inexpensive hiking and snorkeling excursions.

Patey's Place, 75-5731 Ala Hou St., Kailua-Kona, HI 96740 tel. 326-7018 or (800) 972-7408 (recently moved from 75-195 Ala Onaona St.), will set you up in a bunk for $15, a private room for $35, or a room with bath and kitchen for $45.

DIANA LASICH HARPER

FOOD AND DRINK

Hawaii is a gastronome's Shangri-La, a sumptuous smorgasbord in every sense of the word. The varied ethnic groups that have come to Hawaii in the last 200 years have each brought their own special enthusiasm and culture—and lucky for all, they didn't forget their cook pots, hearty appetites, and exotic taste buds. The Polynesians who first arrived found a fertile but barren land. Immediately they set about growing taro, coconuts, and bananas, and raising chickens, pigs, fish, and even dogs, though consumption of the latter was reserved for the nobility. The harvests were bountiful and the islanders thanked the gods with the traditional feast called the luau. The underground oven, the *imu,* baked most of the food. Participants were encouraged to feast while relaxing on straw mats and enjoying the *hula* and various entertainments. The luau is as popular as ever, and a treat that's guaranteed to delight anyone with a sense of eating adventure.

The missionaries and sailors came next; their ships' holds carried barrels of ingredients for the puddings, pies, dumplings, gravies, and roasts—

the sustaining "American foods" of New England farms. The mid-1800s saw the arrival of boatloads of Chinese and Japanese peasants, who wasted no time making rice instead of bread the staple of the islands. The Chinese added their exotic spices, cooking complex Sichuan dishes as well as workers' basics like chop suey. The Japanese introduced *shoyu* (soy sauce), sashimi, boxed *(bento)* lunches, delicate tempura, and rich, filling noodle soups. The Portuguese brought their luscious Mediterranean dishes of tomatoes, peppers and plump, spicy sausages; nutritious bean soups; and mouth-watering sweet treats like *malasadas* (holeless donuts) and *pao dolce* (sweet bread). Koreans carried crocks of zesty *kimchi,* and quickly fired up barbecue pits for *pulgogi,* a traditional marinated beef cooked over an open fire. Filipinos served up their delicious *adobo* stews—fish, meat, or chicken in a rich sauce of vinegar and garlic.

Recently, Thai and Vietnamese restaurants have been offering their irresistible dishes next door to restaurants serving fiery burritos from Mexico and elegant marsala cream sauces from

France. The ocean breezes of Hawaii not only cool the skin but waft with them some of the most delectable aromas on earth, to make the taste buds tingle and the spirit soar.

THE CUISINES OF HAWAII

Hawaiian cuisine, the oldest in the islands, consists of wholesome, well-prepared, and delicious foods. All you have to do on arrival is notice the size of some of the local boys (and women) to know immediately that food to them is indeed a happy and serious business. An oft-heard island joke is that "local men don't eat until they're full; they eat until they're tired." Many Hawaiian dishes have become standard fare at a variety of restaurants, eaten at one time or another by anyone who spends time in the islands. Hawaiian food in general is called *kaukau;* cooked food is *kapahaki,* and something broiled is called *kaola.* Any of these prefixes on a menu will let you know that Hawaiian food is served. Usually inexpensive, it will definitely fill you and keep you going.

Traditional Favorites
In old Hawaii, although the sea meant life, many more people were involved in cultivating beautifully tended garden plots of taro, sugarcane, breadfruit, and various sweet potatoes *(uala)* than with fishing. They husbanded pigs and barkless dogs *(ilio),* and prized *moa* (chicken) for their feathers and meat, but found eating the eggs repulsive. Their only farming implement was the *o'o,* a sharpened hardwood digging stick. The Hawaiians were the best farmers of Polynesia, and the first thing they planted was taro, a tuberous root that was created by the gods at the same time as humans. This main staple of the old Hawaiians was made into poi. Every luau will have poi, a glutinous purple paste made from pounded taro root. It comes in liquid consistencies referred to as one-, two-, or three-finger poi. The fewer fingers you need to eat it, the thicker it is. Poi is one of the most nutritious carbohydrates known, but people unaccustomed to it find it bland and tasteless. Some of the best, fermented for a day or so, has an acidic bite. Poi is made to be eaten *with* something, but locals who love it pop it in their mouths and smack their lips.

Those unaccustomed to it will suffer constipation if they eat too much.

A favorite popular dessert is *haupia,* a custard made from coconut. *Limu* is a generic term for edible seaweed, which many people still gather from the shoreline and eat as a salad, or mix with ground *kukui* nuts and salt as a relish. A favorite Hawaiian snack is *opihi,* small shellfish (limpets) that cling to rocks. People gather them, always leaving some on the rocks for the future. Cut from the shell and eaten raw by all peoples of Hawaii, they sell for $150 per gallon in Honolulu—a testament to their popularity. A general term that has come to mean hors d'oeuvres in Hawaii is *pu pu.* Originally the name of a small shellfish, it is now used for any finger food. A traditional liquor made from ti root is *okolehao.* It literally means "iron bottom," reminiscent of the iron blubber pots used to ferment it.

Luau
The following is a listing of the luau available on the Big Island at the present time. For full descriptions including prices, menus, and times, see the listings in the appropriate district chapters. The luau include: **The Kona Hilton Resort,** tel. 329-3111 (p. 256); **The Royal Waikoloan,** tel. 885-6789 (pp. 295-296); **King Kamehameha Kona Beach Hotel,** tel. 329-2911 (p. 256); **Kona Village Resort,** tel. 325-5555 (p. 256); **Mauna Kea Beach Resort,** tel. 822-7222 (pp. 301-303).

TROPICAL FRUITS AND VEGETABLES

Some of the most memorable taste treats from the islands require no cooking at all: the luscious tropical and exotic fruits and vegetables sold in markets and roadside stands or just found hanging on trees, waiting to be picked. Make sure to experience as many as possible. The general rule in Hawaii is that you are allowed to pick fruit on public lands, but it should be limited to personal consumption. The following is a sampling of some of Hawaii's best produce.

Bananas
No tropical island is complete without them. There are over 70 species in Hawaii, with hundreds of variations. Some are for peeling and eating while others are cooked. A "hand" of ba-

Hawaiian family eating poi

A. PLUM, CIRCA 1846 (HAWAII STATE ARCHIVES)

nanas is great for munching, backpacking, or picnicking. Available everywhere—and cheap.

Avocados

Brought from South America, avocados were originally cultivated by the Aztecs. They have a buttery consistency and nutty flavor. Hundreds of varieties in all shapes and colors are available fresh year-round. They have the highest fat content of any fruit next to the olive.

Coconuts

What tropical paradise would be complete without coconuts? Indeed, these were some of the first plants brought by the Polynesians. When a child was born, a coconut tree was planted to provide fruit for the child throughout his or her lifetime. Truly tropical fruits, coconuts know no season. Drinking nuts are large and green, and when shaken you can hear the milk inside. You get about a quart of fluid from each. It takes skill to open one, but a machete can handle anything. Cut the stem end flat so that it will stand, then bore a hole into the pointed end and put in a straw or hollow bamboo. Coconut water is slightly acidic and helps balance alkaline foods. Spoon meat is a custardlike gel on the inside of drinking nuts. Sprouted coconut meat is also an excellent food. Split open a sprouted nut, and inside is the yellow fruit, like a moist sponge cake. "Millionaire's salad" is made from the heart of a coconut palm. At one time an entire tree was cut down to get to the heart,

which is just inside the trunk below the fronds and is like an artichoke heart except that it's about the size of a watermelon. In a downed tree, the heart stays good for about two weeks.

Breadfruit

This island staple provides a great deal of carbohydrates, but many people find the baked, boiled, or fried fruit bland. It grows all over the islands and is really thousands of little fruits growing together to form a ball.

Mangos

These are some of the most delicious fruits known to humans. They grow wild all over the islands; the ones on the leeward sides of the islands ripen April-June, while the ones on the windward sides can last until October. They're found in the wild on trees up to 60 feet tall. The problem is to stop eating them once you start!

Papayas

This truly tropical fruit has no real season but is mostly available in the summer. Papayas grow on branchless trees and are ready to pick as soon as any yellow appears. Of the many varieties, the "solo papaya," meant to be eaten by one person, is the best. Split them in half, scrape out the seeds and have at them with a spoon.

Passion Fruit

Known by their island name of *lilikoi,* passion fruit make excellent juice and pies. The small yellow fruit (similar to lemons but smooth-skinned) is mostly available in summer and fall. Many grow wild on vines, waiting to be picked. Slice off the stem end, scoop the seedy pulp out with your tongue, and you'll know why they're called "passion fruit."

Guavas

These small, round, yellow fruits are abundant in the wild, where they ripen from early summer to late fall. Considered a pest—so pick all you want. A good source of vitamin C, they're great for juice, jellies, and desserts.

Macadamia Nuts

The king of nuts was brought from Australia in 1892. Now it's the state's fourth-largest agricultural product. Available roasted, candied, or buttered.

Litchis

Called nuts but really small fruit with thin red shells, litchis have sweet, juicy white flesh when fresh and appear nutlike when dried.

Potpourri

Along with the above, you'll find pineapples, oranges, limes, kumquats, thimbleberries, and blackberries in Hawaii, as well as carambolas, wild cherry tomatoes, and tamarinds.

FISH AND SEAFOOD

Anyone who loves fresh fish and seafood has come to the right place. Island restaurants specialize in seafood, and it's available everywhere. Pound for pound, seafood is one of the best dining bargains on the Big Island. You'll find it served in every kind of restaurant, and often

breadfruit

common banana

the fresh catch-of-the-day is proudly displayed on ice in a glass case. The following is a sampling of the best.

Mahimahi

This excellent eating fish is one of the most common and least expensive in Hawaii. It's referred to as "dolphin" but is definitely a fish, not a mammal. Mahimahi can weigh 10-65 pounds; the flesh is light and moist. This fish is broadest at the head. When caught it's a dark olive color, but after a while the skin turns iridescent shades of blue, green, and yellow. It can be served as a main course or as a patty in a fish sandwich.

A'u

This true island delicacy is a broadbill swordfish or marlin. It's expensive even in Hawaii because the damn thing's so hard to catch. The meat is moist and white and truly superb. If it's offered on the menu, order it. It'll cost a bit more, but you won't be disappointed.

Ono

Ono means "delicious" in Hawaiian so that should tip you off to the taste of this wahoo, or king mackerel. *Ono* is regarded as one of the finest eating fishes in the ocean, and its flaky white meat lives up to its name.

Manini

These five-inch fish are some of the most abundant in Hawaii and live in about 10 feet of

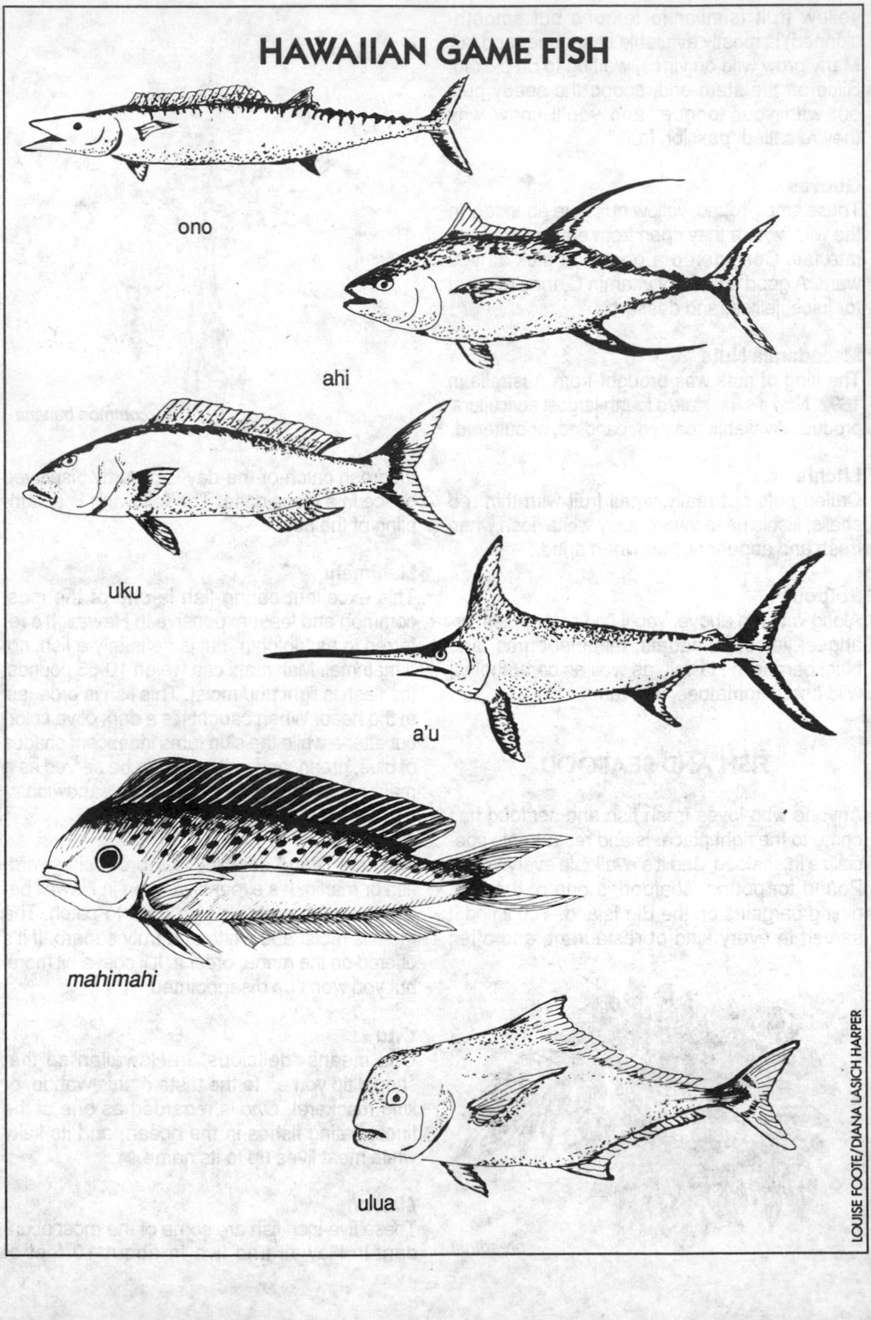

HAWAIIAN GAME FISH

ono

ahi

uku

a'u

mahimahi

ulua

LOUISE FOOTE/DIANA LASICH HARPER

water. They school and won't bite a hook but are easily taken with spear or net. Not often on menus, but they're favorites with local people who know best.

Ulua

This member of the crevalle jack family ranges 15-100 pounds. Its flesh is white and has a steaklike texture. Delicious and often found on the menu.

Uku

This gray snapper is a favorite with local people. The meat is light and firm and grills well.

Ahi

A yellowfin tuna with distinctive pinkish meat, *ahi* is a great favorite cooked or served raw in sushi bars.

Moi

This is the Hawaiian word for "king." The fish has large eyes and a sharklike head. Considered one of the finest eating fishes in Hawaii, it's best during the autumn months.

Seafood Potpourri

Other island seafoods found on menus include *opihi*, a small shellfish (limpet) that clings to rocks and is considered one of the best island delicacies, eaten raw; *aloalo*, similar to tiny lobsters; crawfish, plentiful in taro fields and irrigation ditches; *ahipalaka*, albacore tuna; various octopuses and squids (calamari); and shark of various types.

A'ama are the ubiquitous little black crabs that you'll spot on rocks and around pier areas. They're everywhere. For fun, local fishermen will try to catch them with poles, but the more efficient way is to throw a fish head into a plastic bucket and wait for the crabs to crawl in and trap themselves. The a'ama are about as big as two fingers and make delicious eating.

Limu is edible seaweed that has been gathered as a garnish since pre-contact times, and is frequently found on traditional island menus. There's no other seaweed except *limu* in Hawaii. Because of this, the heavy, fishy-ocean smell that people associate with the sea but which is actually that of seaweed is absent in Hawaii.

UNIQUE ISLAND DRINKS

To complement the fine dining in the islands, bartenders have been busy creating their own tasty concoctions. The standard range of beers, wines, and well drinks is served in Hawaii, but for a real treat you should try mixed drinks inspired by the islands. Most look very innocent because they come in pineapples, coconut shells, or tall frosted glasses. They're often garnished with little umbrellas or sparklers, and most have enough fruit in them to give you your vitamins for the day. Rum is used as the basis of many of them; it's been an island favorite since it was introduced by the whalers of last century. Here are some of the most famous: Mai Tai, a mixture of light and dark rum, orange curaçao, orange and almond flavoring, and lemon juice; Chi chi, a simple concoction of vodka, pineapple juice, and coconut syrup—a real sleeper because it tastes like a milkshake; Blue Hawaii, vodka and blue curaçao; Planter's Punch, light rum, grenadine, bitters, and lemon juice—a great thirst quencher; and Singapore Sling, a sparkling mixture of gin and cherry brandy with lemon juice.

Local Brews

Maui Lager is a premium, all-natural beer brewed in Wailuku at the Pacific Brewing Company by brothers Klaus and Aloysius Klink. The non-pasteurized beer follows the strict German *Reinheitsgebot* ("Purity Law") which calls for only barley, water, hops, and yeast. Another locally brewed beer is **Primo.** At one time brewed only in Hawaii, it's also made on the Mainland now. It's a serviceable American brew in the German style, but like others, it lacks that full, hearty flavor of the European beers.

Coffee

Kona coffee is the only coffee grown in America. It comes from the Kona District of the Big Island and it is a rich, aromatic, truly fine coffee. If it's offered on the menu, have a cup.

Drinking Laws

There are no state-run liquor stores; all kinds of spirits, wines, and beers are available in markets and shops, generally open during normal business hours, seven days a week. The drinking age is 21, and no towns are "dry." Legal hours for serving drinks depend on the type of establishment. Hours generally are: hotels, 6 a.m.-4 a.m.; discos, and nightclubs where there is dancing, 10 a.m.-4 a.m.; bars, lounges where there is no dancing, 6 a.m.-2 a.m. Most restaurants serve alcohol, and in many that don't, you can bring your own.

MUNCHIES AND ISLAND TREATS

Certain finger foods, fast foods, and island treats are unique to Hawaii. Some are meals in themselves, others are snacks. Here are some of the best and most popular.

Pu Pu
Pronounced as in "Winnie the Pooh Pooh," these are little finger foods and hors d'oeuvres. They can be anything from crackers to cracked crab. Often, they're given free at lounges and bars and can even include chicken drumettes, fish kebabs, and tempura. At a good display of them you can have a free meal.

Crackseed
A sweet of Chinese origin, crackseed is preserved and seasoned fruits and seeds. Favorites include coconut, watermelon, pumpkin seeds, mango, plum, and papaya. Distinctive in taste, they take some getting used to, but make great trail snacks. Available in all island markets. Also look for dried fish (cuttlefish) on racks, usually near the crackseed. These are nutritious and delicious and make a great snack.

Shave Ice
This real island institution makes the Mainland "snow cone" melt into insignificance. Special machines literally shave ice to a fluffy consistency. It's mounded into a paper cone, and your choice from dozens of exotic island syrups is generously poured over it. Given, a straw and spoon, you just slurp away.

Malasadas And Pao Dolce
Two sweets from the Portuguese, malasadas are holeless donuts and pao dolce is sweet bread. Sold in island bakeries, they're great for breakfast or as treats.

Lomi Lomi Salmon
This salad of salmon, tomatoes, and onions with garnish and seasonings often accompanies "plate lunches" and is featured at buffets and luaus.

MONEY-SAVERS

Only one thing is better than a great meal: a great meal at a reasonable price. The following are island institutions and favorites that will help you eat well and keep prices down.

Kaukau Wagons
These are lunch wagons, but instead of slick, stainless-steel jobs, most are old delivery trucks converted into portable kitchens. Some say they're a remnant of WW II, when workers had to be fed on the job; others say that the meals they serve were inspired by the Japanese bento, a boxed lunch. You'll see the wagons parked along beaches, in city parking lots, or on busy streets. Usually a line of local people will be placing their orders, especially at lunchtime—a tip-off that the wagon serves delicious, nutritious island dishes at reasonable prices. They might have a few tables, but basically they serve food to go. Most of their filling meals are about $3.50, and they specialize in the "plate lunch."

Plate Lunch
One of the best island standards, these lunches give you a sampling of authentic island food that can include teriyaki chicken, mahimahi, lau lau, and lomi salmon, among others. They're on paper or styrofoam plates, are packed to go, and usually cost less than $3.50. Standard with a plate lunch is "two-scoop rice" and a generous dollop of macaroni or other salad. Full meals, they're great for keeping down food costs and for instant picnics. Available everywhere, from kaukau wagons to restaurants.

Saimin
Special "saimin shops," as well as restaurants, serve this hearty, Japanese-inspired noodle soup on their menu. Saimin is a word unique to Hawaii. In Japan, these soups would be called ramin or soba, and it's as if the two were combined into saimin. A large bowl of noodles in broth, stirred with meat, chicken, fish, or veg-

DIANA LASICH HARPER

The coconut was very important to the Hawaiians and every part was utilized. A tree was planted when a child was born as a prayer for a good food supply throughout life. The trunks were used for building homes and heiau and carved into drums to accompany hula. The husks became bowls, utensils, and even jewelry. 'Aha, sennit rope braided from the husk fiber, was renowned as the most saltwater-resistant natural rope ever made.

etables, costs only a few dollars and is big enough for an evening meal. The best place to eat saimin is in a local hole-in-the-wall shop run by a family.

Tips

Even some of the island's best restaurants in the fanciest hotels offer "early-bird specials"— the regular-menu dinners offered to diners who come in before the usual dinner hour, which is approximately 6 p.m. You pay as little as half the normal price, and can dine in luxury on some of the best foods. The specials are often advertised in the "free" tourist books, which might also include coupons for two-for-one

meals or limited dinners at much lower prices. Just clip them out.

FOOD STORES AND SUPERMARKETS

Groceries and supplies can be purchased in almost every town on the island. Many of the markets in the smaller towns also sell a limited supply of sundries and dry goods. The general rule is: the smaller the market, the higher the prices. The largest and least expensive stores with the biggest selections are found in Hilo and Kailua-Kona. The following is a sampling of what you'll find. More extensive listings are found under "Shopping" in the individual district chapters.

Supermarkets in Hilo include **Food Fair,** 194 Kilauea Ave.; **Safeway,** 333 Kilauea Ave.; **Foodland** at Puainako Shopping Center; **Mall Foods** in Kaikoo Mall; **Pick and Pay,** Hilo Shopping Center. In Kona, **K. Tanaguchi Market** at Kona Coast Shopping Center and **Food for Less** in Lanihau Center, are two of the main supermarkets. **KTA Supermarket** is at the Keauhou Village Mall, at the extreme south end of Ali'i Drive.

Around The Island

These smaller markets should meet your needs as you travel around the Big Island. Along the eastern Hamakua Coast you'll find **Ishigo's General Store** in Honomu Village en route to Akaka Falls. Further north along Route 24 in Honokaa are **T. Kaneshiro Store** and **K.K. Market.** In Kukuihaele, the last village before Waipio Valley, look for the **Last Chance Market.**

In Waimea, **Sure Save Supermarket** is at the Parker Ranch Center. Meat lovers can't go wrong at the **Kamuela Meat Market,** also at the center, selling Parker Ranch beef at hometown prices. On the Kohala Peninsula look for **Kohala Market** in Kawaihae, **M. Nakahara** for general supplies and liquor in Hawi, and Kapaau's **Union Market** for a good assortment of grains, nuts, fruit, and locally made pastries and breads.

In Hilo, shop **Da Store,** which offers groceries and sundries, open 24 hours, at 776 Kilauea Ave. South of Hilo you'll find in Pahoa Town **Pahoa Cash and Carry.** Along the Puna coast is the **Kalapana General Store.** In Volcano Village try **Kilauea Store** along Route 11 just before entering Hawaii Volcanoes National Park.

South of Kailua-Kona is **Casa De Emdeko Liquor and Deli,** just south of town center. **Kamigaki Store** and **Sure Save** are in Kealakekua. **Shimizu Market** is south on Route 11 in Honaunau. Farther south between mile markers 77 and 78 you'll find the very well-stocked **Ocean View General Store.** In the Kau District look for **Wong Yuen Market** in Waiohinu, and **Pick and Pay** in Naalehu, which bills itself as the southernmost market in the United States.

Health Food, Fruit Stores, And Farmers' Markets
Abundant Life Natural Foods is in downtown Hilo at 90 Kamehameha Hwy. at the corner of Waianuinui Street. On Saturday morning, check out the **farmers' market** along Kamehameha Ave. fronting the bay, in the center of the downtown area. For a real treat visit the early morning (over by 8 a.m.) **Suisan Fish Auction** at 85 Lihiwai St. in Hilo.

Kona keeps you healthy with **Kona Healthways** in the Kona Coast Shopping Center. In Honokaa try the **Homestead Market and Cafe** for herbs, bulk foods, dairy products, and vitamins. The **Aloha Village Store,** just next door to the Aloha Cafe in Kainalu, sells gifts, sundries, and natural foods. In Kealakekua look for the well-stocked **Ohana O Ka Aina Food Co-op.** In Naalehu the **Naalehu Fruit Stand** is a favorite with local people for its fresh fruit, grains, minerals, vitamins, and health foods. While heading south from Hilo to Volcanoes, stop along Route 11 at **Keaau Natural Foods;** or in Pahoa at **Pahoa Natural Groceries,** which specializes in organic fruits and juices and is one of the finest health food stores on the Big Island.

A **farmers' market** held in Waimea every Saturday, 7:30 a.m.-noon is where local farmers come to sell their produce, much of which is organic. Look for a dozen or so stalls in the parking lot of the Hawaiian Homelands Building located along Route 19, about two miles east of town center heading toward Honokaa. (For full details see p. 316.)

GETTING THERE

With the number of visitors each year approaching six million, and double that number of travelers just passing through, the state of Hawaii is one of the easiest places in the world to get to . . . by plane. About 10 large U.S. airlines (and other small ones) fly to and from the islands; about the same number of foreign carriers, mostly from Asia and Oceania, touch down on a daily basis. In 1978, airlines were "deregulated." In 1984, the reign of the Civil Aeronautics Board (CAB), which controlled exactly which airlines flew where and how much they could charge, ended. Routes, prices, and schedules were thrown open to free competition. Airlines that had previously monopolized preferred destinations found competitors prying loose their strangleholds. Thus, Hawaii is now one of the most hotly contested air markets in the world. The competition between carriers is fierce, and this makes for "sweet deals" and a wide choice of fares for the money-wise traveler. It also makes for pricing chaos. It's impossible to quote airline prices that will hold true for more than a month, if that long. But it's comforting to know that flights to Hawaii are cheaper today than they have been in years, and mile for mile are one of the best travel bargains in the industry. Familiarize yourself with the alternatives at your disposal so you can make an informed travel selection. Now more than ever, you should work with a sharp travel agent who's on your side.

Almost all travelers to the Big Island arrive by air. A few lucky ones come by private yacht, and in season the cruise ship SS *Constitution* docks in Hilo on Sunday mornings, then sails around the island to Kailua. For the rest, the island's two major airports are at Hilo and Kailua-Kona, with a few secondary strips here and there. Almost every flight to the Big Island

has a stopover, mostly in Honolulu, but these are efficient and at no extra cost. The following should help you plan your arrival.

Note: Handicapped travelers, please see p. 146.

Categories Of Airlines

There are two categories of airlines that you can take to Hawaii: **domestic,** meaning American-owned, and **foreign**-owned. An American law, penned at the turn of the century to protect American shipping, says that "only" an American carrier can transport you to and from two American cities. In the airline industry, this law is still very much in effect. It means, for example, that if you want a roundtrip between San Francisco and Honolulu, you *must* fly on a domestic carrier, such as United or American. If, however, you are flying from San Francisco to Tokyo, you are at liberty to fly a "foreign" airline such as Japan Air Lines, and you may even have a stopover in Hawaii, but you must continue to Tokyo or some other foreign city and cannot fly JAL back to San Francisco. Canadians have no problem flying Canadian Pacific roundtrip from Toronto to Honolulu because this route does not connect two American cities, and so it is with all foreign travel to and from Hawaii. Travel agents know this, but if you're planning your own trip be aware of this fact; if you're traveling roundtrip it must be on a domestic carrier.

Kinds Of Flights

The three kinds of flights are the "milk run," direct, and nonstop. Milk runs are the least convenient. On these, you board a carrier, say in your home town, fly it to a gateway city, change planes and carriers, fly on to the West Coast,

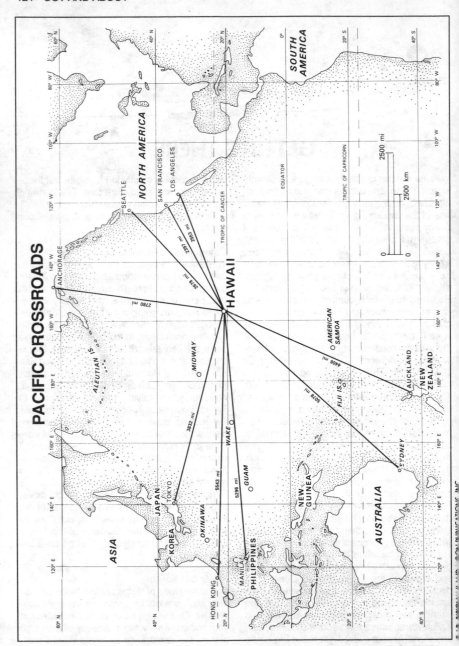

PACIFIC CROSSROADS

change again, and then fly to Hawaii. They're a hassle—your bags have a much better chance of getting lost, you waste time in airports, and to top it off, they're not any cheaper. Avoid them if you can.

On direct flights you fly from point A to point B without changing planes; it doesn't mean that you don't land in between. Direct flights do land usually once to board and deplane passengers, but you sit cozily on the plane along with your luggage and off you go again. Nonstop is just that, but can cost a bit more. You board and when the doors open again you're in Hawaii. All flights from the West Coast gateway cities are nonstop "God willing," because there is only the Pacific in between!

Travel Agents

At one time people went to a travel agent the same way they went to a barber or beautician, loyally sticking with one. Most agents are reputable professionals who know what they're doing. They should be members of the American Society of Travel Agents (ASTA) and licensed by the Air Traffic Conference (ATC). Most have the inside track on the best deals, and they'll save you countless hours calling 800 numbers and listening to elevator music while on hold. Unless you require them to make very special arrangements, their services are free— they are paid a commission by the airlines and hotels that they book for you.

If you've done business with a travel agent in the past, and were satisfied with the services and prices, by all means stick with him or her. If no such positive rapport exists, then shop around. Ask friends or relatives for recommendations; if you can't get any endorsements go to the Yellow Pages. Call two or three travel agents to compare prices. Make sure to give all of them the same information and to be as precise as possible. Tell them where and when you want to go, how long you want to stay, which class you want to travel, and any special requirements. Write down their information. It's amazing how confusing travel plans can be when you have to keep track of flight numbers, times, prices, and all the preparation info. When you compare, don't look only for the cheapest price. Check for convenience in flights, amenities of hotels, and any other fringe benefits that might be included. Then make your choice of agent, and if

he or she is willing to give you individualized service, stick with that agent from then on.

Agents become accustomed to offering the same deals to many clients because they're familiar with the arrangements and because the deals have worked well in the past. Sometimes these are indeed the best, but if they don't suit you, don't be railroaded into accepting them. Any good agent will work with you. After all, it's your trip and your money.

Package Tours

For the independent traveler, practical package deals that include only flight, car, and lodging are okay. Agents put these together all the time and they just might be the best, but if they don't suit you, make arrangements separately. A package *tour* is totally different. On these you get your hand held by an escort, eat where they want you to eat, go where they want you to go, and watch Hawaii slide by your bus window. For some people, especially older folks or groups, this might be the way, but everyone else should avoid the package tour. You'll see Hawaii best on your own, and if you want a tour you can arrange one there, often cheaper. Once arrangements have been made with your travel agent, make sure to take all receipts and letters of confirmation (hotel, car) with you to Hawaii. They probably won't be needed, but if they are, nothing will work better in getting results.

Mainland And International Fares

There are many categories of airline fares, but only three apply to the average traveler: first class, coach, and excursion (APEX). Traveling **first class** seats you in the front of the plane, gives you free drinks and movie headsets, a wider choice of meals, more leg room, and access to VIP lounges, if they exist. There are no restrictions, no penalties for advance-booking cancellations or rebooking of return flights, and no minimum-stay requirements.

Coach, the way that most people fly, is totally adequate. You sit in the plane's main compartment behind first class. Your seats are comfortable, but you don't have as much leg-room or as wide a choice of meals. Movie headsets and drinks cost you a few dollars, but that's about it. Coach offers many of the same benefits as first class and costs about 30% less. You can buy tickets up until takeoff; you have no restrictions on minimum or maximum stays; you receive liberal stopover privileges, and you can cash in your return ticket or change your return date with no penalties.

Excursion or advance payment excursion (APEX) fares are the cheapest. You are accommodated on the plane exactly the same as if you were flying coach. There are, however, some restrictions. You must book and pay for your ticket in advance (7-14 days). At the same time, you must book your return flight, and under most circumstances you can't change either without paying a penalty. Also, your stopovers are severely limited and you will have a minimum/maximum stay period. Only a limited number of seats on any one plane are set aside for APEX fares, so book as early as you can. Also, if you must change travel plans, you can go to the airport and get on as a standby passenger using a discounted ticket, even if the airline doesn't have an official standby policy. There's always the risk that you won't get on, but you do have a chance, as well as priority over an actual standby customer.

Standby is exactly what its name implies: you go to the airport and wait around to see if any flights going to Hawaii have an empty seat. You can save some money, but cannot have a firm itinerary or limited time. Since Hawaii is such a popular destination, standbys can wait days before catching a plane. A company called **Stand Bys Ltd.** offers an up-to-the-minute newsletter and an 800 number which gives you information on charter flights that haven't sold out. The service costs $45 per year, but you can save 15-60% on most tickets. Write to Stand Bys Ltd., 26711 Northwestern Hwy., Southfield, MI 48034, tel. (313) 352-4876.

Active and retired **military personnel** and their dependents are offered special fares on airlines and in military hostels. An excellent resource book listing all of these special fares and more is *Space-A* ($11.75 for book and 1st-class postage), available from Military Travel News, Box 9, Oakton, VA 22124. Plenty of money-saving tips.

Charters

Charter flights were at one time only for groups or organizations that had memberships in travel clubs. Now they're open to the general public. A charter flight is an entire plane or a "block" of seats purchased at a quantity discount by a charter company and then sold to customers. Because they are bought at wholesale prices, charter fares can be the cheapest available. As in package deals, only take a charter flight if it is a "fly only," or perhaps includes a car. You don't need one that includes a guide and a bus. Most importantly, make sure that the charter company is reputable. They should belong to the same organizations (ASTA and ATC) as most travel agents. If not, check into them at the local chamber of commerce.

More restrictions apply to charters than to any other flights. You must pay in advance. If you cancel after a designated time, you can be penalized severely or lose your money entirely. You cannot change departure or return dates and times. However, up to 10 days before departure the charter company is legally able to cancel, raise the price by 10%, or change time and dates. They must return your money if cancellation occurs, or if changed arrangements are unacceptable to you. Mostly they are on the up-and-up and flights go smoothly, but there are horror stories. Be careful. Be wise. Investigate!

Tips

Flights from the West Coast take about five hours; you gain two hours over Pacific Standard Time when you land in Hawaii. From the East Coast it takes about 11 hours and you gain five hours over Eastern Standard Time. Try to fly Mon.-Thurs., when flights are cheaper and easier to book. Pay for your ticket as soon as your plans are firm. If prices go up there is no charge added, but merely booking doesn't guarantee the lowest price. Make sure that airlines, hotels, and car agencies get your phone number too, not only your travel agent's, in case any problems with availability arise (travel agents are often closed on weekends). It's not necessary, but it's a good idea to call and reconfirm flights 24-72 hours in advance.

First-row (bulkhead) seats are good for people who need more legroom, but bad for watching the movie. Airlines will give you special meals (vegetarian, kosher, low cal, low salt) often at no extra charge, but you must notify them in advance. If you're "bumped" from an overbooked flight, you're entitled to a comparable flight to your destination within one hour. If more than an hour elapses, you get denied-boarding compensation which goes up proportionately with the amount of time you're held up. Sometimes this is cash or a voucher for another flight to be used in the future. You don't have to accept what an airline offers on the spot, if you feel they aren't being fair.

When To Go
The prime tourist season starts two weeks before Christmas and lasts until Easter. It picks up again with summer vacation in early June and ends once more in late August. If possible, avoid these times of year. Everything is usually booked solid and prices are inflated. Hotel, airline, and car reservations, which are a must, are often hard to coordinate. You can save 10-50% and a lot of hassling if you go in the artificially created "off season," September to early December, and mid-April (after Easter) until early June. You'll not only find the prices better, but the beaches, hikes, campgrounds and even restaurants will be less crowded. The people will be happier to see you, too.

Traveling With Children
Fares for children ages 2-12 are 50% of the adult fare; children under two not occupying a seat travel free. If you're traveling with an infant or active toddler, book your flight well in advance and request the bulkhead seat or first row in any section and a bassinet if available. Many carriers have fold-down cribs with restraints for baby's safety and comfort. Toddlers appreciate the extra space provided by the front-row seats. Be sure to reconfirm, and arrive early to ensure this special seating. On long flights you'll be glad that you took these extra pains.

Although most airlines have coloring books, puppets, etc., to keep your child busy, it's always a good idea to bring your own. These can make the difference between a pleasant flight and a harried ordeal. Also, remember to bring baby bottles, formula, diapers, and other necessities, as many airlines may not be equipped with exactly what you need. Make all inquiries ahead of time so you're not caught unprepared.

Baggage
You are allowed two free pieces of luggage and a carry-on bag. The two main pieces can weigh up to 70 pounds each; an extra charge is levied for extra weight. The larger bag can have an overall added dimension (height plus width plus length) of 62 inches; the smaller, 55 inches. Your carry-on must fit under your seat or in the overhead storage compartment. Purses and camera bags are not counted as carry-ons and may be taken aboard. Surfboards and bicycles are about $15 extra. Although they make great mementos, remove all previous baggage tags from your luggage; they can confuse handlers. Attach a sturdy holder with your name and address on the handle, or use a stick-on label on the bag itself. Put your name and address inside the bag, and the address where you'll be staying in Hawaii if possible. Carry your cosmetics, identification, money, prescriptions, tickets, reservations, change of underwear, camera equipment, and perhaps a change of shirt or blouse in your carry-on.

Visas
Entering Hawaii is like entering anywhere else in the U.S. Foreign nationals must have a current passport and proper visa, an ongoing or return air ticket, and sufficient funds for the proposed stay in Hawaii. Canadians do not need a visa or passport, but must have proper identification such as passport, driver's license, or birth certificate.

Leaving Hawaii
Remember that before you leave Hawaii for the mainland, all of your bags are subject to an **agricultural inspection,** a usually painless procedure taking only a minute or two. To facilitate your departure, leave all bags unlocked until after inspection. There are no restrictions on beach sand, coconuts, dried flower arrangements, fresh flower *lei*, pineapples, certified pest-free plants, seashells, seed *lei*, and wood roses. However, avocado, litchi, and papaya must be treated before departure. Some other restricted items are berries, fresh gardenias, roses, jade plants, live insects, snails, cotton, plants in soil, soil itself, and sugarcane.

BIG ISLAND ARRIVALS

The Airports
The largest and only international airport on the Big Island is **Hilo International Airport,** tel. 935-0809, which services Hilo and the eastern

half of the island. It's a modern facility with full amenities and its runways can handle all jumbo jets. The two-story terminal has an information center, restaurant, a number of vendors (including *lei* shops), and lockers. Most major car-rental agencies have booths outside the terminal; a taxi for the three-mile ride to town costs about $6.50. The airport features 20 acres of landscaped flowers and an assortment of fountains and waterfalls supplied by rainwater collected on the terminal's roof.

Keahole Airport, tel. 329-2484, is nine miles north of Kailua-Kona and handles the air traffic for Kona. The terminal is a series of open-sided, Polynesian-style buildings. Here too are lockers, food, visitor information, various vendors, and most car-rental agencies. The Gray Line limousine can take you to Kailua for under $10, while a private cab to your hotel is $15 or more.

Waimea-Kohala Airport, tel. 885-4520, is just outside Waimea (Kamuela). There are few amenities and no public transportation to town. **Upolu Airport,** tel. 889-9958, is a lonely strip on the extreme northern tip of the island, with no facilities whatsoever. Both are serviced only on request by small charter airlines.

Nonstop Flights

United Airlines operates the only nonstop flight to the Big Island from the Mainland. The San Francisco flight departs daily at 8:50 a.m. and arrives at Keahole Airport on the Kona coast at 11:16 a.m. In the past during peak season, United has run a flight to Hilo International Airport, but it's an on-and-off affair depending on the number of travelers. It's also interesting to note that the Hilo airport is an international one, and most island flights landed there in the past. Now, with the Kona Coast gaining popularity, many domestic flights have shifted to that side of the island.

Stopover Flights

All major carriers have arrangements for getting you to the Big Island. American carriers such as Hawaiian Air, Delta, Continental, and American, along with foreign carriers like Canadian Pacific, Qantas, and Japan Airlines, land at Honolulu. There they have an inter-line agreement with island carriers, including Hawaiian Air and Aloha Airlines, which then take you to

the Big Island. This sometimes involves a plane change, but your baggage can be booked straight through. Hawaiian Air has expanded to Mainland flights from San Francisco and Los Angeles, with connecting flights in Honolulu to Kona. They offer the added convenience of dealing with just one airline.

Interisland Carriers

Getting to and from the Big Island via the other islands is easy and convenient. The only effective way for most visitors to travel between the Hawaiian islands is by air. Luckily, Hawaii has excellent air transportation that boasts one of the industry's safest flight records. The following airlines have competitive prices, with interisland flights at about $75 each way. You can also save money (about $15) if you **take the first or last daily scheduled flight.** This offer usually applies only to flights to and from Honolulu, but do check because the policy often changes. Another alternative is to **purchase a booklet of six flight vouchers.** You save about $7 per ticket, and they are *transferable.* Just book a flight as normal and present the filled-in voucher to board the plane. Vouchers are perfect for families or groups of friends, and can be purchased at any ticket office or at Honolulu International Airport.

Hawaiian Air, tel. (800) 367-5320 nationwide, (800) 882-8811 statewide, offers the most flights. From Honolulu to Kona, 17 flights (about 40 minutes) are spread throughout the day from approximately 5:40 a.m. to 7:05 p.m. The same scheduling applies to Hilo, except that there are slightly fewer flights, the last departing Honolulu at 7:15 p.m. Hawaiian Air also offers daily flights from Kauai, Molokai, Lanai, and Maui to both Hilo and Kona. Most are aboard DC-9 jet aircraft, with some on the four-prop Dash Transits. About the same number of flights from Hilo and Kona *to* Honolulu and the above destinations are spread throughout the day.

Aloha Airlines, tel. (800) 367-5250, 935-5771 Big Island, also services the Big Island with flights from the neighboring islands. Their 24 daily Honolulu-Kona runs start at 5:40 a.m., with the last at 7 p.m.; 16 Honolulu-to-Hilo flights depart throughout the day, 5:35 a.m.-6:35 p.m. Aloha flies from Kauai to Hilo and Kona with a dozen or so flights to each between approximately 6:30 a.m. and 6:30 p.m. Maui flights to

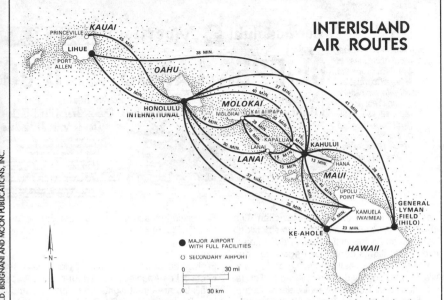

INTERISLAND AIR ROUTES

MAJOR AIRPORT WITH FULL FACILITIES
SECONDARY AIRPORT

Hilo and Kona are much fewer, with usually only four flights per day, two in the morning and two in the afternoon.

Aloha Island Air, tel. (800) 323-3345 nationwide, (800) 652-6541 statewide, offers scheduled flights to and from Honolulu, Princeville on Kauai, Molokai, and Lanai; and from Kahului, Kapalua, and Hana airports on Maui. There are three flights from Honolulu, with the first at 6:10 a.m. and the last at 5 p.m. Flights to and from the other destinations are scheduled at one or two per day and often involve a stopover.

Big Island Air, tel. 329-4868 or (800) 367-8047, ext. 207, operates out of Kailua-Kona and has a regularly scheduled flight between Kona and Hilo on the Big Island only. The RT flight leaves and returns daily between 11:00 a.m. and noon. Check for specifics. Big Island Air also features jet charter service, and flight-see tours around the Big Island.

DOMESTIC CARRIERS

The following are the major domestic carriers to and from Hawaii. The planes used are primarily DC-10s and 747s, with a smaller 727 flown now and again. A list of the "gateway cities" from which they fly direct and nonstop flights is given, but "connecting cities" are not. All flights, by all carriers, land at Honolulu International Airport except the limited direct flights to Maui and Hawaii. Only the established companies are listed. Entrepreneurial small airlines such as the now-defunct Hawaii Express pop up now and again and specialize in dirt-cheap fares. There is a hectic frenzy to buy their tickets and business is great for a while, but then the established companies lower their fares and the gamblers fold.

Hawaiian Air

One of Hawaii's own domestic airlines has entered the Mainland market. They operate a daily flight from Los Angeles and San Francisco to Honolulu, with periodic flights from Anchorage, Las Vegas, Portland, and Seattle. The "common fare" ticket price includes an ongoing flight to any of the Neighbor Islands, and if you're leaving Hawaii, a free flight from a Neighbor Island to the link-up in Honolulu. Senior-citizen discounts for people age 60 or older are offered on trans-

Pan American Airlines, now out of business in the Pacific, opened Hawaii to mass air travel with this historic flight on Wednesday, April 17, 1935. The flight from Alameda Airport to Pearl Harbor took 19 hours and 48 minutes.

The Honolulu Advertiser EXTRA
Hawaii's Territorial Newspaper

79TH. YEAR, NO. 17,324—14 PAGES   HONOLULU, TERRITORY OF HAWAII U.S.A., WEDNESDAY MORNING, APRIL 17, 1935.   PRICE FIVE CENTS.

CLIPPER LANDS AT 8:00

Thousands See Flight's Start At Golden Gate

Heavily - Laden Ship In Graceful Takeoff from Bay Waters; Routine Job to Crew

An Early Morning Caller

Reaches Honolulu At 7:04; Cruises Over Island Until Crowds Arrive At Air Base

Giant Plane Sets New Record for Westbound Hop; Could Easily Have Made Better Time But Delayed Landing for Spectators

---

Pacific and interisland flights. Hawaiian Air's trans-Pacific schedule features flights between Honolulu and points in the South Pacific nearly every day: flights depart for Pago Pago and American Samoa, half continuing on to Apia, Western Samoa, and the rest flying to Tonga, with additional flights to New Zealand, Guam, Tahiti, and Rarotonga. Hawaiian Air offers special discount deals with Dollar rental cars and select major-island hotels. Contact Hawaiian Air at (800) 367-5320 mainland, (800) 882-8811 in Hawaii.

United Airlines

Since their first island flight in 1947, United has become top dog in flights to Hawaii. Their Mainland routes connect over 100 cities to Honolulu. The main gateways are direct flights from San Francisco, Los Angeles, San Diego, Seattle, Portland, Chicago, New York, Denver, and Toronto. They also offer direct flights to Maui from San Francisco, Los Angeles, and Chicago, and from Los Angeles to the Big Island. United offers a number of packages, including flight and hotel on Oahu, and flight, hotel, and car on the Neighbor Islands. They inter-line with Aloha Airlines and deal with Hertz rental cars. They're the "big guys" and they intend to stay that way—their packages are hard to beat. Call (800) 241-6522.

American Airlines

American offers direct flights to Honolulu from Los Angeles, San Francisco, Dallas, and Chicago. They also fly from Los Angeles and San Francisco to Maui, with a connection in Honolulu. Call (800) 433-7300.

Continental

Flights from all Mainland cities to Honolulu connect via Los Angeles and San Francisco. Also available are direct flights from Australia and New Zealand to Honolulu. Call (800) 525-0280 or (800) 231-0856 for international information.

Northwest

Northwest flies from Los Angeles, San Francisco, and Portland via Seattle. There are onward flights to Tokyo, Osaka, Okinawa, Manila, Hong Kong, Taipei, and Seoul. Call (800) 225-2525.

Delta Airlines

In 1985, Delta entered the Hawaiian market; when it bought out Western Airlines its share became even bigger. They have nonstop flights to Honolulu from Dallas/Ft. Worth, Los Angeles, San Francisco, and San Diego; and now flights to Kahului, Maui, via Los Angeles or Honolulu. Call (800) 221-1212.

FOREIGN CARRIERS

The following carriers operate throughout Oceania but have no U.S. flying rights. This means that in order for you to vacation in Hawaii using one of these carriers, your flight must originate or terminate in a foreign city. You can have a stopover in Honolulu with a connecting flight to a Neighbor Island. For example, if you've purchased a flight on Japan Air Lines from San Francisco to Tokyo, you can stop in Hawaii, but you must then carry on to Tokyo. Failure to do so will result in a stiff fine, and the balance of your ticket will not be refunded.

Canadian Airlines International
Nonstop flights from Canada to Honolulu originate in Vancouver, Toronto, and Calgary; nonstop Pacific flights go to Fiji, Auckland, and Sydney, with connecting flights to other Pacific cities. Call (800) 426-7007.

Air New Zealand
Flights link New Zealand, Australia, and Fiji with Los Angeles via Honolulu. Also offered are a remarkable APEX fare from Los Angeles to New Zealand, with stops in Honolulu and Fiji; and a Super Pass fare that lets you stop in eight cities between Los Angeles and Australia. Occasionally, other special fares are offered. Call (800) 262-1234 for current information.

Japan Air Lines
The Japanese are the second-largest group, next to Americans, to visit Hawaii. JAL flights to Honolulu originate in Tokyo, Nagoya, and Osaka. There are no JAL flights between the Mainland and Hawaii. Call (800) 525-3663.

Philippine Airlines
Philippine Airlines flies between Los Angeles or San Francisco and Manila via Honolulu. Connections in Manila are available to most Asian cities. Call (800) 435-9725.

Qantas
Daily flights depart from San Francisco and Los Angeles for Sydney via Honolulu. Stopovers are possible in Fiji and Tahiti. Call (800) 622-0850.

China Airlines
Routes from Los Angeles to Taipei with stopovers in Honolulu and Tokyo are possible, but flights are not available year-round. Connections from Taipei to most Asian capitals. Call (800) 227-5118.

Korean Air
Korean Air offers some of the least expensive flights to Asia. Flights leave only from Los An-

geles, stop in Honolulu, then continue either directly to Seoul or stop over in Tokyo. Connections to many Asian cities. Call (800) 421-8200.

Air Tungaru
Limited flights from Kiribati to Honolulu via Christmas Island and Tarawa. In Hawaii, call 735-3994.

Air Nauru
The South Pacific's richest island offers flights throughout Polynesia, including most major islands, with connections to Japan, Taipei, Hong Kong, Manila, Singapore, and Australia. In Hawaii, call 531-9766.

TRAVEL BY SHIP

American Hawaii Cruises
This American cruise ship company operates two 800-passenger ships, the SS *Independence* and the SS *Constitution*. These ships offer similar seven-day itineraries that circumnavigate and call at the four main islands. Their fares range from an inside "thrifty cabin" at $1095 to a luxury owner's suite for $3950. Children under 16 are often given special rates and cruise free June-Sept. when they share a cabin with their parents. You board the ship in Honolulu after a plane flight to the islands arranged by American Hawaii Cruises. Each ship is a luxury seagoing hotel and gourmet restaurant; swimming pools, health clubs, movies, and nightclubs are all part of the amenities. For details contact: American Hawaii Cruises, 550 Kearny St., San Francisco, CA 94108, tel. (800) 765-7000; from Canada call collect (415) 392-9400.

Alternatives
Other companies offering varied cruises include **P&O Lines**, which operates the *Sea Princess* through the South Pacific, making port at Honolulu on its way from the West Coast once a year.

Royal Cruise Line out of Los Angeles, or Auckland alternatively, sails the *Royal Odyssey*, which docks in Honolulu on its South Pacific and Orient cruise, $2200-4000.

The **Holland America Line** sails the *Rotterdam* on its 108-day Grand Circle cruise, departing Fort Lauderdale, passing around South America, and calling at Honolulu as it heads for Asia. Prices are $20,000-70,000. Call (800) 426-0327.

American
Hawaii
Cruises'
SS Independence

AMERICAN HAWAII CRUISES

Society Expeditions offers a 42-day cruise throughout the South Pacific departing from Honolulu. Fares range $3000-9000. Call (800) 426-7794.

Information
Most travel agents can provide information on the above cruise lines. If you're especialy interested in traveling by freighter, contact: **Freighter Travel Club of America,** Box 12693, Salem, OR 97309; or **Ford's Freighter Travel Guide,** Box 505, 22151 Clarendon St., Woodland Hills, CA 91367.

TOUR COMPANIES

Many tour companies advertise packages to Hawaii in large city newspapers every week. They offer very reasonable airfares, car rentals, and accommodations. Without trying, you can get roundtrip airfare from the West Coast and a week in Hawaii for $400-500 using one of these companies. The following companies offer great deals and have excellent reputations. This list is by no means exhaustive.

Note: For a list of **ecotours** and excursions available *in* Hawaii see "Getting Around." For ecotours *to* Hawaii see below.

SunTrips
This California-based tour and charter company sells vacations all over the world. They're pri-marily a wholesale company, but will work with the general public. SunTrips often works with American Trans-Air, tel. (800) 225-9920, when flying to Hawaii. American Trans-Air answers their phones Mon.-Fri. during normal business hours only. When you receive your SunTrip tickets, you are given discount vouchers for places to stay that are convenient to the airport of departure. Many of these hotels have complimentary airport pickup service, and will allow you to park your car, free of charge, for up to 14 days, which saves a considerable amount on airport parking fees. SunTrips does not offer assigned seating until you get to the airport. They recommend that you get there two hours in advance, and they ain't kidding! This is the price you pay for getting such inexpensive air travel. SunTrips usually has a deal with a car-rental company. Remember that everyone on your incoming flight is offered the same deal, and all make a beeline for the rental car's shuttle van after landing and securing their baggage. If you have a traveling companion, work together to beat the rush by leaving your companion to fetch the baggage and heading directly for the van as soon as you arrive. Pick your car up, then return for your partner and the bags. Even if you're alone, you could zip over to the car-rental center and then return for your bags without having them sit very long on the carousel. Contact SunTrips, 100 Park Center, Box 18505, San Jose, CA 95158, tel. (800) 662-9292, (800) 786-8747 in California, 941-2697 in Honolulu.

Council Travel Services

These full-service, budget-travel specialists are a subsidiary of the nonprofit Council on International Educational Exchange, and the official U.S. representative to the International Student Travel Conference. They'll custom-design trips and programs for everyone from senior citizens to college students. Bona fide students have extra advantages, however, including eligibility for the International Student Identification Card (CISC), which often gets you discount fares and waived entrance fees. Groups and business travelers are also welcome. For full information, write to the main offices at Council Travel Services, 205 E. 42nd St., New York, NY 10017 (212) 661-1450, or 919 Irving St. #102, San Francisco, CA 94122, tel. (415) 566-6222. Other offices are in Austin, Berkeley, Boston, Davis, Long Beach, Los Angeles, Miami, Portland, San Diego, and Seattle.

S.T.A. Travel

You don't have to be a student to avail yourself of their services. Their West Coast office is at 7202 Melrose Ave., Los Angeles, CA 90046 (213) 934-8722. S.T.A. also maintains offices in New York, Boston, Cambridge, Philadelphia, and Washington, as well as throughout Australia and Europe; they also have affiliates in Toronto and Vancouver.

Nature Expeditions International

These quality tours have nature as the theme. Trips are 15-day, four-island, natural-history expeditions, with emphasis on plants, birds, and geology. Their guides are experts in their fields and give personable and attentive service. Contact Nature Expeditions International at 474 Willamette, Box 11496, Eugene, OR 97440, tel. (503) 484-6529 or (800) 869-0639.

Ocean Voyages

This unique company offers seven- and 10-day itineraries aboard a variety of yachts in the Hawaiian Islands. The yachts, equipped to carry 2-10 passengers, ensure individualized sail training. The vessels sail throughout the islands, ex-

ploring hidden bays and coves, and berth at different ports as they go. This opportunity is for anyone who wishes to see the islands in a timeless fashion, thrilling to sights experienced by the first Polynesian settlers and Western explorers. For rates and information contact Ocean Voyages, 1709 Bridgeway, Sausalito, CA 94965, tel. (415) 332-4681.

Island Holiday Tours

This established, Hawaii-based company offers flights with American and United, and rental cars through Budget. Arrangements can also be made for tours, luaus, helicopter rides, etc., on all islands. Contact Island Holiday Tours, 2255 Kuhio Ave., Honolulu, HI 96815, tel. (800) 448-6877.

Pleasant Hawaiian Holidays

A California-based company specializing in Hawaii, Pleasant Hawaiian Holidays makes arrangements for flights, accommodations, and transportation only. At 2404 Townsgate Rd., Westlake Village, CA 91361, tel. (800) 242-9244.

EcoTours To Hawaii

Sierra Club Trips offers Hawaii trips for nature lovers who are interested in an outdoor experience. Various trips include hikes over Maui's Haleakala, a kayak trip along the Na Pali Coast of Kauai, and a family camping spree in Kauai's Kokee region. All trips are led by experienced guides and are open to Sierra Club members only ($33 per year to join). For information contact the Sierra Club Outing Department, 730 Polk St., San Francisco, CA 94109, tel. (415) 776-2211.

Earthwatch allows you to become part of an expeditionary team dedicated to conservation and the study of the natural environment. An expedition might include studying dolphins in Kewalo Basin Marine Mammal Laboratory, or observing the ubiquitous mongoose from a hut high atop Mauna Kea. Basically, you become an assistant field researcher—your lodgings might be a dorm room at the University of Hawaii, and your meals might come from a remote camp kitchen. Fees vary and are tax deductible. If you are interested in this learning experience, contact Earthwatch, 680 Mt. Auburn St., Box 403-P, Watertown, MA 02272, tel. (617) 926-8200.

Backroads, 1516 Fifth St., Suite PR, Berkeley, CA 94710, tel. (510) 527-1555, (800) 462-2848, arranges easy-on-the-environment bicycle and hiking trips to the Big Island. Basic tours include: six-day hiking/camping tour $698; six-day hiking/inn tour $1295; eight-day bicycle/inn tour $1495; and five-day bicycle/camping tour $649. Prices include hotel/inn accommodations or tent when applicable, most meals, and professional guide service. Airfare is not included, and bicycles and sleeping bags can be rented (b.y.o. okay!) for reasonable rates.

Far Horizons, Box 1529, 16 Fern Ln., San Anselmo, CA 94960, tel. (800) 552-4575, specializes in cultural discovery trips. A 12-day trip visits the islands of Hawaii, Lanai, and Oahu. Led by archaeologist Dr. Georgia Lee, an expert in Polynesian rock art, the expedition features stops at Hawaii's most famous *heiau,* petroglyph fields, museums, and historical homes. The cost is $3695 per person and includes trans-Pacific and internal flights, accommodations, ground transportation, most meals, and entry fees.

Crane Tours, 15101 Magnolia Blvd., Sherman Oaks, CA 91403, tel. (800) 653-2545, owned and operated by Bill Crane, has been taking people kayaking and backpacking to the Big Island, Maui, and Kauai since 1976. Basic prices for these eco-adventures start at $650, with the most expensive tour around $800 (airfare not included).

Note: For **ecotours** *in* Hawaii see "Getting Around."

GETTING AROUND

The first thing to remember when traveling on the Big Island is that it *is* big, over four times larger than Rhode Island. A complete range of vehicles is available for getting around, everything from helicopters to mopeds. Hawaii, like Oahu, has good public transportation. Choose the conveyance that fits your style, and you should have no trouble touring the Big Island.

CAR RENTALS

When you arrive at any of Hawaii's airports, you'll walk the gauntlet of car-rental booths and courtesy phones shoulder-to-shoulder along the main walkways. Of the three categories of car-rental agencies in Hawaii, each has its own advantage. The first category is comprised of the big international firms like Dollar, Hertz, Avis, and Budget. These big guys are familiar and easy to work with, sometimes offer special fly/drive deals with airlines, and live up to their promises.

Hawaii has spawned a good crop of statewide car-rental agencies such as Robert's and Holiday Hawaii. These companies and their cars are also reliable, are easy to book through a travel agent, and give good service. Their bar-gain prices and special deals make them worth a call when price-shopping.

The third category is the local entrepreneurial rental agencies. Their deals and cars can range, like rummage-sale treasures, from great finds to pure junk. If nothing is moving from their lot on the day you arrive, you might get a real bargain. Unfortunately, mixed in this category is a hodgepodge of fly-by-nights. Some of these are small but adequate. Others are a rip-off; their cars are bad, their service is worse, and they have more hidden costs than a Monopoly board.

Car-rental Tips

The best way to tour the island is in a rented car, but keep these tips in mind. Most car companies charge you a fee if you rent the car in Hilo and drop it off in Kona, and vice versa. The agencies are prejudiced against the Saddle Road and the spur road leading to South Point, both of which offer some of the *most* spectacular scenery on the island. Their prejudice is unfounded because both roads are paved, generally well maintained, and no problem if you take your time. They'll claim the insurance will not cover you if you have a mishap on these roads. A good automobile policy at home will cover you in a rental car, but definitely check this before you take off. It's even possible, but not recommended, to drive to the top of Mauna Kea if there is no snow. Plenty of signs to the summit say "4WD only"; heed them, not so much for going up, but for needed braking power coming down (see p. 180). Don't even hint of these intentions to the car-rental agencies, or they won't rent you a car.

No way whatsoever should you attempt to drive down to Waipio Valley in a car! The grade is unbelievably steep, and only a 4WD compound first gear can make it. Put simply, you have a good chance of being killed if you try it in a car.

Gas stations are farther apart than on the other islands, and sometimes they close very early. As a rule, fill up whenever the gauge reads half full.

Both General Lyman Field (Hilo Airport) and Keahole Airport (Kona) have a gauntlet of car-rental booths and courtesy phones outside the terminals.

Requirements

A variety of requirements are imposed on the renter by car agencies, but the most important clauses are common. Some of the worst practices being challenged are: no rentals to people under 25 and over 70, and no rentals to military personnel or Hawaiian residents! Before renting, check that you fulfill the requirements. Generally, you must be 21, although some agencies rent to 18-year-olds, while others still require you to be 25. You must possess a valid driver's license, with licenses from most countries accepted, but if you are not American, get an International Driver's License to be safe. You should have a major credit card in your name. This is the easiest way to rent a car. Some companies will take a deposit, but it will be very stiff. It could easily be $50 per day on top of your rental fees and sometimes much more. In addition, they may require a credit check on the spot, complete with phone calls to your employer and bank. If you damage the car, charges will be deducted from your deposit, and the car company itself determines the extent of the damages. Some companies *will not* rent you a car without a major credit card in your name, no matter how much of a deposit you are willing to leave.

When To Rent

On this one, you'll have to make up your own mind, because it's a "bet" that you can either win or lose big. But it's always good to know the odds before you plop down your money. You can reserve your car in advance when you book your air ticket, or play the field when you get there. If you book in advance, you'll obviously have a car waiting for you, but the deal that you made is the deal that you'll get—it may or may not be the best around. On the other hand, if you wait, you can often take advantage of excellent on-the-spot deals. However, you're betting that cars are available. You might be totally disappointed and not be able to rent a car at all, or you might make a honey of a deal.

If you're arriving during the peak seasons of Christmas, Easter and late summer vacation, *absolutely book your car in advance*. They are all accounted for during this period, and even if you can find a junker from a fly-by-night, they'll price-gouge you mercilessly. If you're going off-peak, you stand a good chance of getting the car you want at the price you want. It's generally best to book ahead, but the majority of car companies have toll-free 800 numbers (listed below). At least call them for an opinion of your chances of getting a car upon your intended arrival.

Rates

If you pick up a car-rental brochure at a travel agency, notice that the prices for Hawaii rentals are about the lowest in the U.S. The two rate options for renting are **mileage** and **flat rate.** A third type, **mileage/minimum,** is generally a bad idea unless you plan to do some heavy-duty driving. Mileage rate costs less per day, but you are charged for every mile driven. Mileage rates are best if you drive less than 30 miles per day—but even on an island that isn't much! The flat rate is best, providing a fixed daily rate and unlimited mileage. With either rate, you buy the gas; don't buy the cheapest because the poor performance from low octane eats up your savings.

Discounts of about 10-15% for weekend, weekly, and monthly rates are available. It's sometimes cheaper to rent a car for the week even if you're only going to use it for five days. Both weekly and monthly rates can be split between Neighbor Islands.

Warning: If you keep your car beyond your contract, you'll be charged the highest daily rate unless you notify the rental agency beforehand. Don't keep your car longer than the contract without notifying the company. They are *quick* to send out their repossession specialists. You might find your car gone, a warrant for your arrest, and an extra charge. A simple courtesy call notifying them of your intentions saves a lot of headaches and hassle.

What Wheels To Rent

The super-cheap rates on the eye-catcher brochures refer to subcompact standard shifts. The price goes up with the size of the car and with an automatic transmission. As with options on a new car, the more luxury, the more you pay. If you can drive a standard shift, get one! They're cheaper to rent and operate. Because many Hawaiian roads are twisty affairs, you'll appreciate the downshifting ability and extra control of a standard shift. AM/FM radios are good to have for entertainment and for weather and surf conditions. If you have the choice, take a car with cloth seats instead of sticky vinyl.

The average price of a subcompact standard shift, without a/c, is $30 p/d, $120 p/w, (add about $8 p/d—$50 p/w—for an automatic) but rates vary widely. Luxury cars are about $10 p/d more, with a comparable weekly rate. Most of the car companies, local and national, offer special rates and deals. These deals fluctuate too rapidly to give any hard-and-fast information. They are common, however, so make sure to inquire. Also, peak periods have "black outs" where normally good deals no longer apply.

Insurance

Before signing your car-rental agreement, you'll be offered "insurance" for around $10 p/d. Since insurance is already built into the contract (don't expect the rental agency to point this out), what you're really buying is a waiver on the deductible ($500-1000), in case you crack up the car. If you have insurance at home, you will almost always have coverage on a rental car, including your normal deductible, but not all policies are the same, so check with your agent. Also, if you haven't bought their waiver, and you have a mishap, the rental agencies will put a claim against your major credit card on the spot for the amount of deductible, even if you can prove that your insurance will cover. They'll tell you to collect from your insurance company because they don't want to be left holding the bag on an across-the-waters claim. If you have a good policy with a small deductible, it's hardly worth paying the extra money for the waiver, but if your own policy is inadequate, buy the insurance. Also, most major credit cards offer complimentary car-rental insurance as an incentive for using their cards to rent the car. Simply call the toll-free number of your credit card company to see if this service is included.

Driving Tips

Protect your children as you would at home with car seats. Their rental prices vary considerably: Alamo offers them free of charge; National charges $3 per day; Hertz needs 48 hours notice; Dollar gives them free but they're not always available at all locations. Almost all the agencies can make arrangements if you give them enough notice. Check before you go and if all else fails, bring one from home.

There are few differences between driving in Hawaii and on the Mainland. Just remember that many people on the roads are tourists and can be confused about where they're going. Since many drivers are from somewhere else, there's hardly a "regular style" of driving in the islands. A farmer from Iowa accustomed to poking along on back roads can be sandwiched between a frenetic New Yorker who's trying to drive over his roof and a super-polite but horribly confused Japanese tourist who normally drives on the left.

In Hawaii, drivers don't honk their horns except to say hello, or in an emergency. It's considered rude, and honking to hurry someone might earn you a knuckle sandwich. Hawaiian drivers reflect the climate: they're relaxed and polite. Oftentimes, they'll brake to let you turn left when they're coming at you. They may assume you'll do the same, so be ready, after a perfunctory turn signal from another driver, for him or her to turn across your lane. The more rural the area, the more apt this is to happen.

It may seem like common sense, but remember to slow down when you enter the little towns strung along the circle-island route. It's easy to bomb along on the highway and flash through these towns, missing some of Hawaii's

best scenery. Also, rural children expect *you* to be watchful, and will assume that you are going to stop for them when they dart out into the crosswalks.

B.Y.O. Car

If you want to bring your own car, write for information to: Director of Finance, Division of Licenses, 1455 S. Beretania St., Honolulu, HI 96814. However, unless you'll be in Hawaii for a bare minimum of six months and will spend all your time on one island, don't even think about it. It's an expensive proposition and takes time and plenty of arrangements. From California, the cost is at least $600 to Honolulu, and an additional $100 to any other island. To save on rental costs, it would be better to buy and sell a car there, or to lease for an extended period.

National Companies

The following are national firms represented at both airports. Kona numbers begin with "329," Hilo with "961" or "935." One of the best national firms with an excellent reputation for service and prices is **Dollar Rent A Car,** tel. 329-2744, 961-2101, (800) 367-7006, (800) 342-7398 in Hawaii. Others include: **National Car Rental,** tel. 329-1674, 935-0891 (800) 227-7368; **Hertz,** tel. 329-3566, 935-2896, (800) 654-3131; **Avis,** tel. 329-1745, 935-1290, (800) 331-1212, (800) 831-8000 in Hawaii; **Budget,** tel. 329-8511, 935-9678, (800) 527-0700; **Alamo,** tel. 329-8896, 961-3343, (800) 327-9633.

Local Companies

The following companies have booths or courtesy phones at the airport(s) (telephone prefixes 326 and 329 are for Kona; 935, 961, and 969 are for Hilo). Sometimes, if business is slow, they'll deal on their prices. Firms include: **Sunshine Rent A Car,** tel. 329-2926, 935-1108, (800) 522-8440; **VIP Car Rental,** tel. 326-9466, 329-7328; **Harper,** 969-1478; **World Rent A Car,** tel. 329-1006; **Ciao Exoticar,** tel. 326-2426. Remember that local companies come and go with regularity, so call first to make sure that they are still in business. Harper and Ciao Exoticar carry 4WD rigs, excellent (necessary!) for a drive up to the summit of Mauna Kea.

PUBLIC TRANSPORTATION

The county of Hawaii maintains the Mass Transportation System (MTS), known throughout the island as the **Hele-On Bus.** For information, schedules, and fares contact the MTS at 25 Aupuni St., Hilo 96720, tel. 961-6722 or 935-8241. The main bus terminal is in downtown Hilo at Mooheau Park, just at the corner of Kamehameha Ave. and Mamo Street. Recently, it's been completely rebuilt and modernized. Like bus terminals everywhere, it has a local franchise of derelicts and down-and-outers, but they leave you alone. What the Hele-On Bus lacks in class, it more than makes up for in *color* and affordability. The Hele-On operates Mon.-Sat. approximately 6 a.m.-6 p.m., depending on the run. It goes just about everywhere on the island—sooner or later—but recently many of the routes have been curtailed. If you're in a hurry then definitely forget about taking it, but if you want to meet the people of Hawaii, there's no better way. The base fare is 50 cents, which increases whenever you go into another zone. You can also be charged an extra $1 for a large backpack or suitcase. Don't worry about that—the Hele-On is one of the best bargains in the country. The routes are far too numerous to mention, but one goes from Kealia, south of Captain Cook, through Kailua, and all the way to Hilo on the east coast via Waimea, Honokaa, and Honomu. This journey covers 110 miles in just over four hours and costs about $8, the most expensive fare in the system. You can take the southern route through Kau, passing through Naalehu and Volcano, and continuing on to Hilo. This trip takes just over two hours and costs $6.

The county also maintains the **Banyan Shuttle** in Hilo. This bus does five runs Mon.-Fri. 9 a.m.-2:55 p.m. The Shuttle costs fifty cents but you can buy a $2 pass for one-day unlimited use. The Shuttle runs from the Hukilau Hotel at the end of Banyan Dr. to the Mooheau Bus Terminal in downtown Hilo. En route it stops at the better hotels, Puainako Town Center, Hilo and Kaikoo malls, Lyman Museum, and Rainbow Falls, where you're allowed 10 minutes for a look.

Kailua-Kona also has the **Ali'i Shuttle** that cruises Ali'i Drive. This red, white, and blue bus runs every 45 minutes, 7:45 a.m.-10 p.m. See p. 233 for details.

Taxis

General Lyman Field in Hilo and Keahole Airport north of Kailua always have taxis waiting for fares. From Hilo's airport to downtown costs about $12, and from Keahole to most hotels along Ali'i Dr. in Kailua is $22. Obviously, a taxi is no way to get around if you're trying to save money. Most taxi companies, both in Kona and Hilo, run sightseeing services for fixed prices. In **Kona** try: Kona Airport Taxi, tel. 329-7779; Paradise Taxi, tel. 329-1234; Marina Taxi, tel. 329-2481. In **Hilo** try: Hilo Harry's, tel. 935-7091; A-1 Bob's Taxi, tel. 959-4800; ABC Taxi, tel. 935-0755; Hawaii Taxi, tel. 959-6359.

Note: Inquire from the County Transit Authority, tel. 935-8241, about money-saving coupons for "shared-ride taxi service." They allow door-to-door taxi service within nine miles of the urbanized areas of Hilo, Waimea, and Kona. Service hours and other restrictions apply.

ALTERNATIVE TRAVEL

Hitchhiking

The old thumb works on the Big Island about as well as anywhere else. Some people hitchhike rather than take the Hele-On Bus not so much to save money but to save time! It's a good idea to check the bus schedule (and routes), and set out about 30 minutes before the scheduled departure. If you don't have good luck, just wait for the bus to come along and hail it down. It'll stop.

Bicycles

Peddling around the Big Island can be both fascinating and frustrating. The roads are well paved, but the shoulders are often torn up. With all the triathletes coming to Hawaii, and all the fabulous, little-trafficked roads, you'd think the island would be great for biking! It is, but you are better off bringing your own bike than renting. If you do rent, instead of a delicate road bike, you're better off getting a **cruiser** or **mountain bike** that can handle the sometimes poor road conditions as well as open up the possibilities of offroad biking. Even experienced mountain bikers should be careful on trails, which are often extremely muddy and rutted.

For rentals, try the following. **Hawaiian Pedals Unlimited,** tel. 329-2294, in the Kona Inn Shopping Plaza, rents mountain bikes at $10.50 p/d for four to seven days, $12 p/d for two to three days, $15 for 24 hours; tandems cost $25 p/d. They also offer tours. **Island Cycle Rentals** is at Jack's Diving Locker at the Kona Inn Plaza, tel. 329-7585. **Dave's Bike and Triathlon Shop,** 75-5626 Kuakini Hwy., Kailua-Kona, tel. 329-4522, rents road bikes at $15 first day, $12 second day, $10 third day, or $60 p/w; they also rent mountain bikes. **Pacific United Rental** at 1080 Kilauea Ave., Hilo, tel. 935-2974, has rentals limited to the Hilo area at $8 p/d for single-speed bikes.

Teo's Safaris in Keaau, just south of Hilo, tel. 982-5221, rents bicycles and leads mountain tours. Rentals for 21-speed mountain bikes are $10 p/d, $15 for 24 hours, $20 two days, or $50 for the week. Teo leads a rainforest ride which includes bike and helmet for $20 (call 24 hours in advance). Teo also has panniers, bike racks, and camping equipment available for people renting his bikes (rates subject to length of rental).

For information on biking in Hawaii, contact **Hawaii Bicycling League,** Box 4403, Honolulu, HI 96813. This nonprofit corporation publishes a monthly newsletter, *Spoke-n-Words,* filled with tips and suggested rides. For those interested in **bicycle touring,** contact one of the following for their specialized bike trips. The owners and tour leaders of **Island Bicycle Adventures,** 569 Kapahulu Ave., Honolulu, HI 96815, tel. 734-0700, or (800) 233-2226, are intimately familiar with bicycle touring and are members of the Hawaii Bicycling League. They offer tours to Maui, the Big Island, and Kauai. **Backroads,** 1516 Fifth St., Suite PR, Berkeley, CA 94710, tel. (510) 527-1555, (800) 462-2848, goes easy on the environment with their bicycle and hiking trips to the Big Island (also see pp. 133-134).

free Kailua-Kona Shuttle

J.D. BISIGNANI

SIGHTSEEING TOURS

Tours are offered that will literally let you cover the Big Island from top to bottom. You can drive it, fly it, dive below it, or sail around it.

Note: For snorkel/scuba, deep-sea-fishing, and horseback-riding tours, see the "Sports And Recreation" section.

Van And Bus Tours
Narrated and fairly tame island tours are operated by **Grayline,** tel. 329-9337 or 935-2835; **Robert's Tours,** tel. 935-2858; **Jack's Tours,** tel. 961-6666; and **Polynesian Tours,** tel. 329-8008. All cost about $50, and all offer a "circle island tour" that takes in Kilauea Caldera.

Four-wheel-drive tours include: **Waipio Valley Shuttle,** tel. 775-7121, offering a two-hour tour down to Waipio Valley ($25) (see pp. 193-194) and a Mauna Kea summit tour ($75); and **H.R.T. Tours** (see p. 91).

Paradise Safaris, tel. 322-2366, Box A-D, Kailua-Kona, 96745, owned and operated by Pat Wright, has been taking visitors on high-adventure trips around the Big Island for the last seven years. Pat, originally from New Mexico, is a professional guide who's plied his trade from the Rockies to New Zealand, and has taken people on trips ranging from mountaineering to white-water rafting. Your comfort and safety, as you roam the Big Island, are assured as you ride in sturdy GMC High Sierra vans with 4WD

and a/c. The premier trip offered by Paradise Safaris is an eight-hour journey to the top of Mauna Kea. Pat not only fills your trip with stories, anecdotes, and fascinating facts during the ride, he tops off the safari by setting up an eight-inch telescope so you can get a personal view of the heavens through the rarified atmosphere atop the great mountain. Pat will pick you up at your hotel in Kailua-Kona at about 4 p.m. If you're staying on the Hilo side, he will meet you at a predetermined spot along the Saddle Road. The price is $105-110, with hot savory drinks and good warm parkas included. Paradise Safaris will also tailor special trips for photography, hiking, astronomy, and shore fishing.

Tour Tapes
For a unique concept, rent Tour Tapes, narrated by Russ Apple, Ph.D., a retired national-park ranger and 1987 winner of the *Historic Hawaii Foundation Award*. Russ dispenses his knowledge about the Big Island as you drive along prescribed routes, mostly in and around Hawaii Volcanoes National Park. Tapes and decks are available in Hilo from the Hilo Hawaiian Hotel, Aston Hawaii Naniloa Resort, and Lyman House Museum. They are also available at the Volcano Art Center.

Helicopter And Air Tours
Air tours are a great way to see the Big Island, but they are expensive especially when the volcano is putting on a mighty display. Expect to

spend a minimum of $135-275 for a front-row seat to watch the amazing light show from the air. Kilauea volcano erupting is like winning the lottery for these small companies, and many will charge whatever the market will bear.

Tip: to get the best view of the volcanic activity, schedule your flight for the morning, and no later than 2 p.m. Later, clouds and fog can set in to obstruct your view.

Volcano Helitours, tel. 967-7578, owned and operated by David Okita, is intimately familiar with the volcano area. Their heliport sits atop Kilauea and is located just off a fairway of the Volcano Golf and Country Club. Rates are extremely competitive, and because your flight originates atop the volcano, you waste no air time going to or from the eruption sites. The helicopter is a four-passenger (all seats have windows) Hughes 500D.

Helicopter flights from Hilo International Airport are very competitively priced, with savings over the companies operating out of Kailua-Kona. Two good companies include **Hilo Bay Air,** tel. 969-1545, and **Io Aviation,** tel. 935-3031. Also try **Kainoa Aviation** from Hilo tel. 961-5591, or **Mauna Kea Helicopters,** tel. 885-6400, which flies from the small Kamuela Airport in Waimea.

At mile marker 75 along Route 19 heading north from Kailua-Kona is the turn-off to Waikaloa Village. Just here is a heliport that services the helicopter companies on the Kona side. One of the major island firms, **Papillon Helicopters,** tel. 329-0551, (800) 367-7095, not only flies from here, but maintains its office here. Prices range from $153 for a 45-50 minute flight along the Kohala Coast, to $295 for a Pele Spectacular that flies you over the volcano, dips low over Waipio Valley, and then runs along the Kohala Coast. All seats cost the same price, but the premier seats are up front with the pilot.

Kenai Helicopters, in a small booth next door to Papillon, tel. 329-7424, (800) 622-3144, is in direct, but friendly, competition with Papillon. Their prices are about the same, but they do have the advantage of being one of the oldest and most knowledgeable helicopter companies on the Big Island. They offer the "Fire and Rain Tour," which includes a rainforest and Puna Coast flyover for $145, and the "Creation of Pele," which takes you over the active volcano zone, past Hilo, up the Hamakua Coast, and back to Waikoloa for $297. A ride with Kenai is a once-in-a-lifetime thrill.

Waipio Valley Shuttle

For fixed-wing air tours try one of the following: **Big Island Air** offers small-plane flights from Keahole Airport, two person minimum, tel. 329-4868. They fly a two-hour circle-island tour in an eight-passenger Cessna 402. This tour passes over the volcanic activity. **Hawaii Airventures,** tel. 329-0014, offers sightseeing and photographic tours from Keahole Airport, as does **Classic Aviation,** tel. 329-8687, (800) 695-8100, who can take you on a number of flying adventures in their open-cockpit biplane. **Hawaii Pacific Aviation,** tel. 961-5591, or **Island Hoppers,** tel. 969-2000, will take you topside from Hilo International Airport.

Ocean Tours

Captain Zodiac, tel. 329-3199, Box 5612, Kailua-Kona, 96745, will take you on a fantastic ocean odyssey beginning at Honokohau Small Boat Harbor just north of Kailua-Kona, from where you'll skirt the coast south all the way to Kealakekua Bay. A Zodiac is a very tough, motorized rubber raft. It looks like a big, horseshoe-shaped inner-tube that bends itself and undulates with the waves like a floating waterbed. These seaworthy craft, powered by twin Mercury 280s, have five separate air chambers for unsinkable safety. They'll take you for a thrilling ride down the Kona coast, pausing along the way to whisk you into sea caves, grottoes and caverns. The Kona coast is also marked with ancient ruins and the remains of villages, which the captains point out, and about which they relate historical anecdotes as you pass by. You stop at Kealakekua Bay, where you can swim and snorkel in this underwater conservation park. Roundtrips departing at 8 a.m., and again at 1 p.m., take about five hours and cost $62 adults, $52 children under 11. Captain Zodiac also provides a light tropical lunch of fresh exotic fruit, taro chips, fruit juice, iced tea, and sodas. All you need are a bathing suit, sun hat, towel, lotion, camera, and sense of adventure.

Atlantis Submarine, tel. 329-6626, allows everyone to live out the fantasy of Captain Nemo on a silent cruise under the waves off Kailua-Kona. After checking in at their office in the King Kamehameha Kona Beach Hotel Mall, you board a launch at Kailua Pier that takes you on a 10-minute cruise to the waiting submarine tethered offshore. You're given all of your safety tips on the way there. As you descend, notice that everything white, including teeth, turns pink, because the ultraviolet rays are filtered out. The only colors that you can see clearly beneath the waves are blues and greens because water is 800 times denser than air and filters out the reds and oranges. Everyone has an excellent seat with a viewing port; there's not a bad seat in the submarine, so you don't have to rush to get on. Don't worry about being claustrophobic either—the sub is amazingly airy and bright, with white space-age plastic on the inside walls, and aircraft-quality air blowers over your seat.

The Atlantis Sub is getting some competition from the **Nautilus II,** tel. 326-2003, a semi-submersible very similar to the famous "ironsides" first used in the Civil War. This high-tech model offers a narrated one-hour tour in its spacious, air-conditioned lower deck. Departures are daily from Kailua Pier.

The *Maile,* berthed at Kawaihae Harbor, Box 44335, Kamuela, HI 96743, tel. (800) 726-SAIL, is a 50-foot Gulfstar sloop available for luxury sailing charters and shorter-term whalewatching, snorkeling, and fishing expeditions. Skippered by Ralph Blancato, a U.S. Coast Guard-certified Master, the sloop offers competitive prices on half- or full-day charters, sunset sails, and long-term rental.

For more conventional sailing and boating adventures, try one of the following. **Captain Beans',** tel. 329-2955, is a Kona institution that will take you aboard its glass-bottom boat daily at 5:15 p.m. from Kailua Pier at $45 adults. During the very tame cruise you'll spot fish, listen to island music, and enjoy a sunset dinner. **Captain Cook VII,** tel. 329-6411, is also a glass-bottom boat. Its tour includes snorkeling and lunch for $25 adults.

Whale-watch Cruises
In season (Nov.-April), these fascinating adventures are provided by **Royal Hawaiian Cruises,** tel. 329-6411. Cruises usually last about three hours and cost $35 adults. Accompanied by naturalists from the University of Hawaii, the educational cruise advertises that you will "see a whale, or get a coupon for another whale watch free." For a day of snorkeling, sailing and whalewatching in season, contact **Kamanu Charters,** tel. 329-2021. From Waikoloa, try **Ocean Sports,** tel. 885-5555; they offer snorkeling and whalewatching cruises with five departures per day.

Ecotourism In Hawaii
The following is a partial list of organizations, both public and private, that offer environmentally sound tours and outings throughout the Hawaiian Islands. (For ecotourism *to* Hawaii, see "Getting There," above.)

American Friends Service Committee, 2426 O'ahu Ave., Honolulu, HI 96822, tel. 988-6266 (Hawaii "Land Seminars").

EcoTours of Hawaii/Hawaiian Walkways, Box 2193, Kamuela, HI 96743, tel. 885-7759 (sea kayaking and mountain biking).

Eye of the Whale/Earthwalk Tours, Box 652, Davisville, RI 02854, tel. (401) 539-2401 (sailing and hiking).

Hawaii Audubon Society, 212 Merchant St., Suite 320, Honolulu, HI 96813, tel. 528-1432.

Hawaii Volcanoes National Park/Interpretation, Box 52, Hawaii Volcanoes National Park, HI 96718, tel. 967-7311 (hikes and talks).

The Nature Conservancy, 1116 Smith St., Suite 201, Honolulu, HI 96817, tel. 537-4508 (hikes).

Sierra Club, Box 3220 Kailua-Kona, HI 96745, tel. (808) 885-3575 (hikes and service trips).

SUE STRANGIO EVERETT

HEALTH AND WELL-BEING

In a recent survey published by *Science Digest,* Hawaii was cited as the healthiest state in the U.S. in which to live. Indeed, Hawaiian citizens live longer than anywhere else in America: men to 74 years and women to 78. Lifestyle, heredity, and diet help with these figures, but Hawaii is still an oasis in the middle of the ocean, and germs just have a tougher time getting there. There are no cases of malaria, cholera, or yellow fever. Because of a strict quarantine law, rabies is also nonexistent. On the other hand, tooth decay, perhaps because of a wide use of sugar and the enzymes present in certain tropical fruits, is 30% above the national average. With the perfect weather, a multitude of fresh-air activities, soothing negative ionization from the sea, and a generally relaxed and carefree lifestyle, everyone feels better there. Hawaii is just what the doctor ordered: a beautiful, natural health spa. That's one of its main drawing cards. The food and water are perfectly safe, and the air quality is the best in the country.

Handling The Sun

Don't become a victim of your own exuberance. People can't wait to strip down and lie on the sand like beached whales, but the tropical sun will burn you to a cinder if you're silly. The burning rays come through easier in Hawaii because of the sun's angle, and you don't feel them as much because there's always a cool breeze. The worst part of the day is 11 a.m.-3 p.m. You'll just have to force yourself to go slowly. Don't worry; you'll be able to flaunt your best souvenir, your golden Hawaiian tan, to your green-with-envy friends when you get home. It's better than showing them a boiled lobster body with peeling skin! If your skin is snowflake white, 15 minutes per side on the first day is plenty. Increase by 15-minute intervals every day, which will allow you a full hour per side by the fourth day. Have faith; this is enough to give you a deep golden, uniform tan.

Haole Rot

A peculiar condition caused by the sun is referred to locally as *haole* rot. It's called this because it supposedly affects only white people, but you'll notice some dark-skinned people with the same condition. Basically, the skin becomes mottled with white spots that refuse to tan. You get a blotchy effect, mostly on the shoulders and back. Dermatologists have a fancy name for it, and they'll give you a fancy prescription with a not-so-fancy price tag to cure it. It's common knowledge throughout the islands that Selsun Blue shampoo has some ingredient that stops the white mottling effect. Just wash your hair with it and then make sure to rub the lather over the affected areas, and it should clear up.

Bugs
Everyone, in varying degrees, has an aversion to vermin and creepy crawlers. Hawaii isn't infested with a wide variety, but it does have its share. Mosquitoes were unknown in the islands until their larvae stowed away in the water barrels of the *Wellington* in 1826 and were introduced at Lahaina. They bred in the tropical climate and rapidly spread to all the islands. They are a particular nuisance in the rainforests. Be prepared, and bring a natural repellent like citronella oil, available in most health stores on the islands, or a commercial product available in all groceries or drugstores. Campers will be happy to have mosquito coils to burn at night as well. Cockroaches are very democratic insects. They hassle all strata of society equally. They breed well in Hawaii and most hotels are at war with them, trying desperately to keep them from being spotted by guests. One comforting thought is that in Hawaii they aren't a sign of filth or dirty housekeeping. They love the climate like everyone else, and it's a real problem keeping them under control.

WATER SAFETY

Hawaii has one very sad claim to fame: more people drown here than anywhere else in the world. Moreover, there are dozens of yearly swimming victims with broken necks and backs or with injuries from scuba and snorkeling accidents. These statistics shouldn't keep you out of the sea, because it is indeed beautiful, benevolent in most cases, and a major reason to go to Hawaii. But if you're foolish, the sea will bounce you like a basketball and suck you away for good. The best remedy is to avoid situations you can't handle. Don't let anyone dare you into a situation that makes you uncomfortable. "Macho men" who know nothing about the power of the sea will be tumbled into Cabbage Patch

dolls in short order. Ask lifeguards or beach attendants about conditions, and follow their advice. If local people refuse to go in, there's a good reason. Even experts get in trouble in Hawaiian waters. Some beaches, such as Waikiki, are as gentle as a lamb and you would have to tie an anchor around your neck to drown there. Others, especially on the north coasts during the winter months, are frothing giants.

While beachcombing, or especially when walking out on rocks, never turn your back to the sea. Be aware of undertows (the waves drawing back into the sea). They can knock you off your feet. Before entering the water, study it for rocks, breakers, reefs, and riptides. Riptides are powerful currents, like rivers in the sea, that can drag you out. Mostly they peter out not too far from shore, and you can often see their choppy waters on the surface. If caught in a "rip," don't fight to swim directly against it; you'll lose and only exhaust yourself. Swim diagonally across it, while going along with it, and try to stay parallel to the shore. Don't waste all your lung power yelling, and rest by floating.

When bodysurfing, never ride straight in; come to shore at a 45° angle. Remember, waves come in sets. Little ones can be followed by giants, so watch the action awhile instead of plunging right in. Standard procedure is to duck under a breaking wave. You can survive even thunderous oceans using this technique. Don't try to swim through a heavy froth and never turn your back and let it smash you. Don't swim alone if possible, and obey all warning signs. Hawaiians want to entertain you and they don't put up signs just to waste money. The last rule is, "If in doubt, stay out."

Yikes!
Sharks live in all the oceans of the world. Most mind their own business and stay away from shore. Hawaiian sharks are well fed—on fish—and don't usually bother with unsavory humans. If you encounter a shark, don't panic! Never thrash around because this will trigger their attack instinct. If they come close, scream loudly.

Portuguese man-o-wars put out long, floating tentacles that sting if they touch you. Don't wash the sting off with fresh water, as this will only aggravate it. Hot salt water will take away the sting, as will alcohol, the drinking or rubbing kind, after-shave lotion, and meat tenderizer (MSG), which can be found in any supermarket or Chinese restaurant.

Coral can give you a nasty cut, and it's known for causing infections because it's a living organism. Wash the cut immediately and apply an antiseptic. Keep it clean and covered, and watch for infection.

Poisonous sea urchins, such as the lacquer-black *wana,* can be beautiful creatures. They are found in shallow tidepools and will hurt you if you step on them. Their spines will break off, enter your foot, and burn like blazes. There are cures. Vinegar and wine poured on the wound will stop the burning. If not available, the Hawaiian solution is urine. It might seem ignominious to have someone pee on your foot, but It'll put the fire out. The spines will disintegrate in a few days, and there are generally no long-term effects.

Hawaiian reefs also have their share of moray eels. These creatures are ferocious in appearance, but will never initiate an attack. You'll have to poke around in their holes while snorkeling or scuba diving to get them to attack. Sometimes this is inadvertent on the diver's part, so be careful where you stick your hand while underwater.

HAWAIIAN FOLK MEDICINE AND CURES

Hawaiian folk medicine is well developed; and its cures for common ailments have been used effectively for centuries. Hawaiian *kahuna* were highly regarded for their medicinal skills, and Hawaiians were by far some of the healthiest people in the world until the coming of the Europeans. Many folk remedies and cures are used to this day and, what's more, they work. Many of the common plants and fruits that you'll encounter provide some of the best remedies. When roots and seeds and special exotic plants are used, the preparation of the medicine is as painstaking as in a modern pharmacy. These prescriptions are exact and take an expert to prepare. They should never be prepared or administered by an amateur.

Common Curative Plants

Arrowroot, for diarrhea, is a powerful narcotic used in rituals and medicines. The pepper plant *(Piper methisticum)* is chewed and the juice is spat into a container for fermenting. Used as a

KUKUI (CANDLENUT)

Reaching heights of 80 feet, the *kukui* (candlenut) was a veritable department store to the Hawaiians, who made use of almost every part of this utilitarian giant. Used as a cure-all, its nuts, bark, or flowers were ground into potions and salves and taken as a general tonic, applied to ulcers and cuts as an effective antibiotic, or administered internally as a cure for constipation or asthma attacks. The bark was mixed with water and the resulting juice was used as a dye in tattooing, tapa-cloth making, and canoe painting, and as a preservative for fishnets. The oily nuts were burned as a light source in stone holders, and ground and eaten as a condiment called *inamona*. Polished nuts took on a beautiful sheen and were strung as *lei*. Lastly, the wood itself was hollowed into canoes and used as fishnet floats.

medicine for urinary tract infections, rheumatism, and asthma, it also induces sleep and cures headaches. A poultice for wounds is made from the skins of ripe bananas. Peelings have a powerful antibiotic quality and contain vitamins A, B, and C, phosphorous, calcium, and iron. The nectar from the plant was fed to babies as a vitamin juice. Breadfruit sap is used for healing cuts and as a moisturizing lotion. Coconut is used to make moisturizing oil, and the juice was chewed, spat into the hand, and used as a shampoo. Guava is a source of vitamins A, B, and C. Hibiscus has been used as a laxative. *Kukui* nut oil makes a gargle for sore throats and a laxative, plus the flowers are used to cure diarrhea. *Noni,* an unappetizing hand-grenade-shaped fruit that you wouldn't want to eat unless you had to, reduces tumors, diabetes, and high blood pressure, and the juice is good for diarrhea. Sugarcane sweetens many concoctions, and the juice of toasted cane was a tonic for sick babies. Sweet potato is used as a tonic during pregnancy, and juiced as a gargle for phlegm. Tamarind is a natural laxative and contains the most acid and sugar of any fruit on earth. Taro has been used for lung infections and thrush, and as suppositories. Yams are good for coughs, vomiting, constipation, and appendicitis.

HELP FOR THE HANDICAPPED

A handicapped or physically disabled person can have a wonderful time in Hawaii; all that's needed is a little pre-planning. The following is general advice that should help your planning.

Commission On Persons With Disabilities

This commission was designed with the express purpose of aiding handicapped people. They are a source of invaluable information and distribute self-help booklets free of charge. Any handicapped person heading to Hawaii should write first or visit their offices on arrival. For the *Aloha Guide To Accessibility* ($3) write or visit the head office at: Commission on the Handicapped, 500 Ala Moana Blvd., Honolulu, HI 96813, tel. 586-8121; on Maui, 54 High St., Wailuku, Maui, HI 96793, tel. 243-5441; on Kauai, 3060 Eiwa St. #207, Lihue, Kauai, HI 96766, tel. 241-3308; on Hawaii, Box 1641, Hilo, HI 96820, tel. 933-7747.

General Information

The key for a smooth trip is to make as many arrangements ahead of time as possible. Tell the transportation companies and hotels you'll be dealing with the nature of your handicap in advance so that they can make arrangements to accommodate you. Bring your medical records and notify medical establishments of your arrival if you'll be needing their services. Travel with a friend or make arrangements for an aide on arrival (see below). Bring your own wheelchair if possible and let airlines know if it is battery-powered; boarding interisland carriers requires steps. No problem: they'll board you early on special lifts, but they must know that you're coming. Many hotels and restaurants accommodate disabled persons, but always call ahead just to make sure.

Hawaii Services

At Hilo Airport there are no facilities for deplaning non-ambulatory people from propeller planes, only from jets and on the jetways. Interisland flights should be arranged only on jets. Ramps and a special elevator provide access in the bi-level terminal. Parking is convenient in designated areas. At Kona airport, boarding and deplaning is possible for the handicapped. Ramps make the terminal accessible. To get around, **Handi-Vans** are available in Hilo, tel. 961-6722. **Kamealoha Unlimited** has specially equipped vans, tel. 966-7244. **Parking permits** are available from the Department of Finance, tel. 961-8231. Medical help, nurses, and companions can be arranged through **Big Island Center for Independent Living,** tel. 935-3777. Doctors are referred by **Hilo Hospital,** tel. 961-4211, and **Kona Hospital,** tel. 322-9311. Medical equipment is available from **Kamealoha Unlimited,** tel. 966-7244; **Medi-Home,** tel. 969-1123; **Pacific Rentall,** tel. 935-2974.

ALTERNATIVE HEALTH CARE

The Big Island is blessed with some of the finest natural healers and practitioners in the state. For a holistic healing experience of body, mind, and soul, the following are highly recommended. For hospitals, drugstores, and medical doctors see "Emergency and Medical Care," p. 151.

At the **School of Hawaiian Lomi Lomi,** Box 221, Captain Cook, HI 96704, tel. 323-2416 or 328-2472, Margaret Machado, assisted by her husband Daniel, provides the finest *lomi lomi* and traditional Hawaiian herbal cures in the islands. Both are renowned *kapuna* who dispense a heavy dose of love and concern with every remedy prescribed.

Acupuncture and Herbs is the domain of Angela Longo. This remarkable woman is not only a superbly trained, licensed practitioner of traditional Chinese medicine and acupuncture, but she covers all bases by holding a Ph.D. in biochemistry from U.C. Berkeley. For a totally

Ms. Angela Longo

holistic health experience, contact Angela at her Waimea/Kamuela office, tel. 885-7886.

Angela's top student, **Karen MacIsaac,** has opened a Chinese herb and acupuncture clinic by appointment only, tel. 329-4393, at 75-5995 Kuakini Hwy., Suite 126, Kailua-Kona, HI 96740.

The **Hawaiian Islands School of Body Therapy,** tel. 322-0048, owned and operated by Peter Wind and Lynn Filkins-Wind, offers state-certified massage courses and mini-courses for the beginning or experienced therapist. A full range of massage, anatomy, and physiology are part of the coursework preparing the student for a Hawaii State License. Programs include a basic massage program taking 150 hours, an advanced massage program of 450 hours, and a third-level course designed for the professional that takes a minimum of one year's intensive study to complete. Under Peter and Lynn's tutelage you'll learn *lomi lomi,* reflexology, hydrotherapy, aroma therapy, trigger point therapy, and treatment therapy. Lynn specializes in treatment therapy, which she teaches by the European, hands-on approach,

while Peter is a hydrotherapist and colonics therapist. They are assisted by Gigi Goochey, the anatomy and physiology instructor. Lynn and Peter are dedicated professionals who have clued-in, body and soul, to the art of healing.

Brain Gym Hawaii, tel. 889-5937, Box 1421, Kapaau, HI, is owned and operated by Jan Ellison, whose motto is, "Movement is the door to learning." A practitioner of educational kinesthesiology, Jan offers classes in how movement relates to performance, and how the practice of "Edu-K" helps you realize your full potential. The practice integrates the body, mind, and spirit, aligning them so as to put you in control of your entire self. Costs for therapy sessions are on a sliding scale, and Jan will arrange to meet you at the time and place of your convenience.

To revitalize those aching muscles and put a spring in your step, visit massage practitioners with magic in their hands: **Kiauhou Massage and Spa** at the Kiauhou Beach Hotel, tel. 322-3441, Room 227 is open Tues., Thurs., and Sat. 10 a.m.-5 p.m., and Mon., Wed., and Fri. 5-8 p.m.

To get that just-right chiropractic adjustment, try **Rodgers Chiropractic Arts** with Howard Rodgers, D.C., in the WOW Building, Kailua, tel. 329-2271; or try **Kohala Chiropractic** with Dr. Bob Abdy, Kamuela, tel. 885-6847. Also in Waimea is **Kohala Coast Massage,** tel. 885-5442, and the **Chiropractic Clinic** of Dr. Kenneth C. Williams, tel. 885-7719, emergency tel. 885-6812.

A wonderful healing center is **Halemana** in Pahoa, tel. 965-7783, where they'll soothe you with acupuncture and massage. For full details, see p. 206.

Academy of Therapeutic Massage, c/o Nancy Kahalewai P.M.T., 197 Kinoole St., Hilo, HI 96720, tel. 935-1405, focuses on pre-licensing programs with an emphasis on sports massage, injury prevention and care, and inner changes of body psychology. Semesters include a summer intensive and regular winter and fall classes. Nancy, a longtime member of the Hawaii Board of Massage Advisory Committee, has been practicing her healing arts in the islands for about 15 years. She not only has the "golden touch" but is a terrific resource for all types of alternative medicines available on the Big Island. All massages, given by students, are completely supervised! This is a great opportunity to receive a quality massage at a reasonable price while visiting Hilo.

SUE STRANGIO EVERETT

WHAT TO TAKE

It's a snap to pack for a visit to the Big Island. Everything is on your side. The weather is moderate and uniform on the whole, and the style of dress is delightfully casual. The rule of thumb is to pack lightly: few items, and light clothing both in color and weight. What you'll need will depend largely on your itinerary and your desires. Are you drawn to the nightlife, the outdoors, or both? If you forget something at home, it won't be a disaster. You can buy everything you'll need in Hawaii. As a matter of fact, Hawaiian clothing, such as muumuus and aloha shirts, is one of the best purchases you can make, both in comfort and style. It's quite feasible to bring only one or two changes of clothing with the express purpose of outfitting yourself while there. Prices on bathing suits, bikinis, and summer wear in general are quite reasonable.

Matters Of Taste
A grand conspiracy in Hawaii adhered to by everyone—tourist, traveler, and resident—is to "hang loose" and dress casual. Best of all, alohawear is just about all you'll need for comfort

and virtually every occasion. The classic muumuu is large and billowy, and aloha shirts are made to be worn outside the pants. The best of both are made of cool cotton. Rayon is a natural fiber that isn't too bad, but polyester is hot, sticky, and not authentic. Not all muumuus are of the "tent persuasion." Some are very fashionable and form-fitted with peek-a-boo slits up the side, down the front, or around the back. *Holomuu* are muumuus fitted at the waist with a flowing skirt to the ankles. They are not only elegant, but perfect for "stepping out."

In The Cold And Rain
Two occasions for which you'll have to consider dressing warmly are visits to mountaintops and boat rides where wind and ocean sprays are a factor. You can conquer both with a jogging suit (sweat suit) and a featherweight, water-resistant windbreaker. If you intend to visit Mauna Kea or Mauna Loa, it'll be downright chilly. Your jogging suit with a hooded windbreaker/raincoat will do the trick for all occasions. If you're going to camp or trek, you should add another

layer, a woolen sweater being one of the best. Wool is the only natural fiber that retains most of its warmth-giving properties even if it gets wet. Several varieties of "fleece" synthetics currently on the market also have this ability. If your hands get cold, put a pair of socks over them. Tropical rain showers can happen at any time so you might consider a fold-up umbrella, but the sun quickly breaks through and the warming winds blow.

Shoes

Dressing your feet is hardly a problem. You'll most often wear zoris (rubber thongs) for going to and from the beach, leather sandals for strolling and dining, and jogging shoes for trekking and sightseeing. A few discos require leather shoes, but it's hardly worth bringing them just for that. If you plan on heavy-duty trekking, you'll definitely want your hiking boots. Lava, especially a'a, is murderous on shoes. Most backcountry trails are rugged and muddy, and you'll need those good old lug soles for traction. If you plan moderate hikes, you might want to consider bringing rubberized ankle supports to complement your jogging shoes. Most drugstores sell them, and the best are a rubberized sock with toe and heel cut out.

Specialty Items

Following is a list of specialty items that you might consider bringing along. They're not necessities but most will definitely come in handy. A pair of binoculars really enhances sightseeing—great for viewing birds and sweeping panoramas, and almost a necessity if you're going whalewatching. A folding, Teflon-bottomed travel iron makes up for cotton's one major shortcoming, wrinkles; you can't always count on hotels to have irons. Nylon twine and miniature clothespins are handy for drying garments, especially bathing suits. Commercial and hotel laundromats abound, but many times you'll get by with hand-washing a few items in the sink. A transistor radio/tape recorder provides news, weather, and entertainment, and can be used to record impressions, island music, and a running commentary for your slide show. Hair dryer: although the wind can be relied upon to dry wet hair, it leaves a bit to be desired in the styling department. An inflatable raft for riding waves, along with flippers, mask

and snorkel, can easily be bought in Hawaii but don't weigh much or take up much space in your luggage. If you'll be camping, trekking, or boating with only seawater available for bathing, take along "Sea Saver Soap," available from good sporting goods stores. This special soap will lather in seawater and rinse away the sticky salt residue with it.

For The Camper

If you don't want to take it with you, all necessary camping gear can be purchased or rented while in Hawaii. Besides the above, you should consider taking the following: framed backpack or the convertible packs that turn into suitcases, daypack, matches in a waterproof container, all-purpose knife, mess kit, eating utensils, flashlight (remove batteries), candle, nylon cord, and sewing kit (dental floss works as thread). Take a first-aid kit containing Band-Aids, all-purpose antiseptic cream, alcohol swabs, tourniquet string, cotton balls, elastic bandage, razor blade, Telfa pads, and a small mirror for viewing private nooks and crannies. A light sleeping bag is good, although your fleecy jogging suit with a ground pad and light blanket or even your rain poncho will be sufficient. Definitely bring a down bag for Haleakala or mountainous areas. In a film container pack a few nails, safety pins, fishhooks, line, and bendable wire. Nothing else does what these do and they're all handy for a million and one uses. (See also pp. 75-76.)

Basic Necessities

As previously mentioned, you really have to consider only two "modes" of dressing in Hawaii: beachwear and casual clothing. The following is designed for the mid-range traveler carrying one suitcase or a backpack. Remember that there are laundromats and that you'll be spending a considerable amount of time in your bathing suit. Consider the following: one or two pairs of light cotton slacks for going out and about, and one pair of jeans for trekking, or better yet, corduroys which can serve both purposes; two or three casual sundresses—muumuus are great; three or four pairs of shorts for beachwear and for sightseeing; four to five short-sleeved shirts or blouses and one long-sleeved; three or four colored and printed T-shirts that can be worn anytime from trekking to strolling; a beach coverup—the short terrycloth type is the best; a brimmed hat for rain and sun—the crushable floppy type is great for purse or daypack; two or three pairs of socks are sufficient, nylons you won't need; two bathing suits (nylon ones dry quickest); plastic bags to hold wet bathing suits and laundry; five to six pairs of underwear; towels (optional, because hotels provide them, even for the beach); a first-aid kit, pocket-size is sufficient; suntan lotion and insect repellent; a daypack or large beach purse. And don't forget your windbreaker, perhaps a shawl for the evening, and an all-purpose jogging suit.

Pets And Quarantine

Hawaii has a very rigid pet quarantine policy designed to keep rabies and other mainland disease from reaching the state. All domestic pets are subject to **90 days' quarantine,** regardless of the fact that they may have current veterinary shot certificates. Unless you are contemplating a move to Hawaii, it is not feasible to take pets. For complete information, contact the Department of Agriculture, Animal Quarantine Division, 99-770 Moanalua Rd., Honolulu, HI 96701, tel. 488-8461.

3

1. Waimea, *paniolo* country (J.D. Bisignani); 2. waterfall at Hawaii Tropical Botanical Gardens (J.D. Bisignani); 3. Waipio Valley (David Stanley)

1. Leslie Miki of Abundant Life Natural Foods, Hilo (J.D. Bisignani);
2. aloha, *paniolo* style (J.D. Bisignani); **3.** motorcycle madonna (J.D. Bisignani)

INFORMATION AND SERVICES

EMERGENCY AND MEDICAL CARE

For police, fire and ambulance, dial **911** from anywhere on the island.

Hospitals: Hilo Hospital, tel. 969-4111; Kona Hospital, tel. 322-9311; Honokaa Hospital, tel. 775-7211; Kohala Hospital, tel. 889-6211; Kau Hospital, tel. 928-8331.

Drugstores: Longs Drugs, Hilo, tel. 935-3357, or Kona, tel. 329-1380; Kona Coast Drugs, Kailua, tel. 329-8886; Village Pharmacy, Waimea, tel. 885-4418.

HAWAII VISITORS BUREAU OFFICES

Big Island HVB Offices
The best information is dispensed by the **Hawaii Visitors Bureau,** 250 Keawe St., Hilo, HI 96720, tel. 961-5797; HVB Kona Branch, 75-5719 W. Ali'i Dr., Kailua-Kona, HI 96740, tel. 329-7787.

Statewide HVB offices include: HVB Administrative Office, Waikiki Business Plaza, 2270 Kalakaua Ave., Suite 801, Honolulu, HI 96815, tel. 923-1811; Maui HVB, 250 Alamaha St., Suite N-16, Kahului, HI 96732, tel. 871-8691; Kauai HVB, 3016 Umi St., Suite 207, Lihue, HI 96766, tel. 245-3971.

North America
Hawaii Visitors Bureaus are: **HVB New York,** Empire State Bldg., Suite 808, New York, NY 10018, tel. (212) 947-0717; **HVB Washington D.C.,** 1511 K St. NW, Suite 415, Washington, D.C. 20005, tel. (202) 393-6752; **HVB Chicago,** 180 N. Michigan Ave., Suite 2210, Chicago, IL 60601, tel. (312) 236-0632; **HVB Los Angeles,** Central Plaza, 3440 Wilshire Blvd., Room 610, Los Angeles, CA 90010, tel. (213) 385-5301; **HVB San Francisco,** Suite 450, 50 California St., San Francisco, CA 94111, tel. (415) 392-8173; **HVB Canada,** 205-1624 56th St., Delta, B.C., Canada V4L 2B1, tel. (604) 943-8555.

European Offices
HVB United Kingdom, 14 The Green, Richmond, TW9 1PX, England, tel. 44-81-332-6969.

HVB Germany, c/o Hans Regh Assoc., Postfach 930 247, Ginnheimer Landstrasse 1, D-6000, Frankfurt, tel. 49-69-70-4013.

HVB Belgium, Rue Couperin, #87 Bis, Boncelles 4100, tel. 32-41-38-1517.

Asia/Pacific Offices
HVB Australia, c/o Walshes World, 92 Pitt St., Sydney, N.S.W. 2000, tel. 61-2-235-0194.

HVB Japan, Hibiya Kokusai Bldg., 11th Fl., 2-2-3 Uchisaiwaicho, Chiyoda-ku, Tokyo 100, tel. 011-81-3-3580-2481.

HVB Malaysia, c/o Pacific World Travel, 2.5 & 2.6 Angkasa Raya Bldg., Jalan Ampag, Kuala Lumpur 50450, tel. 60-3-244-8449.

The "HVB Warrior" is posted alongside the roadway, marking sites of cultural and historical importance.

HVB Hong Kong, Suite 3702-A, EIE Tower, Bond Centre, Queensway, Central, Hong Kong, tel. 852-526-0387.

HVB Korea, c/o Travel Press, 2nd Fl., Westin Chosun Hotel, C.P.O. Box 6445, Seoul 100-070, tel. 82-2-757-6781.

HVB Singapore, c/o Pacific Leisure, 3 Seah St., #01-04, Singapore 0718, tel. 65-338-1612.

HVB Thailand, c/o ADAT Sales, 8th Fl., Maneeya Center Bldg., 518/5 Ploenchit Rd., Bangkok 10330, tel. 66-2-255-6838.

HVB New Zealand, c/o Walshes World, 87 Queen St., 2nd Fl., Dingwall Bldg., Auckland, tel. 64-9-379-3708.

HVB Taiwan, c/o Federal Transportation Co., 8th Fl., Nanking E. Road, Section 3, Taipei, tel. 886-2-507-8133.

OTHER INFORMATION SOURCES

The **State Visitor Information** centers at the airports, tel. 935-1018 (Hilo) or 329-3423 (Kona), are good sources of information available on arrival.

The **Chamber of Commerce** can be consulted in Hilo, 180 Kinoole St., Hilo, HI 96720, tel. 935-7178; or in Kailua-Kona, 75-5737 Kuakini Hwy., Suite 207, Kailua-Kona, HI 96740, tel. 329-1758.

For all kinds of up-to-the-minute information, including sports (both local and national), weather, surf report, and news, call 935-1666 and then enter a four-number code as instructed (free 24 hours a day).

Receive 24-hour recorded information regarding volcanic activity by calling 967-7977.

MONEY AND FINANCES

Currency

U.S. currency is among the drabbest in the world. It's all the same size and color; those unfamiliar with it should spend some time getting acquainted so that they don't make costly mistakes. U.S. coinage in use is: $.01, $.05, $.10, $.25, $.50, and $1 (uncommon); paper currency is $1, $2 (uncommon), $5, $10, $20, $50, $100. Bills larger than $100 are not in common usage.

Banks

Full-service banks tend to open slightly earlier than Mainland banks, at 8:30 a.m. Monday-Friday. Closing is at 3 p.m., except for late hours on Friday when most banks remain open until 6 p.m. Of most value to travelers, banks sell and cash traveler's checks, give cash advances on credit cards, and exchange and sell foreign currency.

Traveler's Checks

Traveler's checks are accepted throughout Hawaii at hotels, restaurants, and car-rental agencies, and in most stores and shops. However, to be readily acceptable they should be in American currency. Some larger hotels that often deal with Japanese and Canadians will accept their currency. Banks accept foreign-currency traveler's checks, but it'll mean an extra trip and inconvenience.

Credit Cards

More and more business is transacted in Hawaii using credit cards. Almost every form of accommodation, shop, restaurant, and amusement accepts them. For renting a car they're almost a must. With "credit card insurance" readily available, they're as safe as traveler's checks and sometimes even more convenient. Don't rely on them completely because there are some establishments that won't accept them, or perhaps won't accept the kind that you carry.

THE METRIC SYSTEM

1 inch = 2.54 centimeters (cm)
1 foot = .304 meters (m)
1 mile = 1.6093 kilometers (km)
1 km = .6124 miles
1 fathom = 1.8288 m
1 chain = 20.1168 m
1 furlong = 201.168 m
1 acre = .4047 hectares
1 sq km = 100 hectares
1 sq mile = 2.59 square km
1 ounce = 28.35 grams
1 pound = .4536 kilograms
1 short ton = .90718 metric ton
1 short ton = 2000 pounds
1 long ton = 1.016 metric tons
1 long ton = 2240 pounds
1 metric ton = 1000 kilograms
1 quart = .94635 liters
1 US gallon = 3.7854 liters
1 Imperial gallon = 4.5459 liters
1 nautical mile = 1.852 km

To compute centigrade temperatures, subtract 32 from Fahrenheit and divide by 1.8. To go the other way, multiply centigrade by 1.8 and add 32.

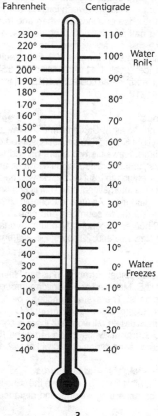

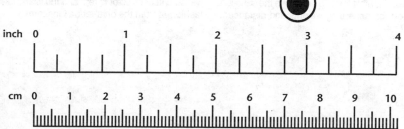

OTHER PRACTICALITIES

Telephone: All-Hawaii Area Code 808

As they do everywhere else in the U.S., long-distance rates go down at 5 p.m. and again at 11 p.m. until 8 a.m. the next morning. From Friday at 5 p.m. until Monday morning at 8 a.m. rates are cheapest. Local calls from public telephones (anywhere on the same island is a local call) cost 25 cents. Calling between islands is a toll call, and the price depends on when and from where you call and for how long you speak. Emergency calls are always free. The area code for the entire state of Hawaii is 808. For directory assistance: local, 1-411; interisland, 1-555-1212; Mainland, 1-area code-555-1212; toll free, (800) 555-1212.

Time Zones

There is no Daylight Saving Time in Hawaii. When Daylight Saving Time is not observed on the Mainland, Hawaii is two hours behind the West Coast, four hours behind the Midwest, and five hours behind the East Coast. Hawaii, being just east of the international date line, is almost a full day behind most Asian and Oceanic cities. Hours behind these countries and cities are: Japan, 19 hours; Singapore, 18 hours; Sydney, 20 hours; New Zealand, 22 hours; Fiji, 22 hours.

Electricity

The same electrical current is in use in Hawaii as on the U.S. Mainland and is uniform throughout the islands. The system functions on 110 volts, 60 cycles of alternating current (AC). Appliances from Japan will work, but there is some danger of burnout, while those requiring the normal European voltage of 220 will not work.

Distance, Weights, And Measures

Hawaii, like all of the U.S., employs the "English method" of measuring weights and distances.

Basically, dry weights are in ounces and pounds; liquid measures are in ounces, quarts, and gallons; and distances are measured in inches, feet, yards, and miles. The metric system, based on units of 10, is known but is not in general use. The conversion chart on p 153 should be helpful.

Reading Material

Make sure to pick up copies of the following free literature. Besides maps and general information, they often include money-saving coupons. Available at most hotels/condos and at all tourist areas, the weekly publications include: *Guide to Hawaii, Spotlight's Big Island Gold,* and *This Week Big Island.* Island newspapers include: *Hawaii-Tribune Herald,* a Hilo publication; and *West Hawaii Today,* published in Kona.

Libraries are located in towns and schools all over the island. The main branch is at 300 Waianuenue Ave., Hilo, tel. 935-5407. They provide all information regarding libraries. In Kailua-Kona, the library is at 75-140 Hualalai Rd., tel. 329-2196. For bookstores, please refer to the "Shopping" section in the Introduction.

Post Office

Branch post offices are found in most major towns. Window service is offered Mon.-Fri. 8:30 a.m.-4 p.m.; some offices are open Saturday 10 a.m.-noon. The following are the main offices: Hilo, tel. 935-2821; Kailua, tel. 329-1927; Captain Cook, tel. 323-3663; Waimea/Kamuela, tel. 885-4026; Volcano, tel. 967-7611; Hawi, tel. 889-5301.

Island Facts

Hawaii has three fitting nicknames: the Big Island, the Volcano Island, and the Orchid Island. It's the youngest, most southerly, and largest (4,038 square miles) island in the Hawaiian chain. Its color is red, and the island *lei* is fashioned from the ohia-lehua blossom.

BOB RACE

HILO

Hilo is a blind date. Everyone tells you what a beautiful personality she has, but . . . But? . . . it rains: 133 inches a year. Mostly the rains come in winter and are limited to predictable afternoon showers, but they do scare some tourists away, keeping Hilo reasonably priced and low key. In spite of, and because of, the rain, Hilo is gorgeous. It's one of the oldest permanently settled towns in Hawaii, and the largest on the windward coast of the island. Hilo's weather makes it a natural greenhouse. Twenty acres of exotic orchids and flowers line the runways at the airport! Botanical gardens and flower farms surround Hilo like a giant *lei,* and shoulder-to-

shoulder banyans canopy entire city blocks. To counterpoint this tropical explosion, Mauna Kea's winter snows backdrop the town. The crescent of Hilo Bay blazes gold at sunrise, while a sculpted lagoon, Asian pagodas, rock gardens, and even a tiny island connected by footbridge line its shores. Downtown's waterfront has the perfect false-front buildings that always need a paint job. They lean on each other like "old salts" that've had one too many. Don't make the mistake of underestimating Hilo, or of counting it out because of its rainy reputation. For most, the blind date with this exotic beauty turns into a fun-filled love affair.

SIGHTS AND BEACHES

SIGHTS

Hilo is a unique town in a unique state in America. You can walk down streets with names like Puueo and Keawe, and they could be streets in Anywhere, U.S.A., with neatly painted houses surrounded by white picket fences. Families live here. There are roots, and traditions, but the

town is changing. Fishermen still come for the nightly ritual of soul-fishing and story-swapping from the bridge spanning the Wailuku River, while just down the street newly arrived chefs prepare Cajun blackened fish at a yuppie restaurant as midnight philosophers sip gourmet coffee and munch sweets next door. Hilo is a classic tropical town. Some preserved buildings, proud again after new face-lifts, are a few stories

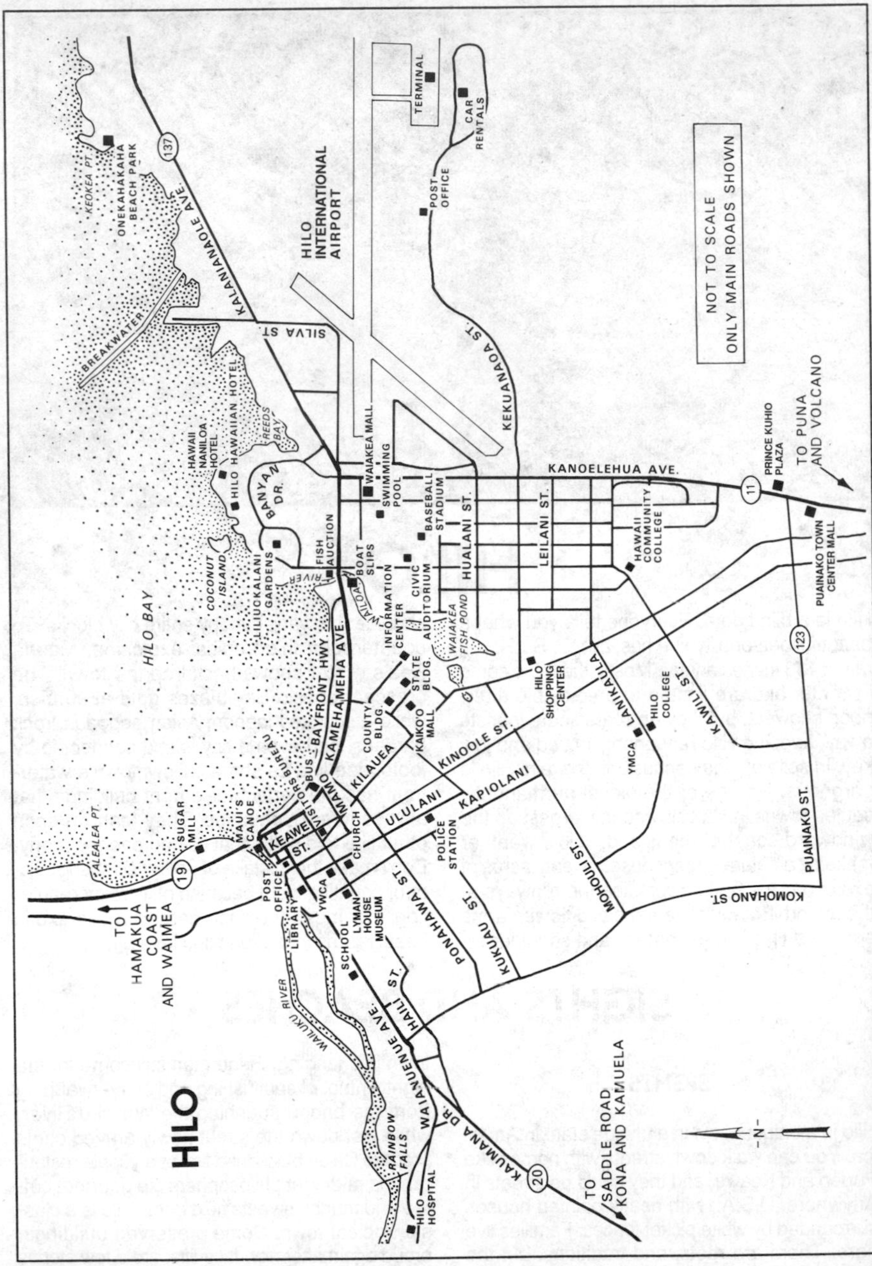

HILO

NOT TO SCALE
ONLY MAIN ROADS SHOWN

TO HAMAKUA COAST AND WAIMEA

HILO BAY

BREAKWATER

KEOKEA PT.

ONEKAHAKAHA BEACH PARK

137

KALANIANAOLE AVE.

SILVA ST.

HILO INTERNATIONAL AIRPORT

TERMINAL

CAR RENTALS

POST OFFICE

KEKUANAOA ST.

KANOELEHUA AVE.

11

PRINCE KUHIO PLAZA

TO PUNA AND VOLCANO

HAWAII NANILOA HOTEL

HILO HAWAIIAN HOTEL

REEDS BAY

BANYAN DR.

COCONUT ISLAND

LILIUOKALANI GARDENS

FISH AUCTION

WAILOA RIVER

BOAT SLIPS

INFORMATION CENTER

CIVIC AUDITORIUM

WAIAKEA FISH POND

WAIAKEA MALL

SWIMMING POOL

BASEBALL STADIUM

HUALANI ST.

LEILANI ST.

HAWAII COMMUNITY COLLEGE

PUAINAKO TOWN CENTER MALL

123

STATE BLDG.

KAIKOO MALL

KINOOLE ST.

HILO SHOPPING CENTER

HILO COLLEGE

YMCA LANAKILA

KAMEHAMEHA AVE.

BAYFRONT HWY.

MAUI'S CANOE

VISITOR BUREAU

BUS

COUNTY BLDG

KILAUEA

ULULANI

CHURCH

KAPIOLANI

POLICE STATION

PANAHAWAI ST.

KUKUAU ST.

MOHOULI ST.

KAMUELA ST.

KAUMANA DR.

PUAINAKO ST.

KOMOHANA ST.

LEALEA PT.

SUGAR MILL

19

KEAWE ST.

POST OFFICE

YWCA

LIBRARY

SCHOOL

LYMAN HOUSE MUSEUM

WAIANUENUE AVE.

WAILUKU RIVER

RAINBOW FALLS

HILO HOSPITAL

20

TO SADDLE ROAD KONA AND KAMUELA

-N-

© 1988 MENEHUNE MAP PUBLICATIONS, INC.

J.D. BISIGNANI

Hilo Bay

tall and date from the turn of the century when Hilo was a major port of entry to Hawaii. Sidewalks in older sections are covered with awnings because of the rains and add a turn-of-the-century gentility. Because Hilo is a town, most Americans can relate to it: it's big enough to have one-way streets and malls, but not so big that it's a metropolis like Honolulu, or so small that it's a village like Hana. You can walk the central area comfortably in an afternoon, but the town does sprawl, and it's *happening*. Teenagers in "boom box" cars cruise the main strip which is lined with fine restaurants, high-tech discos, and mom-and-pop shops. There's even a down-and-out section where guys hunker down in alleyways, smoking cigarettes and peering into the night. But in the still night, there's the deep-throated sound of a ship's foghorn, a specter of times past when Hilo was a vibrant port. Hilo is the opposite of Kailua-Kona both spiritually and physically. There, everything is running super fast, a clone of Honolulu. In Hilo the old beat, the old music, that feeling of a tropical place where rhythms are slow and sensual still exist. Hilo nights are alive with sounds of the tropics and the heady smell of fruits and flowering trees wafting on the breeze. Hilo still remains what it always was—a town, a place where people live.

Hilo is the eastern hub of the island. Choose a direction, and an hour's driving puts you in a time-lost valley deep in *paniolo* country, or on the blackness of a recent lava flow, or above the steaming fumaroles of Hawaii Volcanoes National Park. In and around town are museums, riverbank fishing, cultural centers, plenty of gardens, waterfalls, a potholed riverbed, and lava caves. Hilo's beaches are small, rocky, and hard to find—perfect for keeping crowds away. Hilo is bite-sized, but you'll need a rental car or the Banyan Shuttle to visit most of the sights around town.

The main thoroughfares through town are Kilauea St., which merges into Keawe St. and runs one-way toward the Wailuku River; and Kinoolo St., which runs one-way away from the river. Basically they feed into each other and make a big loop through the downtown area. Kamehameha Ave. fronts the town area and runs along the bay.

Lyman Mission House And Museum
The preserved New England-style homestead of David and Sarah Lyman, Congregationalist missionaries who built it in 1839, is the oldest frame building still standing on the Big Island. Lyman House, at 276 Haili St., Hilo, HI 96720, tel. 835-5021, open Mon.-Sat. 9 a.m.-5 a.m., Sun. 1-4 p.m., admission $4.50 adults, $2.50 children 6-18, opened as a museum in 1932! In 1856, a second story was added, which provided more room and a perfect view of the harbor. In 1926, Haili St. was extended past the home, and at that time the Wilcox and Lyman families had the house turned parallel to the street so that it would front the entrance.

The furniture is authentic "Sandwich Isles" circa 1850, the best pieces fashioned from koa. Much of it has come from other missionary homes, although many pieces belonged to the original occupants.

The floors, mantels, and doors are deep, luxurious koa. The main door is a "Christian door," built by the Hilo Boys Boarding School. The top panels form a cross and the bottom depicts an open Bible. Many of the artifacts on the deep windowsills are tacked down because of earthquakes. One room was used as a schoolroom/dayroom where Mrs. Lyman taught arithmetic, map-making, and proper manners. The dining room holds an original family table that was set with the "Blue Willow" china seen in a nearby hutch. Some of the most interesting exhibits are of small personal items like a music box that still plays, and a collection of New England autumn leaves that Mrs. Lyman had sent over to show her children what that season was like. Upstairs are bedrooms that were occupied by the parents and the eight children (six were boys). Their portraits hang in a row. Mrs. Lyman kept a diary and faithfully recorded eruptions, earthquakes, and tsunamis. Scientists still refer to it for some of the earliest recorded data on these natural disturbances. The master bedroom has a large bed with pineapples carved into the bedposts, crafted by a ship's carpenter who lived with the family for about eight months. The bedroom mirror is an original, in which many Hawaiians received their first surprised look at themselves. A nursery holds a cradle used by all eight children. It's obvious that the Lymans did not live luxuriously, but they were comfortable in their new island home.

Next door to the Lyman House, in a modern two-story building, is the museum. The first floor is designated the **Island Heritage Gallery.** The entry is a replica of a Hawaiian grass house, complete with thatched roof and floor mats. Nearby are Hawaiian tools: hammers of clinkstone, chisels of basalt, and state-of-the-art "stone age" polishing stones with varying textures used to rub bowls and canoes to a smooth finish. Hawaiian fiberwork, the best in Polynesia, is the next display. As well as coconut and pandanus, the Hawaiians used the pliable air root of the *ie'ie*. The material, dyed brown or black, was woven into intricate designs. You'll also see fishhooks, stone lamps, mortars and pes-

Rainbow Falls

J.D. BISIGNANI

tles, *lomi lomi* sticks, even a display on *kahuna*, with a fine text on the *kapu* system. Pre-contact displays give way to kimonos from Japan, a Chinese herbal medicine display, and a nook dedicated to Filipino heritage. Saying good-bye is a bust of Mark Twain, carved into a piece of the very monkeypod tree that he planted in Waiohinu in 1866.

Upstairs is the **Earth Heritage Gallery.** The mineral and rock collection here is rated one of the top 10 in the entire country, and by far the best in Polynesia. Marvel at thunder eggs, agates, jaspers, India blue mezolite, aquamarine lazurite from Afghanistan, and hunks of weirdly shaped lava. These displays are the lifelong collection of the great-grandson of the original Rev. Lyman. Anything coming from the earth can be exhibited here: shells named and categorized from around the world, petrified wood, glass paperweights, crystals, and Chinese artifacts. Other exhibits explain the geology and volcanology of Kilauea and Mauna Kea, and an entire section is dedicated to the vanishing flora and fauna of Hawaii. The museum is an educational delight.

Natural Sites And Walking Tour

Start your tour of Hilo by picking up a pamphlet/ map entitled *Discover Downtown Hilo, A Walking Tour of Historic Sites,* free at most restaurants, hotels, and shops. This self-guiding pamphlet takes you down the main streets and back lanes where you discover the unique architecture of Hilo's glory days. The majority of the vintage buildings have been restored and the architecture varies from the continental style of the Hawaiian Telephone Building to the Zen Buddhist Taishoji Shoto Mission.

A remarkable building is the old police station just across from Kalakaua Park. Behind it, in a classic plantation building, is the home of the **East Hawaii Culture Center,** a nonprofit organization which supports local arts and hosts varying festivals, performances, and workshops throughout the year (see p. 99).

After you leave the Lyman Museum, it's a short walk over to Hilo's library, 300 Waianuenue Avenue. Sitting at the entrance are two large stones. The larger is called the **Naha Stone,** known for its ability to detect any offspring of the ruling Naha clan. The test was simple: place a baby on the stone, and if the infant remained silent, he or she was Naha; if the baby cried, he or she wasn't. It is believed that this 7,000-pound monolith was brought from Kauai by canoe and placed near Pinao Temple in the immediate vicinity of what is now Wailuku Dr. and Keawe Street. Kamehameha the Great supposedly fulfilled a prophecy of "moving a mountain" by budging this stone. The smaller stone is thought to be an entrance pillar of the Pinao Temple. Just behind the library is the Wailuku River. Pick any of its bridges for a panoramic view down to the sea. Often, local fishermen try their luck from the Wailuku's grassy banks. The massive boulder sitting in the river's mouth is known as Maui's Canoe.

A few miles out of town, heading west on Waianuenue Ave., are two natural spectacles definitely worth a look. Just past Hilo High School a sign directs you to Wailuku River State Park. Here is **Rainbow Falls,** a most spectacular yet easily visited natural wonder. You'll look down on a circular pool in the river below that's almost 100 feet in diameter; cascading into it is a lovely waterfall. The falls deserve their name because as they hit the water below, their mists throw flocks of rainbows into the air. Underneath the falls is a huge cavern. Most people are content to look from the vantage point near the parking lot, but if you walk to the left a stone stairway leads to a private viewing area directly over the falls. Here the river, strewn with volcanic boulders, pours over the edge. Follow the path for a minute or so along the bank to a gigantic banyan tree and a different vantage point.

Follow Waianuenue Ave. for two more miles past Hilo Hospital to the heights above town. A sign to turn right onto Pee Pee Falls Street points to the **Boiling Pots.** Usually no one is here. At the parking lot is an emergency phone and toilets. Follow the path past No Swimming signs to an overlook. Indented into the riverbed below are a series of irregularly shaped holes that look as though a peg-legged giant left his peg prints in the hot lava. Seven or eight resemble naturally bubbling Jacuzzis. Turn your head upriver to see Pee Pee Falls, a gorgeous, five-spouted waterfall. You'll have this area to yourself, and it's great for a quiet picnic lunch.

Around Banyan Drive

If your Hilo hotel isn't situated along Banyan Dr., go there. This bucolic road skirts the edge of the Waiakea Peninsula that sticks out into Hilo Bay. Lining the drive is an almost uninterrupted series of banyans forming a giant hedgerow, while the fairways and greens of the Banyan Golf Course take up the center of the tiny peninsula. Park your car at one end and take a 15-minute stroll through this parklike atmosphere; the banyans have been named for well-known American luminaries. Boutiques and a variety of restaurants sit in the coolness under the trees.

Liliuokalani Gardens are formal Japanese-style gardens located along the west end of Banyan Drive. Meditatively quiet, they offer a beautiful view of the bay. **Coconut Island** just offshore is connected by a footbridge leading from the gardens. Along the footpaths are pagodas designed for relaxing, *torii* gates, stone lanterns, and half-moon bridges spanning a series of ponds and streams. Few people visit, and if it weren't for the striking fingers of black lava and coconut trees, you could easily be in Japan.

Suisan Fish Market is at the corner of Banyan Dr. and Lihiwai St., which crosses Kame-

Suisan Fish Auction is
perfect for bargains
and local color.

hameha Avenue. This fish auction draws island fishermen of every nationality. The auctioneer's staccato is pure pidgin. Restaurateurs, housewives, and a smattering of tourists gather by 7:30 a.m. to eyeball the catch of the day. Boats tie up and fishermen talk quietly about the prices. Next door, a small snack shop sells sandwiches and piping-hot coffee. Grab a cup and walk over to the gardens through a nearby entrance—you'll have them to yourself.

Cross Lihiwai St. heading south. **Waiakea Pond,** a brackish lagoon where people often fish, is on your right. To the left are **Hoolulu County Park, Civic Center Auditorium,** and a city nursery brimming with orchids. The **Culture Center Nihon** is here too, at 123 Lihiwai St.; it displays artwork and cultural exhibits from Japan. The center is also a restaurant and sushi bar, with a special room set aside for the "tea ceremony." (For more details see "Food" in the "Practicalities" section.)

On the opposite side of Waiakea Fish Pond (drive down Kamehameha Ave. and make a left onto Pauahi St. since no bridges cross), you'll find **Wailoa Information Center** dispensing all manner of brochures and pamphlets on Hilo and Big Island activities. The walls of this 10-sided building are used to display works of local artists and cultural/historic exhibits, changed on a monthly basis. Across the parking lot in a grassy area is the Tsunami Memorial, dedicated to those who lost their lives in the devastating tidal waves that raked the island.

Volcanic stone, inlaid with blue and green tile, has been laid to form a circular wall that undulates and peaks like a wave. It's worth a look.

Hilo's Gardens

Hilo's greatest asset is its flowers. Its biggest cash crops are orchids and anthuriums. Flowers grow everywhere, but to see them in a more formalized way, visit one of the following nurseries in and around town. Most have excellent prices for floral arrangements sent back to the Mainland. They'll do a Hawaiian bouquet with heliconia, anthuriums, and orchids for around $25 including shipping. The flowers arrive neatly packaged but unassembled, with a picture of the arrangement so that you can put them together yourself. These hearty cut flowers will look fresh and vibrant for as long as two weeks, so a few days in the mail won't hurt them. (Also see "Hawaii Tropical Botanical Gardens," p. 164.)

Hilo Tropical Gardens and Gallery, (formerly Kong's Floraleigh), 1477 Kalanianaole Ave., Hilo, HI 96720, tel. 935-4957, is open daily 9 a.m.-5 p.m. The admission price of $3 (children under 12 free) includes a free cup of Kona coffee. Here you can go on a self-guided tour through the gardens; all plants have been labeled. Everything's here: plumeria, lipstick trees, anthuriums, orchids, birds of paradise, even pineapples, coconuts, and papayas. You can purchase all manner of dried and fresh-cut flowers, seeds, packaged plants, seedlings, and corsages. The Gallery Gift Shop features art and local crafts of the Big Island, including prints, books, wood items and pottery. The "no-pressure" salespeople are courteous and friendly. Shipping purchases is no problem.

Along Kilauea Ave., between Lanikaula and Kawili streets, the Department of Natural Resources, Division of Forestry maintains the **Hilo Arboretum,** open Mon.-Fri. 7:45 a.m.-4:30 p.m., closed Sat., Sun., and holidays; free. This tree nursery contains most of the trees present in Hawaii, including indigenous and imported specimens. The office will provide you with a mimeographed sheet entitled "Hilo Nursery Arboretum." It's basically a self-guided tour, but the clerks will warn you that it's not very good. It attempts to name the trees by matching them with points on the map as you pass by, instead of referring to signs on each specimen. However, the trees are magnificent and you will have this quiet area virtually to yourself. Originally the site was an animal quarantine station operated by the Territory of Hawaii; the 19.4 acres of the arboretum were established in 1920 by Brother Mathias Newell. Brother Newell was a nurseryman employed by the Catholic boys' school in Hilo. At that time the Division of Forestry was already actively introducing plant species from all over the world. For the 40 years from 1921-61 the department was engaged in the development and maintenance of arboretums consisting primarily of plant species from Australia and Africa. Arboretum sites ranged from sea level to Mauna Kea. Plant materials were exchanged and thousands of breadfruit cuttings were exported. Over 1,000 different tree species and 500 different fruit trees were field tested. Here at the Hilo Arboretum over 1,000 trees were planted. A few trees such as the paper bark and some pines are more than 50 years old. Presently a small number of timber species are grown for reforestation purposes. Essentially the Hilo site is utilized for the propagation of rare and endangered plant species, for research, and for experimental pursuits.

Nani Mau Gardens are some of the largest in and around Hilo, and touring these spectacular displays is well worth an afternoon. Located at 421 Makalika St. (off Route 11), Hilo, HI 96720, tel. 959-3541, the gardens are open daily 8:30 a.m.-5 p.m. Admission is $5, golf cart for touring $6. The gardens consist of 20 sculpted acres; 33 more are being developed. More than a botanical garden, Nani Mau is a "floral theme park" designed as a tourist attraction. Walks throughout the garden are very tame but very beautiful; umbrellas are provided during rainy weather, which adds its own dripping, crystalline charm to the experience. Plants are labeled in English, Latin, and Japanese. The gardens are a huge but ordered display of flowers, flowering trees, and shrubbery. The wildly colored plumage of tropical birds here and there competes with the colors of the exotic blooms. The gardens are broken off into separate areas: fruit orchards, heliconia garden, ginger garden, anthurium garden, orchid garden, orchid pavilion, gardenia garden, and bromeliad garden. The new 33 acres include an annual garden, white-sand beach, small volcano, picture garden for photos, and orchids and more orchids. It also features floral sculptures, a small reflective pond, and an assortment of flowers and shrubs laid out in geometric patterns, hearts, mountains, and even "aloha" and "Hilo Hawaii" spelled out with flowers. The tourist shop and snack area is exactly like a Japanese *omiyage* (souvenir) shop. No wonder, since it's owned by Japanese, and the tour buses coming here are all filled with Japanese. If you enjoy a clean, outdoor experience surrounded by magnificent flowers, this is the place.

Tanaka's is an excellent nursery from which to buy and to send flowers. They call themselves Jewel Box Orchids and also The Orchidarium, Hawaii Inc., at 524 Manono St., Hilo, HI. It's off the main track. Follow Route 11 toward Volcano, make a right on Kekuanaoa St., and go down four blocks to Manono. Make a right and they're a few hundred yards down on the left. For beautiful orchids at unbeatable prices, search them out.

While in the neighborhood, visit **Paradise Plants** at 575 Hinano St., tel. 935-4043, a complete garden center specializing in indoor-outdoor plants and tropical fruit trees. They send orchids and other live flowers to the Mainland. Also featured are a large gift area with gifts from around the world. While browsing, check out their free orchid garden, which ranks as Hilo's oldest.

Kualoa Farms is at the corner of Mamaki (off Route 11) and Kealakai streets, tel. 959-4565, open daily 8 a.m.-4 p.m. A guided tour takes you over some of the 62 acres planted in anthuriums, ti plants, torch gingers, and macadamia and papaya orchards.

Nani Mau Gardens

Mauna Loa Macadamia Nut Factory is located along Mauna Loa Rd., eight miles out of Hilo on Route 11 heading towards Volcanoes National Park. Head down the drive until you come to the visitor center. Inside will be a free video explaining the development and processing of macadamia nuts in Hawaii. Take a self-guided tour through the orchards, where all trees and plants are identified. Then return to the snack shop for mac-nut goodies like ice cream and cookies. The gift shop has a wide assortment of mac-nut items at considerably lower prices than anywhere else on the island.

Panaewa Rainforest Zoo

Not many travelers can visit a zoo in such a unique setting where the animals virtually live in paradise. The road to the zoo is a trip in itself, getting you back into the country. Follow Route 11 toward Volcanoes National Park for a few miles until you see the sign pointing down Mamaki St. to the zoo. On a typical weekday, you'll have the place to yourself. The zoo, operated by the Department of Parks and Recreation, is open Mon.-Fri. 9 a.m.-4 p.m., Sat. 11 a.m.-2 p.m., gates locked at 4:15 p.m., closed Christmas and New Year's Day. Admission is free.

Here you have the feeling that the animals are not "fenced in" so much as you are "fenced out." The collection includes ordinary and exotic animals from around the world. You'll see a giant anteater from Costa Rica, pygmy hippos from Africa, and a wide assortment of birds like pheasants and peacocks. The zoo is also a botanical garden with many of the trees, shrubs, and ferns labeled. The zoo hosts many endangered animals indigenous to Hawaii like the Laysan duck, Hawaiian coot, *pueo,* Hawaiian gallinule, and even a feral pig in his own stone mini-condo. There are some great iguanas and mongooses, lemurs, and an aviary section with exotic birds like yellow-fronted parrots and blue and gold macaws. The central area is a tigers' playground; a tall fence marks this rather large area where tigers still rule their domain. It's got its own pond and tall grasses that make the tigers feel at home, but also make them hard to spot.

A touching spot is the **Astronaut Grove,** in memory of the astronauts who were killed on the regrettable explosion of the space shuttle *Challenger.* All are remembered, especially Ellison Onizuka, a native son of the Big Island. The zoo makes a perfect side trip for families or for anyone wishing to get off the beaten track.

Scenic Drive

Route 19 heading north from Hilo toward Honokaa is a must, with magnificent inland and coastal views one after another. (See "Hamakua Coast," p. 185, for full coverage of the northern section leading to Waipio.) Only five minutes from Hilo, you'll come to Papaikou town. Look for a small convenience store on the right. Just here is a road posted as a scenic drive which dips down toward the coast. Take it! Almost immediately a sign says "Narrow Winding Road,

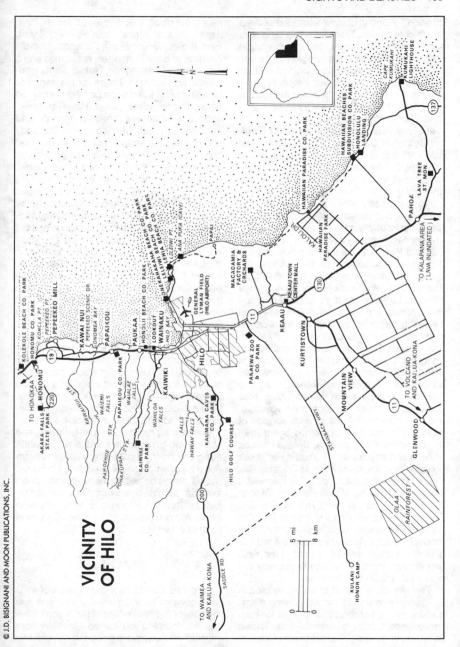

© J.D. BISIGNANI AND MOON PUBLICATIONS, INC.

VICINITY OF HILO

20 MPH," letting you know what kind of area you're coming into. Start down this lane past some very modest homes, and into the jungle that covers the road like a living green tunnel. Prepare for tiny bridges crossing tiny valleys. Stop, and you can almost hear the jungle growing. For those who have heard of the road to Hana, Maui, the Scenic Drive is a mini-version of what it has to offer.

In a few minutes you'll come to **Hawaii Tropical Botanical Gardens,** tel. 964-5233, open daily 8:30 a.m.-5:30 p.m., with the last shuttle van departing for the garden from the registration area at 4:30 p.m. Admission is $12, children under 16 free. Remember that the $12 entrance fee not only allows you to walk through the best-tamed tropical rainforest on the Big Island, but helps preserve the area in perpetuity. The gardens were established in 1978 when Dan and Pauline Lutkenhouse purchased the property in order to educate the public to the beauty of tropical plants in their natural setting. The gardens have been open for viewing since 1984. Mr. Lutkenhouse, a retired San Francisco businessman, purchased the 25-acre valley and personally performed the work that transformed it into one of the most exotic spots in all of Hawaii. The locality was amazingly beautiful but inaccessible because it was so rugged. Through a personal investment of nearly $1 million and six painstaking years of toil aided only by two helpers, he hand-cleared the land, built trails and bridges, developed an irrigation system, acquired more than 2,000 different species of trees and plants, and established one mile of scenic trails and a large water lily lake stocked with *koi* and tropical fish. A shuttle van takes you on a five-minute ride down to Onomea Bay where the gardens are located. Onomea was a favorite spot with the Hawaiians, who came to fish and camp for the night. The valley was a fishing village called Kahlili in the early 1800s. Later on it became a rough-water seaport used for shipping sugarcane and other tropical products. Recently, a remake of *Lord of the Flies* was filmed here, and it's easy to see why the area made the perfect movie set.

The van drops you off at a staging area in the garden where you'll find self-guiding maps, drinking water, restrooms, umbrellas for your convenience, and jungle perfume—better known as mosquito repellent! Plants from the four corners of the globe, including Iran, Central China, Japan, tropical Africa, India, Borneo, Brazil, East Indies, South Pacific Islands, tropical America, and the Philippines, are named with a full botanical description. Native plants from Hawaii are included. Listen for the songs of birds: the white-tailed tropic bird, black-crowned heron, Pacific golden plover, Hawaiian hawk, Japanese white eye, common mynah, and northern cardinal. Choose one of the aptly named trails like Ocean Trail or Waterfall Trail and lose yourself in the beauty of the surroundings. You are in the middle of a tamed jungle, walking along manicured paths. Stroll the Ocean Trail down to the sea, where the rugged coastline is dramatically pummeled by frothy waves. You can hear the waves entering submerged lava caves, where they blow in and out like a giant bellows. Away from the sea you'll encounter screened gazebos filled with exotic birds like cockatoos from Indonesia and blue-fronted Amazon parrots. Walk the inland trails past waterfalls, streams, a bamboo grove, and innumerable flowers. For at least a brief time you get to feel the power and beauty of a living Garden of Eden.

Hawaiian Artifacts, just a minute down Scenic Drive past the gardens, is a shop owned and operated by Paul Gephart, tel. 964-1729, open Mon.-Sat. 9 a.m.-5 p.m. Paul creates wood sculptures mainly from koa and ohia that he turns into whales, dolphins, birds, and poi bowls. Here's also a small but tasteful collection of jewelry and seashells, all at very decent prices.

Continue for another two to three miles, and you'll come to a wooden bridge with a white railing overlooking a cascading mountain stream with a big swimming hole. Great for a freshwater dip, but always be careful: these streams can be torrential during a heavy rain. The side road rejoins Route 19 at Papeeko, a workers' village where you can get gas or supplies. (For points north see "Hamakua Coast," p. 185.)

BEACHES

If you define a beach as a long expanse of white sand covered by a thousand sunbathers and their beach umbrellas, then Hilo doesn't have any. If a beach, to you, can be a smaller, more intimate affair where a good but not gigantic

Richardson Beach

J.D. BISIGNANI

number of tourists and families can spend the day on pockets of sand between fingers of black lava, then Hilo has plenty. Hilo's best beaches all lie to the east of the city along Kalanianaole Ave., which runs six miles from downtown Hilo to its dead end at Leleiwi Point. Not all beaches are clearly marked, but they are easily spotted by cars parked along the road or in makeshift parking lots.

Hilo Bayfront Park is a thousand yards of black sand that narrows considerably as it runs west from the Wailoa River toward downtown. At one time it went all the way to the Wailuku River and was renowned throughout the islands for its beauty, but commercialism of the harbor has ruined it. By the 1960s, so much sewage and industrial waste had been pumped into the bay that it was considered a public menace, and then the great tsunami came. Reclamation projects created the Wailoa River State Recreation Area at the east end, and shorefront land became a buffer zone against future inundation. Few swimmers come to the beach because the water is cloudy and chilly, but the sharks don't seem to mind! The bay is terrific for fishing and picnicking, and the sails of small craft and windsurfers can always be seen. It's a perfect spot for canoe races, and many local teams come here to train. Notice the judging towers and canoe sheds. Toward the west end, near the mouth of the Wailuku River, surfers catch long rides during the winter months, entertaining spectators.

Coconut Island Park is reached by footbridge from a spit of land just outside Liliuokalani Gardens. It was at one time a *pu'uhonua* ("place of refuge") opposite a human sacrificial *heiau* on the peninsula side. Coconut Island has restrooms, a pavilion, and picnic tables shaded by tall coconut trees and ironwoods. A favorite picnic spot for decades, it has a diving tower and a sheltered natural pool area for children. The only decent place to swim in Hilo Bay, it also offers the best panorama of the city, bay, and Mauna Kea beyond.

Reeds Bay Beach Park is on the east side of the Waiakea Peninsula at the end of Banyan Drive. It too is technically part of Hilo Bay, and offers good swimming, though the water is notoriously cold because of a constantly flowing freshwater spring. Most people just picnic here, and fishermen frequent the area.

Keaukaha Beach, located on Puhi Bay, is the first in a series of beaches as you head east on Kalanianaole Avenue. Look for Baker Ave. and pull off to the left into a parking area near an old pavilion. This is a favorite spot with local people, who swim at "Cold Water Pond," a spring-fed inlet at the head of the bay. A sewage treatment plant fronts the western side of Puhi Bay. Much nicer areas await just up Kalanianaole Avenue.

Onekahakaha Beach Park has it all: safe swimming, white-sand beach, lifeguards, all amenities, and camping. Turn left onto Machida Ln. and park in the lot of Hilo's favorite "family" beach, although very recently a number of local homeless people have been living in this area. Swim in the large, sandy-bottomed pool protected by the breakwater. Outside the breakwater the currents can be fierce and drownings have been recorded. Walk east along the shore to find an undeveloped area of the park with many small tidal pools. Beware of sea urchins.

James Kealoha Park is next; people swim, snorkel, and fish, and during winter months it's a favorite surfing spot. A large grassy area is shaded by trees and a picnic pavilion. Just offshore is an island known as Scout Island because local boy scouts often camp here. This entire area was known for its fishponds, and inland, just across Kalanianaole Ave., is Loko'aka Pond, a commercial operation providing the best mullet on the island.

Leleiwi Beach Park lies along a lovely residential area carved into the rugged coastline. Part of the park is dedicated to the Richardson Ocean Center, and the entire area is locally called **Richardson's Beach.** Look for Uwau St., just past the Mauna Loa Shores Condo, and park along the road here. Look for a fancy house surrounded by tall coconut trees and follow the pathway through the grove. Use a shower that's coming out of the retaining wall surrounding the house. Keep walking until you come to a seawall. A tiny cove with a black-sand beach is the first in a series. This is a terrific area for snorkeling, with plenty of marinelife. Walk east to a natural lava breakwater. Behind it are pools filled and flushed by the surging tide. The water breaks over the top of the lava and rushes into the pools, making natural Jacuzzis. This is one of the most picturesque swimming areas on the island. At Leleiwi Beach Park proper (three pavilions), the shore is open to the ocean and there are strong currents; it's best to head directly to Richardson's.

Lehia Park is the end of the road. When the pavement stops, follow the dirt track until you come to a large, grassy field shaded by a variety of trees. This unofficial camping area has no amenities whatsoever. A series of pools like those at Richardson's are small, sandy-bottomed, and safe. Outside of the natural lava breakwater, currents are treacherous. Winter often sends tides surging inland here, making Lehia unusable. This area is about as far away as you can get and still be within a few minutes of downtown Hilo.

PRACTICALITIES

ACCOMMODATIONS

Accommodations in Hilo are hardly ever booked out, and they're reasonably priced. Sounds great, but many hotels have "gone condo" to survive while others have simply shut their doors, so there aren't as many as there once were. During the Merrie Monarch Festival (late April), the entire town is booked solid! The best hotels are clustered along Banyan Dr., with a few gems tucked away on the city streets.

Banyan Drive Hotels

The following hotels lie along Banyan Drive. They range from moderate to deluxe; all are serviced by the Banyan Shuttle (see pp. 138-139).

Prices at the classy **Hilo Hawaiian Hotel,** 71 Banyan Dr., Hilo, HI 96720, tel. 935-9361 or (800) 272-5275, start at $99-122; all rooms have a/c, phone, and TV, plus there's a pool. The Hilo Hawaiian occupies the most beautiful grounds of any hotel in Hilo. From the vantage of the hotel's colonnaded veranda, you overlook formal gardens, Coconut Island, and Hilo Bay. Designed as a huge arc, the hotel's architecture blends well with its surroundings and expresses the theme set by Hilo Bay, that of a long, sweeping crescent. The hotel buffet, especially the Friday and Saturday seafood version, is absolutely out of this world (see "Queen's Court" below). As a deluxe hotel, the Hilo Hawaiian is the best that Hilo has to offer.

Hawaii Naniloa Hotel, 93 Banyan Dr., Hilo, HI 96720, tel. 969-3333 or (800) 442-5845, is a massive, 386-room hotel offering deluxe accommodations. Rates start at $96 standard, $119 superior, $144 deluxe with private balcony. Private suites are available from $189. A third person costs $15 additional; children under 17 sharing with parents are free. They offer a/c, TV, hotel parking, restaurant, and a pool setting—just above the lava—that is the nicest in Hilo. The original hotel dates back over 60 years and has built up a fine reputation for value and service. The Hawaii Naniloa has recently undergone extensive renovations and is now as beautiful as ever.

Uncle Billy's Hilo Bay Hotel is sandwiched between much larger hotels at 87 Banyan Dr., Hilo, HI 96720, tel. 961-5818 or (800) 367-5102. Rooms here begin at $59 d (including breakfast for two), $69 for a kitchenette, and $74 for a room-and-car package. The Hilo Bay's blue metal roof and orange louvered shutters make it look a bit like "Howard Johnson's Meets Polynesia." The lobby's rattan furniture and thatched long-house theme is pure '50s-kitsch Hawaii. There is parking and a pool, all rooms are clean and air-conditioned, and each one has a TV and phone. The hotel offers excellent value for the money. Uncle Billy's Polynesian Marketplace, where you can buy everything from beer to sundries, is part of the complex.

You can't miss the orange-and-black **Hilo Seaside Hotel,** 126 Banyan Dr., tel. 935-0821 or (800) 367-7000. This is the budget hotel on Banyan Drive. It's island-owned by the Kimi family, and like the others in this small chain, it's clean and well kept and has Polynesian-inspired decor. Room prices are $49 standard, $59 superior, $66 deluxe, and $76 kitchenette. Add approximately $20 for a room/car package. Ask about off-season rates, and they will sometimes offer a better rate depending on the amount of business at the time. The grounds are laid out around a central courtyard and the pool is secluded away from the street. At this family-style hotel with a motel atmosphere, the friendly staff goes out of its way to make you feel welcome.

The **Country Club Condo Hotel,** 121 Banyan Dr., tel. 935-7171, is a basic hotel/condo with very reasonable rates. Standard rooms are $39, deluxe ocean $59, one-bedroom suites $80. Weekly and monthly rates are available. Since this is a condo hotel, the rooms vary from unit to unit, but most have either double beds or a queen-sized bed.

Downtown Hotels

The following hotels are found along Hilo's downtown streets. Some are in quiet residential areas, while others are along busy thoroughfares. They are moderately to inexpensively priced.

*John Alexander of the
Dolphin Bay Hotel*

J.D. BISIGNANI

Dolphin Bay Hotel is a sparkling little gem—simply the best hotel bargain in Hilo, one of those places where you get more than you pay for. It sits on a side street in the Puueo section of town at the north end of Hilo Bay: 333 Iliahi St., Hilo, HI 96720, tel. 935-1466. John Alexander, the owner/manager, is at the front desk every day. He's a font of information about the Big Island, and will happily dispense advice on how to make your day-trips fulfilling. The hotel was built by his father, who spent years in Japan, and you'll be happy to discover this influence when you sink deep into the *ofuro*-type tubs in every room. All 18 units have full modern kitchens. Rates are single studio apartment $39 s, $49 d; superior $49 s, $59 d; one bedroom $69 d; two-bedroom, fully furnished unit $79 d, $10 additional guest. Deluxe units upstairs have open-beam ceilings and lanais, and with three spacious rooms feel like apartments. No swimming pool or a/c, but there are color TVs and fans with excellent cross ventilation. The grounds and housekeeping are immaculate. Hotel guests can partake of free bananas, papayas, and other exotic fruits found in hanging baskets in the lobby, as well as free coffee. Weekly rates range from $315 for a studio to $525 for a two-bedroom deluxe. Make reservations, because everyone who has found the Dolphin Bay comes back again and again.

The Wild Ginger Inn, at 100 Puueo St., Hilo, HI 96720, tel. 935-5556, (800) 882-1887, is a refurbished plantation-style hotel, painted shocking pink and green, that bills itself as a bed-and-breakfast inn. An open-aired lobby leads to an encircling veranda overlooking the central courtyard area, with a view of the bay in the distance. Each of the wainscoted rooms, very basic but very clean, has a refrigerator, private shower-bath, cross ventilation, and one double and one twin bed. A double hammock and vintage chairs in the lobby area are for your relaxation. Rates are standard room $39 d, deluxe rooms with cable TV $49-59, special weekly and monthly rates, and extra person $10. The homestyle Hawaiian buffet is terrific: guava-passion juice, milk, local coffee with macadamia nuts, granola, yogurt, muffins, hard-boiled eggs, island fruits in season, turkey-ham, cheese, and toast. The inn is completely nonsmoking with a special area provided for smokers in the garden. The Wild Ginger Inn, with a friendly staff and good service, is an excellent choice for budget accommodations, and gives more than full value for the money.

The Hilo Hotel is downtown at 142 Kinoole St., Hilo, HI 96720, tel. 961-3733. This vintage hotel originally opened in 1888 and was managed by Uncle George Lycurgus, who was more famous as manager of Volcano House. The present buildings date from 1955, and although additions have been made over the years, a sense of nostalgia lingers. Basic rooms in the old wing, all with phone and fridge, are $39-45; deluxe new-wing suites, quieter and with a/c, are $85-115. A big front porch is great for relaxing, and complimentary coffee is served at the pool every morning. The Hilo Hotel is also home to the Fuji Restaurant (see p. 175). This is a classic hotel where you get full value for your money, and where the staff takes pride in doing things the right way.

The **Iolani Hotel,** 193 Kinoole St., Hilo, HI 96720, and the **Kamaaina Hotel** at 110 Haili St., are your basic fleabag dives. You can get a room at either for about $30 per night or $135 p/w if you can find someone to check you in. For information contact Mrs. Beatie at The Surplus Store, 284 Keawe St., tel. 935-6398, only after noon. She doesn't seem overly anxious to rent these rooms, so you'll have to persevere.

Arnott's Lodge, 98 Apapane Rd., Hilo, HI 96720, tel. 969-7097, (800) 368-8752 Mainland, (800) 953-7773 Hawaii, is a very reasonably priced hostel offering a dormitory bunk for $15, and semiprivate rooms with shared bath, kitchen, and living room for $26 s, $36 d. Arnott's also offers inexpensive hiking and snorkel excursions.

If a hotel is not your style, and if you would appreciate something a little more . . . well, homey, try **Holmes' Sweet Home B&B,** at 107 Koula St., Hilo, HI 96720, tel. 961-9089, the residence of John and Charlotte Holmes. Located on a quiet cul-de-sac with a view of Hilo Bay, the home provides two rooms priced $60-70 (no credit cards) that feature their own private entrances, baths, and guest refrigerator and microwave. A continental breakfast is included.

FOOD

Inexpensive Dining

Named after the famous all-Japanese fighting battalion that even predated the famous "442," the **Cafe 100,** at 969 Kilauea Ave., open Mon.-Thurs. 6:45 a.m.-8:30 p.m., Fri.-Sat. until 9:30 p.m., is a Hilo institution. The Miyashiro family has been serving food at their indoor-outdoor restaurant here since the late '50s. Although the *loco moco,* a cholesterol atom bomb containing a hamburger and egg atop rice smothered in gravy, was invented at Hilo's Lincoln Grill, the Cafe 100, serving it since 1961, has actually patented this belly-buster and turned it into an art form. There are the regular loco moco, the teriyaki loco, the sukiyaki loco, the

hot dog loco, the *oyako* loco, and for the health conscious, the mahi loco. With a few exceptions, they cost $2 or less. So, if your waistline, the surgeon general, and your arteries permit, this is *the* place to have one. Breakfast choices include everything from bacon and eggs to coffee and donuts, while lunches feature beef stew $3.75, mixed plate $3.95, fried chicken $3.25, and an assortment of sandwiches from teri-beef to a good old BLT for $2 or so. Make your selection and sit at one of the picnic tables under the veranda to watch the people of Hilo go by.

All trips to Hilo must include a brief stop at **Low's International Food,** long occupying the corner of Kilauea and Ponahawai streets, tel. 969-6652, open daily except Wednesday, 9 a.m.-8 p.m., where *everyone* comes for the unique bread. Some of the more fanciful loaves are made from taro, breadfruit, guava, mango, passion fruit, coconut, banana, pumpkin, and cinnamon. The so-you-want-to-taste-it-all rainbow bread is a combination of taro, guava, and sweetbread. Loaves cost $4.25-5.25, and arrangements can be made to ship them home by Federal Express. Lunches, most under $5, range from their famous pot-roast pork tail with black bean sauce to turkey plate to lamb curry stew. Choose a table under the pavilion and enjoy your picnic in downtown Hilo.

Jasper's Espresso Cafe at 110 Kalakaua, tel. 969-6686, is open daily for lunch and dinner 11 a.m.-7:45 p.m., Fri. and Sat. until 9:45 p.m., and for Sunday brunch 9 a.m.-2 p.m. It is not only a politically correct, community-oriented restaurant housed in a vintage bakery building from the 1920s, but also has the most ceiling fans per square foot in Hilo, and the town's most elegant toilet (worth a visit regardless of whether nature is calling!). Jasper, the owner, serves "food with an attitude," and tries to keep it organic, island-fresh, mostly vegetarian, and wholesome. Racks hold environmental and peace-oriented magazines that you can browse while sipping espresso and listening to quiet acoustic guitar most evenings, or poetry on Fridays. The menu offers garden salad of mixed greens $2.50 (with soup $7.25), Caesar salad $5.50 (with soup $8.25), garden burger $5.50, or a good old crunchy peanut butter sandwich $2 (half orders available). The best deal, however, is an order of pinto beans and brown rice ($3.75) made more savory with toppings of salsa, sour cream, cheese, onions, and jalapeños (add 50 cents). Desserts are scrumptious: homemade Hilo ice cream, chocolate-caramel-macadamia nut cake $3.50, and brownies made with cream cheese, mac nut, chocolate, and peanut butter $1.50. Jasper's is a terrific spot to relax and catch up on world events at the same time. Prices are unbeatable, and the service is friendly.

Mun Cheong Lau is a cheap Chinese joint in downtown Hilo at 172 Kilauea Ave., tel. 935-3040 (takeout too), open daily 11 a.m.-11 p.m., closed Tuesday. If you want to eat with "the people," this is the spot. Soups on the front of the menu are $3.50; those on the back are $2.50, and are about the same except that they don't contain noodles. The servings are generous. Entrees like crispy chicken in oyster sauce for under $5 are delicious at any price. Seafoods include abalone with vegies for $3.40, abalone with black mushrooms $4.50, and shrimp with corn $3.75. A variety of pork or beef dishes are all priced under $3.50, while pineapple spareribs are $2.70 and boneless chicken with mushrooms is $3.75. These are full plates served with steamed rice, 60 cents extra if you want fried rice. For under $4 you can fill up in this place. It's clean, service is friendly, and the dining experience, while certainly not fancy, is definitely authentic.

Owned and operated by Dotty and Rey Frasco, **Dotty's Coffee Shop and Restaurant,** tel. 959-6477, at the Puainako Town Center, is open for breakfast daily 7-11 a.m., for lunch Mon.-Sat. 10:30 a.m.-2 p.m., and for dinner Mon.-Thurs. 5-8 p.m., Fri. 5-9 p.m. Dotty's is an institution where local people come for the large and hearty portions. Breakfast is known for the corned beef hash and eggs and for French toast made with thick slices of sweet bread from Punaluu covered with real maple or coconut syrup at $3.75. Lunch favorites are grilled chicken supreme with mushrooms and Swiss cheese $4.65, or Dotty's ultimate steak sandwich with slices of sirloin, sautéed mushrooms, onions, and Swiss cheese on a grilled potato roll $5.65. Those in the know come from around the island to dine on Dotty's famous oven-roasted turkey, fresh catch of the day, barbecued pork ribs with their own smoke-flavored sauce, and an amazing combination plate for $9.85 that gives you a choice of two: top sirloin, teriyaki steak, ribs, scampi, sautéed shrimp, or the catch-of-the-

day. Fresh vegetables, real mashed potatoes, and homemade soups (great chowder on Friday) come with all full meals. The decor is "American standard" with a formica counter and leatherette booths. Check out the black-and-white photos hanging on the walls.

Ting Hao Mandarin Kitchen is a family affair run by Alice Chang and her sister, also in the Puainako Town Center, tel. 959-6288, open weekdays 11 a.m.-8:30 p.m., weekends 5-8:30 p.m. Seek them out for a mouth-watering, home-cooked meal. The two most expensive items on the menu are Seafood Treasure for $6, and half a tea-smoked duck for $7; all others are under $5. Service is slow due to individual-order cooking, and those in the know pick up a handout menu and call to place their orders 30 minutes before arriving. Also at Puainako Town Center is **Five Spice** with an assortment of *bento* for under $4 and quick snacks like chili and rice $1.90, and chili dogs $1.95.

Bear's Coffee Shop, at 106 Keawe, tel. 935-0708, just down the street from Roussel's, is an upscale coffee shop renowned for its breakfast, served daily 7-11:30 a.m. It features Belgian waffles (made from malted flour) and an assortment of egg dishes for $2.95. Lunch is hearty sandwiches of turkey, pastrami, chicken fillet, tuna, or ham for under $5, along with a small but zesty selection of Mexican food as well as salads. Beverages include Italian sodas, homemade lemonade, and a large selection of coffee, cappuccino, and caffe latte from their full espresso bar. All perfect with desserts like carrot cake, Bear's brownies, cheesecake, and pies. A great place to relax, read the morning paper, and watch Hilo life go by.

Kay's Family Restaurant, at 684 Kilauea Ave., tel. 969-1776, open Tues.-Sun. 5 a.m.-2 p.m. and 5-9 p.m., can't be beat for a good square meal of Asian, Hawaiian, or American standards. Sandwich favorites like hamburgers, fish burgers, grilled cheese, and tuna are all under $3. Large bowls of saimin and wonton soups are under $4. Their grilled plates, like Korean barbecued beef or *kalbi* (short ribs), are cooked over an open wood fire and are delicious. Combo plates of their grilled offerings are $5.95 for one choice, $6.95 for two choices, and $7.95 for three choices, and include rice, miso soup, four kinds of kimchi, and vegetables. Kay's isn't much to look at, with leatherette booths and formica tables, but it's a winner.

The **Ichiban Deli,** at 415 Kilauea Ave., across from the Hilo Hongwanji Temple, open Tues.-Sat. 7 a.m.-2 p.m. and 5-8:30 p.m., takeout available, is a basic Japanese-Hawaiian-American restaurant with breakfast like eggs with bacon or link sausage or corned beef hash $3.35, and lunches like fried chicken or spareribs, each at $4.25. The Japanese meals are standards like *bento* or tempura for under $5. No decor at all, but the prices are very reasonable.

Satsuki's, along the 200 block of Keawe St., receives the highest recommendation because when local people want a good meal at an inexpensive price they head here. Open for lunch 10 a.m-2 p.m., dinner 4:30-9 p.m., closed Tuesday. Specialties are oxtail soup, the lunch special for $4.25, and the Okinawa *soba* plate lunch for only $3.95. Dinner specials are beef teriyaki for $5.70, *tonkatsu* $5.65, and fish teriyaki $7.50. Plenty of traditional favorites like *donburi* and *nabemono.* All meals come with miso soup, Japanese pickles and condiments, rice, and tea. No decor, but spotlessly clean and friendly. Excellent food at excellent value.

Sachi's Gourmet, only a few seconds away at 250 Keawe St., open Mon. 8 a.m.-2 p.m. only, Tues.-Sat. 8 a.m.-2 p.m. and dinner 5-9 p.m., Sun. dinner only 5-9 p.m., is the same type of restaurant as Satsuki's, with its own loyal local clientele. The food is excellent here, too, and the prices are unbeatable. You'll walk away stuffed on traditional Japanese food for about $8 for a full meal.

Dick's Coffee House in the Hilo Shopping Center, tel. 935-2769, is American standard with a Hawaiian twist. Open daily 7 a.m.-7 p.m., Sun. 7-10:30 a.m., this place could be Smalltown, U.S.A., where the walls are covered with pennants, except that the waitresses wear outrageously colorful, Hawaiian-style uniforms. Excellent prices for decent food—full meals with soup, salad, dessert, and coffee go for $4.50.

Hukilau Restaurant at the Hilo Seaside Hotel (see above), 136 Banyan Way, is open daily 7 a.m.-1 p.m. and 4-9 p.m. For breakfast you can have steak and eggs $6.95, fish and eggs $2.95, two eggs and toast $1.85, ham omelette $2.75, or a full choice of hotcakes and waffles at reasonable prices. The lunch menu offers a choice of Reuben sandwich, steak and rice,

baked chicken, or hamburger deluxe; each choice comes with a buffet salad bar for a fixed price of $5.25. The dinner menu is reasonable with T-bone steak $10.95, steak and lobster $14.95, oven roast prime rib $9.95, or the captain's platter (fried fish, shrimp, scallops, and oysters) for $9.95. All dinners come with soup of the day and salad bar. The decor is orange Naugahyde booths and brown formica tables. Some of the vegetables come out of a can, and the deep-fried offerings have enough grease to clog the Alaska pipeline, but the view of Hilo Bay is exceptional and helps with digestion.

The **New China Restaurant,** at 510 Kilauea Ave., tel. 961-5677, open daily 10 a.m.-10 p.m., serves basic Chinese combo plates of chicken, duck, pork, beef, and seafood. The most expensive seafood on the menu is $7 for abalone and Chinese mushrooms. Special plates include steamed chicken with ginger, onion sauce, and steamed rice for $3.80; beef broccoli and crispy chicken for $2.80. Not much class—almost like a McDonald's of Chinese food—but it's bright, shiny, and sparkly.

When a Hilo resident wants a plate lunch, and that's saying something, they go to **Hilo Lunch Shop,** at the corner of Kalanikoa and Piilani, open daily except Sunday 6:15 a.m.-1:30 p.m. At this very basic restaurant, you pick and choose each separately priced item for your plate: tempura 90 cents; mahimahi 50 cents; vegetables 45 cents; for about $3 your plate will be huge. A minute away is **Snappy's Korean Barbecue,** a fairly new restaurant where dishes are priced well under $5.

Down Piilani, just at the Kentucky Fried Chicken, make a right onto Hinano St. and in a minute you'll see **Don's Grill,** tel. 935-9099, open daily except Monday 10:30 a.m.-9 p.m., and to 10 p.m. on Friday. This American/Hawaiian restaurant is known for good food at reasonable prices. Inside find wood-trimmed blue formica tables in a very modern yet functionally tasteful setting. Breakfast starts with two eggs and toast $2.50, omelettes $4.95, and on weekends only, sweet bread French toast $2.75. Lunch can be taco salad $4.95, Philadelphia cheese steak $5.95, club sandwich $4.50, or your own burger creation starting at $4.25. Entrees are barbecued ribs, pork chops, or fillet of fish, all priced under $6. There's homemade pie, cheesecake, and pudding to top off your meal. Don's is a basic American standard restaurant where you can get a good square meal for a good price.

Stratton's at 121 Banyan Dr., tel. 961-6815, is a sports bar/restaurant where many of the local people go for a few laughs and a few beers. The breakfast menu, offered daily 6:30-11 a.m., includes two large eggs and choice of sausage, ham, Portuguese sausage, or Spam along with toast, rice, or hash browns $4.25; mahimahi and eggs $4.50; breakfast special $2.95; and a full pancake breakfast for only $3.95. Lunch, served daily 11 a.m.-3 p.m., includes specials like teriyaki beef $5.65, and captain's platter (a combination of shrimp, oysters, and mahimahi) $7.95; or sandwiches like roast beef with sautéed onions $5.65 and a good old BLT $4.95. (Also see the following "Entertainment" section).

Fast Foods And Snacks

Okay! For those who must, **McDonald's** is at 88 Kanoelehua Ave. and 177 Ululani St., and **Pizza Hut,** which actually has a decent salad bar, is at 326 Kilauea Avenue. Fast-food junkies will be totally happy at the **Puainako Town Center,** where glass and formica cubes hold endless boxes of munchies from **McDonald's, Pizza Hut, Subway Sandwiches, and Taco Bell.**

On Banyan Dr. just outside of the Hilo Hawaiian Hotel, get delicious scoops of ice cream in island flavors like macadamia nut at the **Ice Cream Factory.** Nearby is the **Banyan Snack Shop,** which dispenses whopping plate lunches like the *loco moco*—two scoops of rice and a hamburger covered in fried egg and gravy—for only $2.75. The breakfast specials here are very cheap too.

The Chocolate Bar, next door to Bear's Coffee Shop (see p. 170) at 98 Keawe St., will tempt you with fine candies and ice cream. Everything's homemade, from Gummi Bears to rolled chocolates. **Hilo Seeds and Snacks** next to Lehua's Restaurant at 15 Waianuenue Ave. sells sandwiches and authentic crackseed. The **Kilauea Preserve Center,** at the corner of Kilauea and Ponahawai streets, also sells authentic crackseed.

Lanky's Pastries and Deli, Hilo Shopping Center, tel. 935-6381, open 6:30 a.m.-9 p.m., deli side from 6 a.m., is a perfect place to head if you have a sweet tooth that *must* be satisfied.

The deli/bakery is especially known for its "long johns"—long, thin sugar donuts filled with custard—but they also have all kinds of baked goods from bread to apple turnovers. Their deli case holds sandwiches priced under $3, along with an assortment of *bento,* perfect for a picnic lunch.

Cathy's Lunch Shop, at 270 Kamehameha Ave., is a tiny little place with two tables, where only a few dollars will get you breakfast, a plate lunch, a hamburger, or even a taco.

Moderately Priced

Restaurant Miwa, at Hilo Shopping Center, 1261 Kilauea Ave., tel. 961-4454, is open daily 10 a.m.-9 p.m., sometimes until 10 p.m. for meals, and until 2 a.m. at the bar. Very beautifully appointed, Miwa is a surprise, especially since it's stuck back in the corner of the shopping center. Enter to find traditional *shoji* screens and wooden tables adorned with fine linens, along with a classic sushi bar. The waitresses wear kimonos, though most are local women, and not necessarily Japanese. The menu is excellent, with appetizers like sake-flavored steamed clams for $4.95 and crab *sunomono* (seaweed, cucumber slices, and crab meat) for $4.25. A specialty is *nabemono,* a hearty and zesty soup/stew, prepared at your table, with a two-order minimum. Traditional favorites popular with Westerners include beef sukiyaki and *shabu shabu* (each $14), and there's also a variety of combination dinners that give you a wider sampling of the menu at good value. Restaurant Miwa is an excellent choice for a gourmet meal at a reasonable price in a congenial setting.

Soontaree Gervais, a native Thai who wears a chef's hat about as big as she is, is the owner of **Soontaree's,** also at the Hilo Shopping Center, tel. 934-SIAM, open for lunch Tues.-Fri. 11 a.m.-2 p.m., dinner Tues.-Sun. 5:30-9 p.m. Here, you can have an excellent Thai meal for a very reasonable price. Although there is no view at all, Soontaree's is nicely furnished with pink and blue tablecloths and full place settings. Like many Thai restaurants, they take care of the vegetarian. Meatless items on the menu are identified by a carrot icon next to them. Appetizers could be curry puff $2.95, chicken satay $6.95, grilled eggplant salad $4.95, or grilled Thai shrimp salad $8.95. Luscious Thai soups range from Thai *Tomyam* (mixed seasonal vegetables) $5.95 to *Tom Kar Gar* (a hearty soup of coconut broth, chicken, and lemongrass) $6.95. Entrees are exciting; choices include Thai barbecued chicken $7.95, an assortment of yellow or red curry $5.95-8.95, and *me grob* (crispy noodles with bay shrimp) $7.95. Desserts include traditional *haupia* (coconut custard Hawaiian style) $1.95 and sticky rice pudding with coconut milk $1.95. Soontaree's offers exotic gourmet food at very reasonable prices in a setting that may not be elegant, but is definitely acceptable for a special meal.

Modern and chic with a checkerboard floor, gray-on-black tables and chairs, ceiling fans, and the calming effect of ferns and flowers, **Cafe Pesto,** at 308 Kamehameha Ave., tel. 969-6640, is open Sun.-Thurs. 11 a.m.-9 p.m., Fri.-Sat. 11 a.m.-10 p.m. One of Hilo's newest restaurants, it offers affordable gourmet food in an unpretentious and comfortable setting. The one-size pizza from their wood-fired oven can be anything from *quatro formaggio* (four cheeses) $5.95 to chicken bianco with wild mushrooms, sun-dried tomatoes and basil cream sauce $9.95. Combined with dinner salads of "wild greens" at $3.50, the pizza or a calzone makes a great meal for two. Delectable yet inexpensive items are *foccacio* with rosemary and Gorgonzola $3.50, *crostini* (fresh bread with a creamy, fresh herb garlic butter) $2.95, and soup of the day for only $3.25. Heartier appetites will be satisfied with bouillabaisse, rich with morsels of lobster, shrimp, fresh fish, clams, garlic, tomatoes, and sweet fennel, served with crusty bread for $12.95; or with chicken Lallo Rosa, a breast of chicken, greens, Maui onions, cherry tomatoes, and coriander dressing for $7.95. Pasta lovers will be happy with ceviche pasta salad $7.95; smoked salmon with fettucine $12.95; and the *delisioso* lobster with *penne,* a delightful mix of noodles, spinach, roasted red peppers, cream sauce, and lobster $14.95. Cafe Pesto also has a brassrailed espresso bar where you can order caffe latte or iced cappuccino to top off your meal.

Fiasco's, a good restaurant and night spot, is at the Waiakea Shopping Center, 200 Kanoelehua St., tel. 935-7666, open Sun.-Thurs. 11 a.m.-10 p.m., weekends to 11 p.m., with dancing 9 p.m. until closing on weekends (see the following "Entertainment" section). Featuring a country inn flavor, Fiasco's has a cobblestoned entrance that leads you to the cozy,

post-and-beam dining room appointed with stout wooden tables and captain's chairs, with semiprivate booths lining the walls. The mahogany bar, a classic with polished lion's-head brass rails, offers comfortable stools and black leather booths. The menu begins with appetizers like fried mozzarella $4.25, escargots $5.95, or a big plate of onion rings at $2.75. Lighter appetites might enjoy the salad bar buffet $6.50, or a taco salad with beef or chicken $6.25 (with refried beans $5.25). Sandwiches range from the croissant club $6.75 to French dip $5.95 to a classic burger $5.25. Entrees include Mexican fare like tacos $6.25 and American standards like rib eye steak or prime rib $14.95. Families can save money with a special children's menu.

Uncle Billy's at the Hilo Bay Hotel along Banyan Dr., tel. 935-0861, is open for breakfast (featuring a $1.99 "aloha special") 6:30-9 a.m., dinner 5-8:30 p.m. Enjoy the free nightly *hula* show 6:30-7:30 p.m. The interior is neo-Polynesian with a Model T Ford as part of the decor. Basically a fish and steak restaurant serving up shrimp scampi for $9.95, steaks for $11, and catch-of-the-day from $7.75—a good, fun place to dine.

Ken's Pancake House is one of a chain but you can have a good meal for a good price (cocktails too). Open 24 hours, it's conveniently located on the way to the airport at 1730 Kamehameha Ave., tel. 935-8711.

Nihon Culture Center, 123 Lihiwai St., tel. 969-1133 (reservations required), presents authentic Japanese meals, an excellent sushi bar, and combination dinners along with cultural and artistic displays. Open daily for breakfast, lunch, and dinner until 9 p.m., sushi bar until 10 p.m.

Reuben's Mexican Restaurant will enliven your palate with its zesty dishes. The food is well prepared and the atmosphere is homey. Beer, wine, and margaritas are available. Open daily 10 a.m.-11 p.m., Sun. 4-9 p.m., 336 Kamehameha Ave., tel. 961-2552. *¡Olé!*

Expensive Restaurants

Queen's Court Restaurant at the Hilo Hawaiian Hotel on Banyan Dr., tel. 935-9361, offers a nightly buffet that is *the* best in Hilo. Connoisseurs usually don't consider buffets to be gourmet quality, but the Queen's Court proves them wrong. Each night has a different food theme but the Friday- and Saturday evening

"Seafood Buffet" would give the finest restaurants anywhere a run for their money. The dining room is grand, with large archways and windows overlooking Hilo Bay. A massive table is laden with fresh island vegetables and 15 different salads. Next on seafood night, you choose from oysters, shrimp, crab, sushi, and sashimi. Then the chefs take over. Resplendent in white uniforms and chef's hats, they stand ready to sauté or broil your choice of fish, which always includes best selections like swordfish or *ono*. Beverages include white, rosé, and rich red wines, plus fresh-squeezed guava and orange juice. The dessert table entices you with fresh fruits and imported cheeses, and dares you to save room for cream pies, fresh-baked cookies, and éclairs. The price is an unbelievable $20.95. Sunday champagne brunch is more of the same quality at $16.95. Make reservations, especially on seafood night, because the Hilo Hawaiian attracts many Hilo residents who love great food.

Roussel's, at 60 Keawe St., tel. 935-5111, open for lunch Mon.-Fri., dinner Mon.-Sat, with service all day in the lounge 11:30 a.m.-10 p.m., closed Sundays, is one of the newest additions to Hilo's upscale dining. The building housing the restaurant—the Bishop Trust Building—dates from the 1920s, and the restaurant is in a section that was formerly a bank. Roussel's is owned by Herbert Roussel, who joined with a Louisiana friend, Spencer Oliver, to create the restaurant. They changed the facade of the building to evoke a New Orleans French Quarter style, but preserved the original hardwood floor and hand-molded plaster walls and ceilings. Also, the vault has been converted to a private dining room, brightened by black-and-white checkered floors, mirrors, track lighting, and drumhead tables and chairs. Roussel's specializes in spicy Cajun food. The shrimp and oyster gumbo are outstanding, as are the blackened fish, crisp on the outside and succulent on the inside. Whet your appetite with escargots and garlic and tomato $6.75, blackened sashimi at market price, or crab and shrimp cocktail $7.50. Delightful salads are greens *beaucoup* (a mixture of romaine and butter leaf lettuce with crumbled blue cheese) $3.75, tempting avocado vinaigrette salad with homemade shallot-vinaigrette dressing $3.25, or Creole Caesar $3.95. Move on to the Cajun

entrees of chicken Pontalba (sautéed boneless chicken breast with bearnaise sauce) $14.95, duck in orange sauce $18.75, or prime rib, seasoned and flash-cooked $19.75. Seafood entrees delight with meunière amandine (boneless fillet sautéed with sliced almonds and brown butter sauce) $13.85; fresh local catch blackened, broiled, or sautéed with white wine; and a Louisiana favorite, shrimp Creole $16.25. The menu also includes vegetarian dishes like pasta in garden vegetables sauté and linguine with vegetables, each $13.45. Choose from an assortment of cakes, pies and mousses, baked daily, complement the meal with a choice wine, and end with a wonderful cognac or armagnac. Roussel's is the place to see and be seen. It's upscale Cajun cooking, down on the bayou here in Hilo.

Sicilian fishermen would feel right at home at **Pescatore Ristorante,** 235 Keawe St., tel. 969-9090, open daily for lunch 11 a.m.-2 p.m., dinner 5:30-9 p.m. and until 10 p.m. Fri. and Saturday. The building housing Pescatore is part of the *Main Street U.S.A. Project* evident in downtown Hilo. The building has had multiple uses over the years, and as part of its colorful past, served as a house of ill repute. Completely redone, it has been transformed into a bright, cheery room with high-backed, red velvet armchairs and formally set tables with green linen tablecloths. Italian-style chandeliers, lace curtains, exposed beams, and koa trim add to the elegance. You can also request a "Portofino Room," a separate area for romance and privacy. Lunch fare begins with antipasto of marinated fish with olive oil, garlic, and vinegar, or of fresh clams, when available. Primo piati can be pollo marsalla $8.95, or scalopini marsalla (tender veal sautéed with mushrooms and onion in a wine sauce) $13.95. If your taste turns to pasta, go for the primavera with fresh vegetables in tomato sauce for a very reasonable $7.95. Or try the putanesca, a famous dish cooked by the Italian ladies of the evening for their clientele; it's made from garlic, anchovies, sun-dried tomatoes, black olives, capers, and olive oil and costs $7.95. For dinner, start with their special minestrone $3.50, or the ensalata of sliced tomatoes, mozzarella, and spinach with Italian vinaigrette dressing $4.95. For a dinner antipasto try the hearts of artichokes sautéed with fresh basil, garlic, and tomatoes, and sprinkled with Parmesan cheese

$5.95. Dinner entrees bring cioppino clasico alla pescatore, swimming with morsels of lobster, mussels, clams, shrimp, fish, and scallops served with garlic bread $24.95; *gamberetti Alfredo* (large shrimp sautéed in butter, garlic, fresh basil, and Parmesan cheese in a white-wine sauce); or *vongole* (steamed clams and choice of red or white clam sauce) $17.95. Pescatore's offers elegant, gourmet dining for reasonable prices.

Lehua's Bar and Restaurant, at 11 Waianuenue Ave., tel. 935-8055, open for lunch 11 a.m.-4 p.m., dinner 5-9:30 p.m., is another upscale restaurant in a restored building. The mood is set with track lighting, Casablanca fans, and an excellent sound system. The decor is gray-on-gray with cane chairs and art deco silverware; the walls hold works of local artists. Owners Mark and Larry, transplanted from Oahu where they spent years in the nightclub business, have joined with Chef Corey Giannalone to create a restaurant inspired by island-style cuisine. Lunch offerings feature Lehua's homemade soup $2.95 per bowl, Caesar salad $4.25, and shrimp Lehua $7.75. Also charbroiled burgers $6.95, club sandwiches $6.95, charbroiled chicken $6.50, and barbecued ribs $7.95. Evenings, dine on appetizers like jumbo prawns $5.25; shrimp Lehua salad $7.25; catch of the day $14.50; and mixed grill of prawns, chicken, and teriyaki steak $16.95. Specialties are angel-hair pasta with fresh tomato, basil, and garlic $7.25; and pork spareribs $9.25. The dinner menu also includes cioppino $15.95, sauté medley of stir-fried vegetables over white or brown rice with teriyaki or oyster sauce $7.95, boneless marinated chicken $9.95, and a whopping 16-ounce porterhouse steak $18.95. Friday and Saturday nights bring live entertainment, mostly jazz and Hawaiian music. Lehua's is upbeat, with delicious food, and fun thrown in for free.

Sandalwood Room is the main restaurant of the Hawaii Naniloa Hotel on Banyan Dr., tel. 935-0831. Here, in an elegant room overlooking the bay and lined with aromatic sandalwood, you can feast on dishes from around the world. Zesty curries, rich French sauces, chops done in wine, and Polynesian-inspired dishes are offered on this full and expensive menu.

Fuji Restaurant, as its name implies, is a Japanese restaurant at the Hilo Hotel, 142 Kinoole St., tel. 961-3733. Specialties are *teppan-*

yaki (beef cut thinly and cooked right at your table), tempura, and various *teishoku* (full meals) at $12-24. From the menu choose barbecued chicken $7.25, *zarusoba* (a traditional Japanese dish of cold buckwheat noodles served with seaweed and a cold dip) $4.25, *tendonburi* (rice topped with shrimp, fish, and vegetable tempura) $7.75, and teriyaki *teishoku* (a full meal) $9.75. Seafood entrees are *ahi teishoku* $7.75, or a *soba* seafood *bento* (a combination box lunch with egg roll, shrimp tempura, grilled fish, cold buckwheat noodles, and potato salad) $10.75. There's even a "ladies' menu" with shrimp tempura, chicken cutlet, potato salad, and egg rolls $9.25, and combination meals like *soba* and seafood *bento* at $13.25. All the chefs are from Japan, and the food is authentic.

KK Tei Restaurant, 1550 Kamehameha Ave., tel. 961-3791, is a favored restaurant of many local people. The centerpiece is a bonsai garden complete with pagodas and arched moon bridges. Cook your own beef, chicken, or fish at your tableside hibachi and dip it into an array of savory sauces—or the chefs will prepare your selection from their full menu of Japanese dishes. Entrees cost about $10 in this unique Asian setting. Those in the know accord this restaurant gourmet status.

Harrington's, at 135 Kalanianaole St., tel. 961-4966, is open nightly for dinner 5:30-10 p.m., Sun. 5:30-9 p.m., lounge open 5:30-closing. The setting couldn't be more brilliant, as the restaurant overlooks the bay. A sunset cocktail or dinner is even more romantic with the melodic strains of live jazz, contemporary, or Hawaiian music playing softly in the background. The continental cuisine features appetizers like shrimp cocktail $7.50, seafood chowder $3.50, mushroom tempura $5.25, escargots in casserole $7.50, and a variety of salads. Special vegetarian dishes like eggplant parmigiana are $12.50, while seafood selections of prawns scampi are $19.95, scallops chardonnay $18.25, and calamari meunière $15.25. Meat and fowl dishes are tempting: Slavic steak $15.50, prime rib au jus $18.95, and chicken marsala $15.25.

Chapman's, tel. 935-7552, at the corner of Laukapu and Piilani streets, is open for lunch Mon.-Fri. 11:30 a.m.-2 p.m., dinner nightly 5:30-10 p.m., Sunday brunch 10:30 a.m.-2 p.m., piano bar Thursday 6-10 p.m., and live lounge music on weekend evenings. Chapman's lunch menu features tortellini chicken salad with spinach, macadamia nuts, cherry tomatoes, fresh mushrooms, strips of chicken breast and Caesar dressing $7.95; Alaskan snow crab salad $9.95; roast beef sandwich $5.95; chicken pesto salad $6.95; Korean ribs $8.95; and various burgers from $5.95. For dinner start with calamari oriental (crispy fried calamari topped with black bean sauce) $5.95, sashimi at market price, or tempura *soba* salad (tender crisp shrimp tempura served atop buckwheat noodles and garnished with daikon, carrots, and cucumbers) $11.95. Entrees are chicken Victoria (sautéed chicken breast topped with chunks of lobster and fresh whole mushrooms) $15.95, Chapman's crab cakes cooked to a light golden crispness and complimented by a louie basil cream sauce served with saffron rice $13.95, or Asian-style rack of lamb $18.95. On a side street, away from downtown Hilo, Chapman's is a good place to dine with the local people at an upscale but casual restaurant.

ENTERTAINMENT

Hilo doesn't have a lot of nightlife, but it's not a morgue either. You can dance, disco, or listen to quiet piano music at a few lounges and hotels around town. **Note:** Since most of these entertainment spots are also restaurants, their addresses and phone numbers can be found above in "Food."

In a classic plantation building behind the old police station, on Kalakaua between Keawe and Kinoole streets, is the **East Hawaii Culture Center,** a nonprofit organization that supports local art by showcasing the works of different artists monthly on a revolving basis in the large entrance hall of the old police station. They also host **Shakespeare in the Park,** a local repertory of performers who stage, direct, design, and enact Shakespearean plays under the large banyan in Kalakaua Park during the month of July. If you're in Hilo at this time, it shouldn't be missed. The Big Island Arts Guild and the Dance Council also meet here. The bulletin board is always filled with announcements of happenings in the local art scene.

Lehua's Bar and Restaurant, 11 Wainuenue Ave., (see p. 175) offers a mixed bag of jazz, Hawaiian, or contemporary music on weekends. Occasionally there is a comedy night. Upbeat vibes with good food as well.

Stratton's at 121 Banyan Dr., tel. 961-6815, becomes a sports bar 3-9 p.m. daily. You can enjoy everything from boxing to football on their big-screen TV. After 9 p.m. until closing, Sun.-Thurs., Stratton's features local singers performing their best *karaoke* tunes, and on Friday and Saturday you can dance your heart out at Stratton's disco. (Also see "Inexpensive Dining" above.)

Hilo has its own little sleaze bar, **The Green Onion,** at 885 Kilauea Ave., where exotic dancers can *sometimes* be coaxed on stage if the clientele takes up a collection and offers them a minimum amount of money. Sound good to you? Things *can't* be that bad!

Chapman's, tel. 935-7552, at the corner of Laukapu and Piilani streets, offers a piano bar Thursday 6-10 p.m., and live lounge music on weekend evenings (see p. 175).

Fiasco's at the Waiakea Shopping Mall, 200 Kanoelehua Ave., tel. 935-7666, swings with a full venue of live music, disco, or comedy on most weekends. Doors open at 9 p.m., with a $2 cover and relaxed dress code.

If you're looking for a night out, you can't beat the **Wai'oli Lounge** at the Hilo Hawaiian Hotel, where there is live music every night ranging from contemporary Hawaiian to rock. **Uncle Billy's** at the Hilo Bay Hotel has two dinner *hula* shows nightly at 6:30 and 7:30 p.m. **Harrington's** (see p. 175), one of Hilo's most romantic night spots, offers live jazz, contemporary, or Hawaiian music nightly. Perfect for dinner or just for relaxing.

Others

To catch a flick try the **Waiakea Theaters** I, II, and III at Waiakea Mall on Kanoelehua Ave., tel. 935-9747; and the **Prince Kuhio Theaters I & II** at the Prince Kuhio Plaza. You'll enjoy great listening on **KIPA Rainbow Radio** (AM 620). This station plays an excellent selection of contemporary music with few commercial interruptions. It sounds the way FM used to. K-BIG FM 98 is worth listening too, and KAOI FM 95 from Maui puts out some really good tunes.

SHOPPING

Shopping Malls

Hilo has the best general-purpose shopping on the island. Stock up on film and food before you do any touring or camping. **Prince Kuhio Plaza,** at 111 E. Puainako, open weekdays 9:30 a.m.-9 p.m., Sat. to 5:30 p.m., Sun. 10 a.m.- 5 p.m., is Hilo's newest and the island's largest shopping mall. Restaurants, jewelry shops, shoe stores, supermarkets, and large department stores like Sears and Liberty House make it a one-stop shopper's paradise. Here too you'll find Longs Drugs for film, and Waldenbooks for an extensive selection of reading material. An older but still full-service shopping center is **Kaiko'o Mall** at 777 Kilauea Ave., which includes a JCPenney, Ben Franklin's, Mall Foods, The Book Gallery, and Longs Drugs. **Hilo Shopping Center** is about one-half mile south on Kilauea Ave. at the corner of Kekuanaoa Street. This smaller mall has only a handful of local shops, but it does have some excellent inexpensive restaurants and a fine pastry shop. **Puainako Town Center** is located at 2100 Kanoelehua Ave. (Route 11 south toward Volcanoes), with lots of shops, Sack 'n' Save Market, and plenty of fast foods. **Waiakea Shopping Plaza,** handy to the airport at 100 Kanoelehua Ave., has a small clutch of stores that include Mail With Us, with full fax and mailing services; Koreana restaurant and lounge; and Fiasco's, a local restaurant known for its nightly entertainment (see above).

For Hilo's real treasures see "Hilo's Gardens," p. 160-162, where you'll find listings for the wonderful commercial flower gardens that surround the city. They are experts at preparing and shipping vibrant and colorful floral arrangements. Prices are reasonable and no other gift says Hawaii like a magnificent bouquet of exotic flowers.

Food Markets

For groceries and supplies try: **Food Fair,** 194 Kilauea Ave.; **Safeway,** 333 Kilauea Ave.; **Sack 'n' Save** at Puainako Town Center; or **Mall Foods** in Kaiko'o Mall. For a real treat visit the early morning (over by 8 a.m.) **Suisan Fish Auction** at 85 Lihiwai Street. A retail fresh-fish market is next door (see pp. 159-160). Also see "Fast Foods and Snacks," p. 172.

Health Food And Fruit Stores

Abundant Life Natural Foods, owned and operated by Leslie Miki since 1977, is in downtown Hilo at 292 Kamehameha Ave., open daily 8:30 a.m.-6 p.m., Sat. until 5 p.m., and Sun. 10 a.m.-2 p.m., tel. 935-7411. The store's kitchen puts out daily specials of soup, salads, sandwiches, and *bento,* all for well under $5, while the shelves are stocked with an excellent selection of fresh fruits and vegies, bulk foods, cosmetics, vitamins, and herbs. The bookshelves cosmically vibrate with a selection of tomes on metaphysics and new-age literature.

On Wednesday and Saturday morning, check out the **farmer's market** along Kamehameha Ave. fronting the bay in the center of the downtown area. Great for bargains and local color.

Bookstores

Hilo has excellent bookstores (also see "Shopping Malls" above). **Basically Books,** downtown at 46 Waianuenue St., tel. 961-0144, has a good selection of Hawaiiana, out-of-print books, and an unbeatable selection of maps. You can get anywhere you want to go with their nautical charts, road maps, and topographical maps. The selection includes sectionals for serious hikers and trekkers. Their collection covers most of the Pacific. They also feature a very good selection of travel books, and flags from countries throughout the world.

The **Book Gallery** at Prince Kuhio Plaza, tel. 959-7744, is a full-selection bookstore featuring Hawaiiana, hardcovers, and paperbacks.

Waldenbooks, also at Prince Kuhio Plaza, tel. 959-6468, open daily 9 a.m.-9 p.m., is the largest and best-stocked bookstore in the Hilo area.

Bookfinders of Hawaii at 150 Haili St., tel. 961-5055, specializes in hard-to-find and out-of-print books. If you want it, they'll get it.

Gifts And Crafts

If you're looking for that special island memento or souvenirs to bring home to family and friends, Uncle Billy covers all the bases and along with everything else offers the **Polynesian Marketplace,** adjacent to the Hilo Bay Hotel. Open daily 8 a.m.-8 p.m., the marketplace sells a lot of good

*one of Hilo's many
vintage buildings*

J.D. BISIGNANI

junk, liquor, and resortwear. The **Hilo Hattie** store at Prince Kuhio Plaza has all you need in island clothing, tourist style. **Hawaiian Handcrafts** at 760 Kilauea Ave., tel. 935-5587, specializes in woodcarvings. Here, Dan DeLuz uses exotic woods to turn out bowls, boxes, and vases, and sells shells from around the Pacific.

Sugawara Lauhala and Gift Shop at 59 Kalakaua St. is a virtually unknown Hilo institution operated by the Sugawara sisters, who have been in business for most of their 70-plus years. They make genuine *lau hala* weavings right on the premises of their character-laden shop. Their best hats sell for $75 up, and they also have baskets from $15. If you are after the genuine article made to last a lifetime, you'll find it here.

The **Crystal Grotto,** at 290 Kamehameha Ave., tel. 935-2284, open weekdays 10 a.m.-5:30 p.m., Sat. until 3:30 p.m., is a metaphysical bookstore filled with crystals, jewelry, videotapes, tarot cards, incense, and oils, and a full line of magnificently crafted beadwork. Different psychic readers are available throughout the week; they specialize in everything from astrology to tarot, with prices around $15 for an introductory reading. Just walking into the shop with its attuned vibes might do anything from balancing your aura to causing a past life regression. You never know, unless, of course, you're a psychic reader.

Old Town Printer and Stationers, at 201 Kinoole St., open weekdays 8 a.m-5 p.m., has been in business for 35 years selling stationery,

office supplies, postcards, notecards, and a terrific selection of calendars.

Sig Zane Design, at 122 Kamehameha Ave., tel. 935-7077, open Mon.-Sat. 9:30 a.m.-5 p.m., is one of the most unique and distinctive shops on the island. Here, owner and designer Sig Zane creates distinctive island wearables in 100% cotton. All designs are not only Hawaiian/tropical, but also chronicle useful and medicinal Hawaiian plants, ancient implements, and *hula* instruments. Zig's wife, Nalani, who helps in the shop, is a *kumu hula* who learned the intricate dance steps from her mother, Edith Kanakaole, a legendary dancer who has been memorialized with a local tennis stadium that bears her name. You can get shirts for $49, dresses around $75, and *pareo* $24, as well as affordable house slippers, sweatshirts, T-shirts, *hapi* coats, and even futon covers. The shelves also hold *lau hala* hats, hand-bound koa notebooks, and basketry made from natural fibers. Outfit yourself from head to toe at Sig's shop and be totally in style and comfort.

Dragon Mama, a lovely boutique at 266 Kamehameha Ave., features natural-fiber futons, fine bedding, wool, cotton fabrics, custom covers, meditation pillows, and Japanese rice paper.

Maile's Hawaii, at 216 Kamehameha Ave., open weekdays 9 a.m.-5 p.m., Sat. until 4 p.m., is a *hula* supply store where the shelves hold *ipu*, flutes, drums, and rattles, along with crafts items and an extensive collection of books on Hawaiiana.

Caravan Town at 194 Kamehameha Ave. is open daily except Sun. 8 a.m.-4:30 p.m., Fri. until 5:30 p.m., and Sat. until 4 p.m. It is one of the most interesting junk stores in Hilo. The shelves hold an internationally eclectic mix of merchandise that includes pendulum clocks, plaster Greek goddesses, luggage, and paper lanterns. Also, the shop specializes in over-the-counter Chinese herbs and medicines purportedly effective for everything from constipation to impotence.

The 100 block of Keawe Ave., between Shipman and Kalakaua streets, is Hilo's **yuppie row.** Designer-shoulder-to-designer-shoulder are the **Chocolate Bar,** with fine handmade temptations; **The Futon Connection,** with baskets, futons, and futon furniture; the **Picture Frame Shop and Cunningham Gallery** for fine arts; and **The Most Irresistible Shop in Hilo,** with Ciao backpacks and bags. Here too is **The Fire Place Store,** featuring coffeepots, Mexican *piñatas,* children's toys, greeting cards, *pareu,* T-shirts, and a good selection of cosmetics.

The other side of yuppie row is downhome Hilo. Some downtown shops along Keawe St. are **Kodani's Florist** for fresh-cut flowers and *lei;* and **Hawaii Sales and Surplus,** featuring raincoats, hats, military supplies, knives, backpacks, rubber rafts, and plenty of old and new military uniforms.

Big Island Estate Jewelry and Pawn Shop, at 164 Kilauea St., open Sun.-Thurs. 10 a.m.-3 p.m., is a must-stop. Inside are the expected cameras and guitars, but you'll also find Japanese miniature dolls, glassware, and *hula* supplies. **Northern Lights Antiques,** diagonally across on Ponahawai St., is another treasure chest overflowing with antiques, curios, lamps, beads, and Asian heirlooms.

The **Modern Camera Center,** at 165 Kiawe St., tel. 935-3279/3150, is one of the few full-service camera shops in Hilo.

SERVICES AND INFORMATION

Emergencies

When in need call: **police** 935-3311; **fire-ambulance** tel. 961-6022; **Hilo Hospital** at 1190 Waianuenue St., tel. 961-4211. Keiko Gido has an office at 140 Kinoole St., where she practices the ancient healing arts of acupuncture and shiatsu and various therapeutic massages.

Information

The following will be helpful: **Hawaii Visitors Bureau,** at the corner of Keawe and Haili streets, tel. 961-5797, open Mon.-Fri. 8 a.m.-noon and 1-4:30 p.m.; and the **Chamber of Commerce,** 180 Kinoole St., tel. 935-7178. Both are good sources of maps and helpful brochures. Also try the **Hilo Public Library,** 300 Waianuenue St., tel. 935-5407; or the **University of Hawaii** in Hilo at 1400 Kapiolani St., tel. 961-9311.

Banks And Post Office

For your money needs try the following: **City Bank** at Kaiko'o Mall, tel. 935-6844; **Central Pacific,** 525 Kilauea Ave., tel. 935-5251; or **First Hawaiian,** 1205 Kilauea Ave., tel. 969-2211.

The central **post office,** open weekdays 9 a.m.-4:30 p.m., Sat. 9 a.m.-12:30 p.m., is an efficiently run, modern post office, clearly marked on the access road to the airport. It is extremely convenient for mailings prior to departure.

*Anthurium
obake variety*

BOB RACE

THE SADDLE ROAD

Slicing west across the Hilo District with a north-ward list is Route 200, the Saddle Road. Everyone with a sense of adventure loves this bold cut across the Big Island along a high valley separating the two great mountains, Mauna Loa and Mauna Kea. Along it you pass explorable caves, a *nene* sanctuary, camping areas, and a spur road leading to the very top of Mauna Kea. Besides, it's a great adventure for anyone traveling between Hilo and Kona. Keep your eyes peeled for convoys of tanks and armored personnel carriers as they sometimes sally forth from Pohakuloa Military Camp.

Getting There
The car-rental companies cringe when you mention the Saddle Road. Some even intimidate you by saying that their insurance won't cover you on this road. They're terrified you'll rattle their cars to death. For the most part these fears are groundless. For a few miles the Saddle Road is corrugated because of heavy use by the military but, by and large, it's a good road, no worse than many others around the island. However, it *is* isolated, and there are no facilities along the way. If you bypass it, you'll miss some of the best scenery on the Big Island. From Hilo,

follow Waianuenue Ave. west past Rainbow Falls. Saddle Road (Route 200) splits left within a mile or two and is clearly marked. If you follow it across the island, you'll intersect Route 190 on which you can turn north to Waimea or south to Kona. For information on professional guide service to the top of Mauna Kea, see p. 140. For skiing expeditions see p. 87.

KAUMANA CAVES

In 1881 Mauna Loa's tremendous eruption created a huge flow of lava. The lava became rivers that crusted over, forming a tube through which molten lava continued to flow. Once the eruption ceased, the lava inside siphoned out, leaving the tube that we now call Kaumana Caves. The caves are only five miles out of Hilo along Route 200, clearly marked next to the road. Oddly enough, they are posted as a fallout shelter. Follow a staircase down into a gray hole draped with green ferns and brightened by wildflowers. You can walk about 50 yards into the cave before you'll need a flashlight. It's a thrill to turn around and look at the entrance, where blazing sunlight shoots through the ferns and wildflowers. The floor of the cave is cemented over for easy walking. Another cave visible across the way is undeveloped and more rugged to explore.

Two miles past Kaumana Caves is **Hilo Municipal Golf Course,** a 5,991-yard, par-72 course where you can golf for under $10.

MAUNA KEA

The lava along both sides of the road is old as you approach Mauna Kea ("White Mountain"). The lowlands are covered with grass, ferns, small trees, and mossy rocks. Twenty-seven miles out of Hilo, a clearly marked road to your right leads to the summit of 13,796-foot Mauna Kea. A sign warns you that this road is rough, unpaved, and narrow, with no water, food, fuel, restrooms, or shelters. Moreover, you can expect winds, rain, fog, hail, snow, and altitude sickness. Intrigued? Proceed: it's not as bad as it sounds. A 4WD vehicle is highly advised, and if there's snow it's impossible without one. A normal rental car isn't powerful enough, mainly because you're gaining more than 8,000 feet of elevation in 15 miles, which plays havoc with carburetors. But the real problem is coming down. For a small car with not very good gearing you're going to be riding your brakes for 15 miles. If they fall, you'll stand a very good chance of becoming a resident spirit of the mountain!

Four miles up you pass **Hale Pohaku** ("House of Stone"), which looks like a ski resort; many of the scientists from the observatory atop the mountain live here. A sign says that you need a permit from the Department of Land and Natural Resources (in Hilo) and a 4WD vehicle to proceed. Actually, the road is graded, banked, and well maintained, with the upper four miles paved so that dust is kept to a minimum to protect the sensitive "eyes" of the telescopes. As you climb, you pass through the clouds to a barren world devoid of vegetation. The earth is a red, rolling series of volcanic cones. You get an incredible vista of Mauna Loa peeking through the clouds and what seems like the entire island lying at your feet. In the distance the lights of Maui flicker. **Lake Waiau,** which unbelievably translates as "Swim Water," is almost at the top at 13,020 feet, making it the third-highest lake in the U.S. If the vistas aren't enough, bring a kite along and watch it soar in the winds of the earth's upper atmosphere. Off to your right is Puu Kahinahina, a small hill whose name means "hill of the silver

sword." It's one of the only places on the Big Island where you'll see this very rare plant. The mountaintop was at one time federal land, and funds were made available to eradicate feral goats, one of the worst destroyers of the silver sword and many other native Hawaiian plants.

Mauna Kea is the only spot in the tropical Pacific that was glaciated. The entire summit of the mountain was covered in 500 feet of ice. Toward the summit, you may notice piles of rock which are the terminal moraine of these ancient glaciers. The snows atop Mauna Kea are unpredictable. Some years it is merely a dusting, while in other years, as in 1982, there was enough snow to ski from late November to late July. The ski run comes all the way down from the summit, giving you about a four-mile trail. For skiing adventures and expeditions, see p. 87.

Here and there around the summit are small caves, remnants of ancient quarries where Hawaiians came to dig a special kind of fired rock that is the hardest in all Hawaii. They hauled roughed-out tools down to the lowlands, where they refined them into excellent implements that became coveted trade items.

Kaumana Caves

A natural phenomenon is the strange thermal properties manifested by the cinder cones that dot the top of the mountain. Only 10 feet or so under their surface is permafrost which dates back 10,000 years to the Pleistocene Epoch. If you drill into the cones for only 10-20 feet and put a pipe in, during daylight hours air will be sucked into the pipe. At night, warm air comes out of the pipe with sufficient force to keep a hat levitating.

Evening brings an incredibly clean and cool breeze that flows down the mountain. The Hawaiians called it the Keihau Wind, whose source, according to ancient legend, is the burning heart of the mountain. To the Hawaiians, this inspiring heavenly summit was the home of Poliahu, The Goddess of Snow and Ice, who vied with the fiery Pele across the way on Mauna Loa for the love of a man. He could throw himself into the never-ending embrace of a mythical ice queen, or of a red-hot mama. Tough choice, poor fellow!

Mauna Kea Observatory Complex

Atop the mountain is a mushroom grove of astronomical observatories, as incongruously striking as a futuristic earth colony on a remote planet of a distant galaxy. The crystal-clear air and lack of dust and light pollution make the Mauna Kea Observatory site *the* best in the world. At close to 14,000 feet, it is above 40% of the earth's atmosphere. Although temperatures generally hover around freezing, there's only 9-11 inches of precipitation annually, mostly in the form of snow. The astronomers have come to expect an average of 325 crystal-clear nights per year, perfect for observation. The state of Hawaii leases the tops of the cinder cones, upon which various institutions from all over the world construct telescopes. These institutions in turn give the University of Hawaii up to 15% of their viewing time. The university sells the excess viewing time for $5,000-10,000 a night, which supports the entire astronomy program and makes a little money on the side. Those who work up here must come down every four days because the thin air seems to make them forgetful and susceptible to making minor calculation errors.

Scientists from around the world book months in advance for a squint through one of these phenomenal telescopes. Teams from Great Britain, The Netherlands, Canada, France, and Japan as well as from the U.S. maintain permanent outposts here. The first telescope that you see on your left is the U.K.'s **James Clark Maxwell Telescope,** a radio telescope with a primary reflecting surface over 15 meters in diameter. It was dedicated by Britain's Prince Philip, who rode all the way to the summit in a Rolls Royce. The **Canada-France-Hawaii Telescope,** built in 1977 for $33 million, was the first to spot Halley's comet in 1983, and still can see it.

1. Ahuena Heiau, Kailua-Kona (David Stanley);
2. idols, Pu'uhonua O Honaunau, Temple of Refuge (J.D. Bisignani);
3. Wood Valley Buddhist Temple (J.D. Bisignani)

1. lantana (J.D. Bisignani); **2.** hapu'u fern (J.D. Bisignani); **3.** orchid (Dr. Greg Leo)

The newest eye to the heavens atop Mauna Kea is the **W.M. Keck Observatory,** completed in March 1993 at a cost of $94 million. The Keck Foundation, a philanthropic organization from Los Angeles, funded the telescope, one of the world's most high tech, powerful, and expensive. Operated by the California Association for Research in Astronomy (CARA), a joint project of the University of California and Cal Tech, the telescope has an aperture of 400 inches and employs entirely new and unique types of technology. The primary reflector is fashioned from a mosaic of 36 hectagonal mirrors, each only three inches thick and six feet in diameter. These "small" mirrors have been very carefully joined together to form one incredibly huge, actively controlled light reflector surface. Each of the mirror segments is separately positionable to an accuracy of a millionth of an inch, and is computer-controlled to bring the heavenly objects into perfect focus. This titanic eyeball has already spotted both the most distant known galaxy and the most distant known object in the universe, 12 and 13 billion light years from earth, respectively. The light received from these objects today was emitted not long after the "Big Bang" creating the universe theoretically occurred. In a very real sense, these scientists are looking back toward the beginning of time!

The Keck Observatory includes a public gallery, closed until mid-1994 due to construction of Keck II, Son of Cyclops. When it is completed and linked with the original Keck telescope, scientists will have an immensely more powerful tool for their earthbound exploration of the heavens.

The entire mountaintop complex is managed by the University of Hawaii. Visitors are welcome to tour the complex and to have a look through the telescopes on special weekends May-September. Reservations are a must; arrangements can be made by calling the **Mauna Kea Support Services** in Hilo at tel. 935-3371. The **Onizuka Visitor Center** at the 9,000-foot level, named in honor of astronaut Ellison Onizuka who died in the Challenger tragedy, is a must-stop for stargazers. It allows visitors a chance to acclimatize to the thin, high-mountain air, another must—a stay of one hour here is recommended before heading up to the 13,796-foot summit. (Because of the high altitude and the remoteness of the mountaintop from emergency medical facilities, children under age 16 are prohibited from venturing to the summit. Those with cardiopulmonary or respiratory problems are also discouraged from attempting the trip.) The visitor center provides the last public restrooms before the summit and is a good place to stock up on water, also unavailable higher up. The visitor center also conducts free stargazing tours. Call 961-2180 for more information.

If you plan on continuing up to the summit, you must provide your own transportation. Observatory personnel suggest calling **Harper Car and Truck Rentals** in Hilo, tel. 969-1478, or **Ciao Rentals** in Kailua-Kona, tel. 326-2426, both of which offer 4WD rentals. Take extra layers of warm clothing—it can snow up there any month of the year—and your camera. Photographers, using fast film, get some of the most dazzling shots *after* sunset. During the gloaming, the light show begins. Look down upon the clouds to see them filled with fire. This heavenly light is reflected off the mountain to the clouds and then back up like a celestial mirror in which you get a fleeting glimpse of the soul of the universe.

MAUNA KEA STATE RECREATION AREA

This area, known as Pohakuloa ("Long Stone"), is five miles west of the Mauna Kea Observatory Road (33 miles from Hilo). The altitude is 6,500 feet and the land begins to change into the rolling grasslands for which this *paniolo* country is famous. Here you'll find a cluster of seven cabins that can be rented (arrange in advance) from the Department of Land and Natural Resources, Division of State Parks, 75 Aupuni St., Hilo, HI 96720, tel. 961-7200. The cabins are completely furnished with cooking facilities and hot showers. You'll need warm clothing, but the days and nights are unusually clear and dry with very little rain. The park is within the Pohakuloa Game Management Area, so expect hunting and shooting in season. A few minutes west is the Pohakuloa Military Camp, whose manuevers can sometimes disturb the peace in this high mountain area. Follow the Saddle Road about 20 miles west to intersect Route 190 on which you can turn right (north) to Waimea—seven miles—or left (south) to Kailua—33 miles.

Birdwatchers or nature enthusiasts should turn into Koa Kipuka, a bite-sized hill just near mile marker 28. (A *kipuka* is a very special area, usually a hill or gully, in the middle of a lava flow that was never inundated by lava and therefore provides an old, original, and established ecosystem.) Look for Powerline Road and Pu'u O'o Volcano Trail. Follow either for a chance to see the very rare *akiapola'au* or *apapane,* and even wild turkeys. For descriptions of these birds, see pp. 18-21.

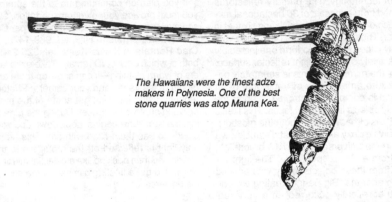

The Hawaiians were the finest adze makers in Polynesia. One of the best stone quarries was atop Mauna Kea.

LOUISE FOOTE

HAMAKUA COAST

Inland the Hamakua Coast is awash in a rolling green sea of sugarcane, while along the shore, cobalt waves foam into razor-sharp valleys where cold mountain streams meet the sea at lonely pebbled beaches. Along a 50-mile stretch of the Belt Road (Route 19) from Hilo to Waipio, the Big Island has grown its cane for 100 years or more. Water is needed for sugar, a ton to produce a pound, and this coast has plenty. Huge flumes once carried the cut cane to the mills. Last century so many Scots worked the plantations hereabouts that Hamakua was called the "Scotch Coast." Now most residents are a mixture of Scottish, Japanese, Filipino, and Por-

tuguese ancestry. Side roads dip off Route 19 into one-family valleys where modest, weather-beaten homes of plantation workers sit surrounded by garden plots on tiny, hand-hewn terraces. These valleys, as they march up the coast, are unromantically referred to as "gulches." From the Belt Road's many bridges, you can trace silvery-ribboned streams that mark the valley floors as they open to the sea. Each is jungle-lush with wildflowers and fruit trees transforming the steep sides to emerald-green velvet.

Special Note: For more on the southern section of the Hamakua Coast, please see "Scenic Drive," pp. 162-164.

HONOMU TO LAUPAHOEHOE

The ride alone, as you head north on the Belt Road, is gorgeous enough to be considered a sight. But there's more! You can pull off the road into sleepy one-horse towns where dogs are safe snoozing in the middle of the road. You can visit a plantation store in Honomu on your way to Akaka Falls, or take a cautious dip at one of the seaside beach parks. If you want solitude, you can go inland to a forest reserve and miles of trails. The largest town on the coast is Honokaa, with supplies, handmade memen-

tos, and a macadamia nut factory. You can veer west to Waimea from Honokaa, but don't. Take the spur road, Route 240, to Waipio Valley, known as the "Valley of Kings," one of the most beautiful in all of Hawaii.

HONOMU AND VICINITY

During its heyday, Honomu ("Silent Bay") was a bustling center of the sugar industry boasting saloons, a hotel/bordello, and a church or two for repentance. Now Honomu is only a stop as you head somewhere else. It's 10 miles north of Hilo and a mile or so inland on Route 220, which leads to Akaka Falls. As you enter Honomu you'll see a string of false-front buildings that are doing a good but unofficial rendition of a living history museum. It's as if the entire town has taken a nap and is about to wake up at any moment. At the south end of town, just at the turn to Akaka Falls, notice the **Odaishasan,** a beautifully preserved Buddhist Temple. Honomu is definitely worth a stop. It takes only five minutes to walk the main street, but those five minutes can give you a glimpse of history that will take you back 100 years.

Practicalities
Before entering town proper you'll spot **Jan's,** a convenience store selling cold beer and groceries. As you enter town look for **The Plate Lunch,** offering sushi, shave ice, sub sandwiches, and frozen bananas, about as downhome

DAVID STANLEY

Akaka Falls

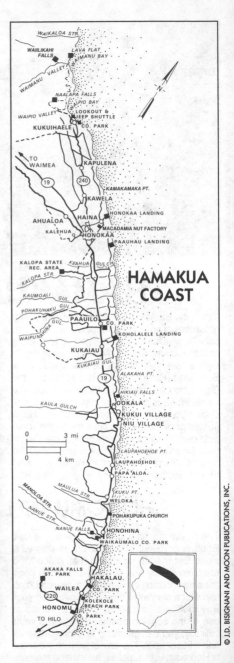

HAMAKUA COAST

© J.D. BISIGNANI AND MOON PUBLICATIONS, INC.

Ishigo's General Store

as you can get. In town at **Akaka Falls Flea Market,** the merchandise changes so you never know what to expect, but they claim "all new quality merchandise at reduced prices." And, in case you're suddenly struck by an irresistible urge for a permanent memento of Honomu, there's even **Akaka Falls Tattoo Club** in town.

As you walk the main street of Honomu, make sure to stop into **Ishigo's General Store,** tel. 963-6128, open Mon.-Fri. 7 a.m.-6 p.m., Sat. and Sun. 7 a.m.-5 p.m., to see a real plantation store still in operation. Owned and operated by Hideo Ishigo, the original store began in 1910 when his forebears, Inokichi Ishigo and his wife Maki, emigrated from Fukuoka, Japan to begin a new life in Hawaii. They began with a bakery, employing recipes that they learned from all the ethnic groups in Hawaii. They passed their knowledge down to their children, who still use the same recipes in the bakery section of the store. The general store section has food, ice cream, sandwiches, and pizza, but the real treats are in the bakery. Here in a self-serve case are familiar munchies like blueberry, pineapple, and coconut turnovers along with taro bread. But according to Mr. Ishigo, the old-timers around here go right for the cream buns and the *anpan* with *adzuki* beans. So if you want to get some *real* local flavor, pick one of these and sit out front sipping a cup of Kona coffee. Mr. Ishigo is very friendly and will "talk story" about Honomu, and may even invite you to a relative's orchid farm in the nearby area. If

he's around, it's an added treat, but you can give yourself a small history course of Honomu by checking out the antiques, mementos, and vintage photos that have been placed around the store. Most photos are of Japanese couples who immigrated to the area. Check out the bottles of *okolehau,* local moonshine, that could easily fuel the space shuttle, and an old HVB roadside warrior that's made of wood.

Next door to Ishigo's, **Akaka Falls Gallery,** tel. 963-6700, is owned and operated by Deborah Jenks, who specializes in island art. Since most of the pieces are on consignment, the gallery display will constantly change, but the philosophy of art based on island themes and created by island artists will remain constant. Part of the gallery is the **Bamboo Cafe,** where you can munch an assortment of sweets and bakery items while enjoying a cup of coffee or espresso from beans prepared by the Big Island's own **Badass Coffee Company** (see pp. 274-275).

Akaka Falls

Follow Route 220 from Honomu past dense sugarcane fields for 3.5 miles to the parking lot of Akaka Falls. From here, walk counterclockwise along a paved "circle route" that takes you through everybody's idea of a pristine Hawaiian valley. For 40 minutes you're surrounded by heliconia, gingers, orchids, ferns, and bamboo groves as you cross bubbling streams on wooden footbridges. Many varieties of plants that would be in window pots anywhere else are giants here, almost like trees. An overlook views Kahuna Falls as it spills into a lush green valley below. The trail becomes an enchanted tunnel through hanging orchids and bougainvillea. In a few moments you arrive at Akaka Falls. The mountain co-operates with the perfect setting, forming a semicircle from which the falls tumble 420 feet in one sheer drop. After heavy rains expect a mad torrent of power; during dry periods marvel at liquid-silver threads forming mist and rain-bows. The area, maintained by the Division of State Parks, is one of the most easily accessi-ble forays into Hawaii's beautiful interior.

Kolekole Beach Park

Look for the first tall bridge (100 feet high) a few minutes past Honomu, where a sign points to a small road that snakes its way down the valley to the beach park below. Amenities in-clude showers, restrooms, grills, electricity, pic-nic tables, and a camping area (county permit). Kolekole is very popular with local people, who use its five pavilions for all manner of special occasions, usually on weekends. A black-sand beach fronts an extremely treacherous ocean. The entire valley was inundated with over 30 feet of water during the great 1946 tsunami. The stream running through Kolekole comes from Akaka Falls, four miles inland. It forms a pool complete with waterfall that is safe for swimming but quite cold.

LAUPAHOEHOE

This wave-lashed peninsula is a finger of smooth *pa'hoehoe* lava that juts into the bay. Located about halfway between Honomu and Honokaa, the valley at one time supported farm-ers and fishermen who specialized in catching turtles. Laupahoehoe was the best boat landing along the coast, and for years canoes and, later, schooners would stop here. A plaque com-memorates the tragic loss of 20 schoolchildren and their teacher who were taken by the great tsunami of 1946. Afterwards, the village was moved to the high ground overlooking the point. Laupahoehoe Beach Park now occupies the low peninsula; it has picnic tables, showers, electricity, and a county camping area. The sea is too rough to swim but many fishermen come

here, along with some daring surfers. Laupa-hoehoe makes a beautiful rest stop along the Belt Road.

Ten miles inland from Laupahoehoe Point along a very rugged jeep trail is **David Dou-glas Historical Monument.** This marks the spot where the naturalist, after whom the Dou-glas fir is named, lost his life under mysterious circumstances. Douglas, on a fact-gathering expedition on the rugged slopes of Mauna Kea, never returned. His body was found at the bot-tom of a deep pit that was used at the time to catch feral cattle. Douglas had spent the previ-ous night at a cabin occupied by an Australian who had been a convict. Many suspected that the Australian had murdered Douglas in a rob-bery attempt and thrown his body into the pit to hide the deed. No hard evidence of murder could be found, and the death was officially termed accidental.

Practicalities

Luckily for all of us traveling the Hamakua Coast, French Canadian Charles Peladeau and his fiancée Judy had a dream. They dreamed of swaying palms, days of bright, sun-splashed beaches, and a vintage 1940s-style diner in which they could prepare food the old-fash-ioned way. *Voilà!* **The Local Cafe,** tel. 962-6669, open weekdays 7:30 a.m.-7:30 p.m., Sat. 10 a.m.-7:30 p.m., Sun. 10 a.m.-5 p.m., is lo-cated in a brightly painted vintage building *in* Laupahoehoe Village between mile markers 24 and 25. Inside, the decor, thanks to Judy, is "modern-classic-chic" appointed with black floor, white wainscoted walls, and turquoise stools, countertop, and ceiling. Musty encyclopedias, dog-eared books, framed photos, and a col-lection of bottles turned translucent with age whisper the faded memories of days gone by. Overhead, lively paintings of "stoned" parrots and stuffed cloth fish, whales, and sharks dan-gle from the ceiling, shouting "Today!" The breakfast menu brings "Charlie's eggs to go," a muffin mounded with egg, ham and cheese $2.25; a three-egg cheese omelette $4.50; and plenty of sweets, treats and side orders. Liv-ing up to its name, the Local Cafe just has to offer a full range of plate lunches like meatball platters, chicken delight, and teriyaki chicken, all for around $5. Burgers and sandwiches include everything from a half-pound beef burger for

*The Local Cafe in
Laupahoehoe*

the very hungry at $4.50, to an assortment of jumbo sandwiches like ham and cheese, or turkey with all the trimmings, for under $4. Charlie, like a true Frenchman—sort of—claims unabashed bragging rights to the Islands' best pizza, served daily from 10:30 a.m. and ranging in price from a small plain pie for $7.95 to Frankie's Delight covered with the works and large enough to feed five for $20.95. Although all of Charlie's food is wholesome and delicious, his pièces de résistance are homemade, deep-dish, fruit and berry pies, topped with homemade ice cream from Hilo (oftentimes gone by early afternoon). Drop in at the Local Cafe and share Charlie's and Judy's dream. You'll be glad that you did!

HONOKAA TO KUKUIHAELE

HONOKAA AND VICINITY

With a population of nearly 2,000, Honokaa ("Crumbling Bay") is the major town on the Hamakua Coast. Here you can continue on Route 19 to Waimea, or take Route 240 through Honokaa and north to Waipio, which you should not miss. First, however, stroll the main street of Honokaa, where a number of shops specialize in locally produced handicrafts. This is also the best place to stock up on supplies or gasoline. The surrounding area is the center of the macadamia nut industry. If you are proceeding north along Route 240, the coastal route heading to Waipio Valley, just past mile-marker 6 on the left, keep an eye peeled for a lava-tube cave right along the roadway. This is just a tease of the amazing natural sights that follow. (See Waipio, p. 193.)

Kalopa State Recreation Area

This spacious natural area is 12 miles north of Laupahoehoe (two miles south of Honokaa), and two miles inland on a well-marked secondary road. Little used by tourists, it's a great place to get away from it all. Hiking is terrific throughout the park on a series of nature trails where much of the flora has been identified. All trails are well marked and vary widely in difficulty. The park provides an excellent opportunity to explore some of the lush gulches of the Hamakua Coast, as well as tent camping (state permit) and furnished cabins that can house up to eight people (see p. 74).

Hawaiian Holiday
Macadamia Nut Factory

This factory, open 9 a.m.-6 p.m., is on a side road that leads from the middle of town down a steep hill toward the sea. A self-guided tour explains how John MacAdams discovered the delicious qualities of these nuts, and how they were named after him. The macadamia nut industry was started in Honokaa when W.H. Purvis, a British agriculturalist who had been working in Australia, brought the first trees to Honokaa in 1881, one of which is still bearing! In

1924, W. Pierre Naquin, then manager of the Honokaa Sugar Co., started the first commercial nut farm in the area. You can buy a large variety of macadamia items, from butters to candies. A delicious and nutritious munchy is a five-ounce, vacuum-packed can of nuts that make a great souvenir or add a special touch to a picnic lunch. The Nut Factory also has a small deli selection and ice cream. Inside the same facility is the **H.R.T. Waipio Tour Desk,** tel. 775-7291, where you can arrange a van or horseback tour through fabulous Waipio (see p. 91).

Practicalities

Centrally located along Route 240 is the **Hotel Honokaa Club.** Contact Marilyn Otake, Manager, Box 185, Honokaa, HI 96727, tel. 775-0678. What it lacks in elegance it makes up for in cleanliness and friendliness. The hotel, mostly used by local people, is old and appears rundown. Upstairs rooms (view and TV) are $42 s, $44 d. The more spartan but very clean downstairs rooms go for $32 s, $35 d, and have their own baths. The hotel dining room serves the best meals in town. Breakfasts are served weekends only 6:30-11 a.m., lunch Mon.-Fri. 11 a.m.-2 p.m., and dinner nightly 5:30-8 p.m. The cooking is home-style with a different dinner special daily, such as a seafood platter $8.75, or lobster and steak $20.95. Specials include rice, potatoes, salad, and coffee. The hotel lounge serves a full range of cocktails and beer daily during lunch and dinner, and depending on business will stay open to 2 a.m.

Local people thought that Jolene was such a good cook, they recently talked her into opening **Jolene's Kau Kau Corner** in downtown Honokaa, tel. 775-9598, open daily except Sunday 10 a.m.- 8 p.m. Most tried-and-true recipes were handed down by her extended family, who also lend a hand in running the restaurant. They currently serve only lunch and dinner, with breakfast a possibility in the near future. The restaurant, located in a vintage storefront, is trim and neat, and the menu includes a variety of plate lunches like beef tips teriyaki $4.95, shrimp plate $5.50, and a steaming bowl of beef stew $4.85. Saimin in two sizes is $1.95 and

$3.50, while most burgers and fries are under $4.50. The dinner menu brings broiled mahimahi $7.75, shrimp tempura $8.25, shrimp and chicken baskets around $5, and the enormous captain's plate of Alaska snow crab leg, shrimp, and New York steak $15.95. Jolene's is as downhome and local as you can get, and what she lacks in atmosphere, she more than makes up for in friendly service, hearty dishes, and reasonable prices. One of the best places to eat along the northern Hamakua Coast!

Dragon Chop Suey, tel. 775-0553, is open daily except Monday 11 a.m.-8 p.m. Along with standard Chinese dishes, it features vegetarian foods like vegetable soup $3.75, vegetarian saimin $3.75, and egg foo young $3.95. Basic Chinese dishes are ginger chicken, pork broccoli chow mein, and pot stickers, all $5-6. Dim sum plate lunches give you a choice of four items for $4.75.

Herb's Place, in downtown Honokaa, is open for breakfast, lunch, and dinner Mon.-Fri. from 5:30 a.m., Sat. from 8:30 a.m., closed Sunday. You get basic meals and cocktails in this little roadside joint.

C.C. Jon's is a plate-lunch, local fast-food stand, just as you enter town. Most of their dishes are under $4.50.

You can pick up supplies and even a few health food items at **T. Kaneshiro Store** and **K.K. Market,** two well-stocked markets in town.

If you are at all interested in the history of Hawaii, make sure to stop by the **The Hawaiian Artifacts Shop** along the main drag in downtown Honokaa. Just look for a carved mermaid and a strobe light blinking you into the shop. This amazing curio and art shop is owned and operated by James and Lokikamakahiki "Loki" Rice. The Rices, both elderly and in failing health, keep no set hours, opening when they feel like it. They're usually there for a few hours in the afternoon, but never before 2 p.m. At first glance the shop may look unauthentic, but once you're inside, that impression quickly melts away. Loki, a full-blooded Hawaiian, was born and raised in Waipio Valley, and James has traveled the Pacific for years. Between the two, the stories from the old days are almost endless. Notice a tiki that serves as a main beam, and two giant shields against the back wall. They belonged to Loki's father, a giant of a man just under seven feet tall and over 450 pounds

who had to have a special coffin made when he was buried on the island of Niihau. Local people bring in their carvings and handicrafts to sell, many of which are *hula* implements and instruments like drums and rattles. Some of the bric-a-brac is from the Philippines or other South Sea islands, but Jim will identify them for you. Mingled in with what seems to be junk are some real artifacts like poi pounders, adzes, and really good drums. Many have come from Loki's family, while others have been collected by the Rices over the years. But the real treasures inside the shop are Jim and Loki, who will share their aloha as long as time permits. Jim is also a **clockmaker** who not only repairs clocks, but makes them as well.

Kamaaina Woodworks, in Honokaa halfway down the hill leading to Hawaiian Holiday Macadamia Nut Factory, tel. 775-7722, is usually open daily except Sunday 9 a.m.-5 p.m., but this depends on the weather, their inclination, and how the spirits are moving on any particular day. The shop is owned and operated by Bill Keb and Roy Mau, talented woodworkers who specialize in fabulous bowls turned from native woods like koa, milo, extremely rare *kou,* and a few introduced woods like mango and Norfolk Island pine. All of the wooden artpieces, priced at $20-1,000, are one-of-a-kind, and are designed to be utilitarian. Less expensive items are koa or milo bracelets $10-20, letter openers $5, and rice paddles $4. When you first enter the shop, don't be surprised if it looks like someone's home with a TV on in the sitting room and glass cases filled with Hawaiian flora and fauna.

On the right, just near the Hotel Honokaa Club, is the **Honokaa Trading Co.,** selling new and used goods, antiques, and collectibles. On the south end of town as you enter, **Seconds To Go,** open daily except Sunday 9:30 a.m.-5 p.m., is owned and operated by Elaine Carlsmith, and is a collectibles and antique shop specializing in Hawaiian artifacts. The shop brims over with articles like classic Hawaiian ties and shirts from the '50s, dancing *hula*-doll lamps, antique hardware and building materials, clawfoot bathtubs, old books, Japanese bowls, a good collection of plates and saucers, and even a ukelele. Elaine also has used fishing gear in case you want to try your luck.

In town, **S. Hasigara** has a few racks of local fashions, and a few bolts of traditional Japanese cloth. Look for the very ethnic **Filipino Store** along the main drag to soak up a cultural experience and to find an array of exotic spices and food ingredients. You can do most of your banking needs at **Bank of Hawaii,** also located in the downtown area. Gas can be purchased at either a **Union 76** or a **Chevron,** both well marked along the main drag.

KUKUIHAELE

For all of you looking for the "light at the end of the tunnel," Kukuihaele ("Traveling Light") is it. On the main road, the **Last Chance** grocery and gas station, open 9 a.m.-6 p.m. daily, stocks basic supplies plus a small assortment of hand-icrafts and gift items. The Last Chance has an excellent selection of domestic and imported beers, along with light snacks for a picnic lunch. The store attendants are friendly and don't mind answering a few questions about the Waipio area if they are not too busy.

Waipio Valley Artworks, tel. 775-0958, open daily 9 a.m.-5 p.m., is an excellent shop in which to pick up an art object. There are plenty of offerings in wood that include carvings and bowls, but the shop also showcases various Hawaii-based artists working in different mediums. Definitely check out inspired prints by Sue Sweard-low, who has tuned in to the soul of Hawaii, and paintings by Carli Oliver and Kim Starr. You'll also find tikis, earrings, basketry made from natural fibers, and ceramics by Robert Joiner and Ann Rathbun. The shop features a snack window serving ice cream, sandwiches, and soft drinks. Out back, a small boutique offers designer T-shirts, alohawear, a smattering of souvenir items, and a fairly extensive collection of books mostly on Hawaiiana. Waipio Valley Artworks is also the meeting place for **Waipio Valley Shuttle,** tel. 775-7121, which will take you down to Waipio Valley (see pp. 193-194).

Accommodations
Waipio Wayside, Box 840, Honokaa, HI 96727, tel. 775-0275, the vintage home of the one-time plantation manager, is now owned and operated by Jackie Horne as a congenial B&B. Look for a white picket fence and two driveways exactly two miles toward Waipio from the Honokaa post office. You enter through double

J.D. BISIGNANI

Jackie Horne at the Waipio Wayside

French doors, onto a rich wooden floor shining with a well-waxed patina. The walls are hand-laid vertical paneling, the prototype that modern paneling tries to emulate. The home contains five double bedrooms ranging in price from $50-80 s, $65-85 d for multiple-night stays; $5 extra for single-night stays; $15 extra person. One large master bedroom is in its own little space out back, but attached to the house. The room, rich with knotty pine, is spacious and airy with plenty of windows. Every bedroom has beautiful curtains that are hand-painted originals by Jackie's friend, Laura Lewis, a local island artist. The back deck, where you will find hammocks in which to rock away your cares, overlooks manicured grounds that gently descend, affording a panoramic view of the coast. Jackie, whose meticulous and tastefully appointed home is straight from the pages of *Ladies' Home Journal,* is also a gourmet cook. Breakfast is sometimes waffles with strawberries and whipped cream, sometimes omelettes and biscuits, with fresh fruit from the property. Beverages are pure Kona coffee, juices, and an assortment of 24 gourmet teas from around the world. A stay at Waipio Wayside is guaranteed to be civilized, relaxing, and affordable.

Hale Kukui, tel. 775-7130, (800) 444-7130, Box 5044, Kukuihaele, HI 96727, owned and operated by William and Sarah McCowatt, is a secluded B&B on four acres perched high on the *pali* from which you get a sweeping view of Waipio Valley and the wide Pacific. Follow the main road *through* Kukuihaele and look for a sign pointing you down a private drive that leads about 200 yards to the comfortable cottage. Inside, the units are tasteful with vaulted ceilings, black ceiling fan, white wicker furniture, and woven wool carpets. The bedroom is large, and the complete kitchen features a two-burner range, refrigerator, sink and preparation area, microwave, table and chairs, and complete utensils. The private lanai has a barbecue grill, and a TV can be provided on request. The grounds

have been improved with a trail that leads down to a semiprivate stream where you'll find a small but refreshing freshwater pool. The units include a self-contained studio and a two-bedroom unit which can be combined into a three-bedroom unit for large families or a group of friends. Rates based on double occupancy are studio (440 square feet, sleeps 2-4) $75; two-bedroom unit (660 square feet, sleeps 4-6) $95; three-bedroom unit (both combined) $150; additional person $10. A five percent discount is offered to members of Greenpeace, the Sierra Club, or any other recognized national environmental organization.

Enjoy the privacy of **Hamakua Hideaway,** Box 5104, Kukuihaele, HI 96727, tel. 775-7425. This B&B is only a 15-minute walk from Waipio Overlook. The entire home, s/d, is $60 daily, with reduced weekly and monthly rates available.

WAIPIO VALLEY

Waipio is the way the Lord would have liked to fashion the Garden of Eden, if he hadn't been on such a tight schedule. You can read about this incredible valley, but you really can't believe it until you see it for yourself. Route 240 ends a minute outside of Kukuihaele at an overlook, and 1,000 feet below is Waipio ("Arching Water"). The valley is a mile across where it fronts the sea at a series of high sand dunes. It's vibrantly green, always watered by Waipio Stream and lesser streams that spout as waterfalls from the *pali* at the rear of the valley. The green is offset by a wide band of black-sand beach. The far side of the valley ends abruptly at a steep *pali* that is higher than the one on which you're standing. A six-mile trail leads over it to Waimanu Valley, smaller, more remote, and more luxuriant.

Travelers have long extolled the amazing abundance of Waipio. From the overlook you can make out the overgrown outlines of garden terraces, taro patches, and fish ponds in what was Hawaii's largest cultivated valley. Every foodstuff known to the Hawaiians once flourished here; even Waipio pigs were said to be bigger than anywhere else. In times of famine, the produce from Waipio could sustain the populace of the entire island (estimated at 100,000

people). On the valley floor and alongside the streams you'll still find avocados, bananas, coconuts, passion fruit, mountain apples, guavas, breadfruit, tapioca, lemons, limes, coffee, grapefruit, and pumpkins. The old fish ponds and streams are alive with prawns, wild pigs roam the interior, and there are abundant fish in the sea.

But the lovingly tended order, most homes, and the lifestyle were washed away in the tsunami of 1946. Now Waipio is unkempt, a wild jungle of mutated abundance. The valley is a neglected maiden with a dirty face and disheveled, windblown hair. Only love and nurturing can refresh her lingering beauty.

Getting There

The road leading down to Waipio is outrageously steep and narrow. If you attempt it in a regular car, it'll eat you up and spit out your bones. Over 20 fatalities have occurred since people started driving it, and it has only been paved since the early 1970s. You'll definitely need 4WD, low range, to make it; downhill vehicles yield to those coming up. There is very little traffic on the road except when surfing conditions are good. Sometimes Waipio Beach has the first good waves of the season and this brings out the surfers en masse. **Waipio Valley**

Waipio Valley

J.D. BISIGNANI

Shuttle, tel. 775-7121, has their office at Waipio Valley Artworks in Kukuihaele. They still have a few super-tough and adventurous open Land Rovers for their 90-minute descent and tour, but mostly you'll ride in air-conditioned comfort in 4WD vans. The tour costs $25.80. Buy your ticket at the Artworks, and then proceed to the Waipio Overlook from where the vans leave every hour on the hour. This is the tamest, but safest, way to enjoy the valley. If you decide to hike down or stay overnight, you can make arrangements for the van to pick you up or drop you off for an added cost. The same company also offers a trip to the top of Mauna Kea.

If you have the energy, the hike down the paved section of the road is just over one mile, but it's a tough mile coming back up! Expect to take three to four hours down and back, adding more time to swim or look around. (For details, see "Camping in Waipio" below.)

ACTIVITIES

For a fun-filled experience guaranteed to please, try horseback riding with **Waipio Naalapa Trail Rides,** tel. 775-0419. Sherri Hannum, a young mother of three who moved to Waipio from Missouri almost 25 years ago, and her husband Mark, own and operate the trail rides. Both are enamored with the valley, and as fate would have it, have become the old-timers of Waipio. They gladly accept the charge of keeping the ancient accounts and oral traditions alive. The adventure begins when Mark picks you up at 9:30 a.m. at Waipio Valley Artworks (see p. 192) in Kukuihaele. You begin a 40-minute 4WD ride down to the ranch, which gives you an excellent tour of the valley in and of itself, since their spread is even deeper into the valley than the end of the line for the commercial valley tour! En route you cross three or four streams, as Mark tells you some of the history and lore of Waipio. When you arrive, Sherri has the horses ready to go. Sherri knows the trails of Waipio intimately. She puts you in the saddle of a surefooted Waipio pony and spends all day telling you legends and stories while leading you to waterfalls, swimming holes, gravesites, and finally a *heiau.* The lineage of the horses of Waipio dates from the late 1700s. They were gifts to the *ali'i* from Capt. George Vancouver. Waipio was especially chosen because the horses were easy to corral and could not escape. Today, over 150 semiwild progeny of the original stock roam the valley floor. Technically, you should bring your own lunch for the ride, since you can't always count on the fruits of Waipio to be happening. But if they are, Sherri will point them out and you can munch to your heart's delight. Tours lasting 2½ hours cost $65 and start at 9:30 a.m. and 1 p.m. Full-day tours can be arranged, but a minimum of two and a maximum of four riders is required. Sorry, no children under 12 or riders weighing more than 230 pounds. Go prepared with long pants, shoes, and swimsuit. A ride with Sherri isn't just an adventure; it's an experience with memories that will last a lifetime.

Waipio Valley Wagon Tour, Box 1340, Honokaa, HI 96727, tel. 775-9518, owned and operated by Peter Tolin, is the newest and one of the most fun-filled ways of exploring Waipio. This surrey-type wagon, which can hold about a dozen people, is drawn by two Tennessee mules. The fascinating two-hour tours depart four times p/d at 9 a.m., 10:30 a.m., 12:30 p.m., and either 2 or 4 p.m. Cost is $35, children under 12 half price, children two and under free. To participate, make reservations 24 hours in advance. Then check in 30 minutes before departure at the Waipio Overlook, where a 4WD vehicle will come to fetch you. The overlook also has a pay phone from which you can call the Wagon Tour to see if there is last-minute room for you, but a space is definitely not guaranteed. Lunch is not included, but if you bring your own, you can walk down to the beach and have a great picnic. The original wagon was built by Peter himself from parts that he ordered from the Mainland. Unfortunately, every part that he ordered broke down over a nine-month trial period. Peter had all new parts made at a local machine shop, only three times thicker than the originals! Now that the wagon has been *Waipionized,* the problems have ceased. The only high-tech aspect of the wagon ride is a set of small loudspeakers through which Peter narrates the history, biology, and myths of Waipio as you roll along.

Special Note

In the summer of 1992, the Bishop Museum requested an environmental impact survey to be done on Waipio Valley because the frequency of visitors to the valley had increased tremendously. Old-time residents were complaining not only about the overuse of the valley, but about the loss of their quiet and secluded lifestyle. Sherri Hannum of Waipio Naalapa Trail Rides and Peter Tolin of Waipio Valley Wagon Tour cooperated fully, and did their best to help in the preservation and reasonable use of one of Hawaii's grandest valleys. They have complied with the regulations imposed by the Bishop Museum even when it meant a significant financial loss to themselves. Because of the impact study, the commercial tours are not allowed to go to the beach area, which is now open to foot

traffic only, and the valley is **closed on Sunday** to commercial tours. Other tour operators, resentful of the Bishop Museum, were not as cooperative as Sherri and Peter, and apparently have put personal gain above the preservation of Waipio.

HISTORY

Legend And Oral History

Waipio is a mystical place. Inhabited for over 1,000 years, it figures prominently in old Hawaiian lore. In the primordial past, Wakea, progenitor of all the islands, favored the valley, and oral tradition holds that the great gods Kane and Kanaloa dallied in Waipio intoxicating themselves on *awa*. One oral chant relates that the demigod Maui, that wild prankster, met his untimely end here by trying to steal baked bananas from these two drunken heavyweights. Lono, god of the Makahiki, came to Waipio in search of

Sherri Hannum of Waipio Naalapa Trail Rides

Nenewe's pool

a bride. He found Kaikilani, a beautiful maiden who lived in a breadfruit tree near **Hiilawe Waterfall,** which tumbles 1,300 feet to the valley below and is Hawaii's highest single falls.

Nenewe, a shark-man, lived near a pool at the bottom of another waterfall on the west side of Waipio that has been recently fenced so that access is no longer available. The pool was connected to the sea by an underwater tunnel. All went well for Nenewe until his grandfather disobeyed a warning never to feed his grandson meat. Once Nenewe tasted meat, he began eating Waipio residents after first warning them about sharks as they passed his sea-connected pool on their way to fish. His constant warnings roused suspicions. Finally, a cape he always wore was ripped from his shoulders, and there on his back was a shark's mouth! He dove into his pool and left Waipio to hunt the waters of the other islands.

Pupualenalena, a *kupua* (nature spirit), takes the form of a yellow dog who can change his size from tiny to huge. He was sent by the chiefs

of Waipio to steal a conch shell that mischievous water sprites were constantly blowing, just to irritate the people. The shell was inherited by Kamehameha and is now in the Bishop Museum. Another dog-spirit lives in a rock embedded in the hillside halfway down the road to Waipio. In times of danger, he comes out of his rock to stand in the middle of the road as a warning that bad things are about to happen.

Finally, a secret section of Waipio Beach is called **Lua o milu,** the legendary doorway to the land of the dead. At certain times, it is believed, ghosts of great *ali'i* come back to earth as "Marchers of the Night," and their strong chants and torch-lit processions fill the darkness in Waipio. Many great kings were buried in Waipio, and it's felt that because of their mana, no harm will come to the people that live here. Oddly enough, the horrible tsunami of 1946 and a raging flood in 1979 filled the valley with wild torrents of water. In both cases, the devastation to homes and the land was tremendous, but not one life was lost. Everyone who still lives in Waipio will tell you that somehow, they feel protected.

The remains of **Paka'alana Heiau** is in a grove of trees on the right-hand side of the beach as you face the sea. It dates from the 12th century and was a "temple of refuge" where *kapu* breakers, vanquished warriors, and the weak and infirm could find sanctuary. The other restored and more famous temple of this type is Pu'uhonua O Honaunau in Kona (see pp. 270-271). Paka'alana was a huge *heiau* with tremendous walls that were mostly intact until the tsunami of 1946. The tidal wave sounded like an explosion when the waters hit the walls of Paka'alana, according to first-hand accounts. The rocks were scattered, and all was turned to ruins. Nearby, **Hanua'aloa** is another *heiau* that is in ruins. Archaeologists know even less about this *heiau*, but all agree that both were healing temples of body and spirit, and the local people feel that their positive mana is part of the protection in Waipio.

Recorded History

Great chiefs have dwelt in Waipio. King Umi-aliloa planted taro just like a commoner, and fished with his own hands. He went on to unite the island into one kingdom in the 15th century. Waipio was the traditional land of Kamehameha the Great, and in many ways was the basis of his earthly and spiritual power. He came here to rest after heavy battles, and offshore was the scene of the first modern naval battle in Hawaii. Here, Kamehameha's war canoes faced those of his nemesis, Keoua. Both had recently acquired cannons bartered from passing sea captains. Kamehameha's artillery was manned by two white sailors, Davis and Young, who became trusted advisors. Kamehameha's forces won the engagement in what became known as the "Battle of the Red-Mouthed Gun."

When Captain Cook came to Hawaii, 4,000 natives lived in Waipio; a century later only 600 remained. At the turn of this century many Chinese and Japanese moved to Waipio and began raising rice and taro. People moved in and out of the valley by horse and mule and there were schools and a strong community spirit. Waipio was painstakingly tended. The undergrowth was kept trimmed and you could see clearly from the back of the valley all the way to the sea. WW II arrived and many people were lured away from the remoteness of the valley by a changing lifestyle and a desire for modernity. The tidal wave in 1946 swept away most of the homes, and the majority of the people pulled up stakes and moved away. For 25 years the valley lay virtually abandoned. The Peace Corps considered it a perfect place to build a compound in which to train volunteers headed for Southeast Asia. This too was abandoned. Then in the late '60s and early '70s a few "back to nature" hippies started trickling in. Most only played "Tarzan and Jane" and moved on, especially after Waipio served them a "reality sandwich" in the form of the flood of 1979.

Waipio is still very unpredictable. In a three-week period from late March to early April of 1989, 47 inches of rain drenched the valley. Roads were turned to quagmires, houses washed away, and more people left. Part of the problem is the imported trees in Waipio. Until the 1940s, the valley was a manicured garden, but now it's very heavily forested. All of the trees that you will see are new; the oldest are mangroves and coconuts. The trees are both a boon and a blight. They give shade and fruit, but when there are floods, they fall into the river, creating log jams that increase the flooding dramatically. Waipio takes care of itself best when humans do not interfere. Now the taro farmers are having problems because the irrigation system for their

crops was washed away in the last flood. But, with hope and a prayer to Waipio's spirits, they'll rebuild, knowing full well that there will be a next time. And so it goes.

Waipio Now

Waipio is at a crossroads. Many of the old people are dying off, or moving topside (above the valley) with relatives. Those who live here learn to accept life in Waipio and genuinely come to love the valley, while others come only to exploit its beauty. Fortunately, the latter underestimate the raw power of Waipio. Developers have eyed the area for years as a magnificent spot in which to build a luxury resort. But even they are wise enough to realize that nature rules Waipio, not man. For now the valley is secure. A few gutsy families with a real commitment have stayed on and continue to revitalize Waipio. The valley now supports perhaps 50 residents. A handful of elderly Filipino bachelors who worked for the sugar plantation continue to live here. About 50 more people live topside, but come down to Waipio to tend their gardens. On entering the valley, you'll see a lotus-flower pond, and if you're lucky enough to be there in December, it will be in bloom. It's tended by an 80-year-old Chinese gentleman, Mr. Nelson Chun, who wades into the chest-deep water to harvest the sausage-linked lotus roots by clipping them with his toes! Margaret Loo comes to

taro

DIANA LASICH HARPER

harvest wild ferns served at the exclusive banquets at the Mauna Kea Beach Resort. Seiko Kaneshiro is perhaps the most famous taro farmer because of his poi factory that produces "Ono Ono Waipio Brand Taro." Another old-timer is Charlie Kawashima, who still grows taro the old-fashioned way, as an art form passed from father to son. He harvests the taro with an *o'o* (digging stick) and after it's harvested cuts off the corm and sticks the *huli* (stalk) back into the ground, where it begins to sprout again in a week or so.

Harrison Kanakoa, recently deceased, mostly lived topside because of failing health in his later years. He was born in a house built in 1881 near Kauiki Heiau, one of the biggest and most powerful *heiau* in the valley. Harrison loved to "talk story," relating tales of when his family was the keeper of the *heiau*. When he was a small boy his grandfather took him to the *heiau*, where he rolled away an entrance stone to reveal a small tunnel that went deep inside. He followed his grandfather in a ways, but his child's courage failed, and he turned away and ran out. He said his grandfather yelled after him something in Hawaiian like "You coward," and refused to show him that place again. In 1952, C.H. Brewer, a very powerful sugarcane company in this area, bulldozed the *heiau* and planted macadamia nuts on top. The trees still bear nuts, but the *heiau* was obliterated.

WAIPIO PRACTICALITIES

Camping In Waipio

For camping in Waipio Valley you must get a permit from the Hamakua Sugar Co., tel. 776-1511. The office is located about 15 minutes from the overlook in Paauilo and you must pick up the permit in person. Camping is allowed in designated areas only on the east side of Waipio Stream. Many hikers and campers have stayed in Waipio overnight without a permit and have had no problem. Remember, however, that most of the land, except for the beach, *is* privately owned.

Waipio Beach, stretching over a mile, is the longest black-sand beach on the island. The surf here can be very dangerous and there are many riptides. During the summer the sands drift to the western side of the valley; in winter

they drift back east. If there is strong wave action, swimming is not advised. It is, however, a good place for surfing and fishing.

The **Waipio Valley Aqueduct Trail,** which follows the clearly marked water system of the recently defunct Hamakua Sugar Plantation, has just opened up to the public. Not overly vigorous, the rather flat trail (except for one spot that requires scrambling down a ladder) skirts the rear of the valley where the natural flora is still thriving. In some places, the sugar company followed an irrigation system laid by native Hawaiians over 1,000 years ago that watered ancient terraces growing wetland taro.

Accommodations

Waipio has a hotel! Owned and operated by Tom Araki, it was built by his dad to serve as a residence for teachers who came to teach at the local school, and was later used for officers of a nearby, now defunct Peace Corps training camp. You'll find eight basic but clean rooms. Light is provided by kerosene lamp, and you must bring your own food to prepare in a communal kitchen. Tom, at 84, is a treasure house of information about Waipio, and a "character" who's more interested in tending his taro patch, telling stories, and drinking wine than he is in running a hotel. His philosophy, which has enabled him to get along with everyone from millionaires to hippies, is a simple "live and let live." The Waipio Hotel has become known and it's even fashionable to stay there. For reservations, write Tom Araki, 25 Malama Pl., Hilo, HI 96720, or call Tom down in Waipio Valley at tel. 775-0368. Expect to pay about $15 per person.

Ever fantasized about running off to a tropical island and living a life of "high" adventure? *The* most secluded accommodation in all of Hawaii is **The Treehouse,** owned and operated by Linda Beech and her partner, Mark Singleton, a technological tinkerer *extraordinaire* who keeps most of the alternative water, phone, and electrical systems up and running. The Treehouse is located deep in Waipio Valley on three acres of land completely surrounded by holdings of the Bishop Museum. Linda or Mark will fetch you from topside in a sturdy 4WD and ferry you across at least five rivers until you come to their idyllic settlement at the foot of Papala Waterfall. Tumbling 1,800 feet over the towering *pali,* the falls provide the water for a hydroelectric power plant (solar backup) that runs everything from stereos to ceiling fans. Linda purchased the land about 25 years ago after returning to Hawaii, the place of her birth. She has had a most interesting life, traveling throughout Asia. In Japan she was a famous personality starring in a very popular and long-running TV sitcom entitled *"Uchi no okasan, tonari no mama-san"* ("The lady of the house and the mama-san next door").

The Treehouse was built in 1972 by master boatbuilders Eric Johnson and Steven Oldfather, who chose a 65-foot monkeypod tree as its perch. Secured by an ingenious "three pin anchoring system," the Treehouse sways like a moored boat, allowing the tree to grow without causing structural damage. It has survived 120 mph winds and has proven to be a most "seaworthy" treehouse. Eric Johnson came back about four years ago to reroof the structure and found it still square and level. Both men have given up professional boatbuilding and have become very famous on the Big Island as custom home builders.

The Treehouse is fascinating, but basic. As you climb the steps, the first landing holds a flushing toilet. Inside, the Treehouse is plain wood and screened windows, not much more. It's very comfortable with island-style furnishings, and provides a full kitchen and all utensils, but it is not luxurious. The luxury is provided by Waipio itself, which floods the interior with golden light and the perfume of tropical flowers wafting on the breeze. All around, the melodious songs of indigenous birds, the ever-present wind, and cascading waters serenade you day and night. If you don't wish to perch high in a tree, Linda also offers **The Hale,** an earthbound but commodious structure where the walls of glass and screen open to the magnificent still-life surrounding you. All guests are invited to use a traditional Japanese *ofuro,* a hot tub, brought back by Linda from her travels in the east. Remember, however, that The Treehouse is a vacation rental, not a B&B, and that you will be required to bring all of your own food and to do your own light housekeeping.

Because The Treehouse, tel. 775-7160 (same as Waipio Valley Wagon Tours), Box 5086, Honokaa, HI 96727, is so remote, it is necessary to make reservations well in advance. Rates at The Treehouse, which can handle two "very friendly" couples, are $200 per couple first day, $150 p/d thereafter, and $25 per additional person over 12 years old. Rates for The Hale, which can sleep up to six, are $75 double occupancy, $25 per additional person. A 50% deposit is requested with the reservation, and a two-week cancellation notice prior to arrival is necessary for a refund. Nature still rules Waipio, and about 10 days per year the streams are flooded and it is impossible to get either in or out. If you can't get in, a prompt refund will be made, and if you're lucky enough to be marooned, complimentary lodging and food will be cordially provided for the duration of your stay.

WAIMANU VALLEY, CAMPING AND HIKING

The hike down to Waipio and over the *pali* to Waimanu Valley 12 miles away is one of the top three treks in Hawaii. You must be fully

Waipio Beach

J.D. BISIGNANI

prepared for camping and in excellent condition to attempt this hike. Also, water from the streams and falls is not always good for drinking due to irrigation and cattle grazing topside; bring purification tablets or boil or filter it to be safe. To get to Waimanu Valley, a switchback trail leads over the *pali* about 100 yards inland from Waipio Beach. The beginning of the switchback trail has a post with a painting that reads "Warning Menehune." Waimanu was bought by the State of Hawaii about 12 years ago, and they are responsible for trail maintenance. The trail ahead is rough, as you go up and down about 14 gulches before reaching Waimanu. At the ninth gulch is a trail shelter. Finally, below is Waimau Valley, half the size of Waipio but more verdant, and even wilder because it has been uninhabited for a longer time. Cross Waimanu Stream in the shallows where it meets the sea. For drinking water (remember to treat it), walk along the west side of the *pali* until you find a likely waterfall. To stay overnight in Waimanu Valley you must have a (free) camping permit available through the Division of Forestry and Wildlife, Box 4849, Hilo, HI 96721, tel. 933-4221, open Tues.-Fri. 8 a.m.-4 p.m., Mon. 10 a.m.-4 p.m. Your length of stay is limited to seven days and six nights. Each of the nine designated campsites has a fireplace and a composting outhouse. Carry out what you carry in!

Early this century, because of economic necessity brought on by the valley's remoteness, Waimanu was known for its *okolehau* (moonshine). Solomon, one of the elders of the community at the time, decided that Waimanu had to diversify for the good of its people. He decided to raise domesticated pigs introduced by the Chinese, who roasted them with spices in rock ovens as a great delicacy. Solomon began to raise and sell the pigs commercially, but when he died, out of respect, no one wanted to handle his pigs, so they let them run loose. They began to interbreed with feral pigs, and after a while there were so many pigs in Waimanu that they ate all the taro, bananas, and breadfruit. The porkers' voracious appetites caused a famine which forced the last remaining families of Waimanu to leave in the late 1940s. Most of the trails that you will encounter are made by wild-pig hunters who still regularly go after Solomon's legacy.

According to oral tradition the first *kahuna lapa'au* (healing doctor) of Hawaii was from Waimanu Valley. His disciples crossed and recrossed Waipio Valley, greatly influencing the development of the area. Some of the *heiau* in Waipio are specifically dedicated to the healing of the human torso; their origins are traced to the healing *kahuna* of Waimanu.

PUNA

The Puna District was formed from rivers of lava spilling from Mauna Loa and Kilauea again and again over the last million years or so. The molten rivers stopped only when they hit the sea, where they fizzled and cooled, forming a chunk of semi-raw land that bulges into the Pacific—marking the state's easternmost point at **Cape Kumukahi.** These titanic lava flows have left phenomenal reminders of their power. **Lava Tree State Monument** was once a rainforest whose giant trees were covered with lava, like hot dogs dipped in batter. The encased wood burned, leaving a hollow stone skeleton. You can stroll through this lichengreen rock forest before you head farther east into the brilliant sunshine of the coast. Little-traveled side roads take you past a multitude of orchid, anthurium, and papaya farms, oases of color in a desert of solid black lava. A lighthouse sits atop Cape Kumukahi, and to the north an ancient paved trail passes beaches where no one ever goes.

Southward is a string of popular beaches—some white, some black. You can camp, swim, surf, or just play in the water to your heart's delight. Villages have gas and food, and all along the coast you can visit natural areas where the sea tortured the hot lava into caves, tubes, arches, and even a natural bathtub whose waters are flushed and replenished by the sea. There are historical sites where petroglyphs tell vague stories from the past, and where generations of families placed the umbilical cords of their newborn into manmade holes in the rock. On Puna's south coast are remains of ancient villages. The park **visitor center** that used to stand just before the beginning of Chain of Craters Road burned down in the summer of 1989 when lava surged across the road, severing this eastern gateway to Volcanoes National Park. (The road is still closed, with no opening scheduled for the near future. See pp. 224-226.) The **Hawaii Belt Road** (Route 11) is a corridor cutting through the center of Puna. It goes through the highlands to Volcanoes National Park, passing well-established villages and scattered housing develop-

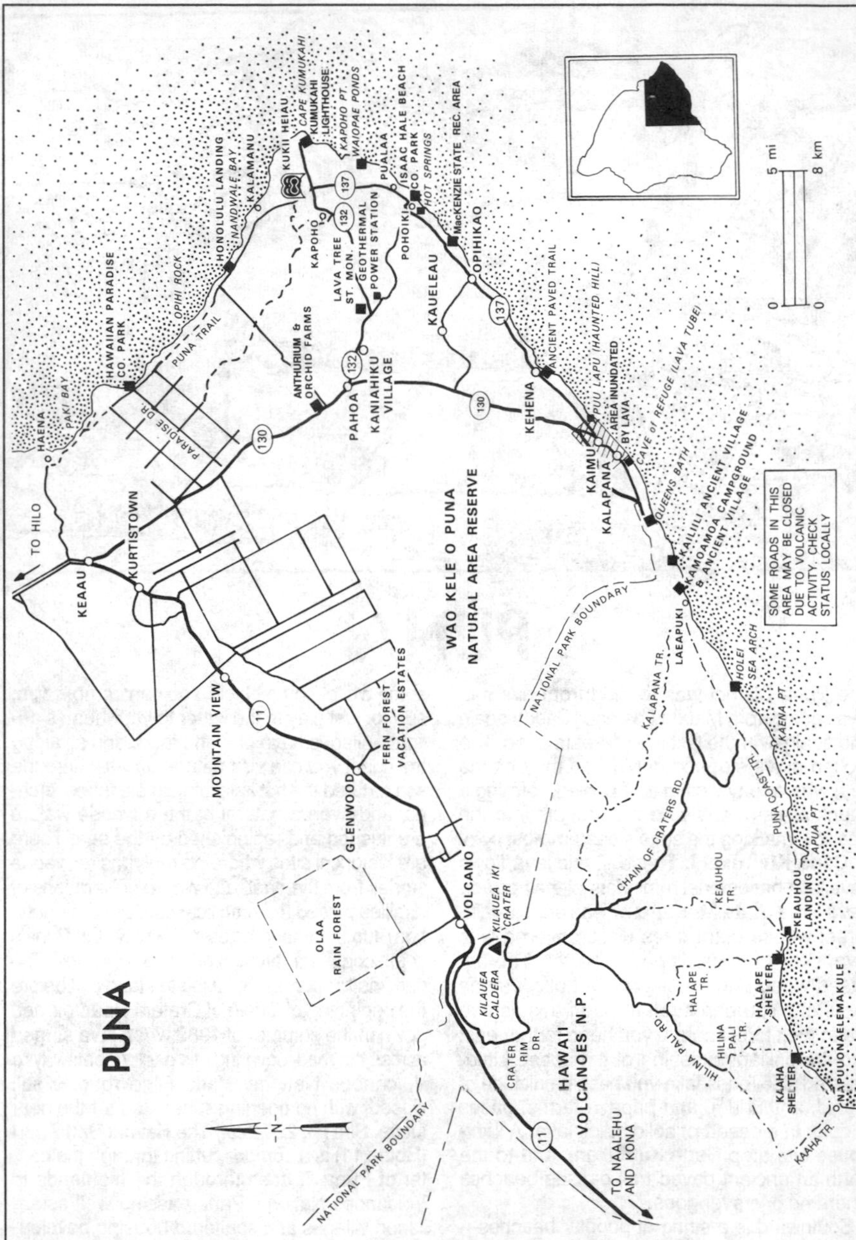
PUNA
TO HILO
HAENA
PAKI BAY
KEAAU
KURTISTOWN
HAWAIIAN PARADISE CO. PARK
PARADISE DR.
PUNA TRAIL
OPIHI ROCK
HONOLULU LANDING
NANAWALE BAY
KALAMANU
KUKII HEIAU
CAPE KUMUKAHI
KUMUKAHI LIGHTHOUSE
KAPOHO PT.
WAIOPAE PONDS
ISAAC HALE BEACH
PUALAA
ISAAC HALE CO. PARK
HOT SPRINGS
MacKENZIE STATE REC. AREA
KAPOHO
LAVA TREE ST. MON.
GEOTHERMAL POWER STATION
POHOIKI
OPIHIKAO
ANTHURIUM & ORCHID FARMS
PAHOA
KANIAHIKU VILLAGE
KAUELEAU
ANCIENT PAVED TRAIL
KEHENA
PUU LAPU (HAUNTED HILL)
AREA INUNDATED BY LAVA
CAVE of REFUGE (LAVA TUBE)
KAIMU
KALAPANA
QUEENS BATH
KAILIILI ANCIENT VILLAGE
KAMOAMOA CAMPGROUND & ANCIENT VILLAGE
LAEAPUKI
HOLEI SEA ARCH
KAENA PT.
PUNA COAST TR.
APUA PT.
KEAUHOU LANDING
HALAPE SHELTER
KAAHA SHELTER
NAPUUONAELEMAKULE
KAAHA TR.
HILINA PALI TR.
HALAPE TR.
KEAUHOU TR.
HILINA PALI RD.
CHAIN OF CRATERS RD.
KALAPANA TR.
NATIONAL PARK BOUNDARY
WAO KELE O PUNA NATURAL AREA RESERVE
MOUNTAIN VIEW
GLENWOOD
FERN FOREST VACATION ESTATES
VOLCANO
OLAA RAIN FOREST
KILAUEA IKI CRATER
KILAUEA CALDERA
CRATER RIM DR.
HAWAII VOLCANOES N.P.
TO NAALEHU AND KONA
N
11
130
132
137
SOME ROADS IN THIS AREA MAY BE CLOSED DUE TO VOLCANIC ACTIVITY. CHECK STATUS LOCALLY
0
5 mi
8 km

ments as new as the lava on which they precariously sit. Back in these hills, new-wave gardeners grow "Puna Butter" *pakalolo,* as wild and raunchy as its name. On the border of Puna and the Kau District to the south is **Hawaii Volcanoes National Park.** Here the goddess Pele resides at Kilauea Caldera, center of one of the world's most active volcanoes.

HAWAII BELT ROAD ~ HILO TO VOLCANOES

Route 11 (Hawaii Belt Road) splits in Keaau and passes through the high mountain villages of Mountain View, Glenwood, and Volcano, then enters Hawaii Volcanoes National Park. It takes a full day and then some to see and appreciate Volcanoes Park, so if "making time" is your main consideration, this is the way to go. The Belt Road, although only two lanes, is straight, well surfaced, and scrupulously maintained. However, if you want much more exciting scenery and a host of natural and historic sites, head south on Route 130 toward Pahoa and the east coast. Route 130 shouldn't be traveled at night, however. In short, if time is on your side, take one day to visit Volcanoes, using the Belt Road for convenience, and another to "Sunday drive" Route 130 along the coast.

KEAAU

Keaau is the first town south of Hilo (10 miles) on Route 11, and although pleasant enough, it's little more than a Y in the road. At the junction of Route 11 and Route 130 is **Keaau Town Center,** a small shopping mall with a handful of variety stores, a laundromat, a post office, restaurants, and a sizable **Ben Franklin's.** Here, the **Sure Save Supermarket** not only has groceries but plenty of sundries and a decent camera department, along with a public fax service.

Food

The local **Dairy Queen,** in the Keaau Town Center, not only makes malts and sundaes but serves breakfast, lunch, and dinner. Plate specials, burgers, and sandwiches like a Reuben with french fries go for $4.95. Next door to the Sure Save Supermarket, the **New Seoul Barbecue,** open daily except Sunday 9 a.m.-9:30 p.m., is an inexpensive, shocking-yellow formi-ca-and-linoleum Korean restaurant offering tasty meals like barbecued beef, chicken, rice, macaroni salad, pickle, and squash jam all for $4.95; or combination plates of steak, chicken, shrimp, sashimi, rice, and macaroni salad for $8.50. Next door is a tiny hole-in-the-wall eatery, **Lunch at Miu's,** that sells an assortment of *manapua* and spring rolls for under $1, steaming bowls of saimin, and plate lunches. For those who want to try an island treat like crackseed or shave ice, visit the center's **Kaeo Krack Seed,** open daily except Sunday 9 a.m.-5 p.m.

Across the street, and a few hundred yards down Route 130, is **Keaau Natural Foods** with a large stock of organic food items, herbs, and grains but no juice or snack bar. However, premade sandwiches like *tempeh* burgers with all the trimmings are $5, and fresh-baked goods are always available.

Tonya's Cafe is a tiny place next door to Keaau Natural Foods; hours are Mon.-Fri. 11 a.m.-7 p.m., closed Saturday and Sunday. Tonya, tiny herself but of big spirit, has surfer specials, sandwiches, and side orders like nachos and tostadas, but the main cuisine is "international vegetarian" featuring an eclectic selection of recipes—anything from Thai to Jamaican. Tonya's is a mix of funky and yuppie in a moderate but tasteful decor where you can read the latest metaphysical tome while eating a frozen yogurt. Her hours can be irregular, but when she's there she serves up some of the best vegetarian food (organic when possible) on this side of the island.

Catty-corner to the shopping mall, just near the red light, look for **Lorenzo's Badass Coffee Bar and Cafe,** open from about 8 a.m. to 10:30 p.m., where you can have an "individually made" cup of coffee or espresso from beans roasted by the Big Island's own Badass Coffee Company (see pp. 274-275). You can also munch on an assortment of bagels and cream cheese $1.50, tuna melt or fish sandwiches $2.95, pizza by the slice, salads—or forget the waistline and go for ice cream and pie. The corner location makes Lorenzo's perfect for people-watching.

A few hundred yards down Route 130 heading toward Pahoa, you'll see **Verna's Drive-In,** and behind it is a small mall with a **Wiki Wiki Mini-Mart.**

MOUNTAIN VILLAGES

South along Route 11, at approximately 10-mile intervals, are Mountain View, Glenwood, and Volcano. **Mountain View** is a village of nurseries specializing in anthuriums. Many of them sport signs inviting you to a free tour. Along Route 11 is a mini-mart and **Verna's Too Snack Shop** serving plate lunches, burgers, and shakes. As you pass through, take a minute to explore the short side-road into the village itself. Every house has a garden of ferns, flowers, and native trees. In the village is **Mt. View Bakery,** home of the famous stone cookies; and the **Mt. View Village Store,** which is fairly well supplied.

Look for a vintage plantation house painted blue between mile markers 12 and 13. This is **Tinny Fisher's Antique Shop,** owned and operated by Charles and Dorothy Wittig. What started as "yard sale treasures" about 10 years ago has turned into a unique curio, antique, and collectibles shop. Open daily except Monday, noon-6 p.m., the shop has all kinds of antiques and collectibles from Asia and Hawaii, including glass balls, Asian furniture, jewelry, and glassware galore. Tinny's also features a good Hawaiiana collection, with artifacts from the ancient days like *kukui* nut lamps, poi pounders, and stone knives.

Glenwood, between mile markers 19 and 20, offers a gas station and **Hirano's General Store** for basic provisions. A few minutes down the road you pass **Akatsuka Tropical Orchids and Flower Gardens,** open daily 8:30 a.m.-5 p.m. If tour buses don't overflow the parking lot, stop in for a look at how orchids are grown or to use the clean restrooms. They offer a complimentary orchid to all visitors. Just before you enter Volcanoes National Park, a sign points to the right down a short side road to **Volcano village** (see pp. 221 and 227-232).

ROUTE 130 AND THE SOUTHEAST COAST

The most enjoyable area in the Puna District is the southeast coast, with its beaches and points of natural and historical interest. If you take Route 130 south from Keaau, in about 12 miles you pass **Pahoa.** As in Keaau, Pahoa is primarily a crossroad. You can continue due south on Route 130 to the seaside villages of **Kaimu** and **Kalapana,** where Route 130 joins coastal Route 137, feeding into Chain of Craters Road which has been buried by recent lava flows and is impassable. (For more information on Chain of Craters Road see pp. 224-226.) Along Route 130, about halfway between Pahoa and Kaimu, look for a small, unobtrusive sign that reads "Scenic Overlook." Pull off and walk toward the sea until you find four hot steam vents. Many local people use them as natural saunas.

You might go directly east from Pahoa along Route 132. This lovely, tree-lined country road takes you past **Lava Tree State Monument,** which shouldn't be missed, and then branches northeast, intersecting Route 137 and terminating at **Cape Kumukahi.** If this seems *too* far out of the way, head down **Pohoiki Road,** just past Lava Tree. You bypass a controversial geothermal power station, then reach the coast at **Isaac Hale Beach Park.** From there, Route 137 heads southwest down the coast to Kalapana, passing the best Puna beaches en route. Fortunately for you, this area of Puna is one of those places where no matter which way you decide to go, you really can't go wrong.

PAHOA AND VICINITY

You can breeze through this "one-street" town, but you won't regret stopping if even for a few minutes. A raised wooden sidewalk passing false-front shops is fun to walk along to get a feeling of the last century. Most of the shops lining it are family-run fruit and vegetable stands supplied by local gardeners. Selections depend upon whether the old pickup truck started and made it to town that day. At one time Pahoa boasted *the* largest sawmill in America. Its buzz saw ripped ohia railway ties for the Santa Fe and other railroads. It was into one of these ties that the *golden spike* uniting the East and West coasts of the Mainland was driven. Many local people earned their livelihood from ohia charcoal that they made and sold all over the island until it was made obsolete by the widespread use of kerosene and gas introduced in the early 1950s. Pahoa's commercial heart went up in flames in 1955. Along the main street was a tofu factory that had a wood-fired furnace. The old fellow who owned the factory banked his fires as usual before he went home for the night. Somehow, they got out of control and burned all the way down to the main alley dividing the commercial district. The only reason the fire didn't jump the alley was because a papaya farmer happened to be around and had a load of water on the back of his truck, which he used to douse the buildings and save the town.

Pahoa is attempting to become part of the *Main Street U.S.A. Project* which will protect and revitalize its commercial center and bring new life to vintage buildings like the Akebono Theater, where classic movies will be shown. Pahoa has one of the highest concentrations of old buildings still standing in Hawaii that are easily accessible. Although it has been by-passed by a new road, make sure to enter the town and stroll along the tiny back roads. The town is attempting to become the anthurium capital of the world, and they have a good start on it. In virtually every garden, surrounded by distinctive lava-rock walls, you'll see black shade mesh under which are magnificent specimens of the normal red flowers, plenty of white ones, a few green, and even black anthuriums.

Lava Tree State Monument

In 1790, slick, fast-flowing *pa'hoehoe* lava surged through this ohia forest, covering the tree trunks from the ground to about a 12- foot level. The moisture inside the trees cooled the lava, forming a hardened shell. At the same time, tremors and huge fissures cracked the earth in the area. When the eruption ended, the still-hot lava drained away through the fissures, leaving the encased tree trunks standing like sentinels. The floor of the forest is so smooth in some areas that the lava seems like asphalt. Each lava tree has its own personality; some resemble totem poles, and it doesn't take much imagination to see old, craggy faces staring back at you. The most spectacular part of the park is near the entrance. Immense trees loom over cavernous cracks *(puka)* in the earth and send their roots, like stilled waterfalls, tumbling down into them. To get to Lava Tree, take Route 132 east from Pahoa for three miles and look for the well-marked entrance on the left. Brochures are available as you enter.

Cape Kumukahi

It's fitting that Kumukahi means "First Begin-ning" since it is the easternmost point of Hawaii

anthuriums under protective shade

and was recognized as such by the original Polynesian settlers. Follow Route 132 past Lava Tree for about 10 miles until it hits the coast, where a lighthouse sits like an exclamation point. Along the way, get an instant course in volcanology: you can easily chart the destructive and regenerative forces at work on Hawaii. At the five-mile marker an HVB Warrior points out the lava flow of 1955. Tiny plants give the lava a greenish cast, and shrubs are already eating into it, turning it to soil. Papaya orchards grow in the raw lava of an extensive flat basin. The contrast between the black, lifeless earth and the vibrant green trees is startling. In the center of the flatland rises a cinder cone, a caldera of a much older mini-volcano unscathed by the modern flows; it is gorgeous with lush vegetation. An HVB Warrior points out the lava flow of 1960, and you can see at a glance how different it was from the flow of five years earlier. When Route 132 intersects Route 137, go straight ahead east down a paved road for two miles to the Cape Kumukahi Lighthouse. People in these parts swear that on the fateful night in 1960 when the nearby village of Kapoho was consumed by the lava flow, an old woman (a favorite guise of Madame Pele) came to town begging for food and was turned away by everyone. She next went to the lighthouse asking for help, and was cordially treated by the lighthouse keeper. When the flow was at its strongest, it came within yards of the lighthouse and then miraculously split, completely encircling the structure but leaving it unharmed as it continued out to sea for a considerable distance.

Practicalities

When you pull into Pahoa you are greeted by the **Pahoa Village Center,** a small shopping center where you'll find a **laundromat** and a video store. Almost adjacent is **The Rib House,** basically counter service offering baby-back ribs, chicken, and burgers at reasonable prices. Here too is **Dairy Queen,** open daily 7 a.m.-8:30 p.m. for breakfast, lunch, and dinner. They serve everything from banana splits to chicken, pizza, and plate lunches. A minute down the road is **Pahoa Cash and Carry** grocery store, **7-Eleven,** and the **Pahoa Casherette,** which are enough for any supplies or incidentals that you may need. Close by is **Pahoa Chop Suey,** a downhome restaurant where you can

eat cheaply; and down the street is **Luquin's Place,** open daily 11 a.m.-9 p.m., tel. 965-9990, a reasonably priced Mexican restaurant that offers enchiladas, burritos, tacos, and combination platters for $5-7.

Pahoa Natural Groceries, tel. 965-8322, open weekdays 9 a.m.-9 p.m., Sun. 9 a.m.-6 p.m., specializing in organic fruits and juices, is one of the finest health food stores on the Big Island. They have an excellent selection of fresh vegies, organic grains, herbs and minerals, and deli items, and a very good bakery selection (see The Bamboo House in the following "Accommodations" section). Adjacent is **The Emporium,** open daily 10 a.m.-6 p.m., with a small but excellent selection of jewelry, Guatemalan clothing, gifts, magazines, and cards. The Emporium also displays artwork, some by local artists, and a colorful selection of rugs. Their shirts and dresses, all 100% cotton, cost $25-50.

Halemana, tel. 965-7783, open Mon.-Fri. 9 a.m.-5 p.m. or by appointment, adjacent to the health food store, is an acupuncture and massage clinic. The acupuncturists are Françoise Hesselink, Jocelyn Mayeux, and Rhonda Ashby. Relax as you lie on the table and breezes blow through the vintage rooms. Let one of these fine practitioners energize and revitalize your spirit and put spring back into your aching muscles.

The **Puna Sands Restaurant,** a block away, makes luscious banana, papaya, or passion fruit smoothies for $2. Sandwiches, all under $5, include roast beef with peppers sautéed in olive oil on a French roll, barbecued ham with homemade sauce, and Italian sausage and peppers with spaghetti sauce. There's also a breakfast special for $1.95. The Pahoa **Coffee Shop** along the main drag specializes in breakfast, but is open for lunch and dinner too. Next door is the **Pahoa Lounge** that rocks with live music every Friday and Saturday night.

Along the elevated boardwalk, you'll spot shops like **Ernie's Produce;** a laundromat; and **T-shirt Boutique,** tel. 965-9776, open daily except Sunday 10 a.m.-4 p.m, where Alva sells tees of all description, from tie-dyed to originals by local artists. Or bring home a permanent souvenir from **Through the Looking Glass, Skin Illusions,** where one hour and $125 will get you an "entry level" tattoo at this fully licensed parlor where only pre-sterilized, single-service utensils and tools are used. Before you decide on a

tree mold formed when lava flowed around a banana tree

tattoo, maybe you should drop in next door at **Pacific Mystics,** a new-age shop, and consult the tarot while browsing among books, crystals, surfboards, and a cosmic smattering of clothes and sunglasses. Up the walk is **Threads,** open daily except Sunday, 10 a.m.-4:30 p.m., where seamstress Mariko Jones will tailor shirts, blouses, and pants to your specifications. She also sells new and used alohawear.

It's a toss-up whether the name **Kukui Hale,** "The Nut House," more aptly describes the characters running this offbeat art shop or the pieces they create, open 10 a.m.-5 p.m. sort of, daily sort of, depending upon their mood. Hanging around the shop are "coconotes" (painted coconuts that can be sent through the mail) for $20 and coconut fiber (sennet) baskets at $20-60. From the ceilings, $12 "angels of the rainforest" (coconuts made into cherubs) smile down upon you. Judith Pearl, one of the owners, also paints mythical renderings of Pele, or whales floating in a pink and azure sky. Next door, look for **Simply Natural,** open daily except Sunday 10:30 a.m.-7:30 p.m., serving sandwiches, shave ice, homemade Hilo ice cream, high-protein shakes, and daily specials like chili and sandwiches. Simply Natural also has a smattering of silver jewelry, penny candy and antiques. Adjacent is **Naung Mai Thai Food,** open daily for lunch and dinner, tel. 965-8186, where you can dine on Thai spring rolls $4.95; red, green, or yellow curried shrimp, chicken, or beef $8.95; or a hearty bowl of Thai chicken-coconut

soup $6.95. A full vegetarian selection, including tofu and eggplant curry $5.95, and rice and noodles $7.95, completes the menu.

One of the best places to eat in Pahoa is **Paradise West Coffee Shop,** tel. 965-9733, open 7 a.m.-2 p.m. daily, breakfast until noon, owned and operated by Dave and Carrie Marry. Dave has a remarkable knowledge of Pahoa's history that he is willing to share if time permits. Breakfast is served with hash browns, rice, and buttermilk biscuits, and includes eggs with bacon $4.95, two eggs with fresh catch priced daily, and their very famous hollandaise sauce that tops eggs Benedict. One of the best deals is *huevos rancheros* with tortillas, beans, and salsa for $3.95. The lunch menu is basic cheeseburgers, tempeh burgers, and turkey sandwiches, all priced under $5.50. The menu changes daily, but you can count on fresh fish, tender steaks, and pasta for $5.95 that can be covered with sun-dried tomatoes, olive oil, parmesan, and fresh basil. They also take care of the vegetarians with tofu scramble and a daily vegie special (see Marry Whales Hotel in the following "Accommodations" section).

Wetlands Saloon, tel. 964-7488, on Pahoa's main street, features live music every weekend that can include local groups like To the Max or Pat Pauline playing everything from rock to blues. Next door is **Koho Okazuya,** open from 7 a.m., a window restaurant serving continental breakfast $2.60, and a variety of lunches like pineapple chicken, beef stew, and hamburger patties. A minute further down the elevated sidewalk is **Da Store** with groceries, a deli case, beer, and liquor.

Let your mind and stomach be soothed with cosmic vibrations and libations at **Huna Ohana,** open daily except Sunday for breakfast 8-11 a.m., lunch 11 a.m.-5:30 p.m., tel. 965-9661. The metaphysical bookstore (open until 6 p.m.) and cafe is owned and operated by Dawn Hurwitz. Vegetarian breakfast dishes include egg soufflé or tofu scramble served with cottage potatoes and multigrain toast at $3.95; bagels and cream cheese $1.75; and an assortment of croissants and special muffins such as purple sweet potato, chocolate zucchini, blueberry, and poppy seed with raspberry filling. Lunch brings pita pizza $3.95, vegie sandwiches $3.50, filling garden burgers (a blend of mushrooms, onions, rolled oats, lowfat mozzarella, brown rice, cottage cheese, eggs, cheddar, bulgur wheat, walnuts and spices) $4.75, or Jamaican patties (a curry pastry turnover with mixed vegie or spinach-and-squash filling) $2. To get those cosmic vibes kicked into high gear, order a cup of espresso, mocha latte, or cappuccino, choose a likely tome from the bookstore section, and kick back on an overstuffed couch or outside in the garden area.

A pipe dream that came true is **The Hawaiian Hemp Company,** open weekdays 10 a.m.-9 p.m., Sun. noon-6 p.m., tel. 965-8600. The shop is filled from floor to ceiling with hemp, one of the oldest and most useful plants known to humanity. The organic, all-hemp products include fanny packs, "Pakaloha" shirts, hip sun hats, shoulder bags, vests, twine, paper, and even hemp oil—nutritionally valuable, with a high concentration of essential fatty acids important to the immune system and in helping to fight cholesterol. Some fashions come from Macao and contain a blend of cotton, while others are made and designed in Hawaii from cloth woven in China. A mini-museum features hemp and its many uses around the world in music, art, medicine, and religious rites, and as a mind-altering drug. For excellent products and a mind-opening education, make sure to stop in at the Hawaiian Hemp Company.

Yo Pizza, tel. 965-7033, open daily except Monday 11 a.m.-10 p.m., uses homemade sauces and dough to make small, medium, and large traditional pizzas costing $4.90-14.90.

They also have Italian Caesar salads $4.50, garden salad $2.75, garlic bread $1.50, and hot, rich cappuccino and espresso, perfect with slices of homemade pie. Lunch can be sub sandwiches $4.50, or you can dine on dinner specials like lasagna or spaghetti and meatballs for $6.50. The decor is "basic pizza parlor" sautéed in olive oil and garlic.

Accommodations

Out behind the Paradise West Coffee Shop (see above) is the **Marry Whales Hotel,** a onetime house of ill repute. Japanese entertainment troupes used to lodge here while performing at one of three major theaters in town. The hotel has 14 rooms, a quiet courtyard filled with flowers and cacti, and a Japanese *ofuro* which is now an outside bath painted by a local artist to look like the inside of an aquarium. The classically designed redwood structure is in remarkably good shape. Monthly rates only are $250-300 including utilities. Shared bathrooms are clean and newly painted but basic. No reservations are accepted because of the limited number of rooms, but always check with Dave at the coffee shop because he knows of other people in the area willing to rent rooms.

Pahoa Natural Groceries (see above) rents **The Bamboo House,** $45 d first night, $35 three nights or more, with rates for four people, just a minute's walk from the store. Small, basic, and clean, it features a bedroom with a queen-sized bed, fold-out couch, private bath, and cable color TV. Write the Bamboo House, Box 1429, Pahoa, HI 96778; or phone the health food store at tel. 965-8322. A 25% deposit is required.

Whittaker's B&B, Box 1324, Pahoa, HI 96778, tel. 965-7015, offers two bedrooms with private baths in a new home located in the Puna rainforest. Each room, large enough for a small family, rents for $50 double, children under 12 free.

KAIMU AND KALAPANA

Special Note

Kaimu and Kalapana have been annihilated by the advancing lava flow. For a full description of **Chain Of Craters Road** see pp. 224-226. Parts of the road are still open, but only *from* Volcanoes National Park.

Sights

Star of the Sea Catholic Church is a small but famous structure better known as **The Painted Church.** An effort to save the historic church from the lava was mounted, and it has been moved. It now sits along the road waiting for a permanent home. A brief history of the area asserts that the now-inundated Kalapana was a spiritual magnet for Roman Catholic priests. Old Spanish documents support evidence that a Spanish priest, crossing the Pacific from Mexico, actually landed very near here in 1555. Father Damien, famous priest of the Molokai Leper Colony, established a grass church about two miles north and conducted a school when he first arrived in the islands in 1864. The present church dates from 1928, when Father Everest Gielen began its construction. Like an inspired but much less talented Michelangelo, this priest painted the ceiling of the church, working mostly at night by oil lamp. Father Everest was transferred to Lanai in 1941, and the work wasn't completed until 1964, when Mr. George Heidler, an artist from Atlanta, Georgia, came to Kalapana and decided to paint the unfinished lower panels in the altar section. The artwork itself can only be described as gaudy but sincere. The colors are wild blues, purples, and oranges. The ceiling is adorned with symbols, portraits of Christ, the angel Gabriel, and scenes from the Nativity. Behind the altar, a painted perspective gives the impression that you're looking down a long hallway at an altar that hangs suspended in air. The church is definitely worth a few minutes at least.

End Of The Road

Just near the lava-inundated village of Kalapana, routes 130 and 137 come to an abrupt halt where Madame Pele has repaved the road with lava. At the end of the line you come to a barricaded area. A bulletin board informs you about the current volcanic activity that has continued virtually unabated since Jan. 1983, when lava fountains soared 1500 feet into the sky and produced a cone over 800 feet tall. The initial lava flow was localized at Puu O'o vent, but after dozens of eruptive episodes it shifted to Kupaianaha, which has continuously produced about half a million cubic yards of lava per day. The lava flows eight miles to the sea, mostly through lava tubes. It has inundated almost

J.D. BISIGNANI

inside The Painted Church

20,000 acres, caused $25 million worth of property damage, and added more than 100 acres of new land to the Puna Coast. (For more information see pp. 216-217.)

A sign strongly warns you against walking out onto the lava. Some hazards that you may encounter are brushfires, smoke, ash, and methane gas, which is extremely explosive. You can also fall through the thin-crusted lava into a tube which will immediately reduce you to a burnt offering to Pele, and unceremoniously deposit your ashes into the sea! New lava can cut like broken glass, and molten lava can be flung through the air by steam explosions, especially near the coastline. Seacliffs collapse frequently, and huge boulders can be tossed several hundred feet into the air. The steam clouds contain minerals that can cause burning eyes, throat and skin irritations, and difficulty in breathing.

If you are still intrigued, realize that you are on the most unstable piece of real estate on the face of the earth. For those maniacs, fools, adventurers, and thrill-seekers who just can't stay away, the walk to the sea takes about 25 minutes. Give yourself up for dead, and proceed. Follow the old roadbed, up and down, over the lava. When you can no longer discern the road, look off to your left and you'll see a large steam cloud rising. Pick your way to it, but don't get too close. Observers say that every day, huge chunks fall off into the sea in this area. As you look back at the mountain you can see heat waves rising from the land upon which you are standing. A camera with a zoom lens or a pair of binoculars accentuates this phenomenon. The whole mountain waves in front of you. As you walk closer to the sea, the lava cools and you can see every type there is: rope lava, lava toes, lava fingers. The tortured flow, that crinkles as you walk over it, has created many imaginative shapes: gargoyles, medieval faces, dolphins, and mythical creatures. At the coast, the lava pours into the sea, creating a white spume of steam lifting 200-300 feet into the air. No other place in the world gives you the opportunity to be the first person to tread upon the earth's newest land.

Practicalities

Keoki's Mart, inland from the former Kaimu black-sand beach, still stands but has been surrounded by lava. As of this writing, it is closed.

Kalani Honua, Box 4500, Kalapana, HI 96778, tel. 965-7828, is an international conference and retreat center, a haven where people come when they truly want to get away from it all. The entrance is located a few miles north of Kalapana on Route 137 between mile markers 17 and 18. Look for a large pink Visitors Welcome sign and proceed until you see the office area and a gift and sundries shop. Depending upon the yearly schedule, they offer a variety of activities that include holistic massage, meditation, yoga, and *lei*-making. Contact them to find out what's happening when you'll be on the Big Island. The grounds have a commune-type atmosphere, with a rain-fed swimming pool, hot tub, Jacuzzi, assembly studios, classrooms, and cedar lodges with kitchen facilities. It's the only place along the Puna Coast that offers lodging and vegetarian fare. Rates are $28 s for a dorm room with shared bath, $52 s and $62 d for a private room with shared bath, $65 s and $75 d for a private room with private bath, guest cottage $85. A conch shell calls you to

breakfast at 8 a.m. and to dinner at 6 p.m. (nonguests welcome). The meals cost $6 and $10 respectively, with a meal ticket pre-purchased at the office. Lights go out at 10:30 p.m., but candles are provided for night owls. Kalani Honua is not for everyone, but if you are looking for unpretentious peace and quiet, there's no better place on the island.

Hale Kipa O Kiana, tel. 965-8661, a modern guesthouse owned and operated by Diana Allegra, is located along Route 137 very close to the now lava-inundated Harry K. Brown Beach Park. Diana is a wonderful cook and loves to do breakfast, which is $5 extra pp and consists of home-baked bread, fresh locally grown fruit, homemade jams, and coffee. The knotty pine guest room, suitable for one or two people, is of open-beam design, is fully carpeted, and has tasteful artwork on the walls. This room features louvered wooden doors, an extra-large closet, desk, private sink, and private bath. Rates are $30 s, $35 d, $10 additional person, and $200 weekly. Accommodations also include use of the massage room complete with dance barre, wall mirror, and a smattering of free weights. The house is styled in a beautiful neo-Hawaiian classical design, and the upstairs, where Diana resides, has a huge porch which extends over the downstairs area, so you have your own lanai with wrought-iron furniture and a chaise lounge. The home overlooks a dramatic landscape of sea and lava, and is only a short walk from two newly formed black-sand beaches.

BEACHES, PARKS, AND CAMPGROUNDS

All of Puna's beaches, parks, and campgrounds lie along coastal Route 137 stretching for 20 miles from Pohoiki to Kamoamoa (recently wiped out by lava flow, see pp. 224-226). Surfers, families, transients, even nude-sunbathing "buffs" have their favorite beaches along this southeast coast. For the most part, swimming is possible, but be cautious during high tide. There is plenty of sun, snorkeling sites, and good fishing, and the campgrounds are almost always available.

Isaac Hale County Beach Park

You can't miss this beach park located on Pohoiki Bay, at the junction of Route 137 and Po-

the Puna Coast

holki Road. Just look for a jumble of boats and trailers parked under the palms. At one time Pohoiki Bay served the Hawaiians as a canoe landing, then later became the site of a commercial wharf for the Puna Sugar Company. It remains the only boat launching area for the entire Puna Coast, used by pleasure boaters and commercial fishermen. Due to this dual role, it's often very crowded. Full amenities include pavilions, restrooms, and showers (county permit). Experienced surfers dodge the rip-current in the center of the bay, and swimming is generally good when the sea is calm. Pohoiki Bay is also one of the best scuba sites on the island. Within walking distance of the salt-and-pepper beach are hot springs that bubble into lava sinks surrounded by lush vegetation. They're popular with tourists and residents, and provide a unique and relaxing way to wash away sand and salt. To find them, face away from the sea and turn left, then look for a small but well-worn path that leads through the jungle. The pools are warm, small, and tranquil. Harmless, tiny brine shrimp nibble at your toes while you soak.

MacKenzie State Recreation Area

This popular state park was named for forest ranger A.J. MacKenzie, highly regarded throughout the Puna District and killed in the area in 1938. The park's 13 acres sit among a cool grove of ironwoods originally planted by MacKenzie. A portion of the old King's Highway, scratched out by prisoners last century as a form of community service, bisects the area. Many people who first arrive on the Big Island hang out at MacKenzie until they can get their start. Consequently, the park receives its share of hard-core types, which has earned it a reputation for rip-offs. Mostly it's safe, but if you're camping, take precautions with your valuables. The entire coastline along MacKenzie is bordered by rugged black-lava seacliffs. Swimming is dangerous, but the fishing is excellent. Be extremely careful when beach-walking, especially out on the fingers of lava; over the years, people have been swept away by freak waves. MacKenzie Park is located along Route 137, two miles south of Isaac Hale. Full amenities and state permits for overnight camping are available.

Puala'a Beach Park

Quietly opened by the County of Hawaii on July 4, 1993, this lovely, 1.3-acre beach park (short on parking) was an ancient fishing village on the boundary of the *ahupua'a* of Leapao'o and Puala'a. Located along the *red road* between Kapoho and Opihikao, the park features a brackish pond warmed by underground volcanic activity. The swimming is safe except for periods of very high surf, and the park is perfect for families with young children.

Kehena

Kehena is actually two pockets of black-sand beach below a low seacliff. Entrance to the beach is marked only by a scenic pulloff on

*Fire and steam mark
the spot where lava
meets the sea.*

Route 137, about five miles south of MacKenzie; usually a half-dozen cars are parked there. At one time Kehena was very popular, and a stone staircase led down to the beach. In 1975 a strong earthquake jolted the area, breaking up the stairway and lowering the beach by three feet. Now access is via a well-worn path, but make sure to wear sneakers because the lava is rough. The ocean here is dangerous, and often pebbles and rocks whisked along by the surf can injure legs. Once down on the beach, head north for the smaller patch of sand, because the larger patch is open to the sea and can often be awash in waves. The black sand is hot, but a row of coconut palms provides shade. The inaccessibility of Kehena makes it a favorite "no-hassle" nude beach with many "full" sunbathers congregating here.

Note: Unfortunately, recent lava flows have completely covered the very popular **Kaimu Beach Park,** also known as Black Sand Beach, and **Harry K. Brown Beach Park.** Now, raw and rugged lava meets the sea to be slowly turned into beach parks for future generations.

HAWAII VOLCANOES NATIONAL PARK

INTRODUCTION

Hawaii Volcanoes National Park (HVNP) is an unparalleled experience in geological grandeur. The western end of the park is the summit of stupendous **Mauna Loa,** the most massive mountain on earth. The park's heart is **Kilauea Caldera,** encircled by 11 miles of **Crater Rim Drive.** At the park visitor center you can give yourself a crash course in geology while picking up park maps and information. Nearby is **Volcano House,** Hawaii's oldest hotel, which has hosted a steady stream of adventurers, luminaries, royalty, and heads of state ever since it opened its doors in the 1860s. Amidst all the natural wonders is a golf course—for those who want to boast they've done it all after hitting a sand wedge from a volcanic fissure. Just down the road is one of Hawaii's last remaining indigenous forests, providing the perfect setting for a bird sanctuary. Mauna Loa Road branches off Crater Rim Drive and ends at a foot trail for the hale and hearty who trek to the 13,677-foot summit.

The rim drive continues past steam vents, sulphur springs, and tortured faultlines that always seem on the verge of gaping wide and swallowing. You can peer into the maw of **Halemaumau Crater,** home of the fire goddess, Pele, and you'll pass **Hawaii Volcano Observatory** (not open to public), which has been monitoring geologic activity since the turn of the century. Nearby is the **Thomas A. Jaggar Museum,** an excellent facility where you can educate yourself on the past and present volcanology of the park. A fantastic walk is **Devastation Trail,** a paved path across a desolate black lava field where gray, lifeless trunks of a suffocated forest lean like old gravestones. Within minutes is **Thurston Lava Tube,** a magnificent natural tunnel *"leid"* by amazingly vibrant fern grottoes at the entrance and exit.

The indomitable power of Volcanoes National Park is apparent to all who come here. Mark Twain, enchanted by his sojourn through Vol-

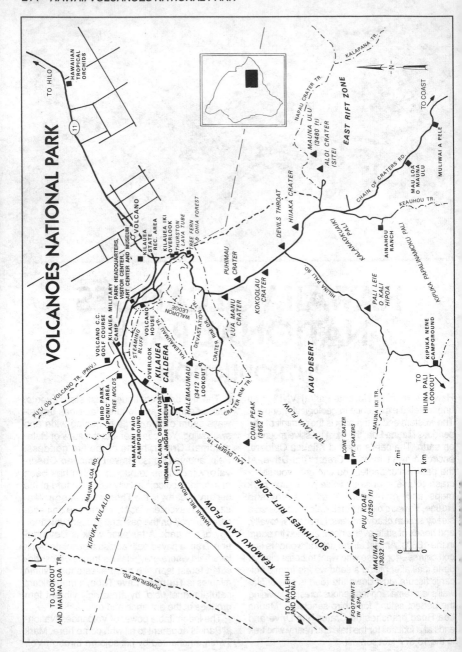

VOLCANOES NATIONAL PARK

1. hibiscus, the state flower (J.D. Bisignani); **2.** pink ginger (Dr. Greg Leo)

1. observatory atop Mauna Kea (J.D. Bisignani); **2.** Honokohau Harbor (J.D. Bisignani)

canoes in the 1860s, quipped, "The smell of sulphur is strong, but not unpleasant to a sinner." Amen brother! Wherever you stop to gaze, realize that you are standing on a thin skin of cooled lava in an unstable earthquake zone atop one of the world's most active volcanoes.

Note: For a description of the villages along Route 11 heading to Volcanoes, please see "Mountain Villages," p. 204.

Geologic History:
Science Versus Madame Pele
The goddess Pele is an irascible old dame. Perhaps it's because she had such a bad childhood. All she wanted was a home of her own where she could house her family and entertain her lover, a handsome chief from Kauai. But her sea goddess sister, Namakaokaha'i, flooded her out wherever she went after Pele seduced her husband, and the pig god, Kama Pu'a, ravished Pele for good measure. So Pele finally built her love nest at Halemaumau Crater at the south end of Kilauea Caldera. Being a goddess obviously isn't as heavenly as one would think, and whenever the pressures of life get too much for Pele, she blows her stack. These tempestuous outbursts made Pele one of the most revered gods in the Hawaiian pantheon because her presence and might were so easily felt.

For a thousand years Pele was appeased by offerings of pigs, dogs, sacred *ohelo* berries (her favorite) and now and again an outcast

man or two (never women) who would hopefully turn her energy from destruction to more comfortable pursuits. Also, if Pele was your family's personal goddess, your remains were sometimes allowed to be thrown into the fire pit as a sign of great respect. In the early 1820s, the chieftess Kapiolani, an ardent convert to Christianity, officially challenged Pele in an attempt to topple her like the other gods of old. Kapiolani climbed down into Pele's crater and ate the sacred *ohelo* berries, flagrantly violating the ageless *kapu*. She then took large stones and defiantly hurled them into the fire pit below while bellowing, "Jehovah is my God. It is He, not Pele, that kindled these flames."

Yet today, most residents, regardless of background, have an inexplicable reverence for Pele. The goddess has modernized her tastes, switching from *ohelo* to juniper berries that she prefers in liquid form as bottles of gin! The Volcano Post Office receives an average of three packages a week containing lava rocks taken by tourists as souvenirs (sometimes 30 per day). Some hold that Pele looks upon these rocks as her children and taking them from her is kidnapping. The accompanying letters implore the officials to return the rocks because ever since the offender brought them home, luck has been bad. The officials take the requests very seriously, returning the rocks with the customary peace offering: a bottle of gin. Many follow-up "thank you" letters have been written to express relief that the bad luck has been lifted. There

river of lava from a recent flow

is no reference in Hawaiian folklore to this phenomenon, although Hawaiians did hold certain rocks sacred. Park rangers will tell you that the idea of "the bad-luck rocks" was initiated a few decades back by a tour bus driver who became sick and tired of tourists getting his bus dirty by piling aboard their souvenirs. *Voilà* another ancient Hawaiian myth! Know, however, that the rocks in Hawaii Volcanoes National Park are protected by federal law, much meaner and more vindictive than Pele ever imagined being.

Pele is believed to take human form. She customarily appears before an eruption as a ravishing beauty or a withered old hag, often accompanied by a little white dog. She expects to be treated cordially, and it's said that she will stand by the roadside at night hitching a ride. After a brief encounter, she departs and seems to mysteriously evaporate into the ether. Kindness on your part is the key; if you come across a strange woman at night, treat her well—it might not help, but it definitely won't hurt.

Eruptions

The first white man atop Kilauea was Rev. William Ellis, who scaled it in 1823. Until the 1920s, the floor of the caldera was exactly what people thought a volcano would be: a burning lake of fire. Then the forces of nature changed, and the fiery lava subsided and hardened over. Today, Kilauea is called the only "drive-in" volcano in the world, and in recent years has been one of the most active, erupting almost continuously since 1983. When it begins gushing, the result is not a nightmare scene of people scrambling away for their lives, but just the opposite; people flock *to* the volcano. Most thrill-seekers are in much greater danger of being run over by a tour bus hustling to see the fireworks than of being entombed in lava. The volcanic action, while soul-shakingly powerful, is predictable and almost totally safe. The Hawaiian Volcano Observatory has been keeping watch since 1912, making Kilauea one of the best-understood volcanoes in the world. The vast volcanic field is creased by rift zones, or natural pressure valves. When the underground magma builds up, instead of *kaboom!* as in Mt. St. Helens, it bubbles to the surface like a spring and gushes out as a river of lava. Naturally, anyone or anything in its path would be burned to a cinder, but scientists routinely walk within a few feet of the still-flowing

lava to take readings. In much the way canaries detect mine gas, longtime lava observers pay attention to their ears. When the skin on top begins to blister, they know that they are too close. The lava establishes a course that it follows much like an impromptu mountain stream caused by heavy rains.

This does not mean that the lava flows are entirely benign, or that anyone should visit the area during an eruption without prior approval by the Park Service. When anything is happening, the local radio stations give up-to-the-minute news, and the Park Service provides a recorded message at tel. 967-7977. In 1790 a puff of noxious gases was emitted from Kilauea and descended on the Kau Desert, asphyxiating a rival army of Kamehameha's that just happened to be in the area. Eighty people died in their tracks. In 1881 a flow of lava spilled toward undeveloped Hilo and engulfed an area within today's city limits. In 1942, a heavy flow came within 12 miles of the city. Still, this was child's play in comparison with the unbelievable flow of 1950. Luckily, this went down the western rift zone where only scattered homes were in its path. It took no lives as it disgorged well over 600 million cubic yards of magma that covered 35 square miles! The flow continued for 23 days and produced seven huge torrents of lava that sliced across the Belt Road in three different areas. At its height, the lava front traveled six miles per hour and put out enough material to pave an eight-lane freeway twice around the world. In 1960, a flow swallowed the town of Kapoho on the east coast. In 1975, Hawaii's strongest earthquake since 1868 caused a tsunami to hit the southeast coast, killing two campers and sinking almost the entire Puna Coast by three feet.

The most recent, and very dramatic, series of eruptions that spectacularly began on Jan. 3, 1983, have continued virtually unabated ever since. Magma bubbled to the surface about two miles away from Pu'u O'o. The gigantic fissure fountained lava and formed Pu'u O'o Cinder Cone that is now 830 feet high and almost 1,000 feet across. Over a 3$\frac{1}{2}$-year period, there were 47 eruptions from this vent. On July 20, 1986 a new fissure, comprised of approximately two miles of fountaining lava, broke upon the surface at Kupaianaha, and has since formed a lava lake about one acre in size and 180 feet deep. At the end of April 1987 all activity suddenly

J.D. BISIGNANI

Pu'u O'o cinder cone

stopped and the lava drained from the lake and tube system, allowing scientists to accurately gauge the depth. About a week later, it all started up again when lava poured back into the lake, went through the tube system, and flowed back down to the ocean. The output is estimated at 650,000 cubic yards per day, which is equal to 55,000 truckloads of cement, enough to cover a football field 38 miles high.

From that point, the flow turned destructive and started taking homes. It moved to the coast in tubes, wiping out Kapaahu, parts of Kalapana, and most of the Royal Gardens Subdivision, with over 70 homes incinerated. In May 1989 it moved into the national park proper, and on June 22, it swallowed the park visitor center at Waha'ula. So far, it has spared Waha'ula Heiau (see pp. 225-226). The destruction has caused over $25 million worth of damage. Many of the homesteaders in the worst areas of the flow were rugged individualists and back-to-nature alternative types who lived in homes that generally had no electricity, running

water, or telephones. The homes were wiped out. Some disreputable insurance companies with legitimate policy holders tried to wiggle out of paying premiums for lost homes, although the policies specifically stipulated loss by lava flow. The insurance companies whined that the 2,000° lava never really touched some of the homes, and therefore, they were exonerated from paying the coverage. Their claims were resoundingly repudiated in the courts, and people were paid for their losses. One gentleman, however, has been forced to continue living in the middle of the lava flow. He's been there from the beginning because his insurance company will not pay if he leaves, claiming that the house was abandoned and therefore not covered. He sits in the middle of the lava plain with the flows all around him. For the last seven years, he's ridden a bicycle out from his house to the road. From there he goes to work and goes about his business, then goes back in on his bicycle. Sometimes in the middle of the night, or while he's gone, a lava flow occurs and he has to wait a couple of days for it to crust over before he can get in and out. Makes you want to rush right out and pay your premium to your caring friends in the insurance business. A prayer to Pele would easily be more effective. There is only one way to treat the power of Hawaii's magnificent volcanoes: not with fear, but with the utmost respect.

Mauna Loa

At 13,677 feet, this magnificent mountain is a mere 117 feet shorter than its neighbor Mauna Kea, which is the tallest peak in the Pacific, and by some accounts, tallest in the world. Measured from its base, 18,000 feet beneath the sea, it would top even Mt. Everest. Mauna Loa is the most massive mountain on earth, containing 10,000 cubic miles of solid, iron-hard lava. This titan weighs more than California's entire Sierra Nevada range! In fact, Mauna Loa ("Long Mountain"), at 60 miles long and 30 wide, occupies the entire southern half of the Big Island, with Volcanoes National Park merely a section of its great expanse.

Special Note

Everything in the park—flora and fauna, rocks, buildings, trails, etc.—is protected by federal law. Be respectful! The *nene,* Hawaii's state bird, is endangered. By feeding these birds, visitors have taught them to stand in parking lots and by the roadside. What appears to be a humane and harmless practice actually helps kill these rare birds. Automobiles running them over has become the leading cause of death of adult birds in the park. Please look, but do not try to approach, feed, or harass the *nene* in any way.

KILAUEA CALDERA

The sights of Hawaii Volcanoes National Park are arranged one after another along **Crater Rim Drive.** Off the beaten track but worth a look are **Mauna Loa Road** (which takes you to places of special interest such as **Tree Molds** and **Bird Park**—10-minute detours) and **Kau Desert Trail,** about eight miles south of the visitor center on the Hawaii Belt Road, Hwy. 11. Most of the sights are the "drive-up" variety, but plenty of major and minor trails lead off here and there.

Admission to the park is $5 per vehicle (good for multiple entry over a seven-day period), $15 for an annual permit, $3 for bicycle traffic, and free to those 62 and over with a *golden age permit.*

Tips
Expect to spend a long full day atop Kilauea to take in all the sights, and never forget that you're on a rumbling volcano where a misstep or loss of concentration at the wrong moment can lead to severe injury, or even loss of life. Try to arrive by 9 a.m. with a picnic lunch to save time and hassles. Kilauea Caldera, at 4,000 feet, is about 10° cooler than the coast. It's often overcast and there can be showers. Wear your walking shoes and bring a sweater and/ or windbreaker. Binoculars, sunglasses, and a hat will also come in handy.

Warning! Small children, pregnant women, and people with respiratory ailments should note that the fumes from the volcano can cause problems. Just stay away from areas of sulfur vents and don't overdo it, and you should be fine.

A very dramatic way to experience the awesome power of the volcano is to take a **helicopter tour.** The choppers are perfectly suited for the up-close maneuverability necessary to get an intimate bird's-eye view. The pilots will fly you over the areas offering the most activity, often dipping low over lava pools, skimming still-glowing flows, and circling the towering steam clouds rising from where lava meets the sea. When activity is really happening, tours are jammed, and prices, like lava fountains, go sky-high. Remember, however, that there is growing resentment by hikers or anyone else trying to have a quiet experience, and that new regulations might limit flights over the lava area. Also, choppers do go down, and it is the park rangers and their rescue units who must go to their aid. (For full details see pp. 140-141.)

VISITOR CENTER AREA

The best place to start is at the Visitors Center/Park Headquarters. The turnoff is clearly marked off Belt Road (Hwy. 11). By midmorning it's jammed, so try to be an early bird. The center is well run by the National Park Service. They offer a free lecture and film about geology and volcanism, with tremendous highlights of past eruptions, and with plenty of detail on Hawaiian culture and natural history. It runs every hour on the hour starting at 9 a.m. Also, a self-guided natural history museum gives more information about the geology of the area, with plenty of exhibits of the flora and fauna. You will greatly enrich your visit if you take a half-hour tour of the museum. Actually the visitor center has been eclipsed by the state-of-the-art information available at the **Thomas A. Jaggar Museum** a few minutes up the road (see p. 220).

For safety's sake, anyone trekking to the backcountry *must* register with the rangers at the visitor center, especially during times of eruption. Do not be foolhardy! There is no charge for camping (see p. 226) and the rangers can give you up-to-the-minute information on trails, backcountry shelters, and cabins. Trails routinely close due to lava flows, tremors, and rock slides. The rangers cannot help you if they don't know where you are. Many day trails leading into the caldera from the rim road are easy walks that need no special preparation. The backcountry trails can be very challenging, and detailed maps (highly recommended) are sold at

J.D. BISIGNANI

friendly and knowledge-able salesperson at the Volcano Art Center

the center along with special-interest geology and natural history publications prepared by the Hawaii Natural History Association. The visitor center is open daily 9 a.m.-5 p.m.; call 967-7311 for trail and camping information, or 967-7977 for a recorded message concerning the latest news on any volcanic activity.

Volcano House

Have you ever dreamed of sleeping with a goddess? Well, you can cuddle up with Pele by staying at Volcano House (for details see p. 231). If your plans don't include an overnight stop, go in for a look. Sometimes this is impossible, because not only do tour buses from the Big Island disgorge here, but tour groups are flown in from Honolulu as well. A stop at the bar provides refreshments and a tremendous view of the crater. Volcano House still has the feel of a country inn, although in reality it's a Sheraton Inn. This particular building dates from the 1940s, but the site has remained the same since a grass hut was perched on the rim of the crater by a sugar planter in 1846. He charged $1 a night. A steady stream of notable visitors has come ever since: almost all of Hawaii's kings and queens dating from the middle of last century, as well as royalty from Europe. Mark Twain was a guest, followed by Franklin Roosevelt. Most recently, a contingent of astronauts lodged here and used the crater floor to prepare for walking on the moon. In 1866 a large grass hut replaced the first, and in 1877 a wooden Vic-

torian-style hotel was built. It is now the Volcano Art Center, and has been moved just across the road. The longest owner/operator of Volcano House was Mr. George Lycurgus, who took over management of the hotel in the 1890s. His son, Nick, followed him and managed the hotel until the 1960s.

Volcano Art Center

Art and history buffs should walk across the street to the Volcano Art Center, tel. 967-7511, which is the original 1877 Volcano House, Hawaii's oldest hotel. You not only get to see some fine arts and crafts, you can take a self-guided tour of this mini-museum, open daily 9 a.m.-5 p.m. A new show featuring one of the many superlative island artists on display is presented monthly. Some prominent artists represented are John Wisnosky, who teaches at University of Hawaii; Chiu Leong, who has a studio nearby where he turns out inspired *raku* pottery; Rick Mills, the best young glass artist in the state; Dietrich Varez, who makes affordable and distinctive woodblock prints; Garron Alexander who does *raku* marinelife; Wilford Yamazawa, another amazing glassworker; Marin Burger, a young artist who lives in Volcano, known as one of the best naturalist painters around; Kathy Long, creator of insightful pencil drawings of local people; Pam Barton, who does whimsical fiber arts; woodworker Jack Straka, famous for his rich turned bowls; and Boone Morrison, the center's founder, a photographer and architect who apprenticed under Ansel Adams. There is also a profusion of less expensive but distinctive items like posters, cards, and earthy basketry made from natural fibers collected locally. One of the functions of the art center is to provide interpretation for the national park. All of the 250-plus artists who exhibit here do works that in some way relate to Hawaii's environment. Volcano Art Center is one of the finest art shops in the entire state, boasting works from the best that the islands have to offer.

CRATER RIM DRIVE

There are so many intriguing nooks and crannies to stop at along Crater Rim Drive that you'll have to force yourself to be picky if you intend to cover the park in one day. Crater Rim Drive is a circular route; it matters little which way you proceed. Take your choice, but the following sights are listed counterclockwise beginning from Kilauea Visitors Center. Your biggest problem will be timing your arrival at the "drive-in" sights to avoid the steady stream of tour buses.

Sulphur Banks
You can easily walk to Sulphur Banks from Volcano Art Center along a 10-minute trail. If you're driving, signs along Rim Drive direct you, and your nose will tell you when you're close. As you approach these fumaroles, the earth surrounding them turns a deep reddish-brown, covered over in yellowish-green sulphur. The rising steam is caused by surface water leaking into the cracks where it becomes heated and rises as vapor. Kilauea releases hundreds of tons of sulphur gases every day, with Sulphur Banks being an example. This gaseous activity stunts the growth of vegetation. And when atmospheric conditions create a low ceiling, the gases sometimes cause the eyes and nose to water. The area is best avoided by those with heart and lung conditions.

Steam Vents
Next you'll come to Steam Vents which are also fumaroles, but without sulphur. The entire field behind the partitioned area steams. The feeling is like being in a sauna. There are no strong fumes to contend with here, just the tour buses. **Kilauea Military Camp** beyond the vent is not

open to the public. The camp serves as an R&R facility for military personnel.

Hawaii Volcano Observatory
This observatory has been keeping tabs on the volcanic activity in the area since the turn of the century. The actual observatory is filled with delicate seismic equipment and is closed to the public, but a lookout nearby gives you a dentist's view into the mouth of Halemaumau Crater ("House of Ferns"), Pele's home. Steam rises and you can feel the power, but until 1924 the view was even more phenomenally spectacular: a lake of molten lava. The lava has since sunk below the surface, which is now crusted over. Scientists do not predict a recurrence in the near future, but no one knows Pele's mind. This is a major stop for the tour buses, but a two-minute saunter along the hiking trail gives you the view to yourself. Information plaques in the immediate area tell of the history and volcanology of the park. One points out a spot from which to observe the perfect shield volcano form of Mauna Loa—most times too cloudy to see. Another reminds you that you're in the middle of the Pacific, an incredible detail you tend to forget when atop these mountains. Here too is Uwekahuna ("Wailing Priest") Bluff, where the *kahuna* made offerings of appeasement to Pele. A Hawaiian prayer commemorates their religious rites.

Thomas A. Jaggar Museum
This newest addition to the national park is located next door to the Hawaiian Volcano Observatory, and offers a fantastic multimedia display of the amazing geology and volcanology of the area. The state-of-the-art museum, complete with a miniseries of spectacular photos on movable walls, topographical maps, inspired paintings, and TV videos, is open 8:30 a.m.-5 p.m. daily, admission free. The expert staff constantly upgrades the displays to keep the public informed on the newest eruptions. The 30-45 minutes that it takes to explore the teaching museum will enhance your understanding of the volcanic area immeasurably. Do yourself a favor and visit this museum before setting out on any explorations.

Moon Walks
A string of interesting stops follows the observatory. One points out the **Kau Desert,** an in-

hospitable site of red-earth plains studded with a few scraggly plants (see p. 223). Next comes the **Southwest Rift,** a series of cracks running from Kilauea's summit to the sea. You can observe at a glance that you are standing directly over a major earthquake fault. Dated lava flows follow in rapid succession until you arrive at **Halemaumau Trail.** The well-maintained trail is only one-quarter mile long and gives an up-close view of the crater. The area is rife with fumaroles and should be avoided by those with respiratory problems. At the end you're treated to a full explanation of Halemaumau. Farther along the road, a roped-off area was once an observation point that caved in. You won't take the ground under your feet for granted! Close by is **Keanakakoi,** a prehistoric quarry from which superior stone was gathered to make tools. It was destroyed by a flow in 1877. If that seems in the remote past, realize that you are now on a section of road that was naturally paved over with lava from a "quickie" eruption in 1982!

Most visitors hike along **Devastation Trail,** which could aptly be renamed "Regeneration Trail." The half mile it covers is fascinating, one of the most-photographed areas in the park. It leads across a field devastated by a tremendous eruption from **Kilauea Iki** ("Little Kilauea") in 1959, when fountains of lava shot 1,900 feet into the air. The area was once an ohia forest that was denuded of limbs and leaves, then choked by black pumice and ash. The vegetation has regenerated since then, and the recuperative power of the flora is part of an ongoing study. Blackberries, not indigenous to Hawaii, are slowly taking over. The good news is that you'll be able to pick and eat blackberries as you hike along the paved trail, but note that the rangers are waging a mighty war against them. Notice that many of the trees have sprouted aerial roots trailing down from the branches: this is total adaptation to the situation, as these roots don't normally appear. As you move farther along the trail, tufts of grass and bushes peek out of the pumice. Then the surroundings become totally barren and look like the nightmare of a nuclear holocaust.

Thurston Lava Tube

If the Devastation Trail produced a sense of melancholy, the Thurston Lava Tube makes you feel like Alice walking through the looking glass. Inside is a fairy kingdom. As you approach, the expected billboard gives you the lowdown on the geology and flora and fauna of the area. Take the five minutes to educate yourself. The paved trail starts as a steep incline which quickly enters a fern forest. All about you are fern trees, vibrantly green, with native birds flitting here and there. As you approach the lava tube, it seems almost manmade, like a perfectly formed tunnel leading into a mine. Ferns and moss hang from the entrance, and if you stand just inside the entrance looking out, it's as if the very air is tinged with green. If there were such things as elves and gnomes, they would surely live here. The walk through takes about 10 minutes, and the tube rolls and undulates through narrow passages and into large "rooms." At the other end, the fantasy world of ferns and moss reappears.

SMALL DETOURS

Volcano Village

You shouldn't miss taking a ride through the village of Volcano, a beautiful settlement with truly charming houses and cottages outlined in ferns. Tiny gravel roads lace the development, which sits virtually atop one of the world's undeniable "power spots." The area is so green and so vibrant that it appears surrealistic. With flowers, ferns, and trees everywhere, it is hard to imagine a more picturesque village in all of America.

Volcano Golf And Country Club

What's most amazing about this course is where it is. Imagine! You're teeing off atop an active volcano surrounded by one of the last pristine forests in the state. At the right time of year, the surrounding ohia turn scarlet when they are in bloom. The fairways are carved from lava, while in the distance Mauna Loa looms. A poor shot, and you can watch your ball disappear down a steam vent. The course began about 70 years ago when a group of local golfers hand-cleared three "greens," placing stakes that served as holes. Later this was improved to sand greens with tin cans for holes, and after an eruption in 1924 blanketed the area with volcanic ash that served as excellent fertilizer, the grass grew and the course became a lush green. After WW II the course was extended to 18 holes, and a clubhouse was added. Finally, Jack Snyder, a well-known course architect, redesigned the course to its present par-72, 6,119-yard layout. Rates are $30 with shared cart. To beat the heavy lunch crowd at Volcano House, try the restaurant at the course, tel. 967-7331 (see p. 232). The course is located just north of the Belt Rd., about two miles west of the park entrance. Phone 967-7550 for more information.

Mauna Loa Road

About 2.5 miles west of the park entrance on the Belt Rd., Mauna Loa road turns off to the north. This road will lead you to the Tree Molds and a bird sanctuary, as well as to the trailhead for the Mauna Loa summit trail. As an added incentive, a minute down this road leaves 90% of the tourists behind.

Tree Molds is an ordinary name for an extraordinary place. Turn off Mauna Loa Rd. soon after leaving the Belt Rd. and follow the signs for five minutes to a cul-de-sac. At the entrance, a billboard tries hard to dramatically explain what occurred here. In a moment, you realize that you're standing atop a lava flow, and that the scattered potholes are entombed tree trunks, most likely the remains of a once-giant koa forest. Unlike at Lava Tree State Monument, where the magma encased the tree and flowed away, the opposite action happened here. The lava stayed put while the tree trunk burned away, leaving 15- to 18-foot-deep holes.

Kipuka Puaulu is a sanctuary for birds and nature lovers who want to leave the crowds behind, just under two miles from Route 11 down Mauna Loa Rd. The sanctuary is an island atop an island. A *kipuka* is a piece of land that is surrounded by lava but has not been inundated by it, leaving the original vegetation and land contour intact. A few hundred yards away, small scrub vegetation struggles, but in the sanctuary the trees form a towering canopy a hundred feet tall. The first sign for Bird Park takes you to an ideal picnic area; the second, 100 yards beyond, takes you to Kipuka Puaulu Loop Trail. As you enter the trail, a bulletin board describes the birds and plants, some of the last remaining indigenous fauna and flora in Hawaii. Please follow all rules. The trail is self guided, and pamphlets describing the stations along the way are dispensed from a box 50 feet down the path. The loop is only one mile long, but to really as-

simile the area, especially if you plan to do any birdwatching, expect to spend an hour minimum. It doesn't take long to realize that you are privileged to see some of the world's rarest plants, such as a small, nondescript bush called *aalii*. In the branches of the towering ohia trees you might see an *elepaio* or an *apapane*, two birds native to Hawaii. Common finches and Japanese white eyes are imported birds that are here to stay. There's a fine example of a lava tube, and an explanation of how ash from eruptions provided soil and nutrients for the forest. Blue morning glories have taken over entire hillsides. Once considered a pest and aggressively eradicated, they have recently been given a reprieve and are now considered good ground cover—perhaps even indigenous. When you do come across a native Hawaiian plant, it seems somehow older, almost prehistoric. If a pre-contact Hawaiian could come back today, he or she would recognize only a few plants and trees even here in this preserve. More than four times as many plants and animals have become extinct in Hawaii in the last 200 years as on the entire North American continent. As you leave, listen for the melodies coming from the treetops, and hope the day never comes when no birds sing.

Mauna Loa Rd. continues westward and gains elevation for approximately 10 miles. At the end of the pavement, at 6,662 feet, you find a parking area and lookout. A trail leads from here to the summit of Mauna Loa. (See following "Camping and Hiking" section.) It takes three to four days to hike. Under no circumstances should it be attempted by novice hikers or those unprepared for cold alpine conditions.

Olaa Track

Off Route 11 close to Volcano village, turn on Wright Rd. (or County Rd. 148) heading toward Mauna Loa (on a clear morning you can see Mauna Kea). Continue for approximately three miles until you see a barbed-wire fence. The fence is distinctive because along it you'll see a profusion of *hapu'u* ferns which are in sharp contrast to the adjacent property. Here is an *ola'a* rainforest, part of the national park and open to the public, although park scientists like to keep it quiet. Be aware that the area is laced with lava tubes. Most are small ankle twisters, but others can open up under you like a glacial crevasse. Here is a true example of a quickly disappearing native forest. What's beautiful about an endemic forest is that virtually all species coexist wonderfully. The ground cover is a rich mulch of decomposing ferns and leaves, fragrant and amazingly soft. This walk is for the intrepid hiker or naturalist who is fascinated by Hawaii's unique foliage.

Remember, trails in this section of the park are poorly marked and quite confusing. You can get lost, and if no one knows that you're in there, it could be life threatening. Also, be aware that you may be trampling native species, and could be inadvertently introducing alien species. The Park Service is trying to bring the area back to its native Hawaiian rainforest condition through eradication of alien plants and elimination of feral pigs.

Kau Desert Trail

Kau Desert Trail starts about eight miles south of the visitor center along Route 11, between mile markers 37 and 38. It's a short hike from the trailhead to the **Kau Desert Footprints.** People going to or from Kailua-Kona can see them en route, but those staying in Hilo should take the time to visit the footprints. The trek across the small section of desert is fascinating, and the history of the footprints makes the experience more evocative. The trail is only 1.6 miles RT and can be hustled along in less than 30 minutes, but allow at least an hour, mostly for observation. The predominant foliage is a red bottlebrush that contrasts with the bleak surroundings—the feeling throughout the area is one of foreboding. You pass a wasteland of *a'a* and *pa'hoehoe* lava flows to arrive at the footprints. A metal fence in a sturdy pavilion surrounds the prints, that look as though they're cast in cement. Actually they're formed from pisolites:

apapane

particles of ash stuck together with moisture, which formed mud that hardened like plaster.

In 1790 Kamehameha was waging war with Keoua over control of the Big Island. One of Keoua's warrior parties of approximately 80 people attempted to cross the desert while Kilauea was erupting. Toxic gases descended upon them and the warriors and their families were enveloped and suffocated. They literally died in their tracks, but the preserved footprints, although romanticism would wish otherwise, were probably made by a party of people who came well after the eruption. This unfortunate occurrence was regarded by the Hawaiians as a direct message from the gods proclaiming their support for Kamehameha. Keoua, who could not deny the sacred signs, felt abandoned and shortly thereafter became a human sacrifice at Puukohola Heiau, built by Kamehameha to honor his war god, Kukailimoku.

CHAIN OF CRATERS ROAD

The Chain of Craters Road that once linked Volcanoes National Park with Kalapana village on the east coast has been severed by an enormous lava flow, and can only be driven from Volcanoes down to where the flow crosses the road near the now-inundated and inaccessible Kamoamoa Campground. Remember that the volcanic activity in this area is unpredictable, and that the road can be closed at a moment's notice. Flying volcanic ash, mixed with the frequent drizzle, can be as slippery as ice. As you head down the road, every bend—and they are uncountable—offers a panoramic vista. There are dozens of pulloffs, many of which are named, like Naulu ("Sea Orchards"); plaques provide geological information about past eruptions and lava flows. The grandeur, power, and immensity of the forces that have been creating the earth from the beginning of time are right before your eyes. The lower part of the road is spectacular. Here, blacker-than-black seacliffs, covered by a thin layer of green, abruptly stop at the sea. The surf rolls in, sending up spumes of seawater. In the distance, steam billows into the air where the lava flows into the sea. At road's end you will find a barricade staffed by park rangers. Heed their warnings. The drive from atop the volcano to the barricade takes about 30 minutes. If you are going in the

evening, when the spectacle is more apparent, bring a flashlight. A ranger will escort you onto the flow, giving an interpretive talk as you walk along. To experience the lava flow from the Kalapana side, see pp. 209-210.

When the road almost reaches the coast, look for a roadside marker that indicates the **Kau Puna Trail.** Just across the road is the **Pu'u Loa Petroglyph Field.** The Kau Puna Trail leads you along the coast, where you can find shelters at Keauhou and Halape. Rain catchment tanks provide drinking water. All campers must register at the Kilauea Visitors Center. In 1975 an earthquake rocked the area, generating a tidal wave that killed two campers; more than 30 others had to be helicoptered to safety. Only registering will alert authorities to your whereabouts in case of a disaster. A number of trails cross in this area and you can take them back up to Chain of Craters Road or continue on a real expedition through the Kau Desert. The Kau Puna Trail requires full trekking and camping gear.

Pu'u Loa Petroglyphs

The walk out to Pu'u Loa Petroglyphs is delightful and highly educational, and only takes one hour. The trail, although it traverses solid lava, is discernible. The tread of feet over the centuries

petroglyphs

J.D. BISIGNANI

HAWAII STATE ARCHIVES

*Ship's artist
Jacques Arago
depicts the harsh
verdict delivered
to a kapu breaker,
circa 1819.*

has discolored the rock. As you walk along, note the *ahu,* traditional trail markers that are piles of stone shaped like little Christmas trees. Most of the lava field leading to the petroglyphs is undulating *pa'hoehoe* and looks like a frozen sea. You can climb bumps of lava, from eight to ten feet high, to scout the immediate territory. Mountainside, the *pali* is quite visible and you can pick out the most recent lava flows—the blackest and least vegetated. As you approach the site, the lava changes dramatically and looks like long strands of braided rope.

The petroglyphs are in an area about the size of a soccer field. A wooden walkway encircles them and ensures their protection. A common motif of the petroglyphs is a circle with a hole in the middle, like a donut; you'll also see designs of men with triangular-shaped heads. Some rocks are entirely covered with designs while others have only a symbolic scratch or two. If you stand on the walkway and trek off at the two o'clock position, you'll see a small hill. Go over and down it, and you will discover even better petroglyphs that include a sailing canoe about two feet high. At the back end of the walkway a sign proclaims that Pu'u Loa meant "Long Hill," which the Hawaiians turned into the euphemism "Long Life." For countless generations, fathers would

come here to place pieces of their infants' umbilical cords into small holes as offerings to the gods to grant long life to their children. Concentric circles were surrounded by the holes that held the umbilical cords. The entire area, an obvious power spot, screams in utter silence, and the still-strong mana is easily felt.

Waha'ula Heiau

Waha'ula Heiau, "Temple of the Red Mouth," radically changed the rituals and practices of the relatively benign Hawaiian religion by introducing the idea of human sacrifice. The 13th century marked the end of the frequent comings and goings between Hawaii and the "Lands to the South" (Tahiti), and began the isolation which would last 500 years until Captain Cook arrived. Unfortunately, this last influx of Polynesians brought a rash of conquering warriors carrying ferocious gods who lusted for human blood before they would be appeased. Paao, a powerful Tahitian priest, supervised the building of Waha'ula and brought in a new chief, Pili, to strengthen the diminished mana of the Hawaiian chiefs due to their practice of intermarriage with commoners. Waha'ula became the foremost *luakini* (human sacrifice) temple in the island kingdom and held this position until the demise of the old ways in 1819. The *heiau* is not at all grandiose, merely an elevated rock platform smoothed over with pebbles.

Note: This entire area is now completely inundated by recent lava flows, and for all intents and purposes, is unreachable. The *heiau* itself is now a small island in a sea of black lava that has so far miraculously escaped destruction. Only Pele's benevolence will continue to save it.

PRACTICALITIES

CAMPING AND HIKING

Campgrounds And Cabins
The main campground in Volcanoes, **Namakani Paio,** clearly marked off Route 11, is situated in a stately eucalyptus grove. There is no charge for tent camping and no reservations are required. A cooking pavilion has fireplaces, but no wood or drinking water are provided. **Cabins** are available through Volcano House (see pp. 219, 231). Each accommodates four people and costs $32 s/d, $6 additional person. A $10 refundable key deposit gives access to the shower and toilet; and a $5 refundable deposit gets you linens, soap, towels, and a blanket (extra sleeping bag recommended). Each cabin contains one double bed and two single bunk beds andan electric light, but no electric outlets. Outside are a picnic table and barbecue grill but you must provide your own charcoal and cooking utensils. Check in at Volcano House at 3 p.m. and check out by noon.

Kipuka Nene is another campground, approximately 10 miles south of Park Headquarters down Hilina Pali Road. Many fewer people camp here and it too is free, with no permit required, but be aware that the campground is subject to closure during the *nene* nesting period, which runs from fall to early winter. You'll find a cooking pavilion and fireplaces, but no firewood or drinking water.

Niaulani Cabin is operated by the Division of State Parks. The cabin is outside the park along Old Volcano Rd., about a half mile south of the Village General Store in Volcano village. The cabin is completely furnished with full kitchen and bathroom facilities. It accommodates up to six people, and the rates are on a sliding scale determined by number of people and length of stay: one person for one day is $10, two people are $14, and six people are $30. Reservations and a deposit are required. For full details write Department of Land and Natural Resources, Divison of State Parks, Box 936, Hilo, HI 96720, tel. 961-7200. Pick up the key at the Divison of State Parks office at 75 Aupuni St., Hilo, 7:45 a.m.-4:30 p.m. Holidays and weekends the key is left at the Hilo Airport information booth.

Hiking
The slopes of Mauna Loa and HVNP are a trekker's paradise. You'll find trails that last for days or for an hour or two. Many have shelters, and those trails that require overnight stays provide cabins. Because of the possibility of an eruption or earthquake, it is *imperative* to check in at Park Headquarters, where you can also pick up current trail info and maps (see p. 218).

The hike to the summit of **Mauna Loa** (13,679 feet) is the most grueling. The trailhead is at the lookout at the end of the pavement of Mauna Loa Road. Hikers in excellent condition can make the summit (RT) in three days, but four would be more comfortable. There is a considerable elevation gain so expect freezing weather even in summer, and snow in winter. Altitude sickness can also be a problem. En route you pass through *nene* country, with a good chance to spot these lava-adapted geese. Fences keep out feral goats, so remember to close gates after you. The first cabin is at Red Hill (10,092 feet) and the second is at the summit. Water is from roof catchment and should be boiled. The summit treats you to a sweeping panorama that includes Haleakala. Mauna Loa's Mokuaweoweo Caldera is over three miles long and has vertical walls towering 600 feet. From November to May, if there is snow, steam rises from the caldera. The trail cabin is on the rim.

The **Crater Rim Loop Trail** begins at Park Headquarters and follows Crater Rim Dr., crossing back and forth a number of times. Hiking the entire 11 miles takes a full day, but you can take it in sections as time and energy permit. It's a well-marked and maintained trail; all you need are warm clothing, water, and determination. For your efforts, you'll get an up-close view of all of the sights outlined along Crater Rim Drlve.

Kilauea Iki Trail begins at the Thurston Lava Tube, or at Park Headquarters via the Waldron Ledge Trail. This five-mile trail generally takes three to four hours as it passes through the center of Kilauea Iki Caldera. It's easy to link up with the Byron Ledge Trail or with the Halemaumau Trail. You can return north to Park Headquarters or continue on either of these two trails to the Halemaumau parking area directly south of Park Headquarters.

Halemaumau Trail provides the best scenery for the effort. It begins at Park Headquarters and descends into Kilauea Caldera, covering six miles (five hours). If possible, arrange to be picked up at the Halemaumau parking area due south of Park Headquarters.

ACCOMMODATIONS, FOOD, AND SHOPPING

If you intend to spend the night atop Kilauea, your choices of accommodations are few and simple. Volcano House provides the only hotel, but cabins are available at the campgrounds, there are plenty of tenting sites, and there is a wonderful assortment of bed and breakfasts.

Kilauea Lodge

This superb addition to the Volcano area, tel. 967-7366, Box 116, Volcano Village, HI 96785, owned and operated by Lorna Larsen-Jeyte and Albert Jeyte, is the premier restaurant and lodge atop Volcano, as well as being one of the very best on the island. The solid stone and timber structure was built in 1938 as a YMCA camp and functioned as such until 1962, when it became a "mom and pop operation," often failing and changing ownership. It faded into the ferns until Lorna and Albert revitalized it in 1987, opening in 1988. The lodge is a classic, with a vaulted, open-beamed ceiling. A warm and cozy "international fireplace" dating from the days of the YMCA camp is embedded with stones and plaques from all over the world, along with coins from countries such as Malaysia, Japan, Singapore, Australia, New Zealand, Finland, Germany, and Italy, to name a few.

The **Kilauea Lodge Restaurant,** open for dinner 5:30-9 p.m. daily, reservations a must, is an extraordinary restaurant serving gourmet continental cuisine at reasonable prices. Choose a seat below the neo-Victorian windows or at a table from which you can view the vibrant green ferns and manicured trees of the grounds. A very friendly and professional staff serves the excellent food prepared by Albert, and starts you off with a fresh "loafette" studded like their fireplace, but with sunflowers and sesame seeds. Appetizers such as mushroom caps stuffed with crab and cheese will titillate your palate. Entrees, ranging $13-26, include soup, salad, and vegetables. Vegetarians will be delighted with Eggplant Supreme, a stew of Mediterranean vegetables served atop fettucine at $13.50, while shrimp tempura at $18.50 adds an Asian touch. Dinner features Seafood Mauna Kea (succulent pieces of seafood served atop a bed of fettucine), and Paupiettes of Beef (prime rib slices rolled around herbs and mushrooms in a special sauce), both for under $20. Always a great choice, the catch-of-the-day is baked, broiled, or sautéed with a savory sauce. Desserts are wonderful, and the meal is topped off with a cup of Irish or Italian coffee.

Kilauea Lodge is also an exquisite inn with an assortment of rooms ranging $85-110, including a complete breakfast for all guests. The architect, Virginia McDonald, a Volcano resident, worked magic in transforming the brooding rooms of the original section into bright, comfortable, and romantic suites. Each bathroom, with vaulted 18-foot ceilings, has a skylight. The sink and grooming area is one piece of Corianne with a light built into it, so that the entire sink area glows. The rooms, all differently appointed, range in decor from Hawaiian-European to Asian with a motif of Japanese fans. Each has a working fireplace, queen-sized bed, and swivel rocking chair. A separate one-bedroom cottage features a wood-burning stove (central heat too), a queen-sized bed, private bath, and small living room with queen-sized pull-out sofa. In 1991, Kilauea Lodge opened seven new units centered around a commodious common room where you can read and snooze by a crackling fire. All rooms in the new section are tastefully furnished with wicker furniture, white curtains, vaulted ceilings, oak trim, Japanese and Hawallan art prlnts, and fluffy quilts to keep off the evening chill. The Kilauea Lodge provides one of the most *civilized* atmospheres in Hawaii in one of its most powerful natural areas. The combination is hard to beat.

Bonnie Goodell's Guest House

This very friendly hideaway, tel. 967-7775, Box 6, Volcano, HI 96785, is on the back roads of Volcano Village. The fully furnished house is designed as a self-sufficient unit where the guests are guaranteed peace and quiet on a lovely six-acre homesite. Bonnie grew up in Hawaii and was for many years the education director for the Honolulu Botanic Gardens. She *knows* her plants and is willing to chat with her guests. The place is particularly good for families. Children have plenty of room to play, while the parents can roam the orchards on the property. The two-story guest home is bright and airy. Enter into a combo living room, kitchen, and dining area with a large bathroom off to the right. Upstairs is a sleeping area with two twin beds and a queen-sized fold-out bed; downstairs is another fold-out bed. Futons can sleep even more. Another cottage, smaller but more luxurious (wheelchair-accessible) is nearing completion. Plans call for a fireplace, and the romantic mood is designed for honeymoon couples who want to be alone. The rate is $50 d, $5 for each additional person, $40 off-season, minimum stay two nights. Sometimes Bonnie will allow an emergency one-night stay if the house is not booked, but she charges $10 extra because the entire house has to be cleaned.

Volcano B&B

This gingerbread house, Hawaiian style, tel. 967-7779, Box 22, Volcano, HI 96785, is owned and operated by Jim and Sandy Pedersen. The home is actually in the old Volcano village, and was originally built in 1912 as a vacation getaway for a local Hawaiian family. Additions and improvements followed over the years until it was purchased by the Pedersens, who have transformed it into a serene mountain bungalow. All windows are original, and along with the vaulted ceilings give the common rooms an open and airy feel. One of the finest features is a lovely sun porch, bedecked in white with blue-trimmed wicker furniture. Morning on the porch is especially beautiful—greet the sunshine and view a garden of ferns, flowers, and

trees. Filling the house at breakfast-time is the homey smell of baking muffins, which you will enjoy with a large bowl of fresh fruit, yogurt-fruit sauce, fluffy golden pancakes that are becoming famous, and 100% pure organic Kona coffee. The B&B has three very comfortable guest rooms. They're small, but rich with the feeling of absolute hominess and relaxation expressed in varying decor. All are immaculate. Rates are $50 s, $55 d, and $65 d with two beds. The second and third floors of the house are dedicated to the guests, with the exception of the kitchen. The Pedersens live below. The common area and sun porch are separated from the living room by two sets of French doors. The living room, equipped with TV and VCR, also serves as a reading room and piano room. The hosts help with small items like coolers, water bottles, and flashlights with which to view the volcano after dark.

Hale Ohia Cottages

Follow a private mountain lane for a few minutes into an enchanted clearing where the artwork of a meticulous Japanese garden surrounds a New England gabled-and-turreted home and its attendant cottages of red-on-brown rough-cut shingles. Once the hideaway of the Dillinghams, an old and influential *kamaaina* family, Hale Ohia, tel. 967-7986, (800) 455-3803, Box 758, Volcano Village, HI 96785, is now owned and operated by Michael D. Tuttle, who recently purchased the property after falling hopelessly in love at first sight. The main house holds the Dillingham Suite ($85), with its own sitting room, bath, fireplace, and glass-covered lanai. Simple and clean, with hardwood floors and wainscoted walls, the home is the epitome of country elegance, Hawaiian style.

Hale Ohia, once the gardener's cottage, has two stories, with the bottom floor occupied by the Iiwi ($60) and Camellia ($65) suites, which are wheelchair-accessible and can be combined for larger groups ($85). Stained-glass windows with a calla lily-and-poppy motif add a special touch, while the low ceilings are reminiscent of the captain's quarters on a sailing ship. The first floor has a full kitchen and a covered lanai complete with barbecue grill that makes it perfect for evening relaxation. Narrow stairs lead to a full bath located on the first landing, from where you get a sweeping view of

J.D. BISIGNANI

Hale Ohia

the grounds while performing your morning meditation. Upstairs opens into a bright and airy parlor and adjacent bedrooms that can sleep five comfortably.

Hale Lehua, once a private study, is secluded down its own lava footpath. Enter to find a wall of windows framing the green-on-green grounds. The interior is cozy with its own fireplace, bamboo and wicker furniture, self-contained bathroom, covered lanai, and partial kitchen with microwave, toaster, and refrigerator. Another "Hale" still unnamed and under construction will feature an outdoor shower, skylight, fireplace, and leaded glass windows through which the surrounding fern forest will emit its emerald radiance.

To make your stay even more delightful, room rates include an "extended" continental breakfast, and guests are welcome to immerse themselves in the bubbling Jacuzzi that awaits you under a canopy of Japanese cedars and glimmering stars.

Chalet Kilauea

Peeking from the *hapuu* fern forest in a manicured glen is **Chalet Kilauea**, tel. 967-7786, (800) 937-7786, Box 998, Volcano Village, HI 96785, where you will be cordially accommodated by owners Lisha and Brian Crawford. Enter the second level of the main house to find a guest living room where you can wile away the hours playing chess, listening to a large collection of CDs, or gazing from the wraparound windows at a treetop view of the surrounding forest, ferns,

and impeccable grounds. Just out the door, a make-over of a one-time Japanese *ofuro* resulted in a gurgling fountain, inside of which a miniature volcano blazes and smokes. (Downstairs is a hot tub and outdoor lounge area, and a black-and-white checkerboard dining room where wrought-iron tables sit before a huge picture window). Breakfasts (changeable daily), friendly and relaxed but with formal table settings, are remarkable: lox and bagels, fresh Volcano onions and tomatoes, macadamia nut or banana pancakes with strawberry topping, fresh papaya and squeezed juices, and Brian's own house blend Kona coffee with a hint of cinnamon.

The main house holds three unique theme rooms (European, African, Asian) that rent for $75 d. The Oriental Jade Room is richly appointed with Chinese folding screens, samurai murals, an Oriental carpet, and jade-green bedspread. Plush terrycloth robes are available for all guests, and a large shared bath of rich blue tile is on the ground level. Connected by a deck to the main house is the Treehouse Suite ($95 d), a two-story unit, with a bath and sitting room downstairs, and a large bedroom on the upper floor. Also on the property are the Ohia Holiday Cottage ($75) and the Hoku Hawaiian House ($100). However, the prize is the very special Hapuu Forest Cabin ($145), nestled at the end of its own driveway and footpath about 50 yards from the main house. The cabin, with a covered porch all around, is post-and-beam with plenty of knotty pine. A 20-foot-high vaulted ceiling, wood-burning stove on a lava-rock base, and Persian carpet help set the cabin's mood. Wherever it is possible to have glass, there is glass! The bathroom has an enormous tub perfect for a couple who wants to sip champagne in pure luxury while throwing open the windows to the night air and the soothing whispers of rustling ferns. A narrow staircase leads to a loft where four skylights allow moonbeams to illuminate the comfy, queen-sized bed. There's a full kitchen (breakfast at the main house included) where you can fix your own meals and snacks, and even a TV if you are so inclined. Lisha and Brian also own and operate **Volcano Reservations,** a B&B reservation service with guest homes available statewide. For complete information see p. 112.

Hale Kilauea

Green pines and native ohia shade Hale Kilauea, tel. 967-7591, Box 28, Volcano, HI 96785, owned and operated by Maurice Thomas. In the main lodge, a central common room is very comfortable with reading materials, fireplace, parlor games, and TV. The spacious and airy rooms in the main lodge, $65-85 d, $15 extra person, all with private baths, are comfortable but not luxurious. Upstairs rooms are more deluxe with plush carpeting, knotty pine trim, refrigerator, small divan, and private lanai. Ask for a room in the rear so that you can overlook the quiet green forest instead of the parking area. Two rooms across from the main building are warm and cozy, although quite small. They are private, and the least expensive at $55. The best deal, however, is a refurbished plantation cottage that sits across the road. The rate is $85 d, with special weekly and monthly rates. The wainscoted cottage provides a small but serviceable kitchen, separate bedroom, and living room that can sleep a few more. Don't expect luxury, but a night in the cottage is a window into Hawaii's past of humble workers in humble homes. With all the rooms, including the cottage, a hearty breakfast of hot and cold cereals, various breads, cheeses, plump sausages, and occasionally quiche, waffles or pancakes is provided.

Lokahi Lodge

Built in 1992 specifically as a B&B by Patrick Dixon and Danny DiCastro, Lokahi Lodge, tel. 985-8647 (on Oahu, Maui and Kauai tel. 922-

6597 or 800-457-6924), Box 7, Volcano, HI 96785, offers quiet country comfort. A rocking-chair veranda, perfect for keeping off sun and showers, completely surrounds the spacious ranch house. Enter into a common sitting room of 16-foot vaulted ceilings where you can relax on overstuffed couches and chairs while warming yourself in front of a red enameled free-standing stove. An old-fashioned, crank-handled telephone hangs on the wall, and an ensemble of organ, piano, and harp awaits anyone inclined to make their own music. A continental breakfast of homemade banana bread, fresh papaya and pineapple, fruit juices, jams, jellies, coffee, and tea assortment is offered at a huge banquet table surrounded by high-backed chairs. The stardust-speckled hallway is lined with vintage *lei* that have been collected by owner Danny DiCastro, a famous *hula* dancer. Rooms, $65 d, $15 extra person, are triple-insulated for guaranteed quiet, are fully carpeted, offer large closets, and have differing decor—for example, billowy paisley curtains and bedspreads with matching wallpaper. Comfortable furniture for private relaxation, tasteful oil prints, and bathrooms with tub, shower, and pedestal sink complete the rooms. For the most privacy request the "yellow or blue rooms" at the far end of the hallway. Each room has a private entrance leading onto the veranda, so that you may come and go without disturbing anyone. Lokahi Lodge definitely lives up to its name, which translates as "peace and harmony."

Carson's Volcano Cottages

Deep in the fern forest, Carson's Volcano Cottages, tel. 967-7683 or (800) 845-LAVA, Box 503, Volcano, HI 96785, owned and operated by Tom and Brenda Carson, offers four B&B rooms, one in its own studio cottage, and the others in a three-room cottage. The accommodations all have private baths, entrances, and decks, and there's a hot tub for use by all on the deck of the main house. Two of the rooms have kitchens. The one-acre property is naturally landscaped with ohia and fern, while moss-covered sculptures of Balinese gods peeking through the foliage escort you through the grounds. The studio cottage, $75 d, a miniature plantation house with corrugated roof, has a kitchen and a bath with skylight. Appointed with fluffy pillows and downy quilts, this would be a perfect rendezvous for a "Victorian lady" and her paramour. The three-room cottage, $70 d per room, has vaulted ceilings, beds with wooden headboards, wicker furniture, and vintage photos on the walls. In one room, the snow-white bedspreads are helped by electric blankets, while a free-standing credenza from the '30s adds a touch of charm. Leaded glass windows open to a private porch. Another room, all in pink, also with its own vaulted ceiling and free-standing wardrobe, is appointed with vintage kitsch bric-a-brac like *hula* dancer glasses and lamps. A retired "lady of the evening" could easily relive all of her memories in this room. Finally, the Oriental Room, striking in black and white, features Balinese masks and a Japanese doll mural. Located at the side of the cottage, this room has a more private entrance and a tiny kitchenette. Tom and Brenda provide a continental breakfast that might include banana bread, French toast, mai tais made with lemon juice, passion fruit juice, bagels and lox, or strawberry crepes. The Carsons also rent out two other homes in the Volcano Village area. One is a vintage two-bedroom home at $85, the other is a one-bedroom cedar home, recently built, that features a living room, full kitchen, bath, and white-pane windows. Another two-bedroom home, in Kapoho, one lot back from the sea, rents for $85.

Volcano House

If you decide to lodge at Volcano House, tel. 967-7321 or (800) 325-3535, Box 53, Hawaii Volcanoes National Park, HI 96718, don't be frightened away by the daytime crowds. They disappear with the sun. Then Volcano House metamorphoses into what it has always been: a quiet country inn. The 37 rooms are comfy but old-fashioned. Who needs a pool or TV when you can look out your window into a volcano caldera? Unfortunately, the management of this venerable hotel has been in a state of flux lately, and there have been reports of indifferent service. Be advised! Room rates are: main building with crater view $131, non-crater view $105, Ohia Wing non-crater view $79, $10 additional person. No charge for children under 12 occupying the same room as their parents. Also see Namakani Paio Cabins, p. 226.

Volcano House Restaurant offers a breakfast buffet, $7.50 pp 7-10:30 a.m. daily, with hot and cold cereals, assorted juices, pancakes topped with ohia berries and macadamia nuts, sweet bread French toast, scrambled eggs, bacon, chili links, and Portuguese sausage. A lighter continental breakfast is $4.50. The lunch buffet ($11 adult, $6.75 child, served daily 11 a.m.-1:30 p.m.), often terribly crowded because of the tour buses, offers salads, fresh fruits, sautéed mahimahi, teriyaki beef, honey-dipped chicken, soft drinks, coffee, and tea. Dinner daily, 5:30-9 p.m., starts with appetizers like sautéed shrimp $6.50 and special salad of the night $6.50. It moves on to entrees like seafood linguine $18.50, filet mignon $19.95, and Volcano House scampi $17.50. Hearty appetites will enjoy the prime rib of beef and shrimp combination at $23. The quality is fair and the prices reasonable; however, the lunchtime buffet is overwhelmingly crowded and should be avoided if possible.

Other Lodging

A B&B with an excellent reputation is **My Island,** tel. 967-7216, Box 100, Volcano, HI 96785. Rates range from a very reasonable $30 s with shared bath to $60 for a double with private bath, and there's even a private studio.

Victoria Rose, a one-room B&B, tel. 967-8026, owned and operated by Louisa and Pat Edie, is a fancy jewelry box done in maroon, pink, and lace, lots of lace. A four-poster "pineapple" bed and a private bath ensure privacy and comfort. Pat is an accomplished astrologer who, on request, will fill your evenings with the stars.

Bonnie Goodell (see above) recommends a similar cottage owned by her friend Beverly Jackson, tel. 967-7986. The setup is just about the same as Bonnie's, except that Beverly's cottage is closer to the road, which makes it more convenient, but a bit less secluded.

Other Food And Shopping

If you are after an exquisite piece of art, a unique memento, or an inexpensive but distinctive souvenir, be sure to visit the **Volcano Art Center** (see pp. 219-220).

You can get away from the crowds and have a satisfying meal at **Volcano Country Club Restaurant** at Volcano Golf Course. The cuisine is quite good. Complete breakfast is served daily 7-10 a.m., a full lunch menu daily 11 a.m.-3 p.m., and light snacks and *pu pu* until 5 p.m. Selections include hearty sandwiches for $6 and under; burgers with trimmings; luncheon N.Y. steak smothered in onions for $7; and a seafood plate with shrimp, fish, and onion rings for $7.75. There is also a good selection of local favorites like *loco moco* and chili with rice for under $6. The bar is well stocked, serving name-brand liquor, exotic drinks, and beer and wine. Next to the Kilauea Lodge, this is the best place for lunch in the area.

A **farmer's market** opens on the first and third Sunday of the month and sells local produce, baked goods, and used books. It's located at the Community Center at the corner of Wright Rd. (the north entrance to the village) and Route 11, between mile markers 26 and 27.

Volcano Store, tel. 967-7210, open 6 a.m.-7 p.m. daily, is in the middle of Volcano village and sells gasoline, film, and a good selection of basic foods. In front are a few **telephone booths,** and just next door is a full-service **post office.**

On the porch of Volcano Store is a **window service restaurant,** open Mon.-Thurs. 8 a.m.-4:30 p.m., Fri.-Sat. until 5 p.m., Sun. until 4 p.m. with seating available. Breakfasts are everything from coffee and a sweet roll to meat and eggs for $3.95, or a special of steak or fish and eggs for $4.99. Lunches are burgers and fries for around $3, and an assortment of plate lunches for under $5.

Behind Volcano Store, **Woodcarver's Corner,** open Wed.-Sun. 10 a.m.-5 p.m., tel. 985-8518, is run by a husband-and-wife team who sell bowls, trays, bracelets, and even totem poles. Prices are good, and the items are a mixture of semi-art and authentic junk.

Just down the road, **Kilauea General Store,** open 6 a.m.-7:30 p.m., Sun. 6:30 a.m.-6:30 p.m., also sells gas, and although it is not as well stocked as a grocery, it does have a deli case, a good stock of beer and liquor, and an excellent community bulletin board.

tree fern

DIANA LASICH HARPER

BOB RACE

KONA

Kona is long and lean, and takes its suntanned body for granted. This district *is* the west coast of the Big Island and lies in the rain shadows of both Mauna Loa and Mauna Kea. You can come here expecting brilliant sunny days and glorious sunsets, and you won't be disappointed; this reliable sunshine has earned Kona the nickname "The Gold Coast." Offshore, the fishing grounds are legendary, especially for marlin that lure game-fishing enthusiasts from around the world. There are actually two Konas, north and south, and both enjoy an upland interior of forests, ranches, and homesteads while most of the coastline is low, broad, and flat. If you've been fantasizing about swaying palms and tropical jungles dripping with wild orchids, you might be in for "Kona shock," especially if you fly directly into Keahole Airport. Around the airport the land is raw black lava that can appear as forbidding as the tailings from an old mining operation. Don't despair. Just north is one of the premier resorts in Hawaii, with a gorgeous white-sand beach lined with dancing coconut palms, and throughout Kona the lava has been transformed into beautiful gardens with just a little love and care.

Kailua-Kona is the heart of North Kona, by far the most developed area in the district. Its **Ali'i Drive** is lined with shops, hotels, and condos, but for the most part the shoreline vista remains intact because most of the buildings are low-rise. To show just how fertile lava can be when tended, miles of multihued bougainvillea and poinsettias line Ali'i Drive like a *lei* that leads to the flowerpot of the **Kona Gardens.** East of town is **Mt. Hualalai** (8,271 feet), where local people still earn a living growing vegetables and taro on small truck farms high in the mountain coolness.

South Kona begins in the town of **Captain Cook.** Southward is a region of diminutive coffee plantations, the only ones in the U.S. The bushes grow to the shoulder of the road and the air is heady with the rich aroma of roasting coffee. Farther south, rough but passable roads branch from the main highway and tumble toward hidden beaches and tiny fishing villages where time just slips away. From north to south, Kona is awash in brilliant sunshine, and the rumble of surf and the plaintive cry of seabirds create the music of peace.

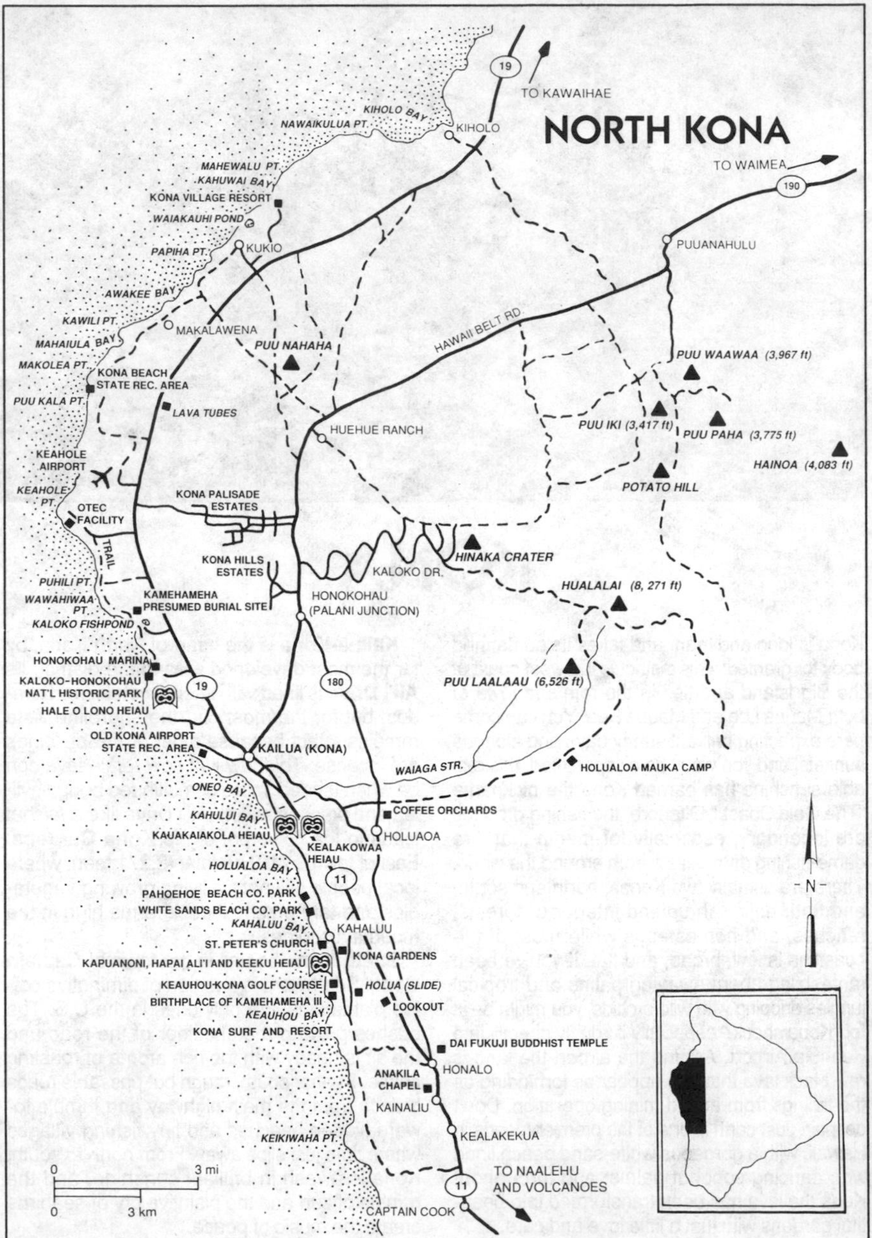

NORTH KONA

TO KAWAIHAE
19

TO WAIMEA
190

KIHOLO BAY
NAWAIKULUA PT.
KIHOLO

MAHEWALU PT.
KAHUWAI BAY
KONA VILLAGE RESORT
WAIAKAUHI POND
PAPIHA PT.
KUKIO

PUUANAHULU

AWAKEE BAY

KAWILI PT.
MAHAIULA BAY
MAKOLEA PT.
KONA BEACH STATE REC. AREA
PUU KALA PT.
MAKALAWENA
PUU NAHAHA

HAWAII BELT RD.

PUU WAAWAA (3,967 ft)

LAVA TUBES

HUEHUE RANCH

PUU IKI (3,417 ft)
PUU PAHA (3,775 ft)

HAINOA (4,083 ft)

KEAHOLE AIRPORT

POTATO HILL

KEAHOLE PT.
OTEC FACILITY

KONA PALISADE ESTATES

HINAKA CRATER

HUALALAI (8,271 ft)

TRAIL

KONA HILLS ESTATES
KALOKO DR.

PUHILI PT.
WAWAHIWAA PT.
KALOKO FISHPOND
KAMEHAMEHA PRESUMED BURIAL SITE
HONOKOHAU (PALANI JUNCTION)

HONOKOHAU MARINA
KALOKO-HONOKOHAU NAT'L HISTORIC PARK
HALE O LONO HEIAU
19

180

PUU LAALAAU (6,526 ft)

OLD KONA AIRPORT STATE REC. AREA
KAILUA (KONA)

WAIAGA STR.

HOLUALOA MAUKA CAMP

ONEO BAY
KAHULUI BAY
KAUAKAIAKOLA HEIAU
KEALAKOWAA HEIAU
HOLUALOA

COFFEE ORCHARDS

HOLUALOA BAY
11

PAHOEHOE BEACH CO. PARK
WHITE SANDS BEACH CO. PARK
KAHALUU BAY
ST. PETER'S CHURCH
KAHALUU

KONA GARDENS

KAPUANONI, HAPAI ALI'I AND KEEKU HEIAU
KEAUHOU-KONA GOLF COURSE
BIRTHPLACE OF KAMEHAMEHA III
KEAUHOU BAY
KONA SURF AND RESORT

HOLUA (SLIDE)
LOOKOUT

DAI FUKUJI BUDDHIST TEMPLE

ANAKILA CHAPEL
HONALO

KAINALIU

KEIKIWAHA PT.

KEALAKEKUA

TO NAALEHU AND VOLCANOES
11

CAPTAIN COOK

-N-

0   3 mi
0   3 km

© J.D. BISIGNANI AND MOON PUBLICATIONS, INC.

KAILUA-KONA AND VICINITY

SIGHTS

The entire Kona District is both old and historic. This was the land of Lono, god of fertility and patron of the Makahiki Festival. It was also the spot where the first missionary packet landed and changed Hawaii forever, and it's been a resort since the 19th century. In and around **Kailua** are restored *heiau,* a landmark lava church, and a royal palace where the monarchs of Hawaii came to relax. The coastline is rife with historical sites: lesser *heiau,* petroglyph fields, and curious amusement rides dating from the days of the Makahiki. Below the town of Captain Cook is **Kealakekua Bay,** the first and main *haole* anchorage in the islands until the development of Honolulu Harbor. This bay's historical significance is overwhelming, alternately being a place of life, death, and hope from where the spirit of Hawaii was changed for all time. Here on the southern coast is a Hawaiian "temple of refuge," restored and made into a National Historical Park. The majority of Kona's sights are strung along Route 11. Except for Kailua-Kona, where a walking tour is perfect, you need a rental car to visit the sights; the Big Island's Hele-On Bus is too infrequent to be feasible. The sights listed below are arranged from Kailua heading south.

Ali'i Shuttle

If you want to concentrate on the scenery and not the driving, take the **Ali'i Shuttle.** Painted red, white, and blue, the bus runs daily every 45 minutes along Ali'i Dr. 7:45 a.m.-10 p.m., and charges $1 each direction. The terminal points are Lanihau Shopping Center on the north end and Kona Surf Resort on the south end, with pickups at major hotels along the way. You can hail the bus and it will stop if possible.

Mokuaikaua Church

Kailua is one of those towns that would love to contemplate its own navel if it could only find it. It doesn't really have a center, but if you had to pick one, it would be the 112-foot steeple of Mokuaikaua ("The trees are felled, now let us

eat") Church. This highest structure in town has been a landmark for travelers and seafarers ever since the church was completed in Jan. 1838. The church claims to be the oldest house of Christian worship in Hawaii. The site was given by King Liholiho to the first Congregationalist missionaries who arrived on the brig *Thaddeus* in 1820. The actual construction was undertaken in 1836 by the Hawaiian congregation under the direction of Rev. Asa Thurston. Much thought was given to the orientation of the structure, designed so the prevailing winds blow through the entire length of the church to keep it cool and comfortable. The walls of the church are fashioned from massive, rough-hewn lava stone, mortared with plaster made from crushed and burned coral that was bound with *kukui* nut oil. The huge cornerstones are believed to have been salvaged from a *heiau* built in the 15th century by King Umi. The masonry is crude but effective—still sound after 150 years.

Inside, the church is extremely soothing, expressing a feeling of strength and simplicity. The resolute beams are native ohia, pegged together and closely resembling the fine beamwork used in barns throughout 19th-century New England. The pews, railings, pulpit, and trim are all fashioned from koa, a rich brown, lustrous wood that begs to be stroked. Although the church is still used as a house of worship, it also has the air of a museum, housing paintings of historical personages instrumental in Hawaii's Christian past. The crowning touch is an excellent model of the brig *Thaddeus,* painstakingly built by the men of the Pacific Fleet Command and presented to the church in 1934. The church is open daily from sunrise to sunset, and volunteer hostesses answer your questions 10 a.m.-noon and 1-3:30 p.m. Mokuaikaua Church is a few hundred yards south of Kailua Pier on the *mauka* side of Ali'i Drive.

Hulihee Palace

Go from the spiritual to the temporal by walking across the street from Mokuaikaua Church and entering Hulihee ("Flight") Palace. This two-story Victorian structure commissioned by Hawaii's first governor, John Kuakini, also dates from

KAILUA-KONA

© J.D. BISIGNANI AND MOON PUBLICATIONS, INC.

1838. A favorite summer getaway for all the Hawaiian monarchs who followed, especially King Kalakaua, it was used as such until 1916. At first glance, the outside is unimpressive, but the more you look the more you realize how simple and grand it is. The architectural lines are those of an English country manor, and indeed Great Britain was held in high esteem by the Hawaiian royalty. Inside, the palace is bright and airy. Most of the massive carved furniture is made from koa. The most magnificent pieces include a huge formal dining table, 70 inches in diameter, fashioned from one solid koa log. Upstairs is a tremendous four-poster bed that belonged to Queen Kapiolani, and two magnificent cabinets that were built by a Chinese convict who was serving a life sentence for smuggling opium. King Kalakaua heard of his talents and commissioned him to build the cabinets. They proved to be so wonderfully crafted that after they were completed the king pardoned the craftsman.

Prince Kuhio, who inherited the palace from his uncle, King Kalakaua, was the first Hawaiian delegate to Congress. He decided to auction off all the furniture and artifacts to raise money, supposedly for the benefit of the Hawaiian people. Providentially, the night before the auction each piece was painstakingly numbered by the royal ladies of the palace, and the name of the person bidding for the piece was dutifully recorded. In the years that followed, the **Daughters of**

Hawaii, who now operate the palace as a museum, tracked down the owners and convinced many to return the items for display. Most of the pieces are privately owned, and because each is unique, the owners wish no duplicates to be made. It is for this reason, coupled with the fact that flashbulbs can fade the wood, that a strict *no photography* policy is enforced.

Delicate and priceless heirlooms on display include a tiger-claw necklace belonging to Kapiolani. You'll also see a portrait gallery of Hawaiian monarchs. Personal and mundane items are on exhibit as well—there's an old report card showing a 68 in philosophy for King Kalakaua—and lining the stairs is a collection of spears reputedly belonging to the great Kamehameha himself.

Hulihee Palace, tel. 329-1877, is on the *makai* side of Ali'i Dr., open daily except Sunday 9 a.m.-4 p.m., last tour at 3:30, admission $4. A hostess knowledgeable in Hawaiiana is usually on duty to answer most questions.

The **Palace Gift Shop,** small but with quality items, is on the grounds next door to the palace. It offers a fine selection of koa sculptures of fish, sharks, and even a turtle, along with Hawaiiana books and postcards. Just outside is a saltwater pond with tropical fish.

Ahuena Heiau

Directly behind the King Kamehameha Kona Beach Hotel, at the north end of "downtown"

Kailua, is the restored Ahuena Heiau. Built around Kamakahonu ("Eye of the Turtle") Beach, it's in a very important historical area. Kamehameha I, the great conqueror, came here to spend the last years of his life, settling down to a peaceful existence after many years of war and strife. The king, like all Hawaiians, reaffirmed his love of the *aina* and tended his own royal taro patch on the slopes of Mt. Hualalai. After he died, his bones were prepared according to ancient ritual on a stone platform within the temple, then taken to a secret burial place just north of town which is believed to be somewhere near Wawahiwaa Point. It was Kamehameha who initiated the first rebuilding of Ahuena Heiau, a temple of peace and prosperity dedicated to Lono, god of fertility. The rituals held here were a far cry from the bloody human sacrifices dedicated to the god of war, Kukailimoku, that were held at Puukohola Heiau, which Kamehameha had built a few leagues north and a few decades earlier. At Ahuena, Kamehameha gathered the sage *kahuna* of the land to discourse in the Hale Mana (main prayer house) on topics concerning wise government and statesmanship. It was here that Liholiho, Kamehameha's son and heir, was educated, and it was here that as a grown man he sat down with the great queens, Keopuolani and Kaahumanu, and broke the ancient *kapu* of eating with women, thereby destroying the old order.

The tallest structure on the temple grounds is the *anuu* (oracle tower), where the chief priest, in deep trance, received messages from the gods. Throughout the grounds are superbly carved *kia akua* (temple images) in the distinctive Kona style, considered some of the finest of all Polynesian art forms. The spiritual focus of the *heiau* was humanity's higher nature, and the tallest figure, crowned with an image of the golden plover, was that of Koleamoku, a god of healing. Another interesting structure is a small thatched hut of sugarcane leaves, Hale Nana Mahina, which means "house from which to watch the farmland." Kamehameha would come here to meditate while a guard kept watch from a nearby shelter. The commanding view from the doorway affords a sweeping panorama from the sea to the king's plantations on the slopes of Mt. Hualalai. Though the temple grounds, reconstructed under the auspices of the Bishop Museum, are impressive, they are only one-third their original size. The *heiau* is open daily 9 a.m.-4 p.m., and admission is free. You can wander around following a self-guided tour, or take the free tour offered by the King Kamehameha Kona Beach Hotel, tel. 329-2911, which includes a tour of their own hotel grounds as well. The hotel portion of the tour includes a walk through the lobby, where various artifacts are displayed, and features an extremely informative botanical tour that highlights the medicinal herbs of old Hawaii. The hotel tours begin at 10 a.m. and 1:30 p.m. Don't miss this excellent educational opportunity, well worth the time and effort!

Ahuena Heiau

While in the area, make sure to visit the **Kailua Pier,** across the street from the *heiau.* Fishing boats are in and out all day, with most charters returning around 5 p.m. You'll have a chance to see some of the marlin for which Kona is noted, but if you have a sympathetic heart or weak stomach it might not be for you. This area is frantic with energy during the various "billfish tournaments" (see "Festivals, Holidays, and Events" in the Introduction) held throughout the year.

Honokohau Marina
Honokohau Harbor, three miles north of Kailua-Kona, is a new boat harbor and deep-sea fishing facility that has eclipsed the old Kailua Pier. The harbor area is full of fishing-oriented shops, and is also home to **Captain Zodiac Cruises** (pp. 141-142) and **Harbor House** (p. 247), formerly Atilla's Bar and Grill, where you can have a yarn with Kona's old salts. Primarily, this is where you come to see huge marlin caught that day, and to talk to the skippers of the deep-sea fishing boats that go after them. (For a description of deep-sea fishing see pp. 78-79.) Be at the harbor at 4 p.m. when all the boats come in every day like clockwork. When you pull into the marina, you'll see a road that goes off to the left. Head that way toward the tan building with a Texaco sign, to where the pier and the weigh-station are located. The huge fish will be hoisted, measured, and photographed while the skippers and their crew clean and prepare the boat for the next day's outing. If you're into deep-sea fishing, this is your chance to pick a likely boat and to get acquainted with the crew.

OTEC Natural Energy Labs
These amazing Ocean Technology facilities are located just south of the airport between mile markers 95 and 94, where you'll find a turnoff heading toward the sea. Incredible things are being done here. For example, cold water from several thousand feet below the surface of the ocean is placed in a turbine with warm surface water, a process that generates electricity and also provides desalinated water. In addition, the cold water is used for raising very un-Hawaiian things such as giant strawberries, lobsters, prawns, abalone, and kelp. Tours are offered Thursdays at 2 p.m. Make sure you call ahead, tel. 329-7341, to ensure a place on a tour.

Liholiho, Kamehameha II

JOHN HAYTER (HAWAII STATE ARCHIVES)

Along Ali'i Drive
Ali'i Dr. heads south from Kailua, passing the majority of Kona's resorts. On the mountain side of the road, a continuous flow of flowers drapes the shoulder like a femme fatale's seductive boa, while seaside the coastline slips along, rugged and bright, making Ali'i Dr. a soothing sight.

At your first stop, near White Sands Beach, look for the historic **Ohana Congregational Church** built in 1855 by Rev. John D. Paris. Services are still held every Sunday at 8 a.m. The base of the church is mostly original lava rock topped with a new roof. The cemetery area is peaceful and quiet and offers a perfect meditative perch from which to scan the coast below. Back on the road, look for signs to Kahaluu Beach Park; pull in and park here. On the rocky northern shore of this bay is **St. Peter's Catholic Church.** Its diminutive size, capped by a blue tin roof that winks at you from amidst the lava like a bright morning glory in an ebony vase, has earned it the nickname **Little Blue Church.** Built in 1889 on the site of an old, partially reclaimed *heiau,* the church is a favorite spot for snapshots. Inside, the epitome of simplicity reigns with bare wood walls and a simple crucifix. The only splash of color is a bouquet of fresh flowers on the altar. To the right of the church as you face it are the remains of **Kuemanu Heiau,** and within a ten-minute walk heading south from the

St. Peter's Church

church along the coast are strung the remains of **Kapuanoni, Hapai Ali'i,** and **Keeku** *heiau.* All are unrestored historical sites that still show signs of being used, and all offer fantastic vantage points from which to view the coast.

Do yourself a favor and visit the grounds of the **Kona Surf Hotel,** which have graciously been opened to the public. You're free to stroll around on your own, and nonguests can take a tour on Wed. and Fri. at 9 a.m. Here are 14 acres of ponds and gardens glorious with the perfumes and blooms of over 30,000 plants, flowers, fruits, and shrubs gathered from throughout Polynesia. To complement the natural setting of the grounds, a profusion of Asian and Hawaiian artwork has been placed here and there. Inside, the main hallways of the hotel's four wings are resplendent with over a million dollars' worth of wall hangings and tapestries. For a special treat, visit in the evening, when the hotel shines spotlights on the water and attracts a flock of manta rays.

A short stroll or a minute's drive south brings you to **Keauhou Bay.** Here you'll find a cluster of historical sites, and the pier for the Fair Winds Snorkel Dive and Charter. Look for a monument marking the birthplace of Kamehameha III in 1814. Local people come to fish from the pier around 5 p.m. for *halalu,* a tough little fish to catch. Ask at the Keauhou Bay Hotel for a free area map. Along the shoreline are a number of partially developed *heiau* sites. You'll also find a *holua,* grass-covered rocks that were slicked with water to form a slide. Hawaiians rode it on wooden sleds, especially during the Makahiki Festival. A small home stuck on a point of land on the edge of the bay is where John Wayne married his wife Pilar in 1954, and marks the site of the first modern house built on the bay

BEACHES AND PARKS

If Kona is short on anything, it is beaches. The ones that it has are adequate and quite striking in their own way, but they tend to be small, few, and far between. Most people expecting a huge expanse of white sands will be disappointed. These beaches do exist on the Big Island's west coast, but they are north of Kailua-Kona in the Kohala District. Kona does, however, have beaches alive with marinelife, providing excellent and safe snorkeling and top-notch tidepooling.

Note: The following are the main beaches in Kailua-Kona and North Kona. For descriptions of South Kona beaches refer to Milolii, Hookena, and Keei, pp. 271-272.

Kamakahonu Beach
You couldn't be more centrally located than at "Eye of the Turtle" Beach. Find it in downtown Kailua-Kona near Kailua Pier and the King Kamehameha Kona Beach Hotel. Local people refer to it as "Kids' Beach" because it is so gentle and perfect for a refreshing dip. Big kids come here to play too, when every year world-class athletes churn the gentle waters into a fury at the start of the Ironman Triathlon. Rent snorkel gear and kayaks for reasonable prices from the **Beach Shack,** located on the beach itself. Restrooms are on the pier.

Old Kona Airport State Recreation Area
In 1970 the old Kona Airport closed and the state of Hawaii turned it into a beach park. To

get there, simply walk along the shoreline for a few hundred yards north of the King Kamehameha Kona Beach Hotel. If driving, follow Ali'i Dr. to the junction just before the North Kona Shopping Center and turn left on the Kuakini Highway Extension. Facilities include showers, restrooms, and picnic area. Parking is unlimited along the old runway. The white-sand beach is sandwiched between water's edge and the runway. You can enter the water at some shallow inlets, but the bottom is often rocky and the waters can be treacherous during high surf. The safest spot is a little sandy cove at the southern end of the beach. Snorkeling is good at the northern end of the beach, and offshore a break makes Old Airport popular with Kona surfers. There is no official camping at the park, but people often do camp at the north end. A heated controversy erupted when a developer purchased the land adjacent to the north end of the park, then closed it to camping. Local fishermen had camped here for years. Protesting in 1981, they raised a tent village named Kukai-limoku, which disbanded when the leaders were arrested for trespassing. It's also disputed whether the developer has claimed eight acres that actually belong to the state. The controversy goes on.

Honokohau Beach

All types of people come to Honokohau Beach, including fishermen, surfers, and snorkelers, but it's primarily known as a **clothes optional beach.** This status has been drastically changing ever since the area officially became part of **Kaloko-Honokohau National Historical Park.** Follow Route 19 north from Kailua-Kona for three miles and turn left on the marked road leading to the Honokohau Small Boat Harbor. Stay to the right and park almost at the end of the access road near the "boat graveyard" in a dirt parking lot. Don't walk straight ahead onto land being claimed by the Pai 'ohana, a local Hawaiian family trying to establish a homestead within the "sovereign jurisdiction of the Kingdom of Hawaii." Instead clamber over the berm, follow the well-worn path into the vegetation, and keep walking for a few minutes to the beach.

This area, more toward Kaloko, was heavily populated during old Hawaiian days, and plenty of archaeological sites—mostly fish ponds, ruins of houses, and a few petroglyphs—are

found along the shoreline. Most of these sites are closed to protect them for posterity; if you come to an archaeological area, obey all posted signs and approach with great care and respect. Remember, it is imperative that you do not touch, disturb, or remove any historical artifacts. The beach offers safe swimming in somewhat shallow water, and except for a composting toilet, has no facilities.

The status of nudity along the beach is changing, and as part of the General Management Plan, the "proposed action" is to make nudity illegal. Camping and open fires, now illegal, are citable offenses under federal regulations. Walk to the north end of the beach, where a trail leads inland through thick vegetation. Follow it to the "Queen's Bath" (officially called the "Anchialine Bath" by the Park Service), a brackish pond surrounded by rock cairns. Because it is under consideration as a historical site, swimming in the pond is not recommended. There's sometimes a ranger back in here, and although the park is officially open, visitation is neither encouraged nor discouraged. On the way out, pause at the active small-boat harbor. Although shark signs are posted, snorkelers frequent the bay.

Kaloko Beach, about a 10-minute hike north of Queen's Bath, has great snorkeling in only 10-20 feet of water. Here, you can explore a series of sea arches. The entire area is a favorite with green sea turtles, who make their presence known mainly in the evenings.

North Kona Beaches

The first beach that you come to heading north from Kailua-Kona is the famous **Pine Trees** surfing beach, located near the OTEC facility (see above) just south of the airport between mile markers 95 and 94. Look for a well-worn dirt road leading to the left away from OTEC, and follow it to Pine Trees. Although famous with surfers and the site of many competitions, Pine Trees (none of which is in evidence) is not a good swimming beach. There are a few one-towel coves along the rocky shoreline where you can gain access to the water, but mostly it's a place from which to observe the action. You can also follow the road toward the OTEC facility until you find a large, sandy, public beach, fronted by rock and coral. Here are a few volleyball nets, a restroom, and some picnic tables.

Recently opened and well marked, **Kona Beach State Recreation Area** is about two miles north of the airport between mile markers 91 and 90. Follow the rugged but passable dirt road for about 1.5 miles to one of the closest beaches to Kailua-Kona. The semi-improved area has a lavatory and dilapidated picnic tables built around palm trees. The land rises before getting to the beach, and to the left are the remains of a concession stand. The swimming here is safe in season, but always be careful.

Before you get to the official parking area for Kona State Beach Park, notice a walking path off to the right. It is a five-minute walk to **Mahaiula Bay.** En route, you'll pass a portable toilet (clean), and about 200 yards further along is magnificent Mahaiula Beach. This crescent of white sand stretches for about 200 yards, with shade trees coming down almost to the water's edge. Completely unimproved and secluded, it's a great beach to "get away from it all" for the day.

Two miles further north, between mile markers 89 and 88, look for a cinder cone whose vegetation has been given a crew cut by the trade winds. Turn here on a very rugged, 4WD-only dirt road that takes you down to **Makalawena Beach.** En route to this totally secluded area, you'll pass over rough lava and coral and eventually come to a gate, where you park. Proceed on foot, and you'll have your choice of three wonderful beaches, ranging in size from 30 to 100 yards long that are all frequented by green sea turtles. Walk to the left past the biggest beach, and look for a path behind it that leads to a brackish but mostly freshwater pond where you can rinse off. Don't be alarmed by the harmless brine shrimp that nibble at your toes. They're much too small to do any real damage. If you do not have 4WD, you can still enjoy this area, but it means a hike of about 30 minutes. Be sure to bring water, especially if you intend to spend the day. From Mahaiula Beach (see above), walk north along a path and in about five minutes you'll come to the remains of an abandoned estate that once belonged to the Magoon Family, longtime island residents and major stockholders in Hawaiian Airlines. The state has purchased this land—which was at one time being eyed by a Japanese firm that wished to build a luxury resort—and it is now, thankfully, in the public domain.

After enjoying your short coastal hike, you will come to Makalawena, where you will be totally secluded. Remember not to take any chances during high surf, since there is no safety supervision whatsoever.

A few minutes farther north, just past the cinder cone, you'll find another road that starts off paved but almost immediately turns to lava and coral. If you have 4WD you can go to the end of the road, and then walk to the beach, but you can also walk for about 15 minutes from the turnout near the highway. The well-worn path leads you to **Kua Bay,** a famous swimming and boogie-boarding beach. Finally, just before you get to the luxury resorts of South Kohala, you'll find **Kiholo Bay** and **Luahinewai Pond,** considered yet another Queen's Bath. Look for a stand of royal palms marking the spot, and follow the rough but passable road down to the beach, where you will find a large round wooden house that once belonged to Loretta Lynn. Close by, a path leads over the lava to a tiny cove made more dramatic by a black-sand beach.

Ali'i Drive Beaches

The following beaches are strung one after the other along Kailua-Kona's Ali'i Drive. The first is **Pahoehoe Beach County Park,** about three miles south of town center. It's not much of a swimming beach, with only one small pocket of white sand next to a low seawall, but it's a handy spot to pull off for a view of the coastline or for a picnic.

White Sands Beach County Park (a.k.a **Magic Sands** or **Disappearing Sands**) is an excellent spot for a dip—if the sand is there. Every year, usually in March and April, the sands are stripped away by heavy seas and currents, exposing rough coral and making the area rugged for the average swimmer. People still come during those months because it's a good vantage point for observing migrating humpback whales. The sands always come back and when they do, the beach is terrific for all kinds of water sports, including bodysurfing and snorkeling. The annual **Magic Sands Bodysurfing Contest** is held during the winter months. The best board surfing is just north of the beach in a break the locals call "Banyans." White Sands' amenities include picnic pavilions, showers, and restrooms, making the beach a favorite spot with local people and tourists.

Kahaluu Beach Park on Kahaluu Bay has always been a productive fishing area. Even today, fishermen come to "throw net." You'll occasionally see large family parties surrounding their favorite fish with a huge *hukilau* net, then sharing their bounty among all participants. Because of this age-old tradition, the area has not been designated a marine conservation district. Kahaluu became a beach park in 1966. This ensured that the people of Kona would always have access to this favorite spot, which quickly became surrounded by commercial development. Amenities include picnic tables, showers, restrooms, even a basketball court. The swimming is very good, but the real attraction is snorkeling. The waters are very gentle and Kahaluu is a perfect place for families or beginning snorkelers. However, stay *within* the bay because a powerful and dangerous rip current lurks outside, and more rescues are made on this beach than on any other in Kona. The shoreline waters are alive with tropical fish: angelfish, parrotfish, the works. Bring bread or cheese with you, and in a minute you'll be surrounded by a live rainbow of colors. Some fish are even bold enough to nip your fingers. It's very curious that when these semi-tame fish spot a swimmer with a spear gun, they'll completely avoid him. They know the difference! Unfortunately, Kahaluu is often crowded, but it is still worth a visit.

ACCOMMODATIONS

Almost all of Kona's accommodations lie along the six miles of Ali'i Dr. from Kailua-Kona to Keauhou. Most hotels/condos fall in the moderate to expensive range, including one superluxury hotel just north of Kailua-Kona. A few inexpensive hotels are scattered here and there along Ali'i Dr., and back up in the hills are a "sleeper" or two that are cheap but decent (see pp. 272-273). The following list should provide you with a good cross section.

Camping Note

It's sad but true: except for the limited beach park in the village of Milolii, 25 miles south of Kailua-Kona, there is *no* official camping in all of the Kona District. Campers wishing to enjoy the Kona Coast must go north to the Kohala District to find a campground, or south to Kau. Some unofficial camping does exist in Kona (see "Beaches And Parks" above), but as always, this generates certain insecurities. Bivouacking for a night or two in any of the unofficial camp spots should be hassle free. Good luck!

Inexpensive

For a reasonable and homey hotel, try the **Kona Tiki,** 75-5968 Ali'i Dr., Box 1567, Kailua-Kona, HI 96745, tel. 329-1425, featuring refrigerators in all rooms (some kitchen units) and complimentary continental breakfast daily. Island fruits and a few old fishing poles are also furnished for the guests. The hotel is close to the road so it's a bit noisy in the day but quiets down at night. Rooms are clean, with ceiling fans, and have been recently refurnished with new curtains and bedspreads of pastel blue. All units face the ocean so everyone gets a view. There's a lovely lanai, a pool, and a trim little garden of raked sand. Prices are $50 s/d, kitchenette unit $55, extra person $6, three-day minimum. Rooms have a/c, but no phones or TVs.

The **Kona Bay Hotel,** at 75-5739 Ali'i Dr., Kailua-Kona, HI 96740, tel. 329-1393 or (800) 367-5102, is a locally owned downtown hotel run by Uncle Billy and his Kona family. Its best feature is the friendly and warm staff. The hotel is a remaining wing of the old Kona Inn, the rest of which was torn down to accommodate the shopping center across the road. The Kona Bay is built around a central courtyard and garden containing the Banana Cafe, pool, and bar. As at Uncle Billy's Hilo Bay Hotel, the motif is "cellophane Polynesian," highlighted by some artificial palms. The rooms are a combination of basic and superior with a/c, TV, green carpeting, one wall papered and the other bare cinder block. Each room has a mini-fridge, and some can be outfitted with kitchenettes. Rates begin at $59 s, $74 d, add $10 for a kitchenette; car-rental package available.

Kona White Sands apartment hotel is a two-story building just across from the famous White (Disappearing) Sands Beach, but all units now appear rented to long-term residents. All units are fully furnished, with electric kitchens, lanai, and cross ventilation; prices run $60/80 s/d, $6 extra person, three-day minimum. For information write Kona White Sands Apartments, Box 594, Kailua-Kona, HI 96745, tel. 329-3210 or (800) 553-5035.

Kona Magic Sands condominium is next door to Jameson's Restaurant at 77-6452 Ali'i Dr., Kailua-Kona, HI 96740, tel. 326-5622. Bookings are made through Kona Vacation Resorts at 77-6435 Kuakini, Kailua-Kona, HI 96740, tel. (800) 367-5168 Mainland, (800) 800-KONA Canada, and 329-6488 locally. Prices start at $65 and $85 nightly for a studio and one-bedroom with substantial savings on weekly and especially monthly rates. You can also call the resident manager at this time, Don Buchnowski, tel. 326-5622, for up-to-the-minute rates and availability. There is a three-night minimum stay and an off-season deal of seven nights for the price of six. The Kona Magic Sands is a landlord-green cinder-block building that is modest, clean, and well maintained. The units are homey and basic with the usual amenities, including TV, parking, cocktail lounge, pool, and maid service on request.

Kona Hukilau Hotel is another downtown hotel at 75-5646 Palani Rd., Kailua-Kona, HI 96740, tel. 367-7000 or (800) 367-7000. It's part of the island-owned Sands, Seaside, and Hukilau chain. Its sister hotel, the **Kona Seaside**, is just up the road; they share pools and other facilities. Most rooms have a/c, cross ventilation, and lanai, but no TV. There's a sun deck and central area with enclosed courtyard and lobby. Prices range from $55 standard to $76 deluxe, double occupancy. A car package adds $10 daily.

Patey's Place, 75-5731 Ala Hou St., Kailua-Kona, HI 96740, tel. 326-7018, (800) 972-7408 (recently moved from 75-195 Ala Onaona St.) is a reasonably priced hostel that will set you up in a bunk for $15 or give you a private room for $35, with bath and kitchen $45.

Moderate

Aston Kona by the Sea, 75-6106 Ali'i Dr., Kailua-Kona, HI 96740, tel. 327-2300 or (800) 922-7866, is a rather new and beautifully situated condominium with extraordinary coastal views. Like many of Kona's properties, it has no beach, but there is a freshwater pool on the premises, and a saltwater pool run by the state only a minute away. From the balcony of your suite overlooking a central courtyard, you can watch the aqua-blue surf crash onto the black lava rocks below. Each spacious one- or two-bedroom unit has two bathrooms, tiled lanai, mod-

ern kitchen complete with dishwasher and garbage disposal, living room with fold-out couch, dining room, color cable TV, and central air. Furniture differs slightly from unit to unit but is always tasteful and often includes rattan with plush cushions, and mauve and earth-toned rugs and walls. Prices are a very reasonable $155-180 for one bedroom, $200-215 for two. Aston Kona by the Sea, like most of the Aston properties, offers excellent value for a peaceful Kona vacation.

Kanaloa at Kona, tel. 322-2272 or (800) 657-7872, 78-261 Manukai St., Kailua-Kona, HI 96740, is situated in an upscale residential area at the southern end of Kailua-Kona and is one of those special places where you feel that you get more than what you pay for. The one- to three-bedroom units are enormous. Big isn't always better, but in this case it is. Each unit comes equipped with a complete and modern kitchen, two baths, a lanai with comfortable outdoor furniture, and a wet bar for entertaining. Rates for the tastefully furnished units range from $125 for one bedroom to $205 for three bedrooms; the rooms can accommodate four and six people respectively at no extra charge. A security officer is on duty, and on the grounds you'll find three pools, lighted tennis courts, Jacuzzis, gas barbecues, an activities desk with free morning coffee, and even a restaurant and cocktail lounge overlooking the black-sand beach. The complex itself is made up of low-rise units around a central courtyard. If you would like to escape the hustle and bustle but stay near the action, the Kanaloa at Kona is the place.

Just down the road from the Kona Surf is the **Kona Lagoon Hotel.** Most rooms feature lanais that overlook a tranquil lagoon, and all have a/c, color TV, and phones. There is a swimming pool, tennis courts, and the nearby Keauhou-Kona Golf Course. Dining and cocktails are provided at the Tonga Room and the Wharf Restaurant, and the Polynesian Long House meeting facility accommodates up to 700 people. Rates begin at a reasonable $58 d, $8 additional person. For information write Kona Lagoon Hotel, 78-6780 Ali'i Dr., Kailua-Kona, HI 96740, tel. 322-2727 or (800) 367-5004.

The **Keauhou Beach Hotel,** tel. 322-3441, (800) 446-8990, 78-6740 Ali'i Dr., Kailua-Kona, HI 96740, is built on a historic site that includes the remains of a *heiau* and a reconstruction of King Kamehameha III's summer cottage. The hotel is famous for its bougainvillea that plummets over the seven-story face of the hotel. Kahaluu Beach Park is adjacent, and the entire area is known for fantastic tidepools. This famous Kona hotel has been undergoing extensive renovation over the past few years, but is open to guests. Rates range from $95 standard up to $400 for a three-bedroom suite. Each has a/c, TV, phone, private lanai, and small refrigerator. The hotel also offers a free shuttle service to local shopping, golfing, and dining.

Casa De Emdeko is a condominium that receives the best possible praise: people who have lodged there once always return. It's a quiet, low-rise condo surrounding a central courtyard with freshwater and saltwater pools, maid service every three days, and a sauna. All units have a/c, full kitchen, and lanai. Prices start at $75 d, $10 extra person, for a garden-view apartment with every seventh night free. Contact Casa De Emdeko at 75-6082 Ali'i Dr., Kailua-Kona, HI 96740, tel. 329-2160 (resident manager); or the booking agent of Kona Vacation Resort, tel. 329-6488 or (800) 367-5168. Office hours are weekdays only 8 a.m.-5 p.m.; check in is at 1 p.m., checkout at 11 a.m. The office is closed on weekends and holidays but special arrangements can be made to accommodate you, and there is a buzzer at the front desk that summons the resident manager.

Kona Islander Inn condominium apartments are well appointed for a reasonable price. Conveniently located within walking distance of downtown Kailua-Kona, they're next door to the Spindrifter Restaurant. The style is "turn-of-the-century plantation" shaded by tall palms. All 100 units have phone, off-road parking, a/c, and TV. For information write Kona Islander Inn, 75-5776 Kuakini Hwy., Kailua-Kona, HI 96740, tel. 329-3181, or Aston Resorts, tel. (800) 367-5124, in Hawaii (800) 342-1551.

Kailua Plantation House, at 75-5948 Ali'i Dr., Kailua-Kona, HI 96740, tel. 329-3727, is a *designed* bed-and-breakfast neo-Victorian home with an island twist. Each different-theme room, prices ranging $120-175, has color cable TV, refrigerator, full bath stocked with Paul Mitchell products, private lanai, a/c and ceiling fans, and soundproofing—there are no common walls, ensuring peace and quiet. The first-floor premier suite, done in shades of pastel blue and white, has its own Jacuzzi, skylights for enjoying the brilliant Kona stars, and a location close enough to the beach that the lapping waves sing you to sleep with a soothing lullaby. Up the central staircase is the rose-colored Victorian Room, dominated by a four-poster bed. Turn-of-the-century furniture includes kerosene-lamp replicas that have been electrified. Another room features a double shower with windows for peering out to sea. The wild Africa Room has a zebra-striped bedspread and black-on-white motif. Rose Singarella, the hostess, takes special care in preparing a healthy breakfast that varies daily. Generous servings always include fresh island fruit and juices, and homemade muffins and cereals. Entrees can be quiches of all sorts, pancakes, or basmati rice.

High above Kailua-Kona on the road to Holualoa, perches **Hale Maluhia B&B,** 76-770 Hualalai Rd., tel. 329-1123, (800) 559-6627, a hideaway lovingly tended by hosts Ken and Ann Smith. Built and furnished in a mixture of rustic Hawaiian with a Victorian twist, the B&B offers accommodations in the main house and two separate cottages. The interiors feature open-beamed ceilings, plenty of natural wood trim, koa cabinets, full kitchens and private baths. There's even a functional working office with a computer, laser printer, and fax machine for those forced to mix business with pleasure. On the property are an outdoor spa, massage table, and two lanai from which to soak in the views; all are wheelchair friendly. Rates begin at $45 for a single bed and shared bath in the main house to $235 for the entire two-bedroom, 3-bath house. The Banyan Cottage is $110, and The Gatehouse $135.

A few reasonably priced and attractive condominium apartments include the following. **Kona Mansion,** a quarter mile from downtown, offers one-bedroom suites for up to four persons $55-60. There's a swimming pool, parking, TV, and maid service on request, with a minimum stay of five nights. Contact Hawaiian Apartment Leasing, 1240 Cliff Dr., Laguna Beach, CA 92651, tel. (714) 497-4253 or (800) 854-8843, or in California tel. (800) 472-8449. **Ali'i Villas,** oceanside just a half mile from Kailua-Kona, offers full kitchens, lanais, TVs, parking, a pool, and barbecues. Rates vary from one-bedroom units at $45 daily, $252 weekly (two to three guests), to two bedrooms (all units waterfront) from $60 daily, $380 weekly (up to four guests). Additional guests cost extra. There is a 20% monthly discount, and every seventh night is free. For bookings, contact Norma C. Edens, Kona Sun Coast Properties, tel. (800) 326-4751. **Kona Billfisher,** tel. (808) 329-9277, near downtown, offers full kitchens, pool, barbecues, limited maid service, and gazebo. One-bedroom units rent from $40 daily for up to four persons, two-bedrooms from $60 for up to six guests. Weekly and monthly rates and discounts. **Kona Plaza,** tel. 329-1132, downtown, has a swimming pool and sun decks and is wheelchair accessible. Daily rates are $40 d, $50 up to four. Weekly, monthly, and off-season rates available.

Expensive

The **Aston Royal Sea Cliff Resort,** winner of an American Automobile Association Three Diamond Award, offers classy condo apartments. The white alabaster building features rooms fronting a central courtyard where you'll find the pool and spa. The unobstructed views of the coast from most rooms are glorious, with sunsets enjoyed on your private lanai a perfect day-ending activity. Full amenities are offered, such as free tennis, daily maid service, two swimming pools, cable color TV, activities desk, jet spa and sauna, and sundries shop. Rates start with a studio at $140, and move to a one-bedroom $160-180, two-bedroom $180-200, and oceanfront villa $400; special 15% rate reduction during the off-season, and a "family plan." Contact Royal Sea Cliff Resort, 75-6040 Ali'i Dr., Kailua-Kona, HI 96740, tel. 329-8021 or (800) 922-7866 Mainland, (800) 445-6633 Canada, (800) 342-1551 Neighbor Islands.

The **Kona Hilton Resort,** tel. 329-3111, (800) 452-4411 in Hawaii, (800) 445-8667, Box 1179, Kailua-Kona, HI 96745, has figuratively and literally become a Kona landmark. The rooms are spacious and each includes a lanai (so protected from public view that it easily serves as an outdoor room). The tennis facilities are superb, and an ocean-fed pool is sheltered from the force of the waves by huge black lava boulders. Rates run from $130 for a standard room to $200 for a deluxe. The hotel, built like rising steps with the floor below larger than the one above, commands a magnificent view from its perch atop a beautiful promontory of black lava.

On the property, you can dine in the **Lanai Restaurant,** the main dining room open for dinner only, or have breakfast and lunch in the Lanai Coffee Shop, which has a beautiful veranda with a magnificent view of the surrounding coastline (for details see p. 252). At both you'll be treated to the wonderful creations of executive chef Hiroshi Omori. The hotel also boasts a mini-shopping mall complete with a sundries store. The **Windjammer,** an open-air bar with nightly entertainment, features jazz and contemporary music throughout the week (see p. 257). The hotel pool, completely refurbished, has an upper kiddies' pool and a lower retiled main pool adjacent to the rolling surf. Between the main building and the beach tower is the coconut grove. The *imu* is fired up every Monday, Wednesday, and Friday, and the luau comes complete with island entertainment that fills the grounds with music and laughter. The tennis courts, attended by hotel pro Adrian Canencia, are lighted for nighttime play, and are open to the public. Costs are a reasonable $6 p/h per court, or $7 for all day; nonguests pay $7 and $9 respectively. Other full-service amenities include a laundry, free parking, beauty salon, babysitters, and no charge for children, regardless of age, if they share a room with their parents. The Kona Hilton keeps alive the tradition of quality service at a quality hotel.

King Kamehameha Kona Beach Hotel is located in downtown Kailua-Kona at 75-5660 Palani Rd., Kailua-Kona, HI 96740, tel. 329-2911 or (800) 367-6060, on a spot favored by Hawaiian royalty; Kamehameha the Great spent the last days of his life here. It's one of the only Kona hotels that has its own beach, adjacent to the restored Ahuena Heiau. The walls of the lobby are lined with artifacts of ancient battles, and a hotel staff member gives historical and botanical tours of the grounds. Rooms (each with a/c, TV, refrigerator, safe, and phone), are appointed in shades of blue with rattan furniture, and each features a lanai with a sweeping panorama of the bay and Mt. Hualalai. Prices range from $105 for a standard room up to $500 for a three-bedroom suite, additional person $20, and children under 18 free when sharing their parents' room. The hotel features restaurants, a famous luau (see p. 256), cocktail lounges, tennis courts, shops, and a pool.

The **Kona Surf Resort,** 78-128 Ehukai St.,

Kailua-Kona, HI 96740, tel. 322-3411, (800) 367-8011, is located at Keauhou Bay, six miles south of Kailua-Kona. The building, comprised of four wings and lined with over $1 million worth of art, is architecturally superb. The impeccable hotel grounds are a magnificent match for the building and are open to the public (see p. 239). The hotel features the **S.S. *James Makee*** restaurant and nightly entertainment in their Puka and Poi Pounder rooms. All 535 rooms have a/c, phones, and TVs. Prices begin at $99 and go to $365 for a suite. There are two swimming pools, lighted tennis courts, and the Keauhou-Kona Golf Course next door, with special rates and starting times for hotel guests.

FOOD

Inexpensive

"So, budget traveler," you've been asking yourself, "which is the best restaurant in town, with the most food at the lowest prices, with that downhome atmosphere?" **The Ocean View Inn**, tel. 329-9998, is it! The gigantic menu of Chinese, American, Japanese, and Hawaiian food is like a mini-directory. Lunch and dinner range $6-12, and a huge breakfast goes for about $3.50. The most expensive dinner is T-bone steak at $12.95. They're open daily except Monday, 6:30 a.m.-2:45 p.m. and 5:30-9:00 p.m., with the bar open 6:30 a.m.-9 p.m. daily. Located across from the seawall near the King Kamehameha Kona Beach Hotel, they're always crowded with local people, a sure sign that the food is good.

Stan's Restaurant, tel. 329-1655, is an open-air establishment one notch up in both price and atmosphere from the Ocean View Inn next door. Here you have a cocktail lounge and a stab at atmosphere with some cozy lighting and rattan furniture. Breakfast is pleasing, with an assortment of island-inspired hotcakes, and a special for $3.95; no lunch is served. Dinner specials, starting at 5 p.m., are hibachi chicken or fillet of mahimahi $7.85, fresh island fish $9.95, and the captain's seafood dinner $11.50. All include salad, rice or whipped potatoes, fresh fruit, and dinner bread. However, the best items are their many Hawaiian foods like *kalua* pig and *lala poi* for under $5. The food is good, but not great, and you generally get a square meal for a very reasonable price.

The **Royal Jade Garden**, tel. 326-7288, open daily 10:30 a.m.-10:30 p.m., in the Lanihau Center, is a Chinese restaurant where you can get an amazing amount of well-prepared food for a moderate price. They have the normal run-of-the-mill chow meins for $5.50-7.50, noodle soups around $5, and meat dishes of chicken, duck, pork, or beef for $5.95-7.50. More expensive items include lobster with black bean sauce for $18.95, and a variety of fresh fish and seafoods for $8 and up. But they have an unbeatable special every night: you choose three entrees plus fried rice or fried noodles for only $5.50 (fewer choices less expensive). It's pre-prepared and placed on a hot table, but it's not cooked to death. You wind up with so much food that the most difficult part is keeping it on your plate. In the Royal Jade there's no decor, but if you are hungry and on a tight budget, this is one of the best values in town.

Yuni's Special Korean Barbecue, tel. 329-3167, also at the Lanihau Center, open daily 9 a.m.-9 p.m., is a basic hot-table-type Korean restaurant where you can enjoy a variety of combo-plates from $4.75. Your choices include *kalbi* beef, barbecued short ribs, and Korean chicken. No decor, but the prices are right, and the dishes make a perfect picnic or lunch.

Kona's **old industrial area,** although it doesn't sound inviting, is a great place to find inexpensive food, along with stores where the *people* shop. To get to the industrial area, head for the airport, and about one minute north of the junction of Route 19 (the airport road) and Palani Rd., make a left on Kaiwi Street. Or follow Kuakini Rd., a major intersection off Palani Rd. just a minute from the sea wall, to Kaiwi Street. The triangle formed by Kaiwi and Kuakini is primarily the old industrial area. The **French Bakery,** Kaahumanu Plaza, 74-5467 Kaiwi St., tel. 326-2688, open weekdays 5:30 a.m.-4 p.m., Saturday 5:30 a.m.-3 p.m., is a budget gourmet deli/restaurant where the food is great and the prices are low. Not only does it have the full range of pastries you would expect, it has wonderful sandwiches like pizza roll with cheese for only $1.25 and with ham or bacon for $1.50. All of the sandwiches are under $4, and the European-style coffee is full-bodied and rich.

Su's Thai Kitchen, in the industrial area (see above) at 74-5588A Pawai Pl. (just off Kaiwi St.), tel. 326-7808, open for lunch week-

1. Devastation Trail (David Stanley),
2. Na Ulu Sea Arches (J.D. Bisignani); **3.** quiet Puna road (J.D. Bisignani)

1. Mookini Heiau (J.D. Bisignani);
2. country life, Hawaiian style (J.D. Bisignani)

days 11 a.m.-2:30 p.m. and for dinner daily 5-9 p.m., is a semi-open-air restaurant with a distinctive touch of southeast Asia. You can sit inside, but choose a spot on the veranda, where there is absolutely no view but where the breezes blow and bamboo curtains are dropped for a feeling of privacy. The extensive menu offers a *pu pu* platter (a combination of all the appetizers including spring roll, shrimp, and chicken sauté served with homemade plum sauce and peanut sauce) for $10.95. Other choices are lightly breaded and pan-fried shrimp combined with fresh mint, lime juice, garlic, and kafir for $8.95; savory Thai soups mostly with a coconut base, with morsels of fish, scallops, or pork $6.95-9.95; salads $4.95-9.95; and a full selection of curries $7.95-9.95. Vegetarians will be happy with vegetable curry, vegetable stir-fry, or sweet-and-sour vegetables. The daily lunch special for $5.95 might be a mini *pu pu* platter; green curry with chicken and eggplant accompanied by a bowl of white rice; or yellow curry with chicken, potatoes, carrots, and onions with a bowl of white rice. The service is friendly, the portions large for the money. Su's is a favorite with local people—the highest recommendation.

A friendly gorilla greets you at the **Pot Belli Deli** (in the industrial area, see above) at 74-5543 Kaiwi St., tel. 329-9454, open weekdays 6 a.m.-4 p.m. The refrigerated deli case holds chicken, ham, or tuna salad sandwiches for $2.65; jumbos of all at $3.95; spinach pie $4.25; and bagels with cream cheese. The shelves hold all the condiments and extras that you would need for a terrific picnic lunch. You can get your order to go, or eat at one of the few booths inside.

Tom Bombadill's menu takes its inspiration from Tolkien's Middle Earth, but its location is a lot noisier, perched over Ali'i Dr. and overlooking the Hilton's tennis courts. They talk about the ocean view, but your neck will have to stretch like the mozzarella on their pizza to see it. The bar pours domestic beers at $2.50, imports at $3.50, and pitchers for $8.50. The menu includes all sorts of hamburgers for under $6; soups $3; and a variety of chicken, fish, and shrimp platters from $6.50. All of these meals are good, but the real specialty is pizza, from $9 up depending upon size and toppings. Open daily 11 a.m.-10 p.m., tel. 329-1292.

Harbor House, formerly Attilla's Bar and Grill, at the Honokohau Small Boat Harbor, tel. 326-4166, open daily 10:30 a.m.-8:30 p.m., features Kona's longest bar. Harbor House is more or less an open-air pavilion, but it is actually quite picturesque as it overlooks the harbor. If you are interested in a charter fishing boat, this is the best place to come to spin a yarn with the local skippers who congregate here nightly at about 4:30 p.m. Over the bar hangs a gigantic 1,556-pound marlin, almost as big as the Budweiser sign. Strategically placed TVs make it a good sports bar, and the jukebox has a great selection of oldies and contemporary tunes. A variety of draft beers from Steinlager to Coors Light come in 16-ounce chilled schooners for only $2.50, with Heineken and Carlsburg $2.75. Sunday and Monday, the frothy schooners are only $2, with the same price daily during happy hour 3-6 p.m. The bill of fare offers grilled bacon cheeseburgers with fries for $6.50, shrimp and chips $6.75, crab-salad sandwich $5, clam chowder $3.25, and chili and rice $4.25. Try their delicious macadamia nut pie for $2.50. Harbor House is one of the truly *colorful* places in Kailua-Kona, and one of the best places to relax and have a hassle-free brew.

Giuseppe's, tel. 329-7888, in the Kailua Bay Inn Shopping Plaza at 75-5699F Ali'i Dr. across from the Kona seawall, open daily except Sunday for lunch 11:30 a.m.-3 p.m. and for dinner 5-9 p.m., serves dishes of savory pasta in a tiny but tasteful restaurant where you can dine in or take out. Lunch specials served until 4 p.m. range from spaghetti marinara for $4.95 to fettucine with artichoke hearts for $6.25. Dinner is *delisioso* with choices like chicken marsala $11.75 and scampi mediterranean $14.25, which includes pasta, dinner salad, and a choice of cheese bread. The minestrone soup served all day for $3.25 per bowl is excellent. The menu is rounded out with a small selection of sandwiches and various dishes from the children's menu for only $3.95. Bring your own beer or wine. During the triathlon, Giuseppe's offers all the pasta you can eat for $10.

Ali'i Sunset Plaza, 75-5799 Ali'i Dr. across from the seawall at the south end of town, has a cluster of inexpensive to moderately priced restaurants that more or less cover the major international cuisines. **King Yee Lau,** tel. 329-

7100, open Mon.-Sat. 11 a.m.-9 p.m., Sun. 4-9 p.m., offers an all-you-can-eat lunch buffet, and the usual Chinese dishes like pressed crisp duck, beef with ginger sauce, and shrimp with seasoned vegetables, all priced under $7.95. Vegetarians can dine on tofu with oyster sauce or a variety of chow mein for under $6.50. **Thai Rin,** tel. 329-2929, open weekdays for lunch 11 a.m.-2:30 p.m., dinner 5-9:30 p.m., weekends dinner only 5-9:30 p.m., fills the air in the small plaza with the aromas of its savory Thai spices. The menu offers spring rolls $4.95; fried noodles Chinese-style $6.95; vegetarian dishes like Thai fried rice $7.95; stir-fried chicken, beef, or pork $7.95; and Thai garlic shrimp or squid $8.95. Thai Rin features a variety of lunch specials for about $5.95. And for a fast snack and a smattering of Hawaiian fare, stop in at **Huli Huli Chicken,** where $5 will get you a plate lunch featuring island barbecued chicken.

Fast Foods And Snacks

At the Kona Inn Shopping Village, try one of the following. **Mrs. Barry's Cookies** are homemade yummies that include macadamia nut, chocolate chip, and peanut butter, gift boxed to send home. Follow your nose to the **Coffee Cantata** and drink a cup in the little courtyard. **Kona Kai Farms Coffee House** features a sampler cup of Kona coffee. **Be Happy Cafe** has plate lunches like beef stew, chicken garlic, teriyaki beef/shrimp combo, and chicken and fries for $5-6.

Around town, the **Bartender's Ocean Breeze** serves up 12-ounce mugs of ice-cold beer for $1 and grill-your-own burgers for $2.75. Other snacks are available on Ali'i Dr., near the Kona Hilton tennis courts, tel. 329-7622. **McGurk's** is a fill-er-up joint next door to Marty's Steak and Seafood in the Kailua Bay Inn Shopping Plaza in downtown Kailua-Kona. They serve an evening special like the Wednesday fish buffet for $6.95 that includes mac-nut coleslaw and french fries. Basically a takeout place with a limited sit-down menu, McGurk's isn't special, but the food is worth the money.

In the Kona Marketplace, **Chili by Max,** open Mon.-Sat. 10 a.m.-8 p.m., Sun. 11 a.m.-8 p.m., is famous for its award-winning oven-baked chili, made with beef or turkey. Also on the bill of fare are kosher hot dogs, chili dogs, chili nachos, baked potatoes, and ice cream.

Across Sarona Rd. from Kona Marketplace and down toward Kuakini Hwy. there's **Subway Sandwiches** a chain selling double-fisted sandwiches to go. On Kuakini Hwy. next to **McDonald's** golden arches is a **7-Eleven,** open 24 hours, and along Palani Rd. is **Taco Bell,** next door to **Pizza Hut,** which is across the road from **Burger King.**

In the **Lanihau Center** along Palani Rd., you can snack at **Gifu Bento,** a sidewalk cafe where you'll find a Japanese-style plate lunch for under $5. **Buns In The Sun,** open Tues.-Sat. 5 a.m.-5 p.m., Sun. 6 a.m.-5 p.m., Mon. to 4 p.m., is a bakery-deli serving everything from croissants to apple turnovers. Also enjoy sandwiches priced at $3.75 to $6.50 while sitting at a few wrought-iron tables under their outdoor canopy. The center also houses **Kentucky Fried Chicken** and **Penguin's Frozen Yogurt** (where you can order a smoothie).

Rocky's Pizza, tel. 322-3223, open daily 11 a.m.-9 p.m. at the Keahou Shopping Village, offers whole pizzas for $9.95-14.95 or slices for $1.75 each. Rocky's also features delicious sub sandwiches like hot pastrami on crusty bread; they are favorites with the locals who like good food at a good price.

In the **Kopiko Plaza,** along Palani Rd. and just down from the Lanihau Center, you'll find **Cynthia's Hawaiian Kitchen** for inexpensive local foods; **Kaminari's,** a cafeteria-style Japanese restaurant with affordable prices; **Domino's Pizza,** for eat in, takeout, or delivery; **Mask,** a bar and grill so new that it hasn't developed a personality yet; and **Kona Mix Plate** for inexpensive plate lunches.

The **Kona Coast Shopping Center,** also along Palani Rd., has a number of small local and ethnic restaurants where you can get inexpensive but savory meals. **Kim's Place,** open weekdays 10 a.m.-8 p.m., Sat. 10 a.m.-4 p.m., closed Sunday, tel. 329-4677, features takeout and catering, and has a few tables with umbrellas; enjoy Korean items like *kalbi, pulgogi,* Korean chicken, and even tempura. Prices for most items are under $5. For the health-conscious, **Kona Health Ways,** open Mon.-Fri. 9 a.m.-7 p.m., Sat. 9 a.m.-6 p.m., Sun. 9:30 a.m.-5 p.m., is a full-service health food store that makes ready-to-eat sandwiches, salads, and soups geared toward the vegetarian. **Mother India,** also in the mall, serves chicken curry

Many of Kailua-Kona's restaurants are found in shopping plazas like the newly built Waterfront Row.

$4.95, lamb curry $5.95, chicken biriani $5.95, and mixed vegetables $4.95.

The Kona Square Shopping Center is home to the very inexpensive **Stumble Inn**. They have breakfast specials for $1.99, and a lunch special. Unfortunately, there is little that's special about their food, but they are open at 5:30 a.m. for those going fishing who need a very early breakfast.

On your way to Pu'uhonua O Honaunau (see "Honalo to Captain Cook and Vicinity" in the section on Central and South Kona) you might consider stopping at **Barry's Nut Farm** along Route 160. They'll give you a free tour of the gardens and nursery, or you can browse for pottery or buy sandwiches and drinks. Open daily 9 a.m.-5 p.m., tel. 328-9930.

Moderate

Cafe Sibu, in the Kona Banyan Court, open daily 11:30 a.m.-9 p.m., tel. 329-1112, is an Indonesian restaurant serving savory marinated meats and vegetables spiced with zesty sauces and flame grilled. The restaurant, across from the seawall under the big banyan tree, has only a few outside tables, and makes a light attempt at decor with a few antique Indonesian masks and *wayang* (Indonesian puppet theater) puppets hanging on the walls. They do, however, win the prize for the most ventilated restaurant in all of Hawaii, with nine ceiling fans whirring in a 10- by 10-foot room! To make the menu even

more varied, the Italian owner offers a daily pasta dish, using recipes over 100 years old that have been handed down by her grandmother. *Delisioso!* If you're hungry, go for the *gado gado* for $9.50, an Indonesian salad layered with spices and peanut sauce that can be dinner for one or a salad entree for two or three. Stir-fried vegetables with chicken or tofu are $9.95; chicken and vegetable curries are $10.50 and $8 respectively; and Balinese chicken marinated in tarragon, garlic, and spices is $10.95. The combination plates are the best deals: you get a stir-fry, chicken curry, and choice of sauté for $11.95. Lunch prices on all of the above are about $2 cheaper. Cafe Sibu serves *the* best and *the* most interesting moderately priced food in Kailua-Kona.

The **Kona Ranch House** is a delightful restaurant with something for everyone. It has two rooms: the family-oriented Paniolo Room, where hearty appetites are filled family style; and the elegant Plantation Lanai, where both palate and sense of beauty are satiated. This restaurant, highlighted by copper drainpipes, brass ceiling fans, wicker furniture, and latticework, all against a natural wood-and-brick background, epitomizes plantation dining. The Kona Ranch House is a classy establishment where you get more than what you pay for. Prices range from reasonable to expensive, and the menus in the two separate rooms reflect this. Open daily 6:30 a.m.-10 p.m., and Sunday for brunch. Reservations are needed for the Plantation Lanai. The restaurant is located two minutes from downtown at the corner of Kuakini Hwy. and Palani Rd., tel. 329-7061.

The **Jolly Roger,** walking distance from downtown at 75-5776 Ali'i Dr., tel. 329-1344 (formerly the Spindrifter), is another Kona restaurant with a remarkable seaside setting. The gently rolling surf lapping at the shore is like free dessert. Full breakfasts are served 6:30 a.m.-noon and start at $4, with waffles and pancakes cheaper. Lunch is served 11 a.m.-4 p.m., dinner 5:30-10 p.m. Sandwiches start at $3; assorted salads are $5; full salad bar is $5.95; and entrees of fresh fish, seafood, and beef are from $10. Happy hour daily, 11 a.m.-6 p.m., features an assortment of *pu pu.* A daily special of steak and eggs Benedict, available 6:30 a.m.-noon, costs $4.75. The decor is bent bamboo with puffy cushions, and the tile-floored veranda has marble-topped tables and white wrought-iron chairs.

Banana Bay Buffet, tel. 329-1393, is located in the courtyard of Uncle Billy's downtown Kona Bay Hotel. Following in the semi-plastic Polynesian tradition of Uncle Billy, they serve a fair to passable buffet for $8.95. A stuffed marlin, seemingly too huge and colorful to be real, gazes down at everyone from the wall. Sometimes free *hula* shows are part of the bargain. Open daily at 6:30 a.m. (breakfast specials $4.95), this restaurant could be an "old reliable" with a touch more care in the food preparation.

Reuben's Mexican Cafe, open daily 11 a.m.-11 p.m., Sun. 3-11 p.m., tel. 329-7031, is tucked away in the downtown Kona Plaza and serves up hefty portions of south-of-the-border fare at good prices. There's a full menu, from *chile rellenos* to *huevos rancheros,* all $5-7. The only "slam" against Reuben's is that the dishes are a bit too tame. Reuben's does have the best prices on imported beers—offering Dos Equis, Corona, and Heineken for only $2.

Marty's Steak and Seafood House, open daily for lunch 11 a.m.-3 p.m., dinner 5-10 p.m., tel. 329-1571, was a former Buzz's Steak House. They serve hefty orders of chops, steaks, fresh fish, and Korean-style barbecued ribs for under $15. Fresh, hot bread and the salad bar are filling and priced reasonably. A nightly buffet special of barbecued beef-back ribs is $12.95, while

crab is $21.95. Sunday nights bring a special of prime rib for $10.95, or a larger cut at $13.95. Marty's has reliable quality and is located upstairs in the Kailua Bay Inn Shopping Plaza. The atmosphere in this open and airy perch overlooking the bay is congenial.

Don Drysdale's Club 53, open daily 10 a.m.-2 a.m., tel. 329-6651, was founded by the famous Dodger pitcher, and in the good sense of the word can best be described as a saloon. The amiable bar and grill serves reasonably priced beer, drinks, and sandwiches until 1 a.m. Sports fans away from home can always catch their favorite events on the bar's TV. Fare includes soup and salads from $2.50, a wide variety of *pu pu* from $4, sandwiches $3-5, plus the special peanut-butter cream pie at $2.35. Drysdale's is one of the most relaxing and casual bars in town, overlooking the bay at the Kona Inn Shopping Village.

Quinn's is Kona's socially eclectic bar and grill where everyone from local bikers to pink-roasted tourists are welcomed. It's also a roost for nighthawks who come here to munch and have a beer when everything else in town is closed. Quinn's, across from the King Kamehameha Kona Beach Hotel, is open daily for lunch 11 a.m.-5:30 p.m. and dinner 5:30 p.m.-1 a.m. (Sunday until 10 p.m.), tel. 329-3822. The local in-crowd comes to the patio for sandwiches, vegetarian specialties, and seafood. The inside bar is cozy, friendly, and sports oriented. For lunch, a gigantic mound of shrimp and crab salad for $8.95 is wonderful. The fresh catch-of-the-day sandwiches with salad for $7.75 are a deal, but they're not always available. Reasonably priced specialties include tenderloin tips sautéed in brandy with onions for $8.95, shrimp and chips for $8.95, and fish and chips for $6.95. Dinner entrees are savory: sautéed scallops $15.95, chicken stir-fry $12.95, and fresh catch sautéed or baked for $18.50 up. All include soup or dinner salad, vegetable, rice, and Quinn's homefried potatoes.

When you enter the Kaloko Industrial Park, just past mile marker 97 heading north from Kailua-Kona, the setting makes you think you're after plumbing supplies. What you'll find is terrific food prepared by one of Hawaii's greatest chefs, at **Sam Choy's Restaurant,** tel. 326-1545, open weekdays 5 a.m.-2 p.m., Sat. 6:30 a.m.-2 p.m., and Wed.-Sat. 5-9 p.m. for dinner, reservations suggested. To get there, make a right along the main road as soon as you enter the industrial park, and pass a gas station (a good place to fuel if you're returning your rental car to the airport). About 50 yards past the gas station, make a left and look for Sam's in a nondescript gray building halfway up the hill on the right. The atmosphere is pleasant enough, but those in the know who have dined on Sam's sumptuous creations, either here or at the Hilton (where he used to be executive chef), come for the food! Breakfasts like the ultimate stew omelette (a three-egg omelette filled with Sam's beef stew) $6, steak and eggs $7.95, or the local favorite of fried rice and egg for $3.50 will keep you going most of the day. The regular menu also includes fresh island fish prepared poke style and then flash-fried for $5.95; Kaloko steak marinated in teriyaki sauce with grilled onions $7.95; and Kaloko noodle mania (chow mein noodles cooked with fresh vegetable and meat and served in a crispy wonton ball) for $6. Or try one of the specials, such as fresh *ahi* sauté $6.75. Local people also come here for the lunch favorites like deep-fried breaded shrimp for $6, or homemade beef stew $5.50. For a gourmet dinner, choose oriental lamb chops with shiitake mushrooms $14.95, vegetable pasta $16.95, macadamia nut chicken breast grilled with papaya and pineapple compote $12.95, or stuffed shrimp Christopher and broiled fillet of beef at $17.95, all with soup and salad. Sam prepares wonderful food, and being a dad himself, he doesn't forget the kids—they have their own menu.

Calling **Bianelli's** "just a pizza shop" is like calling a Ferrari "just a car." Although they make pizza, and it is superb, they also have a full deli counter and plenty of delicious lunch and dinner entrees, all of which they deliver. Bianelli's is located at the Pine Plaza at 75-240 Nani-Kailua, between Hualalai Rd. and the Kona Belt Rd., tel. 326-4800. Specialty sandwiches like a Philly steak are scrumptious, and meals like manicotti, a variety of spaghetti dishes, and lasagna are all well under $10. Bianelli's makes their own pizza dough, and they offer pizza pies ranging from $7.95 for a hand-tossed, New York-style mini-pizza to an exotic pie smothered in garlic and herb sauce, layered with Parmesan and buffalo-milk-mozzarella cheeses, and topped with whole peeled tomatoes and fresh herbs for around $15.95. Vegetarian pizza topped with artichoke hearts, eggplant, sun-dried tomatoes, and Maui onions costs about $14. The wine cellar is outstanding, with over 64 different selections ranging from California merlot to French pinot noir; prices range from about $14 to over $200 per bottle. Bianelli's also has a tremendous selection of domestic and imported beers. Open daily 4-10 p.m., this restaurant is small but tastefully decorated in Italian-American style with the mandatory red-checkered tablecloths. The food and service are excellent. *Delisioso!*

Kona Amigos, tel. 326-2840, across the seawall in downtown Kailua-Kona at 75-5669 Ali'i Dr., is open daily 11 a.m.-midnight. This bar and restaurant features Mexican cuisine, with special dishes like crab enchiladas for $13.50, or enchilada rancheros for $10.50. Less expensive but savory items include a fiesta tostada $8.75, chile rellenos $10.50, and the Miss Manaloa (roasted pork rolled in a flour tortilla) $10.50. The southwestern Caesar salad for $8.95 comes with either grilled chicken breast or grilled fresh fish.

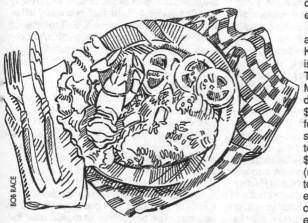

BOB RACE

Sit on the veranda to people-watch or to survey the entire harbor area. In season, the Kona Triathlon starts and finishes in front of this restaurant.

Kaminari's, open Mon.-Sat. 5:30-9 p.m., tel. 326-7799, is an authentic and moderately priced Japanese restaurant located in the Kopiko Plaza along Palani Rd. just near the Lanihau Center. The decor is functional cafeteria style, and the menu includes *tempura or tonkatsu donburi* (deep-fried shrimp, vegetables, and pork cutlet atop rice) $7; an assortment of *teishoku*, including soup, salad, pickles, and rice for $11.80; *sashimi* priced daily; Japanese-style steak $13.80; and *yakitori* (grilled chicken) $5.50.

Expensive

The **Lanai Restaurant** at the Kona Hilton Resort, tel. 329-3111, offers premier dining 5-9:30 p.m. in a magnificent setting. Executive chef Hiroshi Omori and his assistant chefs start you off with sashimi for $8.95, or jumbo shrimp cocktail for $7.95. Soups are Kona's best seafood chowder at $4.95, or old-fashioned Portuguese soup for $4.25, which you can combine with the gourmet salad bar for an excellent yet moderately priced meal. Seafood from sautéed mahi-mahi Eurasian style (tender white fillets of seasoned fish sautéed in shiitake mushroom shoyu butter sauce) to sizzling lobster tail, comes with rice pilaf and fresh vegetables. Entrees include prime rib $19.95 and pineapple smoked pork loin $12.95. The phenomenally hungry can order the Ali'i Platter (not on the menu, daily quote), which comes laden with *sashimi,* shrimp, crab claws, sirloin steak, chicken macadamia, *kalua* pig, chicken *sate,* sliced lobster, and a personal beach boy or two to help lift you from your chair. Choose a table in the richly appointed dining room, or perch on the veranda for an outdoor setting. A remodeling done in 1985 lifted the floor 12 inches so that everyone is ensured a spectacular view through the wraparound windows. The Hilton's Sunday champagne brunch is considered the best in Kailua-Kona by local people (see p. 245). Seatings are 9 a.m.-12:30 p.m., with reservations strongly recommended. The Kona Hilton's Lanai Restaurant offers truly fine dining in an elegant hotel. If you're into something simpler in a casual setting, try the hotel's **Lanai Coffee Shop,** open daily for breakfast, lunch, and dinner. The breakfast menu ranges from steak and eggs for $9.85 to Belgian waffles smothered in nuts, berries, and fresh fruits for $7.25. Lunch could be an assortment of burgers and sandwiches priced under $8, or a crisp chef's salad laden with ham, roast beef, and turkey for $7.75.

Oui oui monsieur, but of course we have zee restaurant *Francais.* It is **La Bourgogne,** tel. 329-6711, open Mon.-Sat. 5:30-10 p.m., located in Kuakini Plaza South, five minutes from downtown Kailua-Kona along Route 11. Guy Chatelard, the original owner of La Bourgogne, has recently sold the restaurant to master chef Ron Gallagher and his manager wife Colleen Moore. Guy stayed on for a transition period, sharing his recipes and food philosophy with Ron and Colleen, who are dedicated to keeping up the fine service and cuisine. For those who just can't live without escargots, shrimp Provençal, or pheasant, you've been saved. How much? Plenty, *mon petit!* Cold and hot appetizers include *pâté du chef* for $6, jumbo shrimp cocktail for $10.50, and mussels baked in garlic butter for $6. Soups of the day are scrumptious: French onion at $4.50, and homemade lobster soup when available at $5.75. For salads, order greens with Roquefort dressing at $3, or Caesar salad for two at $8. Titillating seafood and poultry entrees feature fresh catch-of-the-day $18.50; jumbo shrimp in butter, parsley, and garlic sauce $21; and sliced breast of roast duck with lemon-orange sauce $15. Meat courses are delectable roast saddle of lamb with creamy mustard sauce $26, or veal in creamy white wine and mushroom sauce $25. Top off your gourmet meal with fresh, made-in-house desserts. This restaurant, small and slightly out of the way, is definitely worth a visit for those who enjoy exceptional food.

Jameson's-by-the-Sea (formerly Dorian's), tel. 329-3195, open weekdays for lunch 11 a.m.-2:30 p.m. and dinner every day 5:30-10 p.m., is located at 77-6452 Ali'i Dr. next to Kona Magic Sands Condo. Jameson's makes a good attempt at elegance with high-backed wicker chairs, crystal everywhere, white linen table settings, and a back-lit fish tank in the entry. The sea foams white and crashes on the shore just outside the restaurant's open windows. The quality of the food is very good, but just shy of gourmet. The bar serves domestic beer for $2.75, imported beer $3.50, well drinks $3, and exotics $5, which you can take to the veranda with some *pu pu* to enjoy the sunset. The lunch menu lists appetizers like sashimi, salmon pâté, fried calamari, and shrimp cocktail, all from $7.95. Jameson's Yokohama soup, which is a hearty fish soup with fresh spinach and cream at $4, could complement a dinner salad for around $3.75 to make a light meal. Lunch sandwiches are hearty fish of the day, grilled ham and cheese, or teriyaki steak for around $8. A number of seafood Louie salads made with crab, shrimp, or other seafood cost around $10. The dinner menu offers the same appetizers but adds a seafood platter with sashimi shrimp and fresh oysters for $9.50. The dinner entrees range from fresh catches like *opakapaka, ono,* and mahimahi at market price, to fried shrimp and scallops with oyster sauce and Chinese pea pods for $16.95. Other full meals include filet mignon with béarnaise sauce for $21.95, veal piccata $21.95, and sesame chicken $15.95. There's also shrimp curry with mango chutney for $16.95. For dessert save room for their assortment of homemade chiffon pies from $4.50.

At **Huggo's Restaurant,** tel. 329-1493, on Ali'i Dr. next door to the Kona Hilton, it's difficult to concentrate on the food because the setting is so spectacular. If you were any closer to the sea, you'd be in it, and of course the sunset is great. Because it is built on a pier, you can actually feel the floor rock. When you are having dinner, ask the waitperson for some bread between courses so that you can feed the fish. Huggo's is open Mon.-Fri. 11:30 a.m.-2:30 p.m. for lunch and 5:30-10 p.m. for dinner, with entertainment most nights (see p. 256). Waiters and waitresses are outfitted in alohawear, and the heavy wooden tables are inlaid with maps of the Pacific. Huggo's executive chef, John Halligan, and the head chef, Peter Bartsch from Switzerland, have created a combination of continental, Hawaiian and Pacific Rim cuisine that is extraordinarily good, and affordable. Lunch is reasonable, with tasties like Huggo's club; or a spicy, hot Italian sandwich prepared with pepperoni and aged Italian salami, Greek olives, and tomatoes for under $9. Huggo's burgers are around $8 and include the classic Huggo (with onions and mushrooms and your choice of Swiss or American cheese), the garden burger (a nonmeat patty with all the trimmings), the fresh catch burger (priced daily), and the teriya-

ki chicken burger. Lunch salads include the Kona Caesar for $7.25 and the Chinese chicken salad for $7.50. Meat-lovers must try Huggo's "almost world famous" barbecued ribs with beans for $7.95—more on your plate than you can eat—served only on Tuesday and Thursday. The dinner menu is superb and starts with fresh *sashimi* (which can be seared on request) about $9; escargots $8.95; and seafood chowder made from clams and fresh fish and seasoned with sherry, cream sauce, and butter, a reasonable $3.50 per cup or $5.25 per bowl. The best entrees come from the sea just outside the door and are priced daily at around $22. A fantastic selection is the stuffed fish, delicious with an exotic blend of tender bay shrimp and dijonaise sauce. The Korean shrimp at $19.95, or the Oriental surprise sautéed in a spicy sauce, are also excellent. Huggo's has been in business for over 25 years, and is consistently outstanding. Enjoy free *pu pu* Mon.-Fri. 4-6 p.m. while sipping a cocktail as the red Kona sun dips into the azure sea.

S.S. *James Makee*, tel. 322-3411, is a fancy continental restaurant at the Kona Surf Hotel. The nautical decor is commemorative of the restaurant's namesake, an old island steamer. The limited menu includes shrimp Kamehameha, teriyaki steak, various veals, and filet mignon. Fresh fish of the day is always well prepared and a good choice. A major part of the minimum $20 pp dining experience is the atmosphere. Open daily for dinner at 6 p.m. by reservation only—of course, matey!

The Kona Inn Restaurant at the Kona Inn Shopping Village, tel. 329-4455, open daily for lunch and dinner, is a lovely but lonely carryover from the venerable old Kona Inn. Part of the deal for tearing down the Kona Inn and putting up the Kona Inn Shopping Village was giving the restaurant a prime location. On entering, notice the marlin over the doorway and a huge piece of hung glass through which the sunset sometimes forms prismatic rainbows. The bar and dining area are richly appointed in native koa and made more elegant with a mixture of turn-of-the-century wooden chairs, high-backed peacock thrones, polished hardwood floors, and sturdy open-beam ceilings. If you want to enjoy the view, try a cocktail and some of the *pu pu* served all day, or try one of the light choices like guacamole and chips $5.95, pasta and chicken salad $7.95, shrimp salad $8.95, or a six-pack of oyster shooters $6.95. Lunch is reasonable: steak sandwich $10.95, or Hawaiian chicken sandwich on whole-wheat bun with pineapple and cheese $6.95. The dinner menu starts with Boston or Manhattan chowder $2.95, and mixed green salad of crisp romaine tossed with Caesar dressing and topped with bay shrimp for a very reasonable $3.95. The specialties are local fish like *ono, ahi, opakapaka* or mahimahi for around $20; and seafood pasta topped with shrimp, scallops and mussels for $18.95. Less expensive selections include stir-fried chicken for $13.95, and chicken chardonnay (chicken lightly sautéed with chardonnay, simmered in a Dijon cream sauce, and served over fettucine with leeks and mushrooms) for $15.95. The Kona Inn Restaurant epitomizes Kona beachside dining and the view is simply superb.

Adjacent is **Fisherman's Landing,** tel. 326-2555, open daily for lunch 11:30 a.m.-5 p.m. in the Captain's Deck section, and dinner 5-10 p.m. in the main dining section. You walk down a cobblestone pathway to a group of five Hawaiian dining huts separated by *koi* ponds and wooden bridges. A bronze cannon sits in a reflecting pool, while a gigantic blue marlin is a still-life billboard promising fresh seafood within. The decor is tasteful: glass fishing floats, bronze lanterns, and bamboo tables and chairs. Entrees at Fisherman's Landing (dinner only) feature fresh catch-of-the-day to $22.95, lobster tail $24.95, scampi Alfredo $17.95, top sirloin $14.95, New York steak $17.95, and shrimp tempura $19.95. Lunch specials served under large shade umbrellas in the open-air Captain's Deck brings cold peel-and-eat shrimp $7.95, skipper's chicken salad and soup $6.95, teriyaki beef skewers $6.95, and pasta with calamari $7.95. There are also plenty of oriental selections. Oyster shooters at $1.95 are great when washed down with mugs of beer. Create your own entertainment every Wednesday 9 p.m.-midnight with *karaoke,* or dance to the live music of Sugar Sugar, Sun.-Thurs. 7:30-11:30 p.m. Fisherman's Landing is a perfect Kona restaurant for a relaxing and romantic evening.

Philip Paolo's, tel. 329-4436, in Waterfront Row at 75-5770 Ali'i Dr., is run by Tim O'Higgin—a true Italian if there ever was one. It is open for lunch daily 11 a.m.-2 p.m., and for dinner at 5:30 p.m. Savory selections include an-

tipasto for two at $11.95, minestrone soup for $3.95, and specialty salads that could make a meal, like scallops, crab, and shrimp marinated in olive oil, garlic, and fresh herbs for $10.95. For lunch, try garlic cheese bread for $2.95, tropical salad $6.95, angel-hair Caesar salad $6.95, hot sandwiches like grilled chicken $7.95, or pasta dishes like linguine with clam sauce $5.95. Dinners are served with pasta sautéed in garlic, olive oil, and fresh herbs. The menu suggests dinner specials for $9.95 that include pasta primavera or angel-hair pasta, served with mushrooms and Maui onions sautéed in spinach-and-cream sauce. Other suggestions are fresh island chicken breast with lemon butter sauce for $12.95, or all-you-can-eat spaghetti with zesty marinara sauce sautéed with fresh tomatoes, onions, olive oil, basil, garlic, and Parmesan cheese for $12.95. More expensive dishes are soft-shell crab for $24.95, veal parmigiana $21.95, chicken parmigiana $15.95, or the house specialties like fettucine Giuseppe (meat sautéed in creamy garlic butter and onions) $18.95. The extensive wine list offers varietals from Italy, France, Australia, and California. The large room is appointed with open-beam ceilings joined by distinctive copper couplings, and Casablanca fans.

Also in Waterfront Row, the **Chart House,** tel. 329-2451, open daily for dinner 5-10 p.m., is part of a small chain of restaurants that have built a good reputation for service, value, and well-prepared food. Primarily, they are a steak and seafood house with most meals costing $16-25. The location is very pleasant, away from the street noise and with a good view of the sea.

Kanazawa-tei, tel. 326-1881, open for dinner daily except Sunday, 6-9:30 p.m. (call to confirm lunch openings), is at 75-5845 Ali'i Dr. across from the Kona Hilton. The Japanese restaurant and sushi bar boasts chefs brought over from Japan. Specialties include sukiyaki, teriyaki, and tempura. The dinner menu lists appetizers like *age* tofu $3.95, small tempura $7.45, and butterfish *misoyaki* $9.95. Evening *bento* are extensive; the *Kanazawa-tei bento* includes tempura, *sashimi, yakimoto, nimono,* rice, miso soup and *tsukemono* for $25.50. Other *bento* are Japanese-style steak for $22.95, *sushi moriwase* (assorted sushi) $25.50, and teriyaki chicken $12.25. Kanazawa-tei is an authentic and gourmet Japanese restaurant.

The Continent meets Asia on a Pacific island by way of the magnificent creations of master chef Daniel Thiebaut at the **Palm Cafe,** Coconut Grove Marketplace, 75-5819 Ali'i Dr., tel. 329-7765, open daily 5:30-10 p.m., reservations suggested. Perched above Ali'i Dr., with the sea in the distance, the restaurant has an elegant interior comfortably done in a soothing green-on-green motif with high-backed chairs, linen tablecloths, large louvered windows, and subdued lighting. Start with seared *ahi* served on a bed of crisp leeks and jicama stir-fry $7.50, or Chinese ravioli stuffed with ground pork, shiitake mushrooms, balsamic vinegar, and ginger butter sauce. Salads range from Big Island field greens with Portuguese sweet bread and croutons for $5.50 to the Palm Cafe Caesar for a very reasonable $4.50. Vegetarians will be pleased with vegetable and tofu tempura $16.50, or timbale of vegetables with a Hawaiian chili curry sauce and brown rice $15. The fresh fish dishes are the best, whether prepared with lemon and cilantro butter; Kona style, with ginger, green onions, shoyu, and hot peanut oil; or with an elegant vinaigrette of Kau orange and benishoga. The fish itself is grilled or steamed; daily quote about $22. Another specialty is baked *ono* with almond sesame crust, papaya, and Kona tomato relish, made piquant with ginger lime sauce. The wine selection is superb and can be counted on to complement the meal perfectly. To top off your meal, choose one of the devilish pastry selections, and end with the Earl Gray Tea liqueur.

The **Kona Beach Restaurant,** tel. 329-2911, at the King Kamehameha Kona Beach Hotel, is open daily for breakfast, lunch, and dinner and is especially known for its Sunday brunch served 9 a.m.-1 p.m. Appetizers include crab cakes for $6.95 and sashimi medley $7.95, while entrees range from kiawe-smoked prime rib of beef at $17.95 to barbecued baby-back ribs for $13.95. More moderately priced pastas are made scrumptious with Cajun prawns or sautéed with herbs and spices. Fresh catch or broiled salmon combined with prime rib is $19.95. Hearty luncheon sandwiches are reasonably priced—served with french fries for under $8. The restaurant itself is tasteful, but the best feature is an unobstructed view of the hotel's beach, especially fine at sunset. Also see "Luaus, Buffets, Etc." below.

Luaus, Buffets, Etc.
The **Keauhou Beach Hotel Buffet,** tel. 322-3441, at the hotel's Ocean Terrace, is legendary. People in the know flock here especially for the *Seafood Prime Rib Buffet* for $19.95, children $9.95, served Fri.-Sun. 5-9 p.m. Fill your plate again and again with Alaskan snow crab legs, prime rib (excellent), seafood Newburg, sautéed mahimahi, fresh teriyaki marlin, deep-fried oysters, New England clam chowder, *sashimi, poki,* and boiled shrimp. They also have a great dessert bar with Boston cream pies, strawberry shortcake, rich double-chocolate carrot cake, and banana cream pie. A Chi-

Chef Sam Choy (left) and assistant

J.D. BISIGNANI

nese buffet is offered Mon.-Thurs. for $12.95, children $8.95, and features roast duck, dim sum, Mandarin salad, and a medley of Cantonese and Sichuan selections. The restaurant has a beautiful view of the coast, and dinner is rounded off with live nightly entertainment.

The **Kona Hilton Luau,** tel. 329-3111, held every Monday, Wednesday, and Friday at the hotel's Coconut Grove, offers an authentic evening of entertainment and feasting, Hawaiian style. The *imu* ceremony begins at 6 p.m. and is followed by an open bar, lavish buffet, and thrilling entertainment for three fun-filled hours. Many supposedly authentic luaus play-act with the *imu*-baked pig, but here it is carved and served to the guests. Prices are adults $36, children under 12, $20, with reservations strongly recommended.

A sumptuous feast is held at the **Kona Village Resort,** just north of Kailua-Kona (see p. 295). It's worth attending this luau just to visit and be pampered at this private hotel beach. Adults pay around $40, children under 12 half-price. Held every Friday, by reservation only, tel. 325-5555. The *imu* ceremony is at 6 p.m., followed by no-host cocktails; the luau and Hawaiian entertainment begin at 8 p.m. Also, limited reservations are accepted during the week for lunch, dinner, and special dinners and buffets.

The **King Kamehameha Kona Beach Hotel,** tel. 329-2911, sways with Hawaiian chants during its famous luau held every Sunday, Tuesday, Wednesday, and Thursday. The pig is placed into the *imu* every morning at 10:15 a.m. and the festivities begin in the evening with a *lei* greeting at 5:30 p.m. and a torch-lighting *imu* pageant at 6:15 p.m.; the luau dinner is served 6:30-9 p.m. Prices are adults $45, children 6-12 $15. Reservations are required. **Kona Beach Restaurant,** tel. 329-2911, also at the King Kamehameha Kona Beach Hotel (see above) features a breakfast buffet at $7.95, Mon.-Sat. 6:30-10:30 a.m., Sun. to 9:30 a.m. As good as the breakfast buffet may be, the restaurant is very famous for its **King's Brunch,** served Sun. 10 a.m-1 p.m., adults $19.95, children 6-12 $9.95. The long tables are laden with fruit, vegetables, pasta salad, peel-and-eat shrimp, omelettes, waffles, hot entrees from fresh catch to sashimi, and desserts so sinful you'll be glad that someone's on their knees praying at Sunday services. Every night of the week brings a different theme

buffet for around $15.95 where you can always count on tempura, shrimp, and prime rib as part of the offerings. Weekends are special because of the scrumptious seafood buffet.

Captain Beans' Dinner Cruise departs Kailua Pier daily at 5 p.m. and returns at 8 p.m. You are entertained while the bar dispenses liberal drinks and the deck groans with all-you-can-eat food. And you get a terrific panorama of the Kona Coast from the sea. You can't help having a good time on this cruise, and if the boat sinks with all that food and booze in your belly, you're a goner—but what a way to go! Minimum age is 18 years, $30 includes tax and tip. Reservations suggested; call 329-2955.

ENTERTAINMENT AND ACTIVITIES

Kona nights come alive mainly in the restaurants and dining rooms of the big hotels. The most memorable experience for most is free: watching the sunset from Kailua Pier, and taking a leisurely stroll along Ali'i Drive. All of the luaus previously mentioned have "Polynesian Revues" of one sort or another, which are generally good, clean, sexy fun, but of course these shows are limited only to the luau guests. For those who have "dancin' feet" or wish to spend the evening listening to live music, there's a small but varied selection from which to choose. **Note:** The hotels and restaurants listed below have been previously mentioned in either the "Accommodations" or "Food" sections, so please refer there for addresses and directions.

Around Town
Huggo's Restaurant, with its romantic waterfront setting along Ali'i Dr. features music 8:30 p.m.-12:30 a.m. The entertainment changes nightly; *karaoke* on Tuesday features Juni Maderas. Excellent local bands like Mango, Nightlife, and Kona Blend offer smooth Jahwaiian and other mellow contemporary sounds with a touch of rock now and again.

The **Keauhou Beach Hotel** soothes you with easy listening, Hawaiian style, nightly at their famous buffet. Weekends bring live bands like Holua, and Nightlife who will rock you with everything from original tunes to classic Hawaiian numbers. Also, Uncle George Naope, a

J.D. BISIGNANI

Enjoy the free spectacle as some of the island's best canoeists come to Kailua Bay to work out every evening.

renowned *kuma hula,* delights audiences with members of his local dance troupe on the Kuakini Terrace, Fri. 11 a.m.-1:30 p.m. and then again 5:30-9:30 p.m., Sat. 5:30-9 p.m., Sun. from 10 a.m.-1 p.m. (usually!).

At the **Kona Surf Resort** a quiet piano tinkles in the S.S. *James Makee* Restaurant 6-11 p.m., or you can glide around the dance floor in the Puka Bar to live music 9 p.m.-closing. More yet! The Poi Pounder Nightclub beats out "top 40" dancin' tunes Tues.-Sat. 9 p.m. until the wee hours.

At the **Kona Hilton** piano bar you can enjoy happy hour 4:30-6 p.m. with free *pu pu* while listening to the mellow piano, which begins at 4:30 p.m. and goes until closing. **Windjammer Lounge,** an open-air bar, features jazz on Sunday, the contemporary sounds of the Silk and Steel band Mon.-Wed., and The Fortunes, a blues and rock-and-roll band Thurs.-Sat. Music nightly 8:30 p.m.-closing.

In downtown Kailua-Kona you can pick your fun at the **King Kamehameha Kona Beach Hotel.** Here, the **Billfish Bar** has live entertainment nightly 6-10:30 p.m., featuring mellow Hawaiian music by Hapalaka. The bar is open 10:30 a.m.-10:30 p.m. with happy hour 5-7 p.m.

Around town, the **Eclipse Restaurant** has dance music 10 p.m.-1:30 a.m. every night. **Jolly Roger Restaurant** offers a variety of live music throughout the week beginning at 8:30 p.m. At the **Keauhou-Kona Golf Course Restaurant** you can enjoy live contemporary Hawaiian music

performed by local artists every evening from 7 p.m. For a quiet beer, sports talk, or just hanging out with the local people try **Quinn's, Drysdale's, Ocean View Inn,** or **Sam's Hideaway,** all in downtown Kailua-Kona.

At **Fisherman's Landing Restaurant,** *karaoke* is presented every Wed. 9 p.m.-midnight. They also have live music and dancing nightly to the tunes of Sugar Sugar, a local dance band; Fri.-Sat. 6-9 p.m. a solo musician plays a mixed bag of country, classic rock-and-roll, and Hawaiian music.

The Tech, one of Kailua-Kona's newest discos and hangouts, is open nightly on the premises of the Poo Ping Restaurant II. The restaurant is located at Kamehameha Square, a small shopping mall a few minutes from town along Kuakini Hwy. leading to the airport. It draws a younger, local crowd, but is friendly and what's happening now.

For movies try the **World Square Theater** in the Kona Marketplace or the **Hualalai Theater** in Kailua-Kona.

The **Aloha Theater** in Kainaliu (see p. 273) has a semi-professional local repertory company, the Aloha Community Theater, that puts on plays about six times per year that run for about three weeks each. Showtime in the completely refurbished and well-appointed theater is usually 8 p.m., and admission is a very reasonable $8 (senior discount). Check the local newspaper or the HVB office, or look for posters here and there around town.

SHOPPING

Shopping Note
Below is an overview of Kona-area malls, including a general idea of what they contain. For specific shops see the sub-categories following, i.e., "Markets, Health Food Stores, Bookstores, Specialty Shops."

Kailua-Kona Malls
The Kailua-Kona area has an abundance of two commodities near and dear to a tourist's heart: sunshine and shopping malls.

One of the largest malls in Kailua is the **Kona Inn Shopping Village** at 75-5744 Ali'i Drive. This shopping village boasts more than 40 shops selling fabrics, fashions, art, fruits, gems and jewelry, photo and music needs, food, and even exotic skins (for particular shops see p. 260).

The **Kona Marketplace** in central Kailua-Kona offers a variety of shops selling everything from burgers to bathing suits. The **Kona Banyan Court,** also in central Kailua-Kona, has a dozen shops with a medley of goods and services. Distinctive shops include: **Kona Fine Woods** for souvenir-quality woodcarvings; **Unison,** a surfing shop with T-shirts, sandals, hats, and boogie boards; and **South Sea Silver Company,** whose name says it all. The most impressive shop in the complex is **Big Island Jewelers,** tel. 329-8571, open Mon.-Sat. 9 a.m.-9 p.m., Sun. 10 a.m.-6 p.m., owned and operated by brothers Flynn and Gale Carpenter, master goldsmiths. The shop motto, "Have your jewelry made by a Carpenter," applies to custom-made jewelry fashioned to their or your personal design. **Big Island Jewelers,** in business for over 10 years, does repairs and also carries a full line of pearls and loose stones that they will mount into any setting you wish. You'll also find **Kailua Bay Inn Shopping Plaza** along Ali'i Dr. and **Akona Kai Mall** across from Kailua Pier.

The **King Kamehameha Kona Beach Hotel Mall,** fully air-conditioned, features a cluster of specialty shops and a Liberty House. One excellent shop is **Kona Kapa,** which features beautiful hand-stitched Hawaiian quilts and less expensive items like throw pillows. Open Mon.-Sat. 9 a.m.-6 p.m., Sun. 9 a.m.-5 p.m., tel. 326-7119, the shop also sells koa wood items from carvings to jewelry boxes. One distinctive item is

a koa wood whale that folds out to form a serving bowl. Also in the mall is **Gifts For All Seasons** (jewelry), **Jafar** (high fashion), and **Tots and Teens** (clothes for children).

The **Lanihau Center,** tel. 329-9333, at 75-5595 Palani Rd., is one of Kailua-Kona's newest shopping meccas. It offers **Longs Drugs** for sundries and photo supplies; an assortment of restaurants (see "Food"); apparel and shoe stores including **Feet First; Waldenbooks,** an excellent all-purpose bookstore; **Radio Shack** for electronic gizmos of all sorts; and **Zac's Photo,** a very friendly and professional photo store (see "Photo Needs" following this section).

Kopiko Plaza, along Palani Rd. just down from the Lanihau Center, is a small mall containing **J.R.'s Music Shop,** where you can purchase records, tapes, and CDs of your favorite artists; **Scott's Knife Center** for a fine piece of cutlery from a carving knife to a Swiss Army knife; **Wall Art and Frame**; a video store; and **Action Sports** for the largest selection of sporting equipment in town. The mall also has a smattering of inexpensive restaurants, both for takeout and eat-in (see "Fast Foods and Snacks" above).

Waterfront Row is a relatively new shopping and food complex at the south end of downtown Kailua-Kona. Built of rough-cut lumber, it's done in period architecture reminiscent of an outdoor promenade in a Boston shipyard at the turn of the century. **Pacific Vibrations,** a surf shop, sells everything from postcards to hats, backpacks, and aloha shirts. **Pleasant Hawaiian Holidays** maintains a booth here from where you can book a wide range of activities. **Crazy Shirts** sells unique island creations, and **Kona Jack's** offers distinctive unisex apparel featuring its logo. Restaurants include the **Chart House** for steaks and seafood, **Philip Paolo's** for Italian cuisine, and **Jolly Roger** for American and Hawaiian cuisine (see "Food" above).

Rawson Plaza, at 74-5563 Kaiwi St., is just past the King Kamehameha Kona Beach Hotel in the industrial area. This practical, no-frills area abounds in "no-name" shops selling everything you'll find in town but at substantial savings.

Kona Coast Shopping Center along Palani Rd. features **Pay 'n' Save** for sundries and everything from scuba gear to styrofoam coolers; **KTA Market** (see below); the **Undercover**

Shop, with fine lingerie; **Hallmark Cards;** and a smattering of clothing, accessory, and shoe stores.

South Of Kailua Malls
If, god forbid, you haven't found what you need in Kailua, or if you suddenly need a "shopping fix," even more malls are south on Route 11. **Keauhou Shopping Village** is at the corner of Ali'i Dr. and Kamehameha III Road. Look for flags waving in the breeze high on the hill marking the entrance. This mall houses apparel shops, restaurants, a post office, and photo-processing booths. You can find all your food and prescription needs at **KTA Supermarket,** the largest in the area. **Keauhou Village Bookshop** is a full-service bookstore. **Kona-kai Cafe,** an espresso and coffee shop open daily 8:30 a.m.-6 p.m., will take care of your sweet tooth and drooping energy; you can also buy a pound or two of fresh Kona coffee there. **Drysdale's** is an indoor/outdoor bar and grill where you can relax over a cold beer or choose from their extensive sandwich menu. Other shops include: the **Showcase Gallery,** for glassware, paintings, ceramics, and local crafts; and **Alapaki's,** for island goods from black coral jewelry to colorful muumuus.

Continuing south on Route 11, you'll spot the **Kainaliu Village Mall** along the main drag.

Food Markets, Etc.
KTA Market is generally the cheapest market in town and is located at the Kona Coast Shopping Center along Palani Road. They're well stocked with sundries; an excellent selection of Asian foods, fresh vegies, fish, and fruit; and a smattering of health food that's mixed in with the normal food items. Sugar Pops and kimchi, anyone? **KTA Supermarket,** open Mon.-Sat. 8 a.m.-10 p.m., Sun. 8 a.m.-9 p.m., is at the Keauhou Village Mall, at the extreme south end of Ali'i Dr. at its junction with Kamehameha III Road. You can save time and traffic hassles by shopping here. The market also offers a full-service pharmacy.

Across the road, **Sack 'n' Save,** in the Lanihau Center, open 24 hours, is one of the main supermarkets in town.

Kona Wine Market, in the small Kamehameha Square Shopping Center, 75-5626 Kuakini Hwy., tel. 329-9400, open daily 10 a.m.-

8 p.m., Sun. noon-4 p.m., is the best wine shop on the Kona coast. They feature an impressive international selection of wine and varietals from California, Italy, Spain, France, Chile, and Australia. Prices range from $4.95 for a table wine to $200 for a bottle of select boutique wine. A large cooler holds a fine selection of beer, both domestic and imported, and the store shelves hold wonderful gourmet munchies like Indian chutney, Sicilian olives, mustards, dressings, marinades, smoked salmon, hearty cheeses, and even pasta imported from Italy.

Casa De Emdeko Liquor and Deli is south of town center at 75-6082 Ali'i Drive. It's well stocked with liquor and groceries, but at convenience-store prices. Other markets include **King Kamehameha Pantry,** tel. 329-9191, selling liquors, groceries, and sundries; and **Keauhou Pantry,** tel. 322-3066, in Keauhou along Ali'i Dr., selling more of the same.

Health Food Stores
Kona keeps you healthy with **Kona Healthways** in the Kona Coast Shopping Center, tel. 329-2296, open Mon.-Fri. 9 a.m.-7 p.m., Sat. 9 a.m.-6 p.m., Sun. 9:30 a.m.-5 p.m. Besides a good assortment of health foods, they have cosmetics, books, and dietary supplements. Vegetarians will like their ready-to-eat sandwiches, salads, and soups. Shelves are lined with teas and organic vitamins. They also have a cooler with organic juices, cheeses, and soy milk. A refrigerator holds organic produce, while bins are filled with bulk grains.

Bookstores
Waldenbooks, in the Lanihau Center on Palani Rd., tel. 329-0015, open Mon.-Thurs. 9:30 a.m.-6 p.m., Fri. 9:30 a.m.-9 p.m., Sun. 10 a.m.-5 p.m., not only has the well-stocked and far-ranging selection that this national chain has become famous for, but also features an in-depth Hawaiiana collection and even some Hawaiian music tapes.

In Kailua-Kona be sure to venture into **Middle Earth Bookshop** at 75-5719 Ali'i Dr., in the Kona Plaza Shopping Arcade, tel. 329-2123, open Mon.-Sat. 9 a.m.-9 p.m., Sun. to 6 p.m. This jam-packed bookstore has shelves laden with fiction, nonfiction, paperbacks, hardbacks, travel books, maps, and Hawaiiana. A great place to browse.

Keauhou Village Bookshop at Keauhou Shopping Village, tel. 322-8111, open Mon.-Sat. 9-6, Sun. 9-5, is a full-service bookstore with plenty of Hawaiiana selections, general reading material, a children's section, and a good travel guide section.

Photo Needs

Zac's Photo, in the Lanihau Center, tel. 329-0006, open 7 a.m.-9 p.m. every day, develops prints in one hour and slides in two days. Zac, a native of Belgium, will even make minor camera repairs free of charge. Prices are very competitive and you can save more by clipping two-for-one and 20% discount coupons from the free tourist brochure, *This Week, Big Island.* **Longs Drugs,** in the same mall, also has excellent prices on film and camera supplies.

Ali'i Photo Hut, in the parking lot in front of Huggo's Restaurant along Ali'i Dr., open daily 7:30 a.m.-5:30 p.m., develops prints and rents underwater cameras. Rental rate is $17.95 for camera plus a roll of 36 exposures. A 20% discount on developing is offered with rental.

The **Kona Photo Center** in the North Kona Shopping Plaza, at the corner of Palani Rd. and Kuakini Hwy., tel. 329-3676, is open Mon.-Sat. 8 a.m.-6 p.m. It is a *real* photography store where you can get lenses, cameras, filters, and even telescopes and binoculars. Their processing is competitive, and they also offer custom developing.

Art And Specialty Shops

In the King Kamehameha Kona Beach Hotel, the **Kona Kapa** sells carvings, jewelry, and magnificent quilts (see p. 245), while **The Shellery** lives up to its name with baubles, bangles, and beads made from shells, along with a selection of fine jewelry and pearls.

Island Togs, tel. 329-2144, is across from the Kona Beach Restaurant at the King Kamehameha Kona Beach Hotel. This long-established shop hidden from the main tourist gauntlet is known by the locals as one of the best places to purchase women's bathing suits and bikinis. They also feature very reasonable prices on resortwear, shorts, and an assortment of tops.

In the World Square Shopping Center visit **Coral Isle Art Shop** for modern versions of traditional Hawaiian carvings. You'll find everything from tikis to scrimshaw, with exceptional-

ly good carvings of sharks and whales for a pricey $75 or so.

Enjoy the beauty of Hawaii with flowers from **Editha's Lei Stand,** located in front of Huggo's Restaurant (see above), open daily 10:30 a.m.-6 p.m. Editha creates lovely *lei* that run from $3.75 for a basic strand to $20 for a magnificent triple *lei.* Editha also does fresh-cut flower arrangements, and she can arrangeme for shipment to the Mainland. Also in the parking lot in front of Huggo's Restaurant, along Ali'i Dr., look for a little truck business called **Nikki's** that sells Kona coffee at $8.49 per pound and macadamia nuts at $6.95 per pound, both decent prices.

At the **Kona Inn Shopping Village** you can buy custom jewelry at **Jim Bill's Gemfire.** Featured at the **T-shirt Company,** a.k.a. **Island Salsa,** are designer tee's that are some of the best in Kona. Prices are normally around $18, but they run specials all the time. You can pick up one-of-a-kind creations by Roberta, the owner/artist, for around $10. **Collectors Fine Art** is a perfect labyrinth of rooms and hallways showcasing the acclaimed works of international artists. Not a shop at which to buy trinkets; prices range from $300 to $250,000 for some of the finer paintings and sculptures by internationally acclaimed artists. **Hula Heaven,** open daily 9 a.m.-9 p.m., is situated in a stone tower dating from 1927 and specializes in vintage Hawaiian shirts and modern reproductions. Prices range from $50 for the "look alikes" to $1000 for the rarest of the classics. Because many of the items on display date from the '40s and '50s, the shop is like a trip back in time. Another distinctive shop is **Crystal Visions** for incense, perfume, metaphysical books, and a large selection of crystals, crystal balls, and pyramids. A sign proclaims, "Shoplifting is bad karma," and a shop assistant claims that the owner looked at her *aura,* not her resume, when she was hired. Crystal Visions also stocks essential oils and small, handmade beaded bags for carrying your precious items. A unique item of interest to travelers might be the azurite spheres for expansion of consciousness and astral travel—in case you have lost your airline tickets or your flight has been delayed. If you're feeling low, and your cosmic vibrations need a boost, come in to Crystal Visions.

At **Kona Inn Flower and Lei** you can pick up flowers to add that perfect touch to a ro-

Editha's Lei Stand

J.D. BISIGNANI

mantic evening. Nearby **Chrestel's Collectibles** has stuffed toys, stuffed pillows, and some clothing. **Kona Inn Jewelry,** for worldwide treasures, is one of the oldest and best-known shops for a square deal in Kona. Owned and operated by Joe Goldscharek and his family, they take time to help you choose just the right gift. Inside you'll find stained-glass hangings, jewelry, fine gemstones, and a collection of hand-painted fish. The family tries to pick unique items from around the world that can be found in no other Kona shop. Be aware that the shop is protected by Mama Cat, a sleeping ball of fur honored with her own postcard, who if you're not careful will purr you to death.

Other shops in the center include: **Flamingo's** for contemporary island clothing and evening wear mainly for women; **Big Island Hat Co.** for headgear ranging from a pith helmets to sombreros; **The Treasury,** specializing in jewelry, T-shirts, beachwear, hats, sunglasses, backpacks, shoulder bags, and postcards; **Tahiti Fabrics,** offering bolts of cloth and a nice collection of Hawaiian shirts; **Alley Gecko's,** showcasing colorful gifts from around the world; and the **Old Hawaiian Gold Co.,** which can bedeck you in gold chains or pearl and coral jewelry.

At the **Kona Marketplace** in the downtown area, look for **Kona Jewelery,** specializing in fine jewelry and ceramics. Good for trinkets is **Kona Bazaar Affordables.** Or pick up a pair of eel-skin cowboy boots at **Lee San's Eelskin.** The jam-packed **Aloha From Kona** specializes in baubles, bangles, postcards, handbags, and purses. In contrast is **Ali'i Nexus,** for fine jewelry, one of the nicest and most low-key shops in town. The **Kona Flea Market** stuck to the rear of the mall sells inexpensive travel bags, shells, beach mats, suntan lotion, and all the junk that you could want. **Island Salsa** features original silk-screened T-shirts, alohawear for the entire family, ladies' evening wear, swimwear, and dinner clothes. **Goodies of Hawaii** sounds like a candy store but they actually sell beach towels, T-shirts, windchimes, wooden postcards, distinctive beach bags, and a good selection of candles and ceramics.

Kona Gold, tel. 327-9373, in the Kailua Bay Inn Shopping Plaza, open daily except Sun. 9 a.m.-9 p.m., has excellent prices on custom-made jewelry by Harold Booton, the goldsmith and proprietor. Harold also imports jewelry from around the world, especially silver, and if it's not on sale, bargaining is definitely okay! The store stocks coral jewelry, a smattering of T-shirts, and lifelike wooden sculptures of whales and marine animals, many of which come from Indonesia. Kona Gold is a perfect shop in which to purchase a lifelong memento at a very reasonable price.

Alapaki's, at Keauhou Shopping Village (see "South of Kailua Malls" above), sells distinctive island arts and crafts. Inside you'll find pink, gold, and black coral jewelry; *lei* of shells and seeds; and *tutu* dolls bedecked in colorful muumuus. Distinctive items include koa bowls, each signed by the artist; and a replica of a Hawaiian double-hulled canoe made of coconut and cloth with traditional crab-claw sails. Original paintings by R.K. McGuire feature Hawaiian animals; basketry, fans, and jewelry made from ironwood needles are by local artist Barb Walls. Some of the finest artworks displayed are feather *lei* by Eloise Deshea and woodcarvings by Thomas Baboza.

For some practical purchases at wholesale prices check out **Kona Jeans** for shirts, tops, footwear, and jeans, at 74-5576 Kaiwi Street. **Liberty House Penthouse** at Keauhou Shopping Village will appeal to bargain hunters. This outlet store sells items that have been cleared and reduced from the famous Liberty House stores. You can save on everything from alohawear to formal dresses.

Kailua Candy Company, in the industrial section (see "Inxpensive" in the "Food" section above) on the corner of Kurakini and Kiawi streets, tel. 329-2522 or (800) 622-2462, is open weekdays 8 a.m.-6 p.m., weekends 10 a.m.-6 p.m. It was recognized as one of the "top 10 chocolate shops in the United States" in the February 1993 issue of *Bon Appetit* magazine. All the chocolates are made of the finest ingredients available, and all would try the willpower of Gandhi, but the specialty is the macadamia nut *honu,* Hawaiian for turtle. The best sampler is the one-pound Kailua Candy Company Assortment, hand-packed with a quarter pound each of *honu,* the award-winning Kona coffee swirl, dark macadamia nut clusters, and white coconut Mauna Kea snowballs. It costs $17.10, or $21 shipped anywhere on the Mainland. Shipping of all the candy is available at the cost of postage plus $1 handling fee; shipments are guaranteed to be in perfect condition or they will be replaced free.

Two shops along Ali'i Dr., diagonally across from Hulihee Palace, are **Noa Noa,** featuring hand-painted, one-of-a-kind original clothing, mostly from Indonesia; and **Hawaiian Wear Unlimited,** where you can pick up alohawear for a very reasonable price. Just up the road, **The Glass Blower,** across from the seawall along Likana Ln., is a very interesting shop where you can watch the artist actually blow the glass. This shop is the perfect place to purchase a distinctive treasure. Next door is **Ululani Fresh Cut Flowers,** a reasonably priced *lei* stand. **Good-**

ies just up the alley has gift boxes of jams and jellies, Maui onion mustard, macadamia nuts, an assortment of coffees, and various perfumes and scents.

Real treasure hunters will love the **Kona Gardens Flea Market** held every Wed. and Sat. 8 a.m-2 p.m. at the road fronting the Kona Botanical Gardens along Ali'i Drive. Unfortunately, this formerly huge flea market is now only a shadow of its former self and is always tottering on the brink of closure. The latest rumor has it moving to the old airport, so check.

SERVICES AND INFORMATION

Emergencies
For **ambulance and fire** assistance call 961-6022; for **police** in Kona communities call 323-2645; the **Kona Hospital** is in Kealakekua, tel. 322-9311. The most convenient **pharmacies** are Kona Coast Drugs in Kailua, tel. 329-8886; and Pay 'n' Save Drugs, tel. 329-3577. For **alternative health care services and massage,** both well established in Kailua-Kona, see pp. 146-147.

Information And Services
An **information gazebo** is open daily 7 a.m.-9 p.m. along the boardwalk in the Kona Inn Shopping Village. They can handle your questions about everything from dining to diving. The **Hawaii Visitors Bureau** maintains an office in the Kona Plaza, at 75-5719 Ali'i Dr., tel. 329-7787. The staff is friendly, helpful, and extremely knowledgeable about touring the Big Island. The **library** is at 75-140 Hualalai Rd., tel. 329-2196. The Hele Mai Laundromat is at the North Kona Shopping Center, at the corner of Kuakini Hwy. and Palani Rd., tel. 329-3494. For more services and info see p. 151.

An excellent **tourist map** that highlights restaurants, accommodations, and businesses is available free at the HVB office and at many shops in Kona and throughout the Big Island. The map is published by the Island Map Company, 159 Kiawe St., Suite 1, Hilo, HI 96720, tel. 934-9007.

Banks, Post Office, Etc.
First Interstate Bank, tel. 329-4481, is at 75-5722 Kuakini Hwy.; **First Hawaiian Bank,** in the Lanihau Center on Palani Rd., can be

reached at tel. 329-2461; **Bank of Hawaii** maintains two area offices, one in Kailua at tel. 329-7033, the other in Kealakekua at tel. 322-9377. The main **post office** is on Palani Rd., tel. 329-1927, just past the Lanihau Center. There is also mail service at the **General Store,** a market along Ali'i Dr. in central Kailua-Kona. **Mail Boxes U.S.A.,** at the Lanihau Center, Palani Rd., open weekdays 8:30 a.m.-6:30 p.m., Sat. to 3 p.m., provides Western Union, a notary public, typing service, money orders, gift wrapping, and the boxing and shipping of parcels.

BOB RACE

CENTRAL AND SOUTH KONA

Kailua-Kona's Ali'i Drive eventually turns up the mountainside and joins Route 11, which in its central section is called the **Kuakini Highway.** This road, heading south, quickly passes the towns of **Honalo, Kainaliu** ("Bail the Bilge"), **Kealakekua,** and **Captain Cook.** You'll have ample opportunity to stop along the way for gas, picnic supplies, or browsing. These towns have some terrific restaurants, specialty shops, and boutiques. At Captain Cook, you can dip down to the coast and visit a working coffee mill, or continue south to **Pu'uhonua O Honaunau,** a reconstructed temple of refuge, the best in the state. Farther south still, little-traveled side roads take you to the sleepy seaside villages of **Hookena** and **Milolii,** where traditional lifestyles are still the norm.

Or for an alternative, instead of heading directly south out of Kailua-Kona on Route 11, take Hualalai Rd. (Route 182) to Route 180, a high mountain road that parallels Route 11 and takes you to the artist community of **Holualoa** from where you get an expansive view of the coastline below.

HOLUALOA

Holualoa ("The Sledding Course") is an undisturbed mountain community perched high above the Kailua-Kona Coast. Get there by taking the spur Route 182 off Route 11 from Kailua-Kona, or by taking Route 180 from Honalo in the south or from Honokohau in the north. Climbing Route 182 affords glorious views of the coast below. Notice the immediate contrast of the lush foliage here with the vegetation of the lowland area. On the mountainside, bathed in tropical mists, are tall forest trees interspersed with banana, papaya, and mango trees. Flowering trees pulsating in the green canopy explode in vibrant reds, yellows, oranges, and purples. If you want to get away from the Kona heat and dryness, head up to the well-watered coolness of Holualoa.

Practicalities

After you wind your way up Route 182 through this verdant jungle area, you suddenly enter the village and are greeted by **Kimura's Lauhala**

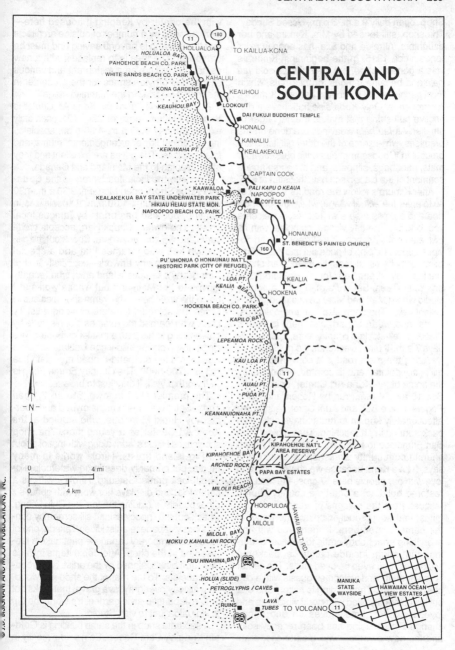

CENTRAL AND
SOUTH KONA

11
180
HOLUALOA
TO KAILUA-KONA
HOLUALOA BAY
PAHOEHOE BEACH CO. PARK
WHITE SANDS BEACH CO. PARK
KAHALUU
KONA GARDENS
KEAUHOU
KEAUHOU BAY
LOOKOUT
DAI FUKUJI BUDDHIST TEMPLE
HONALO
KAINALIU
KEALAKEKUA
KEIKIWAHA PT.
CAPTAIN COOK
KAAWALOA
PALI KAPU O KEAUA
NAPOOPOO
KEALAKEKUA BAY STATE UNDERWATER PARK
COFFEE MILL
HIKIAU HEIAU STATE MON.
NAPOOPOO BEACH CO. PARK
KEEI
HONAUNAU
ST. BENEDICT'S PAINTED CHURCH
160
PU'UHONUA O HONAUNAU NAT'L
HISTORIC PARK (CITY OF REFUGE)
KEOKEA
LOA PT.
KEALIA
KEALIA BEACH
HOOKENA
HOOKENA BEACH CO. PARK
KAPILO BAY
LEPEAMOA ROCK
KAU LOA PT.
AUAU PT.
PUOA PT.
KEANANUIONAHA PT.
KIPAHOEHOE NAT'L
AREA RESERVE
KIPAHOEHOE BAY
ARCHED ROCK
PAPA BAY ESTATES
HAWAII BELT RD.
MILOLII BEACH
HOOPULOA
MILOLII
MILOLII BAY
MOKU O KAHAILANI ROCK
PUU HINAHINA BAY
MANUKA
STATE
WAYSIDE
HAWAIIAN OCEAN
VIEW ESTATES
HOLUA (SLIDE)
PETROGLYPHS / CAVES
*LAVA
TUBES*
TO VOLCANO
11
RUINS

-N-

0   4 mi
0   4 km

Shop, open daily 9 a.m.-5 p.m., closed Sunday. The shop, still tended by Mrs. Kimura and her daughters, Alfreida and Ella, has been in existence since 1915. In the beginning, Kimura's was a general store, but they always sold *lau hala* and became famous for their hats, which local people would make and barter to Kimura's for groceries. Only *Kona-side* hats have a distinctive pull-string that makes the hat larger or smaller. All *lau hala* weavings are done on the premises, while some of the other gift items are brought in. Choose from authentic baskets, floor mats, handbags, slippers, and of course an assortment of the classic sun hats that start at $35.

After Kimura's follow the road for a minute or so to enter the actual village, where the **post office** and a cross atop a white steeple welcome you to town. The tiny village, complete with its own elementary school, is well kept, with an obvious double helping of pride put into this artists' community by its citizens. Numerous art shops line the main street. Look for the **Holualoa Galery,** open Tues.-Sat. 10 a.m.-5 p.m., a pottery studio where Matt and Mary Levine produce excellent *raku*. The shop also features paintings, prints, and wearable art. Just here is **Paul's Place,** a well-stocked country store, open weekdays 7 a.m.-8 p.m., weekends 8 a.m.-8 p.m.

Along the main road is a converted coffee mill, gaily painted and decorated, and currently the home of the **Kona Art Center,** open Tues.-Sat. 10 a.m.-4 p.m., run by Robert and Carol Rogers. Uncle Bob and Aunt Carol, as they are affectionately known to many, have extensive backgrounds in art teaching. They moved from San Francisco to Holualoa in 1965 and began offering community workshop classes. Carol says, "I love Kona because we share, care, and love with our people here." Across the road is a restored building, a one-time country church rescued from the ravages of weather and termites, that now proudly displays the works of the center's members. In here you will find everything from hobby crafts to serious renderings that might include paintings, basketry, sculptures, and even tie-dyed shirts. The center is very friendly and welcomes guests with a cup of Kona coffee. The building is rickety and old, but it's obviously filled with good vibrations and love. However, time moves on and things change. The building has been recently sold, and the new owners—who tried to cooperate

with the center by keeping it housed here—were advised by a number of outside architects that the building is beyond saving and must be torn down. The idea is to replace it with a new center that will house a restaurant and various shops, and provide space for the art center in the rear. This is all in the planning stage.

Across the road from the Kona Art Center is **Vahlia's Flower Shop,** tel. 324-1421, open daily except Sunday 9:30 a.m.-4:30 p.m., specializing in tropical flower arrangements, mums, and fresh *maile lei*. The prices are excellent and they offer shipping to the Mainland and Canada.

Opposite the Holualoa Library is the **Country Frame Shop,** open Mon.-Fri. 9:30 a.m.-4:30 p.m., Sat. 9:30 a.m.-1:30 p.m. It specializes in framing, but also has prints by famous local artists. The owner, Chuck Hart, accepts credit cards and will ship anywhere. Check out the distinctive koa wood frames that add a special island touch to any artwork—especially that of **Kim Starr,** a famous island artist who recently moved to the Mainland but whose works still grace the walls here. The frame shop also showcases the splendid furniture of wood artist Ty Lake, who learned the rudiments of his trade by apprenticing to his dad, a master carpenter. Ty's high-backed chairs, tulip-legged tables, and stout sideboards in rich, hand-rubbed mountain koa sell for $700-5000. The Country Frame Shop is well worth a visit, if only just to browse.

The premier shop in town, **Studio 7,** open Tues.-Sat. 10 a.m.-4 p.m., is owned and operated by Hiroki Morinoue, who studied at the Kona Art Center as a young man. The shop showcases Hiroki's work along with that of about 35 Big Island artists. Hiroki works in many media, but primarily does large watercolors or woodblock prints. Setsuko, Hiroki's wife, is a ceramicist and displays her work with about six other potters, including the famous Chiu Leong. Check out the "neoclassical" silkscreen by contemporary Japanese artist Hideo Takeda, one of seven contemporary Japanese printmakers represented in the shop. Affordable items include free-form bowls, signed by the artist, and wooden bracelets. To the rear of the shop is a wooden walkway over gray lava gravel that looks out onto a Japanese-style garden. It's worth the trip to Holualoa just to visit Studio 7.

A separate shop in the same building is **Goldsmithing by Sam Rosen.** Sam works mostly in gold, silver, and precious stones, but will work in coral if it's unusual. He can also supply the stones from his collection, which includes amazing specimens like malachite and polyhedroid, a quartz from Brazil. All works have a distinctive island theme.

The **Kona Hotel,** along Holualoa's main street, tel. 324-1155, primarily rents its 11 units to local people who spend the work-week in Kailua-Kona's seaside resorts and then go home on weekends. They are more than happy, however, to rent to any visitor passing through, and are a particular favorite with Europeans. The Inaba family opened the hotel in 1926, and it is still owned and operated by Goro Inaba and his wife Yayoko, who will greet you at the front desk upon arrival. A clean room with bare wooden floors, a bed and dresser, and a shared bath down the hall goes for $18-28. Call ahead for reservations. No meals are served, but Mrs. Inaba will make coffee in the morning if you wish. The hotel is simple, clean, and safe.

The enticing aroma of rich coffee has been wafting on the breeze in this mountain community ever since the **Holuakoa Cafe,** owned and operated by Meggi Worbach, opened its doors in mid-1992. Just up the hill from the Kona Hotel, the cafe, open Mon.-Sat. 6:30 a.m.-5 p.m., Thurs. 7-10 p.m. (hours vary) for live music, tel. 322-2233, serves wonderful sticky-buns, bagels, muffins, and coffee and espresso from mocha frappés to double cappuccinos. Other offerings include smoothies, juices, and herbal teas. The cafe also serves as a revolving art gallery for local artists who may include Bob Smith, known for carving koa canoe paddles in the ancient tradition; and Pamela Coulton-Thomas, creator of distinctive postcards and a famous poster entitled *Shadow Dance.* The cafe displays a few boutique and souvenir items, including jewelry from Indonesia, perfume, massage oils, and a smattering of wooden art pieces. You can sit inside at a table, perch at the counter, or enjoy your coffee and pastry alfresco on the veranda, from where the two-block metropolis of Holualoa sprawls at your feet.

HONALO TO CAPTAIN COOK AND VICINITY

The following mountainside communities lie along a five-mile strip of Route 11, and if it weren't for the road signs, it would be difficult for the itinerant traveler to know where one village ends and the next begins. However, if you are after budget accommodations, unique boutique shopping, inexpensive island cuisine, and some off-the-beaten-track sightseeing, you won't be disappointed.

When leaving Holualoa, and if heading for Captain Cook and points south, stay on Route 180, the Mamalahoa Highway, a gorgeous road that gives great views from the heights.

Note: The following are the sights that you will encounter along routes 180 and 11. For ac-

Royal Kona Coffee Mill and Museum

commodations and food, and shopping in the villages along this route, see those sections following this one.

Fuku Bonsai Center

About three miles south of Holualoa on Route 180, you come to the Fuku Bonsai Gardens, open daily 8 a.m.-5 p.m., tel. 322-9222, offering a self-guided tour, $5 pp. A series of nine gardens over an improved path covers a 3.5-acre area and depicts the evolution of different types of bonsai, which traces its *roots* to ancient China. All plants are labeled. A souvenir shop allows you to purchase a living memento that can be shipped home. You can also follow the path to a ceramics studio, where artist-in-residence Jon Pacini creates earthy *raku*.

Near the Fuku Bonsai Center is a cutoff to Route 11, the main highway, but if you continue straight, you'll come to Keauhou and an understocked general store that for some inexplicable reason has a large inventory of bicycle parts. Open most days 9:30 a.m.-5 p.m., it's a good place to get a cold drink, and that's about it.

Honalo

This dot on the map is at the junction of routes 11 and 180. Not much changes here, and the town is primarily known for **Dai Fukuji Buddhist Temple** along the road. It's open daily 9 a.m.-4:30 p.m., free. Inside are two ornate altars; feel free to take photos but please remember to remove your shoes. There's a **Circle K** for sundries, food, and gasoline; and **Teshima's Inn and Restaurant,** an old standby for budget travelers (see the following "Practicalities" section).

Royal Kona Coffee Mill And Museum

In the town of Captain Cook, **Napoopoo Road** branches off Route 11 and begins a roller-coaster ride down to the sea, where it ends at Kealakekua Bay. En route it passes the well-marked Royal Kona Coffee Mill. Along the way you can't help noticing the trim coffee bushes planted along the hillside. Many counterculture types have taken up residence in semi-abandoned "coffee shacks" throughout this hard-pressed economic area, but the cheap, idyllic, and convenience-free life isn't as easy to arrange as it once was. The area is being "rediscovered" and getting more popular. For those just visiting, the tantalizing smell of roasting coffee and the lure of a "free cup" are more than enough stimulus to make you stop. Mark Twain did! The museum is small, of the nontouchable variety with most exhibits behind glass. Mostly they're old black-and-white prints of the way Kona coffee country used to be. Some heavy machinery is displayed out on the back porch. The most interesting is a homemade husker built from an old automobile. While walking around be careful not to step on a couple of lazy old cats so lethargic they might as well be stuffed. Perhaps a cup of the local "java" in their milk bowl would put a spring in their feline step! Inside, more or less integrated into the museum, is a small gift shop. You can pick up the usual souvenirs, but the real treats are gourmet honeys, jellies, jams, candies, and of course coffee. Buy a pound of Royal Kona Blend for about $6, or 100% Royal Kona for around $10. Actually, it's cheaper at other retail outlets and supermarkets around the island, but you can't beat the freshness of getting it right from the source. Refill anyone? The museum is open daily 8 a.m.-4:30 p.m., tel. 328-2511. Mailing address: Mauna Kea Coffee Co., Box 829, Captain Cook, HI 96704.

Kealakekua Bay

Continue down Napoopoo Rd. through the once-thriving fishing village of Napoopoo ("Holes"), now just a circle on the map with a few houses fronted by neat gardens. At road's end, you arrive at Kealakekua ("Road of the God") Bay. Relax a minute and tune in all your sensors because you're in for a treat. The bay is not only a **Marine Life Conservation District** with a fine beach and top-notch snorkeling (see "Napoopoo Beach County Park" following), but it drips with history. *Mauka,* at the parking lot, is the well-preserved **Hikiau Heiau,** dedicated to the god Lono, who had long been prophesied to return from the heavens to this very bay to usher in a "new order." Perhaps the soothsaying *kahuna* were a bit vague on the points of the new order, but it is undeniable that at this spot of initial contact between Europeans and Hawaiians, great changes occurred that radically altered the course of Hawaiian history.

The *heiau* is carved into the steep *pali* that form a well-engineered wall. From these heights the temple priests had a panoramic view of the ocean to mark the approach of Lono's "floating

Captain Cook's Monument

Island," heralded by tall white tapa banners. The *heiau* platform was meticulously backfilled with smooth, small stones; a series of stone footings, once the bases of grass and thatch houses used in the religious rites, is still very much intact. The *pali* above the bay is pocked with numerous burial caves that still hold the bones of the ancients.

Captain James Cook, leading his ships *Resolution* and *Discovery* under billowing white sails, entered the bay on the morning of Jan. 17, 1778, during the height of the Makahiki Festival, and the awestruck natives were sure that Lono had returned. Immediately, traditional ways were challenged. An old crew member, William Watman, had just died, and Cook went ashore to perform a Christian burial atop the *heiau*. This was, of course, the first Christian ceremony in the islands, and a plaque at the *heiau* entrance commemorates the event. On Feb. 4, 1778, a few weeks after open-armed welcome, the goodwill camaraderie that had developed between the English voyagers and their island hosts turned sour, due to terrible cultural misunderstandings. The sad result was the death of Captain Cook. During a final conflict, this magnificent man, who had resolutely sailed and explored the greatest sea on earth, stood helplessly in knee-deep water, unable to swim to rescue-boats sent from his waiting ships. Hawaiians, provoked to a furious frenzy because of an unintentioned insult, beat, stabbed, and clubbed the great captain and four

of his marines to death. (For a full accounting of these events, see pp. 26-29.) A 27-foot obelisk of white marble erected to Cook's memory in 1874 "by some of his fellow countrymen" is at the far northern end of the bay. Another plaque is dedicated to Henry Opukahaia, a young native boy taken to New England, where he was educated and converted to Christianity. Through impassioned speeches begging for salvation for his pagan countrymen, he convinced the first Congregationalist missionaries to come to the islands in 1820.

The land around the monument is actually under British rule, somewhat like the grounds of a foreign consulate. Once a year, an Australian ship comes to tend it, and sometimes local people are hired to clear the weeds. The monument fence is fashioned from old cannons topped with cannon balls. Here too is a bronze plaque often awash by the waves that marks the exact spot where Cook fell. You can see the marble obelisk from the *heiau,* but actually getting to it is tough. Expert snorkelers have braved the mile swim to the point, but be advised it's through open ocean, and Kealakekua Bay is known for sharks that come in during the evening to feed. A rugged jeep/foot trail leads down the *pali* to the monument, but it's poorly marked and starts way back near the town of Captain Cook, almost immediately after Napoopoo Road branches off from Route 11. If you opt for this route, you'll have to backtrack to visit the coffee museum and the *heiau* side of the bay.

Kona Historical Society Museum

The main building of the Kona Historical Society Museum was originally a general store built in the mid-1800s by local landowner and businessman H.L. Greenwell using native stone and lime mortar made from burnt coral. Now on both the Hawaiian and national registers of historic places, the building served many uses, including the warehousing and packaging of sweet oranges raised by Greenwell, purported to be the largest, sweetest, and juiciest in the world. The Kona Museum, Box 398, Captain Cook, HI 96704, tel. 323-3222, is open weekdays 9 a.m.-3 p.m. and every second Sat. 10 a.m.-2 p.m.; admission is by donation. To get there, as you approach Kealakekua along Route 11, look on the right for a sign that reads "Kona Meat Company Market." Pull into this road and follow it around to the back of the meat market, where you will find the parking lot for the museum.

The main artifact is the building itself, but inside, you will find a few antiques like a surrey and glassware, and the usual photographic exhibit with themes like coffee-growing—part of the legacy of Kona. The basement of the building houses archives filled with birth and death records of local people, photographs both personal and official, home movies, books, and maps, most of which were donated by the families of Kona. The archives are open to the public by appointment only. According to the director, Jill Olsen, the main purpose of the Historical Society is the preservation of Kona's history and the dissemination of historical information. Sometimes the society sponsors lectures and films (nominal charge), which are listed in the local newspapers. They also offer 4WD tours of the Kona area ($55) three times per year, usually in March, July, and November, and a historical boat tour in late January ($20) that takes you from Kailua-Kona south along the coast. There is no fixed schedule, but if you are in the area during those times of year, it would be well worth the trouble to contact the museum to find out if these excellent tours are being offered.

Napoopoo Beach County Park

Kealakekua Bay has been known as a safe anchorage since long before the arrival of Captain Cook, and still draws boats of all descriptions. The area, designated a **Marine Life Conservation District,** lives up to its title by being an excellent scuba and snorkeling site. Organized tours from Kailua-Kona often flood the area with boats and divers, but the ocean expanse is vast and you can generally find your own secluded spot to enjoy the underwater show. If you've just come for a quick dip or to enjoy the sunset, look for beautiful, yellow-tailed tropic birds that frequent the bay. Napoopoo Beach County Park has full amenities, including showers, picnic tables, and restrooms.

Heading For Pu'uhonua O Honaunau

This historical park, the main attraction in the area, shouldn't be missed. Though it was once known as City of Refuge Park, the official name is coming into more use in keeping with the emergence of Hawaiian heritage. The best way to get there is to bounce along the four miles of coastal road from Kealakekua Bay. En route, you pass a smaller, more rugged road to **Keei;** this side trip ends at a black-sand canoe launch area and a cozy white-sand beach good for swimming. A channel to an underwater grotto has been sliced through the coral. On the shore are the remains of Kamaiko Heiau, where humans were once sacrificed.

The other, more direct way to Pu'uhonua O Honaunau is Route 160 at Keokea, where it branches off Route 11 at mile marker 104. Whether you are going or coming this way, make sure to take a five-minute side trip off Route 160 to **St. Benedict's Painted Church.** This small house of worship is fronted by latticework, and with its gothic-style belfry looks like a little castle. Inside, a Belgian priest, John Berchman Velghe, took house paint and, with a fair measure of talent and religious fervor, painted biblical scenes on the walls. His masterpiece is a painted illusion behind the altar that gives you the impression of being in the famous Spanish cathedral in Burgos. Father John was pastor here from 1899 until 1904, during which time he did these paintings, similar to others that he did in small churches throughout Polynesia. Before leaving, visit the cemetery to see its petroglyphs and homemade pipe crosses.

Pu'uhonua O Honaunau
National Historical Park

The setting of Pu'uhonua O Honaunau couldn't be more idyllic. It's a picture-perfect cove with many paths leading out onto the sea-washed lava flow. The tall royal palms surrounding this compound shimmer like neon against the black lava so prevalent in this part of Kona. Planted for this purpose, these beacons promised safety and salvation to the vanquished, weak, and war-tossed, as well as to the *kapu*-breakers of old Hawaii. If you made it to this "temple of refuge," scurrying frantically ahead of avenging warriors or leaping into the sea to swim the last desperate miles, the attendant *kahuna*, under pain of their own death, had to offer you sanctuary. *Kapu*-breakers were particularly pursued because their misdeeds could anger the always moody gods, who might send a lava flow or tidal wave to punish all. Only the *kahuna* could perform the rituals that would bathe you in the sacred mana, and thus absolve you from all wrongdoing. This *pu'uhonua* ("temple of refuge") was the largest in all Hawaii, and be it fact or fancy, you can feel its power to this day.

The temple complex sits on a 20-acre finger of lava bordered by the sea on all sides. A massive, 1,000-foot-long mortarless wall, measuring 10 feet high and 17 feet thick, borders the site on the landward side and marks it as a temple of refuge. Archaeological evidence dates use of the temple from the mid-16th century, and some scholars argue that it was a well-known sacred spot as much as 200 years earlier. Actually, three separate *heiau* are within the enclosure. In the mid-16th century, Keawe, a great chief of Kona and the great-grandfather of Kamehameha, ruled here. After his death, he was entombed in **Hale O Keawe Heiau** at the end of the great wall, and his mana reinfused the temple with cleansing powers. For 250 years the *ali'i* of Kona continued to be buried here, making the spot more and more powerful. Even the great Queen Kaahumanu came here seeking sanctuary. As a 17-year-old bride, she refused to submit to the will of her husband, Kamehameha, and defied him openly, often wantonly giving herself to lesser chiefs. To escape Kamehameha's rampage, she made for the temple. Kaahumanu chose a large rock to hide under, and she couldn't be found until her pet dog barked and gave her away. Kaahumanu was coaxed out only after a lengthy intercession by Capt. George Vancouver, who had become a friend of the king. The last royal personage buried here was a son of Kamehameha who died in 1818. Soon afterwards, the "old re-

ligion" of Hawaii died and the temple grounds were abandoned but not entirely destroyed. The foundations of this largest city of refuge in the Hawaiian Islands were left intact.

In 1961, the National Park Service opened Pu'uhonua O Honaunau after a complete and faithful restoration was carried out. Careful consultation of old records and vintage sketches from early ships' artists gave the restoration a true sense of authenticity. Local artists used traditional tools and techniques to carve giant ohia logs into faithful renditions of the temple gods. They now stand again, protecting the *heiau* from evil. One of the most curious is a god-figure, with his maleness erect, glaring out to sea as if looking for some voluptuous mermaid. All the buildings are painstakingly lashed together in the Hawaiian fashion, but with nylon rope instead of traditional cordage, which would have added the perfect touch. Entrance to the park is $1, children under 16 free. Stop at the visitor center to pick up a map and brochure for a self-guided tour. Exhibits line a wall, complete with murals done in heroic style. Push a button and the recorded messages give you a brief history of Hawaiian beliefs and the system governing daily life. Educate yourself; the visitor center, tel. 328-2326, is open daily 7:30 a.m.-5:30 p.m. Rangers give tours 10 a.m.-3:30 p.m. The beach park section (see below) is open 6 a.m.-midnight. Follow the refuge wall toward the northwest to a large, flat rock perfect for lying back and watching the sun set.

Hookena

If you want to see how the people of Kona still live, visit Hookena. A mile or two south of the Pu'uhonua O Honaunau turnoff, or 20 miles south of Kailua-Kona, take a well-marked spur road *makai* off Route 11 and follow it to the sea. The village is in a state of disrepair, but a number of homey cottages and some semi-permanent tents are used mostly on weekends by local fishermen. Hookena also boasts a beach park with showers and picnic tables but no potable water or camping. For drinking water, a tap is attached to the telephone pole near the beginning of your descent down the spur road. The black-sand (actually gray) beach is broad, long, and probably *the* best in South Kona for both swimming and bodysurfing. If the sun gets too hot, plenty of palms lining the beach pro-

J.D. BISIGNANI

secluded Hookena Beach

vide not only shade but a picture-perfect setting. Until the road connecting Kona to Hilo was finally finished in the 1930s, Hookena shipped the produce of the surrounding area from its bustling wharf. At one time, Hookena was the main port in South Kona and even hosted Robert Louis Stevenson when he passed through the islands in 1889. Part of the wharf still remains, and nearby a fleet of outrigger fishing canoes is pulled up on shore. The surrounding cliffs are honeycombed with burial caves. If you walk a half mile north, you'll find the crumpled walls and steeple of Maria Lanakila Church, leveled in an earthquake in 1950. The church was another "painted church," done by Father John Velghe in the same style as St. Benedict's.

Milolii

This active fishing village is approximately 15 miles south of Pu'uhonua O Honaunau. Again, look for signs to a spur road off Route 11 heading *makai.* The road, leading through bleak lava flows, is extremely narrow but worth the detour. Milolii ("Fine Twist") earned its name from times past when it was famous for producing *'aha,* a sennit made from coconut-husk fibers; and *olona,* a twine made from the *olona* plant and best for fishnets. This is one of the last villages in Hawaii where traditional fishing is the major source of income and where old-timers are heard speaking Hawaiian. Fishermen still use small outrigger canoes, now powered by outboards, to catch *opelu,* a type of mackerel that schools in these waters. The method of catching the *opelu* has remained unchanged for centuries. Boats gather and drop packets of chum made primarily from poi, sweet potatoes, or rice. No meat is used so sharks won't be attracted. In the village, a small, understocked store is operated by Willie Kaupiko, though the whole family pitches in. Milolii has a **beach park** that is a favorite with local people on the weekends. Technically, it's a county park (permit), but no one checks. Tents are pitched in and around the parking lot, just under the ironwoods at road's end. Notice that a number of them appear to be semi-permanent. There are flushing toilets, a basketball court, and a brackish pond in which to rinse off, but no drinking water, so bring some. Swimming is safe inside the reef and the tidepooling in the area is some of the best on the south coast. A 15-minute trail leads south to Honomalino Bay where a white-sand beach is secluded and great for swimming. But always check with the local people first about conditions!

ACCOMMODATIONS AND FOOD

Accommodations

So you came to Kona for the sun, surf, and scenery and couldn't care less about your room so long as it's clean and the people running the hotel are friendly? Well, you can't go wrong with any of the following out-of-the-mainstream hotels. They're all basic, but not fleabags. At all of these inexpensive hotels, it is very important to get your rooms first thing in the morning, if you don't have reservations. They are very, very, tough to get into. People know about them, so the rooms are at a premium.

Manago Hotel in Captain Cook has been in the Manago family for 75 years, and anyone who puts his name on a place and keeps it there that long is doing something right. The old section of the hotel along the road is clean but a little worse for wear, and doesn't impress much because it looks like a storefront. Walk in to find a bridgeway into a garden area that's open, bright, and secluded away from the road. The rates with common bath are $22 s, $25 d, $28 t. First-floor rooms with private bath and lanai run $35 s, $38 d, $41 t. For $50-53, extra person $3, you're accommodated in the new wing, where you have a lanai and private bath and can train your eyes to catch the brilliance of the Kona sunset by practicing looking at the orange floor and pink furniture. Psychedelic! The views of the Kona Coast from the hotel grounds are terrific. You can dine in a restaurant in the old section, open for breakfast 7-9 a.m., lunch 11 a.m.-2 p.m., dinner 5-7:30 p.m., closed Monday, where people come from all over the island for the legendary pork chop dinners. For information, write to: Herald Manago, c/o Manago Hotel, Box 145, Captain Cook, Kona, HI 96704, tel. 323-2642.

Teshima's Inn, tel. 322-9140, is a small, clean, family-run hotel in the mountain village of Honalo at the junction of routes 180 and 11. Operated by Mr. and Mrs. Harry Teshima and family, it's somewhat like a Japanese *minshuku* with all rooms fronting a Japanese garden. To be sure of getting a room, call three days to a week in advance, and to reserve you must send at least one night's deposit. If you just turn up, you have a slim chance of getting one of the 11 rooms, five of which are generally rented long term. Check in is at the restaurant section, which is closed 2-5 p.m., so time your arrival accordingly. The rooms at $20 s, $30 d, $250-300 monthly, are spartan but very clean.

Howard and Marge Abert's B&B in Kealakekua, tel. 322-2405, is a friendly place where the home's bottom floor is given over to the guests. Both former Peace Corps volunteers, the Aberts are now retired and have taken up tropical gardening, as well as opening their home to travelers.

The Dragonfly Ranch, Box 675, Honaunau, HI 96762, tel. 328-9570, (800) 487-2159, owned and operated by David and Barbara Link, offers "tropical fantasy lodging" at a country estate. Rooms are remarkable and range from the "Hale in the Trees" to the "Honeymoon Suite" featuring an outdoor water bed. All rooms include a wet bar and refrigerator, private outdoor shower, cable TV, stereo, and small Hawaiiana library. Rates run $70 for a suite in the main house, $120 for the Redwood Cottage and Writer's Studio, and $160 for the Honeymoon Suite (substantial discounts for longer stays).

Food
All of the restaurants in this section happen to fall in the inexpensive range. None merits a special trip, but all are worth a stop if you're hungry when you go by. Some are great, especially for breakfast and brunch. For markets and health food stores, see the following "Shopping" section.

Teshima's Restaurant, tel. 322-9140, open daily 6:30 a.m.-1:45 p.m. and 5-9:30 p.m., at the junction of routes 11 and 180 in the mountain village of Honalo, is just like the small, clean, and homey Teshima's Inn that adjoins it. Here, in unpretentious surroundings, you can enjoy a full American, Hawaiian, or Japanese lunch for about $6.50, a filling daily special for $7, and dinner at $7.50-11. Another specialty is a *bento*, a box lunch for $5 that includes riceballs, luncheon meat, fried fish, teriyaki beef, *kamaboku* (fish cake), and Japanese roll. If you're interested in a good square meal, you can't go wrong.

Aloha Theater Cafe, open daily 8 a.m.-8 p.m., tel. 322-3383, is part of the lobby of the Aloha Theater in Kainaliu. The enormous breakfasts ($4-8) feature locally grown eggs, homemade muffins, and potatoes. Lunchtime sandwiches, $5-8.50, are super-stuffed with varied morsels from tofu and avocado to vegetarian tempeh burgers. There's also a variety of soups and salads and Mexican dishes like a quesadilla *especial* for $7.50. Full dinners like fresh *ahi* and *ono* are $13.95, filet mignon goes for $15.95, and pasta and shells are $12.95. For a snack choose from an assortment of homemade baked goods that you'll enjoy with an espresso or cappuccino. Order at the counter first (table service for dinner), and then sit on the lanai that overlooks a bucolic scene of cows at a watering trough, with the coast below. This is an excellent place to have breakfast or to pick up a picnic lunch on your way south. Also, check out the bulletin board for local happenings, sales, services, and the like.

The Korner Pocket Bar and Grill, tel. 322-2994, serving lunch and dinner weekdays 11

An outrigger canoe sits along a South Kona beach as in pre-contact times.

J.D. BISIGNANI

a.m.-10 p.m., until midnight Fri. and Sat., is a family-oriented/friendly biker bar where you can get excellent food at very reasonable prices. To get there, turn left off Route 11 in Kealakekua onto Halekii St. between the 76 Gas Station and McDonald's, and look for the Korner Pocket in the small shopping center on the left. Start with *pu pu* like twice-baked potato for $1.50, calamari strips $4.25, chicken hot wings $4.95, and chilled shrimp cocktail $5.95. Grill selections are a poolroom burger $4.95, mahimahi sandwich $5.50, or scrumptious bistro burger of grilled beef on crusty sourdough topped with fresh mushrooms sautéed in wine garlic sauce $6.50. Dinners are tempting: garlic scampi $12.95; chicken aiko accented with zesty Japanese sauce of lemon, apple, laurel, and spices; and prime rib eight ball, their encore entree at $10.95. The complete bar is well stocked with wines and spirits, or you can wash down your sandwich with an assortment of draft beers. The Korner Pocket looks as ordinary as a Ford station wagon, both inside and out, but the food is surprisingly good, and the owners, Paul and Judy, are very friendly.

Just beyond **McDonald's** golden arches as you enter Kealakekua, look for the **Canaan Deli,** a luncheonette with an Italian flair. The owners, Gigi and Guy Gambone, hail from Philadelphia, and bring the *back east* deli tradition of a lot of food for little money along with them. You can't go wrong with a Philly cheese-steak sub for $5.50, or a 12-inch lunch pizza for only $6. All sauces, breads, and the pizza dough are homemade.

There are very few places in Captain Cook where you can get a meal. On the right as you enter town is a takeout restaurant with barbecued ribs, chicken, hot biscuits, coleslaw, and salad. You can also try **Hong Kong Chop Suey** in the Ranch Center, which is as basic as can be with most items at $5, including sides. Also, try the legendary pork chop dinner served at the **Manago Hotel** restaurant in downtown Captain Cook (see "Accommodations" above).

SHOPPING

Kainaliu

Next door to the Aloha Cafe, **Aloha Village Store,** sells gifts, sundries, and natural foods. It's a well-stocked health food store with a good selection of powders, herbs, spices, and fresh produce, and a dairy case with organic foodstuffs. The bulletin board is great for letting you know what's happening, especially alternatively, in the area.

Badass Coffee Company, tel. 322-9196, open daily 7:30 a.m.-6 p.m., is a coffee and espresso bar where they roast their own beans on the premises in a *Royal No. 4 Roaster* manufactured in 1910, probably the last operational roaster of its type left in the state. Pure Kona coffee of the best grade sells for $9.95 per pound. After watching the roasting, take your cup of coffee and a homemade pastry to the rear of the shop, where you'll find an indoor stone grotto area away from the noise of the street.

Crystal Star Gallery specializes in cosmic vibrations and how to get in tune with them. You can feel the vibes as soon as you walk into this lavender-and-purple shop stocked with alluring crystals for channeling and massage, plus crystal balls and two racks filled with new-age books.

The Blue Ginger Gallery, tel. 322-3898, open Mon.-Sat. 9 a.m.-5 p.m., showcases the art of owners Jill and David Bever, as well as artists' works from all over the island. David creates art pieces in stained glass, fused glass, and wood. The small but well-appointed shop brims over with paintings, ceramics, sculptures, woodworking, and jewelry. A rack holds one-of-a-kind clothing items like sarongs and aloha shirts. Jill paints on silk, creating fantasy works in strong primary colors. The Blue Ginger Gallery is a perfect place to find a memorable souvenir of Hawaii.

At the south end of town, in the new, small C.H. Aina Shopping Center, is **Ohana O Ka Aina Food Co-op,** open 9 a.m.-6 p.m. weekdays, 10 a.m.-5 p.m. Saturday. This full-range health food store serves freshly made sandwiches from their deli. You can buy fresh orange and ginger lemonade made on the premises. The co-op, the last of its kind in Hawaii, has a large supply of herbs, plenty of vitamins and minerals, a smattering of fresh produce, and an excellent assortment of bulk grains.

Oshima's General Store is well stocked with cameras and film, drugs, fishing supplies, magazines, and some wines and spirits. Also in town are a **Ben Franklin's, Ace Hardware,** and **Kimura's Market,** a general grocery store with some sundries.

Kealakekua

Elizabeth Harris and Co., tel. 323-2447, is open Mon.-Fri. 9 a.m.-5 p.m., and displays shirts, T-shirts, and dresses made by 13 local seamstresses and artists who come in to showcase their works. You'll be greeted by the manager, Mary Harper, who'll be sitting behind a Singer sewing machine or hand-painting shirts. Take a look at the ceramics and glasswork as well. A great stop for truly distinctive clothing.

Right next door to the Kona Central Union Church is **Changing Hands,** a resale shop

Lance of Tropical Temptations

owned by Norma Hand that specializes in vintage clothing, glassware, and mostly Hawaiian antiques and bric-a-brac. Open weekdays 10:30 a.m.-4:30 p.m., occasionally Saturday, you can pick up a treasure ranging in cost from a dollar or two to a few hundred.

The **Kahanahou Hawaiian Foundation,** tel. 322-3901, deals in ancient Hawaiian handicrafts, including masks, *hula* drums, and *hula* accoutrements. This nonprofit organization serves as an apprenticeship school for native Hawaiians who are trying to revitalize traditional arts. Unfortunately, no one seems to be in attendance in the shop, and you are instructed to ring the buzzer. A sign says, "If you're just here to browse and to kill time don't kill ours; we can't afford the luxury." That sets the tone of your greeting when someone finally appears to scowl at you. Obviously the foundation is not into preserving aloha.

The Grass Shack, a.k.a. Little Grass Shack, open Mon.-Sat. 9 a.m.-5 p.m., sometimes Sun-

*the Blue Ginger Gallery
in Captain Cook*

J.D. BISIGNANI

day noon-5 p.m., tel. 323-2877, is an institution in Kealakekua. It looks like a tourist trap, but don't let that stop you from going in and finding some authentic souvenirs, most of which come from the area, the workshop next door, or rehabilitation centers around the island. The items *not* from Hawaii are clearly marked with a big orange sign that says, "Sorry These Items Were Not Made In Hawaii." But the price is right. There are plenty of trinkets and souvenir items, as well as a fine assortment of artistic pieces, especially wooden bowls, *hula* items, and Hawaiian masks. A shop specialty is items made from curly koa. Each piece is signed with the craftsperson's name and the type of wood used. One of the artisans displayed here is master woodworker Jack Straka. Items are also made from Norfolk pine and milo. A showcase holds jewelry and tapa cloth imported from Fiji. The shop is famous for its distinctive *lau hala* hats, the best hat for the tropics.

Tropical Temptations, tel. 326-2007, open Mon.-Sat. 10 a.m.-5 p.m., is housed in a gaily painted yellow and green building. Climb the steps to the porch, where you'll find a service buzzer that will summon owner and chief tempter Lance Dassance, who will smile a welcome into his candy kitchen. Remember, however, that most of the business is wholesale, and not really set up for drop-in visitors. Lance turns the best available grade of local fruits, nuts, and coffee beans into delicious candies. The fresh-fruit process uses no preservatives, additives,

waxes, or extenders, and no sugars except in the chocolate, which is the best grade possible. A slow-drying process is used, so as few nutrients as possible are lost. A shop specialty is candy made from rare white pineapple, which grows for only eight weeks per year. Lance, if not too busy, will be happy to take you on a tour of the facility. He takes a personal pride in making the best candy possible and stresses that he uses only fruit ripened in the last 24 hours. Tropical Temptations, the healthiest candy store in Hawaii, has an outlet booth in Kailua-Kona at the Kona Inn Shopping Village.

Konakai Coffee Farms has a tasting room and restaurant at the south end of Kealakekua. They produce and serve cups of Kona coffee plain, or as espresso, cappuccino, and caffe latte. Check the racks of fresh-roasted pure Kona coffee at about $12 per pound.

The **Kamigaki Store** is also in Kealakekua, and **Sure Save** is in Kealakekua Shopping Center.

Captain Cook
Next door to the Manago Hotel, just as you're entering town, is **Country Store Antiques.** Owned and operated by E.L. Mahre, open Mon.-Fri. 9 a.m.-3 p.m., it's filled to the brim from back to front. Inside you'll find kerosene lamps, dolls, glassware, old bottles, and Hawaiian antique jewelry. The shop is more like a museum than an antique store. There are plenty of purse- and suitcase-sized items that will travel well and make lasting mementos of your trip. On the other

side of the Manago Hotel is the **Manaloa Gallery and Thrift Store,** another bric-a-brac shop filled with art objects and curiosities.

The **Kealakekua Ranch Center,** in Captain Cook, is a two-story mall with fashions, food, and general supplies. Here you'll find a True Value hardware store, Ben Franklin's, and Sure Save Supermarket.

Other Shopping

A row of international flags waving along the roadside might lure you into **Kona Plantation Coffee,** an upscale tourist trap. They offer free coffee 8 a.m.-6 p.m., and the prices on the souvenir-quality items are cheaper than in Kailua-Kona. Poor from the elevated platforms to the coast below before entering. Inside you'll find Kona coffee, T-shirts, carved coconuts, towels, beads, and paper *lei.* Ask them for directions to the lava tube that you are allowed to tour free of charge. Exotic caged birds are also part of the experience.

Bong Brothers, about a mile past the Kona Country Fair, is an authentic fruit store. Check it out for the atmosphere and the fresh local fruit. The **Shimizu Market** is south on Route 11 in Honaunau. Farther south between mile markers 77 and 78 you'll find the very well-stocked **Ocean View General Store,** tel. 929-9966, which sells groceries, snacks, and gas. It's the last place to stock up before Naalehu, at the southern tip of the island.

BOB RACE

KAU

The Kau District is as simple and straightforward as the broad, open face of a country gentleman. It's not boring, and it does hold pleasant surprises for those willing to look. Formed entirely from the massive slopes of Mauna Loa, the district presents some of the most ecologically diverse land in the islands. The bulk of it stretches 50 miles from north to south and almost 40 miles from east to west, tumbling from the snowcapped mountain through the cool green canopy of highland forests. At lower elevations it becomes pastureland of belly-deep grass ending in blistering-hot black sands along the coast that are encircled by a necklace of foamy white sea. At the bottom of Kau is **Ka Lae** ("South Point"), the southernmost tip of Hawaii and the southernmost point in the U.S. It lies at a latitude 500 miles farther south than Miami and twice that below Los Angeles. Ka Lae was probably the first landfall made by the Polynesian explorers on the islands. A variety of archaeological remains supports this belief.

Most people dash through Kau on the Hawaii Belt Road, heading to or from Volcanoes National Park. Its main towns, **Naalehu** and **Pahala,** are little more than pit stops. The Belt Road follows the old Mamalahoa Trail where, for centuries, nothing moved faster than a contented man's stroll. Kau's beauties, mostly tucked away down secondary roads, are hardly given a look by most unknowing visitors. If you take the time and get off the beaten track, you'll discover black- and green-sand beaches, the world's largest macadamia nut farm, Wild West rodeos, and an electricity farm sprouting windmill generators. The upper slopes and broad pasturelands are the domain of hunters, hikers, and *paniolo,* who still ride the range on sure-footed horses. In Kau are sleepy plantation towns that don't even know how quaint they are, and beach parks where you can count on finding a secluded spot to pitch a tent. Time in Kau moves slowly, and aloha still forms the basis of day-to-day life.

1. Lilioukalani Gardens, Hilo (J.D. Bisignani);
2. coastal Route 137 (J.D. Bisignani)

1. banner butterfly fish (Dr. Greg Leo); **2.** i'iwi (Dr. Greg Leo);
3. moray eel (Dr. Greg Leo); **4.** lauwiliwilinukunukuoioi: the name is bigger than the fish (Dr. Greg Leo)

SIGHTS AND BEACHES

The following sights are listed from west to east along Route 11, with detours down secondary roads indicated whenever necessary. The majority of Kau's pleasures are accessible by standard rental car, but many secluded coastal spots can be reached only by 4WD. For example, **Kailiki,** just west of Ka Lae, was an important fishing village in times past. A few archaeological remains are found here, and the beach has a green cast due to the lava's high olivine content. Few tourists ever visit; only hardy fishermen come here to angle the coastal waters. Spots of this type abound, especially in Kau's remote sections. But civilization has found Kau as well: when you pass mile marker 63, look down to the coast and notice a stand of royal palms and a large brackish pond. This is Luahinivai Beach, one of the finest on the island, where country and western star Loretta Lynn has built a fabulous home. Those willing to abandon their cars and to hike the sparsely populated coast or interior of Kau are rewarded with areas unchanged and untouched for generations.

Manuka State Wayside

If hoofing it or 4WDing isn't your pleasure, consider a stop at Manuka State Wayside, 12 miles before you get to South Point Rd. and just inside the Kau District. This civilized scene has restrooms, pavilions, and trails through manicured gardens surrounded by an arboretum. Shelter camping (no tents) is allowed on the grounds. All plants are identified. This is an excellent rest or picnic stop. The forested slopes above Manuka provide ample habitat for introduced, and now totally successful, colonies of wild pigs, pheasants, and turkeys. Some popular hiking areas are covered in the Volcanoes National Park section (see pp. 226-227). Be advised that the entire district is subject to volcanic activity and, except where indicated, has no water, food, shelter, or amenities.

South Point

The Hawaiians simply called this Ka Lae, "The Point." Some scholars believe Polynesian sailors made landfall here as early as A.D. 150, and that their amazing exploits became navigating legend long before colonization began. A paved, narrow, but passable road branches off from Route 11 approximately six miles west of Naalehu, and drops directly south for 12 miles to land's end. Luckily the shoulders are firm, so you can pull over to let another car go by. The car-rental agencies warn against using this road, but their fears are unfounded. You proceed through a flat, treeless area trimmed by free-ranging herds of cattle and horses: more road obstacles to be aware of. Suddenly, incongruously, huge mechanical windmills appear, beating their arms against the sky. This is the **Kamoa Wind Farm.** Notice that this futuristic experiment at America's most southern point uses windmills made in Japan by Mitsubishi! The trees here are bent over by the prevailing wind, demonstrating the obviously excellent wind-power potential of the area. Farther along, a road sign informs you that the surrounding countryside is controlled by the **Hawaiian Homeland Agency,** and that you are forbidden to enter. That means that you are not welcome on the land, but you do have right-of-way on the land.

Here the road splits left and right. Go right until road's end, where you'll find a parking area usually filled with the pickup trucks of local fishermen. Walk to the cliff and notice attached ladders that plummet straight down to where the fishing boats are anchored. Local skippers moor their boats here and bring supplies and their catch up and down the ladders. Proceed south along the coast for only five minutes and you'll see a tall white structure with a big square sign on it turned sideways like a diamond. It marks the true "South Point," the southernmost tip of the United States. Proceed to the sea and notice the tidepools, a warning that the swells can come high onto the rocks, and that you can be swept away if you turn your back on *moana.* Usually, a few people are line fishing for crevalle or pompano. The rocks are covered with Hawaiian dental floss—monofilament fishing line that has been snapped. Survey the mighty Pacific and realize that the closest continental landfall is Antarctica, 7,500 miles to the south.

Back at the Hawaiian Homes sign, follow the road left and pass a series of WW II barracks

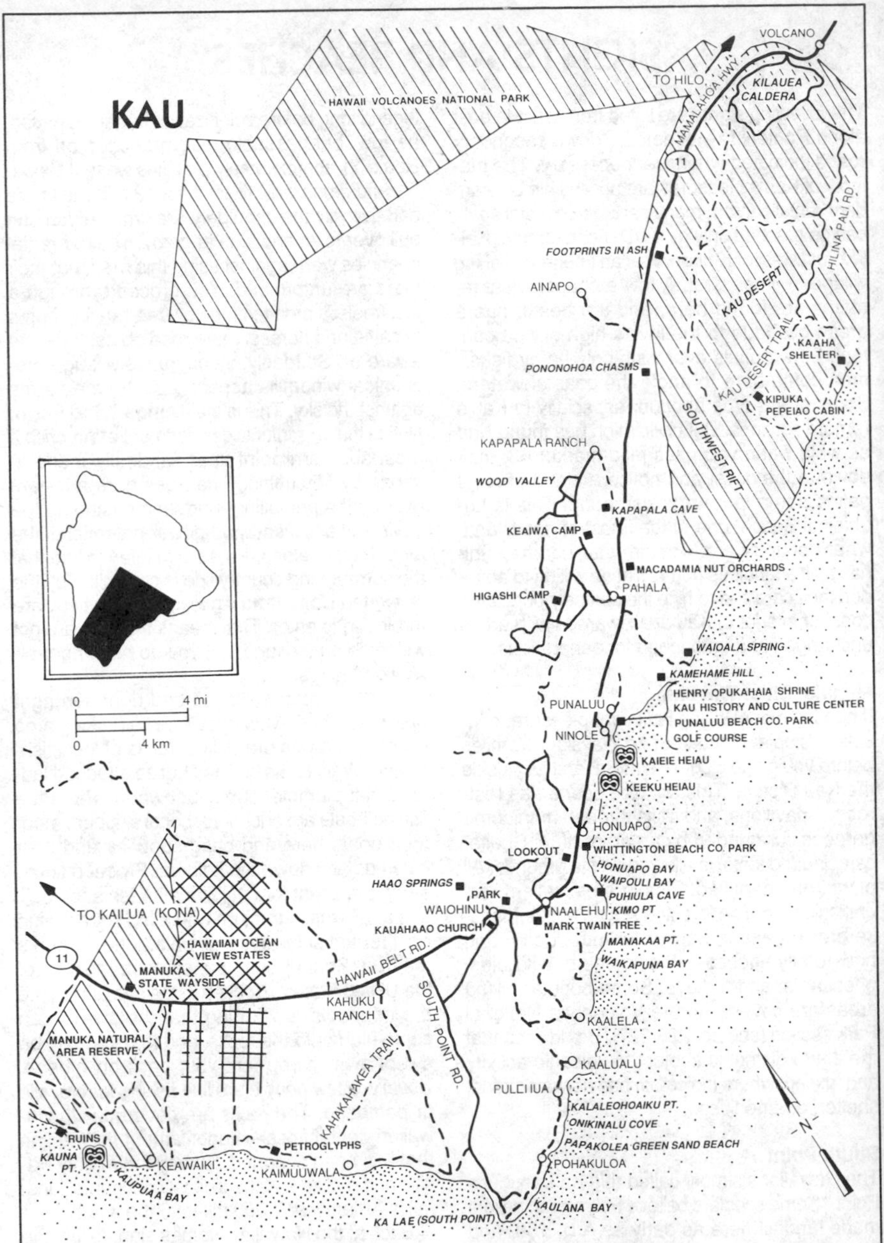

KAU

HAWAII VOLCANOES NATIONAL PARK

TO HILO

MAUNA LOA HWY

VOLCANO

KILAUEA CALDERA

11

HILINA PALI RD.

FOOTPRINTS IN ASH

AINAPO

KAU DESERT

KAU DESERT TRAIL

KAAHA SHELTER

PONONOHOA CHASMS

SOUTHWEST RIFT

KIPUKA PEPEIAO CABIN

KAPAPALA RANCH

WOOD VALLEY

KAPAPALA CAVE

KEAIWA CAMP

MACADAMIA NUT ORCHARDS

HIGASHI CAMP

PAHALA

WAIOALA SPRING

KAMEHAME HILL

HENRY OPUKAHAIA SHRINE
KAU HISTORY AND CULTURE CENTER
PUNALUU BEACH CO. PARK
GOLF COURSE

PUNALUU

NINOLE

KAIEIE HEIAU

KEEKU HEIAU

HONUAPO

WHITTINGTON BEACH CO. PARK

LOOKOUT

HONUAPO BAY
WAIPOULI BAY
PUHIULA CAVE

HAAO SPRINGS

PARK

TO KAILUA (KONA)

WAIOHINU

NAALEHU

KIMO PT.

KAUAHAAO CHURCH

MARK TWAIN TREE

MANAKAA PT.

WAIKAPUNA BAY

11

HAWAIIAN OCEAN
VIEW ESTATES

MANUKA
STATE WAYSIDE

HAWAII BELT RD.

KAHUKU RANCH

SOUTH POINT RD.

KAALELA

MANUKA NATURAL
AREA RESERVE

KAALUALU

KAHAKAHAKEA TRAIL

PULEIIUA

KALALEOHOAIKU PT.

ONIKINALU COVE

PAPAKOLEA GREEN SAND BEACH

RUINS

KAUNA PT.

KEAWAIKI

PETROGLYPHS

KAIMUUWALA

POHAKULOA

AUPUAA BAY

KA LAE (SOUTH POINT)

KAULANA BAY

0   4 mi
0   4 km

N

wind farm at South Point

being reclaimed by nature. This road, too, leads to a parking area and a boat ramp where a few seaworthy craft are bobbing away at their moorings. Walk toward the the navigational marker and you may notice small holes drilled into the stone. These were used by Hawaiian fishermen to secure their canoes to shore by long ropes while the current carried them a short way offshore. In this manner, they could fish without being swept away. Today fishermen still use these holes, but instead of canoes they use floats or tiny boats to carry only their lines out to sea. The *ulua*, tuna, and *ahi* fishing is renowned throughout this area. The fishing grounds here have always been extremely fertile, and thousands of shell and bone fishhooks have been found throughout the area. Scuba divers say that the rocks off South Point are covered with broken fishing line that the currents have woven into wild macrame.

When the *kona* winds blow out of the South Pacific, South Point takes it on the chin. The weather should always be a consideration when you visit. In times past, any canoe caught in the wicked currents was considered lost. Even today, only experienced boaters brave South Point, and only during fine weather.

There is no official camping or facilities of any kind at South Point, but plenty of boat owners bivouac for a night to get an early start in the morning. The lava flow in this area is quite old and grass-covered, and the constant winds act like a natural lawn mower.

Green Sand Beach

From the boat ramp, a footpath leads east toward Kaulana Bay. All along here are remnants of pre-contact habitation, including the remains of a *heiau* foundation. If you walk for three miles, you'll come to Papakolea, better known as Green Sand Beach. The lava in this area contains olivine, a green semiprecious stone that weathered into sandlike particles distributed along the beach. The road heading down to Green Sand Beach is incredible. It begins as a very rugged jeep trail, and disintegrates from there. Do not attempt this walk unless you have close-toed shoes. Thongs will not make it. You're walking into the wind going down, but it's not a rough go—there's no elevation gain to speak of. The lava in the area is *a'a,* weathered and overlaid by a rather thick ground cover. Follow the road, and after 10 minutes, the lava ends and rich, green pastureland begins. An ancient eruption deposited 15-18 feet of ash right here, and the grasses grew.

Continue for approximately 35 minutes, until you see what is obviously an eroded cinder cone at the edge of the sea. (About 15 minutes back, you'll have noticed an area where many 4WDs have pulled off at an overlook. That isn't it!) Peer over the edge to see the beach with its definite green tinge. This is the only *beach* along the way, so it's hard to mistake. Getting down to it is absolutely treacherous. You'll be scrambling over tough lava rock, and you'll have to make drops of four to five feet in certain spots.

black sands of Punaluu

J.D. BISIGNANI

The best approach is to go over the edge as soon as you come to the cinder cone area; don't walk around to what would be the south point of the caldera where the sand is. Once you get over the lip of heavy-duty rock, the trail down is not so bad. When you begin your descent, notice overhangs, almost like caves, where rocks have been piled up to extend them. These rocked-in areas make great shelters, and you can see remnants of recent campfires in spots perfect for a night's bivouac.

Green Sand Beach definitely lives up to its name, but don't expect emerald green. It's more like an army green, a dullish khaki green. Down at the beach, be very aware of the wave action. Watch for at least 15 minutes to be sure breakers are not inundating the entire beach. Then you can walk across it, but stay close to the lava rock wall. The currents can be wicked here and you should only enter the water on very calm days. No one is around to save you, and you don't want to wind up as flotsam in Antarctica.

Waiohinu
Back on the highway, as you head east toward Naalehu, you pass through the tiny town of Waiohinu. A tall church steeple welcomes you to town just after you wiggle your way down a long hill to the coast. There's nothing remarkable about this village, except that as you pass through you'll be seeing an example of the real Hawaiian lifestyle as it exists today. Just past the well-marked Shirakawa Motel (see the following

"Accommodations" section) on the *mauka* side of the road is the **Mark Twain Monkeypod Tree.** Unfortunately, Waiohinu's only claim to fame except for its undisturbed peace and quiet blew down in a heavy windstorm in 1957. Part of the original trunk, carved into a bust of Twain, is on display at the Lyman House Museum in Hilo. Now, a few shoots have begun sprouting from the original trunk and in years to come the Monkeypod Tree will be an attraction again.

Naalehu
Next you come to sizable Naalehu, the largest town in the area and the most southern town in the U.S. Naalehu is lush. Check out the overhanging monkeypod trees. They form a magnificent living tunnel as you go down Route 11 through the center of town. Between Naalehu and Punaluu, the coastal area is majestic. You've left the mountains behind and stretching out into the aqua-blue sea is a tableland of black lava with waves crashing against it, a surrealistic seascape that seems to go on forever.

Whittington Beach Park
Three miles north of Naalehu, just past mile marker 61, is a county park with full amenities and camping. This park is tough to spot from the road because it's not clearly marked. As you're coming down a steep hill from Naalehu you'll see a bridge at the bottom. Turn right and you're there. The park is a bit run down, but never crowded. If you follow the dirt roads to

its undeveloped sections you encounter many old ruins from the turn of the century when Honuapo Bay was an important sugar port.

Ninole And Punaluu

Just east of Naalehu is Whittington Beach Park, followed by Ninole, where you'll find Punaluu Beach Park (mile marker 56), famous for its black-sand beach (see below). Punaluu was an important port during the sugar boom of the 1880s and even had a railroad. Notice the tall coconut palms in the vicinity, unusual for Kau. Punaluu means "Diving Spring," so-named because freshwater springs can be found on the floor of the bay. Native divers once paddled out to sea, then dove with calabashes that they filled with fresh water from the underwater springs. This was the main source of drinking water for the region.

Ninole is also home to the **Seamountain Resort and Golf Course,** built in the early 1970s by a branch of the C. Brewer Company. The string of flat-topped hills in the background is the remains of volcanoes that became dormant about 100,000 years ago. In sharp contrast with them is **Loihi Seamount,** 20 miles offshore and about 3,000 feet below the surface of the sea. This very active submarine volcano is steadily building, and should reach the surface in the next thousand years or so. Near Ninole is **Hokuloa Church,** which houses a memorial to Henry Opukahaia, the Hawaiian most responsible for encouraging the first missionaries to go to Hawaii to save his people from damnation.

Punaluu Beach Park

Between Pahala and Naalehu is Punaluu Beach Park, a county park (permit) with full amenities. Here you'll find a pavilion, bathrooms, telephone, and open camping area. During the day there are plenty of tourists around, but at night the beach park empties, and you virtually have it to yourself. Punaluu boasts some of the only safe swimming on the south coast, but that doesn't mean that it can't have its treacherous moments. Head for the northeast section of the beach near the boat ramp. Stay close to shore because a prevailing rip current lurks just outside the bay. Just near the beach is **Joe and Pauline's Curio Shop.** If you have time, stop in; these people have a reputation for being more interested in offering aloha than in selling you a

trinket. **Ninole Cove Park,** part of the Seamountain Resort, is within walking distance and open to the public. For day use, you might consider parking near the pro shop. As you walk to the beach from here you pass a freshwater pond, quite cold but good for swimming.

Pahala

Eight miles east of Ninole and 22 miles from Volcanoes is Pahala, clearly marked off Route 11. The Hawaii Belt Road flashes past this town, but if you drive into it, heading for the tall stack of the Kau Sugar Co., you'll find one of the best-preserved examples of a classic sugar town in the islands. It was once gospel that sugar would be "king" in these parts forever, but the huge stone stack of the sugar mill puffs erratically, while in the background the whir of a modern macadamia nut-processing plant breaks the stillness. Another half hour or so of driving from Pahala puts you in Hawaii Volcanoes National Park (for Kau Desert Footprints, see p. 223).

Wood Valley Temple

Also known as Nechung Drayang Ling, "Island of Melodious Sound," the Wood Valley Temple, tel. 928-8539, Box 250, Pahala, HI 96777, is true to its name. This Tibetan Buddhist temple sits like a sparkling jewel surrounded by the emerald-green velvet of its manicured grounds. To get there, enter Pahala Village, proceed to the stop sign in the village center, and turn right onto Pikake Street. The road will open up into a very wide cane road where you should be aware of monstrous cane trucks that can lumber down it at any moment. Proceed for five miles until you come to a Y, where you go left. Follow this small road for a few hundred yards through an aromatic stand of majestic eucalyptus trees and look for two tall prayer poles on the right; pull into the parking lot and you'll see the temple, gaily painted red, yellow, orange, and green, glistening on top of the hill. Here Marya and Miguel, the caretakers and administrators, will greet you if they are not off on one of their frequent trips to Asia.

Buddha gave the world essentially 84,000 different teachings to pacify, purify, and develop the mind. In Tibetan Buddhism there are four major lineages, and this temple, founded by Tibetan master Nechung Rinpoche, is a classic

Be aware of huge cane trucks that lumber along the side roads.

J.D. BISIGNANI

synthesis of all four. Monks and scholars from different schools of Buddhism are periodically invited to come and lecture as resident teachers. The Dalai Lama came in 1980 to dedicate the temple, and many lama have come since then. Two affiliate temples are located in Dharamsfala, India and in Lhasa, Tibet. Programs vary, but people genuinely interested in Buddhism come here for meditation and soul-searching as well as for peace, quiet, relaxation, and direction. Morning and evening services at 7 a.m. and 7 p.m. are led by Debala, the Tibetan monk in residence. Formal classes depend upon which invited teacher is in residence (write ahead for a schedule of programs).

The retreat facility is called the Tara Temple and at one time housed a Japanese Shingon Temple in Pahala. When the Shingon sect moved to a new facility in Kona, this building was abandoned and given to Wood Valley Temple. A local contractor moved it to its present location, cranked it up one story, and built the dormitories underneath. The grounds, hallowed and consecrated for decades, already held a Nichiren temple, the main temple here today,

that was dismantled in 1919 and rebuilt on its present site to protect it from lowland flooding. Rates at the retreat facility are private room $25 s, $150 s weekly, $35 d, $210 d weekly. A bunk in the dorm is $15 with use of a large communal kitchen and shared bath. Definitely call or write to make reservations, since you could be disappointed if you just turn up!

The majority of the flowering and fruit trees on the premises are imports. Plenty of parishioners are into agriculture, and there is a strong movement by the temple members to slowly replant the grounds with native vegetation that they collect from various sites in and around Pahala. The grounds, like a botanical garden, vibrate with life and energy. Buddhism strives for its followers to become wise and compassionate people. The focus of the temple is to bring together all meditation and church groups in the community. Plenty of local Christian and Buddhist groups use the nonsectarian facilities. Any group that is spiritually, socially, and community oriented and that has a positive outlook is welcome. Wood Valley Temple can't promise *nirvana,* but they can point you to the path.

PRACTICALITIES

One thing you won't be hassled with in the Kau District is deciding on where to eat or spend the night. The list is short and sweet.

ACCOMMODATIONS

The **Shirakawa Motel,** tel. 929-7462, Box 467, Naalehu, HI 96772, is a small, clean, comfortable hotel where your peace and quiet are guaranteed. Open since 1928, it is run by a Japanese family as quiet and unobtrusive as *ninja.* Prices are a reasonable $27 s, $36 s with kitchen, $40 d with kitchen, with a 10% discount for a one-week stay, 15% for longer. You'll be greeted by two dogs—Rex, a Doberman pinscher, and Kai, a golden Lab—both of whom have given up aggression and opted for the "hang loose, no worries" island lifestyle.

Seamountain Resort at Punaluu, tel. 928-8301 or (800) 367-8047, Box 340, Pahala, HI 96777, is a condominium/hotel complex. Prices range from a studio at $67 to a two-bedroom apartment for $114 (two-day minimum stay). Because of its rural location, Seamountain can offer deluxe accommodations for moderate prices. Your condo unit will be a low-rise, Polynesian-inspired bungalow with a shake roof. Outside your door are the resort's fairways and greens, backdropped by the spectacular coast. If you're after peace and quiet, Seamountain is hard to beat. Besides golf, amenities include a nearby restaurant, tennis courts, pool, and weekly maid service.

Becky's Bed & Breakfast, tel. 929-9690 or (800) 235-1233, Box 673, Naalehu, HI 96772, about 100 yards past the theater on the left, is owned and operated by Becky and Chuck McLinn. Available in this modest but cheery 60-year-old home is a spacious room with a queen bed and private bath for $50 s, $60 d; a room with two double beds and private bath at $55 s, $65 d; and a room with queen bed and shared bath $45 s, $55 d, additional person $10. There is no official policy, but if you'll be staying four nights or longer, a discount can be arranged. To help you relax, the B&B features a backyard deck with a barbecue grill, inviting hammock, and hot tub to unjangle nerves. Becky serves a full breakfast of juice, fruit, and either Hawaiian French toast or hotcakes with bacon or sausage.

South Point Bed & Breakfast, tel. 929-7466, HC1 92-1408 Donala Dr., Captain Cook, HI 96704,, is owned and operated by Bruce and Robin Hall. They offer rooms at $55 d, with a discount for longer stays.

For unique and distinctive accommodations see **Wood Valley Temple,** pp. 283-284.

FOOD AND SHOPPING

The Kau Drive-in Restaurant is open for breakfast, lunch, and dinner. You pass it on the left between mile markers 78 and 77, just near a Texaco gas station. The food is simple but good, and makes a perfect lunch.

a local favorite

J.D. BISIGNANI

*Seamountain
Golf Club Resort*

J.D. BISIGNANI

A mile further south is **South Point Bar and Restaurant,** tel. 929-9343, which has been changing owners regularly but is making a valiant effort to stay open. The restaurant is open for dinner Wed.-Fri. 5-8 p.m., and for breakfast Sat.-Sun. 8 a.m.-1 p.m. Wednesday is Mexican night. On the other evenings you can expect barbecued boneless chicken $9.95, steak dinner $15.95, and an assortment of burgers and sandwiches. The bar is open weekdays noon-8 p.m., and weekends 8 a.m.-8 p.m. The South Point Bar and Restaurant is the only place to stop for food until you get to Naalehu.

Kau Ice and Fishing Center in Waiohinu offers fresh local fish that would make a perfect self-prepared meal for anyone heading back to a condo in Kailua-Kona. Just down the road, you can pick up supplies at **Wong Yuen General Store and Gas Station,** open Mon.-Sat. 8:30 a.m.-5 p.m., Sun. to 3 p.m., tel. 929-7223.

Naalehu Shopping Center is along the road at the west end of town. In the small complex you'll find Food Mart, Ed's Laundromat, and **Greensan's Shop,** where you can pick up sandwiches and plate lunches.

As you are entering the west side of town, a large, easily spotted sign on the left marks the **Punaluu Bake Shop and Visitor's Center,** open daily 9 a.m.-5 p.m. The bake shop, tempting with all kinds of pastries, is especially known for its *pao dolce,* sweet bread. Park and follow a cement pathway to the retail shop for baked goods, coffee, and a smattering of souvenirs.

In **Naalehu** you can gas yourself or your car at the **Luzon Liquor Store,** open Mon.-Sat. 7 a.m.-7:30 p.m., Sun. till 6 p.m., closed Tues., tel. 929-7103. For a quick sandwich or full meal try the **Naalehu Coffee Shop,** open daily, tel. 929-7238. Many of the local people call this restaurant Roy's, after the owner's first name. The menu is typical island cuisine with a Japanese flavor; the best item is the fresh fish from local waters. The restaurant is basic and clean, with most meals on the menu around $7. They also have a wide assortment of souvenirs and tourist junk, and a large *koi* pond outside. Look for the big yellow building just near the shopping center as you enter town.

Naalehu Fruit Stand, tel. 929-9009, open Mon.-Thurs. 9 a.m.-6:30 p.m., Fri. and Sat. till 7 p.m., Sun. till 5 p.m., is a favorite with local people, always a tip-off that the food is great. Along with fresh fruit, they sell submarines, hot dogs, pizza, salads, sodas, teas, coffee, and a good selection of grains, minerals, vitamins, and health foods. The owners, John and Dorene Santangelo, are very friendly and willing to give advice about touring the Kau area. This is the best place on the south coast for a light meal or picnic lunch.

Across the road from the Naalehu Fruit Stand, notice the baseball park. Here **Lilly's Plate Lunch** serves hearty sandwiches and island favorites ready to go.

In **Pahala Village** (see p. 283) you'll find the basics like a gas station, small shopping center, post office, Bank of Hawaii, Mizumo's Superette, and a takeout plate lunch restaurant.

SPORTS AND ACTIVITIES

The only organized sporting facility in Kau is at the Seamountain Resort. Here you'll find four unlit tennis courts and a 6,106-yard, 18-hole, par-72 course. Greens fees are $30, cart $16, and clubs $10.

The **Southern Star Theater** is a large building on the left as soon as you drive into Naalehu. It's a classic old-time theater usually open on weekends, adults $3.25, children $1.75.

The best **sailboarding** in the area is at Kaulana Bay. Head down South Point Rd. (see pp. 279-281), and about a half mile before you get to the windmills is a passable dirt road to the left. You can only see about half a mile down it when you first start out, but keep going. Pass through cattle gates and make absolutely sure to close them behind you. When you get to the bay, go to the left-hand side for the best entry. Remember that down here, no help is available, and you are totally on your own!

Kau Windsurfing in Naalehu, next to the Naalehu Fruit Stand, rents and sells sailboards, fins, snorkels, and masks.

BOB RACE

SOUTH KOHALA

The Kohala District is the peninsular thumb in the northwestern portion of the Big Island. At its tip is **Upolu Point,** only 40 miles from Maui across the **Alenuihaha Channel.** Kohala was the first section of the Big Island to rise from beneath the sea. The long-extinct volcanoes of the Kohala Mountains running down its spine have been reduced by time and the elements from lofty, ragged peaks to rounded domes of 5,000 feet or so. Kohala is divided into North and South Kohala. South Kohala boasts *the* most beautiful swimming beaches on the Big Island, along with good camping and world-class hotels. Inland is **Waimea** (Kamuela), the *paniolo* town and center of the massive Parker Ranch. Founded last century by John Parker, its 200,000 acres on the western slopes of Mauna Kea now make it the largest privately owned ranch in America.

Getting There From Hilo

If you're approaching Kohala from Hilo or the east side of the island, you can take two routes. **The Saddle Road** (Route 200) comes directly west from Hilo and bypasses Mauna Kea and the Observatory Road. This very scenic road has the alluring distinction of being the least favorite route of the car-rental agencies. The Saddle Road intersects Route 190, where you can turn north for six miles to Waimea, or south for 32 miles to Kailua-Kona (see p. 180). **Route 19,** the main artery connecting Hilo with the west coast, changes its "locally known" name quite often, but it's always posted as Route 19. Directly north from Hilo as it hugs the Hamakua Coast it's called the "Hawaii Belt Road." When it turns west in Honokaa, heading for Waimea, it's called the "Mamalahoa Highway." From Waimea directly west to Waikui on the coast Route 19 becomes "Kawaihae Road," and when it turns due south along the coast heading for Kailua-Kona its moniker changes again to "Queen Kaahumanu Highway." The routes heading to Kohala from Kailua-Kona are discussed in the following sections. Many are "sights" in and of themselves, with lovely panoramas and leisurely back-lane rides.

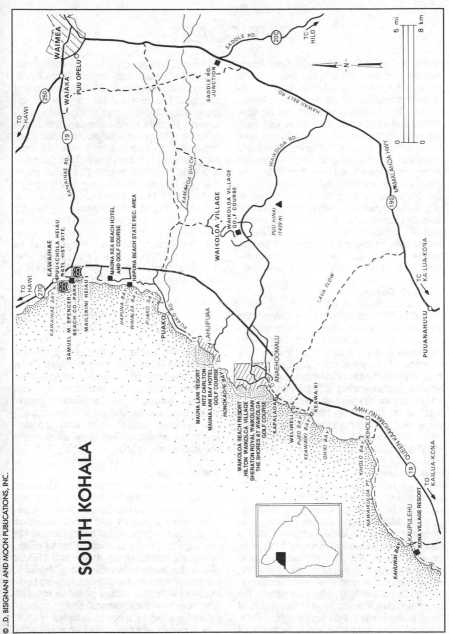

SOUTH KOHALA

THE COAST

The shoreline of South Kohala, from Anaehoomalu Bay north to Kawaihae Bay, is rich in perhaps the finest super-deluxe resorts in the state. This coast's fabulous beaches are known not only for swimming and surf, but for tidepooling and awe-inspiring sunsets as well. Also, the two main beaches offer camping and even rental cabins. There are little-disturbed and rarely visited archaeological sites, expressive petroglyph fields well off the beaten track, the educational **Puukohola Heiau,** and even a rodeo. No "towns" lie along the coast, in the sense of a laid-out community with a main street and attendant businesses and services. The closest facsimile is Kawaihae, with a small cluster of restaurants, shops, and gas station. Waikoloa Village also provides some services, with exclusive boutique shopping in the resorts.

Route 19, Queen Kaahumanu Highway

As you begin heading north from Kailua-Kona on coastal Route 19 (Queen Kaahumanu Highway), you leave civilization behind. There won't be a house or any structures at all, and you'll understand why they call it the "Big Island." Perhaps to soften the shock of what's ahead, magnificent bushes loaded with pink and purple flowers line the roadway for a while. Notice too that friends and lovers have gathered and placed white coral rocks on the black lava, forming pleasant graffiti messages such as "Aloha Mary" and "Love Kevin."

Suddenly you're in the midst of enormous flows of old *a'a* and *pa'hoehoe* as you pass through a huge and desolate lava desert. At first it appears ugly and uninviting, but the subtle beauty begins to grow. On clear days you can see Maui floating on the horizon, and *mauka* looms the formidable presence of Mauna Kea streaked by sunlight filtering through its crown of clouds. Along the roadside, wisps of grass have broken through the lava. Their color, a shade of pinkish gold, is quite extraordinary, and made more striking juxtaposed against the inky-black lava. Caught by your headlights at night, or especially in the magical light of dusk, the grass wisps come alive, giving the illusion of

wild-haired gnomes rising from the earth. In actuality, it's fountain grass imported from Africa.

Around mile marker 70, the land softens and changes. The lava is older, carpeted in rich green grass appearing as rolling hills of pastureland. No cows are in evidence, but be aware of "Kona nightingales," wild jackasses that roam throughout this area and can be road hazards. Also, these long, flat stretches of road can give you "lead foot." Be careful! The police patrol this strip heavily, using unmarked cars (high-performance Trans Ams and the like are favorites) and looking for unsuspecting tourists who have been "road hypnotized." From Kailua-Kona to the Royal Waikoloan Hotel at Anaehoomalu is about 30 miles, with another 10 miles to the Mauna Kea Beach Hotel near Kawaihae. If you're day-tripping to the beaches, expect to spend an hour each way.

SIGHTS AND NEARBY COMMUNITIES

The following sights, beaches, and accommodations are listed from south to north. Since most of the accommodations of South Kohala are themselves sights, and lie on the best beaches, make sure to cross-reference the following sections. All, except for Waikoloa Village, lie along coastal Route 19, which is posted with mile markers, so finding the spots where you want to stop is easy.

Waikoloa Road

If you're interested in visiting Waimea (Kamuela) as well as seeing the South Kohala coast, you might consider turning right off Route 19 between mile markers 74 and 75 onto Waikoloa Road. This is a great deal of territory to cover in one day! This route cuts inland for 13 miles, connecting coastal Route 19 with inland Route 190, which leads to Waimea. About halfway, you pass the planned and quickly growing community of **Waikoloa Village** (about six miles inland from Waikoloa Resorts) that is unfortunately heralded by a condo complex of stark gray in neo-Alcatraz design which would aptly

the wide expanses
of Kohala

be called "Prisoners of Paradise" but is mis-named "The Greens." Try to overlook them, and head for the village itself, which is low-rise and quite tasteful.

The village is serviced by the **Waikoloa Highlands Center**, a small but adequate shopping mall with a gas station, full-service supermarket, Bank of Hawaii, Straw Hat Pizza, postal service store, small medical center, and a few restaurants and shops. This is also the home of **Waikoloa Stables**, tel. 883-9335, which hosts a number of rodeos and Wild West shows (see p. 91). They offer saddle horses and a variety of trail rides for the visitor. Here too is the **Waikoloa Village Golf Course**, tel. 883-9621, a private course open to the public. You can chase that little white ball for par 72 over 6,316 yards for about $40 including cart.

In the village you'll find **Waikoloa Villas**, Box 3066, Waikoloa Village Station, Kamuela, HI 96743, tel. (800) 367-7042 or 883-8855 on the Big Island. Rates are one bedroom $65-80 d, two bedrooms $85-95 d, three bedrooms (loft) $105-115 d, $8 extra person, two-night minimum stay. Amenities include swimming pool, nearby golf, and weekly maid service. All units are fully furnished with complete kitchens. The condo offers a money-saving condo/car package.

Puako

This alluring area is located *makai* on a side road off Route 19 about four miles south of Kawaihae. Hawaiians lived here in times past, but a modern community has been building along the three miles of Puako Bay since the 1950s. A thin ribbon of white sand runs the length of the beach that provides fair swimming, good fishing and snorkeling, and terrific tidepooling. Sunsets here are magnificent and you'll usually have a large stretch of beach to yourself, but remember your flashlight for the walk back because there's no lighting. Near-shore scuba diving is excellent, with huge caverns and caves to explore, and a colorful concentration of coral and marinelife.

Along Puako Road is **Hokuloa Church**, built by Rev. Lorenzo Lyons in 1859. This musically talented reverend mastered the Hawaiian language and composed lovely ballads such as "Hawaii Aloha," which has become the unofficial anthem of the islands. Follow the road through the village to where it ends at a green gate; this is the beginning of **Puako Petroglyphs**; farther on is the adjacent site known as **Anaeho'omalu**. The beach path leading to the rock carvings takes about 20 minutes each way. Access is also available by way of a well-marked self-guiding trail starting from the Mauna Lani Resort area. Any of the large hotels here offer brochures and information concerning the petroglyph fields. The markings are considered some of the finest and oldest in Hawaii, but carvings of horses and cattle signify ongoing art that happened long after Westerners appeared. Circles outlined by a series of small holes belonged to families who placed the umbilical cords of their infants into these indentations to tie them to the *aina* and give them strength for a long and good life. State archaeologists and anthropologists have reported a deterioration of the site due to vandalism, so please look, but don't deface and stay on all established paths.

Puukohola Heiau

Don't miss this completely restored Hawaiian temple, a National Historical Site located one mile south of Kawaihae where coastal Route 19 turns into Route 270 heading into North Kohala. This site, covering 77 acres, includes **Mailekini Heiau** and the nearby **John Young House** site. Administered by the National Park Service, it is open daily 7:30 a.m.-4 p.m.; admission is free. As you enter, pick up a map highlighting the main points of interest. It's worthwhile checking out the visitor center, where Ranger Benjamin Saldua and others provide excellent information. Puukohola ("Whale Hill") received its name either because the hill itself resembles a whale, or because migrating whales pass very close offshore every year. It was fated to become a hill of destiny.

Kamehameha I built this *heiau* in 1790 on the advice of Kapoukahi, a prophet from Kauai who said that Kamehameha would unify all the islands only after he built a temple to his wargod Kukailimoku. Kamehameha complied, building this last of the great Hawaiian *heiau* from mortarless stone that when finished measured 100 by 224 feet. The dedication ceremony of the *heiau* is fascinating history. Kamehameha's last rival was his cousin, Keoua Kuahuula. This warlike chief, through prophecy and advice from his own *kahuna,* realized that it was Kamehameha who would rise to be sovereign of all the islands. Kamehameha invited him to the dedication ceremony, but en route Keoua, in preparation for the inevitable outcome, performed a death purification ceremony by circumcising his own penis. When his canoes came into view, they were met by a hail of spears and musket balls. Keoua's body was carried to Kukailimoku's altar. Kamehameha became the unopposed sovereign of the Big Island and, within a few years, of all of Hawaii.

Near the *heiau* is the house site of John Young, an English seaman who became a close adviser to Kamehameha, who dubbed him Olohana, "All Hands." Young taught the Hawaiians

HAWAII STATE ARCHIVES

John Young by ship's artist A. Pellion

how to use cannons and muskets and fought alongside Kamehameha in many battles. He turned Mailekini Heiau into a fort, and over a century later it was used during WW II by the U.S. Army as an observation area. Young became a respected Hawaiian chief and grandfather of Queen Emma. He's one of only two white men buried at the Royal Mausoleum in Nuuanu Valley on Oahu.

Kawaihae Town

The port marks the northern end of the South Kohala coast. Here Route 19 turns eastward toward Waimea, or turns into Route 270 heading up the coast into North Kohala. Kawaihae town is basically utilitarian, with wharfs and fuel tanks. A service cluster has a shop or two.

BEACHES, PARKS, AND CAMPGROUNDS

Anaehoomalu Bay

After almost 30 miles of the transfixing monochrome blackness of Kohala's lava flows, a green standout of palm trees beckons in the distance. Between mile markers 76 and 77, on the Waikoloa Resorts road, another well-marked access road heads *makai* to the Royal Waikoloan Hotel and historic Anaehoomalu Bay. The bay area, with its freshwater springs, coconut trees, blue lagoon, and white-sand beach, is a picture-perfect seaside oasis. Between the large coconut grove and the beach are two well-preserved fish ponds where mullet was raised *only* for consumption by the royalty who lived nearby or were happening by in seagoing canoes. Throughout the area along well-marked trails are **petroglyphs,** a segment of the cobblestoned **King's Highway,** and numerous archaeological sites including house sites and some hard-to-find burial caves. The white-sand beach is open to the public, with access, parking, and beautiful lava stone showers/bathhouses. Although the sand is a bit grainy, the swimming, snorkeling, scuba, and windsurfing are fine. A walk north along the bay brings you to an area of excellent tidepools and waters heavily populated by marinelife. The next beach north is at Puako Bay (see pp. 291-292).

Holoholokai Beach Park

Located near the Ritz-Carlton Mauna Lani Hotel on a well-marked access road, the picturesque beach park, open to the public daily 6:30 a.m.-7 p.m., is improved with a bathhouse, running water, picnic tables, and resort-quality landscaping. Unfortunately, the beach itself is mostly coral boulders with only tiny pockets offering very limited water access. However, the park is used very little and is perfect for relaxing under a palm tree or for a leisurely stroll to explore the many tidepools.

Hapuna Beach State Recreation Area

Approximately 12 miles north of Anaehoomalu is the *second*-best, but most accessible, white-sand beach on the island. (The best, Kauna'oa, is listed next.) **Camping** is available in six A-frame screened shelters that rent for approximately $7 per night pp and accommodate up to four. Provided are sleeping platforms (no bedding), electric outlets, cold-water showers, and toilets in separate comfort stations, plus a shared range and refrigerator in a central pavilion. Check in at 2 p.m., checkout at 10 a.m. The A-frames are very popular, so reservations and deposit are required. You can receive full information by contacting the Division of State Parks, Box 936 (75 Aupuni St.), Hilo, HI 96720, tel. 933-4200. However, reservations are made by contacting the concessionaire, Hawaii Untouched Parks & Recreation Inc., Box 390962,

Kailua-Kona, HI 96739, tel. 882-1095. There is unofficial camping south along **Waialea Bay** that you can get to by walking or taking the turnoff at mile marker 69.

Hapuna Beach is wide and spacious, almost 700 yards long by 70 wide in summer, with a reduction by heavy surf in winter. A lava finger divides the beach into almost equal halves. During good weather the swimming is excellent, but a controversy rages because there is no lifeguard here. During heavy weather, usually in winter, the rips are fierce, and Hapuna has claimed more lives than any other beach park on all of Hawaii! At the north end is a small cove almost forming a pool that is always safe, a favorite with families and children. Many classes in beginning scuba and snorkeling are held in this area, and shore fishing is good throughout. At the south end, good breaks make for tremendous bodysurfing (no boards allowed), and those familiar with the area make spectacular leaps from the seacliffs.

Kauna'oa Beach

Better known as **Mauna Kea Beach** because of the nearby luxury hotel of the same name, Kauna'oa is less than a mile north of Hapuna Beach and is considered to be the best beach on the Big Island. In times past, it was a nesting and mating ground for green sea turtles, and although these activities no longer occur because of human pressure on the habitat, turtles still visit the south end of the beach. Mauna Kea Beach is long and wide, and the sandy bottom makes for excellent swimming. It is more sheltered than Hapuna, but can still be dangerous. Hotel beach boys, always in attendance, are unofficial lifeguards who have saved many unsuspecting tourists. During high surf, the shoreline is a favorite with surfers. All beaches in Hawaii are public, but *access* to this beach was won only by a lawsuit against the Mauna Kea Beach Hotel in 1973. The ruling forced the hotel to open the beach to the public, which they did in the form of 10 parking spaces, a right of way, public shower, and toilet facilities. To keep the number of nonguests down, only 10 parking passes are handed out each day on a first-come, first-served basis. Pick them up at the guardhouse as you enter the hotel grounds. These entitle you to spend the day on the beach, but on weekends they're gone by 9:30 a.m. You can wait for someone to leave and then get the

the secluded beach at
Kona Village Resort

J.D. BISIGNANI

pass, but that's unreliable. The hotel also issues
a pass for a one-hour visit to the hotel grounds
(overstaying results in a $10 fine). You can use
this pass to drop off family, friends, beach para-
phernalia, and picnic supplies, then park at Hapuna and return via an easy mile-long **nature
trail** connecting Hapuna and Mauna Kea beaches, the route used by the majority of people unable to get a pass. Also, the hotel issues a "food
and drink" pass that entitles you to stay as long
as you wish, if you get it validated at one of the
restaurants or snack bars. So as long as you're in
there, you might as well use the beach for the
price of a soft drink. In time the hotel will catch on,
so test the waters before winding up with a fine.

Spencer Beach County Park
Look for the entrance a minute or two past
Puukohola Heiau on Route 19 just before en-
tering Kawaihae. Trails lead from the beach

park up to the *heiau*, so you can combine a
day at the beach with a cultural education. The
park is named after Samuel Mahuka Spencer,
a longtime island resident who was born in
Waimea, served as county mayor for 20 years,
and died in 1960 at Honokaa. The park provides pavilions, restrooms, cold-water showers, electricity, picnic facilities, and even tennis courts. Day use is free, but tent and trailer
camping is by county permit only, at $1 p/d
(see p. 74). Spencer Beach is protected from
wind and heavy wave action by an offshore
reef and by breakwaters built around Kawaihae Bay. These make it the safest and best
swimming beach along South Kohala's shore
and a favorite with local families with small children. The wide, shallow reef is home to a wide
spectrum of marinelife, making the snorkeling
easy and excellent. The shoreline fishing is
also excellent.

PRACTICALITIES

RESORTS AND ACCOMMODATIONS

Except for a few community-oriented restaurants in Waikoloa Village, and a few reasonably priced roadside restaurants in Kawaihae, all of the food in South Kohala is served in the elegant but expensive restaurants of the luxury hotels. These hotels also provide the **entertainment** along the coast, mostly in the form of quiet musical combos and dinner shows. The **shopping,** too, is in the exclusive boutiques found in the hotel lobbies and mini-malls. The following hotels lie along coastal Route 19 and are listed from south to north. For more "Practicalities" listings please see "Sights and Nearby Communities" above.

Kona Village Resort
So you want to go "native," and you're dreaming of a "little grass shack" along a secluded beach? No problem! The Kona Village Resort is a once-in-a-lifetime dream experience. Located on Kahuwai Bay, a picture-perfect cove of white sand dotted with coconut palms, the village lies seven miles north of the airport, surrounded by 12,000 open acres promising seclusion. The accommodations, called "beachcomber hales," are individual renditions of thatch-roofed huts found throughout Polynesia. They are simple but luxurious, and in keeping with the idea of getting away from it all have no TVs, radios, or telephones. All, however, do have ceiling fans and louvered windows to let the tropical breezes blow through. Beds are covered with distinctive quilts and pillows. Each hut features a wet bar, fridge, coffee-making machine, and extra-large bathroom. Your Do Not Disturb sign is a coconut that you place upon your private lanai, and messages are hand-delivered and placed in a basket, also on the lanai. At one time you had to fly into the hotel's private airstrip, but today you can arrive by car. You enter by an access road that leads through the tortured black lava fields of South Kohala. Don't despair! Down by the sea you can see the shimmering green palm trees as they beckon you to the resort. Kona

Village gives you your money's worth, with tennis, Ping-Pong, *lei* greetings, water sports, and a variety of cocktail parties and luaus. Guided tours are also offered to the many historic sites in the area. Rates start at $295 s, $370 d, full American plan (three meals). There is a strict reservations and refund policy, so check. For information, contact Kona Village Resort, Box 1299, Kailua-Kona, HI 96740, tel. 325-5555 or (800) 367-5290.

Meals are served in the Hale Moana, the main dining room; and at the Halemoana Terrace, where a luncheon buffet is served daily 12:30-2 p.m. (reservations recommended for dinner). At Hale Ookipa "House of Hospitality," a luau is held on Friday nights, and a steak-fry every Wednesday. The restaurants are open to non-hotel guests; a buffet lunch costs $24 pp..

A public tour is offered weekdays from 11 a.m. that includes a 15-acre petroglyph field on the property that you can inspect if you make prior arrangements. You will be instructed to meet a tour guide at the main gate at about 10:50 a.m. The hotel manager is Fred Dewar, who's been at the facility since 1966, along with most of his highly professional and seasoned personnel. They take pride in the hotel and do everything to help you have a rewarding, enjoyable, and relaxing stay at this premier resort. The Kona Village is a Hawaiian classic that deserves its well-earned reputation for excellence.

Royal Waikoloan Hotel
The Sheraton chain wanted to enter the luxury hotel market with a splash, so in 1981 they opened the $70-million, 545-room Sheraton Royal Waikoloan Hotel. They found the perfect spot at Anaehoomalu Bay (between mile markers 77 and 78), and produced a class act. The hotel lobby is a spacious open-air affair, beautifully appointed in koa and objets d'art. All rooms are tastefully decorated and provide a/c, color TV, king-sized beds, and private lanai. Rates range $100-155 s/d for a standard, $250 for a cabana, and $550 for a suite; $20 additional person. For reservations, write: Royal Waikoloan, HCO2 Box 5300, Waikoloa, HI 96743, tel. 885-6789, Mainland tel. (800) 462-

6262. On the superbly kept grounds are six tennis courts, numerous ponds, and a swimming pool. Special features include a small shopping arcade with a dozen or so choice shops, horseback riding, and free shuttle service throughout Waikoloa. The focal points, however, are two marvelous golf courses designed by Robert Trent Jones, Jr. He learned his trade from his dad, whose masterpiece is just up the road at the Mauna Kea Resort.

You have a choice of dining facilities. The **Garden Cafe** features American cuisine, open daily for breakfast, lunch, and dinner. The atmosphere is relaxed and the prices are affordable for such a hotel. **The Tiare** offers elegant dining in elegant surroundings for elegant prices. The continental cuisine includes shrimp nouvelle, rack of lamb, lobster, and roast duckling served to the melodious notes of an accomplished harpist. Open Wed.-Sun. 6:30-10 p.m., tel. 885-6789, reservations recommended. The **Royal Terrace** opens its doors to the sea for breakfast and provides island entertainment with dinner nightly 6:30-10:30 p.m. Featured are nightly theme buffets which can be anything from seafood to Chinese. Expensive.

The Shores at Waikoloa

The Shores at Waikoloa are secluded luxury condominiums nestled away in the planned community of Waikoloa at HCO2, Box 5460, Waikoloa, HI 96743, tel. 885-5001; for reservations phone Aston Hotel and Resorts, tel. (800) 922-

7866 Mainland, (800) 445-6633 Canada, (800) 321-2558 Hawaii. To get there, turn off Route 19 into well-marked Waikoloa at mile marker 76, and proceed straight ahead past the King's Shops, a small shopping area. Keep going for a few minutes and you will come to a sign that says "Condominiums," and another marker that points you to "The Shores at Waikoloa." Enter through a security gate to see the peaceful and beautifully manicured grounds of the low-rise condominium. A few minutes away are the best beaches on Hawaii and all of the activities offered by the large luxury hotels, if you wish to participate. The condominium offers an "activities desk" where you can arrange a snorkeling or sailing excursion or hire a babysitter. A swimming pool and Jacuzzi are open untill 10 p.m., and two complimentary tennis courts (and a few rackets too) are available. The condos are decorated by the individual owners so each room is unique, but there are guidelines and standards so that every unit is tastefully and comfortably decorated, mostly in an island motif. All units are extremely spacious, with many boasting marble and terra-cotta floors, huge bathrooms with double tubs, showers, and sinks, full modern kitchens, and light and airy sitting rooms complete with state-of-the-art entertainment centers. Rates range $165 for a one-bedroom to $295 for a two-bedroom golf villa. Low season brings a 25% reduction, and The Shores offers an unbeatable low-season "golf package" of $145 per night and one round of free golf (usually $95) at

hale *at Kona Village Resort*

J.D. BISIGNANI

either of Waikoloa's two superb courses: the Beach Course, designed by Robert Trent Jones, Jr., and the King's Course, designed by Tom Wieskopf and Jay Morrish. If you are after a luxury vacation within a vacation where you can get away from it all after you've gotten away from it all, The Shores at Waikoloa is a superb choice.

The Ritz-Carlton Mauna Lani

In a tortured field of coal-black lava made more dramatic by free-form pockets of jade-green lawn rises the ivory-white Ritz-Carlton Mauna Lani, at One N. Kaniku Dr., Kohala Coast, HI 96743, tel. 885-2000 or (800) 845-9905. A rolling drive lined with *haku lei* of flowering shrubs entwined with stately palms leads to the open-air porte cochere. Enter to find koa and marble reflecting the diffused and soothing light of the interior. Straight ahead, off the thrust-proscenium Sunset Terrace, a living blue-on-blue still-life of sea and sky is perfectly framed. Nature, powerful yet soothing, surrounds the hotel. Stroll the grounds where gentle breezes always blow, and where the ever-present surf is the back beat of a melody created by trickling rivulets and falling waters as they meander past a magnificent pool and trimmed tropical gardens of ferns and flowers.

The hallways and lobbies, opening from the central area like the delicate ribs of a geisha's fan, are all delightfully elegant with comfortable parlor settings of wonderful soft couches attended by stout tables and portly credenzas. Overhead hang magnificent cut-crystal chandeliers of differing designs. The floors, fringed by marble and covered with luxurious Persian carpets, lead past museum-quality displays of porcelains, sculptures, antiques of all descriptions, and the fine needlework of Hawaiian quilts. On the walls hang 18th- and 19th-century oil paintings—many of tall-masted ships that sail the imagination into Hawaii's proud seafaring past—and in the main hallway just past the concierge desk is a model, executed in the most minute detail, of a three-masted ship under full sail. Koa-paneled elevators have their own chandeliers and Persian rugs, and every set of stairs has a velvety smooth koa banister carved with the pineapple motif, the Hawaiian symbol of hospitality.

Located in two, six-story wings off the main reception hall, the 541 hotel rooms, each with its own private lanai and sensational view, are a

lush interior of the Ritz-Carlton Mauna Lani

mixture of kings, doubles, and suites. Done in neutral tones, the stylish and refined rooms feature handcrafted quilts, twice-daily room attendance, turn-down service complete with a complimentary orchid and Ghirardelli chocolates, remote-control color TV, 24-hour room service, fully stocked honor bar, and in-room safe. Wardrobes, hung with plush terry robes and plump satin hangers, feature automatic lights, along with steam irons and small ironing boards. The spacious marble bathrooms, with wide, deep tubs, separate commodes, and shower stalls are appointed with dressing and vanity mirrors, double sinks, hair dryers, and name-brand grooming products. Rates begin at $285 for a garden view to $455 for a deluxe ocean-front room (low-season rates available). The Ritz Carlton Club, an exclusive floor with its own concierge, offers extra amenities—$495 will get you a room as well as continental breakfast, light lunch, cocktails, cordials, and a full spread of evening hors d'oeuvres. Suites range from an executive one-bedroom to the magnificent Ritz-Carlton Suite and cost $625-2800.

The hotel offers first-rate guest services, amenities, and activities that include a small shopping mall with everything from sundries to designer boutiques, complimentary shuttle to and from Waikoloa's famous championship golf courses, bag storage, 11 tennis courts (with seven lit for evening play), complimentary use of fitness center and snorkel equipment, an enormous swimming pool and sun deck, bicycles for short tours, safe-deposit boxes, on-property car rental, a comfortable amphitheater showing first-run movies, and babysitting. **Ritz Kids** is a special instructional day-camp program for children ages 4-12. Reasonably priced and offered half or full days, Ritz Kids includes lunch and matinee movies, and lets kids engage in a variety of fascinating activities such as making shell jewelry, stringing *lei*, exploring petroglyphs, painting, and playing Hawaiian games and water sports.

Dining at the Ritz can be everything from poolside casual (burgers and fries) to haute cuisine (fine delectables from around the world.) The executive chef, Amy Ferguson-Ota, a native Texan, and her talented staff create sumptuous dishes, combining island ingredients like guava, passion fruit, thimbleberries, and papaya with wild boar, fresh *ahi,* and free-range chicken. The result is a unique cuisine *"mai ka aina a me ke kai,"* "from land and sea." **The Dining Room,** where you will be comfortable in tasteful resortwear, is open Tues.-Sat. 6:30-9:30 p.m., with mellow Hawaiian music from 7 p.m. It is Chef Ferguson-Ota's signature restaurant. The cosmopolitan room, with coved ceiling, gorgeous chandelier, and massive floral centerpiece, is relaxed and comfortable. Tables covered with snow-white linen bear the familiar Ritz cobalt-blue-trimmed plates and crystal. Appetizers range from chicken consommé with angel-hair pasta and enoki mushrooms $12 to Maine lobster in an herbed vinaigrette $22. Entrees from $34 include sautéed Black Angus beef in a three-peppercorn sauce, and roasted squab breast.

At **The Grill,** open for dinner 6:30-9:30 p.m., cocktails and dancing until closing, the dishes are beef and seafood Hawaiian style. Whet your palate with fresh Pacific oysters, sashimi, or carpaccio $12-16, and move on to breadfruit vichyssoise or island seafood chowder for about $7. Salads range from a traditional Caesar to Maui onions and Waimea tomatoes for about

$7. Entrees include a wonderful selection of fresh island fish that are grilled, roasted, or poached in banana curry, saffron herb sauce, or black bean and Kau lime butter. Beef dishes include tenderloin, veal medallions, or Kahua prime rib for under $35. Specialties are rack of lamb; Hawaiian Fisherman's stew (wonderful!); and lobster, scallops, and prawns in a Riesling herb sauce. Fresh pasta topped with grilled shrimp, or linguine with smoked chicken, go for around $22.

The Cafe is open daily for breakfast and dinner. Sunday brunch, 10 a.m.-2 p.m., costs $24.50 adults, $12.50 children ages 5-12. The Cafe is a casual restaurant featuring Pacific Rim and American standard fare, and including both a children's and a you-can-run-but-you-can't-hide fitness menu. Prices for standard complete breakfasts are $14-20; the fitness breakfast $11; and a Japanese breakfast of grilled fish, miso soup, steamed rice, and pickles $18. Meal selections include pasta, California-style pizza, lamb chops, and Thai green chicken curry with eggplant. Those annoyingly-thin-why-don't-you-stay-home-anyway fitness fanatics can graze on spicy peppered shrimp salad, followed by chilled carrot soup. The Cafe features Hawaiian music nightly, and *hula* nightly except Sunday.

The poolside **Ocean Bar and Grill,** open daily for lunch, is the hotel's most casual restaurant, where you dine alfresco in a garden setting. Offerings range from healthful salads to jumbo hot dogs with fries. House specialties are Kahua beef chili and rice, and charbroiled chicken breast. The Ocean Bar and Grill also serves fresh pasta, scrumptious desserts, and pizzas with eclectic toppings like Peking duck, smoked chicken, and Puna goat cheese. And at your feet a perfect crescent white-sand beach opens to the great Pacific.

Mauna Lani Bay Hotel

As soon as you turn off Route 19, the entrance road, trimmed in purple bougainvillea, sets the mood for this $70-million, 350-room hotel that opened in 1983. The per-unit cost of $200,000 was the most ever spent in Hawaii up to that time, and it shows in the oversized rooms emphasizing relaxation and luxury, the majority with an ocean view. The hotel has a tennis garden with 10 courts, a lovely beach and lagoon area, a health spa, exclusive shops, and swimming pools. Enter through a great portico, whose blue tile floor, a mimic of the ever-present sea and sky, immediately begins creating a sense of sedate but beautiful grandeur. Below is a central courtyard, where full-sized palms sway amidst a lava-rock water garden; cascading sheets of clear waters splash through a series of *koi* ponds, making naturally soothing music. A short stroll leads you through a virtual botanical garden to a white-sand beach perfect for island relaxation.

Surrounding the hotel is the marvelous **Francis I'i Brown Golf Course,** whose artistically laid out fairways, greens, and sand traps make it a modern landscape sculpture. The course is carved from lava, with striking ocean views in every direction. It's not a tough course, though it measures 6,813 yards, par 72. Greens fees are expensive, with preferred starting times given to hotel guests. (Call the Pro Shop at 882-7255 for more information.)

The Mauna Lani's rooms begin at $275 garden view to $425 oceanfront, with suites from $725 and royal bungalows for $2500-3000 (includes a personal chef, valet, live-in maid, and swimming pool). The hotel also offers ocean villas starting at $350 for one bedroom to $550 for three bedrooms, weekly and monthly rates available and three-night minimum required. For full information, contact: Mauna Lani Bay Hotel, One Mauna Lani Dr., Kohala Coast, HI 96743, tel. 885-6622 or (800) 367-2323, in Hawaii tel. (800) 992-7987.

Le Soleil, the hotel's award-winning signature restaurant, offers imaginative Mediterranean cuisine, dinner only, 6:30-9:30 p.m. (jackets for men required). Starters can be *ahi* carpaccio or a half lobster roasted with enoki and shiitake mushrooms. Entrees starting at $30 are superb and can be anything from steamed *opakapaka* in a fennel saffron broth to grilled lamb chops in a zesty anchovy garlic puree. But the finest culinary delight is the ever-changing "Chef's Tasting Menu," a five-course extravaganza for $65 that offers delectables like Thai spiced clam soup, grilled scallops on a bed of greens flavored with a sweet-and-sour ginger vinaigrette, fillet of beef with a crab-and-wild-mushroom polenta cake, and a specially prepared dessert.

The **Bay Terrace,** open daily for breakfast, lunch, and dinner, offers the most casual but still superb dining. Daily offerings include everything from full-course breakfasts to dinner entrees like rack of lamb. Weekend nights feature a fabulous seafood buffet that shouldn't be missed, and the Sunday brunch served 11:30 a.m.-2 p.m. is legendary.

The **Canoe House,** open daily for dinner, delights with Pacific Rim cuisine. Not as formal as Le Soleil, this oceanfront restaurant features special *pu pu* like roast Chinese duck with avocado salsa, nori-wrapped tempura *ahi* with soy-mustard sauce and tomato-ginger relish, and a variety of soups and salads like corn chowder made with red Thai curry and coconut milk, and a house salad of organically grown greens. Main dishes tantalize: baked Hawaiian swordfish in a Thai-curry crab crust on a crispy potato pillow with fennel chive vinaigrette, Bangkok-grilled half-of-chicken on a Korean-style salad, and pan-roasted lamb chop with macadamia nut-coconut-honey crust and star anise sauce.

The **Ocean Grill,** where you'll be comfortable in bathing suit and cover-up, serves lunches and cocktails, while **Knickers,** located at the golf clubhouse and known for its sunsets, open daily 6:30 a.m.-9:30 p.m., is a full-service restaurant serving everything from ham-and-eggs to pasta with shrimp and capers. **The Gallery,** on the grounds at the Racquet Club, is an award-winning dinner restaurant and probably the least expensive fine-dining restaurant at the resort. Here, you can dine on medallions of pork tenderloin or wild-mushroom tortellini for under $20.

Hilton Waikoloa Village

At the Hilton Waikoloa Village (formerly Hyatt Regency Waikoloa), 69-425 Waikoloa Beach Dr., Kamuela, HI 96743, tel. 885-1234 or (800) 445-8667, the idea was to create a reality so beautiful and naturally harmonious that anyone who came here, sinner and saint alike, would be guaranteed a glimpse of paradise.

The architecture, "fantasy grand," is subdued and understated, not gaudy. The three main towers, each enclosing a miniature fern-filled botanical garden, are spread over the grounds almost a mile apart and are linked by pink flagstone walkways, canals navigated by hotel launches, and a quiet, space-age tram. Everywhere sculptures, art treasures, and brilliant flowers soothe the eyes. Songs of rare tropical birds and the wind whispering through a bamboo forest create the natural melody that surrounds you. You can swim in a private lagoon accompanied by dolphins, dine in magnificent restaurants, explore surrounding ranchlands, or just let your cares slip away as you lounge in perfect tranquility.

From Keahole (Kona) airport, travel north on Route 19 for about 15 minutes. Look for mile marker 76, and turn beachside toward Waikoloa. Follow the roadway through the lava fields until you arrive at the hotel. Valets will park your car.

Inside, attention to the smallest detail is immediately apparent. Elevators are done in rich woods and burnished brass. An alcove may hold a dozen superbly hand-carved puppets from Indonesia. Halls are bedecked with chandeliers, marble-topped tables, and immense floral displays. Even cigarette receptacles are artworks: large Asian pots or ceramic dolphins with mouths agape, filled with black sand.

A museum promenade displays a Hawaiiana collection of carved koa bowls and feather *lei,* along with carvings from Thailand, paintings from Japan, and porcelains from China. Fantastic pots, taller than a person, are topped with two handles of gold elephant faces and tusks. Look through archways at perfectly framed grottoes harboring *koi* ponds and waterfalls. Sit on royal thrones and benches next to intricately carved credenzas and tables and simply delight at the beauty.

Rooms are luxurious, and pampering is complete. In the evening a silver plate arrives. On it are three truffles rolled in nuts and a small conch shell made of white chocolate. Two mini-bottles hold macadamia and coffee liqueurs. Turn-down service brings more chocolate, flowers, and a Hawaiian legend card. Fluffy robes and Japanese *yukata* (lounging robes) are provided in every room.

The hotel's restaurants are culinary extravaganzas, and every taste is provided for. **Waters Edge** is formal, serving continental cuisine; **Donatello's** features classic Italian; **Cascades** is a Polynesian buffet; **Imari** serves traditional Japanese fare; **Kona Provision Co.** specializes in steak and seafood, and the hotel's bars, lounges, and casual poolside dining options are surprisingly moderately priced.

The beach fronting the property offers excellent snorkeling, while three gigantic pools and a series of lagoons are perfect for water activities and sunbathing.

Take the amazing "Behind the House" tour of the facility (free). You are led below ground, deep into the heart of the hotel, where you get to see how everything works. An underground service roadway, complete with stop signs and traffic cops, runs for over a mile and is traveled by employees on bicycles and motorized utility carts. As you pass offices with signs that read *Wildlife Director, Curator of Art, Astronomer,* you come to realize how distinctive an undertaking the hotel is. Next come the florist shop,

the dolphin pool at the Hilton

J.D. BISIGNANI

J.D. BISIGNANI

*Artwork surrounds you at the
Hilton Waikoloa Village.*

the butcher, the baker, the laundry (with more output than any other laundry in the state of Hawaii—22 pounds of linen go in each room) and wardrobe, responsible for outfitting the hotel's 2,000 employees. You're given staggering figures: 750,000 gallons of fresh water is needed for the pools; over 18 million gallons of seawater is pumped through the canals daily; each motor launch costs $300,000; the 41 chandeliers weigh over 24 tons; the hotel's 300 computers are linked by over 28 miles of cable. On and on, the statistics match the magnificence of what you see.

With all this splendor, still, the most talked-about activity at the hotel is **Dolphin Quest.** A specially constructed saltwater pond, 65 times larger than federal regulations require, is home to Atlantic bottlenose dolphins from Florida's Gulf Coast where they're found in bays and lagoons living most of their lives in water 16-20 feet deep. Here, their pond is 22 feet deep in the center, 350 feet long, and contains 2.5 million gallons of naturally filtered seawater.

Daily, on a lottery basis, guests are chosen to "interact with the dolphins." Dolphin Quest is trying to steer the program away from the concept of "swimming with dolphins," and more toward an educational experience. The program was founded by two highly respected marine veterinarians, Drs. Jay Sweeney and Rae Stone, both prominent in their field for their efforts to protect and preserve marine mammal populations. It was their idea to bring a new experience to the public in which the interaction was from the dolphin's point of view. Instead of a typical stadium-type setting where the dolphins are performers and the people are spectators, they created something more natural so the dolphins would enjoy the experience as much as the people.

Here you don't ride the dolphins and they don't do tricks for you. In the half-hour session, typically 10 minutes are spent in the free pool, where people wade in chest-deep water with the dolphins gliding by. If the dolphins want to be petted they stop, if not they move past like a torpedo. The rest of the time you spend on the dock, where you are given information concerning not only dolphins, but all marinelife and human interdependence with it. The experience is voluntary on the dolphins' part—*they* choose to swim with *you* as a guest in their domain.

Much of the proceeds from the program goes toward marine research. Recently, a team from the University of California at Santa Cruz was housed, funded, and provided with boats to investigate a way to save the more than 100,000 spinner dolphins that are caught in tuna nets every year.

This futuristic and fantastic hotel complex, a relative newcomer to the scene, has set a new standard against which all future resorts will be measured. Of course, as you would expect, all this luxury comes at a price; rates are $250-350 standard, $390-415 deluxe, $575-3000 suites. But experience and time will surely mature the Hilton Waikoloa Village into one of the finest resorts on earth.

The Mauna Kea Beach Resort
Note: As this book went to press, it was announced that this hotel will be closed for renovation from July 1994 through December 1995. The resort's beach, tennis courts, and golf course

the Mauna Kea Beach Resort, an enclave of class and elegance along the Kohala coast

will remain open during that time.

This hotel has set the standard of excellence along Kohala's coast ever since former Hawaii Governor William Quinn interested Laurence Rockefeller in the lucrative possibilities of building a luxury hideaway for the rich and famous. Beautiful coastal land was leased from the Parker Ranch, and the resort opened in 1965. The Mauna Kea was the only one of its kind for a few years until the other luxury hotels were built along this coast.

The hotel's classic, trendsetting **golf course** designed by the master, Robert Trent Jones, has been voted among America's 100 greatest courses and as Hawaii's finest. Also, *Tennis Magazine* includes the hotel among the "50 greatest U.S. tennis resorts." The hotel itself is an eight-story terraced complex of simple, clean-cut design. The grounds and lobbies showcase over 1,000 museum-quality art pieces from throughout the Pacific, and over a half-million plants add greenery and beauty to the surroundings. The landings and lobbies, open and large enough to hold full-grown palm trees, also display beautiful tapestries, bird cages with their singing captives, and huge copper pots on polished brick floors. The Mauna Kea offers a modified American plan (breakfast and dinner), the best beach on the island, and its own dive boat for seagoing adventure. Million-dollar condos also grace the grounds. Guests tend to come back year after year. The beautifully appointed rooms, starting at $260 d (European Plan, no

meals), $25 extra person, are free of TVs, but feature an extra-large lanai and specially made wicker furniture. For full information contact Mauna Kea Beach Resort, One Mauna Kea Beach Dr., Kohala Coast, HI 96743, tel. 882-7222 or (800) 882-6060.

Sumptuous dining is presented by Chef Jean-Marc Heim in the **Batik Room**, dinner nightly 7-10 p.m., where the Sri Lankan-inspired decor adds a touch of Eastern mystery and romance. Intricate *batik* tapestries, brass liner plates, and regal *houdah* (elephant thrones) set the mood for the exotic menu. Begin your feast with Italian-inspired ravioli stuffed with abalone and wild mushrooms $13.25, or with island *ahi* tartar cake $12.50. Soups ranging from a light beef consommé with truffles to lobster bisque armagnac cost $4.50-6.75. Entrees, magnificent creations from around the world starting at $26, include roasted duck in a papaya and coriander sauce; a variety of island fish grilled, steamed and sautéed; and zesty Thai curries made from beef, lamb, chicken, or shrimp. A titillating dessert is chocolate soufflé topped with macadamia nuts, champagne sauce, Grand Marnier, or fresh blueberries.

The Garden, another of the hotel's fine dining restaurants, open daily for dinner 6:30-9 p.m., and now under the skillful hand of Chef Bruce MacVicar, set the standards in the mid-1980s when it was one of the first restaurants to offer Hawaiian regional cuisine. The Garden starts you with appetizers like Trio of Island Sashimi, and Poke with lime rice cake for $12.75, or the famous "Firecracker," deep-fried salmon wrapped in *nori* and garnished with a hot-and-sour chili dip at $8.25. Soups and salads are rock lobster with won ton $6.25, Waimanu chowder made with smoked chicken and sweet Maui onions $5.50, Kamuela spinach with papaya seed dressing $6.50, and hearts of Waimea butter lettuce in a papaya, avocado, and lilikoi dressing $5.50. Entrees range from red prawns in coconut curry $32, to sugarcane-and kiawe-grilled free-range veal, and coffee-smoked rack of lamb. Also in keeping with the Hawaiian regional theme are grilled rare *ahi* steaks and breast of range chicken with Waipio taro pancakes. Desserts like the banana chocolate mousse Napoleon would have soothed even the most belligerent at Waterloo.

The Terrace, informal and alfresco, serves breakfast, lunch, and dinner. Breakfast is either à la carte—from a simple continental breakfast to a traditional American with eggs, potatoes, juice, and bacon—or a lavish buffet offering fresh fruits, cereals, French toast, Belgian waffles, the finest and most delectable breakfast meats, steaming pots of Kona coffee, pineapple crepes, and even *huevos rancheros*. Lunch can similarly be à la carte—Paniolo steak sandwiches or Cobb salad, for example—or a magnificent buffet of chilled seafood, sashimi, salmon, steaks, chops, lox, a cornucopia of island fruits and vegetables, and a dessert bar. Dinner offers starters like *fritto misto,* shrimp cocktail, or Mediterranean Caesar salad, all from $7. Sweet onion soup or brown bean soup with orzo are sure to please. Entrees are a variety of pasta dishes or grilled lamb chops, medallions of fresh *ono,* veal t-bone, or jumbo prawns for under $30.

For light fare and quick snacks try the hotel's beachside **Hau Tree Cafe,** serving lunch and cocktails 11:30 a.m.-3:30 p.m.; or **The 19th Hole,** adjoining the pro shop, where you can snack on everything from burgers to sushi daily 11 a.m.-4:30 p.m. The Mauna Kea is also famous for its Saturday-evening **clambake** at the Hau Tree Cafe, where you can feast on Maine lobster, garlic shrimp, and sumptuous steamed clams while the sun sets to the melodious strains of musician extraordinaire George Kahumoku and Friends. Tuesday is extra special, featuring the Mauna Kea's world-famous

Old Hawaiian Aha'aina Luau. As the sun sends blazing shafts of red and gold over the Luau Gardens at North Pointe, you dine on island favorites like *laulau, hulihuli* pork, Korean short ribs, island-grown steaks, and snow crab claws. The evening entertainment includes a torch lighting ceremony, traditional *hula* presented by *kumu hula* Nani Lim Yap, and the dramatic Samoan fire dance.

Puako Beach Apartments
Puako village has the only reasonably priced accommodations in this diamond-studded neck of the woods. The 38 modern units go for $50-$120 (four bedrooms), $5 extra person. All units have a kitchen, laundry facilities, lanai, and twice-weekly maid service. There is ample parking, TV, and a swimming pool. Write Puako Beach Apartments, 3 Puako Beach Dr., Kamuela, HI 96743, tel. 882-7711.

FOOD, SHOPPING, AND ENTERTAINMENT

The following is a list of the very limited food, shopping, and entertainment in South Kohala, independent of that offered at the luxury resorts, hotels, and condominiums. Please refer to "Resorts and Accommodations" above for coverage of these topics at the hotels.

King's Shops
The planned resort community of Waikoloa has its own small but adequate shopping center, The King's Shops, tel. 885-8811, open daily 9:30 a.m.-9:30 p.m., that features over 40 different shops and restaurants, along with entertainment (see below), special events, and a **tourist information center.** A number of the shops feature Hawaiian artifacts, with museum-quality exhibits displayed here and there, and even some petroglyphs that offer a link to the mythology of ancient Hawaii. Some of the shops include: **Benetton's** and **Crazy Shirts** for distinctive tops, shirts, and tees; **Zac's** for your photo needs; **Ocean Splash** for everything from masks and snorkels to boogie boards; **Tutu Nene** for women's fine clothing and art objects; **Liberty House** for department-store merchandise; **Whaler's General Store** for light groceries and sundries; **Waikoloa Hat Company** for lids of all

descriptions, but especially those made from natural fibers. **Noa Noa** has an excellent selection of imported fashions from throughout Southeast Asia, especially Indonesia. Fabrics range from rayon to silk; the batik prints were individually designed. Excellent prices. **Endangered Species** welcomes you with a python overhead. Most items, from T-shirts to sculptures, have an animal or floral motif. A portion of the proceeds from all sales goes to the World Wildlife Foundation. **Tiki Trading Post** is a terrific shop featuring mainly island-stylish men's clothing. Inside are jogging shorts, T-shirts, sweatshirts, aloha shirts, and even some shoes. Their motto, "Dress like you live here," says it all.

Restaurants at the King's Shops include: **Hama Yu Japanese Restaurant,** open daily 11:30 a.m.-2 p.m. and 5:30-9 p.m. Choose appetizers ($4.50-7) like soft-shell crab, *yakitori*, and a variety of sashimi and sushi. Dinners include tempura $24, Japanese steak $26, and *tonkatsu* $19. For a smaller and more moderately priced meal try **Hawaiian Chili by Max,** a window restaurant where you can have a variety of chilies and hot dogs, all well prepared and health conscious.

Kawaihae Center

The Kawaihae Shopping Center can take care of your rudimentary shopping needs. It sits at the Y-junction of routes 19 and 270 and is situated so that the upper floors face Route 19 and the lower floors are along Route 270. There's a **7-Eleven** convenience store, **Kohala Kollections** for artwork and antiques, the **Cactus Tree** for alohawear, and **Tropical Dreams** for homemade ice creams and sorbets. Restaurants are on both levels (see following). Across the road are a **76 gas station** and **Laau's Fish Market** (open Mon.-Sat. 6 a.m.-6 p.m.).

Kohala Divers

Located along Route 270 in Kawaihae, open daily 8 a.m.-5 p.m., tel. 882-7774, Kohala Divers offers scuba certification for $300, snorkel rentals for $10 (24 hours), and scuba rentals for $22. They lead two-tank dives for $75, and will take snorkelers along if they have room on the boat ($15). It's a bit far to go from Kailua-Kona, but they offer big savings, and they're the only dive company along the Kohala coast.

Blue Dolphin

In Kawaihae Village along Route 270 is a takeout-window restaurant, the Blue Dolphin, run by a husband-and-wife team, tel. 882-7771, open 10 a.m.-3 p.m. weekdays. Their limited menu features lemonade made from organically grown island lemons, and plate lunches like teriyaki beef $4.95, sautéed mahimahi $5.50, and a mixed plate for $4.95. If you're heading north and want to picnic along the way, the Blue Dolphin will fill the bill.

Cafe Pesto

Who'd expect a yuppie upscale restaurant in the sleepy village of Kawaihae? Cafe Pesto, tel. 882-1071, open Sun.-Thurs. 11 a.m.-9 p.m., Fri.-Sat. 11 a.m.-10 p.m., has a chic interior design with black-and-white checkerboard flooring and black-and-white tables. The bold gourmet menu tantalizes you with starters like *crostini* (French bread with a fresh, creamy herb garlic butter) $2.95 and freshly made soups from $3.25. Daily specials might be scallop-and-Brie bisque $6.95, wild green salad $3.50, blue Caesar salad $3.95, or Greek pasta salad $6.95. Pasta dishes are scrumptious: smoked-salmon pasta with spinach, capers, sun-dried tomatoes and fettucine in saffron cream sauce $12.95; or chipotle shrimp and hot Calibrese sausage, red onions, and sweet peppers over cilantro-tossed linguine $13.95. Lunch, served 11 a.m.-4 p.m., brings an assortment of hot sandwiches that includes everything from smoked ham to a chicken pita for under $8. Cafe Pesto also serves gourmet pizza with crust and sauces made fresh daily. Among their best pizzas are shiitake mushrooms and artichokes with rosemary and Gorgonzola sauce, seafood pesto pizza, and pizza luau, all ranging in price from $5.95 for a small to $16.95 for a large (also served by the slice for $2). Cafe Pesto is *the* perfect place to stop for a civilized lunch as you explore the Kohala coast.

Tres Hombres Beach Grill

Pancho Villa in aloha shirt and sombrero and riding a surfboard (!) would be instantly at home in Tres Hombres, tel. 882-1031, located in the Kawaihae Center, open 11:30 a.m.-midnight, dinners to 9 p.m. on weekdays, and to 10 p.m. weekends. Besides being a south-of-the-border restaurant, run by Popeye, an old-time waterman from Southern California, Tres Hombres is an unofficial surfing museum filled with a fine collection of surfboards and surfing memorabilia donated by such legendary greats as Dewey Weber, Greg Knoll, and Jack Wise. Some of the tables are fashioned from wooden surfboards made of balsa wood with mahogany striping, others from green-and-white Mexican tiles. Bar stools are of provincial Mexican design topped with leather. The bamboo-appointed interior has a relaxed tropical effect. The extensive menu, presented on a miniature surfboard, offers savories like nachos $7.95, quesadillas $6.95, and a selection of rolled tacos $6.95. Salads include Caesar $5.95, and chicken taco salad (easily a full meal) $10.95. For combination dinners you have your choice of Mexican favorites like enchiladas, chile rellenos, tostadas, and burritos, for $9.95. Full-dinner entrees can be roasted chicken $11.95; steak, shrimp, or chicken fajitas $14.95; or simple but delicious fish tacos $11.95. The full bar serves not only all the island favorites, but adds special concoctions like K-38s, Swamis, and Popeye's grog, with *pu pu* served 3-6 p.m. daily. Relax with an ice-cold margarita on the lanai of this tastefully casual restaurant, and experience an excellent change of pace from the luxury hotels just down the road.

Golf Cart Vendor

You can actually buy a well-made sandwich, hot dog with all the trimmings, and a variety of soft drinks and beer from the strategically placed and gaily canopied Golf Cart Vendor at the Mauna Lani Resort Golf Course. Follow Kaniku Dr. toward the Ritz-Carlton Hotel and look for the access road pointing to Holoholokai Beach Park. Follow it, and in about 100 yards just where the golf cart track crosses the road, look to the right for the cart. This makes a perfect stop if you're heading to the Puako Petroglyphs or to the beach park. The sandwiches, fairly hearty, are under $4, the hot dogs $2.50, and the beer, soda and snacks are priced amazingly right for this exclusive neck of the woods!

Entertainment

Free entertainment is offered at the **King's Shops** at Waikoloa every Thurs. 6-8 p.m., when local musicians come to perform contemporary Hawaiian music. The Royal Waikoloan Hotel offers *pu pu* and refreshments at the event for a nominal charge. The evening is popular with both tourists and local people, and is an excellent chance to have fun Hawaiian style.

BOB RACE

WAIMEA (KAMUELA)

Waimea is in the South Kohala District. But because of its inland topography of high mountain pasture, mostly covering Mauna Kea's western slopes, Waimea could be considered a district in its own right. It also has a unique culture inspired by the range-riding *paniolo* of the expansive **Parker Ranch**. This spread, founded early last century by John Palmer Parker, dominates the heart and soul of the region. Waimea revolves around ranch life and livestock. A herd of rodeos and "Wild West shows" are scheduled throughout the year. But a visit here isn't one-dimensional. In town are home accommodations and inspired country dining. For fun and relaxation there's a visitor and ranch center; Puuopelu, the Parker mansion and art collection; a wonderful museum operated by John Parker's great-great granddaughter and her husband; a litany of historic shrines and churches; and an abundance of fresh-air and wide-open spaces, the latter not so easily found in the islands.

The town is split almost directly down the center—the east side is the wet side, and the west is the dry side. Houses on the east side are easy to find and reasonable to rent; houses on the dry side are expensive and usually unavailable. You can literally walk from verdant green fields and tall trees to dry desert in a matter of minutes. This imaginary line also demarcates the local social order: upper-class ranch managers (dry), and working-class *paniolo* (wet). However, the air of Waimea, refreshed and cooled by fine mists *(kipuupuu)*, combines with only 20 inches of rainfall a year into the best mountain weather in Hawaii. Waimea is equally known as Kamuela, the Hawaiianized version of Samuel, after one of John Parker's grandsons. Kamuela is used as the post office address, so as not to confuse Waimea with a town of the same name on the island of Kauai. The village is experiencing a growth spurt. In 1980 it had no traffic lights and was home to about 2,000 people. Now the population has grown fivefold and there are traffic jams. Waimea is modernizing, and its cowboy backwoods character is rapidly changing.

Getting There

The main artery connecting Waimea and Kailua-Kona is Route 190, also known as the Hawaii Belt Road. This stretch is locally called the Mamalahoa Highway. From Kailua-Kona, head out on Palani Road until it turns into Route 190. As you gain elevation heading into the interior, look

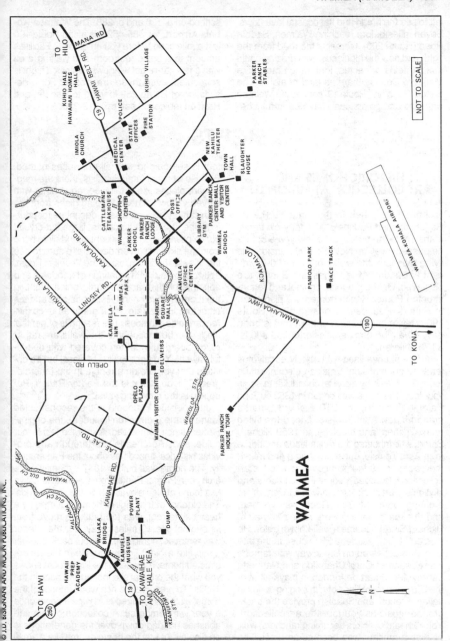

WAIMEA

NOT TO SCALE

© J.D. BISIGNANI AND MOON PUBLICATIONS, INC.

left to see the broad and flat coastal lava flows. Seven miles before reaching Waimea, Saddle Road (Route 200) intersects the road from the right, and now the highlands, with grazing cattle amidst fields of cactus, look much more like Marlboro Country than the land of aloha. The Saddle Road and Route 19, connecting Waimea with Hilo and points east, have been fully de-scribed on p. 180 and p. 288. The **Waimea-Ko-hala Airport,** tel. 885-4520, is along Route 190 just a mile or so before you enter town. Facilities amount to a basic restroom and waiting area with a few car-rental windows. Unless a flight is scheduled, even these are closed. For a de-scription of Route 250 leading to Kapaau and Hawi on the coast, see pp. 319-320.

SIGHTS

HISTORIC HOMES AND ART COLLECTION AT PUUOPELU

Richard Smart, heir to the fantastic Parker Ranch, opened Puuopelu, a century-old family mansion, to the public just a few years before he passed away on Nov. 12, 1992. Inside this living museum, the works of over 100 promi-nent artists, including Degas and Renoir, are displayed. On the grounds, original and recon-structed Parker Ranch homes are also open to visitors. Puuopelu is located along Route 190 a few minutes south of town and is open daily 10 a.m.-5 p.m., admission $7.50 adults, $3.75 children.

A formal drive lined with stately eucalyptus leads to the mansion. Enter an elegant sitting room illuminated by a crystal chandelier to begin your tour. The home was begun in 1852 by John Palmer Parker II. In 1910 Richard Smart's grandmother, Aunt Tootsie, added the living room, kitchen, and fireplace. In 1969 Richard Smart, who inherited the ranch lands and home from Aunt Tootsie, gutted the home and raised the ceiling to 19 feet to accommodate his art collection. He added elegant French doors and skylights. Part of the kitchen was converted into a dining room, the Gold Room was created, and the koa doorways were raised to match. Richard Smart became a well-known actor. He studied at the Pasadena Playhouse in the late '20s, and appeared on Broadway with famous names such as Carol Channing and Nannette Fabray. Mr. Smart performed in plays all over the U.S., and recordings of him singing songs in Italian, French, and Spanish provide the back-ground music as you tour the art collection. You've heard of actors becoming ranchers; well, he was a rancher who became an actor. The tour is self guided with all art pieces named. Besides works of famous artists, there are mag-nificent pieces like a tall wooden cabinet with carved yellow Chinese Peiping glass from the 19th century, silver tea sets, decanters for pour-ing wine at elegant functions, large cut-crystal punch bowls, and magnificent chandeliers hung from the skylights overhead. Make sure to see the little side bedroom, called the Venetian Room, aptly decorated with paintings of gondolas and appointed with treasures from Venice. Lighting the room are two chandeliers, one pink and the other turquoise. Here, the filigreed art-deco mir-rors are also fabulous. The feeling is of genteel elegance, but notice that the walls are rather rough board and battten covered with beauti-ful artwork. You get a feeling of class, but it's ob-vious that you are on a ranch. In the emerald-green kingdom that is the Parker Ranch, Pu-uopelu is the crowning jewel.

Just outside Puuopelu is the reconstructed **Mana Home** (admission included), the original Parker Ranch homestead. A knowledgeable tour guide, Judy Apo, leads you through and pro-vides historical anecdotes about the Parker fam-ily. The home was built in 1847 by family patri-arch John Palmer Parker from the durable native koa found at high elevations on the ranch lands. The exterior of the original home, covered by a heavy slate roof, was too brittle to move from its original site 12 miles away, but the interior was removed, numbered, and put back together again like a giant jigsaw puzzle in the recon-structed home. A model in the living room shows you what the original site looked like back in the 1800s. To preserve the rich wood interior of the home, all that's required is to wipe it down once a year with lemon oil. A collection of fine cal-abashes handed down over the generations is on display. At first the home seems like a small cabin, just what you'd expect from the 1850s, but in actuality it's a two-story home with one bedroom downstairs and three upstairs.

The Parker dynasty (see "Parker Ranch Visitor Center," following, for more information) began when John Palmer Parker jumped ship and married Kipikani, the granddaughter of Kamehameha. They bought two acres of land for $10, and Parker with his two sons built the Mana Home. In later years Kipikani, being the granddaughter of the king, received 640 acres. The two sons, John Palmer Parker II and Ebenezer, who were by then married, built two homes on it, and as children came, added more rooms in the sprawling New England tradition. They also built one large community kitchen, at which the entire family cooked and dined. A replica shows how the home grew over the years, and it is a good indicator of how the Parker fortunes grew along with it. As the children's children got older, they needed a schoolhouse, so they built one at the corner of the original site. It still stands and is maintained by a *paniolo* and his family who live there. Unfortunately, many members of the Parker family died young. The first-born, John Palmer Parker II, married Hanai. His brother, Ebenezer, married Kilea, a woman from Maui, who bore him four children. One of their boys was Samuel Parker, known in Hawaiian as Kamuela, the co-name of Waimea. Samuel married Napela, and together they had nine children. Samuel's father Ebenezer died at age 26 after swallowing the bone of a flubber (a little bird the size of a pigeon) that punctured his intestine. Kilea could never get over his death and visited his grave daily. Finally, she decided that she wanted to return to her family on Maui. She was advised by the people of the island not to go because of rough seas. Kilea did not heed the advice, and along with her entourage was lost at sea. Meanwhile, John Palmer Parker II and Hanai gave birth to only one boy who died within 12 months. Childless, they adopted one of their nephew Samuel's nine children as a *hanai* child in a practice that continues to this day. He was the fifth child, John, who became John Palmer Parker III and who later married Elizabeth Dowsick, known as Aunt Tootsie. They had one girl, Thelma Parker, before John III died of pneumonia at age 19. Aunt Tootsie raised Thelma as a single parent, and somehow managed to purchase Samuel Park-

a modern paniolo of Waimea

er's and his eight children's half of the ranch. Thelma Parker married Gillian Smart. They had one boy, Mr. Richard Smart, before his mother Thelma died at age 20 of tuberculosis. Aunt Tootsie literally took the bull by the horns to keep the ranch going, and when she passed away in 1943 she left everything to her grandson Richard. The ranch prospered under his ownership and spread to its present 225,000 acres with 50,000 head of cattle that supply fully one-third of the beef in the Hawaiian Islands.

SIGHTS IN TOWN

Hale Kea

On 11 emerald-green rolling acres, typical of *paniolo* country, sits **Hale Kea** ("White House"), tel. 885-6094, the restored residence of the top hand on the Parker Ranch. Located on Kawaihae Rd. before you enter Waimea from Kohala, Hale Kea is open daily at 10 a.m. Admission is free, and a shuttle van from the Kohala coast is available by reservation. On the premises are boutique shops, art galleries, and **Hartwell's Restaurant** (see "Food" and "Shopping" following). Built in 1897 for the Parker Ranch's first manager, A.W. Carter, the residence served the Carter family for a total of 60 years in this capacity; 35 years for A.W., and then another 25 years for his son, Hartwell Carter, who took over as manager.

You enter through a large, breeze-catching veranda, which leads into a formal parlor and sitting room. Here velveteen chairs, wicker furniture from 1899, and a baby grand piano bring genteel civility to the heart of a hard-working ranch. The veranda, sprinkled with dining tables and chairs, and most of the rooms in the main house serve as dining rooms for the restaurant. Feel free to wander around and look at the displays. One of the larger rooms is a formal private dining room with a striking blue carpet and a huge table that could comfortably seat more than a dozen diners. An intimate room called the "Library" was built by Laurence Rockefeller in 1969, and is appointed in rich koa and lined with a collection of rare tomes and sporting arms. Another informal room is the "Paniolo," with heavy, well-worn tables and chairs where you can almost smell the coffee brewing and bacon sizzling as the cowboys prepared to meet the day. Every room holds usable antiques, furniture, fixtures, and artifacts that are still very serviceable and in use.

Leave the main house and amble around out back, where modest outbuildings that once served as bunkhouses, stables, and storage sheds now house unique shops selling original artwork, designer clothing, and "souvenirs Hawaii." The grounds are made more lovely with rose, flower, and vegetable gardens, and with a gazebo perfect for a soothing contemplation of this striking upcountry land.

Parker Ranch Visitor Center And Museum

This is the first place to stop while in town. The visitor center, at the Parker Ranch Shopping Center, is open daily 9 a.m.-4 p.m., tel. 885-7655, adults $5, children $3.75 (joint admission to Puuopelu available). After spending an hour at the center's two museums and taking in the slide presentation, you'll have a good overview of the history of the Parker Ranch and, by extension, Waimea. Exhibits at the **John Palmer Parker Museum** depict the history and genealogy of the six generations of Parkers who have owned the ranch. At the entrance is a photo of the founder, John Parker, a seaman who left Newton, Massachusetts, on a trading vessel in 1809 and landed in Kealakekua, becoming a fast friend of Kamehameha the Great. Parker, then only 19, continued his voyages, returning in 1814 and marrying Kipikane, a chieftess and granddaughter of Kamehameha. In the interim, domesticated cattle, a present from Captain Vancouver to Kamehameha, had gone wild due to neglect and were becoming a dangerous nui-

Ranch life still dominates Waimea.

J.D. BISIGNANI

1. the Puna coast (J.D. Bisignani); 2. moody Pololu Valley (J.D. Bisignani)

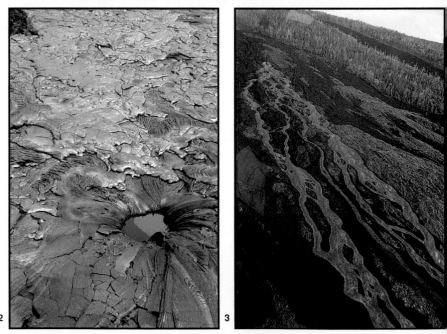

1. awesome volcanic power, 1989 eruption (U.S. Geological Survey, J.D. Griggs); **2.** lava pool (J.D. Bisignani); **3.** rivulets of lava make their way to the sea (J.D. Bisignani)

sance all over the Big Island. Parker was hired to round up the best of them and to exterminate the rest. While doing so, he chose the finest head for his own herd. In 1847 King Kamehameha III divided the land by what was known as the Great *Mahele,* and John Parker was granted Royal Deed No. 7, for a two-acre parcel on the northeast slopes of Mauna Kea. His wife, being royal born, was entitled to 640 acres, and with these lands and tough determination, the mighty 225,000-acre Parker Ranch began. It remains the largest privately owned ranch in the U.S., and on its fertile pastures over 50,000 cattle and 1,000 horses are raised.

In the museum, old family photos include one of Rev. Elias Bond, who presided over the Christian marriage of Parker and his Hawaiian wife in 1820. Preserved also are old Bibles, clothing from the era, and an entire koa hut once occupied by woodcutters and range riders. There are fine examples of quilting, stuffed animals, an arsenal of old weapons, and even a vintage printing press. A separate room is dedicated to **Duke Kahanamoku,** the great Hawaiian Olympian and "Father of Modern Surfing." Inside are paddles he used; his bed and dresser; legions of the medals, cups, and trophies he won; and even Duke's walking sticks. The 15-minute video in the comfortable **Thelma Parker Theater** begins whenever enough people have assembled after going through the museum. The video presents a thorough and professional rendition of the Parker Ranch history, along with sensitive glimpses of ranch life of the still very active *paniolo.*

Imiola Church

Head east on Route 19 to "church row," a cluster of New England-style structures on the left, a few minutes past the Parker Ranch Shopping Center. Most famous among them is Imiola ("Seeking Life") Church. It was built in 1857 by the Rev. Lorenzo Lyons, who mastered the Hawaiian language and translated some of the great old Christian hymns into Hawaiian, as well as melodic Hawaiian chants into English. The current minister is a friendly and urbane man, Rev. Bill Hawk, a new arrival who is assisted by his wife Sandra. The yellow clapboard church with white trim would be at home along any New England village green. When you enter, you'll notice an oddity: the pulpit is at the near

side and you walk around it to face the rear of the church. The walls and ceilings are of rich brown koa, but the pews, supposedly of the same lustrous wood, have been painted pink! The hymnals contain many of the songs translated by Father Lyons. Outside is a simple monument to Rev. Lyons, along with a number of his children's gravesites. A tour of the church is free, and definitely worth the time.

Kamuela Museum

The Kamuela Museum, largest privately owned museum in Hawaii, is a fantastic labor of love. For the octogenarian owners, founders, and curators, Albert and Harriet Solomon, it's a vocation that began in 1968 and fulfilled a prophecy of Albert's grandmother, who was pure Hawaiian and a renowned *kahuna* from Pololu Valley. When Albert was only eight years old, his grandmother foretold that he would build "a great longhouse near three mountains and that he would become famous, visited by people from all over the world." This prediction struck him so much that he wrote it down and kept it throughout his life. When grown, he married Harriet, the great-great granddaughter of John Palmer Parker, and the two lived in Honolulu for most of their adult lives, where Albert was a policeman. For 50 years the Solomons collected, collected, and collected! Harriet, being a Parker, was given heirlooms by family members which are also on exhibit. The museum is west of town center on Route 19—50 yards after the junction with Route 250 heading toward Hawi. The museum, dedicated to Mary Ann Parker, John Parker's only daughter, is open every day of the year 8 a.m.-5 p.m., tel. 885-4724, admission $5, children under 12, $2.

As you enter, the screen door bangs like a shot to signal Albert and Harriet that another visitor has arrived. Although the tour is self guided, Mrs. Solomon directs you through the museum, almost like a stern "schoolmarm" who knows what's best for you, but actually she's a sweetheart who has plenty of time for her guests and is willing to "talk story." Inside it's easy to become overwhelmed as you're confronted with everything from sombreros to a stuffed albatross, moose head, and South American lizard. An extensive weapons collection includes Khyber rifles, Japanese machine guns, swords, and knives. If you enjoy Hawaiiana, there's *kahili* and *konane* boards, poi pounders, stone sinkers and hooks, wooden surfboards, and a very unique "canoe buster." The museum has a few extremely rare stone idols and a good collection of furniture from the Hawaiian nobility, including Prince Kuhio's council table. Antiques of every description include Japanese and Hawaiian feathered fans, carved Chinese furniture, a brass diving helmet, some of the first Hawaiian Bibles, and even buffalo robes used by the pioneers. Everywhere are old photos commemorating the lives of the Parkers down through the years. Before you leave, go into the front room, where the view through a huge picture window perfectly frames a pond and three round-topped mountains in *paniolo* country.

PRACTICALITIES

ACCOMMODATIONS

As far as staying in Waimea is concerned, you won't be plagued with indecision. Of the two hotels in town, both are basic and clean, one inexpensive and the other upscale.

The **Kamuela Inn,** tel. 885-4243, Box 1994, Kamuela, HI 96743, a one-time basic cinder-block motel with 19 units, has been transformed into a bright and airy 31-unit boutique hotel. It is located down a small cul-de-sac off Route 19 just before Opelu Rd. Office hours are 7:15 a.m.-8 p.m., but a key and instructions will be left for late arrivals. The new owner, Carolyn Cascavilla, takes personal pride in the hotel, and offers each guest a complimentary continental breakfast. The small but pleasant grounds are appointed with flowers and manicured trees and you'll find a swing to lull you into relaxation. A new wing features the deluxe "Executive Suite" and a "Penthouse" where Governor John Waihee, among other dignitaries, has found peace and quiet. The new wing is comfortable and tasteful with hardwood floors, queen-sized beds, a full kitchen, and a small anteroom that opens onto a private lanai, perfect for a quiet morning breakfast. The Penthouse is upstairs, and breaks into two joinable units that can accommodate up to six guests. The basic motel rooms are small, neat, and tidy with twin beds with wicker headboards, private bathrooms, and color TV, but no a/c (not needed) or phones. Prices range from $54 s for a basic room to $165 for the deluxe suites.

The **Parker Ranch Lodge,** tel. 885-4100, Box 458, Kamuela, HI 96743, is located along Lindsey Rd. in "downtown" Waimea, but don't let "downtown" fool you because it's very quiet. The rooms, most with kitchenettes and vaulted ceilings, have full baths, and are well appointed with rich brown carpeting, large writing desks, easy chairs, phones, and TVs. The barn-red board-and-batten inn sits off by itself and lives up to being in *paniolo* country by giving the impression of a gentleman's bunkhouse. Rates are $74 standard, $85.15 for a kitchenette unit, $10 additional person.

FOOD

Inexpensive/Moderate
The Bread Depot, tel. 885-6354, in the Opelo Plaza along Route 19, open daily for breakfast 7-11 a.m., lunch 11:30 a.m.-4 p.m. (Sat. until 3 p.m.), and dinner Tues.-Sat. 5-9 p.m., is a pizza/sandwich shop and bakery *extraordinaire!* Deli sandwiches are the classics like pastrami, honey ham, and vegie bean served on a variety of fresh-baked breads for $4.95. Daily specials can be vegie lasagna $5.75, or a sliced turkey (real) sandwich on *paniolo* bread with roasted potatoes for $7.95. On the lighter side is an assortment of homemade soups and salads for around $4.50. The dinner menu is freshly baked honey-crust pizza and calzone, but what pizza and calzone! Some mouth-watering offerings are duck-sausage pizza with Madeira whole-grain mustard sauce, sun-dried tomatoes, spinach, and roasted garlic; or Thai chicken pizza with ginger-marinated chicken breast, green onions, and bean sprouts. Each costs under $10. The plump calzones can be stuffed vegetarian-style with brie, spinach, mushrooms, eggplant and red onions, or with chorizo sausage, peppers, tomato, cilantro, sour cream, and marinara sauce, both priced under $9. The Bread Depot offers budget-gourmet casual dining where the quality and preparation of the food is first rate.

One of the cheapest places in Waimea to get good standard American/Hawaiian food is the **Kamuela Drive-In Deli**. This no-nonsense eatery, frequented by local people, is next door to the Parker Ranch Shopping Center. They get the folks in these parts started at 5 a.m. with a hearty breakfast for under $5. Plate lunches of teriyaki beef and the like sell for $5-6. If you're into food and not atmosphere, this is the place.

Auntie Alice's, tel. 885-6880, open daily 6 a.m.-6 p.m., is a small restaurant/bakery in the Parker Ranch Shopping Center serving homemade pies and breakfast for under $5, with hefty sandwiches around $6.

Massayo's is another basic eatery open daily 5 a.m.-3 p.m., where you can get hearty breakfasts and plate lunches with an Asian twist for $4-5. It's in the Hayashi Building near the Kamuela Inn along Route 19 heading west out of town.

For mid-range fare try **Great Wall Chop Suey** at the Waimea Center along the Mamalahoa Hwy. (Route 19), tel. 885-7252, open daily except Wednesday 11 a.m.-8:30 p.m., lunch 11 a.m.-3 p.m. Its appealing selection of standard Chinese dishes includes a lunch special of one, two, or three choices for $3.95, $4.95, and $5.95, respectively. Dinner specials are an all-you-can-eat buffet at $6.95, and fresh *manapua* made daily. For entrees try a variety of beef, chicken, and pork dishes all around $5.50, or lobster with black bean sauce at $12.50, the most expensive item on the menu.

Also in the Waimea Center is **Young's Kalbi**, a Korean restaurant open daily except Monday, 10:30 a.m.-9 p.m., that serves dishes like *kalbi* chicken, shrimp tempura, oyster-sauce chicken, and spicy pork, all priced under $6.

Cattleman's Steakhouse, tel. 885-4077, next door to the Waimea Center along Route 19 heading east, is a terrific place to soak up the local scene and to enjoy basic but hearty food. At this recently renovated restaurant, the menu is steak and more steak, all from the Parker Ranch. Tuesday-Sat. 3-5:30 p.m. they have the *Pau Hana* Relaxer (happy hour). Also *karaoke* Tues. and Wed., Hawaiian music Thurs. by Smitty and Charlie, and everything from country to rock 'n' roll by groups like Ecstasy on the weekends. The bill of fare starts with scampi or sautéed mushrooms $6.95, and moves on to peppercorn steak, steak Diane, steak and scampi, or New York steak $17.95. Other entrees include Hawaiian chop steak $15.95, chicken oriental $15.95, seafood pasta $17.95, and baked manicotti $15.95. A limited children's menu helps keep prices down, with everything under $10. The soup-and-salad buffet is just $9.95. Cattleman's Steakhouse is not a *great* restaurant, but the service is friendly, and the scene couldn't be more authentic.

Paniolo Country Inn, tel. 885-4377, in town center, open daily for breakfast 7-11 a.m., lunch 11 a.m.-5 p.m., dinner 5-8:45 p.m., specializes in full breakfasts, flame-broiled steaks, burgers, and plate lunches. Breakfast selections include omelettes with one item $3.75, and the *wikiwiki* breakfast of English muffin, banana bread or wheat toast, coffee, and small fruit juice $3.25. Lunches can be the Rodeo Special (a bun heaped with pepperoni, salami, bell peppers, mushrooms, and onions and smothered with pizza sauce and melted cheese) $5.95, or the Paniolo Country (a sandwich made with layers of spiced ham, turkey breast, bacon, tomato, onion, melted cheese, mayonnaise, and sprouts) $6.50. Hamburgers range from $5.75 for a regular burger to $6.95 for the deluxe with the works. Soups and salads are $4.25, the paniolo taco salad $6.25, and the tostada grande salad $6.95. Plate lunches are standards like teriyaki short ribs $7.25, while a dinner plate could be top sirloin $12.50. The Paniolo Country Inn even has pizza, and a children's menu to keep prices down. The food is wholesome, the atmosphere American standard, and the service prompt and friendly.

Don's Pake Kitchen, about two miles east of town on Route 19, open daily 10 a.m.-9 p.m., has a good reputation for food at reasonable prices even though most of their selections are of the steam-table variety. Chef's specials are ginger beef, oyster chicken, and shrimp-sauce pork all priced under $6. Steamed rice sold by the pint is $1.20. Don's also specializes in large pans of food that can feed entire families. Next door is **The Vegetable Stop,** open Mon., Wed., Sat. 9 a.m.-5 p.m. Most of the best vegies and fruits, homegrown but not necessarily organic, are gone by noon.

Fine Dining

One of the best benefits of Waimea's coming of age is the number of excellent restaurants that have recently opened. The competition among gourmet-food establishments is stiff, so each one tries to find its culinary niche.

The Edelweiss on Route 19 across from the Kamuela Inn is Waimea's established gourmet restaurant, where chef Hans-Peter Hager, formerly of the super-exclusive Mauna Kea Beach Hotel, serves gourmet food in rustic but elegant surroundings. The Edelweiss is open Tues.-Sat. for lunch 11:30 a.m.-1:30 p.m. and for dinner 5-9:30 p.m., tel. 885-6800. Inside, heavy posts and beams exude that "country feeling," but fine crystal and pure white tablecloths let you know you're in for some superb dining. The wine cellar is quite extensive, with selections of domestic, French, Italian, and German wines. Affordable lunches include offerings like soup, turkey sandwiches, and chicken salad in papaya for under $8.50. Dinner starts with melon with prosciutto at $4.95, escargot for $5.75, onion soup at $4.25, and Caesar salad for $4.25. Some Edelweiss specialties are sautéed veal, lamb, beef, and bacon with pfefferling for $19.50; roast duck braised with a light orange sauce at $17.50; half spring chicken diablo at $15.50; and of course German favorites like Wiener schnitzel at $16.50, and roast pork and sauerkraut for $15.50. The cooking is rich and delicious; the proof a loyal clientele who return again and again.

Gentlemen ranchers and their ladies love **The Parker Ranch Broiler,** open daily for lunch 11 a.m.-2 p.m. in the dining room and 2-3 p.m. in the bar (limited menu), dinner 5-10 p.m., in the Parker Ranch Shopping Center, tel. 885-7366. Put on your best duds and sashay into the cushy green-velvet saloon, or into the tasteful koa-paneled main dining area. Local lunchtime favorites include Hawaiian chopped steak $7.95, teriyaki beef plate $8.75, and Hawaiian beef stew $8.95. For lighter fare try the Caesar salad, Parker Ranch chef salad, or fiesta taco salad, each for $7.95. Soups are reasonable at $3.75 per bowl—there is always Portuguese bean soup, and a soup du jour. Start dinner with appetizers like escargots $7.95, sautéed mushrooms $5.75, and Chinese chicken salad $8.95. Fulfilling the name of Parker Ranch Broiler, the chef chooses the best cuts of Parker Ranch beef to create a variety of savory meat dishes such as top sirloin $14.95, or a 12-ounce New York cut $19.95. Other entrees include Pulehu

chicken $14.95, shrimp scampi and seafood linguine, and even the fresh fish of the day at market price. Even if you don't dine here, it's worth a trip to the bar just for the atmosphere and to immerse yourself in one of the traditions of "*Paniolo* Country."

Merriman's, tel. 885-6822, open for Sunday brunch 10:30 a.m.-1:30 p.m., lunch weekdays 11:30 a.m.-1:30 p.m., dinner 5:30-9 p.m., in the Opelo Shopping Center along Route 19, has been receiving a great deal of praise from travelers and residents alike for its excellent food. The restaurant, like a small house from the outside, is stylish with pink and gray tablecloths, multicolored Fiestaware settings, and black- or pink-cushioned chairs of bent bamboo. Chef Peter Merriman creates classical European and American haute cuisine from local ingredients like Kohala lamb, Parker Ranch beef, Waimea lettuce, Puna goat cheese, and vine-ripened tomatoes. The menu changes every few months, but perennial appetizer favorites are corn and Kahuku shrimp fritters $6.75, vine-ripened Lokelani tomatoes with Maui onions $4.50, and spinach salad with balsamic vinaigrette dressing $4.50. Lunch fare is coconut grilled chicken with peanut dipping sauce and rice $5.75; grilled eggplant with Puna goat cheese, basil, and hot sauce $5.75; and grilled papaya salad with shrimp and peanuts for $8.50. Entrees are superb: Oahu chicken ginger-grilled with Indonesian peanut sauce $14.50; seafood sausage, chicken, fish, and shellfish in a saffron sauce at $21.50; and Thai-style shrimp curry for $21.50. Vegetarians can graze on linguine with tomato capers and snow peas $13.50, or on stir-fried vegetables with spicy curry for $12.50. Some of the most delicious offerings, however, are the fresh catch at market price, prepared in various gourmet styles including wrapped in *nori* and sautéed with *wasabi,* or herb-marinated and grilled with mango-lime sauce, banana, mango, and coconut relish. Merriman's is destined to become a Big Island classic. Enjoy!

Dine in turn-of-the-century elegance at **Hartwell's Restaurant,** located at **Hale Kea,** the one-time country estate of the Parker Ranch's manager (for complete details see pp. 310-311). The restaurant, tel. 885-6094, is open daily for lunch 11 a.m.-3:30 p.m., dinner 5-9:30 p.m., Sunday brunch 10 a.m.-3 p.m. A free shuttle bus is available by reservation from the Kohala Coast resorts. Choose your dining-room style, which can range from "downhome country" to "landed gentry," from any of the converted rooms of the New England-style rambling home. The lunch menu offers the chef's kettle, an edible bread bowl filled with a hearty stew or tangy chili for $6.95, oriental salad made from grilled marinated chicken breast tossed with fried wonton $9.95, or the restaurant's famous baby-back ribs basted in barbecue sauce and served with cornbread and coleslaw. Sunday brunch is a full choice from the breakfast menu for $11.95-14.95. Light suppers are presented 5-6:30 p.m. with entrees like herbed breast of chicken for $14.95 and veal scallopini $17.95. Full dinners start with appetizers like Chesapeake Bay crab cakes $6.95, grilled shrimp $7.95, and a variety of soups and salads from $4.95. For an entree choose Alaska king crab, New York sirloin, or island fresh lamb raised in Kau, all $20-25.

SHOPPING

Shops And Boutiques

Waimea's accelerated growth can be measured by the shopping centers springing up around town. One new center, still under construction across from the Parker Ranch Shopping Center, has some people concerned, as it will surround the Spencer House, a classical home from the ranch period. People were not thrilled when this area was denuded of its stately trees to accommodate the shopping center.

There is shopping in and around town, but the greatest concentration of shops is at the **Parker Ranch Shopping Center,** with over 30 specialty stores selling shoes, apparel, sporting goods, toys, and food. The **Parker Ranch Store** sells boots, cowboy hats, shirts, skirts, and buckles and bows. Many handcrafted items are made on the premises. Open daily, tel. 885-4977. **Setay,** a unique fine-jewelry shop, sells china, crystal, silver, and gold, tel. 885-4127. **Panda Imports,** tel. 885-8558, offers colorful handwoven cotton imports from Guatemala—everything from baby clothes to hammocks. Here too you'll find **Ben Franklin's,** for sundries; **Keep In Touch,** with books and stationery; and **Honolulu Sporting Goods,** to name just a few.

The **Waimea Center,** most stores open weekdays 9 a.m.-5 p.m. and Sat. 10 a.m.-5 p.m., well marked along the Mamalahoa Hwy. near McDonald's, is the town's newest shopping mall. Among its shops you will find a **KTA Superstore** with everything from groceries to pharmaceuticals; **Zac's Photo** for developing and all photo needs; **Kona Fashion Club** for women's apparel; the **Men's Shop,** whose name says it all; **Kamuela Kids** for children's clothing; **Postmart** for all mailing and packaging needs including fax service; **Rhythm and Reading** with tapes, CDs, records, videos, and gifts; **Capricorn Book Store** for a fine selection of reading materials ranging from magazines to best-sellers; and the **Competitive Edge Triathalon Center,** an excellent sporting goods store featuring bicycles, swimming gear, and Rollerblades. The Waimea Center also has some fast-food eateries like **TCBY Yogurt** and **Subway Sandwiches** for a fast sandwich. Two inexpensive restaurants are **Great Wall Chop Suey** and **Young's Kalbi,** a Korean restaurant (see "Food" above for a description).

Make sure to tour **Hale Kea,** the converted but preserved country estate of the Parker Ranch's manager (for complete details see pp. 309-311). The "White House," tel. 885-6094, and its distinctive boutique shops are open daily from 10 a.m. Admission is free, and complimentary shuttle from the Kohala Coast resorts is available by reservation. In the rambling home, appointed with period furniture and *paniolo* memorabilia, and in the attendant outbuildings, you will find: **Grande Gems and Galleries** offering fine jewelry and original artwork; **Noa Noa,** a shop with a reputation for designer clothes from Southeast Asia made of materials from rayon to silk at excellent prices; **Tutu Nene** for women's fashions; and the **Island Heritage Collection** for a distinctive gift by an island artisan.

Around town try: **Waimea Design Center** along Route 19, tel. 885-6171, offering Asian handicrafts and Hawaiian koa bowls and furniture; or **The Warehouse,** a small shopping complex whose specialty shops sell books, coffees, spices, flowers, and alohawear, tel. 885-7905.

The **Rosetta Stone,** on Route 19, about two miles out of town toward Hilo, tel. 885-7211, open Tues.-Sat. 10 a.m.-6 p.m., Sun. and Mon. noon-6 p.m., owned and operated by Suzanne Collins, vibrates with new-age books on metaphysics.

Shelves are stocked with minerals, jewelry, incense, music, and sacred artifacts from around the world. Shoppers will find elegant hairpieces, fantastic boas, baskets filled with stones from around the world, tarot cards, the *I-ching*, smudging sticks, and a few tie-dye dresses. Just walking in can help balance your aura, while the fair prices will help balance your budget!

Parker Square Shopping Mall, along Route 19 heading west from town center, has a collection of fine boutiques and shops. Here, the **Gallery of Great Things,** tel. 885-7706, open Mon.-Sat. 9 a.m.-5 p.m., really is loaded with great things. Inside you'll find novelty items like a carousel horse, silk dresses—pricey at $200— straw hats, koa paddles for $700, a Persian *kris* for $425, vintage kimonos, an antique water jar from the Chiang Mai area of northern Thailand for $925, Japanese woodblock prints, enormous bronze fish that once fit the entranceway of a palatial estate, and less expensive items like shell earrings for $8 and koa hair sticks for $4. The Gallery of Great Things, with its museum-quality items, is definitely worth a browse. Also in the mall, **Waimea Body Works** features swimsuits and outdoor gear for the active traveler. **Gifts in Mind** has novelty items and a very good selection of aloha shirts and dresses. **Mango Ranch** sells duds for cowpokes, including bow ties, fancy shirts, and cowboy hats. **Bentley's** specializes in ceramics and tableware. **Noa Noa** imports its fashions from Indonesia, offering beautiful batik creations mostly for women, but there are some items for men. Don't let the name **Waimea General Store** fool you. It mostly sells sundries with plenty of stationery, children's games, stuffed toys, and books on Hawaiiana.

Opelo Plaza, along Route 19 heading west from town center, is one of Waimea's newest shopping malls. It features **Gallery of the Pacific** as well as **The Bread Depot** and **Merriman's,** two of Waimea's best restaurants in their categories (see "Food" above).

Food Markets And Sundries
For **food shopping** at the Parker Ranch Shopping Center there's **Sure Save Supermarket; Kamuela Meat Market,** featuring fine cuts of Parker Ranch beef; and **Big Island Natural Foods,** selling snacks, sundries, lotions, potions, notions, and coffee.

The **Circle K** convenience store, with food items and gasoline, is located along Route 19 heading west out of town.

A **farmer's market** is held in Waimea every Sat. 7:30 a.m.-noon, when local farmers come to sell their produce, much of which is organic. Look for a dozen or so stalls in the parking lot of the Hawaiian Homelands Building located along Route 19 about two miles east of town center heading toward Honokaa. In one of the first stalls is Marie McDonald, a Hawaiian woman (don't let the name fool you) who is an expert at fashioning of *haku lei,* a beautiful and intricate form of *lei*-making with multiple strands of intertwined flowers and ferns. Ms. McDonald and her daughter, who often helps at the stand, will take time to "talk story" and to inform you about medicinal herbs and some of the unique produce found at the market.

SERVICES AND INFORMATION

Entertainment
There ain't much happening around the old town entertainment-wise, but **free** *hula lessons* are given at the Parker Ranch Visitor Center on Monday afternoons. Enjoy live music and dancing nightly at **Cattleman's Steakhouse** (see above).

Emergency/Health
Police can be be reached at 885-7334, **ambulance and fire** at 961-6022.

Physicians are available at Lucy Henriques Medical Center, tel. 885-7921.

Chiropractic care is available from Dr. Bob Abdy at **Kohala Chiropractic,** tel. 885-6847, open Mon., Wed., Fri. 9 a.m.-noon, and 2-5 p.m.; Tues. and Thurs. 9 a.m.-1 p.m. Dr. Abdy's office is in a small shopping center across from the Edelweiss restaurant, west of town on Route 19. He has an excellent reputation. In the Ironwood Center, east of town on Route 19 (across from the Circle K) is **Hamakua Kohala Coast Massage,** tel. 885-5442, and the **Chiropractic Clinic** of Dr. Kenneth C. Williams, tel. 885-7719.

Angela Longo, Ph.D., tel. 885-7886, located in the Kamuela Office Center, is a practitioner of **acupuncture** and a Chinese herbalist. Angela, who graduated from U.C. Berkeley with a Ph.D. in biochemistry, combines principles from both East and West into a holistic approach to health and well-being. Besides attending to her demanding practice, Angela is a devoted single parent and a classical Indian dancer who performs at special functions around the island. She is one of the most amazing health practitioners in the entire state.

Dr. Richard Leibman is a **naturopathic physician,** in town at 885-4611.

Information/Services

The **post office** is located in the Parker Ranch Shopping Center. Mailing address for Waimea is Kamuela, so as not to confuse it with the Waimeas on Oahu and Kauai.

The **Waimea visitor center** is west of town along Route 19, almost directly across from the Opelo Shopping Center. They hand out free maps and brochures of the area and provide public restrooms.

The **Chock Inn Launderette** is west on Route 19, tel. 885-4655.

BOB RACE

NORTH KOHALA

Jungle trees with crocheted shawls of hanging vines stand in shadowed silence as tiny stores and humble homes abandoned by time melt slowly back into the muted North Kohala earth. This secluded region changes very little, and very slowly. It also has an eastward list toward the wetter side of the island, so if you're suffering from "Kona shock" and want to see flowers, palms, banana trees, and Hawaiian jungle, head for the north coast. Here the island of Hawaii lives up to its reputation of being not only big, but bold and beautiful as well.

North Kohala was the home of Kamehameha the Great. From this fiefdom he launched his conquest of all the islands. The shores and lands of North Kohala are rife with historical significance, and with beach parks where no one but a few local people ever go. Here cattle were introduced to the islands in the 1790s by Captain Vancouver, an early explorer and friend of Kamehameha. Among North Kohala's cultural treasures are **Lapakahi State Historical Park,** a must-stop offering "touchable" exhibits that allow you to become actively involved in Hawaii's traditional past; and **Puukohola Heiau,** one of the last great traditional temples built in Hawaii. Northward is **Kamehameha's birth-**

place—the very spot. And within walking distance is **Mookini Heiau,** one of the oldest in Hawaii and still actively ministered by the current generation of a long line of *kahuna.*

Hawi is a sugar town whose economy recently turned sour when the sugar company drastically cut back its local operations. Hawi is making a comeback, along with this entire northern shore, which has seen an influx of small, boutique-like businesses and art shops. In **Kapaau,** a statue of Kamehameha I peering over the chief's ancestral dominions fulfills an old *kahuna* prophecy. On a nearby side road stands historic **Kalahikiola Church,** established in 1855 by Rev. Elias Bond. On the same side road is the old **Bond Homestead,** the most authentic yet virtually unvisited missionary home in all of Hawaii. Financially strapped, but lovingly tended by the remaining members of the Bond family, it's on the National Historical Record, and even rents *the* cheapest rooms on all of the Big Island. The main coastal road ends at **Pololu Valley Lookout,** where you can overlook one of the premier taro-growing valleys of old Hawaii. A walk down the steep *pali* into this valley is a walk into timelessness, with civilization disappearing like an ebbing tide.

NORTH KOHALA

© J.D. BISIGNANI AND MOON PUBLICATIONS, INC.

Getting There

In Kawaihae, at the base of the North Kohala peninsula, Route 19 turns east and coastal Route 270, known as the Akoni Pule Highway, heads north along the coast. It passes through both of North Kohala's two major towns, Hawi and Kapaau, and ends at the *pali* overlooking Pololu Valley. All the historical sites, beach parks, and towns in the following sections are along this route, listed from south to north.

Route 250, the back road to Hawi, is a delightful country lane that winds through gloriously green grazing lands for almost 20 miles along the leeward side of the Kohala Mountains. It begins in the western outskirts of

Waimea and ends in Hawi on the far north coast. One of the most picturesque roads on the island, it's dotted with mood-setting cactus and small "line shacks." Suddenly vistas open to your left, and far below are expansive panoramas of rolling hills tumbling to the sea. At mile marker 8 is **Von Holt Memorial Park,** a scenic overlook perfect for a high mountain picnic. Past here at mile marker 13 is **Ironwood Outfitters,** a horse ranch and riding stable owned and operated by Judy Ellis. Trail rides with Ms. Ellis through this upland *paniolo* country are among the best that you can find on the island (see p. 91). Around mile marker 19, keep your eyes peeled for a herd of llamas on the left. At the coast, Route 250 splits. Right takes you to Ka-paau, and left to Hawi. If you're coming along the coastal Route 270 from Kapaau toward Hawi, look for K. Naito's store, and make a left there to go back over Route 250 to Waimea; you don't have to go all the way to Hawi to catch Route 250.

Upolu Airport, tel. 889-9958, is a lonely strip at Upolu Point, the closest spot to Maui. A sign points the way at mile marker 20 along coastal Route 270. Here, you'll find only a bench and a public telephone. The strip is serviced only on request by the small propeller planes of charter and commuter airlines.

SIGHTS, BEACHES, AND TOWNS

KAWAIHAE COAST

Lapakahi State Historical Park

This 600-year-old reconstructed Hawaiian fish-ing village, combined with adjacent **Koai'e Cove Marine Conservation District,** is a standout hunk of coastline 12 miles north of Kawaihae. Gates are open daily 8 a.m.-4 p.m., when park guides are in attendance. Some-times, especially on weekends, they take the day off; and it's okay to park outside the gate and take the self-guided tour, although the guides' knowlegeable anecdotes make the tour much more educational.

The small grass shack near some *lau hala* trees at the entrance stocks annotated brochures and yellow water jugs. As you walk counter-clockwise around the numbered stations, you pass canoe sheds and a fish shrine dedicated to Ku'ula, to whom the fishermen always dedicated a portion of their catch. A salt-making area demon-strates how the Hawaiians evaporated seawater by moving it into progressively smaller "pans" carved in the rock. There are numerous home-sites along the wood-chip trail. Particularly in-teresting to children are exhibits of games like *konane* (Hawaiian checkers) and *ulimika* (a form of bowling using stones) that the children are encouraged to try. Throughout the area, all trees, flowers, and shrubs are identified, and as an extra treat, migrating whales come close to shore Dec.-April. Don't leave without finding a shady spot and taking the time to look out to sea. For information write Lapakahi State Park, Box 100, Kapaau, HI 96755, tel. 889-5566.

Mahukona And Kapaa Beach Parks

Mahukona Beach County Park is a few min-utes north of Lapakahi down a well-marked side road. As you approach, notice a number of abandoned buildings and warehouses; Mahu-kona was once an important port from which the Kohala Sugar Co. shipped its goods. Still there is a pier with a hoist used by local fisher-men to launch their boats. The harbor is filled with industrial debris which makes for some good underwater exploring, and snorkeling the offshore reef is rewarded with an abundance of sealife. Swimming off the pier is also good, but all water activities are dangerous during winter months and high surf. Picnic facilities in-clude a large pavilion and tables; a large green tank holds drinking water. There are also cold-water showers and restrooms, and electricity is available in the pavilion. Although numerous signs close to the pavilion say No Camping, both tent and trailer camping are allowed with a county permit near the parking lot.

Kapaa Beach County Park is five minutes farther north. Turn *makai* on a side road and cross a cattle grate as you head toward the sea. This park is even less visited than Mahukona. The rocky beach makes water entry difficult. It's primarily for day use and fishing, but there are showers, a restroom, and a pavilion. Camp-ing is allowed with a county permit. Neither of these two beaches is spectacular, but they are secluded and accessible. If you're interested in a very quiet spot to contemplate a lovely panora-ma of Maui in the distance, this is it.

Mookini Heiau And
Kamehameha's Birthplace

At mile marker 20 turn down a one-lane road to Upolu Airport. Follow it until it reaches the dead end at the runway. Turn left here on a *very* rough dirt road to Mookini Heiau. This entire area is one of the most rugged and isolated on the Big Island, with wide, windswept fields; steep sea-cliffs; and pounding surf. Pull off at any likely spot along the road and keep your eyes peeled

J.D. BISIGNANI

konane *board*

for signs of cavorting humpback whales that frequent this coast yearly Nov.-May. After bumping down the road for about two miles look for a tall transmission tower pointing its bony metal finger skyward that marks the road to the *heiau*. Sometimes the road is closed with a locked gate and you'll have to walk five minutes uphill to gain access, but if the gate is open, you can drive in.

Only *ali'i* came to the *heiau* to purify themselves and worship, sometimes offering human sacrifices. In 1963, Mookini Heiau was the first Hawaiian site to be listed in the National Historical Sites Registry. Legend says that the very first temple at Mookini was built as early as A.D. 480. This incredible date implies that Mookini must have been built immediately upon the arrival of the first Polynesian explorers, who many scholars maintain arrived in large numbers a full two centuries later. More believable oral history relates that the still-standing foundation of the temple was built by the Tahitian high priest Paao, who came with conquering warriors from the south in the 12th century, bringing the powerful mana of the fierce war-god Kukailimoku. The oral tale relates that the stones for the temple were fitted in a single night, passed hand to hand by a human chain of 18,000 warriors for a distance of 14 miles from Pololu Valley. They created an irregular rectangle measuring 125 by 250 feet, with 30-foot-high and 15-foot-thick walls all around.

When you visit the *heiau,* pick up a brochure from a box at the entrance (often empty); if none

is available, a signboard nearby gives general information. Notice that the leeward stones are covered in lichens, giving them a greenish cast and testifying to the age of the *heiau*. Notice a huge, flat stone near another embedded in the ground with the menacing atmosphere of a sacrificial altar. Nearby is a clone of the famous "Phallic Rock" on Molokai. Please be respectful as you walk around, as this temple is still in use, and stay on the designated paths that are cordoned off by woven rope. To the rear is an altar area where recent offerings are often seen; the floor of the temple is carpeted with well-placed stones and tiny green plants that give a natural mosaic effect. For at least eight and perhaps 15 centuries, members of the Mookini family have been the priests and priestesses of the temple. Today, the inherited title of *kahuna nui* rests with Leimomi Mookini Lum, a nearby resident. The entire *heiau* is surrounded by a wavelike hump, perhaps the remnant of an earlier structure, that resembles a castle moat. Be sure to visit the nearby "little grass shack," one of the best examples of this traditional Hawaiian architecture in the islands. Check how sturdy the walls are, and what excellent protection is provided by the grass-shingled roof. Also, be aware of the integration of its stone platform and how perfectly suited the shack is to provide comfort against the elements in Hawaii. Look through the door at a timeless panorama of the sea and surf.

A minute from the *heiau* along the dirt road, an HVB Warrior points to Kamehameha's birthplace, **Kamehameha Akahi Aina Hanau.** The entrance to the area is at the back side, away from the sea. Inside the low stone wall, that always seems to radiate heat, are some large boulders believed to be the actual "birthing stones" where the high chieftess Kekuiapoiwa, wife of the warrior *ali'i* Keoua, gave birth to Kamehameha sometime around 1752. This male child, born as his father prepared a battle fleet to invade Maui, would grow to be the greatest of the Hawaiian chiefs—a brave, powerful, but lonely man, like the flat plateau upon which he drew his first breath. The temple's ritual drums and haunting chants dedicated to Ku were the infant's first lullabies. He would grow to accept Ku as his god, and together they would subjugate all of Hawaii. In this expansive North Kohala area, Kamehameha was confronted with unencumbered vistas and sweeping views of neighboring islands, unlike most Hawaiians, whose outlooks were held in check by the narrow, confining, but secure walls of steep-sided valleys. Only this man with this background could rise to become "The Lonely One," high chief of a unified kingdom.

HAWI, KAPAAU, AND VICINITY

Hawi
As you come into Hawi along Route 270, you'll see a line of false-front buildings leaning shoulder-to-shoulder like patient old men knowing that something *will* happen. One of the buildings is an ancient movie theater that still shows films. Introducing you to the town are Sacred Heart Church and Hawi Jodo Buddhist Mission, two lovely temples of worship and symbols of Hawaii's diversified spirituality. In the middle of town, Route 250, crossing the Kohala Mountains from Waimea, intersects the main road.

Hawi was once a bustling sugar town that boasted four movie theaters in its heyday. In the early 1970s, the Kohala Sugar Co. pulled up stakes, leaving the one-industry town high and dry. Still standing is the monumental stack of the sugarworks, a dormant reminder of what once was. The people of Hawi have always had grit, and instead of moving away they're hanging in and doing a good job of revitalizing their town. Spirit, elbow grease, and paint are their chief allies. Toughing it out is a handful of local shops selling food and household goods, an information center, a hotel (the only functional one in North Kohala), a restaurant or two, a pizza parlor, and some remarkable crafts shops and boutiques (see below).

Kapaau
Kapaau is a sleepy community, the last town for any amenities on Route 270 before you reach the end of the line at Pololu Overlook. There's a gas station, grocery store, library, bank, and police station. Most young people have moved away seeking economic opportunity, but the old folks remain, and macadamia

Mookini Heiau

nuts are bringing some vitality back into the area. Here too, but on a smaller scale than in Hawi, local artists and some new folks are starting shops and businesses catering to tourists. The main attraction in town is **Kamehameha's Statue,** in front of the Kapaau Courthouse. The statue was commissioned by King Kalakaua in 1878, at which time an old *kahuna* said that the statue would feel at home only in the lands of Kamehameha's birth. Thomas Gould, an American sculptor living in Italy, was hired to do the statue, and he used John Baker, a part Hawaiian and close friend of Kalakaua, as the model. Gould was paid $10,000 to produce the remarkable and heroic sculpture, which was sent to Paris to be bronzed. It was freighted to Hawaii, but the ship carrying the original statue sank just off Port Stanley in the Falkland Islands, and the nine-ton statue was thought lost forever. With the insurance money, Gould was recommissioned and he produced another statue that arrived in Honolulu in 1883, where it still stands in front of the Judiciary Building. Within a few weeks, however, a British ship arrived in Honolulu, carrying the original statue that had somehow been salvaged and unceremoniously dumped in a Port Stanley junkyard. The English captain bought it there and sold it to King Kalakaua for $850. There was only one place where the statue could be sent: to the then-thriving town of Kapaau in the heart of Kamehameha's ancestral homelands. Every year, on the night before Kamehameha Day, the statue is freshly painted with a new coat of house paint; the bronze underneath remains as strong as the great king's will.

Kamehameha County Park, down a marked side road, has a full recreation area, including an Olympic pool open to the public, basketball courts, and weight rooms in the main building along with outside tennis courts with night lighting and a driving range. There is a kiddie area, restrooms, and picnic tables, all free.

Kalahikiola Church

A few minutes east of town an HVB Warrior points to a county lane leading to Kalahikiola Congregational Church. The road is delightfully lined with palm trees, pines, and macadamias like the formal driveway that it once was. Pass the weathering buildings of the **Bond Estate** and follow the road to the church on the hill.

original Kamehameha statue

J.D. BISIGNANI

This church was built by Rev. Elias Bond and his wife Ellen, who arrived at Kohala in 1841 and dedicated the church in 1855. Rev. Bond and his parishioners were determined to overcome many formidable obstacles in building Kalahikiola ("Life from the Sun") Church, so that they could "sit in a dry and decent house in Jehovah's presence." They hauled timber for miles, quarried and carried stone from distant gulches, raised lime from the sea floor, and brought sand by the jarful all the way from Kawaiahae to mix their mortar. After two years of backbreaking work and $8,000, the church finally stood in God's praise, 85 feet long by 45 wide. The attached bell tower, oddly out of place, looks like a shoe box standing on end topped by four mean-looking spikes. Note that the doors don't swing, but slide—some visitors leave because they think it's locked. Inside, the church is dark and cool, and inexplicably the same type of spikes as on the bell tower flank both sides of the altar. There is also a remarkable koa table. Pamphlets (25 cents) describe the history of the church.

The Bond Estate

The *most* remarkable and undisturbed missionary estate still extant in Hawaii is the old Bond Homestead and its attendant buildings including the now defunct but renovated Kohala Girls School. The estate is kept up by 10 surviving cousins of the Bond family, who have recently formed the nonprofit Iole Mission Homestead Foundation. Chaired by Mrs. Noreen Alexander of Honolulu, the Foundation is dedicated to preserving the home and opening it and the surrounding grounds to public tours in the very near future. It's already on the National Historical Register. However, age and the loss of that caring touch of a family actually living in the home have taken their toll. The Foundation is refurbishing the home and strengthening the basic structure so that this venerable old house can take the extra stress created by the traffic of future visitors. Until the renovations are completed, the Bond Estate is closed to the public; please remember this. Mr. Walter Fruitiger, a North Kohala resident and board member of the Foundation, has graciously dedicated his time to answering questions concerning the future visitation of the Bond Estate. If you have any questions or interest in future developments, please contact Mr. Fruitiger at 889-5267. Note, however, that you can rent a room in the refurbished Kohala Girls school for the cheapest rates in Hawaii (see p. 326).

When you enter the grounds, the clock turns back 100 years. The first buildings were completed in 1841 by Rev. Isaac Bliss, who preceded Elias and Ellen Bond. The main buildings, connected in New England farm fashion, have steep-pitched roofs designed to keep off the "back east" snows. They worked equally well here to keep rainwater out, as they were originally covered with thatch. The original furniture and family possessions are placed as if the residents were out for the afternoon, although the family has not lived in the house since 1925, when it was occupied by Dr. Benjamin Bond. In the majority of missionary homes and museums in Hawaii, suitable period furniture had to be purchased or replicas made to fill the house, but here it is all original! The homey dining and writing room is dominated by a large table that can take six leaves because the Bonds never knew how many there would be for dinner—four, or 60 who might have landed by schooner in the middle of the afternoon. A full set of dishes waits undisturbed in the sideboard. A cozy little parlor has comfortable wicker rocking chairs and a settee under a photo of Elias Bond himself. The reverend built the settee and most of the furniture in the house. His furniture from New England arrived on a ship after he did, but because it was Sabbath, the reverend refused to have it unloaded. Unfortunately, the ship caught fire and all the Bonds personal possessions were lost. In the kitchen area a refrigerator dating from the '20s looks like a bank vault. It ran on electricity from a generator on the homestead that was frequently used by local plantation owners to recharge their batteries. Off in a side room, an old wooden bathtub is as sound as the day it was built. In Rev. Bond's bedroom is a crocheted "primer" dated 1817, made by his sister Eliza who died before he came to Hawaii; he brought it as a memento and it still hangs on the wall. Upstairs are two large rooms in disrepair, which contain a treasure trove of antiques. Notice too, the sturdy, barn-style architecture of pegs and beams.

The small wing attached to the main house, called "The Cottage," was built when Dr. Benjamin Bond was first married. The family ate together in the main house, using the cottage as a Victorian bedroom and sitting room that now abounds with photos and antiques. The attached bathroom was once a summerhouse that was dragged to the present location by a steam tractor, then plumbed. As you look around, you'll feel that everything is here except for the people.

Keokea Beach Park

Two miles past Kapaau toward Pololu you pass a small fruit stand and an access road heading *makai* to secluded Keokea Beach County Park. The park, on the side of the hill going down to the sea, is very picturesque and luxuriant. It is a favorite spot of North Kohala residents, especially on weekends, but receives little use during the week. The rocky shoreline faces the open ocean, so swimming is not advised except during summer calm. There are a pavilion, restrooms, showers, and picnic tables. A county permit is required for tent and trailer camping.

Pololu Valley

POLOLU VALLEY AND BEYOND

Finally you come to Pololu Valley Overlook. Off to the right is a small home belonging to Bill Sproat, a man of mixed Hawaiian ancestry and a longtime resident of Pololu. Bill, whose vim and vigor belie his 81 years, was a mule skinner throughout the area for 50 years. He is a treasure house of knowledge and homespun wisdom, and still speaks fluent Hawaiian. His mother was a Hawaiian who became a schoolteacher down in Pololu, and his dad was an adventurer who came to Hawaii in the 1890s. Bill's grandmother was a *kahuna* who lived in the valley and never converted to Christianity. Most of the folks feared her dark powers, but not Bill who, although a strong Christian, learned much about Hawaii and its ways from his grandmother. If Bill is in his yard, perhaps tending a mule, make sure to stop and talk with him.

It's about 12 miles from Pololu to Waipio Valley, with five U-shaped valleys in between, including Honokea and Waimanu, two of the largest. From the lookout it takes about 15 minutes to walk down to the floor of Pololu. The trail is well maintained as you pass through a heavy growth of *lau hala,* but it can be slippery when wet. At the bottom is a gate that keeps grazing animals in; make sure to close it after you! **Kohala Ditch,** a monument to labor-intensive engineering, is to the rear of these valleys. It carried precious water to the sugar plantations. Pololu and the other valleys were once inhabited and were among the richest wet taro plantations of old Hawaii. Today, abandoned and neglected, they have been taken over by introduced vegetation. The black-sand beach fronting Pololu is lined with sand dunes, with a small sandbar offshore. The rip current here can be very dangerous, so enter the water only in summer months. The rip fortunately weakens not too far from shore; if you're caught, go with it and ride the waves back in. Many people hike into Pololu for seclusion and back-to-nature camping. Make sure to boil the stream water before drinking. Plenty of wild fruits can augment your food supply, and the shoreline fishing is excellent. The trails leading eastward to the other valleys are in disrepair and should not be attempted unless you are *totally* prepared, and better yet, accompanied by someone who knows the terrain.

PRACTICALITIES

ACCOMMODATIONS

You won't spend a lot of time wondering where you'll be staying in North Kohala. If you don't intend to camp, you can count your lodging options on one hand, without even using your thumb.

The **Kohala Village Inn and Restaurant** (formerly the Kohala Lodge) at 55-514 Hawi Rd., tel. 889-0419, changed hands recently. Newly renovated, it has a quiet little courtyard, restaurant, and TVs in some rooms. The 18 rooms are a reasonable $45-55 s, a large double room that sleeps five goes for $72. Weekly rates are available.

Hawaiian Plantation House (Aha Hui Hale), Box 10, Hawi, HI 96719, tel. 889-5523, was once a plantation manager's house. The white clapboard structure sits on four lush acres, letting its two-bedroom suites for $65 d, $10 extra person, communal kitchen.

The manager of the Iole Development Corp., tel. 889-5217 or 889-6989, rents modest rooms in the old **Kohala Girls School** section of the Bond Estate (p. 324). These buildings are very old, but the conveniences and amenities have been upgraded. Basically, you'll have to take care of yourself as no housekeeping services are provided. The manager *prefers* renting these rooms to school and civic organizations, but he will rent to travelers if they are the right sort, which translates as clean, quiet, and respectful! Rates are $275 per month, with shared bath and kitchen. Daily rates available upon request.

Wo On Gallery and Guest House, tel. 889-5002, owned and operated by Leslie Patten, Box 1065, Kapaau, HI 96755, is a rustic lodging in Halawa. Leslie has opened a gallery dedicated to local artists in the historic Wo On ("Harmony and Peace") General Store that served the Chinese community during plantation days. To the rear of the gallery is an attached, fully furnished, one-room apartment, complete with kitchen. The unit, which can sleep four, rents for $50 daily, $250 weekly, and $800 monthly.

Breakfast is rarely provided due to Leslie's hectic schedule, which includes minding twin daughters, but a steaming pot of Gevalia coffee is always offered. Next door is lovely and historically significant Tong Wo Cemetery and Temple, well worth a visit.

RESTAURANTS

The **Kohala Village Inn and Restaurant** (formerly Honey's Country Kitchen) at 55-514 Hawi Rd., tel. 889-0105, serves local style/continental food. It's open for breakfast and lunch Tues.-Fri. 6:30 a.m.-2 p.m., Sat. 7 a.m.-2 p.m., Sun. 8 a.m.-1 p.m., and for dinner Fri.-Sat. 5-9 p.m.

Ohana Pizza & Beer Garden, tel. 889-5888, also in downtown Hawi, features very good pizza for $5.50-10.75 depending upon size and toppings. This clean, friendly restaurant also offers hefty sandwiches for $2.95, and pasta dinners (like homemade lasagna) served with dinner salad and homemade garlic bread for $6. Salads are $1.50, and homemade garlic bread $1. You can order wine or a chilled domestic beer for $1.75, or an import for $2.50. The staff of local people is friendly and hospitable. A great place to pick up a picnic lunch.

Mits Drive-In, tel. 889-6474, is a small roadside restaurant in Kapaau where you can pick up a fast hamburger, hot dog, soft drink, or snack. Inexpensive.

Don's Family Deli, tel. 889-5822, open daily for breakfast and lunch until 6 p.m., across the street from the Kamehameha Statue in Kapaau, is a taste of New York in North Kohala. How can a visit to tropical paradise be complete without bagels and lox, lasagna, or a thick slice of quiche? Don's features Dreyer's ice cream, coffee and cappuccino, and homemade biscotti filled with nuts and that zesty anisette flavor. Don Rich, a longtime Kohala resident, will also fix you up with a tofu or mahimahi burger, and offers a wide selection of meats and breads if you prefer to make your own picnic lunch.

Tropical Dreams Gourmet Shop, in bustling downtown Kapaau, open daily 10 a.m.-5 p.m., Sun. 1-5 p.m., serves freshly made ice cream (macadamia is great), and fresh fruit sorbet in season.

SHOPPING

For food shopping try: **Union Market,** tel. 889-6450, along Route 270 coming into Kapaau, which sells not only general merchandise and meats, but also a hefty assortment of grains, nuts, fruits, and locally made pastries and breads. **H. Naito** is a general grocery, dry goods, and fishing supplies store in Kapaau, tel. 889-6851. Also in Kapaau, **Kohala Spirits,** open Mon.-Sat. 10 a.m.-10 p.m., stocks a fairly wide range of liquor, beer, and wine. **K. Takata** is a well-stocked grocery store in Hawi, tel. 889-5261. **Kohala Health Food,** in downtown Hawi, tel. 889-0277, is open daily except Sunday 10:30 a.m.-6:30 p.m.; its shelves are filled with herbs, vitamins, minerals, and local organic produce when available.

For a special treat try **Tropical Dreams,** a locally owned company in Kohala that handmakes gourmet macadamia nut butters. Some of their mouth-watering butters are flavored with Kona coffee, chocolate, or lehua honey. Contact Tropical Dreams for their full brochure at Box 557, Kapaau, HI 96755, tel. 889-5386, (800) 548-8050. Gift package assortments a specialty.

In Kapaau, across from the Kamehameha statue, is **Ackerman Gallery,** open daily 9 a.m.-5:30 p.m., tel. 889-5971, owned and operated by artist Gary Ackerman. Besides showcasing his own sensitive, island-inspired paintings, he displays local pottery, carvings, and one-of-a-kind jewelry. He also carries a smattering of artwork from throughout the Pacific. The artwork selections are tasteful, but expensive. You can also choose a reasonably priced gift item, especially from the handmade jewelry section. Make sure to check out the beautiful hand-blown glass display by a local artist named Yamazawa.

The distinctive, iridescent glaze is achieved by using volcanic cinders—you can bring home a true island memento that includes a bit of Madame Pele herself. Almost next door is **Kohala Sporting,** with a selection of boogie boards, T-shirts, and hunting licenses.

Gary has expanded and has opened another **Ackerman Gallery** also in Kapaau across from Tropical Dreams. This lovely gallery, housed in a turn-of-the-century building, showcases the fine art of local island artists like Greg Pontius, Kelly Dunn (magnificent bowls), and Gary Ackerman (inspired painting).

Hana Koa is a woodworking shop owned by artist Don Wilkinson, who learned the trade of making fine antique furniture replicas from his father. His excellent work, primarily in koa, focuses on the early-20th-century period. Don, a friendly storehouse of information, lives along Route 250 heading in from Waimea, tel. 889-6444.

Hale Wood, tel. 889-5075, in Hawi across from the launderette, open mostly by appointment, is owned and operated by husband-and-wife team Buck and Juli, woodworker and finisher, respectively. They work mostly in koa, fashioning hope chests, coat racks, and glass-tiled tables. A small gift shop offers some reasonably priced items like curly koa chop sticks for $5. Some of their pricier items bear tags for their "Friend to a Tree" program, that promises a purchase and planting of a koa tree in your name.

Another local artist is **David Gomes,** tel. 889-5100, a guitar and ukulele maker. He works in koa and other woods and does inlay in shell, abalone, and wood. His beautiful instruments take four to six months to complete. His small shop is located about a half mile on the Kapaau side of the junction of routes 270 and 250. Next door is a hobby and crafts store.

In Hawi, **Dawn's,** tel. 889-5112, open daily except Sunday 9 a.m.-5 p.m., sells sports clothes, T-shirts, and alohawear. The **Heritage Tree** is a specialty *hula* supply store in Kapaau across from the Kamehameha statue. If you're looking for a small variety of traditional arts and crafts, this shop is worth a stop.

SERVICES AND INFORMATION

The **Kohala Visitor Center** dispenses maps, information, and aloha. It's open daily and located just near the junction of routes 270 and 250 in Hawi. Next door is the local **laundromat,** a semi-open-aired affair that can be used

just about all the time. **Police** can be reached at 889-6225, emergency **fire** and **ambulance** at 961-6022.

The area **post office** is a new and large facility on Route 270 between Hawi and Kapaau just near the H. Naito Store.

The full-service **Kamehameha Pharmacy** is along Route 270 in downtown Kapaau.

BOOKLIST

INTRODUCTORY

Aloha, The Magazine of Hawaii and the Pacific. Honolulu, HI: Davick Publications. Subscription, P.O. Box 27810, San Diego, CA 92128. This excellent bimonthly magazine is much more than just slick and glossy photography. Special features may focus on sports, the arts, history, flora and fauna, or just pure island adventure. *Aloha* is equally useful as a "dream book" for those who wish that they could visit Hawaii, and as a current resource for those actually going. One of the best for an overall view of Hawaii, and well worth the subscription price.

Barrow, Terrence. *Incredible Hawaii.* Rutland, VT: Tuttle, 1974. Illustrated by Ray Lanternman. A pocket-sized compilation of oddities, little-known facts, trivia, and superlatives regarding the Hawaiian Islands. Fun, easy reading, and informative.

Cohen, David, and Rick Smolan. *A Day in the Life of Hawaii.* New York: Workman, 1984. On Dec. 2, 1983, 50 of the world's top photojournalists were invited to Hawaii to photograph a variety of normal-life incidents occurring on that day. The photos are excellently reproduced, and are accompanied by a minimum of text.

Day, A.G., and C. Stroven. *A Hawaiian Reader.* New York: Appleton, Century, Crofts, 1959. A poignant compilation of essays, diary entries, and fictitious writings that takes you from the death of Captain Cook through the "statehood services."

Emphasis International. *On the Hana Coast.* Honolulu: Emphasis International Ltd., 1983. Text by Ron Youngblood. Sketches of the people, land, legends, and history of Maui's northeast coast. Beautifully illustrated with line drawings, vintage photos, and modern color work. Expresses true feeling and insight into people and things Hawaiian by letting them talk for themselves. An excellent book capturing what's different and what's universal about the people of the Hana District.

Friends of the Earth. *Maui, The Last Hawaiian Place.* New York: Friends of the Earth, 1970. A pictorial capturing the spirit of Maui in 61 contemporary color plates along with a handful of historical illustrations. A highly informative as well as beautiful book printed in Italy.

Hawaii Magazine. 1400 Kapiolani Blvd., Suite B, Honolulu, HI 96814. Covers the Hawaiian Islands like a tropical breeze. Feature articles on all aspects of life in the islands with special departments on travel, happenings, exhibits, and restaurant reviews. Up-to-the-minute information, and a fine read.

Hopkins, Jerry. *The Hula.* Ed. Rebecca Crockett-Hopkins. Hong Kong: APA Productions, 1982. Page after page of this beautifully illustrated book sways with the dynamic vibrancy of ancient Hawaii's surviving artform. Hopkins leads you from dances performed and remembered only through legends to those of past and present masters captured in vintage and classic photos. For anyone interested in the history and spirit of Hawaii portrayed in its unique style of expressive motion.

Island Heritage Limited. *The Hawaiians.* Norfolk Island, Australia: Island Heritage Ltd., 1970. Text by Gavan Daws and Ed Sheehan. Primarily a "coffee table" picture book that lets the camera do the talking with limited yet informative text.

Judd, Gerritt P., comp. *A Hawaiian Anthology.* New York: MacMillan, 1967. A potpourri of observations from literati such as Twain and Stevenson who have visited the islands over the years. Also, excerpts from ordinary people's journals and missionary letters from early times down to a gleeful report of the day that Hawaii became a state.

Krauss, Bob. *Here's Hawaii.* New York: Coward, McCann Inc., 1960. Social commentary in a series of humorous anecdotes excerpted from this newspaperman's column from the late '60s. Dated, but in essence still useful because people and values obviously change very little.

Lueras, Leonard. *Surfing, The Ultimate Pleasure*. New York: Workman Publishing, 1984. An absolutely outstanding pictorial account of Hawaii's own sport—surfing. Vintage and contemporary photos are surrounded by well-researched and written text. Bound to become a classic.

McBride, L.R. *Practical Folk Medicine of Hawaii*. Hilo, HI: Petroglyph Press, 1975. An illustrated guide to Hawaii's medicinal plants as used by the *kahuna lapa'au* (medical healers). Includes a thorough section on ailments, diagnosis, and the proper folk remedy to employ. Illustrated by the author, a renowned botanical researcher and former ranger at Volcanoes National Park.

Michener, James A. *Hawaii*. New York: Random House, 1959. Michener's fictionalized historical novel has done more to inform *and* misinform readers about Hawaii than any other book ever written. A great tale with plenty of local color and information that should be read for pleasure and not considered fact.

Naturist Society Magazine. P.O. Box 132, Oshkosh, WI 54920. This excellent magazine not only uncovers bathing-suit-optional beaches throughout the islands, giving tips for naturists visiting Hawaii, but also reports on local politics, environment, and conservation measures from the health-conscious nudist point of view. A fine publication.

Piercy, LaRue. *Hawaii, This and That*. Hilo, HI: Petroglyph Press, 1981. Illustrated by Scot Ebanez. A 60-page book filled with one-sentence facts and oddities about all manner of things Hawaiian. Informative, amazing, and fun to read.

Rose, Roger G. *Hawaii: The Royal Isles*. Honolulu: Bishop Museum Press, 1980. Photographs, Seth Joel. A pictorial mixture of artifacts and luminaries from Hawaii's past. Includes a mixture of Hawaiian and Western art depicting island ways. Beautifully photographed with highly descriptive accompanying text.

Wilkerson, James A., M.D., ed. *Medicine for Mountaineering*. 3rd ed. Seattle: The Mountaineers, 1985. Don't let the title fool you. Although the book focuses on specific health problems that may be encountered while mountaineering, it is the best first-aid and general health guide available today. Written by doctors for the layperson to use until help arrives, it is jampacked with easily understandable techniques and procedures. For those intending extended treks, it is a must.

HISTORY/POLITICAL SCIENCE

Albertini, Jim, et al. *The Dark Side of Paradise, Hawaii in a Nuclear War*. Honolulu: cAtholic Action of Hawaii. Well-documented research outlining Hawaii's role and vulnerability in a nuclear world. This book presents the antinuclear and antimilitary side of the political issue in Hawaii.

Apple, Russell A. *Trails: From Steppingstones to Kerbstones*. Honolulu: Bishop Museum Press, 1965. "Special Publication #53" is a special-interest archaeological survey focusing on the trails, roadways, footpaths, and highways and how they were designed and maintained throughout the years. Many "royal highways" from pre-contact Hawaii are cited.

Ashdown, Inez MacPhee. *Old Lahaina*. Honolulu: Hawaiian Service Inc., 1976. A small, pamphlet-type book listing most of the historical attractions of Lahaina town, past and present. Ashdown is a life-long resident of Hawaii and gathered her information firsthand by listening to and recording stories of ethnic Hawaiians and old *kamaaina* families.

———. *Ke Alaloa o Maui*. Wailuku, HI: Kamaaina Historians Inc., 1971. A compilation of the history and legends of sites on the island of Maui. Ashdown was at one time a "lady in waiting" for Queen Liliuokalani and has since been proclaimed Maui's "Historian Emeritus."

Bell, Roger. *Last Among Equals: Hawaiian Statehood and American Politics*. Honolulu: University of Hawaii, 1984. Documents Hawaii's long and rocky road to statehood, tracing political partisanship, racism, and social change.

Cameron, Roderick. *The Golden Haze*. New York: World Publishing, 1964. An account of Capt. James Cook's voyages of discovery throughout the South Seas. Uses original diaries and journals for an "on the spot" reconstruction of this great seafaring adventure.

Daws, Gavan. *Shoal of Time, A History of the Hawaiian Islands*. Honolulu: University of Hawaii Press, 1968. A highly readable history of Hawaii dating from its "discovery" by the Western world down to its acceptance as the 50th state. Good insight into the psychological make-up of the influential characters who formed Hawaii's past.

Department of Geography, University of Hawaii. *Atlas of Hawaii*. 2nd ed. Honolulu: University of Hawaii Press, 1983. Much more than an atlas filled with reference maps, it also contains commentary on the environment, culture, and sociology of Hawaii, plus a gazetteer and statistical tables. Actually a mini-encyclopedia.

Feher, Joseph. *Hawaii: A Pictorial History*. Honolulu: Bishop Museum Press, 1969. Text by Edward Joesting and O.A. Bushnell. An oversized tome laden with annotated historical and contemporary photos, prints, and paintings. Seems like a big "school book," but extremely well done. If you are going to read one survey about Hawaii's historical, social, and cultural past, this is the one.

Fuchs, Lawrence. *Hawaii Pono*. New York: Harcourt, Brace and World, 1961. A detailed, scholarly work presenting an overview of Hawaii's history, based upon psychological and sociological interpretations. Encompasses most socio-ethnological groups, from native Hawaiians to modern entrepreneurs. A must for social historical background.

Handy, E.S., and Elizabeth Handy. *Native Planters in Old Hawaii*. Honolulu: Bishop Museum Press, 1972. A superbly written, easily understandable scholarly work on the intimate relationship of pre-contact Hawaiians and the *aina* (land). Much more than its title implies, the book should be read by anyone seriously interested in Polynesian Hawaii.

The Hawaii Book. Chicago: J.G. Ferguson, 1961. Insightful selections of short stories, essays, and historical and political commentaries by experts specializing in Hawaii. Good choice of photos and illustrations.

Hawaiian Children's Mission Society. *Missionary Album*. Honolulu: Mission Society, 1969. Firsthand accounts of the New England missionaries sent to Hawaii and instrumental in its conversion to Christianity. Downhome stories of daily life's ups and downs.

Heyerdahl, Thor. *American Indians in the Pacific*. London: Allen and Unwin Ltd., 1952. Theoretical and anthropological accounts of the influence on Polynesia of the Indians along the Pacific coast of North and South America. Fascinating reading, with unsubstantiated yet intriguing theories presented.

Ii, John Papa. *Fragments of Hawaiian History*. Honolulu: Bishop Museum, 1959. Hawaii's history under Kamehameha I as told by a Hawaiian who actually experienced it.

Joesting, Edward. *Hawaii: An Uncommon History*. New York: W.W. Norton Co., 1972. A truly uncommon history told in a series of vignettes relating to the lives and personalities of the first white men in Hawaii, Hawaiian nobility, sea captains, writers, and adventurers. Brings history to life. Absolutely excellent!

Lee, William S. *The Islands*. New York: Holt, Rinehart, 1966. A socio-historical set of stories concerning *malihini* (newcomers) and how they influenced and molded the Hawaii of today.

Liliuokalani. *Hawaii's Story By Hawaii's Queen*. Rutland, VT: Tuttle, 1964. A moving personal account of Hawaii's inevitable move from monarchy to U.S. Territory by its last queen, Liliuokalani. The facts can be found in other histories, but none provides the emotion or point of view as expressed by Hawaii's deposed monarch. A "must read" to get the whole picture.

Nickerson, Roy. *Lahaina, Royal Capital of Hawaii*. Honolulu: Hawaiian Service, 1978. The story of Lahaina from whaling days to present, spiced with ample photographs.

Smith, Richard A., et al., eds. *The Frontier States.* New York: Time-Life Books, 1968. Short and concise comparisons of the two newest states: Hawaii and Alaska. Dated information, but good social commentary and an excellent appendix suggesting tours, museums, and local festivals.

Takaki, Ronald. *Plantation Life and Labor in Hawaii, 1835-1920.* Honolulu: University of Hawaii Press, 1983. A perspective of plantation life in Hawaii from a multiethnic viewpoint. Written by a nationally known island scholar.

MYTHOLOGY AND LEGENDS

Beckwith, Martha. *Hawaiian Mythology.* Honolulu: University of Hawaii Press, 1970. Forty-five years after its original printing, this work remains *the* definitive text on Hawaiian mythology. Ms. Beckwith compiled this book from many sources, giving exhaustive cross-references to genealogies and legends expressed in the oral tradition. If you are going to read one book on Hawaii's folklore, this should be it.

Colum, Padraic. *Legends of Hawaii.* New Haven: Yale University Press, 1937. Selected legends of old Hawaii reinterpreted, but closely based upon the originals.

Elbert, S., comp. *Hawaiian Antiquities and Folklore.* Honolulu: Univerity of Hawaii Press, 1959. Illustrated by Jean Charlot. A selection of the main legends from Abraham Fornander's great work, *The Polynesian Race.*

Melville, Leinanai. *Children of the Rainbow.* Wheaton, IL: Theosophical Publishing, 1969. A book on higher spiritual consciousness attuned to nature, which was the basic belief of pre-Christian Hawaii. The appendix contains illustrations of mystical symbols used by the *kahuna.* An enlightening book in many ways.

Thrum, Thomas. *Hawaiian Folk Tales.* Chicago: McClurg and Co., 1907. A collection of Hawaiian tales from the oral tradition as told to the author from various sources.

Westervelt, W.D. *Hawaiian Legends of Volcanoes.* Boston: Ellis Press, 1916. A small book

concerning the volcanic legends of Hawaii and how they related to the fledgling field of volcanism at the turn of the century. The vintage photos alone are worth a look.

NATURAL SCIENCES

Abbott, Agatin, Gordon MacDonald, and Frank Peterson. *Volcanoes in the Sea.* Honolulu: University of Hawaii Press, 1983. A simplified yet comprehensive text covering the geology and volcanism of the Hawaiian Islands. Focuses upon the forces of nature (wind, rain, and surf) that shape the islands.

Boom, Robert. *Hawaiian Seashells.* Honolulu: Waikiki Aquarium, 1972. Photos, Jerry Kringle. A collection of 137 seashells found in Hawaiian waters, featuring many found nowhere else on earth. Broken into categories with accompanying text including common and scientific names, physical descriptions, and likely habitats. A must for shell collectors.

Brock, Vernon, and W.A. Gosline. *Handbook of Hawaiian Fishes.* Honolulu: University of Hawaii Press, 1960. A detailed guide to most of the fishes occurring in Hawaiian waters.

Carlquist, Sherwin. *Hawaii: A Natural History.* New York: Doubleday, 1970. Definitive account of Hawaii's natural history.

Carpenter, Blyth, and Russell Carpenter. *Fish Watching in Hawaii.* San Mateo, CA: Natural World Press, 1981. A color guide to many of the reef fish found in Hawaii and often spotted by snorkelers. If you're interested in the kinds of fish you'll see, this guide will be very helpful.

Fielding, Ann, and Ed Robinson. *An Underwater Guide to Hawaii.* Honolulu: University of Hawaii Press, 1987. If you've ever had a desire to snorkel/scuba the living reef waters of Hawaii and to be familiar with what you're seeing, get this small but fact-packed book. The amazing array of marinelife found throughout the archipelago is captured in glossy photos with accompanying informative text. Both the scientific and common names of specimens are given. This book will enrich your underwater experience and serve as an easily understood reference guide for many years.

Hamaishi, Amy, and Doug Wallin. *Flowers of Hawaii.* Honolulu: World Wide Distributors, 1975. Close-up color photos of many of the most common flowers spotted in Hawaii.

Hawaii Audubon Society. *Hawaii's Birds.* Honolulu: Hawaii Audubon Society, 1981. A field guide to Hawaii's birds, listing the endangered indigenous species, migrants, and introduced species that are now quite common. Color photos with text listing distribution, description, voice, and habits. Excellent field guide.

Hosaka, Edward. *Shore Fishing in Hawaii.* Hilo, HI: Petroglyph Press, 1984. Known as the best book on Hawaiian fishing since 1944. Receives the highest praise because it has born and bred many Hawaiian fishermen.

Hubbard, Douglass, and Gordon MacDonald. *Volcanoes of the National Parks of Hawaii.* Volcanoes, HI: Hawaii Natural History Assoc., 1982. The volcanology of Hawaii, documenting the major lava flows and their geological effect on the state.

Island Heritage Limited. *Hawaii's Flowering Trees.* Honolulu: Island Heritage Press. A concise field guide to many of Hawaii's most common flowering trees. All color photos with accompanying descriptive text.

Kay, E. Alison, comp. *A Natural History of the Hawaiian Islands.* Honolulu: University of Hawaii Press, 1972. A selection of concise articles by experts in the fields of volcanism, oceanography, meteorology, and biology. An excellent reference source.

Kuck, Lorraine, and Richard Togg. *Hawaiian Flowers and Flowering Trees.* Rutland, VT: Tuttle, 1960. A classic field guide to tropical and subtropical flora illustrated in watercolor. A "to the point" description of Hawaiian plants and flowers with a brief history of their places of origin and their introduction to Hawaii.

Merlin, Mark D. *Hawaiian Forest Plants, A Hiker's Guide.* Honolulu: Oriental Publishing,

1980. A companion guide for trekkers into Hawaii's interior. Full-color plates identify and describe the most common forest plants encountered.

————*Hawaiian Coastal Plants.* Honolulu: Oriental Publishing, 1980. Color photos and botanical descriptions of many of the plants and flowers found growing along Hawaii's varied shorelines.

Merrill, Elmer. *Plant Life of the Pacific World.* Rutland, VT: Tuttle, 1983. The definitive book for anyone planning a botanical tour to the entire Pacific Basin. Originally published in the 1930s, it remains a tremendous work.

Nickerson, Roy. *Brother Whale, A Pacific Whalewatcher's Log.* San Francisco: Chronicle Books, 1977. Introduces the average person to earth's greatest mammals. Provides historical accounts, photos, and tips on whale-watching. Well written, descriptive, and the best "first time" book on whales.

Sohmer, S.H., and R. Gustafson. *Plants and Flowers of Hawaii.* Honolulu: University of Hawaii Press, 1987. Sohmer and Gustafson range the vegetation zones of Hawaii, from mountains to coast, introducing you to the wide and varied floral biology of the islands. They give a good introduction to the history and uniqueness of the evolution of Hawaiian plantlife. Beautiful color plates are accompanied by clear and concise plant descriptions, with the scientific and common Hawaiian names listed.

Stearns, Harold T. *Road Guide to Points of Geological Interest in the Hawaiian Islands.* Palo Alto, CA: Pacific Books, 1966. The title is almost as long as this handy little book that lets you know what forces of nature formed the island's scenery.

Van Riper, Charles, and Sandra van Riper. *A Field Guide to the Mammals of Hawaii.* Honolulu: Oriental Publishing. A guide to the surprising number of mammals introduced into Hawaii. Full-color pages document description, uses, tendencies, and habitat. Small and thin, makes a worthwhile addition to any serious trekker's backpack.

TRAVEL

Morey, Kathy *Kauai Trails,* Berkeley: Wilderness Press, 1991. Morey's books are specialized, detailed trekker's guides to Hawaii's outdoors. Complete with useful maps, historical references, official procedures, and descriptions of plants and animals you might encounter along the way. If you're focused on hiking, these are the best to take along. Big Island, Maui, and Oahu Trails in the works. Inquire!

Riegert, Ray. *Hidden Hawaii.* Berkeley, CA: And/Or Press, 1982. Ray offers a "user-friendly" guide to the islands.

Stanley, David. *South Pacific Handbook.* 5th ed. Chico, CA: Moon Publications, 1993. The model upon which all travel guides should be based. Simply the best book in the world for travel throughout the South Pacific.

Sutton, Horace. *Aloha Hawaii.* New York: Doubleday, 1967. A dated but still excellent guide to Hawaii providing sociological, historical, and cultural insight. Horace Sutton's literary style is the best in the travel guide field. Entertaining reading.

Thorne, Chuck. *The Diver's Guide to Maui.* Kahului, HI: Maui Dive Guide, 1984. A no-nonsense snorkeler's and diver's guide to Maui waters. Extensive maps, descriptions, and "straight from the shoulder" advice by one of Maui's best and most experienced divers. A must for all levels of divers and snorkelers.

Thorne, Chuck, and Lou Zitnik. *A Diver's Guide to Hawaii.* Kihei, HI: Hawaii's Diver's Guide, 1984. An expanded diver's and snorkeler's guide to the waters of the six main Hawaiian Islands. Complete list of maps with full descriptions, tips, and ability levels. A must for all levels of snorkelers and divers.

Warner, Evie, and Al Davies. *Bed and Breakfast Goes Hawaiian* Kapaa, HI: Island Bed and Breakfast, 1990. A combination bed-and-breakfast directory and guide to sights, activities, events, and restaurants on the six major islands.

COOKING

Alexander, Agnes. *How to Use Hawaiian Fruit.* Hilo, HI: Petroglyph Press, 1984. A full range of recipes using delicious and different Hawaiian fruits.

Fitzgerald, Donald, et al., eds. *The Pacific House Hawaii Cookbook.* Pacific House, 1968. A full range of Hawaiian cuisine, including recipes for traditional Chinese, Japanese, Portuguese, New England, and Filipino dishes.

Gibbons, Euell. *Beachcombers Handbook.* New York: McKay Co., 1967. An autobiographical account of this world-famous naturalist as a young man living off the land in Hawaii. Great tips on spotting and gathering naturally occurring foods, survival advice, and recipes. Unfortunately, the lifestyle described is long outdated.

Margah, Irish, and Elvira Monroe. *Hawaii, Cooking with Aloha.* San Carlos, CA: Wide World, 1984. Island recipes including *kalua* pig, *lomi* salmon, and hints on decor.

LANGUAGE

Boom, Robert, and Chris Christensen. *Important Hawaiian Place Names.* Honolulu: Boom Enterprises, 1978. A handy, pocket-sized book listing most of the major island place-names and their translations.

Elbert, Samuel. *Spoken Hawaiian.* Honolulu: University of Hawaii Press, 1970. Progressive conversational lessons.

Elbert, Samuel, and Mary Pukui. *Hawaiian Dictionary.* Honolulu: University of Hawaii, 1971. The best dictionary available on the Hawaiian language. The *Pocket Hawaiian Dictionary* is a condensed version, which is less expensive and adequate for most travelers with a general interest in the language.

GLOSSARY

Words marked with an asterisk (*) are used commonly throughout the islands.

a'a—rough clinker lava. *A'a* has become the correct geological term to describe this type of lava found anywhere in the world.

ahupua'a—pie-shaped land divisions running from mountain to sea that were governed by *konohiki*, local *ali'i* who owed their allegiance to a reigning chief

aikane—friend; pal; buddy

aina—land; the binding spirit to all Hawaiians. Love of the land is paramount in traditional Hawaiian beliefs.

akamai—smart; clever; wise

akua—a god, or simply "divine." You'll hear people speak of their family or personal *amakua* (ancestral spirit). Favorites are the shark or the *pueo* (Hawaiian owl).

ali'i—a Hawaiian chief or noble

aloha*—the most common greeting in the islands; can mean both hello or goodbye, welcome or farewell. It can also mean romantic love, affection, or best wishes.

amakua—a personal or family spirit, usually an ancestral spirit

aole—no

auwe—alas; ouch! When a great chief or loved one died, it was a traditional wail of mourning.

halakahiki—pineapple

hale*—house or building. Often combined with other words to name a specific place such as Haleakala ("House of the Sun") or Hale Pai ("printing house")

hana*—work; combined with *pau* means end of work or quitting time

hanai—literally "to feed." Part of the true aloha spirit. A *hanai* is a permanent guest, or an adopted family member, usually an old person or a child. This is an enduring cultural phenomenon in Hawaii, in which a child from one family (perhaps that of a brother or sister, and quite often one's grandchild) is raised as one's own without formal adoption.

haole*—a word that at one time meant foreigner, but which now means a white person or Caucasian. Many etymological definitions have been put forth, but none satisfies everyone. Some feel that it signified a person without a background, because the first white men could not chant their genealogies as was common to Hawaiians.

hapa*—half, as in a mixed-blooded person being referred to as *hapa haole*

hapai*—pregnant; used by all ethnic groups when a *keiki* is on the way

haupia*—a coconut custard dessert often served at luaus

heiau*—a traditional Hawaiian temple. A platform made of skillfully fitted rocks, upon which structures were built and offerings made to the gods.

holomuu*—an ankle-length dress that is much more fitted than a muumuu, and which is often worn on formal occasions

hono—bay, as in Honolulu ("Sheltered Bay")

ho'oilo—traditional Hawaiian winter that began in November

hoolaulea—any happy event, but especially a family outing or picnic *hoomalimali*—sweet talk; flattery

huhu—angry; irritated

hui—a group; meeting; society. Often used to refer to Chinese businesspeople or family members who pool their money to get businesses started.

hukilau—traditional shoreline fish-gathering in which everyone lends a hand to *huki* (pull) the huge net. Anyone taking part shares in the *lau* (food). It is much more like a party than hard work, and if you're lucky you'll be able to take part in one.

hula—a native Hawaiian dance in which the rhythm of the islands is captured by swaying hips and stories told by lyrically moving hands. A *halau* is a group or school of *hula*.

huli huli—barbecue, as in *huli huli* chicken

i'a—fish in general. *I'a maka* is raw fish.

imu—underground oven filled with hot rocks and used for baking. The main cooking feature at luaus, used to steam-bake pork and other succulent dishes. The tending of the *imu* was traditionally for men only.

ipo—sweetheart; lover; girlfriend or boyfriend

kahili—a tall pole topped with feathers, resembling a huge feather duster. It was used by an *ali'i* to announce his or her presence.

kahuna—priest; sorcerer; doctor; skillful person. *Kahuna* had tremendous power in old Hawaii which they used for both good and evil. The *kahuna ana'ana* was a feared individual because he practiced "black magic" and could pray a person to death, while the *kahuna lapa'au* was a medical practitioner bringing aid and comfort to the people.

kai—the sea. Many businesses and hotels employ *kai* as part of their name.

kalua—roasted underground in an *imu*. A favorite island food is *kalua* pork.

kamaaina—a child of the land; an old-timer; a longtime island resident of any ethnic background; a resident of Hawaii or native son or daughter. Hotels and airlines often offer discounts called "*kamaaina* rates" to anyone who can prove island residency.

kanaka—man or commoner; later used to distinguish a Hawaiian from other races. Tone of voice can make it a derisive expression.

kane—means man, but actually used to signify a relationship such as husband or boyfriend. Written on a door it means "Men's Room."

kaola—any food that has been broiled or barbecued

kapu—forbidden; taboo; keep out; do not touch

kapuna—a grandparent or old-timer; usually means someone who has gained wisdom. The statewide school system now invites *kapuna* to talk to the children about the old ways and methods.

kaukau—slang word meaning food or chow; grub. Some of the best food in Hawaii comes from the "*kaukau* wagons," trucks that sell plate lunches and other morsels.

kauwa—a landless, untouchable caste once confined to living on reservations. Members of this caste were often used as human sacrifices at *heiau*. Calling someone *kauwa* is still considered a grave insult.

kava—a mildly intoxicating traditional drink made from the juice of chewed awa root, spat into a bowl, and used in religious ceremonies

keiki—child or children; used by all ethnic groups. "Have you hugged your *keiki* today?"

kiawe—an algaroba tree from South America commonly found in Hawaii along the shore. It grows a nasty long thorn that can easily puncture a tire. Legend has it that the trees were introduced to the islands by a misguided missionary who hoped the thorns would coerce natives into wearing shoes. Actually, they are good for fuel, as fodder for hogs and cattle, and for re-forestation, none of which you'll appreciate if you step on one of their thorns or flatten a tire on your rental car!

kokua—help. As in "Your *kokua* is needed to keep Hawaii free from litter."

kona wind*—a muggy subtropical wind that blows from the south and hits the leeward side of the islands. It usually brings sticky hot weather and one of the few times when air-conditioning will be appreciated.

konane—a traditional Hawaiian game, similar to checkers, played with pebbles on a large flat stone used as a board

koolau—windward side of the island

kukui—a candlenut tree whose pods are polished and then strung together to make a beautiful *lei*. Traditionally the oil-rich nuts were strung on the rib of a coconut leaf and used as a candle.

kuleana—homesite; the old homestead; small farms. Especially used to describe the small spreads on Hawaiian Homes Lands on Molokai.

Kumulipo*—ancient Hawaiian genealogical chant that records the pantheon of gods, creation, and the beginning of humankind

la—the sun. Often combined with other words to be more descriptive, such as *La*haina ("Merciless Sun") or Haleakala ("House of the Sun").

lanai*—veranda or porch. You'll pay more for a hotel room if it has a lanai with an ocean view.

lani—sky or the heavens

lau hala*—traditional Hawaiian weaving of mats, hats, etc., from the prepared fronds of the pandanus (screw pine)

lei*—a traditional garland of flowers or vines. One of Hawaii's most beautiful customs. Given at any auspicious occasion, but especially when arriving or leaving Hawaii.

lele—the stone altar at a *heiau*

limu—edible seaweed of various types. Gathered from the shoreline, it makes an excellent salad. It's used to garnish many island dishes and is a favorite at luaus.

lomi lomi—traditional Hawaiian massage; also, raw salmon made into a vinegared salad with chopped onion and spices

lua*—the toilet; the head; the bathroom

luakini—a human-sacrifice temple. Introduced to Hawaii in the 13th century at Wahaula Heiau on the Big Island.

luau*—a Hawaiian feast featuring poi, *imu*-baked pork, and other traditional foods. Good ones provide some of the best gastronomical delights in the world.

luna—foreman or overseer in the plantation fields. They were often mounted on horseback and were renowned either for their fairness or cruelty. They represented the middle class, and served as a buffer between plantation workers and white plantation owners.

mahalo*—thank you. *Mahalo nui* means "big thanks" or "thank you very much."

mahele—division. The "Great Mahele" of 1848 changed Hawaii forever when the traditional common lands were broken up into privately owned plots.

mahimahi*—a favorite eating fish. Often called a dolphin, but a mahimahi is a true fish, not a cetacean.

mahu—a homosexual; often used derisively like "fag" or "queer"

maile—a fragrant vine used in traditional *lei*. It looks ordinary but smells delightful.

makaainana—a commoner; a person "belonging" to the *aina* (land), who supported the *ali'i* by fishing and farming and as a warrior

makai*—toward the sea; used by most islanders when giving directions

make—dead; deceased

malihini*—newcomer; tenderfoot; recent arrival

malo—the native Hawaiian loincloth. Never
worn anymore except at festivals or pageants.

mana*—power from the spirit world; innate energy of all things animate or inanimate; the grace
of god. Mana could be passed on from one person to another, or even stolen. Great care was
taken to protect the *ali'i* from having their mana
defiled. Commoners were required to lie flat on
the ground and cover their faces whenever a
great *ali'i* approached. *Kahuna* were often employed in the regaining or transference of mana.

manauahi—free; gratis; extra

manini—stingy; tight. A Hawaiianized word
taken from the name of Don Francisco *Marin,*
who was instrumental in bringing many fruits
and plants to Hawaii. He was known for never
sharing any of the bounty from his substantial
gardens on Vineyard Street in Honolulu.

mauka*—toward the mountains; used by most
islanders when giving directions

mauna—mountain. Often combined with other
words to be more descriptive, such as Mauna
Kea ("White Mountain").

mele—a song or chant in the Hawaiian oral tradition that records the history and genealogies of
the *ali'i*

menehune—the legendary "little people" of
Hawaii. Like leprechauns, they are said to have
shunned humans and possess magical powers. Stone walls said to have been completed in
one night are often attributed to them. Some
historians argue that they actually existed and
were the aboriginals of Hawaii, inhabiting the
islands before the coming of the Polynesians.

moa—chicken; fowl

moana*—the ocean; the sea. Many businesses
and hotels as well as places have *moana* as
part of their name.

moe—sleep

moolelo—ancient tales kept alive by the oral
tradition and recited only by day

muumuu*—a "Mother Hubbard," an ankle-
length dress with a high neckline introduced by
the missionaries to cover the nakedness of the
Hawaiians. It has become fashionable attire for
almost any occasion in Hawaii.

nani—beautiful

nui—big; great; large; as in *mahalo nui* (thank
you very much)

ohana—a family; the fundamental social division; extended family. Now used to denote a
social organization with grass-roots overtones,
as in the "Protect Kahoolawe Ohana."

okolehau—literally "iron bottom"; a traditional
booze made from ti root. *Okole* means "rear
end" and *hau* means "iron," which was descriptive of the huge blubber pots in which *okolehau*
was made. Also, if you drink too much it'll surely knock you on your *okole.*

ono*—delicious; delightful; the best. *Ono ono*
means "extra or absolutely delicious."

opihi—a shellfish or limpet that clings to rocks
and is gathered as one of the islands' favorite *pu
pu.* Custom dictates that you never remove all of
the *opihi* from a rock; some are always left to
grow for future generations.

opu—belly; stomach

pa'hoehoe*—smooth, ropey lava that looks like
burnt pancake batter. *Pa'hoehoe* is now the
correct geological term used to describe this
type of lava found anywhere in the world.

pakalolo—marijuana; the state's most productive cash crop

pake—a Chinese person. Can be derisive, depending on tone in which it is used. It is a bastardization of the Chinese word meaning "uncle."

pali*—a cliff; precipice. Hawaii's geology makes them quite common. The most famous are the *pali* of Oahu where a major battle was fought.

paniolo*—a Hawaiian cowboy. Derived from the Spanish *espaniola*. The first cowboys brought to Hawaii during the early 19th century were Mexicans from California.

papale—hat. Except for the feathered helmets of the *ali'i* warriors of old Hawaii, hats were generally not worn. However, once the islanders saw their practical uses and how fashionable they were, they began weaving them from various materials and quickly became experts at manufacture and design.

pau*—finished; done; completed. Often combined into *pau hana,* which means end of work or quitting time.

pa'u—long split skirt often worn by women when horseback riding. Last century, an island treat was *pa'u* riders in their beautiful dresses at Kapiolani Park in Honolulu. The tradition is carried on today at many of Hawaii's rodeos.

pilau—stink; bad smell; stench

pilikia—trouble of any kind, big or small; bad times

poi*—a glutinous paste made from the pounded corm of taro which ferments slightly and has a light sour taste. Purplish in color, it's a staple at luaus, where it is called "one-, two-, or three-finger" poi, depending upon its thickness.

pono—righteous or excellent

pua—flower

puka*—a hole of any size. *Puka* is used by all island residents, whether talking about a pinhole in a rubber boat or a tunnel through a mountain.

punalua—the tradition of sharing mates in practice before the missionaries came. Western seamen took advantage of it, and this led to the spreading of contagious diseases and eventually to the ultimate demise of the Hawaiian people.

punee*—bed; narrow couch. Used by all ethnic groups. To recline on a *punee* on a breezy lanai is a true island treat.

pu pu*—an appetizer; a snack; hors d'oeuvres; can be anything from cheese and crackers to sushi. Oftentimes, bars or nightclubs offer them free.

pupule—crazy; nuts; out of your mind

pu'u—hill, as in Pu'u Ulaula ("Red Hill")

tapa*—a traditional paper cloth made from beaten bark. Intricate designs were stamped in using beaters, and natural dyes added color. The tradition was lost for many years but is now making a comeback, and provides some of the most beautiful folk art in the islands.

taro*—the staple of old Hawaii. A plant with a distinctive broad leaf that produces a starchy root. It was brought by the first Polynesians and was grown on magnificently irrigated plantations. According to the oral tradition, the life-giving properties of taro hold mystical significance for Hawaiians, since it was created by the gods at about the same time as humans.

ti—a broad-leafed plant that was used for many purposes, from plates to *hula* skirts (never grass). Especially used to wrap religious offerings presented at the *heiau*.

tutu*—grandmother; granny; older woman. Used by all as a term of respect and endearment.

ukulele*—*uku* means "flea" and *lele* means "jumping," so literally "jumping flea"—the way the Hawaiians perceived the quick finger movements used on the banjo-like Portuguese folk instrument called a *cavaquinho*. The ukulele quickly became synonymous with the islands.

wahine*—young woman; female; girl; wife. Used by all ethnic groups. When written on a door it means "Women's Room."

wai—fresh water; drinking water

wela—hot. *Wela kahao* is a "hot time" or "making whoopee."

wiki*—quickly; fast; in a hurry. Often seen as *wiki wiki* (very fast), as in "Wiki Wiki Messenger Service."

ACCOMMODATIONS INDEX

RESTAURANT INDEX

INDEX

Page numbers in **boldface** indicate the primary reference. *Italicized* page numbers
indicate information found in captions, charts, callouts, illustrations, or maps.

ABOUT THE AUTHOR

Joe Bisignani is a fortunate man because he makes his living doing the two things that he likes best: traveling and writing. Joe has been with Moon Publications since 1979 and is the author of *Japan Handbook*, *Kauai Handbook*, *Hawaii Handbook*, *Oahu Handbook*, and *Maui Handbook*. When not traveling, he makes his home in Northern California.

ABOUT THE COVER ARTIST

Artist Roy Gonzalez Tabora, whose art is featured on all the covers of the Hawaii handbooks series, was born into a family of painters. At the age of twenty, already an accomplished realist painter, he continued his education and received his degree in fine arts from the University of Hawaii. He never simply copies from a photograph or relies solely upon his imagination, choosing instead to render an artful blend using his heart and his mind to produce what are considered some of the finest and most unforgettable seascapes in the world. He is currently represented by Kahn Galleries, 4569 Kukui St., Kapaa, HI 96746, tel. (808) 822-5281, fax (808) 822-2756.

MOON HANDBOOKS—THE IDEAL TRAVELING COMPANIONS

Open a Moon Handbook and you're opening your eyes and heart to the world. Thoughtful, sensitive, and provocative, Moon Handbooks encourage an intimate understanding of a region, from its culture and history to essential practicalities. Fun to read and packed with valuable information on accommodations, dining, recreation, plus indispensable travel tips, detailed maps, charts, illustrations, photos, glossaries, and indexes, Moon Handbooks are ideal traveling companions: informative, entertaining, and highly practical.

To locate the bookstore nearest you that carries Moon Travel Handbooks or to order directly from Moon Publications, call: (800) 345-5473, Monday-Friday, 9 a.m.-5 p.m. PST.

THE PACIFIC/ASIA SERIES

BALI HANDBOOK   by Bill Dalton
Detailed travel information on the most famous island in the world. 428 pages.   **$12.95**

BANGKOK HANDBOOK   by Michael Buckley
Your tour guide through this exotic and dynamic city reveals the affordable and accessible possibilities. Thai phrasebook. 214 pages.   **$10.95**

BLUEPRINT FOR PARADISE: How to Live on a Tropic Island   by Ross Norgrove
This one-of-a-kind guide has everything you need to know about moving to and living comfortably on a tropical island. 212 pages.   **$14.95**

FIJI ISLANDS HANDBOOK   by David Stanley
The first and still the best source of information on travel around this 322-island archipelago. Fijian glossary. 198 pages.   **$11.95**

INDONESIA HANDBOOK   by Bill Dalton
This one-volume encyclopedia explores island by island the many facets of this sprawling, kaleidoscopic island nation. Extensive Indonesian vocabulary. 1,000 pages.   **$19.95**

JAPAN HANDBOOK   by J.D. Bisignani
In this comprehensive new edition, award-winning travel writer J.D. Bisignani offers to inveterate travelers, newcomers, and businesspeople alike a thoroughgoing presentation of Japan's many facets. 950 pages.   **$22.50**

MICRONESIA HANDBOOK: Guide to the Caroline, Gilbert, Mariana, and Marshall Islands
by David Stanley
Micronesia Handbook guides you on a real Pacific adventure all your own. 345 pages.   **$11.95**

NEW ZEALAND HANDBOOK   by Jane King
Introduces you to the people, places, history, and culture of this extraordinary land. 571 pages.
$18.95

OUTBACK AUSTRALIA HANDBOOK   by Marael Johnson
Australia is an endlessly fascinating, vast land, and *Outback Australia Handbook* explores the
cities and towns, sheep stations, and wilderness areas of the Northern Territory, Western
Australia, and South Australia. Full of travel tips and cultural information for adventuring,
relaxing, or just getting away from it all. 355 pages.   **$15.95**

PHILIPPINES HANDBOOK   by Peter Harper and Evelyn Peplow
Crammed with detailed information, *Philippines Handbook* equips the escapist, hedonist, or
business traveler with thorough coverage of the Philippines's colorful history, landscapes, and
culture. 600 pages.   **$17.95**

SOUTHEAST ASIA HANDBOOK   by Carl Parkes
Helps the enlightened traveler discover the real Southeast Asia. 873 pages.   **$21.95**

SOUTH KOREA HANDBOOK   by Robert Nilsen
Whether you're visiting on business or searching for adventure, *South Korea Handbook* is an
invaluable companion. Korean glossary with useful notes on speaking and reading the
language. 548 pages.   **$14.95**

SOUTH PACIFIC HANDBOOK   by David Stanley
The original comprehensive guide to the 16 territories in the South Pacific. 740 pages.   **$19.95**

TAHITI-POLYNESIA HANDBOOK   by David Stanley
All five French-Polynesian archipelagoes are covered in this comprehensive guide by
Oceania's best-known travel writer. 235 pages.   **$11.95**

THAILAND HANDBOOK   by Carl Parkes
Presents the richest source of information on travel in Thailand. 568 pages.   **$16.95**

THE HAWAIIAN SERIES

BIG ISLAND OF HAWAII HANDBOOK   by J.D. Bisignani
An entertaining yet informative text packed with insider tips on accommodations, dining, sports
and outdoor activities, natural attractions, and must-see sights. 350 pages.   **$13.95**

HAWAII HANDBOOK   by J.D. Bisignani
Winner of the 1989 Hawaii Visitors Bureau's Best Guide Award and the Grand Award for
Excellence in Travel Journalism, this guide takes you beyond the glitz and high-priced hype and
leads you to a genuine Hawaiian experience. Covers all 8 Hawaiian Islands. 879 pages.   **$15.95**

KAUAI HANDBOOK   by J.D. Bisignani
Kauai Handbook is the perfect antidote to the workaday world. Hawaiian and pidgin glossaries.
236 pages.   **$9.95**

MAUI HANDBOOK   by J.D. Bisignani
"No fool-'round" advice on accommodations, eateries, and recreation, plus a comprehensive
introduction to island ways, geography, and history. Hawaiian and pidgin glossaries. 350 pages.
$11.95

OAHU HANDBOOK   by J.D. Bisignani
A handy guide to Honolulu, renowned surfing beaches, and Oahu's countless other diversions.
Hawaiian and pidgin glossaries. 354 pages.   **$11.95**

THE AMERICAS SERIES

ALASKA-YUKON HANDBOOK   by Deke Castleman and Don Pitcher
Get the inside story, with plenty of well-seasoned advice to help you cover more miles on less money. 384 pages.   **$14.95**

ARIZONA TRAVELER'S HANDBOOK   by Bill Weir
This meticulously researched guide contains everything necessary to make Arizona accessible and enjoyable. 505 pages.   **$14.95**

BAJA HANDBOOK   by Joe Cummings
A comprehensive guide with all the travel information and background on the land, history, and culture of this untamed thousand-mile-long peninsula. 356 pages.   **$13.95**

BELIZE HANDBOOK   by Chicki Mallan
Complete with detailed maps, practical information, and an overview of the area's flamboyant history, culture, and geographical features, *Belize Handbook* is the only comprehensive guide of its kind to this spectacular region. 263 pages.   **$14.95**

BRITISH COLUMBIA HANDBOOK   by Jane King
With an emphasis on outdoor adventures, this guide covers mainland British Columbia, Vancouver Island, the Queen Charlotte Islands, and the Canadian Rockies. 381 pages.
$15.95

CANCUN HANDBOOK   by Chicki Mallan
Covers the city's luxury scene as well as more modest attractions, plus many side trips to unspoiled beaches and Mayan ruins. Spanish glossary. 257 pages.   **$12.95**

CATALINA ISLAND HANDBOOK: A Guide to California's Channel Islands
by Chicki Mallan
A complete guide to these remarkable islands, from the windy solitude of the Channel Islands National Marine Sanctuary to bustling Avalon. 245 pages.   **$10.95**

COLORADO HANDBOOK   by Stephen Metzger
Essential details to the all-season possibilities in Colorado fill this guide. Practical travel tips combine with recreation—skiing, nightlife, and wilderness exploration—plus entertaining essays. 416 pages.   **$17.95**

COSTA RICA HANDBOOK   by Christopher P. Baker
Experience the many wonders of the natural world as you explore this remarkable land. Spanish-English glossary. 574 pages.   **$17.95**

IDAHO HANDBOOK   by Bill Loftus
A year-round guide to everything in this outdoor wonderland, from whitewater adventures to rural hideaways. 275 pages.   **$12.95**

JAMAICA HANDBOOK   by Karl Luntta
From the sun and surf of Montego Bay and Ocho Rios to the cool slopes of the Blue Mountains, author Karl Luntta offers island-seekers a perceptive, personal view of Jamaica. 230 pages.
$14.95

MONTANA HANDBOOK by W.C. McRae and Judy Jewell
The wild West is yours with this extensive guide to the Treasure State, complete with travel practicalities, history, and lively essays on Montana life. 393 pages. **$13.95**

NEVADA HANDBOOK by Deke Castleman
Nevada Handbook puts the Silver State into perspective and makes it manageable and affordable. 400 pages. **$14.95**

NEW MEXICO HANDBOOK by Stephen Metzger
A close-up and complete look at every aspect of this wondrous state. 375 pages. **$14.95**

NORTHERN CALIFORNIA HANDBOOK by Kim Weir
An outstanding companion for imaginative travel in the territory north of the Tehachapis. 765 pages. **$19.95**

OREGON HANDBOOK by Stuart Warren and Ted Long Ishikawa
Brimming with travel practicalities and insiders' views on Oregon's history, culture, arts, and activities. 461 pages. **$15.95**

PACIFIC MEXICO HANDBOOK by Bruce Whipperman
Explore 2,000 miles of gorgeous beaches, quiet resort towns, and famous archaeological sites along Mexico's Pacific coast. Spanish-English glossary. 428 pages. **$15.95**

TEXAS HANDBOOK by Joe Cummings
Seasoned travel writer Joe Cummings brings an insider's perspective to his home state. 483 pages. **$13.95**

UTAH HANDBOOK by Bill Weir
Weir gives you all the carefully researched facts and background to make your visit a success. 445 pages. **$14.95**

WASHINGTON HANDBOOK by Dianne J. Boulerice Lyons and Archie Satterfield
Covers sights, shopping, services, transportation, and outdoor recreation, with complete listings for restaurants and accommodations. 433 pages. **$13.95**

WYOMING HANDBOOK by Don Pitcher
All you need to know to open the doors to this wide and wild state. 495 pages. **$14.95**

YUCATAN HANDBOOK by Chicki Mallan
All the information you'll need to guide you into every corner of this exotic land. Mayan and Spanish glossaries. 391 pages. **$14.95**

THE INTERNATIONAL SERIES

EGYPT HANDBOOK   by Kathy Hansen
An invaluable resource for intelligent travel in Egypt. Arabic glossary. 522 pages.   **$18.95**

MOSCOW-ST. PETERSBURG HANDBOOK   by Masha Nordbye
Provides the visitor with an extensive introduction to the history, culture, and people of these two great cities, as well as practical information on where to stay, eat, and shop. 260 pages. **$13.95**

NEPAL HANDBOOK   by Kerry Moran
Whether you're planning a week in Kathmandu or months out on the trail, *Nepal Handbook* will take you into the heart of this Himalayan jewel. 378 pages.   **$12.95**

NEPALI AAMA   by Broughton Coburn
A delightful photo-journey into the life of a Gurung tribeswoman of Central Nepal. Having lived with Aama (translated, "mother") for two years, first as an outsider and later as an adopted member of the family, Coburn presents an intimate glimpse into a culture alive with humor, folklore, religion, and ancient rituals. 165 pages.   **$13.95**

PAKISTAN HANDBOOK   by Isobel Shaw
For armchair travelers and trekkers alike, the most detailed and authoritative guide to Pakistan ever published. Urdu glossary. 478 pages.   **$15.95**

STAYING HEALTHY IN ASIA, AFRICA, AND LATIN AMERICA
by Dirk G. Schroeder, Sc D, MPH
Don't leave home without it! Besides providing a complete overview of the health problems that exist in these areas, this book will help you determine which immunizations you'll need beforehand, what medications to take with you, and how to recognize and treat infections and diseases. Includes extensively illustrated first-aid information and precautions for heat, cold, and high altitude. 200 pages.   **$10.95**

TIBET HANDBOOK: A PILGRIMAGE GUIDE
by Victor Chan
This remarkable book is both a comprehensive trekking guide to mountain paths and plateau trails, and a pilgrimage guide that draws on Tibetan literature and religious history. 1104 pages. **$30.00**

MOONBELTS

Made of heavy-duty Cordura nylon, the Moonbelt offers maximum protection for your money and important papers. This all-weather pouch slips under your shirt or waistband, rendering it virtually undetectable and inaccessible to pickpockets. One-inch-wide nylon webbing, heavy-duty zipper, one-inch quick-release buckle. Accommodates traveler's checks, passport, cash, photos. Size 5 x 9 inches. Black.   **$8.95**

**New travel handbooks may be available that are not on this list.
To find out more about current or upcoming titles,
call us toll-free at (800) 345-5473.**

IMPORTANT ORDERING INFORMATION

FOR FASTER SERVICE: Call to locate the bookstore nearest you that carries Moon Travel
Handbooks or order directly from Moon Publications:

(800) 345-5473 • **Monday-Friday** • **9 a.m.-5 p.m. PST** • **fax (916) 345-6751**

PRICES: All prices are subject to change. We always ship the most current edition. We will let
you know if there is a price increase on the book you ordered.

SHIPPING & HANDLING OPTIONS: 1) Domestic UPS or USPS first class (allow 10 working
days for delivery): $3.50 for the first item, 50 cents for each additional item.

Exceptions:
   • **Moonbelt** shipping is $1.50 for one, 50 cents for each additional belt.
   • Add $2.00 for same-day handling.
   • UPS 2nd Day Air or Printed Airmail requires a special quote.
   • International Surface Bookrate (8-12 weeks delivery):
      $3.00 for the first item, $1.00 for each additional item. Note: Moon Publications cannot
      guarantee international surface bookrate shipping.

FOREIGN ORDERS: All orders that originate outside the U.S.A. must be paid for with either
an International Money Order or a check in U.S. currency drawn on a major U.S. bank based
in the U.S.A.

TELEPHONE ORDERS: We accept Visa or MasterCard payments. Minimum order is
US$15.00. Call in your order: (800) 345-5473, 9 a.m.-5 p.m. Pacific Standard Time.

ORDER FORM

Be sure to call (800) 345-5473 for current prices and editions or for the name of the bookstore nearest you that carries Moon Travel Handbooks • 9 a.m.–5 p.m. PST
(See important ordering information on preceding page)

Name: _____ Date: _____

Street: _____

City: _____ Daytime Phone: _____

State or Country: _____ Zip Code: _____

QUANTITY	TITLE	PRICE

Taxable Total_____

Sales Tax (7.25%) for California Residents_____

Shipping & Handling_____

TOTAL_____

Ship: ☐ UPS (no PO Boxes) ☐ 1st class ☐ International surface mail

Ship to: ☐ address above ☐ other _____

Make checks payable to: **MOON PUBLICATIONS, INC.** P.O. Box 3040, Chico, CA 95927-3040 U.S.A. We accept Visa and MasterCard. **To Order:** Call in your Visa or MasterCard number, or send a written order with your Visa or MasterCard number and expiration date clearly written.

Card Number: ☐ **Visa** ☐ **MasterCard**

☐ ☐ ☐ ☐ ☐ ☐ ☐ ☐ ☐ ☐ ☐ ☐ ☐ ☐ ☐ ☐

Exact Name on Card: _____

expiration date:_____

signature_____

S/94

WHERE TO BUY THIS BOOK

BOOKSTORES AND LIBRARIES:
Moon Publications Handbooks are sold worldwide. Please write
our sales manager for a list of wholesalers and distributors in
your area that stock our travel handbooks.

TRAVELERS:
We would like to have Moon Publications Handbooks available
throughout the world. Please ask your bookstore to write or
call us for ordering information. If your bookstore will not order
our guides for you, please write or call for a free catalog.

**MOON PUBLICATIONS, INC.
P.O. BOX 3040
CHICO, CA 95927-3040 U.S.A.
TEL: (800) 345-5473
FAX: (916) 345-6751**

TRAVEL MATTERS

Travel Matters is Moon Publications' biannual newsletter. It provides today's traveler with
timely, informative travel news and articles.

You'll find resourceful coverage on:

- **Money**—What does it cost? Is it worth it?
- **Low impact travel**—tread lightly travel tips
- **Special interest travel**—cultural tours,
  environmental excursions, outdoor recreation,
  adventure treks, and more
- **Travel styles**—families, seniors, disabled travelers,
  package and theme tours
- **Consumer reviews**—books, language aids, travel
  gadgets, products, and services
- **Facts and opinions**—reader's letters and Moon
  Handbook author news
- **Moon Handbook booklist**—the latest titles and
  editions, and where and how to purchase them

To receive a free copy of *Travel Matters*, write Moon Publications Inc., P.O. Box 3040,
Chico, CA 95927-3040, or call toll-free (800) 345-5473.

Hawaii, A Dollar Destination

We're the Hawaii specialist. We've got exciting new Chrysler cars like this Lebaron convertible at rates that will keep you smiling. And, our friendly island service is everywhere you want to be on Oahu, Maui, Kauai, Big Island, Molokai and Lanai. Make Dollar Rent A Car your destination in Hawaii.

On Oahu: 944-1544
Toll-free from the neighbor islands: 1-800-342-7398
Worldwide reservations: 1-800-800-4000

Dollar features quality products of the Chrysler Corporation
like the Chrysler Lebaron convertible and other fine cars. ★

Right On The Airport.
Right On The Money.℠